Merriam-Webster's
easy learning
Complete Spanish

Grammar + Verbs + Vocabulary

Merriam-Webster, Incorporated
Springfield, Massachusetts, USA

Developed in association with **Collins**

Published by Collins
An imprint of HarperCollins Publishers
Westerhill Road
Bishopbriggs
Glasgow G64 2QT

Second edition 2016

ISBN 978-0-00-814173-8

10 9 8 7 6 5

© HarperCollins Publishers 2009, 2016

Typeset by Davidson Publishing Solutions,
Glasgow

Printed in Italy by GRAFICA VENETA S.p.A.

If you would like to comment on any aspect
of this book, please contact us at the given
address or online.
E-mail: dictionaries@harpercollins.co.uk
 www.facebook.com/collinsdictionary
 @collinsdict

Acknowledgements
We would like to thank those authors and
publishers who kindly gave permission for
copyright material to be used in the Collins
Corpus. We would also like to thank Times
Newspapers Ltd for providing valuable data.

MANAGING EDITOR
Maree Airlie

CONTRIBUTORS
Cordelia Lilly
Eduardo Vallejo

FOR THE PUBLISHER
Gerry Breslin
Hannah Dove
Chloe Osborne

BASED ON:
Collins Easy Learning Spanish Grammar
Collins Easy Learning Spanish Verbs
Collins Easy Learning Spanish Vocabulary

Contents

Note on trademarks
Entered words which we have reason to believe constitute trademarks have been designated as such. However, neither the presence nor the absence of such designation should be regarded as affecting the legal status of any trademark.

Foreword for language teachers

Merriam-Webster's Easy Learning Complete Spanish is designed to be used with both young and adult learners, as a group reference book to complement your course book during classes, or as a recommended text for self-study and homework/coursework.

The text is intended for learners from beginner to intermediate and advanced levels, and therefore its content and vocabulary have been matched to the needs of students at each level.

The approach aims to develop knowledge and understanding of grammar and to improve the ability of learners to apply it by:

- defining parts of speech at the start of each major section with examples in English to clarify concepts
- minimizing the use of grammar terminology and providing clear explanations of terms both within the text and in the **Glossary**
- illustrating points with examples (and their translations) based on topics and contexts which are relevant to beginner and intermediate course content

The text helps your students develop positive attitudes to grammar learning by:

- giving clear, easy-to-follow explanations
- prioritizing content according to relevant specifications for learner levels
- sequencing points to reflect course content, e.g. verb tenses
- highlighting useful **Tips** to deal with common difficulties
- summarizing **Key points** at the end of sections to consolidate learning

In addition to fostering success and building a thorough foundation in Spanish grammar, the optional **Grammar Extra** sections will encourage and challenge your learners to further their studies to higher and advanced levels.

The blue pages in the middle section of the book contain **Verb Tables** and a **Verb Index** which students can use as a reference in their work.

Finally the **Vocabulary** section in the last part of the book provides thematic vocabulary lists which can either be used for self-study or as an additional teaching resource.

Introduction for students

Whether you are starting to learn Spanish for the very first time, brushing up on topics you have studied in class, or studying to improve your mastery of the language, *Merriam-Webster's Easy Learning Complete Spanish* is here to help. This easy-to-use guide takes you through all the basics you will need to speak and understand modern, everyday Spanish.

Newcomers can sometimes struggle with the technical terms they come across when they start to explore the grammar of a new language. This book explains how to come to grips with all the parts of speech you will need to know, using simple, jargon-free language.

The text is divided into sections, each dealing with a particular area of grammar. Each section can be studied individually, as numerous cross-references in the text guide you to relevant points in other sections of the book for further information.

Every major section begins with an explanation of the area of grammar covered in the pages that follow. For quick reference, these definitions are also collected together on pages viii–xii in a glossary of essential grammar terms.

> **What is a verb?**
> A **verb** is a 'doing' word which describes what someone or something does, what someone or something is, or what happens to them, for example, *be*, *sing*, *live*.

Each grammar point in the text is followed by simple examples of real Spanish, complete with English translations, thus helping you to understand the rules. Underlining has been used in examples throughout the text to highlight the grammatical point being explained.

➤ In orders and instructions telling someone <u>TO DO</u> something, the pronoun is attached to the end of the verb to form one word.

Ayúda<u>me</u>.	Help me.
Acompáña<u>nos</u>.	Come with us.

In Spanish, as with any foreign language, there are certain pitfalls which have to be avoided. **Tips** and **Information** notes throughout the text are useful reminders of the things that often trip learners up.

Key points sum up all the important facts about a particular area of grammar, saving you time when you are reviewing and helping you focus on the main grammatical points.

If you think you would like to continue your Spanish studies at a higher level, check out the **Grammar Extra** sections. These are intended for advanced students who are interested in knowing a little more about the structures they will come across as they widen their exposure to the language.

The blue pages in the middle of the book contain **Verb Tables**, where 120 important Spanish verbs (both regular and irregular) are fully conjugated. Examples show you how to use these verbs in a sentence. You can look up any common verb in the **Verb Index** on pages 460–464 to find a cross-reference to a model verb.

Finally, the **Vocabulary** section at the end of the book is divided into 50 topics, followed by a list of supplementary vocabulary.

Glossary of Grammar Terms

ABSTRACT NOUN a word used to refer to a quality, idea, feeling or experience, rather than a physical object, for example, *size, reason, happiness*. Compare with **concrete noun**.

ACTIVE a form of the verb that is used when the subject of the verb is the person or thing doing the action, for example, *I wrote a letter*. Compare with **passive**.

ADJECTIVE a 'describing' word that tells you more about a person or thing, such as their appearance, color, size or other qualities, for example, *pretty, blue, big*.

ADVERB a word usually used with verbs, adjectives or other adverbs that gives more information about when, where, how or in what circumstances something happens or to what degree something is true, for example, *quickly, happily, now, extremely, very*.

AGREE in the case of adjectives and pronouns, to have the correct word ending or form according to whether what is referred to is masculine, feminine, singular or plural; in the case of verbs, to have the form which goes with the person or thing carrying out the action.

APOSTROPHE s an ending ('s) added to a noun to show who or what someone or something belongs to, for example, *Danielle's dog, the doctor's wife, the book's cover*.

ARTICLE a word like *the, a* and *an*, which is used in front of a noun. See also **definite article, indefinite article**.

AUXILIARY VERB a verb such as *be, have* or *do* used with a main verb to form tenses, negatives and questions.

BASE FORM the form of the verb without any endings added to it, for example, *walk, have, be, go*.

CARDINAL NUMBER a number used in counting, for example, *one, seven, ninety*. Compare with **ordinal number**.

CLAUSE a group of words containing a verb.

COMPARATIVE an adjective or adverb with *-er* on the end of it or *more* or *less* in front of it that is used to compare people, things or actions, for example, *slower, less important, more carefully*.

COMPOUND NOUN a word for a living being, thing or idea, which is made up of two or more words, for example, *can opener, railway station*.

CONCRETE NOUN a word that refers to an object you can touch with your hand, rather than to a quality or idea, for example, *ball, map, apples*. Compare with **abstract noun**.

CONDITIONAL a verb form used to talk about things that would happen or would be true under certain conditions, for example, *I would help you if I could*. It is also used to say what you would like or need, for example, *Could you give me the bill?*

CONJUGATE to give a verb different endings according to whether you are referring to *I, you, they* and so on, and according to whether you are referring to the present, past or future, for example, *I have, she had, they will have*.

CONJUGATION a group of verbs which have the same endings as each other or change according to the same pattern.

CONJUNCTION a word such as *and, because* or *but* that links two words or phrases of a similar type or two parts of a sentence, for example, *Diane and I have been friends for years; I left because I was bored*.

CONSONANT a letter that isn't a vowel, for example, *b, f, m, s, v* and so on. Compare with **vowel**.

CONTINUOUS TENSE a verb tense formed using *to be* and the *-ing* form of the main verb, for example, *They're swimming* (present continuous); *He was eating* (past continuous).

DEFINITE ARTICLE the word *the*. Compare with **indefinite article**.

DEMONSTRATIVE ADJECTIVE one of the words *this, that, these* and *those* used with a noun to refer to particular peope or things, for example, *this woman, that dog*.

DEMONSTRATIVE PRONOUN one of the words *this, that, these* and *those* used instead of a noun to point out people or things, for example, *That looks fun*.

DIRECT OBJECT a noun or pronoun used with verbs to show who or what is acted on by the verb. For example, in *He wrote a letter* and *He wrote me a letter*, *letter* is the direct object. Compare **indirect object**.

DIRECT OBJECT PRONOUN a word such as *me, him, us* and *them* which is used instead of a noun to stand in for the person or thing most directly affected by the action expressed by the verb. Compare with **indirect object pronoun**.

ENDING a form added to a verb, for example, *go → goes*, and to adjectives and nouns depending on whether they refer to masculine, feminine, singular or plural things.

EXCLAMATION a word, phrase or sentence that you use to show you are surprised, shocked, angry and so on,

for example, *Wow!; How dare you!; What a surprise!*

FEMININE a form of noun, pronoun or adjective that is used to refer to a living being, thing or idea that is not classed as masculine.

FUTURE a verb tense used to talk about something that will happen or will be true.

GENDER whether a noun, pronoun or adjective is feminine or masculine.

GERUND a verb form in English ending in *-ing*, for example, *eating, sleeping*.

IMPERATIVE the form of a verb used when giving orders and instructions, for example, *Shut the door!; Sit down!; Don't go!; Let's eat*.

IMPERFECT one of the verb tenses used to talk about the past, especially in descriptions, and to say what was happening or used to happen, for example, *It was sunny at the weekend; We were living in Spain at the time; I used to walk to school*. Compare to **preterite**.

IMPERSONAL VERB a verb whose subject is *it*, but where the *it* does not refer to any specific thing, for example, *It's raining; It's 10 o'clock*.

INDEFINITE ADJECTIVE one of a small group of adjectives used to talk about people or things in a general way, without saying who or what they are, for example, *several, all, every*.

INDEFINITE ARTICLE the words *a* and *an*. Compare with **definite article**.

INDICATIVE ordinary verb forms that aren't subjunctive, such as the present, preterite or future. Compare with **subjunctive**.

INDEFINITE PRONOUN a small group of pronouns such as *everything, nobody* and *something*, which are used to refer to people or things in a general way, without saying exactly who or what they are.

INDIRECT OBJECT a noun or pronoun used with verbs to show who benefits or is harmed by an action. For example, in *I gave the carrot to the rabbit*, *the rabbit* is the indirect object and *the carrot* is the direct object. Compare with **direct object**.

INDIRECT OBJECT PRONOUN a pronoun used with verbs to show who benefits or is harmed by an action. For example, in *I gave him the carrot* and *I gave it to him*, *him* is the indirect object and *the carrot* and *it* are the direct objects. Compare with **direct object pronoun**.

INDIRECT QUESTION a question that is embedded in another question or instruction such as *Can you tell me what time it is?*; *Tell me why you did it*. Also used for reported speech such as *He asked me why I did it*.

INDIRECT SPEECH the words you use to report what someone has said when you aren't using their actual words, for example, *He said that he was going out*. Also called **reported speech**.

INFINITIVE a form of the verb that hasn't any endings added to it and doesn't relate to any particular tense. In English the infinitive is usually shown with *to*, as in *to speak, to eat*.

INTERROGATIVE ADJECTIVE a question word used with a noun, for example, *What instruments do you play?*; *Which shoes do you like?*

INTERROGATIVE PRONOUN one of the words *who, whose, whom, what* and *which* when they are used instead of a noun to ask questions, for example, *What's that?*; *Who's coming?*

INTRANSITIVE VERB a type of verb that does not take a direct object,

for example, *to sleep, to rise, to swim*. Compare with **transitive verb**.

INVARIABLE used to describe a form which does not change.

IRREGULAR VERB a verb whose forms do not follow a general pattern. Compare with **regular verb**.

MASCULINE a form of noun, pronoun or adjective that is used to refer to a living being, thing or idea that is not classed as feminine.

NEGATIVE a question or statement which contains a word such as *not, never* or *nothing*, and is used to say that something is not happening, is not true or is absent, for example, *I never eat meat; Don't you love me?* Compare with **positive**.

NOUN a 'naming' word for a living being, thing or idea, for example, *woman, desk, happiness, Andrew*.

NOUN GROUP, NOUN PHRASE a word or group of words that acts as the subject or object of a verb, or as the object of a preposition, for example, *my older sister; the man next door; that big house on the corner*.

NUMBER used to say how many things you are referring to or where something comes in a sequence. See also **ordinal number** and **cardinal number**. Also the condition of being singular or plural.

OBJECT a noun or pronoun which refers to a person or thing that is affected by the action described by the verb. Compare with **direct object**, **indirect object** and **subject**.

OBJECT PRONOUN one of the set of pronouns including *me, him* and *them*, which are used instead of the noun as the object of a verb or preposition. Compare with **subject pronoun**.

ORDINAL NUMBER a number used to indicate where something comes in an order or sequence, for example, *first, fifth, sixteenth*. Compare with **cardinal number**.

PART OF SPEECH a word class, for example, *noun, verb, adjective, preposition, pronoun*.

PASSIVE a form of the verb that is used when the subject of the verb is the person or thing that is affected by the action, for example, *we were told*.

PAST PARTICIPLE a verb form which is used to form perfect and pluperfect tenses and passives, for example, *watched, swum*. Some past participles are also used as adjectives, for example, *a broken watch*.

PAST PERFECT see **pluperfect**.

PERFECT a verb form used to talk about what has or hasn't happened, for example, *I've broken my glasses; We haven't spoken about it*.

PERSON one of the three classes: the first person (*I, we*), the second person (*you* singular and *you* plural), and the third person (*he, she, it* and *they*).

PERSONAL PRONOUN one of the group of words including *I, you* and *they* which are used to refer to you, the people you are talking to, or the people or things you are talking about.

PLUPERFECT one of the verb tenses used to describe something that had happened or had been true at a point in the past, for example, *I'd forgotten to finish my homework*. Also called **past perfect**.

PLURAL the form of a word which is used to refer to more than one person or thing. Compare with **singular**.

POSITIVE a positive sentence or instruction is one that does not contain a negative word such as *not*. Compare with **negative**.

POSSESSIVE ADJECTIVE one of the words *my, your, his, her, its, our* or *their*, used with a noun to show who it belongs to.

POSSESSIVE PRONOUN one of the words *mine, yours, hers, his, ours* or *theirs*, used instead of a noun to show who something belongs to.

PREPOSITION is a word such as *at, for, with, into* or *from*, which is usually followed by a noun, pronoun or, in English, a word ending in *-ing*. Prepositions show how people and things relate to the rest of the sentence, for example, *She's at home; a tool for cutting grass; It's from David*.

PRESENT a verb form used to talk about what is true at the moment, what happens regularly, and what is happening now, for example, *I'm a student; I travel to college by train; I'm studying languages*.

PRESENT PARTICIPLE a verb form in English ending in *-ing*, for example, *eating, sleeping*.

PRETERITE a verb form used to talk about actions that were completed in the past in Spanish. It often corresponds to the ordinary past tense in English, for example, *I bought a new bike; Mary went to the store on Friday; I typed two reports yesterday*.

PRONOUN a word which you use instead of a noun, when you do not need or want to name someone or something directly, for example, *it, you, none*.

PROPER NOUN the name of a person, place, organization or thing. Proper nouns are always written with a capital letter, for example, *Kevin, Boston, Europe, Newsweek*.

QUESTION WORD a word such as *why, where, who, which* or *how* which is used to ask a question.

RADICAL-CHANGING VERBS in Spanish, verbs which change their stem or root in certain tenses and in certain persons.

REFLEXIVE PRONOUN a word ending in -self or -selves, such as *myself* or *themselves*, which refers back to the subject, for example, *He hurt himself*; *Take care of yourself*.

REFLEXIVE VERB a verb where the subject and object are the same, and where the action 'reflects back' on the subject. A reflexive verb is used with a reflexive pronoun such as *myself, yourself, herself*, for example, *I washed myself*; *He shaved himself*.

REGULAR VERB a verb whose forms follow a general pattern or the normal rules. Compare with **irregular verb**.

RELATIVE PRONOUN a word such as *that, who* or *which*, when it is used to link two parts of a sentence together.

REPORTED SPEECH see **indirect speech**.

SENTENCE a group of words which usually has a verb and a subject. In writing, a sentence begins with a capital and ends with a period, question mark or exclamation mark.

SIMPLE TENSE a verb tense in which the verb form is made up of one word, rather than being formed from *to have* and a past participle or *to be* and an *-ing* form; for example, *She plays tennis*; *He wrote a book*.

SINGULAR the form of a word which is used to refer to one person or thing. Compare with **plural**.

STEM the main part of a verb to which endings are added.

SUBJECT a noun or pronoun that refers to the person or thing doing the action or being in the state described by the verb, for example, *My cat doesn't drink milk*. Compare with **object**.

SUBJECT PRONOUN a word such as *I, he, she* and *they* which carries out the action described by the verb. Pronouns stand in for nouns when it is clear who is being talked about, for example, *My brother isn't here at the moment. He'll be back in an hour.* Compare with **object pronoun**.

SUBJUNCTIVE a verb form used in certain circumstances to indicate some sort of feeling, or to show doubt about whether something will happen or whether something is true. It is only used occasionally in modern English, for example, *If I were you, I wouldn't bother; So be it.*

SUPERLATIVE an adjective or adverb with -est on the end of it or *most* or *least* in front of it that is used to compare people, things or actions, for example, *thinnest, most quickly, least interesting*.

SYLLABLE consonant+vowel units that make up the sounds of a word, for example, *ca-the-dral* (3 syllables), *im-po-ssi-ble* (4 syllables).

TENSE the form of a verb which shows whether you are referring to the past, present or future.

TRANSITIVE VERB a type of verb that takes a direct object, for example, *to spend, to raise, to waste*. Compare with **intransitive verb**.

VERB a 'doing' word which describes what someone or something does, is, or what happens to them, for example, *be, sing, live*.

VOWEL one of the letters *a, e, i, o* or *u*. Compare with **consonant**.

Nouns

What is a noun?
A **noun** is a 'naming' word for a living being, thing or idea, for example,
woman, *desk*, *happiness*, *Andrew*.

Using nouns

➤ In Spanish, all nouns are either <u>masculine</u> or <u>feminine</u>. This is called their <u>gender</u>. Even words for things have a gender.

➤ Whenever you are using a noun, you need to know whether it is masculine or feminine as this affects the form of other words used with it, such as:

- adjectives that describe it
- articles (such as **el** or **una**) that go before it

➡ *For more information on **Articles** and **Adjectives**, see pages 10 and 19.*

➤ You can find information about gender by looking the word up in a dictionary. When you come across a new noun, always learn the word for *the* or *a* that goes with it to help you remember its gender.

- **el** or **un** before a noun usually tells you it is masculine
- **la** or **una** before a noun tells you it is feminine

➡ *For exceptions to these rules, see **Articles**, page 11.*

➤ We refer to something as <u>singular</u> when we are talking about just one of them, and as <u>plural</u> when we are talking about more than one. The singular is the form of the noun you will usually find when you look a noun up in the dictionary. As in English, nouns in Spanish change their form in the plural.

➤ Adjectives, articles and pronouns are also affected by whether a noun is singular or plural.

Tip
Remember that you have to use the right word for *the*, *a* and so on according to the gender of the Spanish noun.

2 Nouns

Gender

1 Nouns referring to people

➤ Most nouns referring to men and boys are <u>masculine</u>.

el hombre	the man
el rey	the king

➤ Most nouns referring to women and girls are <u>feminine</u>.

la mujer	the woman
la reina	the queen

➤ When the same word is used to refer to either men/boys or women/girls, its gender usually changes depending on the sex of the person it refers to.

el estudiante	the (male) student
la estudiante	the (female) student
el belga	the Belgian (man)
la belga	the Belgian (woman)

Grammar Extra!

Some words for people have only <u>one</u> possible gender, whether they refer to a male or a female.

la persona	the (male *or* female) person
la víctima	the (male *or* female) victim

➤ In English, we can sometimes make a word masculine or feminine by changing the ending, for example, English<u>man</u> and English<u>woman</u> or *prince* and *princess*. In Spanish, very often the ending of a noun changes depending on whether it refers to a man or a woman.

el camarero	the waiter
la camarera	the waitress
el empleado	the employee (*male*)
la empleada	the employee (*female*)
el inglés	the Englishman
la inglesa	the Englishwoman

> **Tip**
>
> Note that a noun ending in **-o** is usually <u>masculine</u>, and a noun ending in **-a** is usually <u>feminine</u>.

⇨ *For more information on **Masculine and feminine forms of words**, see page 5.*

2 Nouns referring to animals

➤ In English we can choose between words like *bull* or *cow*, depending on the sex of the animal. In Spanish too there are sometimes separate words for male and female animals.

el toro	the bull
la vaca	the cow

➤ Sometimes, the same word with different endings is used for male and female animals.

el perr<u>o</u>	the (male) dog
la perr<u>a</u>	the (female) dog, bitch
el gat<u>o</u>	the (male) cat
la gat<u>a</u>	the (female) cat

> **Tip**
>
> When you do not know or care what sex the animal is, you can usually use the masculine form as a general word.

➤ Words for other animals don't change according to the sex of the animal. Just learn the Spanish word with its gender, which is always the same.

el sapo	the toad
el hámster	the hamster
la cobaya	the guinea pig
la tortuga	the tortoise

3 Nouns referring to things

➤ In English, we call all things – for example, *table, car, book, apple* – 'it'. In Spanish, however, things are either <u>masculine</u> or <u>feminine</u>. As things don't divide into sexes the way humans and animals do, there are no physical clues to help you with their gender in Spanish. Try to learn the gender as you learn the word.

➤ There are lots of rules to help you. Certain endings are usually found on masculine nouns, while other endings are usually found on feminine nouns.

4 Nouns

➤ The following ending is usually found on __masculine nouns__.

Masculine ending	Examples
-o	el **libro** the book el **periódico** the newspaper BUT: la **mano** the hand la **foto** the photo la **moto** the motorbike la **radio** the radio (*although in parts of Latin America, it is* el **radio**)

➤ The following types of word are also masculine.

- names of the days of the week and the months of the year

  Te veré el lunes.   I'll see you on Monday.

- the names of languages

  el inglés   English

  el español   Spanish

  Estudio el español.   I'm studying Spanish.

- the names of rivers, mountains and seas

  el Ebro   the Ebro

  el Everest   Everest

  el Atlántico   the Atlantic

➤ The following endings are usually found on __feminine nouns__.

Feminine ending	Examples
-a	la **casa** the house la **cara** the face BUT: el **día** the day el **mapa** the map el **planeta** the planet el **tranvía** the streetcar and many words ending in **-ma** (el **problema** the problem, el **programa** the program, el **sistema** the system, el **clima** the climate)
-ción -sión	la **lección** the lesson la **estación** the station la **expresión** the expression
-dad -tad -tud	la **ciudad** the city la **libertad** freedom la **multitud** the crowd

For further explanation of grammatical terms, please see pages viii-xii.

Grammar Extra!

Some words have different meanings depending on whether they are masculine or feminine.

Masculine	Meaning	Feminine	Meaning
el capital	the capital (meaning *money*)	la capital	the capital (meaning *city*)
el cometa	the comet	la cometa	the kite
el cura	the priest	la cura	the cure
el guía	the guide (*man*)	la guía	the guidebook; the guide (*woman*)

Invirtieron mucho capital.   They invested a lot of capital.
Viven en la capital.   They live in the capital.

4 Masculine and feminine forms of words

➤ Like English, Spanish sometimes has very different words for males and females.

el hombre	the man
la mujer	the woman
el rey	the king
la reina	the queen

➤ Many Spanish words can be used to talk about men or women simply by changing the ending. For example, if the word for the male ends in -o, you can almost always make it feminine by changing the -o to -a.

el amigo	the (male) friend
la amiga	the (female) friend
el hermano	the brother
la hermana	the sister
el empleado	the (male) employee
la empleada	the (female) employee
el viudo	the widower
la viuda	the widow

Note that some words referring to people end in -a in the masculine as well as in the feminine. Only the article (el or la, un or una) can tell you what gender the noun is.

el dentista	the (male) dentist
la dentista	the (female) dentist
el deportista	the sportsman
la deportista	the sportswoman

6 Nouns

➤ Many masculine nouns ending in a consonant (any letter other than a vowel) become feminine by adding an **-a**.

el español	the Spanish man
la española	the Spanish woman
el profesor	the (male) teacher
la profesora	the (female) teacher

> ## Tip
>
> If the last vowel of the masculine word has an accent, this is dropped in the feminine form.
>
> | | |
> |---|---|
> | **un** inglés | an Englishman |
> | **una** inglesa | an Englishwoman |
> | **un** francés | a Frenchman |
> | **una** francesa | a Frenchwoman |
>
> ⇨ *For more information about **Spelling** and **Stress**, see pages 196 and 200.*

Key points

✔ The ending of a Spanish word often helps you work out its gender: for instance, if a word ends in **-o**, it is probably masculine; if it ends in **-a**, it is probably feminine.

✔ These endings generally mean that the noun is feminine: **-ción, -sión, -dad, -tad, -tud**

✔ Days of the week and months of the year are masculine. So are languages, mountains and seas.

✔ You can change the ending of some nouns from **-o** to **-a** to make a masculine noun feminine.

Forming plurals

1 Plurals ending in -s and -es

➤ In English we usually make nouns plural by adding an -s to the end (*garden* → *gardens*; *house* → *houses*), although we do have some nouns which are <u>irregular</u> and do not follow this pattern (*mouse* → *mice*; *child* → *children*).

Tip

Remember that you have to use **los** (for <u>masculine nouns</u>) or **las** (for <u>feminine nouns</u>) with plural nouns in Spanish. Any adjective that goes with the noun also has to agree with it, as does any pronoun that replaces it.

⇨ *For more information on* **Articles**, **Adjectives** *and* **Pronouns**, *see pages* 10, 19 *and* 41.

➤ To form the plural in Spanish, add **-s** to most nouns ending in a vowel (*a, e, i, o* or *u*) which doesn't have an accent.

el libro	the book
<u>los</u> **libro**<u>s</u>	the books
el hombre	the man
<u>los</u> **hombre**<u>s</u>	the men
la profesora	the (female) teacher
<u>las</u> **profesora**<u>s</u>	the (female) teachers

➤ Add **-es** to singular nouns ending in a consonant (any letter other than a vowel).

el profesor	the (male) teacher
<u>los</u> **profesor**<u>es</u>	the (male/male and female) teachers
la ciudad	the town/city
<u>las</u> **ciudad**<u>es</u>	the towns/cities

ℹ Note that some foreign words (that is, words which have come from another language, such as English) ending in a consonant just add **-s**.

el disc-jockey	the DJ
<u>los</u> **disc-jockey**<u>s</u>	the DJs

8 Nouns

➤ Words ending in **-s** which have an unstressed final vowel do not change in the plural.

el paraguas	the umbrella
los paraguas	the umbrellas
el lunes	(on) Monday
los lunes	(on) Mondays

⇨ *For more information on* **Stress**, *see page 200.*

➤ Most singular nouns ending in an accented vowel add **-s** in the plural, but those ending in **í** (and sometimes **ú**) usually have two possible plurals: with **-es** or **-s**.

el café	the café
<u>los</u> **café<u>s</u>**	the cafés
el sofá	the sofa
<u>los</u> **sofá<u>s</u>**	the sofas
el jabalí	the boar
<u>los</u> **jabalí<u>es</u>** *or* **jabalí<u>s</u>**	the boars

---

Grammar Extra!

When nouns are made up of two separate words, they are called <u>compound nouns</u>, for example, **el abrelatas** (meaning *the can opener*) and **el hombre rana** (meaning *the frogman*). Some of these nouns don't change in the plural, for example, **los abrelatas**, while others do, for example, **los hombre<u>s</u> rana**. It is always best to check in a dictionary to see what the plural is.

---

2 Spelling changes with plurals ending in -es

➤ Singular nouns which end in an accented vowel and either **-n** or **-s** drop the accent in the plural.

la canció<u>n</u>	the song
las cancio<u>nes</u>	the songs
el autobú<u>s</u>	the bus
los autobu<u>ses</u>	the buses

➤ Singular nouns of more than one syllable which end in **-en** and don't already have an accent, add one in the plural.

el examen	the exam
los exá<u>menes</u>	the exams

el joven	the youth
los jóvenes	young people

➤ Singular nouns ending in **-z** change to **-c** in the plural.

la luz	the light
las lu<u>ces</u>	the lights
la vez	the times
las ve<u>ces</u>	the times

⇨ *For further information on **Spelling** and **Stress**, see pages 196 and 200.*

3 Plural versus singular

➤ A few words relating to clothing that are plural in English can be singular in Spanish.

<u>una</u> **braga**	(a pair of) panties
<u>un</u> **slip**	(a pair of) underpants
<u>un</u> **pantalón**	(a pair of) pants

➤ A few common words behave differently in Spanish from the way they behave in English.

un mueble	a piece of furniture
unos muebles	some furniture
una noticia	a piece of news
unas noticias	some news
un consejo	a piece of advice
unos consejos	some advice

Key points

✔ Add **-s** to form the plural of a noun ending in an unaccented vowel.

✔ Add **-es** to form the plural of most nouns ending in a consonant.

✔ Drop the accent when adding plural **-es** to nouns ending in an accented vowel + **-n** or **-s**.

✔ Add an accent when adding plural **-es** to words of more than one syllable ending in **-en**.

✔ Change **-z** to **-c** when forming the plural of words like **luz**.

✔ A few common words are plural in English but not in Spanish.

Articles

> **What is an article?**
> In English, an **article** is one of the words *the*, *a*, and *an* which is given in front of a noun.

Different types of article

➤ There are two types of article:

- the <u>definite</u> article: *the* in English. This is used to identify a particular thing or person.

    I'm going to <u>the</u> supermarket.
    That's <u>the</u> woman I was talking to.

- the <u>indefinite</u> article: *a* or *an* in English, whose plural is *some* or *any* (or no word at all). This is used to refer to something unspecific, or that you do not really know about.

    Is there <u>a</u> supermarket near here?
    I need <u>a</u> day off.

For further explanation of grammatical terms, please see pages viii-xii.

The definite article: el, la, los and las

1 The basic rules

➤ In English, there is only <u>one</u> definite article: *the*. In Spanish, you have to choose between <u>four</u> definite articles: **el**, **la**, **los** and **las**. Which one you choose depends on the noun which follows.

➤ In Spanish, all nouns (including words for things) are either masculine or feminine – this is called their <u>gender</u>. And just as in English they can also be either singular or plural. You must bear this in mind when deciding which Spanish word to use for *the*.

⇨ *For more information on **Nouns**, see page 1.*

➤ **el** is used before <u>masculine singular nouns</u>.

<u>el</u> niño	the boy
<u>el</u> periódico	the newspaper

➤ **la** is used before <u>feminine singular nouns</u>.

<u>la</u> niña	the girl
<u>la</u> revista	the magazine

> ### Tip
> To help you speak and write correct Spanish, always learn the <u>article</u> or the <u>gender</u> together with the noun when learning vocabulary. A good dictionary will also give you this information.

➤ **los** and **las** are used before <u>plural nouns</u>. **los** is used with masculine plural words, and **las** is used with feminine plural words.

<u>los</u> niños	the boys
<u>las</u> niñas	the girls
<u>los</u> periódicos	the newspapers
<u>las</u> revistas	the magazines

i Note that you use **el** instead of **la** immediately before a feminine singular word beginning with **a** or **ha** when the stress falls on the beginning of the word. This is because **la** sounds wrong before the '*a*' sound. <u>BUT</u> if you add an adjective in front of the noun, you use **la** instead, since the two '*a*' sounds do not come next to each other.

<u>el</u> agua helada	the icy water
<u>el</u> hacha afilada	the sharp ax
<u>la</u> misma agua	the same water
<u>la</u> mejor hacha	the best ax

2 a and de with the definite article

➤ If **a** is followed by **el**, the two words become **al**.

al cine	to the movies
al empleado	to the employee
al hospital	to the hospital
Vio **al** camarero	He saw the waiter.

➤ If **de** is followed by **el**, the two words become **del**.

del departamento	of/from the department
del autor	of/from the author
del presidente	of/from the president

3 Using the definite article

➤ **el**, **la**, **los** and **las** are often used in Spanish in the same way as *the* is used in English. However, there are some cases where the article is used in Spanish but not in English.

➤ The definite article <u>IS</u> used in Spanish:

- when talking about people, animals and things in a general way

Me gustan los animales.	I like animals.
Están subiendo los precios.	Prices are going up.
Me gusta el chocolate.	I like chocolate.
No me gusta el café.	I don't like coffee.
El azúcar es dulce.	Sugar is sweet.

- when talking about abstract qualities, for example, *time, hope, darkness, violence*

El tiempo es oro.	Time is money.
Admiro la sinceridad en la gente.	I admire honesty in people.

[i] Note that the definite article is <u>NOT</u> used in certain set phrases consisting of **tener** and a noun or after certain prepositions.

tener hambre	to be hungry	(*literally: to have hunger*)
sin duda	no doubt	(*literally: without doubt*)
con cuidado	carefully	(*literally: with care*)

⇨ *For more information on **Prepositions**, see page 178.*

- when talking about colors

El azul es mi color favorito.   Blue is my favorite color.

- when talking about parts of the body – you do not use *my, your, his* and so on as you would in English

Tiene los ojos verdes.   He's got green eyes.
No puedo mover las piernas.   I can't move my legs.

i Note that possession is often shown by a personal pronoun in Spanish.

La cabeza me da vueltas.   My head is spinning.
Lávate las manos.   Wash your hands.

⇨ *For more information on **Personal pronouns**, see page 42.*

- when using someone's title – for example, *Doctor, Mr* – but talking ABOUT someone rather than to them

El doctor Vidal no está.   Dr Vidal isn't here.
El señor Pelayo vive aquí.   Mr Pelayo lives here.

- when talking about institutions, such as school or church

en el colegio   at school
en la universidad   at college
en la iglesia   at church
en el hospital   in the hospital
en la cárcel   in prison

- when talking about meals, games or sports

La cena es a las nueve.   Dinner is at nine o'clock.
Me gusta el tenis.   I like tennis.
No me gusta el ajedrez.   I don't like chess.

- when talking about days of the week and dates, where we use the preposition *on* in English

Te veo el lunes.   I'll see you on Monday.
Los lunes tenemos muchos deberes.   We have a lot of homework on Mondays.
Nací el 17 de marzo.   I was born on 17 March.

- when talking about the time

Es la una.   It's one o'clock.
Son las tres.   It's three o'clock.
Son las cuatro y media.   It's half past four.

- when talking about prices and rates

Cuestan dos dólares <u>la</u> docena.   They cost two dollars a dozen.
Cobra 200 pesos <u>la</u> hora.   He charges 200 pesos an hour.

- with an adjective on its own to specify which one or ones

A él le gustan estas cortinas   He likes these curtains but I'm
pero yo voy a comprar <u>las rojas</u>.   going to buy <u>the red ones</u>.

i The adjective must agree with the noun it refers to.

Key points

✔ Before masculine singular nouns → use **el**.
✔ Before feminine singular nouns → use **la**.
✔ Before feminine singular nouns starting with stressed **a** or **ha** → use **el**.
✔ Before masculine plural nouns → use **los**.
✔ Before feminine plural nouns → use **las**.
✔ a + el → al
✔ de + el → del
✔ There are some important cases when you would use a definite article in Spanish when you wouldn't in English; for example, when talking about:
  - things in a general way
  - abstract qualities
  - colors
  - parts of the body
  - someone with a title in front of their name
  - institutions
  - meals, games or sports
  - the time, days of the week and dates (*using the preposition <u>on</u> in English*)
  - prices and rates
  - with an adjective on its own to mean *the red one, the thick ones* and so on

---

The indefinite article: un, una, unos and unas

1 The basic rules

➤ In English, the indefinite article is *a*, which changes to *an* when it comes before a vowel or a vowel sound, for example, *an apple*. In the plural, we use *some* or *any*.

➤ In Spanish, you have to choose between <u>four</u> indefinite articles: **un**, **una**, **unos** and **unas**. Which one you choose depends on the noun that follows.

➤ In Spanish, all nouns (including words for things) are either masculine or feminine – this is called their <u>gender</u>. And, just as in English, they can also be either singular or plural. You must bear this in mind when deciding which Spanish word to use for *a*.

➡ *For more information on **Nouns**, see page 1.*

➤ **un** is used before <u>masculine singular nouns</u>.

un niño	a boy
un periódico	a newspaper

➤ **una** is used before <u>feminine singular nouns</u>.

una niña	a girl
una revista	a magazine

➤ **unos** is used before <u>masculine plural nouns</u>.

unos niños	some boys
unos periódicos	some newspapers

➤ **unas** is used before <u>feminine plural nouns</u>.

unas niñas	some girls
unas revistas	some magazines

ℹ️ Note that you use **un** instead of **una** immediately before a feminine singular word beginning with **a** or **ha** when the stress falls on the beginning of the word. This is because **una** sounds wrong before the 'a' sound. <u>BUT</u> if you add an adjective in front of the noun, you use **una** instead, since the two 'a' sounds do not come next to each other.

un ave migratoria	a migratory bird
una extensa área	a wide area

2 Using the indefinite article

➤ The indefinite article is often used in Spanish in the same way as it is in English. However, there are some cases where the article is not used in Spanish but is in English, and vice versa.

➤ The indefinite article is <u>NOT</u> used in Spanish:

- when you say what someone's job is

Es profesor.	He's <u>a</u> teacher.
Mi madre es enfermera.	My mother is <u>a</u> nurse.

- after **tener**, **buscar**, or **llevar (puesto)** when you are only likely *to have*, *be looking for* or *be wearing* one of the items in question

No tengo coche.	I don't have <u>a</u> car.
¿Llevaba sombrero?	Was he wearing <u>a</u> hat?

[i] Note that when you use an adjective to describe the noun, you <u>DO</u> use an article in Spanish too.

Es <u>un</u> buen médico.	He's <u>a</u> good doctor.
Tiene <u>una</u> novia española.	He has a Spanish girlfriend.
Busca <u>un</u> piso pequeño.	He's looking for a little apartment.

➤ The indefinite article is <u>NOT</u> used in Spanish with the words **otro**, **cierto**, **cien**, **mil**, **sin**, and **qué**.

otro libro	another book
cierta calle	<u>a</u> certain street
cien soldados	<u>a</u> hundred soldiers
mil años	<u>a</u> thousand years
sin casa	without <u>a</u> house
¡Qué sorpresa!	What <u>a</u> surprise!

➤ The indefinite article <u>IS</u> used in Spanish but <u>NOT</u> in English when an abstract noun, such as **inteligencia** (meaning *intelligence*) or **tiempo** (meaning *time*) has an adjective with it.

Posee <u>una</u> gran inteligencia.	He possesses great intelligence.

Key points

✔ Before masculine singular nouns → use **un**.

✔ Before feminine singular nouns → use **una**.

✔ Before feminine singular nouns starting with stressed **a** or **ha** → use **un**.

✔ Before masculine plural nouns → use **unos**.

✔ Before feminine plural nouns → use **unas**.

✔ You do not use an indefinite article in Spanish for saying what someone's job is.

✔ You do not use an indefinite article in Spanish with the words **otro**, **cierto**, **cien**, **mil**, **sin**, and **qué**.

For further explanation of grammatical terms, please see pages viii-xii.

The article lo

➤ Unlike the other Spanish articles, and articles in English, **lo** is <u>NOT</u> used with a noun.

➤ **lo** can be used with a masculine singular adjective or past participle (the **-ado** and **-ido** forms of regular verbs) to form a noun.

<u>Lo único</u> que no me gusta …	The only thing I don't like …
Esto es <u>lo importante</u>.	That's the important thing.
<u>Lo bueno</u> de eso es que …	The good thing about it is that …
Sentimos mucho <u>lo ocurrido</u>.	We are very sorry about what happened.

⇨ *For more information on the **Past participle**, see page 115.*

➤ **lo** is also used in a number of very common phrases:

- **a lo mejor** — maybe, perhaps
  <u>A lo mejor</u> ha salido. — Perhaps he's gone out.

- **por lo menos** — at least
  Hubo <u>por lo menos</u> cincuenta heridos. — At least fifty people were injured.

- **por lo general** — generally
  <u>Por lo general</u> me acuesto temprano. — I generally go to bed early.

➤ **lo** can also be used with **que** to make **lo que** (meaning *what*).

Vi <u>lo que</u> pasó.	I saw what happened.
<u>Lo que</u> más me gusta es nadar.	What I like best is swimming.

Grammar Extra!

lo can be used with **de** followed by a noun phrase to refer back to something the speaker and listener both know about.

<u>Lo de tu hermano</u> me preocupa mucho.	<u>That business with your brother</u> worries me a lot.
<u>Lo de ayer</u> es mejor que lo olvides.	It would be best to forget <u>what happened yesterday.</u>

lo can be used with an adjective followed by **que** to emphasize how big/small/beautiful and so on something is or was. The adjective must agree with the noun it describes.

No sabíamos <u>lo pequeña que</u> era la casa.	We didn't know <u>how small</u> the house was.
No te imaginas <u>lo simpáticos que</u> son.	You can't imagine <u>how nice</u> they are.

lo can also be used in a similar way with an adverb followed by **que**.

Sé <u>lo mucho que</u> te gusta la música.	I know <u>how much</u> you like music.

Key points

✔ **lo** is classed as an article in Spanish, but is not used with nouns.

✔ You can use **lo** with a masculine adjective or past participle to form a noun.

✔ You also use **lo** in a number of common phrases.

✔ **lo que** can be used to mean *what* in English.

Adjectives

> **What is an adjective?**
> An **adjective** is a 'describing' word that tells you more about a person or thing, such as their appearance, color, size or other qualities, for example, *pretty*, *blue*, *big*.

Using adjectives

➤ Adjectives are words like *clever*, *expensive* and *silly* that tell you more about a noun (a living being, thing or idea). They can also tell you more about a pronoun, such as *he* or *they*. Adjectives are sometimes called 'describing words'. They can be used right next to a noun they are describing, or can be separated from the noun by a verb like *be*, *look*, *feel* and so on.

> a <u>clever</u> girl
> an <u>expensive</u> coat
> a <u>silly</u> idea
> He's just being <u>silly</u>.

➟ For more information on **Nouns** and **Pronouns**, see pages 1 and 41.

➤ In English, the only time an adjective changes its form is when you are making a comparison.

> She's <u>cleverer</u> than her brother.
> That's the <u>silliest</u> idea I've ever heard!

➤ In Spanish, however, most adjectives <u>agree</u> with what they are describing. This means that their endings change depending on whether the person or thing you are referring to is masculine or feminine, singular or plural.

> **un chico <u>rubio</u>**   a fair boy
> **una chica <u>rubia</u>**   a fair girl
> **unos chicos <u>rubios</u>**   some fair boys
> **unas chicas <u>rubias</u>**   some fair girls

➤ In English adjectives come <u>BEFORE</u> the noun they describe, but in Spanish you usually put them <u>AFTER</u> it.

> **una casa <u>blanca</u>**   a <u>white</u> house

➟ For more information on **Word order with adjectives**, see page 24.

Making adjectives agree

1 Forming feminine adjectives

➤ The form of the adjective shown in dictionaries is generally the masculine singular form. This means that you need to know how to change its form to make it agree with the person or thing it is describing.

➤ Adjectives ending in -o in the masculine change to -a for the feminine.

mi hermano <u>pequeño</u>	my little brother
mi hermana <u>pequeña</u>	my little sister

➤ Adjectives ending in any vowel other than -o (that is: *a, e, i* or *u*) or ending in a vowel with an accent on it do <u>NOT</u> change for the feminine.

el vestido <u>verde</u>	the green dress
la blusa <u>verde</u>	the green blouse
un pantalón <u>caqui</u>	some khaki pants
una camisa <u>caqui</u>	a khaki shirt
un médico <u>iraquí</u>	an Iraqi doctor
una familia <u>iraquí</u>	an Iraqi family

➤ Adjectives ending in a consonant (any letter other than a vowel) do <u>NOT</u> change for the feminine except in the following cases:

- Adjectives of nationality or place ending in a consonant add -a for the feminine. If there is an accent on the final vowel in the masculine, they lose this in the feminine.

un periódico <u>inglés</u>	an English newspaper
una revista <u>inglesa</u>	an English magazine
el equipo <u>francés</u>	the French team
la cocina <u>francesa</u>	French cooking
el vino <u>español</u>	Spanish wine
la lengua <u>española</u>	the Spanish language

ⓘ Note that these adjectives do not start with a capital letter in Spanish.

- Adjectives ending in -or in the masculine usually change to -ora for the feminine.

un niño <u>encantador</u>	a charming little boy
una niña <u>encantadora</u>	a charming little girl

[i] Note that a few adjectives ending in **-or** used in comparisons – such as **mejor** (meaning *better, best*), **peor** (meaning *worse, worst*), **mayor** (meaning *older, bigger*), **superior** (meaning *upper, top*), **inferior** (meaning *lower, inferior*) as well as **exterior** (meaning *outside, foreign*) and **posterior** (meaning *rear*) do not change in the feminine.

- Adjectives ending in **-án**, **-ón** and **-ín** in the masculine change to **-ana**, **-ona** and **-ina** (without an accent) in the feminine.

un gesto <u>burlón</u>	a mocking gesture
una sonrisa <u>burlona</u>	a mocking smile
un hombre <u>parlanchín</u>	a chatty man
una mujer <u>parlanchina</u>	a chatty woman

➤ Adjectives ending in a consonant but which do not fall into the above categories do <u>NOT</u> change in the feminine.

un chico <u>joven</u>	a young boy
una chica <u>joven</u>	a young girl
un final <u>feliz</u>	a happy ending
una infancia <u>feliz</u>	a happy childhood

2 Forming plural adjectives

➤ Adjectives ending in an unaccented vowel (*a, e, i, o* or *u*) in the singular add **-s** in the plural.

el <u>último</u> tren	the last train
los <u>últimos</u> trenes	the last trains
una casa <u>vieja</u>	an old house
unas casas <u>viejas</u>	some old houses
una chica muy <u>habladora</u>	a very chatty girl
unas chicas muy <u>habladoras</u>	some very chatty girls
una pintora <u>francesa</u>	a French (woman) painter
unas pintoras <u>francesas</u>	some French (women) painters
una mesa <u>verde</u>	a green table
unas mesas <u>verdes</u>	some green tables

➤ Adjectives ending in a consonant in the masculine or feminine singular add **-es** in the plural. If there is an accent on the <u>FINAL</u> syllable in the singular, they lose it in the plural.

un chico muy <u>hablador</u>	a very chatty boy
unos chicos muy <u>habladores</u>	some very chatty boys
un pintor <u>francés</u>	a French painter
unos pintores <u>franceses</u>	some French painters

un examen <u>fácil</u>	an easy exam
unos exámenes <u>fáciles</u>	some easy exams
la tendencia <u>actual</u>	the current trend
las tendencias <u>actuales</u>	the current trends

➤ **-z** at the end of a singular adjective changes to **-ces** in the plural.

un día <u>feliz</u>	a happy day
unos días <u>felices</u>	happy days

Tip

When an adjective describes a mixture of both masculine and feminine nouns, use the <u>masculine plural</u> form of the adjective.

El pan y la fruta son <u>baratos</u>. Bread and fruit are cheap.

Grammar Extra!

Adjectives ending in an accented vowel in the singular usually add **-es** in the plural.

un médico iran<u>í</u>	an Iranian doctor
unos médicos iran<u>íes</u>	some Iranian doctors

---

3 Invariable adjectives

➤ A small number of adjectives do not change in the feminine or plural. They are called <u>invariable</u> because their form <u>NEVER</u> changes, no matter what they are describing. These adjectives are often made up of more than one word – for example **azul marino** (meaning *navy blue*) – or come from the names of things – for example **naranja** (meaning *orange*).

las chaquetas <u>azul marino</u>	navy-blue jackets
los vestidos <u>naranja</u>	orange dresses

4 Short forms for adjectives

➤ The following adjectives drop the final **-o** before a <u>masculine singular noun</u>.

bueno	→	buen	→	un <u>buen</u> libro	a good book
malo	→	mal	→	<u>mal</u> tiempo	bad weather
alguno	→	algún	→	<u>algún</u> libro	some book
ninguno	→	ningún	→	<u>ningún</u> hombre	no man
uno	→	un	→	<u>un</u> día	one day
primero	→	primer	→	el <u>primer</u> hijo	the first child
tercero	→	tercer	→	el <u>tercer</u> hijo	the third child

For further explanation of grammatical terms, please see pages viii-xii.

[i] Note that the adjectives **alguno** and **ninguno** add accents when they are shortened to become **algún** and **ningún**.

➤ **grande** (meaning *big, great*) is shortened to **gran** before a <u>singular noun</u>.

un gran actor	a great actor
una gran sorpresa	a big surprise

➤ **ciento** (meaning *a hundred*) changes to **cien** before all <u>plural nouns</u> as well as before **mil** (meaning *thousand*) and **millones** (meaning *millions*).

cien años	a hundred years
cien millones	a hundred million

[i] Note that you use the form **ciento** before other numbers.

ciento tres	one hundred and three

➪ *For more information on **Numbers**, see page 206.*

Grammar Extra!

➤ **cualquiera** drops the final **a** before singular nouns.

<u>cualquier</u> **día**	any day
a <u>cualquier</u> **hora**	any time

Key points
✔ Most Spanish adjectives change their form according to whether the person or thing they are describing is masculine or feminine, singular or plural.
✔ In Spanish, adjectives usually go after the noun they describe.
✔ Don't forget to make adjectives agree with the person or thing they describe – they change for the feminine and plural forms:
un chico español
una chica española
unos chicos españoles
unas chicas españolas
✔ Some adjectives never change their form.
✔ Some adjectives drop the final -o before a masculine singular noun.
✔ **grande** and **ciento** also change before certain nouns.

Word order with adjectives

➤ When adjectives are used right beside the noun they are describing, they go BEFORE it in English. Spanish adjectives usually go AFTER the noun.

una corbata <u>azul</u>	a <u>blue</u> tie
una palabra <u>española</u>	a <u>Spanish</u> word
la página <u>siguiente</u>	the <u>following</u> page
la hora <u>exacta</u>	the <u>precise</u> time

➤ When you have two or more adjectives after the noun, you use **y** (meaning *and*) between the last two.

un hombre alto <u>y</u> delgado	a tall, slim man

➤ A number of types of Spanish adjectives go BEFORE the noun:

- demonstrative adjectives

  <u>este</u> sombrero   this hat

- possessive adjectives (**mi**, **tu**, **su** and so on)

  <u>mi</u> padre   my father

- numbers

  <u>tres</u> días   three days

- interrogative adjectives

  <u>¿qué</u> hombre?   which man?

- adjectives used in exclamations

  ¡<u>Qué</u> lástima!   What a pity!

- indefinite adjectives

  <u>cada</u> día   every day

- shortened adjectives

  <u>mal</u> tiempo   bad weather

➤ Some adjectives can go both <u>BEFORE</u> and <u>AFTER</u> the noun, but their meaning changes depending on where they go.

Adjective	Before Noun	Examples	After Noun	Examples
antiguo	former	**un antiguo colega** a former colleague	old, ancient	**la historia antigua** ancient history
diferente	various	**diferentes idiomas** various languages	different	**personas diferentes** different people
grande	great	**un gran pintor** a great painter	big	**una casa grande** a big house
medio	half	**medio melón** half a melon	average	**la nota media** the average mark
mismo	same	**la misma respuesta** the same answer	self, very, precisely	**yo mismo** myself **eso mismo** precisely that
nuevo	new	**mi nuevo coche** my new car (= *new to me*)	brand new	**unos zapatos nuevos** some (brand) new shoes
pobre	poor (= *wretched*)	**esa pobre mujer** that poor woman	poor (= *not rich*)	**un país pobre** a poor country
viejo	old (= *long-standing*)	**un viejo amigo** an old friend	old (= *aged*)	**esas toallas viejas** those old towels

Grammar Extra!

In Spanish, you can use **el/la/uno/una** with an adjective where in English you'd use *the tall one, a red one* and so on.

La camiseta verde está bien pero prefiero <u>la roja</u>.	The green T-shirt is OK but I prefer the red one.
¿Quieres una taza grande o <u>una pequeña</u>?	Would you like a big cup or a small one?
A él le gustan los edificios modernos pero yo prefiero <u>los antiguos</u>.	He likes modern buildings but I prefer old ones.

[i] The adjective must agree with the noun it refers to.

Key points

✔ Most Spanish adjectives go after the noun.
✔ Certain types of adjectives in Spanish go before the noun.
✔ Some adjectives can go before or after the noun – the meaning changes according to the position in the sentence.

Comparatives and superlatives of adjectives

1 Making comparisons using comparative adjectives

> **What is a comparative adjective?**
> A **comparative adjective** in English is one with -er on the end of it or more or less in front of it, that is used to compare people or things, for example, cleverer, less important, more beautiful.

➤ In Spanish, to say something is *cheaper, more expensive* and so on, you use **más** (meaning *more*) before the adjective.

Esta bicicleta es <u>más barata</u>.	This bicycle is cheaper.
La verde es <u>más cara</u>.	The green one is more expensive.

➤ To say something is *less expensive, less beautiful* and so on, you use **menos** (meaning *less*) before the adjective.

La verde es <u>menos cara</u>.	The green one is less expensive.

➤ To introduce the person or thing you are making the comparison with, use **que** (meaning *than*).

Es <u>más</u> alto <u>que</u> yo.	He's taller than me.
La otra bicicleta es <u>más</u> cara <u>que</u> esta.	The other bicycle is more expensive than this one.
Esta bicicleta es <u>menos</u> cara <u>que</u> la otra.	This bicycle is less expensive than the other one.

Grammar Extra!

When *than* in English is followed by a verbal construction, use <u>de lo que</u> rather than **que** alone.

Está <u>más</u> cansada <u>de lo que</u> parece.	She is more tired than she seems.

---

2 Making comparisons using superlative adjectives

> **What is a superlative adjective?**
> A **superlative adjective** in English is one with -est on the end of it or *most* or *least* in front of it, that is used to compare people or things, for example, thinnest, most beautiful, least interesting.

➤ In Spanish, to say something is *the cheapest*, *the most expensive* and so on, you use **el/la/los/las** (+ noun) + **más** + adjective.

el caballo **más viejo**	the oldest horse
la casa **más pequeña**	the smallest house
los hoteles **más baratos**	the cheapest hotels
las manzanas **más caras**	the most expensive apples
¿Quién es **el más alto**?	Who's the tallest?

➤ To say something is *the least expensive*, *the least intelligent* and so on, you use **el/la/los/las** (+ noun) + **menos** + adjective.

el hombre **menos simpático**	the least likeable man
la niña **menos habladora**	the least talkative girl
los cuadros **menos bonitos**	the least attractive paintings
las empleadas **menos trabajadoras**	the least hardworking (female) employees
¿Quién es **el menos trabajador**?	Who's the least hardworking?

Típ

In phrases like *the cleverest girl in the school* and *the tallest man in the world*, you use **de** to translate *in*.

el hombre más alto **del** mundo   the tallest man **in** the world

---

3 | **Irregular comparatives and superlatives**

➤ Just as English has some irregular comparative and superlative forms – *better* instead of '*more good*', and *worst* instead of '*most bad*' – Spanish also has a few irregular forms.

Adjective	Meaning	Comparative	Meaning	Superlative	Meaning
bueno	good	**mejor**	better	**el mejor**	the best
malo	bad	**peor**	worse	**el peor**	the worst
grande	big	**mayor**	older	**el mayor**	the oldest
pequeño	small	**menor**	younger	**el menor**	the youngest

Este es **mejor** que el otro.	This one is better than the other one.
Es **el mejor** de todos.	It's the best of the lot.
Hoy me siento **peor**.	I feel worse today.
la peor alumna de la clase	the worst student in the class

ℹ️ Note that **mejor**, **peor**, **mayor** and **menor** don't change their endings in the feminine. In the plural, they become **mejores**, **peores**, **mayores** and **menores**. Don't forget to use **el**, **la**, **los** or **las** as appropriate, depending on whether the person or thing described is masculine or feminine, singular or plural.

Tip

más grande and **más pequeño** are used mainly to talk about the actual size of something.

Este plato es <u>más grande</u> que aquel.	This plate is bigger than that one.
Mi casa es <u>más pequeña</u> que la tuya.	My house is smaller than yours.

mayor and **menor** are used mainly to talk about age.

mis hermanos <u>mayores</u>	my older brothers
la hija <u>menor</u>	the youngest daughter

---

4 Other ways of making comparisons

➤ To say *as ... as* (for example, *as pretty as, not as pretty as*) you use **tan ... como** in Spanish.

Pedro es <u>tan</u> alto <u>como</u> Miguel.	Pedro is as tall as Miguel.
No es <u>tan</u> guapa <u>como</u> su madre.	She isn't as pretty as her mother.
No es <u>tan</u> grande <u>como</u> yo creía.	It isn't as big as I thought.

Grammar Extra!

You use **tanto** with a noun rather than **tan** with an adjective in some expressions. This is because in Spanish you would use a noun where in English we would use an adjective.

Pablo tiene <u>tanto</u> miedo <u>como</u> yo.	Pablo is as frightened as I am.
Yo no tengo <u>tanta</u> hambre <u>como</u> tú.	I'm not as hungry as you are.

➤ To make an adjective stronger, you can use **muy** (meaning *very*).

Este libro es <u>muy</u> interesante.	This book is very interesting.

For further explanation of grammatical terms, please see pages viii-xii.

Grammar Extra!

For even more emphasis, you can add **-ísimo** (meaning *really, extremely*) to the end of an adjective. Take off the final vowel if the adjective already ends in one. For example, **delgado** (meaning *thin*) becomes **delgadísimo** (meaning *really thin*).

Se ha comprado un coche <u>carísimo</u>.	He's bought himself a really expensive car.
Está <u>delgadísima</u>.	She's looking really thin.

If you add **-ísimo**, you need to take off any other accent. For example, **fácil** (meaning *easy*) becomes **facilísimo** (meaning *extremely easy*) and **rápido** (meaning *fast*) becomes **rapidísimo** (meaning *extremely fast*).

Es <u>facilísimo</u> de hacer.	It's really easy to make.
un coche <u>rapidísimo</u>	an extremely fast car

When the adjective ends in **-co**, **-go** or **-z**, spelling changes are required to keep the same sound. For example, **rico** (meaning *rich*) becomes **riquísimo** (meaning *extremely rich*) and **feroz** (meaning *fierce*) becomes **ferocísimo** (meaning *extremely fierce*).

Se hizo <u>riquísimo</u>.	He became extremely rich.
un tigre <u>ferocísimo</u>	an extremely fierce tiger

⇨ *For more information on **Spelling** and **Stress**, see pages 196 and 200.*

Key points

✔ Comparative adjectives in Spanish are formed by:
  - **más** + adjective + **que**
  - **menos** + adjective + **que**

✔ Superlative adjectives in Spanish are formed by:
  - **el/la/los/las** + **más** + adjective
  - **el/la/los/las** + **menos** + adjective

✔ There are a few irregular comparative and superlative forms in Spanish.

✔ You can use **tan ... como** to say *as ... as*.

✔ To make an adjective stronger, use **muy**.

Demonstrative adjectives

> **What is a demonstrative adjective?**
> A **demonstrative adjective** is one of the words *this, that, these* and *those* used with a noun in English to point out a particular thing or person, for example, *this* woman, *that* dog.

1 Using demonstrative adjectives

➤ Just as in English, Spanish demonstrative adjectives go <u>BEFORE</u> the noun. Like other adjectives in Spanish, they have to change for the feminine and plural forms.

	Masculine	Feminine	Meaning
Singular	este	esta	this
	ese	esa	that (*close by*)
	aquel	aquella	that (*further away*)
Plural	estos	estas	these
	esos	esas	those (*close by*)
	aquellos	aquellas	those (*further away*)

➤ Use **este/esta/estos/estas** (meaning *this/these*) to talk about things and people that are near <u>you</u>.

<u>Este</u> bolígrafo no escribe.	This pen isn't working.
Me he comprado <u>estos</u> libros.	I've bought these books.

➤ Use **ese/esa/esos/esas** and **aquel/aquella/aquellos/aquellas** (meaning *that/those*) to talk about things that are further away.

<u>Esa</u> revista es muy mala.	That magazine is very bad.
¿Conoces a <u>esos</u> señores?	Do you know those gentlemen?
No le gusta <u>aquella</u> muñeca.	She doesn't like that doll.
Siga usted hasta <u>aquellos</u> árboles.	Carry on until you reach those trees (over there).

2 ese or aquel?

➤ In English we use *that* and *those* to talk about anything that is not close by, but in Spanish you need to be a bit more precise.

➤ Use **ese/esa/esos/esas**:

- to talk about things and people that are nearer to the person you are talking to than to you

ese papel en el que escribes	that paper you're writing on
¿Por qué te has puesto **esas** medias?	Why are you wearing those tights?

- to talk about things and people that aren't very far away

No me gustan **esos** cuadros.	I don't like those pictures.

➤ Use **aquel/aquella/aquellos/aquellas** to talk about things that are further away

Me gusta más **aquella** mesa.	I prefer that table (over there).

Grammar Extra!

You should use **ese/esa/esos/esas** when you are talking about a definite date, month or year.

¿1999? No me acuerdo de dónde pasamos las vacaciones **ese año.	1999? I can't remember where we went on vacation that year.

You should use **aquel/aquella/aquellos/aquellas** when you are talking about something in the past and not mentioning a definite date.

aquellas vacaciones que pasamos en Francia	those vacations we had in France

---

Key points

✔ <u>this</u> + noun = **este/esta** + noun

✔ <u>these</u> + noun = **estos/estas** + noun

✔ <u>that</u> + noun = **ese/esa** + noun (*when the object is not far away from you or the person you're talking to*)

✔ <u>that</u> + noun = **aquel/aquella** + noun (*when the object is more distant*)

✔ <u>those</u> + noun = **esos/esas** + noun (*when the objects are not far away from you or the person you're talking to*)

✔ <u>those</u> + noun = **aquellos/aquellas** + noun (*when the objects are more distant*)

Interrogative adjectives

> **What is an interrogative adjective?**
> An **interrogative adjective** is one of the question words and expressions used with a noun such as *which, what, how much* and *how many*; for example, *Which shirt are you going to wear?; How much time have we got?*

➤ In Spanish the interrogative adjectives are **qué** (meaning *which* or *what*) and **cuánto/cuánta/cuántos/cuántas** (meaning *how much/how many*). Note that like all other Spanish question words, **qué** and **cuánto** have accents on them.

➤ **¿qué?** (meaning *which?* or *what?*) doesn't change for the feminine and plural forms.

¿Qué libro te gusta más?	Which book do you like best?
¿Qué clase de diccionario necesitas?	What kind of dictionary do you need?
¿Qué instrumentos tocas?	What instruments do you play?
¿Qué ofertas has recibido?	What offers have you received?

➤ **¿cuánto?** means the same as *how much?* in English. It changes to **¿cuánta?** in the feminine form.

¿Cuánto dinero te queda?	How much money have you got left?
¿Cuánta lluvia ha caído?	How much rain have we had?

[*i*] Note that with **gente** (meaning *people*), which is a feminine singular noun, **cuánta** must be used.

¿Cuánta gente ha venido?	How many people came?

➤ **¿cuántos?** means the same as *how many?* in English. It changes to **¿cuántas?** in the feminine plural.

¿Cuántos bolígrafos quieres?	How many pens would you like?
¿Cuántas personas van a venir?	How many people are coming?

> *Tip*
> Don't forget to add the opening upside-down question mark in Spanish questions.

Grammar Extra!

In English we can say, *Tell me what time it is*, *He asked me how much sugar there was* and *I don't know which dress to choose* to express doubt, report a question, or ask a question in a roundabout or indirect way. In Spanish you can use **qué** and **cuánto/cuánta/cuántos/cuántas** in the same way.

Dime <u>qué</u> hora es.	Tell me what time it is.
Me preguntó <u>cuánto</u> azúcar había.	He asked me how much sugar there was.
No sé <u>qué</u> vestido escoger.	I don't know which dress to choose.
No sé a <u>qué</u> hora llegó.	I don't know what time she arrived.
Dime <u>cuántas</u> postales quieres.	Tell me how many postcards you'd like.

Adjectives used in exclamations

➤ In Spanish **¡qué...!** is often used where we might say *What a ...!* in English.

¡Qué lástima!	What a pity!
¡Qué sorpresa!	What a surprise!

> *Tip*
>
> Don't forget to add the opening upside-down exclamation mark in Spanish exclamations.

Grammar Extra!

¡qué...! combines with **tan** or **más** and an adjective in Spanish to mean *What (a) ...!* in English.

¡Qué día tan *or* **más bonito!**	What a lovely day!
¡Qué tiempo tan *or* **más malo!**	What awful weather!
¡Qué pasteles tan *or* **más ricos!**	What delicious cakes!

In Spanish **cuánto/cuánta/cuántos/cuántas** can be used to mean *What a lot of ...!* in English.

¡Cuánto dinero!	What a lot of money!
¡Cuánta gente!	What a lot of people!
¡Cuántos autobuses!	What a lot of buses!
¡Cuánto tiempo!	What a long time!

Possessive adjectives (1)

> **What is a possessive adjective?**
> In English a **possessive adjective** is one of the words *my, your, his, her, its, our* or *their* used with a noun to show that one person or thing belongs to another.

➤ Like other adjectives in Spanish, possessive adjectives have to change for the feminine and plural forms.

Singular		Plural		Meaning
masculine	feminine	masculine	feminine	
mi	mi	mis	mis	my
tu	tu	tus	tus	your (*belonging to someone you address as* **tú**)
su	su	sus	sus	his; her; its; your (*belonging to someone you address as* **usted**)
nuestro	nuestra	nuestros	nuestras	our
vuestro	vuestra	vuestros	vuestras	your (*belonging to people you address as* **vosotros/vosotras**)
su	su	sus	sus	their; your (*belonging to people you address as* **ustedes**)

⇨ For more information on **Ways of saying 'you' in Spanish**, see page 44.

¿Dónde está <u>tu</u> hermana?	Where's your sister?
José ha perdido <u>su</u> cartera.	José has lost his wallet.
¿Dónde están <u>nuestros</u> pasaportes?	Where are our passports?
¿Por qué no traéis a <u>vuestros</u> hijos?	Why don't you bring your children?
Mis tíos están vendiendo <u>su</u> casa.	My uncle and aunt are selling their house.

> *Tip*
>
> Possessive adjectives agree with what they describe <u>NOT</u> with the person who owns that thing.
>
> **Pablo ha perdido <u>su</u> bolígrafo.** Pablo has lost his pen.
> **Pablo ha perdido <u>sus</u> bolígrafos.** Pablo has lost his pens.

ℹ️ Note that possessive adjectives aren't normally used with parts of the body. You usually use the <u>definite article</u> instead.

Tiene <u>los</u> ojos verdes.	He's got green eyes.
No puedo mover <u>las</u> piernas.	I can't move my legs.

➪ *For more information on **Articles**, see page 10.*

> ### Tip
>
> As **su** and **sus** can mean *his, her, its, your* or *their*, it can sometimes be a bit confusing. When you need to avoid confusion, you can say the Spanish equivalent of *of him* and so on.
>
> | | | | |
> |---|---|---|---|
> | <u>su</u> casa | → | **la casa <u>de él</u>** | his house *(literally: the house of him)* |
> | <u>sus</u> amigos | → | **los amigos <u>de usted</u>** | your friends *(literally: the friends of you)* |
> | <u>sus</u> coches | → | **los coches <u>de ellos</u>** | their cars *(literally: the cars of them)* |
> | <u>su</u> abrigo | → | **el abrigo <u>de ella</u>** | her coat *(literally: the coat of her)* |
>
> ➪*For more information on **Personal pronouns**, see page 42.*

> ### Key points
> ✔ The Spanish possessive adjectives are:
> - **mi/tu/su/nuestro/vuestro/su** with a masculine singular noun
> - **mi/tu/su/nuestra/vuestra/su** with a feminine singular noun
> - **mis/tus/sus/nuestros/vuestros/sus** with a masculine plural noun
> - **mis/tus/sus/nuestras/vuestras/sus** with a feminine plural noun
>
> ✔ Possessive adjectives come before the noun they refer to. They agree with what they describe, rather than with the person who owns that thing.
>
> ✔ Possessive adjectives are not usually used with parts of the body. Use **el/la/los** or **las** as appropriate instead.
>
> ✔ To avoid confusion, it is sometimes clearer to use **el coche de él/ella/ellas/ellos/usted** and so on rather than **su coche**.

Possessive adjectives (2)

➤ In Spanish, there is a second set of possessive adjectives, which mean *(of) mine, (of) yours* and so on. Like other adjectives in Spanish, they change in the feminine and plural forms.

Singular		Plural		Meaning
masculine	feminine	masculine	feminine	
mío	mía	míos	mías	mine/of mine
tuyo	tuya	tuyos	tuyas	yours/of yours (*belonging to* **tú**)
suyo	suya	suyos	suyas	his/of his; hers/of hers; of its; yours/of yours (*belonging to* **usted**)
nuestro	nuestra	nuestros	nuestras	ours/of ours
vuestro	vuestra	vuestros	vuestras	yours/of yours (*belonging to* **vosotros/as**)
suyo	suya	suyos	suyas	theirs/of theirs; yours/of yours (*belonging to* **ustedes**)

➪ *For more information on **Ways of saying 'you' in Spanish**, see page 44.*

un amigo <u>mío</u>	a (male) friend of mine, one of my (male) friends
una revista <u>tuya</u>	a magazine of yours, one of your magazines
una tía <u>suya</u>	an aunt of his/hers/theirs/yours, one of his/her/their/your aunts
una amiga <u>nuestra</u>	a (female) friend of ours, one of our friends
¿De quién es esta bufanda? – Es <u>mía</u>.	Whose scarf is this? – It's mine.

[*i*] Note that unlike the other possessive adjectives, these adjectives go AFTER the noun they describe.

un amigo <u>vuestro</u>	a (male) friend of yours, one of your friends

> ## Tip
>
> Possessive adjectives agree with what they describe <u>NOT</u> with the person who owns that thing.
>
> **Estos apuntes son <u>míos</u>.**   These notes are mine.

Grammar Extra!

mío/mía and so on are also used in exclamations and when addressing someone. In this case they mean the same as *my* in English.

¡Dios <u>mío</u>!	My God!
amor <u>mío</u>	my love
Muy señor <u>mío</u>	Dear Sir
hija <u>mía</u>	my dear daughter

Indefinite adjectives

> **What is an indefinite adjective?**
> An **indefinite adjective** is one of a small group of adjectives used to talk about people or things in a general way without saying exactly who or what they are, for example, *several*, *all*, *every*.

➤ In English indefinite adjectives do not change, but in Spanish most indefinite adjectives change for the feminine and plural forms.

Singular		Plural		Meaning
masculine	feminine	masculine	feminine	
algún	alguna	algunos	algunas	some; any
cada	cada			each; every
mismo	misma	mismos	mismas	same
mucho	mucha	muchos	muchas	a lot of
otro	otra	otros	otras	another; other
poco	poca	pocos	pocas	little; few
tanto	tanta	tantos	tantas	so much; so many
todo	toda	todos	todas	all; every
		varios	varias	several

<u>algún</u> día	some day
el <u>mismo</u> día	the same day
las <u>mismas</u> películas	the same movies
<u>otro</u> coche	another car
<u>mucha</u> gente	a lot of people
<u>otra</u> manzana	another apple
<u>pocos</u> amigos	few friends

i Note that you can never use **otro** (meaning *other* or *another*) with **un** or **una**.

¿Me das <u>otra</u> manzana?	Will you give me another apple?
¿Tienes <u>otro</u> jersey?	Have you got another jumper?

> *Tip*
>
> *Some* and *any* are usually not translated before nouns that you can't count like bread, butter, water.
>
> | | |
> |---|---|
> | Hay pan en la mesa. | There's some bread on the table. |
> | ¿Quieres café? | Would you like some coffee? |
> | ¿Hay leche? | Is there any milk? |
> | No hay mantequilla. | There isn't any butter. |

➤ **todo/toda/todos/todas** (meaning *all* or *every*) can be followed by:

- a definite article (**el**, **la**, **los**, **las**)

Han estudiado durante <u>toda la</u> noche.	They've been studying all night.
Vienen <u>todos los</u> días.	They come every day.

- a demonstrative adjective (**este**, **ese**, **aquel** and so on)

Ha llovido <u>toda esta</u> semana.	It has rained all this week.

- a possessive adjective (**mi**, **tu**, **su** and so on)

Pondré en orden <u>todos mis</u> libros.	I'll sort out all my books.

- a place name

Lo sabe <u>todo Madrid</u>.	The whole of Madrid knows it.

⇨ *For more information on **Articles**, **Demonstrative adjectives** and **Possessive adjectives**, see pages 10, 30 and 35.*

➤ As in English, Spanish indefinite adjectives come <u>BEFORE</u> the noun they describe.

las <u>mismas</u> películas	the same movies

Key points

✔ Like other adjectives, Spanish indefinite adjectives (such as **otro** and **todo**) must agree with what they describe.

✔ They go before the noun to which they relate.

Pronouns

> **What is a pronoun?**
> A **pronoun** is a word you use instead of a noun, when you do not need
> or want to name someone or something directly, for example, *it*, *you*, *none*.

➤ There are several different types of pronoun:
- <u>Personal pronouns</u> such as *I*, *you*, *he*, *her* and *they*, which are used
  to refer to you, the person you are talking to, or other people and things.
  They can be either <u>subject pronouns</u> (*I*, *you*, *he* and so on) or <u>object
  pronouns</u> (*him*, *her*, *them*, and so on).
- <u>Possessive pronouns</u> like *mine* and *yours*, which show who someone or
  something belongs to.
- <u>Indefinite pronouns</u> like *someone* or *nothing*, which refer to people or things
  in a general way without saying exactly who or what they are.
- <u>Relative pronouns</u> like *who*, *which* or *that*, which link two parts of a
  sentence together.
- <u>Interrogative pronouns</u> like *who*, *what* or *which*, which are used in
  questions.
- <u>Demonstrative pronouns</u> like *this* or *those*, which point things or people
  out.
- <u>Reflexive pronouns</u>, a type of object pronoun that forms part of Spanish
  reflexive verbs like **lavarse** (meaning *to wash*) or **llamarse** (meaning
  to be called).

⇨ *For more information on **Reflexive verbs**, see page 91.*

➤ Pronouns often stand in for a noun to save repeating it.
>   I finished my homework and gave <u>it</u> to my teacher.
>   Do you remember Jack? I saw <u>him</u> this weekend.

➤ Word order with personal pronouns is usually different in Spanish and English.

Personal pronouns: subject

> **What is a subject pronoun?**
> A **subject pronoun** is a word such as *I*, *he*, *she* and *they*, that carries out the action expressed by the verb. Pronouns stand in for nouns when it is clear who or what is being talked about, for example, *My brother isn't here at the moment. He'll be back in an hour.*

1 Using subject pronouns

➤ Here are the Spanish subject pronouns:

Singular	Meaning	Plural	Meaning
yo	I	nosotros (*masculine*)	we
tú	you	nosotras (*feminine*)	we
él	he	vosotros (*masculine*)	you
ella	she	vosotras (*feminine*)	you
usted (Vd.)	you	ellos (*masculine*)	they
		ellas (*feminine*)	they
		ustedes (Vds.)	you

i Note that there is an accent on **tú** (*you*) and **él** (*he*) so that they are not confused with **tu** (*your*) and **el** (*the*).

> *Tip*
> The abbreviations **Vd**. and **Vds**. are often used instead of **usted** and **ustedes**.

➤ In English we use subject pronouns all the time – *I walk, you eat, they are going*. In Spanish you don't need them if the verb endings and context make it clear who the subject is. For example **hablo español** can only mean *I speak Spanish* since the **-o** ending on the verb is only used with *I*. Similarly, **hablamos francés** can only mean *we speak French* since the **-amos** ending is only used with *we*. So the subject pronouns are not needed in these examples.

Tengo un hermano.	*I've got a brother.*
Tenemos dos coches.	*We've got two cars.*

[i] Note that **usted/Vd.** and **ustedes/Vds**. are often used for politeness, even if they are not really needed.

¿Conoce usted al señor Martín?	Do you know Mr Martín?
Pasen ustedes por aquí.	Please come this way.

⇨ *For more information on **Ways of saying 'you' in Spanish**, see page 44.*

➤ Spanish subject pronouns are normally only used:
- for emphasis

¿Y tú qué piensas?	What do you think about it?
Ellos sí que llegaron tarde.	They really did arrive late.

- for contrast or clarity

Yo estudio español pero él estudia francés.	I study Spanish but he studies French.
Él lo hizo pero ella no.	He did it but she didn't.

- after **ser** (meaning *to be*)

Soy yo.	It's me.
¿Eres tú?	Is that you?

- in comparisons after **que** and **como**

Enrique es más alto que yo.	Enrique is taller than I am or than me.
Antonio no es tan alto como tú.	Antonio isn't as tall as you (are).

⇨ *For more information on **Making comparisons**, see page 26.*

- on their own without a verb

¿Quién dijo eso? – Él.	Who said that? – He did.
¿Quién quiere venir? – Yo.	Who wants to come? – I do.

- after certain prepositions

entre tú y yo	between you and me

⇨ *For more information on **Pronouns after prepositions**, see page 54.*

[i] Note that *it* used as the subject, and *they* referring to things, are <u>NEVER</u> translated into Spanish.

¿Qué es? – Es una sorpresa.	What is it? – It's a surprise.
¿Qué son? – Son abrelatas.	What are they? – They are can openers.

2 Ways of saying 'you' in Spanish

➤ In English we have only <u>one</u> way of saying *you*. In Spanish, there are <u>several</u> words to choose from. The word you use depends on:
  • whether you are talking to one person or more than one person
  • whether you are talking to a friend or family member, or someone else.

➤ If you are talking to one person <u>you know well</u>, such as a friend, a young person or a relative, use **tú**. In Spain **tú** is also used when talking to someone your own age even if you don't know them very well.

➤ If you are talking to one person <u>you do not know so well</u>, such as your teacher, your boss or a stranger, it is safest to use the polite form, **usted**. In Latin America **usted** is often used no matter how well you know the person.

➤ If you are talking to <u>more than one person</u> you know well, use **vosotros** (or **vosotras**, if you are talking to women only) in Spain. Use **ustedes** instead in Latin America.

➤ Use **ustedes** if you are talking to more than one person <u>you do not know so well</u>.

> *Tip*
>
> Remember that adjectives describing **tú** and **usted** should be feminine if you're talking to a woman or girl, while adjectives describing **ustedes** should be feminine plural if you're talking to women or girls only.

3 Using the plural subject pronouns

➤ When you are talking about males only, use **nosotros**, **vosotros** or **ellos**.

Nosotros no somos italianos. <u>We</u> are not Italian.

➤ When you are talking about females only, use **nosotras**, **vosotras** or **ellas**.

Hablé con mis hermanas. I spoke to my sisters.
Ellas estaban de acuerdo conmigo. <u>They</u> agreed with me.

➤ When you are talking about both males and females, use **nosotros**, **vosotros** or **ellos**.

Ellos sí que llegaron tarde. <u>They</u> really did arrive late.

Key points

✔ The Spanish subject pronouns are: **yo**, **tú**, **él**, **ella**, **usted** in the singular, and **nosotros/nosotras**, **vosotros/vosotras**, **ellos/ellas**, **ustedes** in the plural.

✔ Don't use the subject pronouns (other than **usted** and **ustedes**) with verbs except for emphasis or clarity.

✔ Make sure you choose the correct form of the verb.

✔ Do use the subject pronouns:
  • after **ser** (meaning *to be*)
  • in comparisons after **que** and **como**
  • in one-word answers to questions.

✔ Choose the word for *you* carefully. Remember to think about how many people you are talking to and your relationship with them when deciding between **tú**, **vosotros**, **vosotras**, **usted** and **ustedes**.

✔ *It* as the subject of the verb, and *they* when it refers to things are NOT translated in Spanish.

✔ Use masculine plural forms (**nosotros**, **vosotros**, **ellos**) for groups made up of men and women.

✔ Remember to make any adjectives describing the subject agree.

Personal pronouns: direct object

> **What is a direct object pronoun?**
> A **direct object pronoun** is a word such as *me*, *him*, *us* and *them*, which is used instead of the noun to stand in for the person or thing most directly affected by the action expressed by the verb.

1 Using direct object pronouns

➤ Direct object pronouns stand in for nouns when it is clear who or what is being talked about, and save having to repeat the noun.

  I've lost my glasses. Have you seen <u>them</u>?

  'Have you met Jo?' – 'Yes, I really like <u>her</u>!'

➤ Here are the Spanish direct object pronouns:

Singular	Meaning	Plural	Meaning
me	me	nos	us
te	you (*relating to* **tú**)	os	you (*relating to* **vosotros/vosotras**)
lo	him it (*masculine*) you (*relating to* **usted** – *masculine*)	los	them (*masculine*) you (*relating to* **ustedes** – *masculine*)
la	her it (*feminine*) you (*relating to* **usted** – *feminine*)	las	them (*feminine*) you (*relating to* **ustedes** – *feminine*)

<u>Te</u> quiero.	I love you.
No <u>los</u> toques.	Don't touch them.

i Note that you cannot use the Spanish direct object pronouns on their own without a verb or after a preposition such as **a** or **de**.

➪ *For more information on **Pronouns after prepositions**, see page 54.*

2 Word order with direct object pronouns

➤ The direct object pronoun usually comes <u>BEFORE</u> the verb.

¿<u>Las</u> ve usted?	Can you see them?
¿No <u>me</u> oís?	Can't you hear me?
Tu hija no <u>nos</u> conoce.	Your daughter doesn't know us.
¿<u>Lo</u> has visto?	Have you seen it?

➤ In orders and instructions telling someone <u>TO DO</u> something, the pronoun joins onto the end of the verb to form one word.

Ayúda<u>me.</u>	Help me.
Acompáña<u>nos.</u>	Come with us.

[*i*] Note that you will often need to add a written accent to preserve the spoken stress when adding pronouns to the end of verbs.

⟹ *For more information on **Stress**, see page 200.*

➤ In orders and instructions telling someone <u>NOT TO DO</u> something, the pronoun does <u>NOT</u> join onto the end of the verb.

No <u>los</u> toques.	Don't touch them.

➤ If the pronoun is the object of an infinitive (the *to* form of the verb) or a gerund (the *-ing* form of the verb), you always add the pronoun to the end of the verb to form one word, unless the infinitive or gerund follows another verb. Again, you may have to add a written accent to preserve the stress.

Se fue después de arreglar<u>lo.</u>	He left after fixing it.
Practicándo<u>lo</u>, aprenderás.	You'll learn by practising it.

⟹ *For more information on **Verbs** and **Gerunds**, see pages 69 and 125.*

➤ Where an infinitive or gerund follows another verb, you can put the pronoun either at the end of the infinitive or gerund, or before the other verb.

Vienen a ver<u>nos</u> *or*	
<u>Nos</u> vienen a ver.	They are coming to see us.
Está comiéndo<u>lo</u> *or*	
<u>Lo</u> está comiendo.	He's eating it.

⟹ *For further information on the **Order of object pronouns**, see page 52.*

3 Special use of lo

➤ **lo** is sometimes used to refer back to an idea or information that has already been given. The word *it* is often missed out in English.

¿Va a venir María? – No lo sé.	Is María coming? – I don't know.
Habían comido ya pero no nos lo dijeron.	They had already eaten, but they didn't tell us.
Yo conduzco deprisa pero él lo hace despacio.	I drive fast but he drives slowly.

Key points

✔ The Spanish direct object pronouns are: **me**, **te**, **lo**, **la** in the singular, and **nos**, **os**, **los**, **las** in the plural.

✔ The object pronoun usually comes before the verb.

✔ Object pronouns are joined to the end of infinitives, gerunds or verbs instructing someone to do something.

✔ If an infinitive or gerund follows another verb, you can choose whether to add the object pronoun to the end of the infinitive or gerund or to put it before the first verb.

✔ **lo** is sometimes used to refer back to an idea or information that has already been given.

Personal pronouns: indirect object

> **What is an indirect object pronoun?**
> An **indirect object pronoun** is used instead of a noun to show the person or thing an action is intended to benefit or harm, for example, *me* in *He gave me a book.; Can you get me a towel?; He wrote to me*.

1 Using indirect object pronouns

➤ It is important to understand the difference between direct and indirect object pronouns in English, as they can have different forms in Spanish.

➤ You can usually test whether an object is a direct object or an indirect one by asking questions about the action using *what* and *who*:

- an indirect object answers the question *who ... to?* or *who ... for?*, equally *what ... to?* or *what ... for?*

   He gave me a book. → *Who did he give the book to?* → me
   (=*indirect object pronoun*)

   Can you get me a towel? → *Who can you get a towel for?* → me
   (=*indirect object pronoun*)

   We got some varnish for it. → *What did you get the varnish for?* → it
   (=*indirect object pronoun*)

- if something answers the question *what* or *who*, then it is the direct object and <u>NOT</u> the indirect object.

   He gave me a book. → *What did he give me?* → a book
   (=*direct object*)

   I saw Mandy. → *Who did you see?* → Mandy
   (=*direct object*)

   We got some varnish for it. → *What did you get?* → some varnish
   (=*direct object*)

i Note that a verb won't necessarily have both a direct and an indirect object.

➤ Here are the Spanish indirect object pronouns:

Singular	Meaning	Plural	Meaning
me	me, to me, for me	**nos**	us, to us, for us
te	you, to you, for you (*relating to* **tú**)	**os**	you, to you, for you (*relating to* **vosotros/vosotras**)
le	him, to him, for him her, to her, for her it, to it, for it you, to you, for you (*relating to* **usted**)	**les**	them, to them, for them you, to you, for you (*relating to* **ustedes**)

➤ The pronouns shown in the table are used instead of using the preposition **a** with a noun.

> **Estoy escribiendo <u>a Teresa</u>.** I am writing to Teresa. →
> **Le estoy escribiendo.** I am writing to her.
> **Compra un regalo <u>a los niños</u>.** Buy the children a present. →
> **Cómprales un regalo.** Buy them a present.

➤ Some Spanish verbs like **mirar** (meaning *to look at*), **esperar** (meaning *to wait for*) and **buscar** (meaning *to look for*) take a direct object, because the Spanish construction is different from the English.

Grammar Extra!

You should usually use direct object pronouns rather than indirect object pronouns when replacing personal **a** + <u>noun</u>.

> **Vi <u>a Teresa</u>.** → **<u>La</u> vi.**   I saw Teresa. → I saw her.

⇨ *For more information on **Personal a**, see page 182.*

---

2 Word order with indirect object pronouns

➤ The indirect object pronoun usually comes <u>BEFORE</u> the verb.

Sofía <u>os</u> ha escrito.	Sophie has written to you.
¿<u>Os</u> ha escrito Sofía?	Has Sofía written to you?
Carlos no <u>nos</u> habla.	Carlos doesn't speak to us.
¿Qué <u>te</u> pedían?	What were they asking you for?

➤ In orders and instructions telling someone <u>TO DO</u> something, the pronoun goes on the end of the verb to form one word.

Respónde<u>me</u>.	Answer me.
Di<u>me</u> la respuesta.	Tell me the answer.

ⓘ Note that you will often need to add a written accent to preserve the spoken stress.

⇨ *For more information on **Stress**, see page 200.*

➤ In orders and instructions telling someone <u>NOT TO DO</u> something, the pronoun does not join onto the end of the verb.

> **No <u>me</u> digas la respuesta.**   Don't tell me the answer.

For further explanation of grammatical terms, please see pages viii-xii.

➤ If the pronoun is the object of an infinitive (the *to* form of the verb) or a gerund (the *-ing* form of the verb), you always add the pronoun to the end of the verb to form one word, unless the infinitive or gerund follows another verb. Again, you may have to add a written accent to preserve the stress.

Eso de darle tu dirección no fue muy prudente.	It wasn't very wise to give him your address.
Gritándole tanto lo vas a asustar.	You'll frighten him by shouting at him like that.

➤ Where an infinitive or gerund follows another verb, you can put the pronoun either at the end of the infinitive or gerund, or before the other verb.

Quiero decirte algo. *or* **Te quiero decir algo.**	I want to tell you something.
Estoy escribiéndole. *or* **Le estoy escribiendo.**	I am writing to him/her.

⇨ *For further information on the **Order of object pronouns**, see page 52.*

> ### Key points
>
> ✔ The Spanish indirect object pronouns are: **me**, **te**, **le** in the singular, and **nos**, **os**, **les** in the plural.
> ✔ They can replace the preposition **a** (meaning *to*) + noun.
> ✔ Like the direct object pronoun, the indirect object pronoun usually comes before the verb.
> ✔ Object pronouns are joined to the end of infinitives, gerunds or verbs instructing someone to do something.
> ✔ If an infinitive or gerund follows another verb, you can choose whether to add the object pronoun to the end of the infinitive or gerund or to put it before the first verb.

Order of object pronouns

➤ Two object pronouns are often used together in the same sentence; for example: *he gave me them* or *he gave them to me*. In Spanish, you should always put the indirect object pronoun <u>BEFORE</u> the direct object pronoun.

Indirect		Direct
me	BEFORE	lo
te		la
nos		los
os		las

Ana <u>os lo</u> mandará mañana.	Ana will send it to you tomorrow.
¿<u>Te los</u> ha enseñado mi hermana? `	Has my sister shown them to you?
No <u>me lo</u> digas.	Don't tell me (that).
Todos estaban pidiéndo<u>telo</u>.	They were all asking you for it.
No quiere prestár<u>nosla</u>.	He won't lend it to us.

➤ You have to use **se** instead of **le** (*to him, to her, to you*) and **les** (*to them, to you*), when you are using the object pronouns **lo**, **la**, **los**, or **las**.

<u>Se</u> lo di ayer.	I gave it to him/her/you/them yesterday.
<u>Se</u> las enviaré.	I'll send them to him/her/you/them.

Key points

✔ When combining two object pronouns, put the indirect object pronoun before the direct object pronoun.

✔ Use **se** as the indirect object pronoun rather than **le** or **les** when there is more than one object pronoun.

For further explanation of grammatical terms, please see pages viii-xii.

Further information on object pronouns

➤ The object pronoun **le** can mean *(to) him*, *(to) her* and *(to) you*; **les** can mean *(to) them* and *(to) you*, and **se** can mean all of these things, which could lead to some confusion.

➤ To make it clear which one is meant, **a él** (meaning *to him*), **a ella** (meaning *to her*), **a usted** (meaning *to you*) and so on can be added to the phrase.

A ella le escriben mucho.	They write to her often.
A ellos se lo van a mandar pronto.	They will be sending it to them soon.

➤ When a noun object comes before the verb, the corresponding object pronoun must be used too.

A tu hermano lo conozco bien. I know your brother well.
(*literally: Your brother I know him well.*)

A María la vemos algunas veces. We sometimes see María.
(*literally: María we see her sometimes.*)

➤ Indirect object pronouns are often used in constructions with the definite article with parts of the body or items of clothing to show who they belong to. In English, we'd use a possessive adjective.

La chaqueta le estaba ancha. His jacket was too loose.
Me duele el tobillo. My ankle's sore.

⇨ *For more information on* **The definite article** *and* **Possessive adjectives**, *see pages 11, 35 and 37.*

➤ Indirect object pronouns can also be used in certain common phrases which use reflexive verbs.

Se me ha perdido el bolígrafo. I have lost my pen.

⇨ *For more information on* **Reflexive verbs**, *see page 91.*

[*i*] Note that in Spain, you will often hear **le** and **les** used instead of **lo** and **los** as direct object pronouns when referring to men and boys. It is probably better not to copy this practice since it is considered incorrect in some varieties of Spanish, particularly Latin American ones.

Pronouns after prepositions

➤ In English, we use *me*, *you*, *him* and so on after a preposition, for example, *he came toward me*; *it's for you*; *books by him*. In Spanish, there is a special set of pronouns which are used after prepositions.

➤ The pronouns used after a preposition in Spanish are the same as the subject pronouns, except for the forms **mí** (meaning *me*) **ti** (meaning *you*), and **sí** (meaning *himself, herself, yourself, themselves, yourselves*).

Singular	Meaning	Plural	Meaning
mí	me	**nosotros**	us (*masculine*)
ti	you	**nosotras**	us (*feminine*)
él	him	**vosotros**	you (*masculine*)
ella	her	**vosotras**	you (*feminine*)
usted (Vd.)	you	**ellos**	them (*masculine*)
sí	himself	**ellas**	them (*feminine*)
	herself	**ustedes (Vds.)**	you
	yourself	**sí**	themselves
			yourselves

Pienso <u>en ti</u>.	I think about you.
¿Son <u>para mí?</u>	Are they for me?
No he sabido nada <u>de él.</u>	I haven't heard from him.
Es <u>para ella</u>.	It's for her.
Iban <u>hacia ellos</u>.	They were going toward them.
Volveréis <u>sin nosotros</u>.	You'll come back without us.
Volaban <u>sobre vosotros</u>.	They were flying above you.

🛈 Note that **mí**, **sí** and **él** each have an accent, to distinguish them from **mi** (meaning *my*), **si** (meaning *if*), and **el** (meaning *the*), but **ti** does not have an accent.

➤ These pronouns are often used for emphasis.

¿A <u>ti</u> no te escriben?	Don't they write to <u>you</u>?
Me lo manda a <u>mí</u>, no a <u>ti</u>.	She's sending it to <u>me</u>, not to you.

➤ **con** (meaning *with*) combines with **mí**, **ti** and **sí** to form:

- **conmigo**   with me

Ven <u>conmigo</u>.	Come with me.

- **contigo**   with you

Me gusta estar <u>contigo</u>.	I like being with you.

- **consigo** with himself/herself/yourself/themselves/yourselves
  Lo trajeron consigo. They brought it with them.

➤ **entre, hasta, salvo, menos** and **según** are always used with the <u>subject pronouns</u> (**yo** and **tú**), rather than with the object pronouns (**mí** and **ti**).

- **entre** between, among
  entre tú y yo between you and me
- **hasta** even, including
  Hasta yo puedo hacerlo. Even I can do it.
- **menos** except
  todos menos yo everybody except me
- **salvo** except
  todos salvo yo everyone except me
- **según** according to
  según tú according to you

⇨ *For more information on **Subject pronouns**, see page 42.*

> ### Key points
> ✔ Most prepositions are followed by the forms: **mí**, **ti**, **sí** and so on.
> ✔ **con** combines with **mí**, **ti** and **sí** to form **conmigo**, **contigo** and **consigo**.
> ✔ **entre, hasta, menos, salvo** and **según** are followed by the subject pronouns **yo** and **tú**.

Possessive pronouns

What is a possessive pronoun?
A **possessive pronoun** is one of the words *mine, yours, hers, his, ours* or *theirs*, which are used instead of a noun to show that one person or thing belongs to another, for example, *Ask Carole if this pen is <u>hers</u>.; <u>Mine's</u> <u>the blue one</u>.*

➤ Here are the Spanish possessive pronouns:

Masculine singular	Feminine singular	Masculine plural	Feminine plural	Meaning
el mío	la mía	los míos	las mías	mine
el tuyo	la tuya	los tuyos	las tuyas	yours (*belonging to* **tú**)
el suyo	la suya	los suyos	las suyas	his; hers; its; yours (*belonging to* **usted**)
el nuestro	la nuestra	los nuestros	las nuestras	ours
el vuestro	la vuestra	los vuestros	las vuestras	yours (*belonging to* **vosotros/vosotras**)
el suyo	la suya	los suyos	las suyas	theirs; yours (*belonging to* **ustedes**)

⇨ *For more information on **Ways of saying 'you' in Spanish**, see page 44.*

Pregunta a Cristina si este bolígrafo es <u>el suyo</u>.	Ask Cristina if this pen is hers.
¿Qué equipo ha ganado, <u>el suyo</u> o <u>el nuestro</u>?	Which team won – theirs or ours?
Mi perro es más joven que <u>el tuyo</u>.	My dog is younger than yours.
Daniel pensó que esos libros eran <u>los suyos</u>.	Daniel thought those books were his.
Si no tienes lápices, te prestaré <u>los míos</u>.	If you haven't got any pencils, I'll lend you mine.
Las habitaciones son más pequeñas que <u>las vuestras</u>.	The rooms are smaller than yours.

For further explanation of grammatical terms, please see pages viii-xii.

Típ

In Spanish, possessive pronouns agree with what they describe, <u>NOT</u> with the person who owns that thing. For example, **el suyo** can mean *his*, *hers*, *yours* or *theirs*, but can only be used to replace a masculine singular noun.

ℹ️ Note that the prepositions **a** and **de** combine with the article **el** to form **al** and **del**, for example, **a** + **el mío** becomes **al mío**, and **de** + **el mío** becomes **del mío**.

Prefiero tu coche <u>al mío</u>.	I prefer your car to mine.
Su coche se parece <u>al vuestro</u>.	His/Her/Their car looks like yours.
Mi piso está encima <u>del tuyo</u>.	My apartment is above yours.
Su colegio está cerca <u>del nuestro</u>.	His/Her/Your/Their school is near ours.

➤ Instead of **el suyo/la suya/los suyos/las suyas**, it is sometimes clearer to say **el/la/los/las de usted**, **el/la/los/las de ustedes**, **el/la/los/las de ellos** and so on. You choose between **el/la/los/las** to agree with the noun referred to.

> **mi libro y <u>el de</u> usted**   my book and yours

➤ **el/la/los/las de** can also be used with a name or other noun referring to somebody.

Juan tiene un coche bonito pero yo prefiero <u>el de</u> Ana.	Juan's got a nice car, but I prefer Ana's.
Ellos tienen una casa bonita pero yo prefiero <u>la del</u> médico.	They've got a nice house but I prefer the doctor's.

Key points

✔ The Spanish possessive pronouns are **el mío**, **el tuyo**, **el suyo**, **el nuestro**, **el vuestro** and **el suyo** when they stand in for a masculine noun. If they stand in for a feminine or a plural noun, their forms change accordingly.

✔ In Spanish, the pronoun you choose has to agree with the noun it replaces, and <u>not</u> with the person who owns that thing.

✔ **el/la/los/las de** are used with a noun or pronoun to mean the *one(s) belonging to* ...

Indefinite pronouns

> **What is an indefinite pronoun?**
> An **indefinite pronoun** is one of a small group of pronouns such as *everything*, *nobody* and *something* which are used to refer to people or things in a general way without saying exactly who or what they are.

➤ Here are the most common Spanish indefinite pronouns:

- **algo**   something, anything

Tengo <u>algo</u> para ti.	I have something for you.
¿Viste <u>algo</u>?	Did you see anything?

- **alguien**   somebody, anybody

<u>Alguien</u> me lo ha dicho.	Somebody told me.
¿Has visto a <u>alguien</u>?	Have you seen anybody?

Tip

Don't forget to use personal **a** before indefinite pronouns referring to people when they are the object of a verb.

¿Viste <u>a</u> alguien?	Did you see anybody?
No vi <u>a</u> nadie.	I didn't see anybody.

⇨ For more information on **Personal a**, see page 182.

- **alguno/alguna/algunos/algunas**   some, a few

<u>Algunos</u> de los niños ya saben leer.	Some of the children can already read.

- **cada uno/una**   each (one), everybody

Le dio una manzana a <u>cada uno</u>.	She gave each one an apple.
¡<u>Cada uno</u> a su casa!	Everybody home!

- **cualquiera**   anybody; any

<u>Cualquiera</u> puede hacerlo.	Anybody can do it.
<u>Cualquiera</u> de las explicaciones vale.	Any of the explanations is valid.

- **mucho/mucha/muchos/muchas**   much; many

<u>Muchas</u> de las casas no tenían jardín.	Many of the houses didn't have a garden.

- **nada** nothing, anything

¿Qué tienes en la mano? – <u>Nada</u>.	What have you got in your hand? – Nothing.
No dijo <u>nada</u>.	He didn't say anything.

- **nadie** nobody, anybody

¿A quién ves? – A <u>nadie</u>.	Who can you see? – Nobody.
No quiere ver a <u>nadie</u>.	He doesn't want to see anybody.

Tip

Don't forget to use personal **a** before indefinite pronouns referring to people when they are the object of a verb.

¿Viste <u>a</u> alguien?	Did you see anybody?
No vi <u>a</u> nadie.	I didn't see anybody.

➡️ *For more information on **Personal a**, see page 182.*

- **ninguno/ninguna** none, any

¿Cuántas tienes? – <u>Ninguna</u>.	How many have you got? – None.
No me queda <u>ninguno</u>.	I haven't any left *or* I have none left.

- **otro/otra/otros/otras** another one; others

No me gusta este modelo. ¿Tienes <u>otro</u>?	I don't like this model. Have you got another?

i Note that you can never put **un** or **una** before **otro** or **otra**.

- **poco/poca/pocos/pocas** little; few

solo unos <u>pocos</u>	only a few

- **tanto/tanta/tantos/tantas** so much; so many

¿Se oía mucho ruido? – No <u>tanto</u>.	Was there a lot of noise? – Not so much.

- **todo/toda/todos/todas** all; everything

Lo ha estropeado <u>todo</u>.	He has spoiled everything.
<u>Todo</u> va bien.	It's all going well.

- **uno ... el otro/una ... la otra** (the) one ... the other

<u>Uno</u> dijo que sí y <u>el otro</u> que no.	One said yes while the other said no.

- **unos ... los otros/unas ... las otras** some ... the others

  Unos cuestan 30 euros, Some cost 30 euros, the others
  los otros 40 euros. 40 euros.

- **varios/varias** several

  Varios de ellos me gustan I like several of them very much.
  mucho.

Tip

Don't forget to make those pronouns that have feminine and plural forms agree with the noun they refer to.

He perdido mi goma pero I've lost my rubber but I've got
tengo otra. another one.

---

[i] Note that **algo**, **alguien** and **alguno** can <u>NEVER</u> be used after a negative such as **no**. Instead you must use the appropriate negative pronouns, **nada**, **nadie**, **ninguno**.

  No veo a nadie. I can't see anybody.
  No tengo nada que hacer. I haven't got anything to do.

➤ You use **nada**, **nadie** and **ninguno** on their own without **no** to answer questions.

  ¿Qué pasa? – Nada. What's happening? – Nothing.
  ¿Quién habló? – Nadie. Who spoke? – Nobody.
  ¿Cuántos quedan? – Ninguno. How many are there left? – None.

➤ You also use **nada**, **nadie** and **ninguno** on their own without **no** when they come before a verb.

  Nada lo asusta. Nothing frightens him.
  Nadie habló. Nobody spoke.
  Ninguno de mis amigos quiso None of my friends wanted to
  venir. come.

⇨ *For more information on **Negatives**, see page 157.*

Key points

✔ Where indefinite pronouns have alternative endings, they must agree with the noun they refer to.

✔ *Anything* is usually translated by **algo** in questions and by **nada** in sentences containing **no**.

✔ *Anybody* is usually translated by **alguien** in questions and by **nadie** in sentences containing **no**.

✔ When **nada**, **nadie** or **ninguno** come <u>after</u> the verb, remember to put **no** before it. When they come <u>before</u> the verb, don't use **no**.

For further explanation of grammatical terms, please see pages viii-xii.

Relative pronouns

> **What is a relative pronoun?**
> In English, a **relative pronoun** is one of the words *who, which* and *that* (and the more formal *whom*) which can be used to introduce information that makes it clear which person or thing is being talked about, for example, *The man who has just come in is Ann's boyfriend.; The vase that you broke was quite valuable.*
> Relative pronouns can also introduce further information about someone or something, for example, *Peter, who is a brilliant painter, wants to study art.; Jane's house, which was built in 1890, needs a lot of repairs.*

1 Relative pronouns referring to people

➤ In English, we use the relative pronouns *who, whom* and *that* to talk about people. In Spanish, **que** is used.

el hombre **que** vino ayer	the man who came yesterday
Mi hermano, **que** tiene veinte años, es mecánico.	My brother, who is twenty, is a mechanic.
el hombre **que** vi en la calle	the man (that) I saw in the street

> ### Tip
>
> In English we often leave out the relative pronouns *who, whom* and *that*. For example, we can say both *the friends that I see most*, or *the friends I see most.*
>
> In Spanish, you can **NEVER** leave out **que** in this way.

➤ When the relative pronoun is used with a <u>preposition</u>, use **el/la/los/las que** or **quien/quienes** which must agree with the noun it replaces; **el que** changes for the feminine and plural forms, **quien** changes only in the plural.

➤ Here are the Spanish relative pronouns referring to people that are used after a preposition:

	Masculine	Feminine	Meaning
Singular	el que quien	la que quien	who, that, whom
Plural	los que quienes	las que quienes	who, that, whom

las mujeres con <u>las que</u> or con <u>quienes</u> estaba hablando	the women (that) she was talking to
La chica de <u>la que</u> or de <u>quien</u> te hablé llega mañana.	The girl (that) I told you about is coming tomorrow.
los niños de <u>los que</u> or de <u>quienes</u> se ocupa usted	the children (that) you look after

i Note that when **de** is used with **el que**, they combine to become **del que**. When **a** is used with **el que**, they combine to become **al que**.

el chico <u>del que</u> te hablé	the boy I told you about
Vive con un hombre <u>al que</u> adora.	She lives with a man she adores.

Tip

In English, we often put prepositions at the end of the sentence, for example, *the man she was talking to*. In Spanish, you can <u>never</u> put a preposition at the end of a sentence.

el hombre <u>con el que</u> or <u>con quien</u> estaba hablando	the man she was talking to

⇨ *For more information on **Prepositions**, see page 178.*

---

2 **Relative pronouns referring to things**

➤ In English, we use the relative pronouns *which* and *that* to talk about things. In Spanish, **que** is used.

la novela <u>que</u> ganó el premio	the novel <u>that</u> or <u>which</u> won the prize
el coche <u>que</u> compré	the car (<u>that</u> or <u>which</u>) I bought

---

Tip

In English, we often leave out the relative pronouns *which* and *that*. For example, we can say both *the house <u>which</u> we want to buy*, or *the house we want to buy*.

In Spanish, you can <u>NEVER</u> leave out **que** in this way.

➤ When the relative pronoun is used with a preposition, use **el/la/los/las que**, which must agree with the noun it replaces. Here are the Spanish relative pronouns referring to things that are used after a preposition:

	Masculine	Feminine	Meaning
Singular	el que	la que	which, that
Plural	los que	las que	which, that

la tienda a <u>la que</u> siempre va	the store (that or which) she always goes to
los temas de <u>los que</u> habla	the subjects he talks about

[i] Note that when **de** is used with **el que**, they combine to become **del que**. When **a** is used with **el que**, they combine to become **al que**.

el programa <u>del que</u> te hablé	the program I told you about
el banco <u>al que</u> fuiste	the bank you went to

➤ The neuter form **lo que** is used when referring to the whole of the previous part of the sentence.

Todo estaba en silencio, <u>lo que</u> me pareció raro.	All was silent, which I thought was odd.

⇨ *For more information on **lo que**, see page 17.*

Tip

In English, we often put prepositions at the end of the sentence, for example, *the store she always goes to*. In Spanish, you can <u>never</u> put a preposition at the end of a sentence.

la tienda <u>a la que</u> siempre va	the store she always goes <u>to</u>
la película <u>de la que</u> te hablaba	the movie I was telling you <u>about</u>

Grammar Extra!

In English we can use *whose* to show possession, for example, *the woman whose son is ill*. In Spanish you use **cuyo/cuya/cuyos/cuyas**; **cuyo** is actually an adjective and must agree with the noun it describes <u>NOT</u> with the person who owns that thing.

> **La mujer, <u>cuyo</u> nombre era Antonia, estaba jubilada.** The woman, whose name was Antonia, was retired.
>
> **el señor en <u>cuya</u> casa me alojé** the gentleman whose house I stayed in

In your reading, you may come across the forms **el cual/la cual/los cuales/las cuales** which are a more formal alternative to **el que/la que/los que/las que** after a preposition.

> **las mujeres con <u>las cuales</u> estaba hablando** the women (that or who) she was talking to
>
> **la ventana desde <u>la cual</u> nos observaban** the window from which they were watching us

el cual/la cual/los cuales/las cuales are also useful to make it clear who you are talking about in other cases where the pronoun does not immediately follow the person or thing it refers to.

> **El padre de Elena, <u>el cual</u> tiene mucho dinero, es ...** Elena's father, who has a lot of money, is ...

---

3 | **Other uses of** el que, la que, los que, las que

➤ You can use **el que, la que, los que, las que** to mean *the one(s) (who/which)* or *those who*.

> **Esa película es <u>la que</u> quiero ver.** That movie is the one I want to see.
>
> **<u>los que</u> quieren irse** those who want to leave

Key points

- ✔ **que** can refer to both people and things in Spanish.
- ✔ In English we often miss out the relative pronouns *who*, *which* and *that*, but in Spanish you can never miss out **que**.
- ✔ After a preposition you use **el que/la que/los que/las que** or **quien/quienes** if you are referring to people; you use **el que/la que/los que/las que** if you are referring to things. **el que** and **quien** agree with the nouns they replace.
- ✔ **a + el que → al que**
  de + el que → del que
- ✔ <u>Never</u> put the preposition at the end of the sentence in Spanish.
- ✔ **el que/la que/los que** and **las que** are also used to mean *the one(s) who/which* or *those who*.

For further explanation of grammatical terms, please see pages viii-xii.

Interrogative pronouns

> **What is an interrogative pronoun?**
> In English, an **interrogative pronoun** is one of the words *who*, *which*, *whose*, *whom*, and *what* when they are used without a noun to ask questions.

➤ These are the interrogative pronouns in Spanish:

Singular	Plural	Meaning
¿qué?	¿qué?	what?
¿cuál?	¿cuáles?	which? which one(s)?; what?
¿quién?	¿quiénes?	who? (*as subject or after a preposition*)
¿cuánto?/¿cuánta?	¿cuántos?/¿cuántas?	how much? how many?

ℹ Note that question words have an accent on them in Spanish.

1 ¿qué?

➤ ¿qué? Is the equivalent of *what?* in English.

¿**Qué** están haciendo?	What are they doing?
¿**Qué** dices?	What are you saying?
¿Para **qué** lo quieres?	What do you want it for?

➤ You can use ¿**por qué?** in the same way as *why?* in English.

| ¿**Por qué** no vienes? | Why don't you come? |

2 ¿cuál?, ¿cuáles?

➤ ¿cuál? and ¿cuáles? are usually the equivalent of *which?* in English and are used when there is a choice between two or more things.

| ¿**Cuál** de estos vestidos te gusta más? | Which of these dresses do you like best? |
| ¿**Cuáles** quieres? | Which (ones) do you want? |

ℹ Note that you don't use **cuál** before a noun; use **qué** instead.

| ¿**Qué** libro es más interesante? | Which book is more interesting? |

⇨ *For more information on **Interrogative adjectives**, see page 32.*

3 | qué es or cuál es?

➤ You should only use **¿qué es ...?** (meaning *what is...?*) and **¿qué son ...?** (meaning *what are...?*) when you are asking someone to define, explain or classify something.

¿Qué es esto?	What is this?
¿Qué son los genes?	What are genes?

➤ Use **¿cuál es ...?** and **¿cuáles son ...?** (also meaning *what is ...?* and *what are ...?*) when you want someone to specify a particular detail, number, name and so on.

¿Cuál es la capital de España?	What is the capital of Spain?
¿Cuál es tu consejo?	What's your advice?

4 | ¿quién?

➤ **¿quién?** and **¿quiénes?** are the equivalent of *who?* in English when it is the subject of the verb or when used with a preposition.

¿Quién ganó la carrera?	Who won the race?
¿Con quiénes los viste?	Who did you see them with?
¿A quién se lo diste?	Who did you give it to?

➤ **¿a quién?** and **¿a quiénes?** are the equivalent of *who(m)?* when it is the object of the verb.

¿A quién viste?	Who did you see? *or* Whom did you see?
¿A quiénes ayudaste?	Who did you help? *or* Whom did you help?

➤ **¿de quién?** and **¿de quiénes?** are the equivalent of *whose?* in English.

¿De quién es este libro?	Whose is this book? *or* Whose book is this?
¿De quiénes son estos coches?	Whose are these cars? *or* Whose cars are these?

5 | ¿cuánto?, ¿cuántos?

➤ **¿cuánto?** (*masculine*) and **¿cuánta?** (*feminine*) are the equivalent of *how much* in English. **¿cuántos?** (*masculine plural*) and **¿cuántas?** (*feminine plural*) are the equivalent of *how many?*

¿Cuánto es?	How much is it?
¿Cuántos tienes?	How many have you got?

For further explanation of grammatical terms, please see pages viii-xii.

Demonstrative pronouns

> **What is a demonstrative pronoun?**
> In English a **demonstrative pronoun** is one of the words *this*, *that*, *these*, and *those* used instead of a noun to point people or things out, for example, *That looks fun*.

1 Using demonstrative pronouns

➤ These are the demonstrative pronouns in Spanish:

	Masculine	Feminine	Neuter	Meaning
Singular	este	esta	esto	this, this one
	ese	esa	eso	that, that one (*close by*)
	aquel	aquella	aquello	that, that one (*further away*)
Plural	estos	estas		these, these ones
	esos	esas		those, those ones (*close by*)
	aquellos	aquellas		those, those ones (*further away*)

➤ The demonstrative pronouns in Spanish have to agree with the noun that they are replacing.

¿Qué abrigo te gusta más? – Este de aquí.	Which coat do you like best? – This one here.
Aquella casa era más grande que esta.	That house was bigger than this one.
estos libros y aquellos	these books and those (over there)
Quiero estas sandalias y esas.	I'd like these sandals and those ones.

2 ¿ese or aquel?

➤ In English we use *that* and *those* to talk about anything that is not close by. In Spanish, you need to be a bit more precise.

➤ Use **ese/esa** and so on to indicate things and people that are nearer to the person you're talking to than to you.

Me gusta más ese que tienes en la mano.	I prefer the one you've got in your hand.

➤ Use **ese/esa** and so on to indicate things and people that aren't very far away.

Si quieres ver una película, podemos ir a esa que dijiste.	If you want to see a movie, we can go and see that one you mentioned.

➤ Use **aquel/aquella** and so on to talk about things that are further away.

Aquella al fondo de la calle es mi casa.	My house is that one at the end of the street.

i The masculine and feminine forms of demonstrative <u>pronouns</u> sometimes have an accent, to distinguish them from demonstrative <u>adjectives</u>:

éste/ésta	this one	**éstos/éstas**	these ones
ése/ésa	that one	**ésos/ésas**	those ones
aquél/aquélla	that one	**aquéllos/aquéllas**	those ones

⇨ *For more information on **Demonstrative adjectives**, see page 30.*

➤ The neuter forms (**esto**, **eso**, **aquello**) are used to talk about an object you don't recognize or about an idea or statement.

¿Qué es <u>eso</u> que llevas en la mano?	What's that you've got in your hand?
No puedo creer que <u>esto</u> me esté pasando a mí.	I can't believe this is really happening to me.
<u>Aquello</u> sí que me gustó.	I really did like that.

i Note that the neuter forms of demonstrative pronouns NEVER have an accent.

Key points

✔ Spanish demonstrative pronouns agree with the noun they are replacing.

✔ Masculine and feminine demonstrative pronouns sometimes have an accent on them in both the singular and the plural.

✔ In Spanish you have to choose the correct pronoun to emphasize the difference between something that is close to you and something that is further away:
  • **este/esta/estos** and **estas** (meaning *this/these*) are used to indicate things and people that are very close.
  • **ese/esa/esos** and **esas** (meaning *that/those*) are used to indicate things and people that are near the person you are talking to or that aren't too far away.
  • **aquel/aquella/aquellos/aquellas** (meaning *that/those*) are used to indicate things and people that are further away.

✔ The neuter pronouns (**esto**, **eso** and **aquello**) are used to talk about things you don't recognize or to refer to statements or ideas. They NEVER have an accent.

Verbs

> **What is a verb?**
> A **verb** is a 'doing' word which describes what someone or something does, what someone or something is, or what happens to them, for example, *be*, *sing*, *live*.

Overview of verbs

➤ Verbs are frequently used with a noun, with somebody's name or, particularly in English, with a pronoun such as *I*, *you* or *she*. They can relate to the present, the past and the future; this is called their <u>tense</u>.

➪ *For more information on **Nouns** and **Pronouns**, see pages 1 and 41.*

➤ Verbs are either:

- **regular**; their forms follow the normal rules
- **irregular**; their forms do not follow normal rules

➤ Almost all verbs have a form called the <u>infinitive</u>. This is a base form of the verb (for example, *walk*, *see*, *hear*) that hasn't had any endings added to it and doesn't relate to any particular tense. In English, the infinitive is usually shown with *to*, as in *to speak*, *to eat*, *to live*.

➤ In Spanish, the infinitive is always made up of just one word (never two as in *to speak* in English) and ends in **-ar**, **-er** or **-ir**: for example, **habl<u>ar</u>** (meaning *to speak*), **com<u>er</u>** (meaning *to eat*) and **viv<u>ir</u>** (meaning *to live*).
All Spanish verbs belong to one of these three types, which are called <u>conjugations</u>. We will look at each of these three conjugations in turn on the next few pages.

➤ Regular English verbs have other forms apart from the infinitive: a form ending in *-s* (*walks*), a form ending in *-ing* (*walking*), and a form ending in *-ed* (*walked*).

➤ Spanish verbs have many more forms than this, which are made up of endings added to a <u>stem</u>. The stem of a verb can usually be worked out from the infinitive.

➤ Spanish verb endings change depending on who or what is doing the action and on when the action takes place. In fact, the ending is very often the only thing that shows you <u>who</u> is doing the action, as the Spanish equivalents of *I*, *you*, *he* and so on (**yo**, **tú**, **él** and so on) are not used very much. So, both **hablo** on its own and **yo hablo** mean *I speak*. Sometimes there is a name or a noun in the sentence to make it clear who is doing the action.

> **<u>José</u> habla español.**   <u>José</u> speaks Spanish.
>
> **<u>El profesor</u> habla español.**   <u>The teacher</u> speaks Spanish.

⇨   *For more information on **Subject pronouns**, see page 42.*

➤ Spanish verb forms also change depending on whether you are talking about the present, past or future, so (**yo**) **habl<u>aré</u>** means *I will speak* while (**yo**) **habl<u>é</u>** means *I spoke*.

➤ Some verbs in Spanish do not follow the usual patterns. These <u>irregular verbs</u> include some very common and important verbs like **ir** (meaning *to go*), **ser** and **estar** (meaning *to be*) and **hacer** (meaning *to do* or *to make*). Other verbs are only slightly irregular, changing their stems in certain tenses.

⇨   *For **Verb Tables**, see the middle section.*

Key points

✔ Spanish verbs have different forms depending on who or what is doing the action and on the tense.

✔ Spanish verb forms are made up of a stem and an ending. The stem is usually based on the infinitive of the verb. The ending depends on who or what is doing the action and on when the action takes place.

✔ Regular verbs follow the standard patterns for **-ar**, **-er** and **-ir** verbs. Irregular verbs do not.

The present tenses

What are the present tenses?
The **present tenses** are the verb forms that are used to talk about what is true at the moment, what happens regularly and what is happening now; for example, I'*m* a student; I *travel* to college by train; I'*m studying* languages.

➤ In English, there are two tenses you can use to talk about the present:

- the present simple tense

  I <u>live</u> here.
  They <u>get up</u> early.

- the present continuous tense

  He <u>is eating</u> an apple.
  You <u>are</u>n't <u>working</u> very hard.

➤ In Spanish, there is also a <u>present simple</u> and a <u>present continuous</u> tense. As in English, the <u>present simple</u> in Spanish is used to talk about:

- things that are generally true

  En invierno <u>hace</u> frío.   It'<u>s</u> cold in winter.

- things that are true at the moment

  Carlos no <u>come</u> carne.   Carlos <u>does</u>n't eat meat.

- things that happen at intervals

  A menudo <u>vamos</u> al cine.   We often <u>go</u> to the cinema.

➤ The <u>present continuous</u> tense in Spanish is used to talk about things that are happening right now or at the time of writing:

  Marta <u>está viendo</u> la televisión.   Marta <u>is watching</u> television.

➤ However, there are times where the use of the present tenses in the two languages is not exactly the same.

⇨ *For more information on the use of the **Present tenses**, see pages 79 and 84.*

The present simple tense

1 Forming the present simple tense of regular -ar verbs

➤ If the infinitive of the Spanish verb ends in -ar, it means that the verb belongs to the first conjugation, for example, hablar, lavar, llamar.

➤ To know which form of the verb to use in Spanish, you need to work out what the stem of the verb is and then add the correct ending. The stem of regular -ar verbs in the present simple tense is formed by taking the infinitive and chopping off -ar.

Infinitive	Stem (without -ar)
hablar (to speak)	habl-
lavar (to wash)	lav-

➤ Now you know how to find the stem of a verb you can add the correct ending. The one you choose will depend on who or what is doing the action.

i Note that as the ending generally makes it clear who is doing the action, you usually don't need to add a subject pronoun such as yo (meaning *I*), tú (meaning *you*) as well.

⇨ *For more information on **Subject pronouns**, see page 42.*

➤ Here are the present simple endings for regular -ar verbs:

Present simple endings	Present simple of hablar	Meaning: to speak
-o	(yo) hablo	I speak
-as	(tú) hablas	you speak
-a	(él/ella) habla	he/she/it speaks
	(usted) habla	you speak
-amos	(nosotros/nosotras) hablamos	we speak
-áis	(vosotros/vosotras) habláis	you speak
-an	(ellos/ellas) hablan	they speak
	(ustedes) hablan	you speak

➤ You use the él/ella (*third person singular*) form of the verb with nouns and with people's names, when you are just talking about one person, animal or thing.

Lydia estudia medicina.	Lydia studies *or* is studying medicine.
Mi profesor me ayuda mucho.	My teacher helps me a lot.

For further explanation of grammatical terms, please see pages viii-xii.

➤ You use the **ellos/ellas** (*third person plural*) form of the verb with nouns and with people's names, when you are talking about more than one person, animal or thing.

Lydia y Carlos estudi<u>an</u> **medicina.**	Lydia and Carlos study *or* are studying medicine.
Mis profesores me ayud<u>an</u> **mucho.**	My teachers help me a lot.

ℹ Note that even though you use the **él/ella** and **ellos/ellas** <u>forms</u> of the verb to talk about things in Spanish, you should <u>never</u> include the pronouns **él**, **ella**, **ellos** or **ellas** themselves in the sentence when referring to things.

Funciona bien.	It works well.
Funcionan bien.	They work well.

⇨ For more information on **Ways of saying 'you' in Spanish**, *see page 44*.

> **Key points**
>
> ✔ Verbs ending in **-ar** belong to the first conjugation. Regular **-ar** verbs form their present tense stem by losing the **-ar**.
>
> ✔ The present tense endings for regular **-ar** verbs are: **-o**, **-as**, **-a**, **-amos**, **-áis**, **-an**.
>
> ✔ You usually don't need to give a pronoun in Spanish as the ending of the verb makes it clear who or what is doing the action.

2 Forming the present simple tense of regular -er verbs

➤ If the infinitive of the Spanish verb ends in **-er**, it means that the verb belongs to the <u>second conjugation</u>, for example, **comer**, **depender**.

➤ The stem of regular **-er** verbs in the present simple tense is formed by taking the <u>infinitive</u> and chopping off **-er**.

Infinitive	Stem (without -er)
comer (*to eat*)	com-
depender (*to depend*)	depend-

➤ Now add the correct ending, depending on who or what is doing the action.

ℹ Note that as the ending generally makes it clear who is doing the action, you usually don't need to add a subject pronoun such as **yo** (meaning *I*) or **tú** (meaning *you*) as well.

⇨ For more information on **Subject pronouns**, *see page 42*.

➤ Here are the present simple endings for regular **-er** verbs:

Present simple endings	Present simple of comer	Meaning: *to eat*
-o	(yo) com<u>o</u>	I eat
-es	(tú) com<u>es</u>	you eat
-e	(él/ella) com<u>e</u>	he/she/it eats
	(usted) com<u>e</u>	you eat
-emos	(nosotros/nosotras) com<u>emos</u>	we eat
-éis	(vosotros/vosotras) com<u>éis</u>	you eat
-en	(ellos/ellas) com<u>en</u>	they eat
	(ustedes) com<u>en</u>	you eat

➤ You use the **él/ella** (*third person singular*) form of the verb with nouns and with people's names, when you are just talking about one person, animal or thing.

> **Juan com<u>e</u> demasiado.**   Juan eats too much.
>
> **Mi padre me deb<u>e</u> 150 pesos.**   My father owes me 150 pesos.

➤ You use the **ellos/ellas** (*third person plural*) form of the verb with nouns and with people's names, when you talking about more than one person, animal or thing.

> **Juan y Pedro com<u>en</u>**   Juan and Pedro eat too much.
> **demasiado.**
>
> **Mis padres me deb<u>en</u> 150 pesos.**   My parents owe me 150 pesos.

[*i*] Note that even though you use the **él/ella** and **ellos/ellas** forms of the verb to talk about things in Spanish, you should <u>never</u> include the pronouns **él**, **ella**, **ellos** or **ellas** themselves in the sentence when referring to things.

> **Depende.**   It depends.

⇨ *For more information on **Ways of saying 'you' in Spanish**, see page 44.*

Key points

✔ Verbs ending in **-er** belong to the second conjugation. Regular **-er** verbs form their present tense stem by losing the **-er**.

✔ The present tense endings for regular **-er** verbs are: **-o, -es, -e, -emos, -éis, -en**.

✔ You usually don't need to give a pronoun in Spanish as the ending of the verb makes it clear who or what is doing the action.

---

3 Forming the present simple tense of regular -ir verbs

➤ If the infinitive of the Spanish verb ends in -ir, it means that the verb belongs to the <u>third conjugation</u>, for example, vivir, recibir.

➤ The stem of regular -ir verbs in the present simple tense is formed by taking the <u>infinitive</u> and chopping off -ir.

Infinitive	Stem (without -ir)
vivir (to live)	viv-
recibir (to receive)	recib-

➤ Now add the correct ending depending on who or what is doing the action.

[i] Note that as the ending generally makes it clear who is doing the action, you usually don't need to add a subject pronoun such as yo (meaning I) or tú (meaning you) as well.

⇨ For more information on **Subject pronouns**, see page 42.

➤ Here are the present simple endings for regular -ir verbs:

Present simple endings	Present simple of vivir	Meaning: to live
-o	(yo) vivo	I live
-es	(tú) vives	you live
-e	(él/ella) vive	he/she/it lives
	(usted) vive	you live
-imos	(nosotros/nosotras) vivimos	we live
-ís	(vosotros/vosotras) vivís	you live
-en	(ellos/ellas) viven	they live
	(ustedes) viven	you live

➤ You use the **él/ella** (third person singular) form of the verb with nouns and with people's names, when you are just talking about one person, animal or thing.

Javier vive aquí.	Javier lives here.
Mi padre recibe muchas cartas.	My father gets a lot of letters.

➤ You use the **ellos/ellas** (third person plural) form of the verb with nouns and with people's names, when you talking about more than one person, animal or thing.

Javier y Antonia viven aquí.	Javier and Antonia live here.
Mis padres reciben muchas cartas.	My parents get a lot of letters.

i Note that even though you use the **él/ella** and **ellos/ellas** forms of the verb to talk about things in Spanish, you should <u>never</u> include the pronouns **él**, **ella**, **ellos** or **ellas** themselves in the sentence when referring to things.

> **Ocurrió ayer.**   It happened yesterday.

⇨ *For more information on **Ways of saying 'you' in Spanish**, see page 44.*

Key points

✔ Verbs ending in **-ir** belong to the third conjugation. Regular **-ir** verbs form their present tense stem by losing the **-ir**.

✔ The present tense endings for regular **-ir** verbs are: - **o**, **-es**, **-e**, **-imos**, **-ís**, **-en**.

✔ You usually don't need to give a pronoun in Spanish as the ending of the verb makes it clear who or what is doing the action.

---

4 Forming the present simple tense of less regular verbs

➤ Many Spanish verbs do not follow the regular patterns shown previously. There are lots of verbs that change their <u>stem</u> in the present tense when the stress is on the stem. This means that all forms are affected in the present simple <u>APART FROM</u> the **nosotros** and **vosotros** forms. Such verbs are often called <u>radical-changing verbs</u>, meaning root-changing verbs.

➤ For example, some verbs containing an **-o** in the stem change it to **-ue** in the present simple for all forms <u>APART FROM</u> the **nosotros/nosotras** and **vosotros/vosotras** forms.

	encontrar *to find*	recordar *to remember*	poder *to be able*	dormir *to sleep*
(yo)	enc**ue**ntro	rec**ue**rdo	p**ue**do	d**ue**rmo
(tú)	enc**ue**ntras	rec**ue**rdas	p**ue**des	d**ue**rmes
(él/ella/usted)	enc**ue**ntra	rec**ue**rda	p**ue**de	d**ue**rme
(nosotros/as)	enc**o**ntramos	rec**o**rdamos	p**o**demos	d**o**rmimos
(vosotros/as)	enc**o**ntráis	rec**o**rdáis	p**o**déis	d**o**rmís
(ellos/ellas/ustedes)	enc**ue**ntran	rec**ue**rdan	p**ue**den	d**ue**rmen

➤ Other verbs containing an **-e** in the stem change it to **-ie** for all forms <u>APART FROM</u> the **nosotros/nosotras** and **vosotros/vosotras** forms.

	cerrar *to close*	pensar *to think*	entender *to understand*	perder *to lose*	preferir *to prefer*
(yo)	cierro	pienso	entiendo	pierdo	prefiero
(tú)	cierras	piensas	entiendes	pierdes	prefieres
(él/ella/usted)	cierra	piensa	entiende	pierde	prefiere
(nosotros/as)	cerramos	pensamos	entendemos	perdemos	preferimos
(vosotros/as)	cerráis	pensáis	entendéis	perdéis	preferís
(ellos/ellas/ustedes)	cierran	piensan	entienden	pierden	prefieren

➤ A few **-ir** verbs containing **-e** in the stem change this to **-i** in the present simple for all forms <u>APART FROM</u> the **nosotros/nosotras** and **vosotros/vosotras** forms.

	pedir *to ask (for)*	servir *to serve*
(yo)	pido	sirvo
(tú)	pides	sirves
(él/ella/usted)	pide	sirve
(nosotros/as)	pedimos	servimos
(vosotros/as)	pedís	servís
(ellos/ellas/ustedes)	piden	sirven

➤ If you are not sure whether a Spanish verb belongs to this group of <u>radical-changing verbs</u>, you can look up the **Verb Tables** in the middle section.

⮕ *For more information on **Spelling**, see page 196.*

*For more information on **Spelling**, see page 196.*

5 | Forming the present simple tense of common irregular verbs

➤ There are many other verbs that do not follow the usual patterns in Spanish. These include some very common and important verbs such as **tener** (meaning *to have*), **hacer** (meaning *to do* or *to make*) and **ir** (meaning *to go*). These verbs are shown in full on the next page.

➤ Here are the present simple tense endings for **tener**:

	tener	Meaning: to have
(yo)	tengo	I have
(tú)	tienes	you have
(él/ella/usted)	tiene	he/she/it has, you have
(nosotros/nosotras)	tenemos	we have
(vosotros/vosotras)	tenéis	you have
(ellos/ellas/ustedes)	tienen	they have, you have

Tengo dos hermanas.	I have two sisters.
No **tengo** dinero.	I don't have any money.
¿Cuántos sellos **tienes**?	How many stamps have you got?
Tiene el pelo rubio.	He has blond hair.

➤ Here are the present simple tense endings for **hacer**:

	hacer	Meaning: to do, to make
(yo)	hago	I do, I make
(tú)	haces	you do, you make
(él/ella/usted)	hace	he/she/it does, he/she/it makes, you do, you make
(nosotros/nosotras)	hacemos	we do, we make
(vosotros/vosotras)	hacéis	you do, you make
(ellos/ellas/ustedes)	hacen	they do, they make, you do, you make

Hago una tortilla.	I'm making an omelet.
No **hago** mucho deporte.	I don't do a lot of sport.
¿Qué **haces**?	What are you doing?
Hace calor.	It's hot.

➤ Here are the present simple tense endings for **ir**:

	ir	Meaning: to go
(yo)	voy	I go
(tú)	vas	you go
(él/ella/usted)	va	he/she/it goes, you go
(nosotros/nosotras)	vamos	we go
(vosotros/vosotras)	vais	you go
(ellos/ellas/ustedes)	van	they go, you go

For further explanation of grammatical terms, please see pages viii-xii.

<u>Voy</u> a Salamanca.	I'm going to Salamanca.
¿Adónde <u>vas</u>?	Where are you going?
No <u>va</u> al colegio.	He doesn't go to school.
No <u>van</u> a vender la casa.	They aren't going to sell the house.

⇨ *For other irregular verbs in the present simple tense, see* **Verb Tables** *in the middle section.*

6 How to use the present simple tense in Spanish

➤ The present simple tense is often used in Spanish in the same way as it is in English, although there are some differences.

➤ As in English, you use the Spanish present simple to talk about:

- things that are generally true

  En verano <u>hace</u> calor.   It's hot in summer.

- things that are true now

  <u>Viven</u> en Guatemala.   They live in Guatemala.

- things that happen all the time or at certain intervals or that you do as a habit

  Marta <u>lleva</u> gafas.   Marta wears glasses.

  Mi tío <u>vende</u> mariscos.   My uncle sells shellfish.

➤ There are some instances when you would use the present simple in Spanish, but you wouldn't use it in English:

- to talk about current projects and activities that may not actually be going on right at this very minute

  <u>Construye</u> una casa.   He's building a house.

- to talk about things that you are planning to do

  El domingo <u>jugamos</u> en León.   We're playing in León on Sunday.

  Mañana <u>voy</u> a Madrid.   I am going to Madrid tomorrow.

- when you use certain time expressions in Spanish, especially **desde** (meaning *since*) and **desde hace** (meaning *for*), to talk about activities and states that started in the past and are still going on now

  Jaime <u>vive</u> aquí <u>desde hace</u> dos años.   Jaime has been living here for two years.

  Daniel <u>vive</u> aquí <u>desde</u> 2009.   Daniel has lived here since 2009.

  <u>Llevo</u> horas esperando aquí.   I've been waiting here for hours.

⇨ *For more information on the use of tenses with* **desde**, *see page 189.*

ser and estar

➤ In Spanish there are two irregular verbs, **ser** and **estar**, that both mean *to be*, although they are used very differently. In the present simple tense, they follow the patterns shown below.

Pronoun	ser	estar	Meaning: *to be*
(yo)	soy	estoy	I am
(tú)	eres	estás	you are
(él/ella/usted)	es	está	he/she/it is, you are
(nosotros/nosotras)	somos	estamos	we are
(vosotros/vosotras)	sois	estáis	you are
(elllos/ellas/ustedes)	son	están	they/you are

➤ **ser** is used:
- with an adjective when talking about a characteristic or fairly permanent quality, for example, shape, size, height, color, material, nationality.

Mi hermano **es** alto.	My brother is tall.
María **es** inteligente.	María is intelligent.
Es rubia.	She's blonde.
Es muy guapa.	She's very pretty.
Es rojo.	It's red.
Es de algodón.	It's made of cotton.
Sus padres **son** italianos.	His parents are Italian.
Es joven/viejo.	He's young/old.
Son muy ricos/pobres.	They're very rich/poor.

- with a following noun or pronoun that tells you what someone or something is

Miguel **es** camarero.	Miguel is a waiter.
Soy yo, Enrique.	It's me, Enrique.
Madrid **es** la capital de España.	Madrid is the capital of Spain.

- to say that something belongs to someone

La casa **es** de Javier.	The house belongs to Javier.
Es mío.	It's mine.

- to talk about where someone or something comes from

Yo **soy** de Santa Clara.	I'm from Santa Clara.
Mi mujer **es** de La Habana.	My wife is from Havana.

- to say what time it is or what the date is

Son las tres y media.	It's half past three.
Mañana es sábado.	Tomorrow is Saturday.

- in calculations

Tres y dos son cinco.	Three and two are five.
¿Cuánto es? – Son dos euros.	How much is it? It's two euros.

- when followed by an infinitive

Lo importante es decir la verdad.	The important thing is to tell the truth.

➾ *For more information on the **Infinitive**, see page 144.*

- to describe actions using the passive (for example *they are made, it is sold*)

Son fabricados en España.	They are made in Spain.

➾ *For more information on the **Passive**, see page 122.*

➤ estar is used:
- to talk about where something or someone is

Estoy en Madrid.	I'm in Madrid.
¿Dónde está Burgos?	Where's Burgos?
Está cerca de aquí.	It's near here.

- with an adjective when there has been a change in the condition of someone or something or to suggest that there is something unexpected about them

El café está frío.	The coffee's cold.
¡Qué guapa estás con este vestido!	How pretty you look in that dress!
Hoy estoy de mal humor.	I'm in a bad mood today.

➾ *For more information on **Adjectives**, see page 19.*

- with a past participle used as an adjective, to describe the state that something is in

Las tiendas están cerradas.	The stores are closed.
No está terminado.	It isn't finished.
El lavabo está ocupado.	The toilet is engaged.
Está roto.	It's broken.

➾ *For more information on **Past participles**, see page 115.*

- when talking about someone's health

¿Cómo **están** ustedes?	How are you?
Estamos todos bien.	We're all well.

- to form continuous tenses such as the present continuous tense

Está comiendo.	He's eating.
Estamos aprendiendo mucho.	We are learning a great deal.

⇨ *For more information on the **Present continuous**, see page 84.*

➤ Both **ser** and **estar** can be used with certain adjectives, but the meaning changes depending on which is used.

➤ Use **ser** to talk about <u>permanent</u> qualities.

Marta **es** muy joven.	Marta is very young.
Es delgado.	He's slim.
Viajar **es** cansado.	Traveling is tiring.
La química **es** aburrida.	Chemistry is boring.

➤ Use **estar** to talk about <u>temporary</u> states or qualities.

Está muy joven con ese vestido.	She looks very young in that dress.
¡**Estás** muy delgada!	You're looking very slim!
Hoy **estoy** cansado.	I'm tired today.
Estoy aburrido.	I'm bored.

➤ **ser** is used with adjectives such as **importante** (meaning *important*) and **imposible** (meaning *impossible*) when the subject is *it* in English.

Es muy interesante.	It's very interesting.
Es imposible.	It's impossible.
Es fácil.	It's easy.

➤ **ser** is used in certain set phrases.

Es igual *or* **Es** lo mismo.	It's all the same.
Es para ti.	It's for you.

➤ **estar** is also used in some set phrases.

- estar de pie — to be standing
  - Juan **está** de pie. — Juan is standing.
- estar de vacaciones — to be on vacation
  - ¿**Estás** de vacaciones? — Are you on vacation?
- estar de viaje — to be on a trip
  - Mi padre **está** de viaje. — My father's on a trip.
- estar de moda — to be in fashion

Las pantallas de plasma están de moda.	Plasma screens are in fashion.

- **estar claro**   to be obvious
  Está claro que no entiendes.   It's obvious that you don't understand.

Grammar Extra!

Both **ser** and **estar** can be used with past participles.

Use **ser** and the past participle in passive constructions to describe an action.

> **Son fabricados en España.**   They are made in Spain.

Use **estar** and the past participle to describe a state.

> **Está terminado.**   It's finished.

⇨ *For more information on **Past participles**, see page 115.*

Key points

✔ **ser** and **estar** both mean *to be* in English, but are used very differently.

✔ **ser** and **estar** are irregular verbs. You have to learn them.

✔ Use **ser** with adjectives describing permanent qualities or characteristics; with nouns or pronouns telling you who or what somebody or something is; with time and dates; and to form the passive.

✔ Use **estar** to talk about location; health; with adjectives describing a change of state; and with past participles used as adjectives to describe states.

✔ **estar** is also used to form present continuous tenses.

✔ **ser** and **estar** can sometimes be used with the same adjectives, but the meaning changes depending on which verb is used.

✔ **ser** and **estar** are both used in a number of set phrases.

The present continuous tense

➤ In Spanish, the present continuous tense is used to talk about something that is happening at this very moment.

➤ The Spanish present continuous tense is formed from the <u>present tense</u> of **estar** and the <u>gerund</u> of the verb. The gerund is the form of the verb that ends in **-ando** (for **-ar** verbs) or **-iendo** (for **-er** and **-ir** verbs) and is the same as the *-ing* form of the verb in English (for example, *walking*, *swimming*).

<u>Estoy</u> traba<u>jando</u>	I'm working.
No <u>estamos</u> com<u>iendo</u>.	We aren't eating.
¿<u>Estás</u> escrib<u>iendo</u>?	Are you writing?

➡ *For more information on **estar** and the **Gerund**, see pages 80 and 125.*

➤ To form the gerund of an **-ar** verb, take off the **-ar** ending of the infinitive and add **-ando**:

Infinitive	Meaning	Stem (without -ar)	Gerund	Meaning
hablar	to speak	**habl-**	**hablando**	speaking
trabajar	to work	**trabaj-**	**trabajando**	working

➤ To form the gerund of an **-er** or **-ir** verb, take off the **-er** or **-ir** ending of the infinitive and add **-iendo**:

Infinitive	Meaning	Stem (without -er/-ir)	Gerund	Meaning
comer	to eat	**com-**	**comiendo**	eating
escribir	to write	**escrib-**	**escribiendo**	writing

Tip

When in doubt, use the present continuous to talk about things that are in the middle of happening right now. Use the present simple tense to talk about activities which are current but which may not be happening at this minute.

Lydia <u>estudia</u> medicina.	Lydia's studying medicine.

➡ *For more information on the **Present simple tense**, see page 72.*

Key points

✔ Use the present continuous in Spanish for actions that are happening right now.

✔ To form the present continuous tense in Spanish, take the present tense of **estar** and add the gerund of the main verb.

The imperative

> **What is the imperative?**
> An **imperative** is a form of the verb used when giving orders and instructions, for example, *Sit down!*; *Don't go!*; *Let's start!*

1 Using the imperative

➤ In Spanish, the form of the imperative that you use for giving instructions depends on:

- whether you are telling someone to do something or not to do something
- whether you are talking to one person or to more than one person
- whether you are on familiar or more formal terms with the person or people

➤ These imperative forms correspond to the familiar **tú** and **vosotros/vosotras** and to the more formal **usted** and **ustedes**, although you don't actually say these pronouns when giving instructions.

⇨ *For more information on **Ways of saying 'you' in Spanish**, see page 44.*

➤ There is also a form of the imperative that corresponds to *let's* in English.

2 Forming the imperative: instructions not to do something

➤ In orders that tell you <u>NOT</u> to do something and that have **no** in front of them in Spanish, the imperative forms for **tú**, **usted**, **nosotros/nosotras**, **vosotros/vosotras** and **ustedes** are all taken from a verb form called the <u>present subjunctive</u>. It's easy to remember because the endings for **-ar** and **-er** verbs are the opposite of what they are in the ordinary present tense.

⇨ *For more information on the **Present tense** and the **Subjunctive**, see pages 71 and 134.*

➤ In regular **-ar** verbs, you take off the **-as**, **-a**, **-amos**, **-áis** and **-an** endings of the present tense and replace them with: **-es**, **-e**, **-emos**, **-éis** and **-en**.

-ar verb	trabajar	to work
tú form	¡no trabajes!	Don't work!
usted form	¡no trabaje!	Don't work!
nosotros/as form	¡no trabajemos!	Let's not work!
vosotros/as form	¡no trabajéis!	Don't work!
ustedes form	¡no trabajen!	Don't work!

86 Verbs

➤ In regular **-er** verbs, you take off the **-es**, **-e**, **-emos**, **-éis** and **-en** endings of the present tense and replace them with **-as**, **-a**, **-amos**, **-áis** and **-an**.

-er verb	comer	to eat
tú form	¡no comas!	Don't eat!
usted form	¡no coma!	Don't eat!
nosotros/as form	¡no comamos!	Let's not eat!
vosotros/as form	¡no comáis!	Don't eat!
ustedes form	¡no coman!	Don't eat!

➤ In regular **-ir** verbs, you take off the **-es**, **-e**, **-imos**, **-ís** and **-en** endings of the present tense and replace them with **-as**, **-a**, **-amos**, **-áis** and **-an**.

-ir verb	decidir	to decide
tú form	¡no decidas!	Don't decide!
usted form	¡no decida!	Don't decide!
nosotros/as form	¡no decidamos!	Let's not decide!
vosotros/as form	¡no decidáis!	Don't decide!
ustedes form	¡no decidan!	Don't decide!

➤ A number of irregular verbs also have irregular imperative forms. These are shown in the table below.

	dar to give	decir to say	estar to be	hacer to do/make	ir to go
tú form	¡no des! don't give!	¡no digas! don't say!	¡no estés! don't be!	¡no hagas! don't do/make!	¡no vayas! don't go!
usted form	¡no dé! don't give!	¡no diga! don't say!	¡no esté! don't be!	¡no haga! don't do/make!	¡no vaya! don't go!
nosotros form	¡no demos! let's not give!	¡no digamos! let's not say!	¡no estemos! let's not be!	¡no hagamos! let's not do/make!	¡no vayamos! let's not go!
vosotros form	¡no deis! don't give!	¡no digáis! don't say!	¡no estéis! don't be!	¡no hagáis! don't do/make!	¡no vayáis! don't go!
ustedes form	¡no den! don't give!	¡no digan! don't say!	¡no estén! don't be!	¡no hagan! don't do/make!	¡no vayan! don't go!

	poner to put	salir to leave	ser to be	tener to have	venir to come
tú form	¡no pongas! don't put!	¡no salgas! don't leave!	¡no seas! don't be!	¡no tengas! don't have!	¡no vengas! don't come!
usted form	¡no ponga! don't put!	¡no salga! don't leave!	¡no sea! don't be!	¡no tenga! don't have!	¡no venga! don't come!
nosotros form	¡no pongamos! let's not put!	¡no salgamos! let's not leave!	¡no seamos! let's not be!	¡no tengamos! let's not have!	¡no vengamos! let's not come!
vosotros form	¡no pongáis! don't put!	¡no salgáis! don't leave!	¡no seáis! don't be!	¡no tengáis! don't have!	¡no vengáis! don't come!
ustedes form	¡no pongan! don't put!	¡no salgan! don't leave!	¡no sean! don't be!	¡no tengan! don't have!	¡no vengan! don't come!

For further explanation of grammatical terms, please see pages viii-xii.

[i] Note that if you take the **yo** form of the present tense, take off the **-o** and add the endings to this instead for instructions <u>NOT TO DO</u> something, some of these irregular forms will be more predictable.

digo	*I say*	→	negative imperative stem	→	**dig-**
hago	*I do*	→	negative imperative stem	→	**hag-**
pongo	*I put*	→	negative imperative stem	→	**pong-**
salgo	*I leave*	→	negative imperative stem	→	**salg-**
tengo	*I have*	→	negative imperative stem	→	**teng-**
vengo	*I come*	→	negative imperative stem	→	**veng-**

3 | Forming the imperative: instructions to do something

➤ In instructions telling you <u>TO DO</u> something, the forms for **usted**, **nosotros** and **ustedes** are exactly the same as they are in negative instructions (instructions telling you not to do something) except that there isn't a **no**.

	trabajar to work	comer to eat	decidir to decide
usted form	¡Trabaje!	¡Coma!	¡Decida!
nosotros/as form	¡Trabajemos!	¡Comamos!	¡Decidamos!
ustedes form	¡Trabajen!	¡Coman!	¡Decidan!

➤ There are special forms of the imperative for **tú** and **vosotros/vosotras** in positive instructions (instructions telling you to do something).

➤ The **tú** form of the imperative is the same as the **tú** form of the ordinary present simple tense, but without the final **s**.

trabajar	→	**¡Trabaja!**
to work		Work!
comer	→	**¡Come!**
to eat		Eat!
decidir	→	**¡Decide!**
to decide		Decide!

⇨ *For more information on the **Present simple tense**, see page 72.*

➤ The **vosotros/vosotras** form of the imperative is the same as the infinitive, except that you take off the final **-r** and add **-d** instead.

trabajar	→	**Trabajad!**
to work		Work!
comer	→	**Comed!**
to eat		Eat!
decidir	→	**Decidid!**
to decide		Decide!

88 Verbs

➤ There are a number of imperative forms that are irregular in Spanish. The irregular imperative forms for **usted**, **nosotros/nosotras** and **ustedes** are the same as the irregular negative imperative forms without the **no**. The **tú** and **vosotros/vosotras** forms are different again.

	dar to give	decir to say	estar to be	hacer to do/make	ir to go
tú form	¡da! give!	¡di! say!	¡está! be!	¡haz! do/make!	¡ve! go!
usted form	¡dé! give!	¡diga! say!	¡esté! be!	¡haga! do/make!	¡vaya! go!
nosotros/as form	¡demos! let's give!	¡digamos! let's say!	¡estemos! let's be!	¡hagamos! let's do/make!	¡vamos! let's go!
vosotros/as form	¡dad! give!	¡decid! say!	¡estad! be!	¡haced! do/make!	¡id! go!
ustedes form	¡den! give!	¡digan! say!	¡estén! be!	¡hagan! do/make!	¡vayan! go!

	poner to put	salir to leave	ser to be	tener to have	venir to come
tú form	¡pon! put!	¡sal! leave!	¡sé! be!	¡ten! have!	¡ven! come!
usted form	¡ponga! put!	¡salga! leave!	¡sea! be!	¡tenga! have!	¡venga! come!
nosotros/as form	¡pongamos! let's put!	¡salgamos! let's leave!	¡seamos! let's be!	¡tengamos! let's have!	¡vengamos! let's come!
vosotros/as form	¡poned! put!	¡salid! leave!	¡sed! be!	¡tened! have!	¡venid! come!
ustedes form	¡pongan! put!	¡salgan! leave!	¡sean! be!	¡tengan! have!	¡vengan! come!

ⓘ Note that the **nosotros/as** form for **ir** in instructions TO DO something is **vamos**; in instructions NOT TO DO something, it is **no vayamos**.

4 Position of object pronouns

➤ An object pronoun is a word like **me** (meaning *me* or *to me*), **la** (meaning *her/it*) or **les** (meaning *to them/to you*) that is used instead of a noun as the object of a sentence. In orders and instructions, the position of these object pronouns in the sentence changes depending on whether you are telling someone TO DO something or NOT TO DO something.

⇨ *For more information on **Object pronouns**, see page 46.*

For further explanation of grammatical terms, please see pages viii-xii.

➤ If you are telling someone <u>NOT TO DO</u> something, the object pronouns go <u>BEFORE</u> the verb.

¡No <u>me lo</u> mandes!	Don't send it to me!
¡No <u>me</u> molestes!	Don't disturb me!
¡No <u>los</u> castigue!	Don't punish them!
¡No <u>se la</u> devolvamos!	Let's not give it back to him/her/them!
¡No <u>les</u> contestéis!	Don't answer them!

➤ If you are telling someone <u>TO DO</u> something, the object pronouns join on to the <u>END</u> of the verb. An accent is usually added to make sure that the stress in the imperative verb stays the same.

¡Explíca<u>melo</u>!	Explain it to me!
¡Perdóne<u>me</u>!	Excuse me!
¡Díga<u>me</u>!	Tell me!
¡Esperémos<u>la</u>!	Let's wait for her/it!

[i] Note that when there are two object pronouns, the indirect object pronoun always goes before the direct object pronoun.

⇨ *For more information on **Stress**, see page 200.*

5 Other ways of giving instructions

➤ For general instructions in instruction leaflets, recipes and so on, use the <u>infinitive</u> form instead of the imperative.

<u>Ver</u> página 9.	See page 9.

➤ **vamos a** with the infinitive is often used to mean *let's.*

<u>Vamos a</u> ver.	Let's see.
<u>Vamos a</u> empezar.	Let's start.

Key points

✔ In Spanish, in instructions <u>not to do</u> something, the endings are taken from the present subjunctive. They are the same as the corresponding endings for **-ar** and **-er** verbs in the ordinary present tense, except that the **-e** endings go on the **-ar** verbs and the **-a** endings go on the **-er** and **-ir** verbs.

✔ For **-ar** verbs the forms are: **no hables** (**tú** form); **no hable** (**usted** form); **no hablemos** (**nosotros/as** form); **no habléis** (**vosotros/as** form); **no hablen** (**ustedes** form)

✔ For **-er** verbs the forms are: **no comas** (**tú** form); **no coma** (**usted** form); **no comamos** (**nosotros/as** form); **no comáis** (**vosotros/as** form); **no coman** (**ustedes** form)

✔ For **-ir** verbs the forms are: **no decidas** (**tú** form); **no decida** (**usted** form); **no decidamos** (**nosotros/as** form); **no decidáis** (**vosotros/as** form); **no decidan** (**ustedes** form)

✔ In instructions <u>to do</u> something, the forms for **usted**, **nosotros/as** and **ustedes** are the same as they are in instructions not to do something.

✔ The forms for **tú** and **vosotros/as** are different:
  ● the **tú** form is the same as the corresponding form in the ordinary present tense, but without the final **-s**: **trabaja**; **come**; **decide**
  ● the **vosotros/as** form is the same as the infinitive but with a final **-d** instead of the **-r**: **trabajad**; **comed**; **decidid**

✔ A number of verbs have irregular imperative forms.

✔ The object pronouns in imperatives go before the verb when telling someone not to do something; they join onto the end of the verb when telling someone to do something.

Reflexive verbs

> **What is a reflexive verb?**
> A **reflexive verb** is one where the subject and object are the same, and where the action 'reflects back' on the subject. It is used with a reflexive pronoun such as *myself, yourself* and *herself* in English, for example, *I washed myself.*;
> *He shaved himself.*

1 Using reflexive verbs

➤ In Spanish, reflexive verbs are much more common than in English, and many are used in everyday language. The infinitive form of a reflexive verb has **se** attached to the end of it, for example, **secarse** (meaning *to dry oneself*). This is the way reflexive verbs are shown in dictionaries. **se** means *himself, herself, itself, yourself, themselves, yourselves* and *oneself*. **se** is called a reflexive pronoun.

➤ In Spanish, reflexive verbs are often used to describe things you do to yourself every day or that involve a change of some sort, for example, going to bed, sitting down, getting angry, and so on. Some of the most common reflexive verbs in Spanish are listed here.

acostarse	to go to bed
afeitarse	to shave
bañarse	to have a bath, to have a swim
dormirse	to go to sleep
ducharse	to have a shower
enfadarse	to get angry
lavarse	to wash
levantarse	to get up
llamarse	to be called
secarse	to get dried
sentarse	to sit down
vestirse	to get dressed

Me baño a las siete y media.	I have a bath at half past seven.
¡Duérmete!	Go to sleep!
Mi hermana **se ducha**.	My sister has a shower.
Mi madre **se enfada** mucho.	My mother often gets angry.
Mi hermano no **se lava**.	My brother doesn't wash.
Me levanto a las siete.	I get up at seven o'clock.
¿Cómo **te llamas**?	What's your name?
¿A qué hora **os acostáis**?	What time do you go to bed?
¡Sentaos!	Sit down!
Nos vestimos.	We're getting dressed.

i Note that **se**, **me** and so on are very rarely translated as *himself*, *myself* and so on in English. Instead of *he dresses himself* or *they bath themselves*, in English, we are more likely to say *he gets dressed* or *they have a bath*.

➤ Some Spanish verbs can be used both as reflexive verbs and as ordinary verbs (without the reflexive pronoun). When they are used as ordinary verbs, the person or thing doing the action is not the same as the person or thing receiving the action, so the meaning is different.

Me lavo.	I wash (myself).
Lavo la ropa a mano.	I wash the clothes by hand.
Me llamo Antonio.	I'm called Antonio.
¡Llama a la policía!	Call the police!
Me acuesto a las 11.	I go to bed at 11 o'clock.
Acuesta al niño.	He puts the child to bed.

Grammar Extra!

Some verbs mean <u>ALMOST</u> the same in the reflexive as when they are used on their own.

Duermo.	I sleep.
Me duermo.	I go to sleep.
¿Quieres ir al cine?	Do you want to go to the movies?
Acaba de ir**se**.	He has just left.

---

2 **Forming the present tense of reflexive verbs**

➤ To use a reflexive verb in Spanish, you need to decide which reflexive pronoun to use. See how the reflexive pronouns in the table on the next page correspond to the subject pronouns.

Subject pronoun	Reflexive pronoun	Meaning
(yo)	me	myself
(tú)	te	yourself
(él) (ella) (uno) (usted)	se	himself herself oneself itself yourself
(nosotros/nosotras)	nos	ourselves
(vosotros/vosotras)	os	yourselves
(ellos) (ellas) (ustedes)	se	themselves yourselves

(Yo) <u>me</u> levanto temprano.	I get up early.
(Él) <u>se</u> acuesta a las once.	He goes to bed at eleven.
Ellos no <u>se</u> afeitan.	They don't shave.

➤ The present tense forms of a reflexive verb work in just the same way as an ordinary verb, except that the reflexive pronoun is used as well.

⇨ *For more information on the Present tense, see page 71.*

➤ The following table shows the reflexive verb **lavarse** in full.

Reflexive forms of lavarse	Meaning
(yo) me lavo	I wash (myself)
(tú) te lavas	you wash (yourself)
(él) se lava (ella) se lava (uno) se lava se lava (usted) se lava	he washes (himself) she washes (herself) one washes (oneself) it washes (itself) you wash (yourself)
(nosotros/nosotras) nos lavamos	we wash (ourselves)
(vosotros/vosotras) os laváis	you wash (yourselves)
(ellos) se lavan (ellas) se lavan (ustedes) se lavan	they wash (themselves) they wash (themselves) you wash (yourselves)

➤ Some reflexive verbs, such as **acostarse**, are irregular. Some of these irregular verbs are shown in the **Verb tables** in the middle section.

3 | Position of reflexive pronouns

➤ In ordinary tenses such as the present simple, the reflexive pronoun goes <u>BEFORE</u> the verb:

<u>Me</u> acuesto temprano.	I go to bed early.
¿Cómo <u>se</u> llama usted?	What's your name?

⇨ *For more information on the **Present simple tense**, see page 72.*

➤ When telling someone <u>NOT TO DO</u> something, you also put the reflexive pronoun <u>BEFORE</u> the verb.

No <u>te</u> levantes.	Don't get up.
¡No <u>os</u> vayáis!	Don't go away!

➤ When telling someone <u>TO DO</u> something, you join the reflexive pronoun onto the end of the verb.

¡Sién<u>tense</u>!	Sit down!
¡Cálla<u>te</u>!	Be quiet!

⇨ *For more information on the **Imperative**, see page 85.*

> *Típ*
>
> When adding reflexive pronouns to the end of the imperative,
> you drop the final **-s** of the **nosotros** form and the final **-d** of the
> **vosotros** form, before the pronoun.
>
> | | |
> |---|---|
> | ¡Vámo<u>nos</u>! | Let's go! |
> | ¡Senta<u>os</u>! | Sit down! |

➤ You always join the reflexive pronoun onto the end of infinitives and gerunds (the **-ando** or **-iendo** forms of the verb) unless the infinitive or gerund follows another verb.

Hay que relajar<u>se</u> de vez en cuando.	You have to relax from time to time.
Acostándo<u>se</u> temprano, se descansa mejor.	You feel more rested by going to bed early.

➤ Where the infinitive or gerund follows another verb, you can put the reflexive pronoun either at the end of the infinitive or gerund or before the other verb.

Quiero bañar<u>me</u> *or* <u>Me</u> quiero bañar.	I want to have a bath.

Tienes que vestirte or **Te tienes que vestir.**	You must get dressed.
Está vistiéndose or **Se está vistiendo.**	She's getting dressed.
¿Estás duchándote? or **¿Te estás duchando?**	Are you having a shower?

⇨ *For more information on **Gerunds**, see page 125.*

[i] Note that, when adding pronouns to the ends of verb forms, you will often have to add a written accent to preserve the stress.

⇨ *For more information on **Stress**, see page 200.*

4 Using reflexive verbs with parts of the body and clothes

➤ In Spanish, you often talk about actions to do with your body or your clothing using a reflexive verb.

Se está secando el pelo.	She's drying her hair.
Nos lavamos los dientes.	We brush our teeth.
Se está poniendo el abrigo.	He's putting on his coat.

[i] Note that in Spanish you do not use a possessive adjective such as *my* and *her* when talking about parts of the body. You use **el**, **la**, **los** and **las** with a reflexive verb instead.

Me estoy lavando las manos.	I'm washing my hands.

⇨ *For more information on **Articles**, see page 10.*

5 Other uses of reflexive verbs

➤ In English we often use a passive construction, for example, *goods are transported all over the world, most of our tea is imported from India and China.* In Spanish, this construction is not used so much. Instead, very often a reflexive verb with **se** is used.

Aquí se vende café.	Coffee is sold here.
Aquí se venden muchos libros.	Lots of books are sold here.
Se habla inglés.	English is spoken here.
En Suiza se hablan tres idiomas.	Three languages are spoken in Switzerland.

[i] Note that the verb has to be singular or plural depending on whether the noun is singular or plural.

⇨ *For more information on the **Passive**, see page 122.*

➤ A reflexive verb with **se** is also used in some very common expressions.

¿Cómo <u>se dice</u> "siesta" en inglés?	How do you say "siesta" in English?
¿Cómo <u>se escribe</u> "Tarragona"?	How do you spell "Tarragona"?

➤ **se** is also used in impersonal expressions. In this case, it often corresponds to *one* (or *you*) in English.

No <u>se puede</u> entrar.	You can't go in.
No <u>se permite</u>.	You aren't or It isn't allowed.

➪ *For more information on **Impersonal verbs**, see page 129.*

➤ **nos**, **os** and **se** are all also used to mean *each other* and *one another*.

<u>Nos</u> escribimos.	We write to one another.
<u>Nos</u> queremos.	We love each other.
Rachel y Julie <u>se</u> odian.	Rachel and Julie hate each other.
No <u>se</u> conocen.	They don't know each other.

Key points

✔ A reflexive verb is made up of a reflexive pronoun and a verb.

✔ The reflexive pronouns are: **me**, **te**, **se**, **nos**, **os**, **se**.

✔ The reflexive pronoun goes before the verb, except when you are telling someone to do something and with infinitives and gerunds.

The future tense

> **What is the future tense?**
> The **future** tense is a verb tense used to talk about something that will happen or will be true in the future, for example, *He'll be here soon; I'll give you a call; What will you do?; It will be sunny tomorrow.*

1 Ways of talking about the future

➤ In Spanish, just as in English, you can often use the present tense to refer to something that is going to happen in the future.

Cogemos el tren de las once.	We're getting the eleven o'clock train.
Mañana voy a Madrid.	I am going to Madrid tomorrow.

➤ In English we often use *going to* with an infinitive to talk about the immediate future or our future plans. In Spanish, you can use the present tense of **ir** followed by **a** and an infinitive.

Va a perder el tren.	He's going to miss the train.
Va a llevar una media hora.	It's going to take about half an hour.
Voy a hacerlo mañana.	I'm going to do it tomorrow.

2 Forming the future tense

➤ In English we can form the future tense by putting *will* or its shortened form *'ll* before the verb. In Spanish you have to change the verb endings. So, just as **hablo** means *I speak*, **hablaré** means *I will speak* or *I shall speak.*

➤ To form the future tense of regular **-ar**, **-er** and **-ir** verbs, add the following endings to the infinitive of the verb: **-é, -ás, -á, -emos, -éis, -án**.

➤ The following table shows the future tense of three regular verbs: **hablar** (meaning *to speak*), **comer** (meaning *to eat*) and **vivir** (meaning *to live*).

(yo)	hablaré	comeré	viviré	I'll speak/eat/live
(tú)	hablarás	comerás	vivirás	you'll speak/eat/live
(él) (ella) (usted)	hablará	comerá	vivirá	he'll speak/eat/live she'll speak/eat/live it'll speak/eat/live you'll speak/eat/live
(nosotros/nosotras)	hablaremos	comeremos	viviremos	we'll speak/eat/live
(vosotros/vosotras)	hablaréis	comeréis	viviréis	you'll speak/eat/live
(ellos/ellas/ustedes)	hablarán	comerán	vivirán	they'll/you'll speak/eat/live

Hablaré con ella.	I'll speak to her.
Comeremos en casa de José.	We'll eat at José's.
No **volverá**.	He won't come back.
¿Lo **entenderás**?	Will you understand it?

i Note that in the future tense only the **nosotros/nosotras** form doesn't have an accent.

> ## Tip
>
> Remember that Spanish has no direct equivalent of the word *will* in verb forms like *will rain* or *will look* and so on. You change the Spanish verb ending instead to form the future tense.

Grammar Extra!

In English, we sometimes use *will* with the meaning of *be willing to* rather than simply to express the future, for example, *Will you wait for me a moment?* In Spanish you don't use the future tense to say this; you use the verb **querer** (meaning *to want*) instead.

¿Me **quieres** esperar un momento, por favor?	Will you wait for me a moment, please?

---

3 | Verbs with irregular stems in the future tense

➤ There are a few verbs that <u>DO NOT</u> use their infinitives as the stem for the future tense. Here are some of the most common.

Verb	Stem	(yo)	(tú)	(él) (ella) (usted)	(nosotros) (nosotras)	(vosotros) (vosotras)	(ellos) (ellas) (ustedes)
decir to say	dir-	diré	dirás	dirá	diremos	diréis	dirán
haber to have	habr-	habré	habrás	habrá	habremos	habréis	habrán
hacer to do/make	har-	haré	harás	hará	haremos	haréis	harán
poder to be able to	podr-	podré	podrás	podrá	podremos	podréis	podrán
poner to put	pondr-	pondré	pondrás	pondrá	pondremos	pondréis	pondrán
querer to want	querr-	querré	querrás	querrá	querremos	querréis	querrán
saber to know	sabr-	sabré	sabrás	sabrá	sabremos	sabréis	sabrán

For further explanation of grammatical terms, please see pages viii-xii.

Verb	Stem	(yo)	(tú)	(él) (ella) (usted)	(nosotros) (nosotras)	(vosotros) (vosotras)	(ellos) (ellas) (ustedes)
salir to leave	saldr-	saldré	saldrás	saldrá	saldremos	saldréis	saldrán
tener to have	tendr-	tendré	tendrás	tendrá	tendremos	tendréis	tendrán
venir to come	vendr-	vendré	vendrás	vendrá	vendremos	vendréis	vendrán

Lo **haré** mañana.	I'll do it tomorrow.
No **podremos** hacerlo.	We won't be able to do it.
Lo **pondré** aquí.	I'll put it here.
Saldrán por la mañana.	They'll leave in the morning.
¿A qué hora **vendrás?**	What time will you come?

🛈 Note that the verb **haber** is only used when forming other tenses, such as the perfect tense, and in the expression **hay** (meaning *there is* or *there are*).

⇨ *For more information on the **Perfect tense** and on **hay**, see pages 115 and 130.*

4 Reflexive verbs in the future tense

➤ The future tense of reflexive verbs is formed in just the same way as for ordinary verbs, except that you have to remember to give the reflexive pronoun (**me**, **te**, **se**, **nos**, **os**, **se**).

Me levantaré temprano.	I'll get up early.

Key points

✔ You can use a present tense in Spanish to talk about something that will happen or be true, just as in English.

✔ You can use **ir a** with an infinitive to talk about things that will happen in the immediate future.

✔ In Spanish there is no direct equivalent of the word *will* in verb forms like *will rain* and *will look*. You change the verb endings instead.

✔ To form the future tense, add the endings **-é**, **-ás**, **á**, **-emos**, **-éis**, **-án** to the infinitive.

✔ Some verbs have irregular stems in the future tense. It is worth learning these.

The conditional

> **What is the conditional?**
> The **conditional** is a verb form used to talk about things that would happen or that would be true under certain conditions, for example, I _would_ help you _if I could_.
> It is also used to say what you would like or need, for example, _Could_ you give me the bill?

1 Using the conditional

➤ You can often recognize a conditional in English by the word _would_ or its shortened form _'d_.

I _would_ be sad if you left.
If you asked him, he_'d_ help you.

➤ You use the conditional for:

- saying what you would like to do

  Me gustaría conocerlo.   I'd like to meet him.

- making suggestions

  Podrías alquilar una bici.   You could hire a bike.

- giving advice

  Deberías hacer más ejercicio.   You should take more exercise.

- saying what you would do

  Le dije que le ayudaría.   I said I would help him.

> _Tip_
>
> There is no direct Spanish translation of _would_ in verb forms like _would be_, _would like_, _would help_ and so on. You change the Spanish verb ending instead.

2 Forming the conditional

➤ To form the conditional of regular **-ar**, **-er**, and **-ir** verbs, add the following endings to the _infinitive_ of the verb: **-ía**, **-ías**, **-ía**, **-íamos**, **-íais**, **-ían**.

➤ The following table shows the conditional tense of three regular verbs: **hablar** (meaning *to speak*), **comer** (meaning *to eat*) and **vivir** (meaning *to live*).

(yo)	hablaría	comería	viviría	I would speak/eat/live
(tú)	hablarías	comerías	vivirías	you would speak/eat/live
(él)	hablaría	comería	viviría	he would speak/eat/live
(ella)				she would speak/eat/live it would speak/eat/live
(usted)				you would speak/eat/live
(nosotros/nosotras)	hablaríamos	comeríamos	viviríamos	we would speak/eat/live
(vosotros/vosotras)	hablaríais	comeríais	viviríais	you would speak/eat/live
(ellos/ellas)	hablarían	comerían	vivirían	they would speak/eat/live
(ustedes)				you would speak/eat/live

Dije que <u>hablaría</u> con ella.	I said that I would speak to her.
Si tuvieras tiempo, <u>comería</u> contigo.	I'd have lunch with you if you had time.
Aquí <u>viviríais</u> más tranquilos.	You'd have a quieter life here.

Tip

Don't forget to put an accent on the **i** in the conditional.

i Note that the endings in the conditional tense are identical to those of the <u>imperfect tense</u> for **-er** and **-ir** verbs. The only difference is that they are added to a different stem.

⇨ *For more information on the **Imperfect tense**, see page 110.*

3 | Verbs with irregular stems in the conditional

➤ To form the conditional of irregular verbs, use the same stem as for the <u>future tense</u>, then add the usual endings for the conditional. The same verbs that are irregular in the future tense are irregular in the conditional.

Verb	Stem	(yo)	(tú)	(él) (ella) (usted)	(nosotros) (nosotras)	(vosotros) (vosotras)	(ellos) (ellas) (ustedes)
decir to say	dir-	diría	dirías	diría	diríamos	diríais	dirían
haber to have	habr-	habría	habrías	habría	habríamos	habríais	habrían
hacer to do/ make	har-	haría	harías	haría	haríamos	haríais	harían
poder to be able to	podr-	podría	podrías	podría	podríamos	podríais	podrían
poner to put	pondr-	pondría	pondrías	pondría	pondríamos	pondríais	pondrían
querer to want	querr-	querría	querrías	querría	querríamos	querríais	querrían
saber to know	sabr-	sabría	sabrías	sabría	sabríamos	sabríais	sabrían
salir to leave	saldr-	saldría	saldrías	saldría	saldríamos	saldríais	saldrían
tener to have	tendr-	tendría	tendrías	tendría	tendríamos	tendríais	tendrían
venir to come	vendr-	vendría	vendrías	<u>vendría</u>	vendríamos	vendríais	vendrían

⇨ For more information on the **Future tense**, see page 97.

    ¿Qué <u>harías</u> tú en mi lugar?   What would you do if you were me?
    ¿<u>Podrías</u> ayudarme?   Could you help me?
    Yo lo <u>pondría</u> aquí.   I would put it here.

ⓘ Note that the verb **haber** is only used when forming other tenses, such as the perfect tense, and in the expression **hay** (meaning *there is/there are*).

⇨ For more information on the **Perfect tense** and on **hay**, see pages 115 and 130.

4 | Reflexive verbs in the conditional

➤ The conditional of reflexive verbs is formed in just the same way as for ordinary verbs, except that you have to remember to give the reflexive pronoun (**me**, **te**, **se**, **nos**, **os**, **se**).

> **Le dije que <u>me levantaría</u>**
> **temprano.**
>
> I told him I would get up early.

Key points

✔ In Spanish, there is no direct equivalent of the word *would* in verb forms like *would go* and *would look* and so on. You change the verb ending instead.

✔ To form the conditional tense, add the endings **-ía**, **ías**, **-ía**, **-íamos**, **-íais**, **-ían** to the infinitive. The conditional uses the same stem as for the future.

✔ Some verbs have irregular stems which are used for both the conditional and the future. It is worth learning these.

The preterite

> **What is the preterite?**
> The **preterite** is a form of the verb that is used to talk about actions that
> were completed in the past in Spanish. It often corresponds to the simple
> past in English, as in I <u>bought</u> a new bike; Mary <u>went</u> to the store on Friday; I <u>typed</u>
> two reports yesterday.

1 Using the preterite

➤ In English, we use the <u>simple past tense</u> to talk about actions:
  - that were completed at a certain point in the past
    I <u>bought</u> a dress yesterday.
  - that were part of a series of events
    I <u>went</u> to the beach, <u>undressed</u> and <u>put on</u> my swimsuit.
  - that went on for a certain amount of time
    The war <u>lasted</u> three years.

➤ In English, we also use the <u>simple past tense</u> to describe actions which
  happened frequently (*Our parents <u>took</u> us swimming in the vacations*), and to
  describe settings (*It <u>was</u> a dark and stormy night*).

➤ In Spanish, the <u>preterite</u> is the most common tense for talking about the past.
  You use the preterite for actions:
  - that were completed at a certain point in the past

    Ayer <u>compré</u> un vestido.   I bought a dress yesterday.
  - that were part of a series of events

    <u>Fui</u> a la playa, me <u>quité</u> la ropa   I went to the beach, undressed and
    y me <u>puse</u> el bañador.   put on my swimsuit.
  - that went on for a certain amount of time

    La guerra <u>duró</u> tres años.   The war lasted for three years.

➤ However, you use the <u>imperfect tense</u> for actions that happened frequently
  (where you could use *used to* in English) and for descriptions of settings.

▷ *For more information on the **Imperfect tense**, see page 110.*

2 Forming the preterite of regular verbs

➤ To form the preterite of any regular **-ar** verb, you take off the **-ar** ending to
  form the stem, and add the endings: **-é, -aste, -ó, -amos, -asteis, -aron**.

For further explanation of grammatical terms, please see pages viii-xii.

➤ To form the preterite of any regular **-er** or **-ir** verb, you also take off the **-er** or **-ir** ending to form the stem and add the endings: **-í**, **-iste**, **-ió**, **-imos**, **-isteis**, **-ieron**.

➤ The following table shows the preterite of three regular verbs: **hablar** (meaning *to speak*), **comer** (meaning *to eat*) and **vivir** (meaning *to live*).

(yo)	habl**é**	com**í**	viv**í**	I spoke/ate/lived
(tú)	habl**aste**	com**iste**	viv**iste**	you spoke/ate/lived
(él) (ella) (usted)	habl**ó**	com**ió**	viv**ió**	he spoke/ate/lived she spoke/ate/lived it spoke/ate/lived you spoke/ate/lived
(nosotros/nosotras)	habl**amos**	com**imos**	viv**imos**	we spoke/ate/lived
(vosotros/vosotras)	habl**asteis**	com**isteis**	viv**isteis**	you spoke/ate/lived
(ellos/ellas) (ustedes)	habl**aron**	com**ieron**	viv**ieron**	they spoke/ate/lived you spoke/ate/lived

<u>Bailé</u> con mi hermana.	I danced with my sister.
No <u>hablé</u> con ella.	I didn't speak to her.
<u>Comimos</u> en un restaurante.	We had lunch in a restaurant.
¿<u>Cerraste la</u> ventana?	Did you close the window?

i Note that Spanish has no direct translation of *did* or *didn't* in questions or negative sentences. You simply use a past tense and make it a question by making your voice go up at the end or changing the word order; you make it negative by adding **no**.

⇨ For more information on **Questions** and **Negatives**, see pages 160 and 157.

Tip

Remember the accents on the **yo** and **él/ella/usted** forms of regular verbs in the preterite. Only an accent shows the difference, for example, between **hablo** *I speak* and **habló** *he spoke*.

3 | Irregular verbs in the preterite

➤ A number of verbs have very irregular forms in the preterite. The table shows some of the most common.

Verb	(yo)	(tú)	(él) (ella) (usted)	(nosotros) (nosotras)	(vosotros) (vosotras)	(ellos) (ellas) (ustedes)
andar to walk	anduve	anduviste	anduvo	anduvimos	anduvisteis	anduvieron
conducir to drive	conduje	condujiste	condujo	condujimos	condujisteis	condujeron
dar to give	di	diste	dio	dimos	disteis	dieron
decir to say	dije	dijiste	dijo	dijimos	dijisteis	dijeron
estar to be	estuve	estuviste	estuvo	estuvimos	estuvisteis	estuvieron
hacer to do, to make	hice	hiciste	hizo	hicimos	hicisteis	hicieron
ir to go	fui	fuiste	fue	fuimos	fuisteis	fueron
poder to be able to	pude	pudiste	pudo	pudimos	pudisteis	pudieron
poner to put	puse	pusiste	puso	pusimos	pusisteis	pusieron
querer to want	quise	quisiste	quiso	quisimos	quisisteis	quisieron
saber to know	supe	supiste	supo	supimos	supisteis	supieron
ser to be	fui	fuiste	fue	fuimos	fuisteis	fueron
tener to have	tuve	tuviste	tuvo	tuvimos	tuvisteis	tuvieron
traer to bring	traje	trajiste	trajo	trajimos	trajisteis	trajeron
venir to come	vine	viniste	vino	vinimos	vinisteis	vinieron
ver to see	vi	viste	vio	vimos	visteis	vieron

ⓘ Note that **hizo** (the **él/ella/usted** form of **hacer**) is spelt with a **z**.

⇨ *For more information on **Spelling**, see page 196.*

For further explanation of grammatical terms, please see pages viii-xii.

Fue a Madrid.	He went to Madrid.
Te **vi** en el parque.	I saw you in the park.
No **vinieron**.	They didn't come.
¿Qué **hizo**?	What did she do?
Se lo **di** a Teresa.	I gave it to Teresa.
Fue en 1999.	It was in 1999.

Típ

The preterite forms of **ser** (meaning *to be*) are the same as the preterite forms of **ir** (meaning *to go*).

➤ Some other verbs are regular EXCEPT FOR the **él/ella/usted** and **ellos/ellas/ustedes** forms (*third persons singular and plural*). In these forms the stem vowel changes.

Verb	(yo)	(tú)	(él) (ella) (usted)	(nosotros) (nosotras)	(vosotros) (vosotras)	(ellos) (ellas) (ustedes)
dormir to sleep	dormí	dormiste	d**u**rmió	dormimos	dormisteis	d**u**rmieron
morir to die	morí	moriste	m**u**rió	morimos	moristeis	m**u**rieron
pedir to ask for	pedí	pediste	p**i**dió	pedimos	pedisteis	p**i**dieron
reír to laugh	reí	reíste	r**i**o	reímos	reísteis	r**i**eron
seguir to follow	seguí	seguiste	s**i**guió	seguimos	seguisteis	s**i**guieron
sentir to feel	sentí	sentiste	s**i**ntió	sentimos	sentisteis	s**i**ntieron

i Note that **reír** also has an accent in all persons APART FROM the **él/ella/usted** and **ellos/ellas/ustedes** (third persons singular and plural) forms.

Antonio **durmió** diez horas.	Antonio slept for ten hours.
Murió en 1066.	He died in 1066.
Pidió paella.	He asked for paella.
¿Los **siguió**?	Did she follow them?
Sintió un dolor en la pierna.	He felt a pain in his leg.
Nos **reímos** mucho.	We laughed a lot.
Juan no se **rio**.	Juan didn't laugh.

➤ **caer** (meaning *to fall*) and **leer** (meaning *to read*) have an accent in all persons apart from the **ellos/ellas/ustedes** form (*third person plural*). In addition, the vowel changes to **y** in the **él/ella/usted** and **ellos/ellas/ustedes** forms (*third persons singular and plural*).

Verb	(yo)	(tú)	(él) (ella) (usted)	(nosotros) (nosotras)	(vosotros) (vosotras)	(ellos) (ellas) (ustedes)
caer to fall	caí	caíste	cayó	caímos	caísteis	cayeron
construir to build	construí	construiste	construyó	construimos	construisteis	construyeron
leer to read	leí	leíste	leyó	leímos	leísteis	leyeron

i Note that **construir** also changes to **y** in the **él/ella/usted** and **ellos/ellas/ustedes** forms (*third persons singular and plural*), but only has accents in the **yo** and **él/ella/usted** forms.

Se <u>cayó</u> por la ventana.	He fell out of the window.
Ayer <u>leí</u> un artículo muy interesante.	I read a very interesting article yesterday.
<u>Construyeron</u> una nueva autopista.	They built a new highway.

4 | Other spelling changes in the preterite

➤ Spanish verbs that end in **-zar**, **-gar** and **-car** in the infinitive change the **z** to **c**, the **g** to **gu** and the **c** to **qu** in the **yo** form (*first person singular*).

Verb	(yo)	(tú)	(él) (ella) (usted)	(nosotros) (nosotras)	(vosotros) (vosotras)	(ellos) (ellas) (ustedes)
cruzar to cross	cru<u>c</u>é	cruzaste	cruzó	cruzamos	cruzasteis	cruzaron
empezar to begin	empe<u>c</u>é	empezaste	empezó	empezamos	empezasteis	empezaron
pagar to pay for	pa<u>gu</u>é	pagaste	pagó	pagamos	pagasteis	pagaron
sacar to take out	sa<u>qu</u>é	sacaste	sacó	sacamos	sacasteis	sacaron

<u>Crucé</u> el río.	I crossed the river.
<u>Empecé</u> a hacer mis deberes.	I began doing my homework.
No <u>pagué</u> la cuenta.	I didn't pay the bill.
Me <u>saqué</u> las llaves del bolsillo.	I took my keys out of my pocket.

For further explanation of grammatical terms, please see pages viii–xii.

ⓘ Note that the change from **g** to **gu** and **c** to **qu** before **e** is to keep the sound hard.

⇨ *For more information on **Spelling**, see page 196.*

5 | Reflexive verbs in the preterite

➤ The preterite of reflexive verbs is formed in just the same way as for ordinary verbs, except that you have to remember to give the reflexive pronoun (**me**, **te**, **se**, **nos**, **os**, **se**).

Me levanté a las siete.   I got up at seven.

Key points

✔ The preterite is the most common way to talk about the past in Spanish.

✔ To form the preterite of regular **-ar** verbs, take off the **-ar** ending and add the endings: **-é**, **-aste**, **-ó**, **-amos**, **-asteis**, **-aron**.

✔ To form the preterite of regular **-er** and **-ir** verbs, take off the **-er** and **-ir** endings and add the endings: **-í**, **-iste**, **-ió**, **-imos**, **-isteis**, **-ieron**.

✔ There are a number of verbs which are irregular in the preterite. These forms have to be learnt.

✔ With some verbs, the accents and spelling change in certain forms.

The imperfect tense

> **What is the imperfect tense?**
> The **imperfect tense** is one of the verb tenses used to talk about the past, especially in descriptions, and to say what was happening or used to happen, for example, *It was sunny at the weekend; We were living in Spain at the time; I used to walk to school.*

1 Using the imperfect tense

➤ In Spanish, the imperfect tense is used:

- to describe what things were like and how people felt in the past

Hacía calor.	It was hot.
No **teníamos** mucho dinero.	We didn't have much money.
Tenía hambre.	I was hungry.

- to say what used to happen or what you used to do regularly in the past

Cada día **llamaba** a su madre.	He used to call his mother every day.

- to describe what was happening or what the situation was when something else took place

Tomábamos café.	We were having coffee.
Me **caí** cuando **cruzaba** la carretera.	I fell over when I was crossing the street.

Grammar Extra!

Sometimes, instead of the ordinary imperfect tense being used to describe what was happening at a given moment in the past when something else occurred interrupting it, the continuous form is used. This is made up of the imperfect tense of **estar** (**estaba**, **estabas** and so on), followed by the **-ando/-iendo** form of the main verb. The other verb – the one that relates the event that occurred – is in the preterite.

Montse **miraba** la televisión *or* Montse **estaba mirando** la televisión cuando sonó el teléfono.	Montse was watching television when the telephone rang.

⇨ *For further information on the **Preterite**, see page 104.*

---

2 Forming the imperfect tense

➤ To form the imperfect of any regular **-ar** verb, you take off the **-ar** ending of the infinitive to form the stem and add the endings: **-aba, -abas, -aba, -ábamos, -abais, -aban**.

For further explanation of grammatical terms, please see pages viii-xii.

➤ The following table shows the imperfect tense of one regular -ar verb: **hablar** (meaning *to speak*).

(yo)	**hablaba**	I spoke I was speaking I used to speak
(tú)	**hablabas**	you spoke you were speaking you used to speak
(él/ella/usted)	**hablaba**	he/she/it/you spoke he/she/it was speaking, you were speaking he/she/it/you used to speak
(nosotros/nosotras)	**hablábamos**	we spoke we were speaking we used to speak
(vosotros/vosotras)	**hablabais**	you spoke you were speaking you used to speak
(ellos/ellas/ustedes)	**hablaban**	they/you spoke they/you were speaking they/you used to speak

ℹ️ Note that in the imperfect tense of -**ar** verbs, the only accent is on the nosotros/nosotras form

Hablaba francés e italiano.	He spoke French and Italian.
Cuando era joven, mi tío trabajaba mucho.	My uncle worked hard when he was young.
Estudiábamos matemáticas e inglés.	We were studying math and English.

➤ To form the imperfect of any regular -**er** or -**ir** verb, you take off the -**er** or -**ir** ending of the infinitive to form the stem and add the endings: -**ía**, -**ías**, -**ía**, -**íamos**, -**íais**, -**ían**.

➤ The following table shows the imperfect of two regular verbs: **comer** (meaning *to eat*) and **vivir** (meaning *to live*).

(yo)	comía	vivía	I ate/lived I was eating/living I used to eat/live
(tú)	comías	vivías	you ate/lived you were eating/living you used to eat/live
(él/ella/usted)	comía	vivía	he/she/it/you ate/lived he/she/it was eating/living, you were eating/living he/she/it used to eat/live, you used to eat/live
(nosotros/nosotras)	comíamos	vivíamos	we ate/lived we were eating/living we used to eat/live
(vosotros/vosotras)	comíais	vivíais	you ate/lived you were eating/living you used to eat/live
(ellos/ellas/ustedes)	comían	vivían	they/you ate/lived they/you were eating/living they/you used to eat/live

[i] Note that in the imperfect tense of **-er** and **-ir** verbs, there's an accent on all the endings.

A veces, <u>comíamos</u> en casa de Pepe.	We sometimes used to eat at Pepe's.
<u>Vivía</u> en un piso en Barcelona.	She lived in a apartment in Barcelona.
Cuando llegó el médico, ya se <u>sentían</u> mejor.	They were already feeling better when the doctor arrived.

Típ

The imperfect endings for **-er** and **-ir** verbs are the same as the endings used to form the conditional for all verbs. The only difference is that, in the conditional, the endings are added to the future stem.

⇨ *For more information on the **Conditional**, see page 100.*

3 | Irregular verbs in the imperfect tense

➤ **ser**, **ir** and **ver** are irregular in the imperfect tense.

	ser	Meaning: to be
(yo)	era	I was
(tú)	eras	you were
(él/ella/usted)	era	he/she/it was, you were
(nosotros/nosotras)	éramos	we were
(vosotros/vosotras)	erais	you were
(ellos/ellas/ustedes)	eran	they were/you were

<u>Era</u> un chico muy simpático.	He was a very nice boy.
Mi madre <u>era</u> profesora.	My mother was a teacher.

	ir	Meaning: to go
(yo)	iba	I went/used to go/was going
(tú)	ibas	you went/used to go/were going
(él/ella/usted)	iba	he/she/it went/used to go/was going, you went/used to go/were going
(nosotros/nosotras)	íbamos	we went/used to go/were going
(vosotros/vosotras)	ibais	you went/used to go/were going
(ellos/ellas/ustedes)	iban	they/you went/used to go/were going

<u>Iba</u> a la oficina cada día.	Every day he would go to the office.
¿Adónde <u>iban</u>?	Where were they going?

	ver	Meaning: to see/to watch
(yo)	veía	I saw/used to see I watched/used to watch/was watching
(tú)	veías	you saw/used to see you watched/used to watch/were watching
(él/ella/usted)	veía	he/she/it saw/used to see he/she/it watched/used to watch/was watching you saw/used to see you watched/used to watch/were watching
(nosotros/nosotras)	veíamos	we saw/used to see we watched/used to watch/were watching
(vosotros/vosotras)	veíais	you saw/used to see you watched/used to watch/were watching
(ellos/ellas/ustedes)	veían	they/you saw/used to see they/you watched/used to watch/were watching

Los sábados, siempre lo **veíamos**.	We always used to see him on Saturdays.
Veía la televisión cuando llegó mi tío.	I was watching television when my uncle arrived.

4 Reflexive verbs in the imperfect tense

➤ The imperfect of reflexive verbs is formed in just the same way as for ordinary verbs, except that you have to remember to give the reflexive pronoun (**me**, **te**, **se**, **nos**, **os**, **se**).

Antes <u>se levantaba</u> temprano.	He used to get up early.

Grammar Extra!

In Spanish, you also use the imperfect tense with certain time expressions, in particular with **desde** (meaning *since*), **desde hacía** (meaning *for*) and **hacía … que** (meaning *for*) to talk about activities and states that had started previously and were still going on at a particular point in the past:

<u>Estaba</u> enfermo desde 2000.	He had been ill since 2000.
<u>Conducía</u> ese coche desde hacía tres meses.	He had been driving that car for three months.
Hacía mucho tiempo que <u>salían</u> juntos.	They had been going out together for a long time.
Hacía dos años que <u>vivíamos</u> en Madrid.	We had been living in Madrid for two years.

Compare the use of **desde**, **desde hacía** and **hacía … que** with the imperfect with that of **desde**, **desde hace**, and **hace … que** with the present.

⇨ *For more information on the use of tenses with **desde**, see page 189.*

> **Key points**
> ✔ To form the imperfect tense of **-ar** verbs, take off the **-ar** ending and add the endings: **-aba, -abas, -aba, -ábamos, -abais, -aban**.
> ✔ To form the imperfect tense of **-er** and **-ir** verbs, take off the **-er** and **-ir** endings and add the endings: **-ía, -ías, -ía, -íamos, -íais, -ían**.
> ✔ **ser**, **ir** and **ver** are irregular in the imperfect.

The perfect tense

> **What is the perfect tense?**
> The **perfect** tense is a verb form used to talk about what has or hasn't happened; for example, *I've broken my glasses; We haven't spoken about it.*

1 Using the perfect tense

➤ In English, we use the perfect tense (*have*, *has* or their shortened forms '*ve* and '*s* followed by a past participle such as *spoken*, *eaten*, *lived*, *been*) to talk about what has or hasn't happened today, this week, this year or in our lives up to now.

➤ The Spanish perfect tense is used in a similar way.

He terminado el libro.	I've finished the book.
¿**Has fregado** el suelo?	Have you washed the floor?
Nunca **ha estado** en Bolivia.	He's never been to Bolivia.
Ha vendido su caballo.	She has sold her horse.
Todavía no **hemos comprado** un ordenador.	We still haven't bought a computer.
Ya se **han ido**.	They've already left.

Grammar Extra!

You may also come across uses of the perfect tense in Spanish to talk about actions completed in the very recent past. In English, we'd use the past simple tense in such cases.

¿Lo **has visto**?	Did you see that?

2 Forming the perfect tense

➤ As in English, the perfect tense in Spanish has two parts to it. These are:

* the <u>present</u> tense of the verb **haber** (meaning *to have*)
* a part of the main verb called the <u>past participle</u>.

3 Forming the past participle

➤ To form the past participle of regular **-ar** verbs, take off the **-ar** ending of the infinitive and add **-ado**.

> **hablar** (*to speak*) → **hablado** (*spoken*)

➤ To form the past participle of regular **-er** or **-ir** verbs, take off the **-er** or **-ir** ending of the infinitive and add **-ido**.

> **comer** (*to eat*) → **comido** (*eaten*)
> **vivir** (*to live*) → **vivido** (*lived*)

4 | The perfect tense of some regular verbs

➤ The following table shows how you can combine the present tense of **haber** with the past participle of any verb to form the perfect tense.

In this case, the past participles are taken from the following regular verbs: **hablar** (meaning *to speak*); **trabajar** (meaning *to work*); **comer** (meaning *to eat*); **vender** (meaning *to sell*); **vivir** (meaning *to live*); **decidir** (meaning *to decide*).

	Present of haber	Past participle	Meaning
(yo)	he	hablado	I have spoken
(tú)	has	trabajado	you have worked
(él/ella/usted)	ha	comido	he/she/it has eaten, you have eaten
(nosotros/nosotras)	hemos	vendido	we have sold
(vosotros/vosotras)	habéis	vivido	you have lived
(ellos/ellas/ustedes)	han	decidido	they/you have decided

Has trabajado mucho.	You've worked hard.
No **he comido** nada.	I haven't eaten anything.

i Note that you should not confuse **haber** with **tener**. Even though they both mean *to have*, **haber** is mainly only used for forming tenses and in certain impersonal expressions such as **hay** and **había** meaning *there is, there are, there was, there were,* and so on.

⇨ *For further information on **Impersonal verbs**, see page 129.*

5 | Verbs with irregular past participles

➤ Some past participles are irregular. There aren't too many, so try to learn them.

abrir (*to open*)	→	**abierto** (*opened*)
cubrir (*to cover*)	→	**cubierto** (*covered*)
decir (*to say*)	→	**dicho** (*said*)
escribir (*to write*)	→	**escrito** (*written*)
freír (*to fry*)	→	**frito** or **freído** (*fried*)
hacer (*to do, to make*)	→	**hecho** (*done, made*)
morir (*to die*)	→	**muerto** (*died*)
oír (*to hear*)	→	**oído** (*heard*)
poner (*to put*)	→	**puesto** (*put*)

For further explanation of grammatical terms, please see pages viii-xii.

romper (*to break*)	→	roto (*broken*)
ver (*to see*)	→	visto (*seen*)
volver (*to return*)	→	vuelto (*returned*)

He abierto una cuenta en el banco.	I've opened a bank account.
No ha dicho nada.	He hasn't said anything.
Hoy he hecho muchas cosas.	I've done a lot today.
Todavía no he hecho los deberes.	I haven't done my homework yet.
Han muerto tres personas.	Three people have died.
¿Dónde has puesto mis zapatos?	Where have you put my shoes?
Carlos ha roto el espejo.	Carlos has broken the mirror.
Jamás he visto una cosa parecida.	I've never seen anything like it.
¿Ha vuelto Ana?	Has Ana come back?

Tip

he/has/ha and so on must <u>NEVER</u> be separated from the past participle. Any object pronouns go before the form of **haber** being used, and <u>NOT</u> between the form of **haber** and the past participle.

No lo he visto.	I haven't seen it.
¿Lo has hecho ya?	Have you done it yet?

---

6 **Reflexive verbs in the perfect tense**

➤ The perfect tense of reflexive verbs is formed in the same way as for ordinary verbs. The reflexive pronouns (**me**, **te**, **se**, **nos**, **os**, **se**) come before **he**, **has**, **ha**, and so on. The table on the next page shows the perfect tense of **lavarse** in full.

Subject pronoun	Reflexive pronoun	Present tense of haber	Past Participle	Meaning
(yo)	me	he	lavado	I have washed
(tú)	te	has	lavado	you have washed
(él) (ella) (uno) (usted)	se	ha	lavado	he has washed she has washed one has washed it has washed you have washed
(nosotros) (nosotras)	nos	hemos	lavado	we have washed we have washed
(vosotros) (vosotras)	os	habéis	lavado	you have washed you have washed
(ellos) (ellas) (ustedes)	se	han	lavado	they have washed they have washed you have washed

Grammar Extra!

Don't use the perfect tense with **desde**, **desde hace** and **hace ... que** when talking about how long something has been going on for. Use the present tense instead.

<u>Está</u> enfermo desde julio.	He has been ill since July.
<u>Conduce</u> ese coche desde hace tres meses.	He has been driving that car for three months.
Hace mucho tiempo que <u>salen</u> juntos.	They have been going out together for a long time.

➪ *For more information on the **Present tense**, see page 72.*

➤ In European Spanish you <u>CAN</u> use the perfect tense in the negative with **desde** and **desde hace**.

No lo <u>he visto</u> desde hace mucho tiempo.	I haven't seen him for a long time.

Key points

✔ The Spanish perfect tense is formed using the present tense of **haber** and a past participle.

✔ In Spanish, the perfect tense is used very much as it is in English.

✔ The past participle of regular **-ar** verbs ends in **-ado**, and the past participle of regular **-er** and **-ir** verbs ends in **-ido**.

✔ Make sure you know the following irregular past participle forms: **abierto, cubierto, dicho, escrito, frito, hecho, muerto, puesto, roto, visto, vuelto**.

For further explanation of grammatical terms, please see pages viii-xii.

The pluperfect or past perfect tense

> **What is the pluperfect tense?**
> The **pluperfect** is a verb tense that is used to talk about what had happened
> or had been true at a point in the past, for example, *I'd forgotten to finish my
> homework.*

1 Using the pluperfect tense

➤ When talking about the past, we sometimes refer to things that had
happened previously. In English, we often use *had* followed by a <u>past participle</u>
such as *spoken, eaten, lived* or *been* to do this. This tense is known as the
<u>pluperfect</u> or <u>past perfect</u> tense.

➤ The Spanish pluperfect tense is used and formed in a similar way.

Ya **habíamos comido** cuando llegó.	We'd already eaten when he arrived.
Nunca lo **había visto** antes de aquella noche.	I'd never seen it before that night.

2 Forming the pluperfect tense

➤ Like the perfect tense, the pluperfect tense in Spanish has <u>two</u> parts to it:

- the imperfect tense of the verb **haber** (meaning *to have*)
- the past participle.

➪ *For more information on the **Imperfect tense** and **Past participles**, see pages 110
and 115.*

➤ The table below shows how you can combine the imperfect tense of **haber**
with the past participle of any verb to form the pluperfect tense. Here, the
past participles are taken from the following regular verbs: **hablar** (meaning
to speak); **trabajar** (meaning *to work*); **comer** (meaning *to eat*); **vender**
(meaning *to sell*); **vivir** (meaning *to live*); **decidir** (meaning *to decide*).

Subject pronoun	Imperfect of haber	Past Participle	Meaning
(yo)	había	hablado	I had spoken
(tú)	habías	trabajado	you had worked
(él/ella/usted)	había	comido	he/she/it/you had eaten
(nosotros/nosotras)	habíamos	vendido	we had sold
(vosotros/vosotras)	habíais	vivido	you had lived
(ellos/ellas/ustedes)	habían	decidido	they/you had decided

No **había trabajado** antes.	He hadn't worked before.
Había vendido su caballo.	She had sold her horse.

➤ Remember that some very common verbs have irregular past participles.

abrir (*to open*)	→	**abierto** (*opened*)
cubrir (*to cover*)	→	**cubierto** (*covered*)
decir (*to say*)	→	**dicho** (*said*)
escribir (*to write*)	→	**escrito** (*written*)
freír (*to fry*)	→	**frito** or **freído** (*fried*)
hacer (*to do, to make*)	→	**hecho** (*done, made*)
morir (*to die*)	→	**muerto** (*died*)
oír (*to hear*)	→	**oído** (*heard*)
poner (*to put*)	→	**puesto** (*put*)
romper (*to break*)	→	**roto** (*broken*)
ver (*to see*)	→	**visto** (*seen*)
volver (*to return*)	→	**vuelto** (*returned*)

No <u>había dicho</u> nada.	He hadn't said anything.
Tres personas <u>habían muerto</u>.	Three people had died.

Tip

había/habías/habían and so on must <u>NEVER</u> be separated from the past participle. Any object pronouns go before the form of **haber** being used, and <u>NOT</u> between the form of **haber** and the past participle.

No lo había visto.	I hadn't seen it.

---

3 Reflexive verbs in the pluperfect tense

➤ The pluperfect tense of reflexive verbs is formed in the same way as for ordinary verbs. The reflexive pronouns (**me**, **te**, **se**, **nos**, **os**, **se**) come before **había**, **habías**, **había**, and so on. The table on the next page shows the pluperfect tense of **lavarse** in full.

Subject pronoun	Reflexive pronoun	Imperfect tense of haber	Past Participle	Meaning
(yo)	me	había	lavado	I had washed
(tú)	te	habías	lavado	you had washed
(él) (ella) (uno) (usted)	se	había	lavado	he had washed she had washed one had washed it had washed you had washed
(nosotros) (nosotras)	nos	habíamos	lavado	we had washed we had washed
(vosotros) (vosotras)	os	habíais	lavado	you had washed you had washed
(ellos) (ellas) (ustedes)	se	habían	lavado	they had washed they had washed you had washed

Grammar Extra!

Don't use the pluperfect with **desde**, **desde hacía** and **hacía ... que** when talking about how long something had been going on for. Use the <u>imperfect</u> instead.

<u>Estaba</u> enfermo desde 2000.	He had been ill since 2000.
<u>Conducía</u> ese coche desde hacía tres meses.	He had been driving that car for three months.
Hacía mucho tiempo que <u>salían</u> juntos.	They had been going out together for a long time.

⇨ *For more information on the **Imperfect tense**, see page 110.*

In European Spanish you <u>CAN</u> use the pluperfect tense in the negative with **desde** and **desde hacía**.

No lo <u>había visto</u> desde hacía mucho tiempo.	I hadn't seen him for a long time.

Key points

✔ The Spanish pluperfect tense is formed using the imperfect tense of **haber** and a past particple.

✔ In Spanish, the pluperfect tense is used very much as it is in English.

✔ The past participle of regular -**ar** verbs ends in -**ado**, while that of regular -**er** and -**ir** verbs ends in -**ido**.

✔ Make sure you know the irregular forms: **abierto**, **cubierto**, **dicho**, **escrito**, **frito**, **hecho**, **muerto**, **puesto**, **roto**, **visto**, **vuelto**.

The passive

> **What is the passive?**
> The **passive** is a verb form that is used when the subject of the verb is the person or thing that is affected by the action, for example, *Mary is liked by everyone; Two children were hurt in an accident; The house was sold*.

1 Using the passive

➤ Verbs can be either <u>active</u> or <u>passive</u>.

➤ In a normal or <u>active</u> sentence, the subject of the verb is the person or thing doing the action described by the verb. The object of the verb is the person or thing that the verb most directly affects.

> Peter *(subject)* wrote *(active verb)* a letter *(object)*.
> Ryan *(subject)* hit *(active verb)* me *(object)*.

➤ Provided the verb has an object, in English, as in Spanish, you can turn an <u>active</u> sentence round to make it a <u>passive</u> sentence by using *to be* followed by a past participle. In this case the person or thing directly affected by the action becomes the subject of the verb.

> A letter *(subject)* was written *(passive verb)*.
> I *(subject)* was hit *(passive verb)*.

➤ To show who or what is responsible for the action in a passive construction, in English you use *by*.

> I *(subject)* was hit *(passive verb)* <u>by</u> Ryan.

➤ You use the passive rather than the active when you want to focus attention on the person or thing <u>affected by</u> the action rather than the person or thing that carries it out.

> <u>John</u> was injured in an accident.

➤ You can also use the passive when you don't know who is responsible for the action.

> Several buses were vandalized.

2 Forming the passive

➤ In English we use the verb *to be* with a <u>past participle</u> (*was painted, were seen, are made*) to form the passive. In Spanish, the passive is formed in exactly the same way, using the verb **ser** (meaning *to be*) and a <u>past participle</u>. When you say who the action is or was done by, you use the preposition **por** (meaning *by*).

➤ *For more information on the **Past participle**, see page 115.*

Son fabricados en España.	They're made in Spain.
Es hecho a mano.	It's made by hand.
Fue escrito por JK Rowling.	It was written by JK Rowling.
La casa fue construida en 1956.	The house was built in 1956.
El cuadro fue pintado por mi padre.	The picture was painted by my father.
El colegio va a ser modernizado.	The school is going to be modernized.

[*i*] Note that the ending of the past participle agrees with the subject of the verb **ser** in exactly the same way as an adjective would.

⇨ *For more information on **Adjectives**, see page 19.*

➤ Here is the preterite of the **-ar** verb **enviar** (meaning *to send*) in its passive form.

Subject pronoun	Preterite of ser	Past Participle	Meaning
(yo)	fui	enviado (masculine) enviada (feminine)	I was sent
(tú)	fuiste	enviado (masculine) enviada (feminine)	you were sent
(él) (ella) (usted)	fue	enviado enviada enviado (masculine) enviada (feminine)	he was sent she was sent you were sent
(nosotros) (nosotras)	fuimos fuimos	enviados enviadas	we were sent we were sent
(vosotros) (vosotras)	fuisteis	enviados enviadas	you were sent you were sent
(ellos) (ellas) (ustedes)	fueron	enviados enviadas enviados (masculine) enviadas (feminine)	they were sent they were sent you were sent you were sent

➤ You can form other tenses in the passive by changing the tense of the verb **ser**.

Future: **serán enviados** they will be sent.
Perfect: **han sido enviados** they have been sent.

➤ Irregular past participles are the same as they are in the perfect tense.

⇨ *For more information on **Irregular past participles**, see page 116.*

3 Avoiding the passive

➤ Passives are not as common in Spanish as they are in English. Spanish native speakers usually prefer to avoid using the passive by:

- using the active construction instead of the passive

La policía <u>interrogó</u> al sospechoso.	The suspect was interrogated by the police.
Su madre le <u>regaló</u> un libro.	He was given a book by his mother.

- using an active verb in the third person plural

<u>Ponen</u> demasiados anuncios en la televisión.	Too many ads are shown on television.

- using a reflexive construction (as long as you don't need to say who the action is done by)

<u>Se fabrican</u> en España.	They're made in Spain.
<u>Se hace</u> a mano.	It's made by hand.
La casa <u>se construyó</u> en 1956.	The house was built in 1956.
Todos los libros <u>se han vendido</u>.	All the books have been sold.

⇨ *For more information on **Reflexive verbs**, see page 91.*

- using an impersonal **se** construction

<u>Se</u> cree que va a morir.	It is thought he will die.

⇨ *For more information on the impersonal **se** construction, see page 133.*

> ## Tip
>
> Active verbs often have both a direct object and an indirect object.
> He gave me (*indirect object*) a book (*direct object*).
> In English, both of these objects can be made the subject of a passive verb; <u>*I* was given a book.</u> or <u>*A book* was given to me</u>.
> In Spanish, an indirect object can <u>NEVER</u> become the subject of a passive verb.

Key points

✔ The passive is formed using **ser** + past participle, sometimes followed by **por** (meaning *by*).

✔ The past participle must agree with the subject of **ser**.

✔ Passive constructions are not as common as they are in English. You can often avoid the passive by using the third person plural of the active verb or by using a reflexive construction.

For further explanation of grammatical terms, please see pages viii-xii.

The gerund

> **What is a gerund?**
> The **gerund** is a verb form ending in -*ing* which is used to form verb tenses, and which in English may also be used as an adjective and a noun, for example, *What are you doing?*; *the setting sun*; *Swimming is easy!*

1 Using the gerund

➤ In Spanish, the gerund is a form of the verb that usually ends in -**ando** or -**iendo** and is used to form continuous tenses.

Estoy trabajando.	I'm working.
Estamos comiendo.	We are eating.

➤ It is used with **estar** to form continuous tenses such as:

- the present continuous

Está fregando los platos.	He's washing the dishes.
Estoy escribiendo una carta.	I'm writing a letter.

⇨ *For more information on the **Present continuous**, see page 84.*

- the imperfect continuous

Estaba reparando el coche.	She was fixing the car.
Estaban esperándonos.	They were waiting for us.

[*i*] Note that continuous tenses should only be used in Spanish to describe action that is or was happening at the precise moment you are talking about.

Grammar Extra!

Sometimes another verb, such as **ir** or **venir** is used instead of **estar** with a gerund in continuous tenses. These verbs emphasize the gradualness or the slowness of the process.

Iba anocheciendo.	It was getting dark.
Eso lo vengo diciendo desde hace tiempo.	That's what I've been saying all along.

➤ The gerund is also used after certain other verbs:

- **seguir haciendo algo** and **continuar haciendo algo** are both used with the meaning of *to go on doing something* or *to continue doing something*.

Siguió cantando or **Continuó cantando.**	He went on singing or He continued singing.
Siguieron leyendo or **Continuaron leyendo.**	They went on reading or They continued reading.

- **llevar** with a time expression followed by the gerund is used to talk about how long someone has been doing something:

Lleva dos años estudiando inglés.	He's heen studying English for two years.
Llevo una hora esperando aquí.	I've been waiting here for an hour.

[*i*] Note that the present tense of **llevar** followed by a gerund means the same as the English *have/has been + -ing*.

➤ **pasar(se)** with a time expression followed by the gerund is used to talk about how long you've spent doing something.

Pasé *or* **Me pasé el fin de semana estudiando.**	I spent the weekend studying.
Pasamos *or* **Nos pasamos el día leyendo.**	We spent the day reading.

➤ Verbs of movement, such as **salir** (meaning *to come out* or *to go out*), **entrar** (meaning *to come in* or *to go in*), and **irse** (meaning *to leave*) are sometimes followed by a gerund such as **corriendo** (meaning *running*) or **cojeando** (meaning *limping*). The English equivalent of **salir corriendo**, **entrar corriendo** or **irse cojeando**, would be *to run out*, *to run in* or *to limp off* in such cases.

Salió corriendo.	He ran out.
Se fue cojeando.	He limped off.

Tip

Use a past participle not a gerund to talk about physical position.

Estaba <u>tumbado</u> en el sofá.	He was lying on the sofa.
Estaba <u>sentada</u>.	She was sitting down.
Lo encontré <u>tendido</u> en el suelo.	I found him lying on the floor.
La escalera estaba <u>apoyada</u> contra la pared.	The ladder was leaning against the wall.

⇨ *For more information on the **Past participles**, see page 115.*

➤ You will also come across the gerund used in other ways. For example:

Los vimos jugando al fútbol.	We saw them playing soccer.
Estudiando, aprobarás.	By studying, *or* If you study, you'll pass.

2 Forming the gerund of regular verbs

➤ To form the gerund of regular -ar verbs, take off the -ar ending of the infinitive to form the stem, and add -ando.

Infinitive	Stem	Gerund
hablar	habl-	hablando
trabajar	trabaj-	trabajando

➤ To form the gerund of regular -er and -ir verbs, take off the -er and -ir ending of the infinitive to form the stem, and add -iendo.

Infinitive	Stem	Gerund
comer	com-	comiendo
vivir	viv-	viviendo

3 The gerund of irregular verbs

➤ Some verbs have an irregular gerund form. You have to learn these.

Infinitives	Meaning	Gerund	Meaning
decir	to say	diciendo	saying
dormir	to sleep	durmiendo	sleeping
freír	to fry	friendo	frying
morir	to die	muriendo	dying
pedir	to ask for	pidiendo	asking for
poder	to be able to	pudiendo	being able to
reír	to laugh	riendo	laughing
seguir	to follow	siguiendo	following
sentir	to feel	sintiendo	feeling
venir	to come	viniendo	coming
vestir	to dress	vistiendo	dressing

➤ In the next group of verbs there is a y rather than the normal i.

Infinitives	Meaning	Gerund	Meaning
caer	to fall	cayendo	falling
creer	to believe	creyendo	believing
leer	to read	leyendo	reading
oír	to hear	oyendo	hearing
traer	to bring	trayendo	bringing
ir	to go	yendo	going

> ## Tip
>
> In English, we often use -ing forms as adjectives, for example, *running water, shining eyes, the following day*. In Spanish, you cannot use the **-ando** and **-iendo** forms like this.
>
> Instead, there are sometimes corresponding forms ending in **-ante** and **-iente** that can be used as adjectives.
>
> | | |
> |---|---|
> | agua <u>corriente</u> | running water |
> | ojos <u>brillantes</u> | shining eyes |
> | Al día <u>siguiente</u>, visitamos Toledo. | The following day we visited Toledo. |
>
> Similarly, in English, we often use the -ing forms as nouns. In Spanish you have to use the <u>infinitive</u> instead.
>
> | | |
> |---|---|
> | **<u>Fumar</u> es malo para la salud.** | <u>Smoking</u> is bad for you. |

4 | Position of pronouns with the gerund

➤ Object pronouns and reflexive pronouns are usually attached to the end of the gerund, although you can also often put them before **estar** in continuous tenses.

Estoy hablándote *or* **<u>Te</u> estoy hablando.**	I'm talking to you.
Está vistiéndose *or* **<u>Se</u> está vistiendo.**	He's getting dressed.
Estaban mostrándoselo *or* **<u>Se lo</u> estaban mostrando.**	They were showing it to him/her/them/you.

(i) Note that you will always have to add an accent to keep the stress in the same place when adding pronouns to the end of a gerund.

➪ *For more information on **Stress**, see page 200.*

> ### Key points
>
> ✔ Use the gerund in continuous tenses with **estar** as well as after **seguir** and **continuar**.
> ✔ Gerunds for **-ar** verbs add **-ando** to the stem of the verb.
> ✔ Gerunds for **-er** and **-ir** verbs usually add **-iendo** to the stem of the verb.
> ✔ **-ando** and **-iendo** gerunds <u>cannot</u> be used as adjectives or nouns.
> ✔ You can attach pronouns to the end of the gerund, or sometimes put them before the previous verb.

Impersonal verbs

> **What is an impersonal verb?**
> An **impersonal verb** is a verb whose subject is *it*, but this 'it' does not refer to
> any specific thing; for example, *It's going to rain; It's nine o'clock.*

1 Verbs that are always used impersonally

➤ There are some verbs such as **llover** (meaning *to rain*) and **nevar** (meaning
  to snow), that are only used in the 'it' form, the infinitive, and as a gerund (the
  -ing form of the verb). These are called <u>impersonal verbs</u> because there is no
  person, animal or thing performing the action.

Llueve.	It's raining.
Está lloviendo.	It's raining.
Va a llover.	It's going to rain.
Nieva.	It's snowing.
Está nevando.	It's snowing.
Nevaba.	It was snowing.
Estaba nevando.	It was snowing.
Mañana nevará.	It will snow tomorrow.

2 Verbs that are sometimes used impersonally

➤ There are also some other very common verbs that are sometimes used
  as impersonal verbs, for example **hacer**, **haber** and **ser**.

➤ **hacer** is used in a number of impersonal expressions relating to the weather:

<u>Hace</u> frío/calor.	It's cold/hot.
Ayer <u>hacía</u> mucho frío/calor.	It was very cold/hot yesterday.
<u>Hace</u> sol/viento.	It's sunny/windy.
Va a <u>hacer</u> sol/viento.	It's going to be sunny/windy.
<u>Hace</u> un tiempo estupendo/ horrible.	It's a lovely/horrible day.

➤ **hacer** is also used in combination with **que** and **desde** in impersonal time
  expressions, to talk about how long something has been going on for or how
  long it is since something happened.

<u>Hace</u> seis meses <u>que</u> vivo aquí. *or* Vivo aquí <u>desde hace</u> seis meses.	I've been living here for six months.

Hace tres años que estudio español *or* Estudio español desde hace tres años.	I've been studying Spanish for three years.
Hace mucho tiempo que no la veo *or* No la veo desde hace mucho tiempo.	I haven't seen her for ages *or* It's been ages since I saw her.
Hace varias semanas que no voy por allí *or* No voy por allí desde hace varias semanas.	I haven't been there for several weeks *or* It's several weeks since I went there.

[*i*] Note the use of the present simple in Spanish in the above examples where in English we'd use the perfect tense or the past tense.

➤ hacer is also used impersonally in the expression (me/te/le) hace falta, which means *it is necessary (for me/you/him)*.

Si hace falta, voy.	I'll go if necessary.
No hace falta llamar.	We/You/I needn't call.
Me hace falta otro vaso más.	I need another glass.
No hace falta ser un experto.	You don't need to be an expert.
No hacía falta.	It wasn't necessary.

[*i*] Note that not all impersonal expressions in Spanish are translated into English using impersonal expressions.

➤ haber too can be used impersonally with the meaning *there is/there are*, *there was/there were*, *there will be*, and so on. It has the special form hay in the present. For the other tenses, you take the third person singular (the 'it' form) of haber in the appropriate tense.

Hay un cine cerca de aquí.	There's a movie theater near here.
Hay dos supermercados.	There are two supermarkets.
No hay bares.	There are no bars.
Había mucho ruido.	There was a lot of noise.
Había muchos coches.	There were a lot of cars.
Hubo un accidente.	There was an accident.
Hubo varios problemas.	There were several problems.
¿Habrá tiempo?	Will there be time?
¿Habrá suficientes sillas?	Will there be enough chairs?

[*i*] Note that you should ALWAYS use the singular form (never the plural), no matter how many things there are.

➤ **haber** is used in the construction **hay que** with an infinitive to talk about actions that need to be taken.

<u>Hay que</u> trabajar más.	We/You need to work harder.
<u>Hay que</u> ser respetuoso.	You/We/One must be respectful.
<u>Habrá</u> que decírselo.	We'll/You'll have to tell him.

➤ **ser** can be used in certain impersonal constructions with adjectives, for example:

- es/era/fue + adjective + infinitive

<u>Es</u> importante ahorrar dinero.	It's important to save money.
<u>Fue</u> torpe hacer eso.	It was silly to do that.
<u>Sería</u> mejor esperar.	It would be better to wait.

- es/era/fue + adjective + **que** + verb

<u>Es cierto que</u> tengo problemas.	It's true that I've got problems.
<u>Es verdad que</u> trabaja mucho.	It's true that he works hard.

[i] Note that when they are used in the negative (**no es cierto que…**; **no es verdad que…**), these expressions have to be followed by the subjunctive.

⇨ *For more information on the **Subjunctive**, see page 134.*

Grammar Extra!

When impersonal expressions that don't state facts are followed by **que** (meaning *that*) and a verb, this verb must be in the <u>subjunctive</u>.

For this reason, the following non-factual impersonal expressions are all followed by the subjunctive:

- **Es posible que…**
  It's possible that … / …might…
  Es posible que ganen.
  They might win.
- **Es imposible que…**
  It's impossible that… / …can't possibly…
  Es imposible que lo sepan.
  They can't possibly know.
- **Es necesario que…**
  It's necessary that… / …need to…
  No es necesario que vengas.
  You don't need to come.
- **Es mejor que…**
  … be better to …
  Es mejor que lo pongas aquí.
  You'd be better to put it here.

⇨ *For more information on the **Subjunctive**, see page 134.*

➤ **ser** is also used impersonally with **de día** and **de noche** to say whether it's day or night.

> **Era de noche cuando llegamos.**   It was night when we arrived.
> **Todavía es de día allí.**   It's still day there.

➡ *For other time expressions with* **ser**, *see page 81.*

➤ **basta con** is used impersonally:

- with a following <u>infinitive</u> to mean *it's enough to/all you need do is*

> **Basta con telefonear para**   All you need do is to phone to
> **reservar un asiento.**   reserve a seat.
>
> **Basta con dar una vuelta por la**   You only need to take a walk round
> **ciudad para...**   the city to ...

- with a <u>noun</u> or <u>pronoun</u> to mean *all you need is* or *all it takes is*

> **Basta con un error para que**   All it takes is one mistake to ruin
> **todo se estropee.**   everything.

➤ **(me) parece que** is used to give opinions.

> **Parece que va a llover.**   It looks as if it's going to rain.
> **Me parece que estás**   I think that you are wrong.
> **equivocado.**

[*i*] Note that when **(me) parece que** is used in the negative, the following verb has to be in the <u>subjunctive</u>.

➡ *For more information on the* **Subjunctive**, *see page 134.*

➤ **vale la pena** is used to talk about what's worth doing.

> **Vale la pena.**   It's worth it.
> **No vale la pena.**   It's not worth it.
> **Vale la pena hacer el esfuerzo.**   It's worth making the effort.
> **No vale la pena gastar tanto**   It's not worth spending so much
> **dinero.**   money.

For further explanation of grammatical terms, please see pages viii-xii.

Grammar Extra!

se is often used in impersonal expressions, especially with the verbs **creer**, **decir**, **poder**, and **tratar**. In such cases it often corresponds to *it*, *one* or *you* in English.

- **Se cree que...**

  It is thought *or* People think that...

  Se cree que es un mito.

  It is thought to be a myth.

- **Se dice que...**

  It is said *or* People say that...

  Se dice que es rico.

  He is said to be rich.

- **Se puede...**

  One can.../People can.../You can...

  Aquí se puede aparcar.

  One can park here.

- **Se trata de...**

  It's a question of .../It's about ...

  No se trata de dinero.

  It isn't a question of money.

  Se trata de resolverlo.

  We must solve it.

 *For more information on **Reflexive verbs**, see page 91.*

Key points

✔ Impersonal verbs and expressions can only be used in the *'it'* form, the infinitive and the gerund.

✔ Impersonal expressions relating to the weather are very common.

✔ Although in English we use *there is* or *there are* depending on the number of people or things that there are, in Spanish **hay**, **había**, **hubo** and so on are used in the singular form only.

✔ Some very common ordinary verbs are also used as impersonal verbs.

The subjunctive

> **What is the subjunctive?**
> The **subjunctive** is a verb form that is used in certain circumstances especially when expressing some sort of feeling or when there is doubt about whether something will happen or whether something is true. It is only used occasionally in modern English, for example, *If I were you, ...*;
> *So be it.; I wish you were here.*

1 Using the subjunctive

➤ Although you may not know it, you will already be familiar with many of the forms of the present subjunctive, as it is used when giving orders and instructions not to do something as well as in the **usted**, **ustedes** and **nosotros** forms of instructions to do something. For example, if you phone someone in Spain, they will probably answer with ¡**diga!** or ¡**dígame!**, an imperative form taken from the present subjunctive of **decir**.

⇨ *For more information on* **Imperatives**, *see page 85.*

➤ In Spanish the subjunctive is used after certain verbs and conjunctions when two parts of a sentence have different subjects.

Tengo miedo de que le ocurra algo.   I'm afraid <u>something</u> may (*subjunctive*) happen to him.

(The subject of the first part of the sentence is *I*; the subject of the second part of the sentence is *something*.).

➤ In English, in a sentence like *We want him/José to be happy*, we use an infinitive (*to be*) for the second verb even though *want* and *be happy* have different subjects (*we* and *him/José*).

➤ In Spanish you cannot do this. You have to use the <u>subjunctive</u> for the second verb.

Queremos que él sea feliz.   We want that he (*subjunctive*) be happy.

Queremos que José sea feliz.   We want that José (*subjunctive*) be happy.

➤ You <u>CAN</u> use an infinitive for the second verb in Spanish when the subject of both verbs is the same.

Queremos ser felices.   We want to be happy.

2 Coming across the subjunctive

➤ The subjunctive has several tenses, the main ones being the <u>present subjunctive</u> and the <u>imperfect subjunctive</u>. The tense used for the subjunctive verb depends on the tense of the previous verb.

For further explanation of grammatical terms, please see pages viii-xii.

⇨ *For more information on **Tenses with the subjunctive**, see page 139.*

➤ In sentences containing two verbs with different subjects, you will find that the second verb is in the subjunctive when the first verb:

- expresses a wish

Quiero que <u>vengan</u>.	I want them to come.
Quiero que se <u>vaya</u>.	I want him/her to go away.
Deseamos que <u>tengan</u> éxito.	We want them to be successful.

- expresses an emotion

Siento mucho que no <u>puedas</u> venir.	I'm very sorry that you can't come.
Espero que <u>venga</u>.	I hope he comes.
Me sorprende que no <u>esté</u> aquí.	I'm surprised that he isn't here.
Me alegro de que te <u>gusten</u>.	I'm pleased that you like them.

➤ If the subject of both verbs is the <u>same</u>, an infinitive is used as the second verb instead of a subjunctive.

➤ Compare the following examples. In the examples on the left, both the verb expressing the wish or emotion and the second verb have the same subject, so the second verb is an <u>infinitive</u>. In the examples on the right, each verb has a different subject, so the second verb is in the <u>subjunctive</u>.

Infinitive construction	Subjunctive construction
Quiero <u>estudiar</u>. I want to study.	**Quiero que José <u>estudie</u>.** I want José to study.
Maite quiere <u>irse</u>. Maite wants to leave.	**Maite quiere que me <u>vaya</u>.** Maite wants me to leave.
Siento no <u>poder</u> venir. I'm sorry I can't come.	**Siento que no <u>puedas</u> venir.** I'm sorry that you can't come.
Me alegro de <u>poder</u> ayudar. I'm pleased to be able to help.	**Me alegro de que <u>puedas</u> ayudar.** I'm pleased you can help.

➤ You will also come across the verb + **que** + subjunctive construction (often with a personal object such as **me**, **te** and so on) when the first verb is one you use to ask or advise somebody to do something.

Sólo te pido que <u>tengas</u> cuidado.	I'm only asking you to be careful.
Te aconsejo que no <u>llegues</u> tarde.	I'd advise you not to be late.

➤ You will also come across the subjunctive in the following cases:

- after verbs expressing doubt or uncertainty, and verbs saying what you think about something that are used with **no**

Dudo que <u>tenga</u> tiempo.	I doubt I'll have time.
No creo que <u>venga</u>.	I don't think she'll come.
No pienso que <u>esté</u> bien.	I don't think it's right.

- in impersonal constructions that show a need to do something

¿Hace falta que <u>vaya</u> Jaime?	Does Jaime need to go?
No es necesario que <u>vengas</u>.	You don't need to come.

- in impersonal constructions that do not express facts

Es posible que <u>tengan</u> razón.	They may be right.

⇨ *For more information on **Impersonal verbs**, see page 129.*

Grammar Extra!

Use the <u>indicative</u> (that is, any verb form that isn't subjunctive) after impersonal expressions that state facts provided they are <u>NOT</u> in the negative.

Es verdad que <u>es</u> interesante.	It's true that it's interesting.
Es cierto que me <u>gusta</u> el café.	It's true I like coffee.
Parece que se <u>va</u> a ir.	It seems that he's going to go.

➤ The subjunctive is used after **que** to express wishes.

¡Que lo <u>pases</u> bien!	Have a good time!
¡Que te <u>diviertas</u>!	Have fun!

➤ The subjunctive is also used after certain conjunctions linking two parts of a sentence which each have different subjects.

- **antes de que**   before

¿Quieres decirle algo antes de que se <u>vaya</u>?	Do you want to say anything to him before he goes?

- **para que**   so that

Es para que te <u>acuerdes</u> de mí.	It's so that you'll remember me.

- **sin que**   without

Salimos sin que nos <u>vieran</u>.	We left without them seeing us.

⇨ *For more information on **Conjunctions**, see page 192.*

> ## Típ
>
> Use **para**, **sin** and **antes de** with the underlined infinitive when the subject of
> both verbs is the <u>same</u>.
>
> **Fue en taxi para no <u>llegar</u> tarde.** He went by taxi so that he
> wouldn't be late.
>
> **Pedro se ha ido sin <u>esperar</u>nos.** Pedro's gone without waiting
> for us.
>
> **Cenamos antes de <u>ir</u> al teatro.** We had dinner before we
> went to the theater.

3 Forming the present subjunctive

➤ To form the present subjunctive of most verbs, take off the **-o** ending of
the **yo** form of the <u>present simple</u>, and add a fixed set of endings.

➤ For **-ar** verbs, the endings are: **-e**, **-es**, **-e**, **-emos**, **-éis**, **-en**.

➤ For both **-er** and **-ir** verbs, the endings are: **-a, -as, -a, -amos, -áis, -an**.

➤ The following table shows the present subjunctive of three regular verbs:
hablar (meaning *to speak*), **comer** (meaning *to eat*) and **vivir** (meaning
to live).

Infinitive	(yo)	(tú)	(él)(ella)(usted)	(nosotros)(nosotras)	(vosotros)(vosotras)	(ellos)(ellas)(ustedes)
hablar to speak	habl<u>e</u>	habl<u>es</u>	habl<u>e</u>	habl<u>emos</u>	habl<u>éis</u>	habl<u>en</u>
comer to eat	com<u>a</u>	com<u>as</u>	com<u>a</u>	com<u>amos</u>	com<u>áis</u>	com<u>an</u>
vivir to live	viv<u>a</u>	viv<u>as</u>	viv<u>a</u>	viv<u>amos</u>	viv<u>áis</u>	viv<u>an</u>

Quiero que <u>comas</u> algo. I want you to eat something.

Me sorprende que no <u>hable</u> inglés. I'm surprised he doesn't speak English.

No es verdad que <u>trabajen</u> aquí. It isn't true that they work here.

➤ Some verbs have very irregular **yo** forms in the ordinary present tense and
these irregular forms are reflected in the stem for the present subjunctive.

Infinitive	(yo)	(tú)	(él) (ella) (usted)	(nosotros) (nosotras)	(vosotros) (vosotras)	(ellos) (ellas) (ustedes)
decir to say	diga	digas	diga	digamos	digáis	digan
hacer to do/make	haga	hagas	haga	hagamos	hagáis	hagan
poner to put	ponga	pongas	ponga	pongamos	pongáis	pongan
salir to leave	salga	salgas	salga	salgamos	salgáis	salgan
tener to have	tenga	tengas	tenga	tengamos	tengáis	tengan
venir to come	venga	vengas	venga	vengamos	vengáis	vengan

Voy a limpiar la casa antes de que <u>vengan</u>.	I'm going to clean the house before they come.

📝 Note that only the **vosotros** form has an accent.

Tip

The present subjunctive endings are the opposite of what you'd expect, as **-ar** verbs have endings starting with **-e**, and **-er** and **-ir** verbs have endings starting with **-a**.

---

4 **Forming the present subjunctive of irregular verbs**

➤ The following verbs have irregular subjunctive forms:

Infinitive	(yo)	(tú)	(él) (ella) (usted)	(nosotros) (nosotras)	(vosotros) (vosotras)	(ellos) (ellas) (ustedes)
dar to give	dé	des	dé	demos	deis	den
estar to be	esté	estés	esté	estemos	estéis	estén
haber to have	haya	hayas	haya	hayamos	hayáis	hayan
ir to go	vaya	vayas	vaya	vayamos	vayáis	vayan
saber to know	sepa	sepas	sepa	sepamos	sepáis	sepan
ser to be	sea	seas	sea	seamos	seáis	sean

No quiero que te <u>vayas</u>.	I don't want you to go.
Dudo que <u>esté</u> aquí.	I doubt if it's here.
No piensan que <u>sea</u> él.	They don't think it's him.
Es posible que <u>haya</u> problemas.	There may be problems.

For further explanation of grammatical terms, please see pages viii-xii.

➤ Verbs that change their stems (<u>radical-changing verbs</u>) in the ordinary present usually change them in the same way in the present subjunctive.

⇨ *For more information on **radical-changing verbs**, see page 76.*

Infinitive	(yo)	(tú)	(él) (ella) (usted)	(nosotros) (nosotras)	(vosotros) (vosotras)	(ellos) (ellas) (ustedes)
pensar to think	<u>piense</u>	<u>pienses</u>	<u>piense</u>	pensemos	penséis	<u>piensen</u>
entender to understand	<u>entienda</u>	<u>entiendas</u>	<u>entienda</u>	entendamos	entendáis	<u>entiendan</u>
poder to be able	<u>pueda</u>	<u>puedas</u>	<u>pueda</u>	podamos	podáis	<u>puedan</u>
querer to want	<u>quiera</u>	<u>quieras</u>	<u>quiera</u>	queramos	queráis	<u>quieran</u>
volver to return	<u>vuelva</u>	<u>vuelvas</u>	<u>vuelva</u>	volvamos	volváis	<u>vuelvan</u>

> **No hace falta que <u>vuelvas</u>.** There's no need for you to come back.
>
> **Es para que lo <u>entiendas</u>.** It's so that you understand.
>
> **Me alegro de que <u>puedas</u> venir.** I'm pleased you can come.

➤ Sometimes the stem of the **nosotros** and **vosotros** forms isn't the same as it is in the ordinary present tense.

Infinitive	(yo)	(tú)	(él) (ella) (usted)	(nosotros) (nosotras)	(vosotros) (vosotras)	(ellos) (ellas) (ustedes)
dormir to sleep	duerma	duermas	duerma	<u>durmamos</u>	<u>durmáis</u>	duerman
morir to die	muera	mueras	muera	<u>muramos</u>	<u>muráis</u>	mueran
pedir to ask for	pida	pidas	pida	<u>pidamos</u>	<u>pidáis</u>	pidan
seguir to follow	siga	sigas	siga	<u>sigamos</u>	<u>sigáis</u>	sigan
sentir to feel	sienta	sientas	sienta	<u>sintamos</u>	<u>sintáis</u>	sientan

> **Queremos hacerlo antes de que nos <u>muramos</u>.** We want to do it before we die.
>
> **Vendré a veros cuando os <u>sintáis</u> mejor.** I'll come and see you when you feel better.

5 Tenses with the subjunctive

➤ If the verb in the first part of the sentence is in the <u>present, future</u> or <u>imperative</u>, the second verb will usually be in the <u>present subjunctive</u>.

> **Quiero** (*present*) **que lo hagas** (*present subjunctive*).
> I want you to do it.
>
> **Iremos** (*future*) **por aquí para que no nos vean** (*present subjunctive*). We'll go this way so that they won't see us.

➤ If the verb in the first part of the sentence is in the <u>conditional</u> or a <u>past tense</u>, the second verb will usually be in the <u>imperfect subjunctive</u>.

Me gustaría (*conditional*) **que llegaras** (*imperfect subjunctive*) **temprano**.
I'd like you to arrive early.

Les pedí (*preterite*) **que me esperaran** (*imperfect subjunctive*).
I asked them to wait for me.

6 Indicative or subjunctive?

➤ Many expressions are followed by the <u>indicative</u> (the ordinary form of the verb) when they state facts, and by the <u>subjunctive</u> when they refer to possible or intended future events and outcomes.

➤ Certain conjunctions relating to time such as **cuando** (meaning *when*), **hasta que** (meaning *until*), **en cuanto** (meaning *as soon as*) and **mientras** (meaning *while*) are used with the <u>indicative</u> when the action has happened or when talking about what happens regularly.

¿Qué dijo cuando te <u>vio</u>?	What did he say when he saw you?
Siempre lo compro cuando <u>voy</u> a España.	I always buy it when I go to Spain.
Me quedé allí hasta que <u>volvió</u> Antonio.	I stayed there until Antonio came back.

➤ The same conjunctions are followed by the <u>subjunctive</u> when talking about a vague future time.

¿Qué quieres hacer cuando <u>seas</u> mayor?	What do you want to do when you grow up? (*but you're not grown up yet*)
¿Por qué no te quedas aquí hasta que <u>vuelva</u> Antonio?	Why don't you stay here until Antonio comes back? (*but Antonio hasn't come back yet*)
Lo haré en cuanto <u>pueda</u> *or* **tan pronto como <u>pueda</u>.**	I'll do it as soon as I can. (*but I'm not able to yet*)

Grammar Extra!

aunque is used with the <u>indicative</u> (the ordinary verb forms) when it means *although* or *even though*. In this case, the second part of the sentence is stating a fact.

Me gusta el francés aunque <u>prefiero</u> el alemán.	I like French although I prefer German.
Seguí andando aunque me <u>dolía</u> la pierna.	I went on walking even though my leg hurt.

aunque is used with the <u>subjunctive</u> when it means *even if*. Here, the second part of the sentence is not yet a fact.

Te llamaré cuando vuelva aunque <u>sea</u> tarde.	I'll call you when I get back, even if it's late.

For further explanation of grammatical terms, please see pages viii-xii.

7 | Forming the imperfect subjunctive

➤ For all verbs, there are <u>two</u> imperfect subjunctive forms that are exactly the same in meaning.

➤ The stem for both imperfect subjunctive forms is the same: you take off the -aron or -ieron ending of the **ellos** form of the preterite and add a fixed set of endings to what is left.

⮕ *For more information on the **Preterite**, see page 104.*

➤ For -ar verbs, the endings are: -ara, -aras, -ara, -áramos, -arais, -aran <u>or</u> -ase, -ases, -ase, -ásemos, -aseis, -asen. The first form is more common.

➤ For -er and -ir verbs, the endings are: -iera, -ieras, -iera, -iéramos, -ierais, -ieran <u>or</u> -iese, -ieses, -iese, -iésemos, -ieseis, -iesen. The first form is more common.

➤ The following table shows the imperfect subjunctive of three regular verbs: **hablar** (meaning *to speak*), **comer** (meaning *to eat*) and **vivir** (meaning *to live*).

Infinitive	(yo)	(tú)	(él) (ella) (usted)	(nosotros) (nosotras)	(vosotros) (vosotras)	(ellos) (ellas) (ustedes)
hablar to speak	hablara	hablaras	hablara	habláramos	hablarais	hablaran
	hablase	hablases	hablase	hablásemos	hablaseis	hablasen
comer to eat	comiera	comieras	comiera	comiéramos	comierais	comieran
	comiese	comieses	comiese	comiésemos	comieseis	comiesen
vivir to live	viviera	vivieras	viviera	viviéramos	vivierais	vivieran
	viviese	vivieses	viviese	viviésemos	vivieseis	viviesen

➤ Many verbs have irregular preterite forms which are reflected in the stem for the imperfect subjunctive. For example:

Infinitive	(yo)	(tú)	(él) (ella) (usted)	(nosotros) (nosotras)	(vosotros) (vosotras)	(ellos) (ellas) (ustedes)
dar to give	diera	dieras	diera	diéramos	dierais	dieran
	diese	dieses	diese	diésemos	dieseis	diesen
estar to be	estuviera	estuvieras	estuviera	estuviéramos	estuvierais	estuvieran
	estuviese	estuvieses	estuviese	estuviésemos	estuvieseis	estuviesen
hacer to do/ make	hiciera	hicieras	hiciera	hiciéramos	hicierais	hicieran
	hiciese	hicieses	hiciese	hiciésemos	hicieseis	hiciesen
poner to put	pusiera	pusieras	pusiera	pusiéramos	pusierais	pusieran
	pusiese	pusieses	pusiese	pusiésemos	pusieseis	pusiesen
tener to have	tuviera	tuvieras	tuviera	tuviéramos	tuvierais	tuvieran
	tuviese	tuvieses	tuviese	tuviésemos	tuvieseis	tuviesen
ser to be	fuera	fueras	fuera	fuéramos	fuerais	fueran
	fuese	fueses	fuese	fuésemos	fueseis	fuesen
venir to come	viniera	vinieras	viniera	viniéramos	vinierais	vinieran
	viniese	vinieses	viniese	viniésemos	vinieseis	viniesen

8 | Forming the imperfect subjunctive of some irregular -ir verbs

➤ In some irregular -ir verbs – the ones that don't have an i in the ellos form of the preterite – -era, -eras, -era, -éramos, -erais, -eran or -ese, -eses, -ese, -ésemos, -eseis, -esen are added to the preterite stem instead of -iera and -iese and so on.

⇨ *For more information on the Preterite, see page 104.*

Infinitive	(yo)	(tú)	(él) (ella) (usted)	(nosotros) (nosotras)	(vosotros) (vosotras)	(ellos) (ellas) (ustedes)
decir to say	dijera	dijeras	dijera	dijéramos	dijerais	dijeran
	dijese	dijeses	dijese	dijésemos	dijeseis	dijesen
ir to go	fuera	fueras	fuera	fuéramos	fuerais	fueran
	fuese	fueses	fuese	fuésemos	fueseis	fuesen

[*i*] Note that the imperfect subjunctive forms of **ir** and **ser** are identical.

Teníamos miedo de que se fuera.   We were afraid he might leave.
No era verdad que fueran ellos.   It wasn't true that it was them.

For further explanation of grammatical terms, please see pages viii-xii.

9 Present indicative or imperfect subjunctive after si

➤ Like some other conjunctions, **si** (meaning *if*) is sometimes followed by the ordinary present tense (the <u>present indicative</u>) and sometimes by the <u>imperfect subjunctive</u>.

➤ **si** is followed by the <u>present indicative</u> when talking about likely possibilities.

Si <u>quieres</u>, te dejo el coche.	If you like, I'll lend you the car. *(and you may well want to borrow the car)*
Compraré un bolígrafo si <u>tienen</u>.	I'll buy a pen if they have any. *(and there may well be some pens)*

➤ **si** is followed by the <u>imperfect subjunctive</u> when talking about unlikely or impossible conditions.

Si <u>tuviera</u> más dinero, me lo compraría.	If I had more money, I'd buy it. *(but I haven't got more money)*
Si yo <u>fuera</u> tú, lo compraría.	If I were you, I'd buy it. *(but I'm not you)*

Tip
You probably need the imperfect subjunctive in Spanish after **si** if the English sentence has *would* in it.

Key points

- ✔ After certain verbs you have to use a subjunctive in Spanish when there is a different subject in the two parts of the sentence.
- ✔ A subjunctive is also found after many impersonal expressions, as well as after certain conjunctions.
- ✔ Structures with the subjunctive can often be avoided if the subject of both verbs is the same. An infinitive can often be used instead.
- ✔ The endings of the present subjunctive in regular **-ar** verbs are: **-e, -es, -e, -emos, -éis, -en**.
- ✔ The endings of the present subjunctive in regular **-er** and **-ir** verbs are: **-a, -as, -a, -amos, -áis, -an**.
- ✔ The endings of the imperfect subjunctive in regular **-ar** verbs are: **-ara, -aras, -ara, -áramos, -arais, -aran** or **-ase, -ases, -ase, -ásemos, -aseis, -asen**.
- ✔ The endings of the imperfect subjunctive in regular **-er** and **-ir** verbs are: **-iera, -ieras, -iera, -iéramos, -ierais, -ieran** or **-iese, -ieses, -iese, -iésemos, -ieseis, -iesen**.
- ✔ Some verbs have irregular subjunctive forms.

The infinitive

What is the infinitive?
The **infinitive** is a form of the verb that hasn't had any endings added to it and doesn't relate to any particular tense. In English, the infinitive is usually shown with *to*, as in *to speak, to eat, to live*.

---

1 Using the infinitive

➤ In English, the infinitive is usually thought of as being made up of two words, for example, *to speak*. In Spanish, the infinitive consists of one word and is the verb form that ends in **-ar**, **-er** or **-ir**, for example, **hablar**, **comer**, **vivir**.

➤ When you look up a verb in the dictionary, you will find that information is usually listed under the infinitive form.

➤ In Spanish, the infinitive is often used in the following ways:

- after a preposition such as **antes de** (meaning *before*), **después de** (meaning *after*)

Después de comer, fuimos a casa de Pepe.	After eating, we went round to Pepe's.
Salió **sin hacer** ruido.	She went out without making a noise.
Siempre veo la tele **antes de acostarme**.	I always watch TV before going to bed.

[i] Note that in English we always use the *-ing* form of the verb after a preposition, for example, *before going*. In Spanish you have to use the infinitive form after a preposition.

- in set phrases, particularly after adjectives or nouns

Estoy **encantada de poder** ayudarte.	I'm delighted to be able to help you.
Está **contento de vivir** aquí.	He's happy living here.
Tengo ganas de salir.	I feel like going out.
No **hace falta comprar** leche.	We/You don't need to buy any milk.
Me dio mucha **alegría verla**.	I was very pleased to see her.
Me da miedo cruzar la carretera.	I'm afraid of crossing the road.

For further explanation of grammatical terms, please see pages viii–xii.

- after another verb, sometimes as the object of it

<u>Debo llamar</u> a casa.	I must phone home.
<u>Prefiero esquiar</u>.	I prefer skiing.
<u>Me gusta escuchar</u> música.	I like listening to music.
<u>Nos encanta nadar</u>.	We love swimming.
¿<u>Te apetece ir</u> al cine?	Do you fancy going to the cinema?

[*i*] Note that, when it comes after another verb, the Spanish infinitive often corresponds to the *-ing* form in English.

- in instructions that are aimed at the general public – for example in cookery books or on signs

<u>Cocer</u> a fuego lento.	Cook on a low heat.
Prohibido <u>pisar</u> el césped.	Don't walk on the grass.

- as a noun, where in English we would use the *-ing* form of the verb

Lo importante es <u>intentarlo</u>.	Trying is the important thing.

[*i*] Note that, when the infinitive is the subject of another verb, it may have the article el before it, particularly if it starts the sentence.

El viajar tanto me resulta cansado.	I find so much travelling tiring.

> ### *Típ*
> Be especially careful when translating the English *-ing* form.
> It is often translated by the infinitive in Spanish.

2 Linking two verbs together

➤ There are three ways that verbs can be linked together when the second verb is an infinitive:

- with no linking word in between

¿Quieres venir?	Do you want to come?
Necesito hablar contigo.	I need to talk to you.

- with a preposition:

ir <u>a</u> hacer algo	to be going to do something
aprender <u>a</u> hacer algo	to learn to do something
dejar <u>de</u> hacer algo	to stop doing something

Voy <u>a</u> comprarme un móvil.	I'm going to buy a mobile.
Aprendimos <u>a</u> esquiar.	We learnt to ski.
Quiere dejar <u>de</u> fumar.	He wants to stop smoking.

[*i*] Note that you have to learn the preposition required for each verb.

- in set structures

tener que hacer algo	to have to do something
Tengo que salir.	I've got to go out.
Tendrías que comer más.	You should eat more.
Tuvo que devolver el dinero.	He had to pay back the money.

3 Verbs followed by the infinitive with no preposition

➤ Some Spanish verbs and groups of verbs can be followed by an infinitive with no preposition:

- **poder** (meaning *to be able to, can, may*), **saber** (meaning *to know how to, can*), **querer** (meaning *to want*) and **deber** (meaning *to have to, must*)

No **puede venir**.	He can't come.
¿**Sabes esquiar**?	Can you ski?
Quiere estudiar medicina.	He wants to study medicine.
Debes hacerlo.	You must do it.

- verbs like **gustar**, **encantar** and **apetecer**, where the infinitive is the subject of the verb

Me gusta estudiar.	I like studying.
Nos encanta bailar.	We love dancing.
¿**Te apetece ir** al cine?	Do you fancy going to the cinema?

- verbs that relate to seeing or hearing, such as **ver** (meaning *to see*) and **oír** (meaning *to hear*)

Nos **ha visto llegar**.	He saw us arrive.
Te **he oído cantar**.	I heard you singing.

- the verbs **hacer** (meaning *to make*) and **dejar** (meaning *to let*)

¡No me **hagas reír**!	Don't make me laugh!
Mis padres no me **dejan salir** por la noche.	My parents don't let me go out at night.

- the following common verbs

decidir	to decide
desear	to wish, want
esperar	to hope
evitar	to avoid
necesitar	to need
odiar	to hate
olvidar	to forget
pensar	to think
preferir	to prefer
recordar	to remember
sentir	to regret

Han **decidido comprarse** una casa.	They've decided to buy a house.
No **desea tener** más hijos.	She doesn't want to have any more children.
Espero poder ir.	I hope to be able to go.
Evita gastar demasiado dinero.	He avoids spending too much money.
Necesito salir un momento.	I need to go out for a moment.
Olvidó **dejar** su dirección.	She forgot to leave her address.
Pienso hacer una paella.	I'm thinking of making a paella.
Siento molestarte.	I'm sorry to bother you.

➤ Some of these verbs combine with infinitives to make set phrases with a special meaning:

- **querer decir**   to mean

  ¿Qué **quiere decir** eso?   What does that mean?

- **dejar caer**   to drop

  Dejó caer la bandeja.   She dropped the tray.

4   Verbs followed by the preposition a and the infinitive

➤ The following verbs are the most common ones that can be followed by **a** and the infinitive:

- verbs relating to movement such as **ir** (meaning *to go*) and **venir** (meaning *to come*)

  Se va **a** comprar un caballo. He's going to buy a horse.

  Viene **a** vernos.   He's coming to see us.

- the following common verbs

aprender a hacer algo	to learn to do something
comenzar a hacer algo	to begin to do something
decidirse a hacer algo	to decide to do something
empezar a hacer algo	to begin to do something
llegar a hacer algo	to manage to do something
llegar a ser algo	to become something
probar a hacer algo	to try to do something
volver a hacer algo	to do something again

Me gustaría aprender a nadar.	I'd like to learn to swim.
No llegó a terminar la carrera.	He didn't manage to finish his degree course.
Llegó a ser primer ministro.	He became prime minister.
No vuelvas a hacerlo nunca más.	Don't ever do it again.

➤ The following verbs can be followed by **a** and a person's name or else by **a** and a noun or pronoun referring to a person, and then by another **a** and an infinitive.

ayudar a alguien a hacer algo	to help someone to do something
enseñar a alguien a hacer algo	to teach someone to do something
invitar a alguien a hacer algo	to invite someone to do something
¿Podrías ayudar a Antonia a fregar los platos?	Could you help Antonia to do the dishes?
Enseñó a su hermano a nadar.	He taught his brother to swim.
Los he invitado a tomar unas copas en casa.	I've invited them over for drinks.

5 | Verbs followed by the preposition de and the infinitive

➤ The following verbs are the most common ones that can be followed by **de** and the infinitive:

aburrirse de hacer algo	to get bored with doing something
acabar de hacer algo	to have just done something
acordarse de haber hecho/ de hacer algo	to remember having done/ to do something
alegrarse de hacer algo	to be glad to do something
dejar de hacer algo	to stop doing something
tener ganas de hacer algo	to want to do something
tratar de hacer algo	to try to do something

Me aburría de no poder salir de casa.	I was getting bored with not being able to leave the house.
Acabo de comprar un móvil.	I've just bought a mobile.
Acababan de llegar cuando...	They had just arrived when...
Me alegro de verte.	I'm glad to see you.
¿Quieres dejar de hablar?	Will you stop talking?
Tengo ganas de volver a España.	I want to go back to Spain.

6 Verbs followed by the preposition con and the infinitive

➤ The following verbs are the most common ones that can be followed by con and the infinitive:

| amenazar con hacer algo | to threaten to do someting |
| soñar con hacer algo | to dream about doing something |

| Amenazó con denunciarlos. | He threatened to report them. |
| Sueño con vivir en España. | I dream about living in Spain. |

7 Verbs followed by the preposition en and the infinitive

➤ The verb quedar is the most common one that can be followed by en and the infinitive:

| quedar en hacer algo | to agree to do something |
| Habíamos quedado en encontrarnos a las ocho. | We had agreed to meet at eight. |

Key points

✔ Infinitives are found after prepositions, set phrases and in instructions to the general public.

✔ They can also function as the subject or object of a verb, when the infinitive corresponds to the -ing form in English.

✔ Many Spanish verbs can be followed by another verb in the infinitive.

✔ The two verbs may be linked by nothing at all, or by a, de or another preposition.

✔ The construction in Spanish does not always match the English. It's best to learn these constructions when you learn a new verb.

Prepositions after verbs

➤ In English, there are some phrases which are made up of verbs and prepositions, for example, to <u>accuse</u> somebody <u>of</u> something, to <u>look forward to</u> something and to <u>rely on</u> something.

➤ In Spanish there are also lots of set phrases made up of verbs and prepositions. Often the prepositions in Spanish are not the same as they are in English, so you will need to learn them. Listed below are phrases using verbs and some common Spanish prepositions.

⇨ *For more information on verbs used with a preposition and the infinitive, see page 147.*

1 | Verbs followed by a

➤ **a** is often the equivalent of the English word *to* when it is used with an indirect object after verbs like **enviar** (meaning *to send*), **dar** (meaning *to give*) and **decir** (meaning *to say*).

dar algo <u>a</u> alguien	to give something to someone
decir algo <u>a</u> alguien	to say something to someone
enviar algo <u>a</u> alguien	to send something to someone
escribir algo <u>a</u> alguien	to write something to someone
mostrar algo <u>a</u> alguien	to show something to someone

⇨ *For more information on **Indirect objects**, see page 49.*

> ### Tip
> There is an important difference between Spanish and English with this type of verb. In English, you can say either *to give something to someone* or *to give someone something*.
> You can <u>NEVER</u> miss out **a** in Spanish in the way that you can sometimes miss out *to* in English.

➤ Here are some verbs taking **a** in Spanish that have a different construction in English.

asistir <u>a</u> algo	to attend something, to be at something
dirigirse <u>a</u> (un lugar)	to head for (a place)
dirigirse a alguien	to address somebody
jugar <u>a</u> algo	to play something (*sports/games*)
llegar <u>a</u> (un lugar)	to arrive at (a place)

oler <u>a</u> algo	to smell of something
parecerse <u>a</u> alguien/algo	to look like somebody/something
subir(se) <u>a</u> un autobús/un coche	to get on a bus/into a car
subir(se) <u>a</u> un árbol	to climb a tree
tener miedo <u>a</u> alguien	to be afraid of somebody

Este perfume huele <u>a</u> jazmín.	This perfume smells of jasmine.
¡De prisa, sube <u>al</u> coche!	Get into the car, quick!
Nunca tuvieron miedo <u>a</u> su padre.	They were never afraid of their father.

⇨ *For verbs such as **gustar**, **encantar** and **faltar**, see **Verbal idioms** on page 154.*

2 Verbs followed by de

➤ Here are some verbs taking **de** in Spanish that have a different construction in English:

acordarse <u>de</u> algo/alguien	to remember something/somebody
alegrarse <u>de</u> algo	to be glad about something
bajarse <u>de</u> un autobús/un coche	to get off a bus/out of a car
darse cuenta <u>de</u> algo	to realize something
depender <u>de</u> algo/alguien	to depend on something/somebody
despedirse <u>de</u> alguien	to say goodbye to somebody
preocuparse <u>de</u> algo/alguien	to worry about something/somebody
quejarse <u>de</u> algo	to complain about something
reírse <u>de</u> algo/alguien	to laugh at something/somebody
salir <u>de</u> (un cuarto/un edificio)	to leave (a room/a building)
tener ganas <u>de</u> algo	to want something
tener miedo <u>de</u> algo	to be afraid of something
trabajar <u>de</u> (camarero/secretario)	to work as (a waiter/secretary)
tratarse <u>de</u> algo/alguien	to be a question of something/to be about somebody

Nos acordamos muy bien <u>de</u> aquellas vacaciones.	We remember that vacation very well.
Se bajó <u>del</u> coche.	He got out of the car.
No depende <u>de</u> mí.	It doesn't depend on me.
Se preocupa mucho <u>de</u> su apariencia.	He worries a lot about his appearance.

3 Verbs followed by con

➤ Here are some verbs taking **con** in Spanish that have a different construction in English:

comparar algo/a alguien <u>con</u> algo/alguien	to compare something/somebody with something/somebody
contar <u>con</u> alguien/algo	to rely on somebody/something
encontrarse <u>con</u> alguien	to meet somebody (*by chance*)
enfadarse <u>con</u> alguien	to get annoyed with somebody
estar de acuerdo <u>con</u> alguien/algo	to agree with somebody/something
hablar <u>con</u> alguien	to talk to somebody
soñar <u>con</u> alguien/algo	to dream about somebody/something
Cuento <u>con</u>tigo.	I'm relying on you.
Me encontré <u>con</u> ella al entrar en el banco.	I met her as I was going into the bank.
¿Puedo hablar <u>con</u> usted un momento?	May I talk to you for a moment?

4 Verbs followed by en

➤ Here are some verbs taking **en** in Spanish that have a different construction in English:

entrar <u>en</u> (un edificio/ un cuarto)	to enter, go into (a building/a room)
pensar <u>en</u> algo/alguien	to think about something/somebody
trabajar <u>en</u> (una oficina/ una fábrica)	to work in (an office/a factory)
No quiero pensar <u>en</u> eso.	I don't want to think about that.

5 Verbs followed by por

➤ Here are some verbs taking **por** in Spanish that have a different construction in English:

interesarse <u>por</u> algo/alguien	to ask about something/somebody
preguntar <u>por</u> alguien	to ask for/about somebody
preocuparse <u>por</u> algo/alguien	to worry about something/somebody

---

For further explanation of grammatical terms, please see pages viii-xii.

Me interesaba mucho <u>por</u> la arqueología.	I was very interested in archaeology.
Se preocupa mucho <u>por</u> su apariencia.	He worries a lot about his appearance.

6 Verbs taking a direct object in Spanish but not in English

➤ In English there are a few verbs that are followed by *at*, *for* or *to* which, in Spanish, are not followed by any preposition other than the personal **a**.

⇨ *For more information on **Personal a**, see page 182.*

mirar algo/a alguien	to look at something/somebody
escuchar algo/a alguien	to listen to something/somebody
buscar algo/a alguien	to look for something/somebody
pedir algo	to ask for something
esperar algo/a alguien	to wait for something/somebody
pagar algo	to pay for something
Mira esta foto.	Look at this photo.
Me gusta escuchar música.	I like listening to music.
Estoy buscando las gafas.	I'm looking for my glasses.
Pidió una taza de té.	He asked for a cup of tea.
Estamos esperando el tren.	We're waiting for the train.
Ya he pagado el billete.	I've already paid for my ticket.
Estoy buscando a mi hermano.	I'm looking for my brother.

Key points

✔ The prepositions used with Spanish verbs are often very different from those used in English, so make sure you learn common expressions involving prepositions in Spanish.

✔ The most common prepositions used with verbs in Spanish are **a**, **de**, **con**, **en** and **por**.

✔ Some Spanish verbs are not followed by a preposition, but are used with a preposition in English.

Verbal Idioms

1 Present tense of gustar

➤ You will probably already have come across the phrase **me gusta...** meaning *I like...* . Actually, **gustar** means literally *to please*, and if you remember this, you will be able to use **gustar** much more easily.

Me gusta el chocolate.	I like chocolate. (*literally: chocolate pleases me*)
Me gustan los animales.	I like animals. (*literally: animals please me*)
Nos gusta el español.	We like Spanish. (*literally: Spanish pleases us*)
Nos gustan los españoles.	We like Spanish people. (*literally: Spanish people please us*)

➤ Even though **chocolate**, **animales**, and so on, come after **gustar**, they are the <u>subject</u> of the verb (the person or thing performing the action) and therefore the endings of **gustar** change to agree with them.

➤ When the thing that you like is <u>singular</u>, you use **gusta** (*third person singular*), and when the thing that you like is <u>plural</u>, you use **gustan** (*third person plural*).

Le gusta Francia.	He/She likes France. (*literally: France pleases him/her*)
Le gustan los caramelos.	He/She likes sweets. (*literally: Sweets please him/her*)

[i] Note that **me**, **te**, **le**, **nos**, **os** and **les**, which are used with **gustar**, are indirect object pronouns.

➪ *For more information on **Indirect object pronouns**, see page 49.*

2 Other tenses of gustar

➤ You can use **gustar** in other tenses in Spanish.

Les gustó la fiesta.	They liked the party.
Les gustaron los fuegos artificiales.	They liked the fireworks.
Te va a gustar la película.	You'll like the movie.
Te van a gustar las fotos.	You'll like the photos.
Les ha gustado mucho el museo.	They liked the museum a lot
Les han gustado mucho los cuadros.	They liked the paintings a lot.

For further explanation of grammatical terms, please see pages viii-xii.

➤ You can also use **más** with **gustar** to say what you prefer.

A mí me <u>gusta más</u> el rojo.	I prefer the red one. (*literally: the red one pleases me more*)
A mí me <u>gustan más</u> los rojos.	I prefer the red ones. (*literally: the red ones please me more*)

3 Other verbs like gustar

➤ There are several other verbs which behave in the same way as **gustar**:

- encantar

Me <u>encanta</u> el flamenco.	I love flamenco.
Me <u>encantan</u> los animales.	I love animals.

- faltar

Le <u>faltaba</u> un botón.	He had a button missing.
Le <u>faltaban</u> tres dientes.	He had three teeth missing.

- quedar

No les <u>queda</u> nada.	They have nothing left.
Solo nos <u>quedan</u> dos kilómetros.	We've only got two kilometers left.

- doler

Le <u>dolía</u> la cabeza.	His head hurt.
Le <u>dolían</u> las muelas.	His teeth hurt.

- interesar

Te <u>interesará</u> el libro.	The book will interest you.
Te <u>interesarán</u> sus noticias.	His news will interest you.

- importar

No me <u>importa</u> la lluvia.	The rain doesn't matter to me. *or* I don't mind the rain.
Me <u>importan</u> mucho mis estudios.	My studies matter to me a lot.

- hacer falta

Nos <u>hace</u> falta un ordenador.	We need a computer.
Nos <u>hacen</u> falta libros.	We need books.

Grammar Extra!

All the examples given above are in the third persons singular and plural as these are by far the most common. However, it is also possible to use these verbs in other forms.

Creo que le <u>gustas</u>.	I think he likes you. (*literally: I think you please him*)

---

4 | Verbal idioms used with another verb

➤ In English you can say I *like playing soccer*, *we love swimming* and so on, and in Spanish you can also use another verb with most of the verbs like **gustar**. However, the verb form you use for the second verb in Spanish is the <u>infinitive</u>.

Le <u>gusta jugar</u> al fútbol.	He/She likes playing soccer.
No me <u>gusta bailar</u>.	I don't like dancing.
Nos <u>encanta estudiar</u>.	We love studying.
No me <u>importa tener</u> que esperar.	I don't mind having to wait.

➪ *For more information on the* **Infinitive**, *see page 144.*

> ### Key points
> ✔ There are a number of common verbs in Spanish which are used in the opposite way to English, for example, **gustar**, **encantar**, **hacer falta**, and so on. With all these verbs, the object of the English verb is the subject of the Spanish verb.
> ✔ The endings of these verbs change according to whether the thing liked or needed and so on is singular or plural.
> ✔ All these verbs can be followed by another verb in the infinitive.

Negatives

> **What is a negative?**
> A **negative** question or statement is one which contains a word such as *not*, *never* or *nothing* and is used to say that something is not happening, is not true or is absent.

1 no

➤ In English, we often make sentences negative by adding *don't*, *doesn't* or *didn't* before the verb. In Spanish you simply add **no** (meaning *not*) before the main verb.

Positive			**Negative**	
Trabaja.	He works.	→	**No trabaja.**	He doesn't work.
Comen.	They eat.	→	**No comen.**	They don't eat.
Salió.	She went out.	→	**No salió.**	She didn't go out.
Lo he visto.	I've seen it.	→	**No lo he visto.**	I haven't seen it.
Sabe nadar.	He can swim.	→	**No sabe nadar.**	He can't swim.

> **Tip**
> <u>NEVER</u> translate *don't*, *doesn't*, *didn't* using **hacer**.

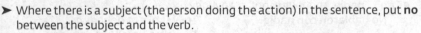

➤ Where there is a subject (the person doing the action) in the sentence, put **no** between the subject and the verb.

Juan <u>no</u> vive aquí.	Juan doesn't live here.
Mi hermana <u>no</u> lee mucho.	My sister doesn't read much.
Mis padres <u>no</u> han llamado.	My parents haven't called.
Él <u>no</u> lo comprenderá.	He won't understand.

[*i*] Note that the Spanish word **no** also means *no* in answer to a question.

➤ Where the subject is only shown by the verb ending, **no** goes before the verb.

<u>No</u> tenemos tiempo.	We haven't got time.
Todavía <u>no</u> ha llegado.	He hasn't arrived yet.
<u>No</u> hemos comido.	We haven't eaten.
<u>No</u> llevará mucho tiempo.	It won't take long.

➤ If there are any object pronouns (for example, **me**, **te**, **lo**, **los**, **le** and so on) before the verb, **no** goes <u>BEFORE</u> them.

<u>No</u> lo he visto.	I didn't see it.
<u>No</u> me gusta el fútbol.	I don't like soccer.

➤ In phrases consisting only of *not* and another word, such as *not now* or *not me*, the Spanish **no** usually goes <u>AFTER</u> the other word.

Ahora <u>no</u>.	Not now.
Yo <u>no</u>.	Not me.
Todavía <u>no</u>.	Not yet.

➤ Some phrases have a special construction in Spanish.

Espero que sí.	I hope so.	→	**Espero que no.**	I hope not.
Creo que sí.	I think so.	→	**Creo que no.**	I don't think so.

2 Other negative words

➤ In Spanish, you can form negatives using pairs and groups of words, as you can in English.

- **no ... nunca**   never *or* not ... ever
  <u>No</u> la veo <u>nunca</u>.

  I never see her *or*
  I don't ever see her.

- **no ... jamás**   never *or* not ... ever
  <u>No</u> la veo <u>jamás</u>.

  I never see her *or*
  I don't ever see her.

- **no ... nada**   nothing *or* not ... anything
  <u>No</u> ha dicho <u>nada</u>.

  He has said nothing *or*
  He hasn't said anything.

- **no ... nadie**   nobody *or* not ... anybody
  <u>No</u> hablaron con <u>nadie</u>.

  They spoke to nobody *or*
  They didn't speak to anybody.

- **no ... tampoco**   not ... either
  Yo <u>no</u> la vi. – Yo <u>tampoco</u>.

  I didn't see her. – Neither did I.
  or I didn't either. *or* Nor did I.

  A él <u>no</u> le gusta el café y a mí <u>tampoco</u>.

  He doesn't like coffee and neither do I.

- **no ... ni ... ni**   neither ... nor
  <u>No</u> vinieron <u>ni</u> Carlos <u>ni</u> Ana.

  Neither Carlos nor Ana came.

- **no ... más**   no longer *or* not ... any more
  <u>No</u> te veré <u>más</u>.

  I won't see you any more.

- **no ... ningún/ninguna** + *noun*   no *or* not ... any
  <u>No</u> tiene <u>ningún</u> interés en ir.

  She has no interest in going.

➤ Most of these negative words can also be used without **no** provided they come before any verb.

Nunca or **Jamás** la veo.	I never see her.
Nadie vino.	No one came.
Ni Pedro **ni** Pablo fuman.	Neither Pedro nor Pablo smokes.
¿Quién te ha dicho eso? – **Nadie**.	Who told you that? - No one.
¿Qué has hecho? – **Nada**.	What have you done? – Nothing.

➤ Sometimes negative expressions combine with each other.

Nunca hacen **nada**.	They never do anything.
Nunca viene **nadie**.	No one ever comes.
No lo haré **nunca más**.	I'll never do it again.
No veo **nunca** a **nadie**.	I never see anyone.

3 Word order with negatives

➤ In English you can put words like *never* and *ever* between *have/has/had* and the past participle, for example, *We have never been to Argentina*. You should <u>NEVER</u> separate **he, has, ha, había** and so on from the past participle of the verb in Spanish.

Nunca hemos estado en Argentina.	We have never been to Argentina.
Nunca había visto **nada** así.	I had never seen anything like this.
Ninguno de nosotros había esquiado **nunca**.	None of us had ever skied.

⇨ *For more information on **Past participles**, see page 115.*

Key points

✔ The Spanish word **no** is equivalent to both *no* and *not* in English.

✔ You can make sentences negative by putting **no** before the verb (and before any object pronouns that are in front of the verb).

✔ Other negative words also exist, such as **nunca**, **nadie** and **nada**. Use them in combination with **no**, with the verb sandwiched in between. Most of them also work on their own provided they go <u>before</u> any verb.

✔ Never insert negative words, or anything else, between **he, has, ha, había** and so on and the past participle.

Questions

> **What is a question?**
> A **question** is a sentence which is used to ask someone about something and which often has the verb in front of the subject. Questions often include a question word such as *why*, *where*, *who*, *which* or *how*.

Asking questions in Spanish

There are three main ways of asking questions in Spanish:

- by making your voice go up at the end of the sentence
- by changing normal word order
- by using a question word

> *Tip*
>
> Don't forget the opening question mark in Spanish. It goes at the beginning of the question or of the question part of the sentence.
>
> **¿No quieres tomar algo?**   Wouldn't you like something to eat or drink?
>
> **Eres inglés, ¿verdad?**   You're English, aren't you?

1 Asking a question by making your voice go up

➤ If you are expecting the answer *yes* or *no*, there is a very simple way of asking a question. You keep the word order exactly as it would be in a normal sentence but you turn it into a question by making your voice go up at the end.

¿Hablas español?	Do you speak Spanish?
¿Es profesor?	Is he a teacher?
¿Hay leche?	Is there any milk?
¿Te gusta la música?	Do you like music?

➤ When the subject (the person or thing doing the action) of the verb is a noun, pronoun or name it can be given before the verb, just as in an ordinary sentence. But you turn the statement into a question by making your voice go up at the end.

¿Tu hermana ha comprado pan?	Did your sister buy any bread?
¿Tú lo has hecho?	Did you do it?
¿Tu padre te ha visto?	Did your father see you?
¿El diccionario está aquí?	Is the dictionary here?

For further explanation of grammatical terms, please see pages viii-xii.

2 | Asking a question by changing word order

➤ When the subject of the verb is specified, another even more common way of asking questions is to change the word order so that the verb comes <u>BEFORE</u> the subject instead of after it.

¿Lo has hecho tú?	Did you do it?
¿Te ha visto tu padre?	Did your father see you?
¿Está el diccionario aquí?	Is the dictionary here?

[i] Note that the position of object pronouns is not affected.

➪ *For more information on **Word order with object pronouns**, see pages 47, 50 and 52.*

Grammar Extra!

If the verb has an object, such as *any bread* in *Did your sister buy any bread?*, the subject usually comes <u>AFTER</u> the object, provided the object is short.

¿Ha compado <u>pan</u> tu hermana?	Did your sister buy any bread?
¿Vio <u>la película</u> tu novio?	Did your boyfriend see the movie?

If the object is made up of several words, the subject goes <u>BEFORE</u> it.

Se han comprado tus padres	Have your parents bought that
<u>aquella casa de que me hablaste?</u>	house you told me about?

When there is an adverbial phrase (*to the party*, *in Barcelona*) after the verb, the subject can go <u>BEFORE OR AFTER</u> the adverbial phrase.

¿Viene <u>a la fiesta</u> Andrés? *or*	Is Andrés coming to the party?
¿Viene Andrés <u>a la fiesta</u>?	

---

3 | Asking a question by using a question word

➤ Question words are words like *when, what, who, which, where* and *how* that are used to ask for information. In Spanish, <u>ALL</u> question words have an accent on them.

¿adónde?	where ... to?
¿cómo?	how?
¿cuál/cuáles?	which?, what?
¿cuándo?	when?
¿cuánto/cuánta?	how much?
¿cuántos/cuántas?	how many?
¿dónde?	where?
¿para qué?	what for?
¿por qué?	why?
¿qué?	what?, which?
¿quién?	who?

> ### Tip
>
> Be careful not to mix up **por qué** (meaning *why*) with **porque** (meaning *because*).

¿**Cuándo** se fue?	When did he go?
¿**Qué** te pasa?	What's the matter?
¿**Qué** chaqueta te vas a poner?	Which jacket are you going to wear?
¿**Cuál** de los dos quieres?	Which do you want?
¿**Cuánto** azúcar quieres?	How much sugar do you want?
¿**Cuánto** tiempo llevas esperando?	How long have you been waiting?

➪ *For more information on question words, see* **Interrogative adjectives** *on page 32 and* **Interrogative pronouns** *on page 65.*

➤ When the question starts with a question word that isn't the subject of the verb, the noun or pronoun (if given) that is the subject of the verb goes <u>AFTER</u> it.

¿De qué color es <u>la moqueta</u>?	What color's the carpet?
¿A qué hora comienza <u>el concierto</u>?	What time does the concert start?
¿Dónde están <u>tus pantalones</u>?	Where are your pants?
¿Adónde iba <u>tu padre</u>?	Where was your father going?
¿Cómo están <u>tus padres</u>?	How are your parents?
¿Cuándo volverán <u>ustedes</u>?	When will you come back?

4 | Which question word to use?

➤ **qué** or **cuál** or **cuáles** can be used to mean *which*:

- always use **qué** before a noun

¿<u>Qué chaqueta</u> te vas a poner?	<u>Which jacket</u> are you going to wear?

- otherwise use **cuál** (*singular*) or **cuáles** (*plural*)

¿<u>Cuál</u> quieres?	<u>Which (one)</u> do you want?
¿<u>Cuáles</u> quieres?	<u>Which (ones)</u> do you want?

➤ **quién** or **quiénes** can be used to mean *who*:

- use **quién** when asking about one person

¿<u>Quién</u> ganó?	<u>Who</u> won?

- use **quiénes** when asking about more than one person

¿<u>Quiénes</u> estaban?	<u>Who</u> was there?

For further explanation of grammatical terms, please see pages viii-xii.

[*i*] Note that you need to put the personal **a** before **quién** and **quiénes** when it acts as an object.

¿A quién viste?	<u>Who</u> did you see?

⇨ *For more information on **Personal a**, see page 182.*

➤ **de quién** or **de quiénes** can be used to mean *whose*:

- use **de quién** when there is likely to be one owner

¿De quién es este abrigo?	<u>Whose</u> coat is this?

- use **de quiénes** when there is likely to be more than one owner

¿De quiénes son estos abrigos?	<u>Whose</u> coats are these?

[*i*] Note that the structure in Spanish is the equivalent of *Whose <u>is</u> this coat?/Whose <u>are</u> these coats?* Don't try putting **¿de quién?** or **¿de quiénes?** immediately before a noun.

➤ **qué**, **cómo**, **cuál** and **cuáles** can all be used to mean *what* although **qué** is the most common translation:

- use **cómo** or **qué** when asking someone to repeat something that you didn't hear properly

¿Cómo *or* **Qué (has dicho)?**	<u>What</u> (did you say)?

- use **¿cuál es ... ?** and **¿cuáles son ... ?** to mean *what is ... ?* and *what/are ... ?* when you aren't asking for a definition

¿Cuál es la capital de Francia?	<u>What's</u> the capital of France?
¿Cuál es su número de teléfono?	<u>What's</u> his telephone number?

- use **¿qué es ... ?** and **¿qué son ... ?** to mean *what is ... ?* and *what are ... ?* when you are asking for a definition

¿Qué son los genes?	<u>What are</u> genes?

- always use **qué** to mean *what* before another noun

¿Qué hora es?	<u>What time</u> is it?
¿Qué asignaturas estudias?	<u>What subjects</u> are you studying?

Tip

You can finish an English question (or sentence) with a preposition such as *about*, for example, *Who did you write to?*; *What are you talking about?* You can <u>NEVER</u> end a Spanish question or sentence with a preposition.

¿Con quién hablaste?	Who did you speak <u>to</u>?

Grammar Extra!

All the questions we have looked at so far have been straight questions, otherwise known as <u>direct questions</u>. However, sometimes instead of asking directly, for example, *Where is it?* or *Why did you do it?*, we ask the question in a more roundabout way, for example, *Can you tell me where it is?* or *Please tell me why you did it*. These are called <u>indirect questions.</u>

In indirect questions in English we say *where <u>it is</u>* instead of *where <u>is it</u>* and *why <u>you did it</u>* instead of *why <u>did you do it</u>*, but in Spanish you still put the subject <u>AFTER</u> the verb.

¿Sabes adónde <u>iba tu padre</u>?	Do you know where your father was going?
¿Puedes decirme para qué <u>sirven los diccionarios</u>?	Can you tell me what dictionaries are for?

The subject also goes <u>AFTER</u> the verb in Spanish when you report a question in indirect speech.

Quería saber adónde <u>iba mi padre</u>.	He wanted to know where my father was going.

[i] Note that you still put accents on question words in Spanish even when they are in indirect and reported questions or when they come after expressions of uncertainty:

No sé <u>qué</u> hacer.	I don't know what to do.
No sabemos <u>por qué</u> se fue.	We don't know why he left.

5 Negative questions

➤ When you want to make a negative question, put **no** before the verb in the same way that you do in statements (non-questions).

¿<u>No</u> vienes?	Aren't you coming?
¿<u>No</u> lo has visto?	Didn't you see it?

➤ You can also use **o no** at the end of a question in the same way that we can ask *or not* in English.

¿Vienes <u>o no</u>?	Are you coming <u>or not</u>?
¿Lo quieres <u>o no</u>?	Do you want it <u>or not</u>?

6 Short questions

➤ In English we sometimes check whether our facts and beliefs are correct by putting *isn't it?*, *don't they?*, *are they?* and so on at the end of a comment. In Spanish, you can add **¿verdad?** in the same way.

Hace calor, ¿<u>verdad</u>?	It's hot, <u>isn't it</u>?
Te gusta, ¿<u>verdad</u>?	You like it, <u>don't you</u>?

For further explanation of grammatical terms, please see pages viii–xii.

| **No te olvidarás, ¿verdad?** | You won't forget, <u>will you</u>? |
| **No vino, ¿verdad?** | He didn't come, <u>did he</u>? |

➤ You can also use **¿no?**, especially after positive comments.

| **Hace calor, ¿no?** | It's hot, <u>isn't it</u>? |
| **Te gusta, ¿no?** | You like it, <u>don't you</u>? |

7 | Answering questions

➤ To answer a question which requires a *yes* or *no* answer, just use **sí** or **no**.

¿Te gusta? – Sí/No.	Do you like it? – Yes, I do/No, I don't.
¿Está aquí? – Sí/No.	Is he here? – Yes he is/No, he isn't.
¿Tienes prisa? – Sí/No.	Are you in a hurry? – Yes, I am/ No, I'm not.
No lo has hecho, ¿verdad? – Sí/No.	You haven't done it, have you? – Yes, I have/No, I haven't.

➤ You can also often answer **sí** or **no** followed by the verb in question. In negative answers this may mean that you say **no** twice.

| **Quieres acompañarme? – Sí, quiero.** | Would you like to come with me? – Yes, I would. |
| **¿Vas a ir a la fiesta? – No, no voy.** | Are you going to the party? – No, I'm not. |

> ### Key points
> ✔ You ask a question in Spanish by making your voice go up at the end of the sentence, by changing normal word order, and by using question words.
> ✔ Question words always have an accent on them.
> ✔ To make a negative question, add **no** before the verb.
> ✔ You can add **¿verdad?** to check whether your facts or beliefs are correct.

Adverbs

What is an adverb?
An **adverb** is a word usually used with verbs, adjectives or other adverbs that gives more information about when, how, where, or in what circumstances something happens, or to what degree something is true, for example, *quickly, happily, now, extremely, very*.

How adverbs are used

➤ In general, adverbs are used together with verbs, adjectives and other adverbs, for example, *act quickly; smile cheerfully; rather ill; a lot happier; really slowly; very well*.

➤ Adverbs can also relate to the whole sentence. In this case they often tell you what the speaker is thinking or feeling.

   Fortunately, Jan had already left.

How adverbs are formed

1 The basic rules

➤ In English, adverbs that tell you how something happened are often formed by adding *-ly* to an adjective, for example, *sweet → sweetly*. In Spanish, you form this kind of adverb by adding **-mente** to the feminine singular form of the adjective.

Masculine adjective	Feminine adjective	Adverb	Meaning
lento	lenta	lentamente	slowly
normal	normal	normalmente	normally

   Habla muy lenta*mente*.   He speaks very slowly.
   ¡Hazlo inmediata*mente*!   Do it immediately!
   Normal*mente* llego a las nueve.   I normally arrive at nine o'clock.

i Note that adverbs <u>NEVER</u> change their endings in Spanish to agree with anything.

> ### *Tip*
> You don't have to worry about adding or removing accents on the adjective when you add **-mente**; they stay as they are.
>
>   **fácil** easy   →   **fácilmente** easily

For further explanation of grammatical terms, please see pages viii-xii.

Grammar Extra!

When there are two or more adverbs joined by a conjunction such as **y** (meaning *and*) or **pero** (meaning *but*), leave out the **-mente** ending on all but the last adverb.

Lo hicieron <u>lenta</u> pero <u>eficazmente</u>. They did it slowly but efficiently.

Use the form **recién** rather than **recientemente** (meaning *recently*) before a past participle (the form of the verb ending in **-ado** and **-ido** in regular verbs).

El comedor está <u>recién</u> pintado. The dining room has just been painted.

⇨ For more information on **Past participles**, see page 115.

In Spanish, adverbs ending in **-mente** are not as common as adverbs ending in *-ly* in English. For this reason, you will come across other ways of expressing an adverb in Spanish, for example, **con** used with a noun or **de manera** used with an adjective.

Conduce <u>con cuidado</u>. Drive carefully.

Todos estos cambios ocurren <u>de manera natural</u>. All these changes happen naturally.

---

2 | Irregular adverbs

➤ The adverb that comes from **bueno** (meaning *good*) is **bien** (meaning *well*). The adverb that comes from **malo** (meaning *bad*) is **mal** (meaning *badly*).

Habla <u>bien</u> el español. He speaks Spanish <u>well</u>.

Está muy <u>mal</u> escrito. It's very <u>badly</u> written.

➤ Additionally, there are some other adverbs in Spanish which are exactly the same as the related masculine singular adjective:

● **alto** (adjective: *high, loud*; adverb: *high, loudly*)

El avión volaba <u>alto</u> sobre las montañas. The plane flew high over the mountains.

Pepe habla muy <u>alto</u>. Pepe talks very <u>loudly</u>.

● **bajo** (adjective: *low, quiet*; adverb: *low, quietly*)

El avión volaba muy <u>bajo</u>. The plane was flying very <u>low</u>.

¡Habla <u>bajo</u>! Speak <u>quietly</u>.

● **barato** (adjective: *cheap*; adverb: *cheaply*)

Aquí se come muy <u>barato</u>. You can eat really <u>cheaply</u> here.

● **claro** (adjective: *clear*; adverb: *clearly*)

Lo oí muy <u>claro</u>. I heard it very <u>clearly</u>.

● **derecho** (adjective: *right, straight*; adverb: *straight*)

Vino <u>derecho</u> hacia mí. He came <u>straight</u> toward me.

- **fuerte** (adjective: *loud, hard*; adverb: *loudly, hard*)

  Habla muy <u>fuerte</u>. He talks very <u>loudly</u>.

  No lo golpees tan <u>fuerte</u>. Don't hit it so <u>hard</u>.

- **rápido** (adjective: *fast, quick*; adverb: *fast, quickly*)

  Conduces demasiado <u>rápido</u>. You drive too <u>fast</u>.

  Lo hice tan <u>rápido</u> como pude. I did it as <u>quickly</u> as I could.

[i] Note that, when used as adverbs, these words do <u>NOT</u> agree with anything.

⇨ *For more information on words which can be both adjectives and adverbs, see page 175.*

Grammar Extra!

Sometimes an <u>adjective</u> is used in Spanish where in English we would use an <u>adverb</u>.

Esperaban <u>impacientes</u>. They were waiting <u>impatiently</u>.

Vivieron muy <u>felices</u>. They lived very <u>happily</u>.

[i] Note that these Spanish <u>adjectives</u> describe the person or thing being talked about and therefore <u>MUST</u> agree with them.

Often you could equally well use an adverb or an adverbial expression in Spanish.

Esperaban <u>impacientemente</u> *or*
con impaciencia. They were waiting <u>impatiently</u>.

Key points

✔ To form adverbs that tell you how something happens, you can usually add **-mente** to the feminine singular adjective in Spanish.

✔ Adverbs don't agree with anything.

✔ Some Spanish adverbs are irregular, as in English.

✔ Some Spanish adverbs are identical in form to their corresponding adjectives; when used as adverbs, they never agree with anything.

For further explanation of grammatical terms, please see pages viii-xii.

Comparatives and superlatives of adverbs

1 Comparative adverbs

What is a comparative adverb?
A **comparative adverb** is one which, in English, has -er on the end of it or more or less in front of it, for example, earlier, later, more/less often.

➤ Adverbs can be used to make comparisons in Spanish, just as they can in English. The comparative of adverbs (more often, more efficiently, faster) is formed using the same phrases as for adjectives:

- **más ... (que)**   more ... (than)
  <u>más</u> rápido <u>(que)</u>   faster (than), more quickly (than)
  Corre <u>más</u> rápido que tú.   He runs faster than you do.

- **menos ... (que)**   less ... (than)
  <u>menos</u> rápido <u>(que)</u>   less fast (than), less quickly (than)
  Conduce <u>menos</u> rápido que tú.   He drives less fast than you do.

2 Superlative adverbs

What is a superlative adverb?
A **superlative adverb** is one which, in English, has -est on the end of it or most or least in front of it, for example, soonest, most/least often.

➤ The superlative of adverbs (the most often, the most efficiently, the fastest) is formed in the same way in Spanish as the comparative, using **más** and **menos**. In this case they mean the most and the least.

María es la que corre <u>más</u> <u>rápido</u>.	Maria is the one who runs (the) fastest.
la chica que sabe <u>más</u>	the girl who knows (the) most
la chica que sabe <u>menos</u>	the girl who knows (the) least
El que llegó <u>menos tarde</u> fue Miguel.	Miguel was the one who arrived least late.

[i] Note that even though comparative and superlative adverbs are usually identical in Spanish, you can tell which one is meant by the rest of the sentence.

3 Irregular comparative and superlative adverbs

➤ Some common Spanish adverbs have irregular comparative and superlatives.

Adverb	Meaning	Comparative	Meaning	Superlative	Meaning
bien	well	**mejor**	better	**mejor**	(the) best
mal	badly	**peor**	worse	**peor**	(the) worst
mucho	a lot	**más**	more	**más**	(the) most
poco	little	**menos**	less	**menos**	(the) least

La conozco mejor que tú.   I know her <u>better</u> than you do.
¿Quién lo hace mejor?   Who does it (the) <u>best</u>?
Ahora salgo más/menos.   I go out <u>more/less</u> these days.

Tip

When saying *more than*, *less than* or *fewer than* followed by a number, use **más** and **menos** <u>de</u> rather than **más** and **menos que**.

más/menos de veinte cajas   more/fewer than twenty boxes

---

[i] Note that in phrases like *it's the least one can expect* or *it's the least I can do*, where the adverb is qualified by further information, in Spanish you have to put **lo** before the adverb.

Es lo menos que se puede esperar.   It's the least one can expect.

4 Other ways of making comparisons

➤ There are other ways of making comparisons in Spanish:

- **tanto como**   as much as

  No lee tanto como tú.   He doesn't read <u>as much as</u> you.

- **tan ... como**   as ... as

  Vine tan pronto como pude.   I came <u>as</u> fast <u>as</u> I could.

Key points

✔ **más** + adverb (+ **que**) = *more* + adverb + (*than*)
✔ **menos** + adverb (+ **que**) = *less* + adverb + (*than*)
✔ **más** + adverb = (*the*) *most* + adverb
✔ **menos** + adverb = (*the*) *least* + adverb
✔ There are a few irregular comparative and superlative adverbs.
✔ There are other ways of making comparisons in Spanish: **tanto como**, **tan ... como**.

For further explanation of grammatical terms, please see pages viii-xii.

Common adverbs

1 One-word adverbs not ending in -mente

➤ There are some common adverbs that do not end in **-mente**, most of which give more information about when or where something happens or to what degree something is true.

- **ahí** there
¡<u>Ahí</u> están!	<u>There</u> they are!

- **ahora** now
¿Dónde vamos <u>ahora</u>?	Where are we going <u>now</u>?

- **allá** there
allá arriba	up <u>there</u>

- **allí** there
<u>Allí</u> está.	<u>There</u> it is.

- **anoche** last night
<u>Anoche</u> llovió.	It rained <u>last night</u>.

- **anteanoche** the night before last
<u>Anteanoche</u> nevó.	It snowed <u>the night before last</u>.

- **anteayer** the day before yesterday
<u>Anteayer</u> hubo tormenta.	There was a storm <u>the day before yesterday</u>.

- **antes** before
Esta película ya la he visto <u>antes</u>.	I've seen this movie <u>before</u>.

- **apenas** hardly
<u>Apenas</u> podía levantarse.	He could <u>hardly</u> stand up.

- **aquí** here
<u>Aquí</u> está el informe.	<u>Here</u>'s the report.

- **arriba** above, upstairs
Visto desde arriba parece más pequeño.	Seen from above it looks smaller.
<u>Arriba</u> están los dormitorios.	The bedrooms are <u>upstairs</u>.

- **atrás** behind

  Yo me quedé <u>atrás</u>. I stayed <u>behind</u>.

- **aun** even

  <u>Aun</u> sentado me duele la
  pierna. <u>Even</u> when I'm sitting down, my
  leg hurts.

- **aún** still, yet

  ¿<u>Aún</u> te duele? Does it <u>still</u> hurt?

Típ

The following mnemonic (memory jogger) should help you
remember when to use **aun** and when to use **aún**:

<u>Even</u> **aun** doesn't have an accent.

aún <u>still</u> has an accent.

aún hasn't lost its accent <u>yet</u>.

- **ayer** yesterday

  <u>Ayer</u> me compré un bolso. I bought a handbag <u>yesterday</u>.

- **casi** almost

  Son <u>casi</u> las cinco. It's <u>almost</u> five o'clock.

- **cerca** near

  El colegio está muy <u>cerca</u>. The school is very <u>near</u>.

- **claro** clearly

  Lo oí muy <u>claro</u>. I heard it very <u>clearly</u>.

- **debajo** underneath

  Miré <u>debajo</u>. I looked <u>underneath</u>.

- **dentro** inside

  ¿Qué hay <u>dentro</u>? What's <u>inside</u>?

- **despacio** slowly

  Conduce <u>despacio</u>. Drive <u>slowly</u>.

- **después** afterwards

  <u>Después</u> estábamos muy
  cansados. We were very tired <u>afterwards</u>.

- **detrás** behind

  Vienen <u>detrás</u>. They're coming along <u>behind</u>.

For further explanation of grammatical terms, please see pages viii-xii.

- **enfrente** opposite
  la casa de enfrente — the house opposite

- **enseguida** straightaway
  La ambulancia llegó enseguida. — The ambulance arrived right away.

- **entonces** then
  ¿Qué hiciste entonces? — What did you do then?

- **hasta** even
  Estudia hasta cuando está de vacaciones. — He studies even when he's on vacation.

- **hoy** today
  Hoy no tenemos clase. — We haven't any lessons today.

- **jamás** never
  Jamás he visto nada parecido. — I've never seen anything like it.

- **lejos** far
  ¿Está lejos? — Is it far?

- **luego** then, later
  Luego fuimos al cine. — Then we went to the movies.

- **muy** very
  Estoy muy cansada. — I'm very tired.

- **no** no, not
  No, no me gusta. — No. I don't like it.

- **nunca** never
  No viene nunca. — He never comes.
  '¿Has estado alguna vez en Argentina?' – 'No, nunca.' — 'Have you ever been to Argentina?' – 'No, never.'

- **pronto** soon, early
  Llegarán pronto. — They'll be here soon.
  ¿Por qué has llegado tan pronto? — Why have you arrived so early?

- **quizás** or **quizá** perhaps
  Quizás está cansado. — Perhaps he's tired.

ℹ️ Note that you use the present subjunctive after **quizás** or **quizá** if referring to the future.

| **Quizás** venga mañana. | Perhaps he'll come tomorrow. |

➡️ *For more information on the **Subjunctive**, see page 134.*

- **sí** yes

  | ¿Te apetece un café? – **Sí**, gracias. | Do you fancy a coffee? – Yes, please. |

- **siempre** always

  | **Siempre** dicen lo mismo. | They always say the same thing. |

- **solo** *or* **sólo** only

  | **Solo** cuesta tres euros. | It only costs three euros. |

- **también** also, too

  | A mí **también** me gusta. | I like it too. |

- **tampoco** either, neither

  | Yo **tampoco** lo compré. | I didn't buy it either. |
  | Yo no la vi. – Yo **tampoco**. | I didn't see her. – Neither did I. |

- **tan** as, so

  | Vine **tan** pronto **como** pude. | I came as fast as I could. |
  | Habla **tan** deprisa **que** no la entiendo. | She speaks so fast that I can't understand her. |

- **tarde** late

  | Se está haciendo **tarde**. | It's getting late. |

- **temprano** early

  | Tengo que levantarme **temprano**. | I've got to get up early. |

- **todavía** still, yet, even

Todavía tengo dos.	I've still got two.
Todavía no han llegado.	They haven't arrived yet.
mejor **todavía**	even better

- **ya** already

  | **Ya** lo he hecho. | I've already done it. |

Tip

The accented form **sólo** (meaning *only*) is sometimes used when there might otherwise be confusion with the adjective **solo** (meaning *alone*, *lonely*, *single*), as in **Sale solo los sábados** (meaning *He only goes out on Saturdays* or *He goes out alone on Saturdays*).

2 Words which are used both as adjectives and adverbs

➤ **bastante**, **demasiado**, **tanto**, **mucho** and **poco** can be used both as adjectives and as adverbs. When they are <u>adjectives</u>, their endings change in the feminine and plural to agree with what they describe. When they are <u>adverbs</u>, the endings don't change.

	Adjective use	Adverb use
bastante enough; quite a lot; quite	Hay <u>bastantes</u> libros. There are enough books.	Ya has comido <u>bastante</u>. You've had enough to eat. Son <u>bastante</u> ricos. They are quite rich.
demasiado too much (*plural*: too many); too	<u>demasiada</u> mantequilla too much butter <u>demasiados</u> libros too many books	He comido <u>demasiado</u>. I've eaten too much. Llegamos <u>demasiado</u> tarde. We arrived too late.
tanto so much (*plural*: so many); so often	Ahora no bebo <u>tanta</u> leche. I don't drink as much milk these days. Tengo <u>tantas</u> cosas que hacer. I've so many things to do.	Se preocupa <u>tanto</u> que no puede dormir. He worries so much that he can't sleep. Ahora no la veo <u>tanto.</u> I don't see her so often now.
mucho a lot (of), much (*plural*: many)	Había <u>mucha</u> gente. There were a lot of people. <u>muchas</u> cosas a lot of things	¿Lees <u>mucho</u>? Do you read a lot? ¿Está <u>mucho</u> más lejos? Is it much further?
poco little, not much, (*plural*: few, not many); not very	Hay <u>poca</u> leche. There isn't much milk. Tiene <u>pocos</u> amigos. He hasn't got many friends.	Habla muy <u>poco</u>. He speaks very little. Es <u>poco</u> sociable. He's not very sociable.

Tip

Don't confuse **poco**, which means *little*, *not much* or *not very*, with **un poco**, which means *a little* or *a bit*.

Come <u>poco</u>.	He eats <u>little</u>.
¿Me das <u>un poco</u>?	Can I have <u>a bit</u>?

➤ **más** and **menos** can also be used both as adjectives and adverbs. However, they NEVER change their endings, even when used as adjectives.

	Adjective use	Adverb use
más more	No tengo <u>más</u> dinero. I haven't any more money. <u>más</u> libros more books	Es <u>más</u> inteligente que yo. He's more intelligent than I am. **Mi hermano trabaja <u>más</u> ahora.** My brother works more now.
menos less; fewer	<u>menos</u> mantequilla less butter **Había <u>menos</u> gente que ayer.** There were fewer people than yesterday.	Estoy <u>menos</u> sorprendida que tú. I'm less surprised than you are. **Trabaja <u>menos</u> que yo.** He doesn't work as hard as I do.

3 Adverbs made up of more than one word

➤ Just as in English, some Spanish adverbs are made up of two or more words instead of just one.

a veces	sometimes
a menudo	often
de vez en cuando	from time to time
todo el tiempo	all the time
hoy en día	nowadays
en seguida	immediately

Key points
✔ There are a number of common adverbs in Spanish which do not end in **-mente**.

✔ **bastante**, **demasiado**, **tanto**, **mucho** and **poco** can be used both as adjectives and as adverbs. Their endings change in the feminine and plural when they are adjectives, but when they are adverbs their endings <u>do not</u> change.

✔ **más** and **menos** can be both adjectives and adverbs – their endings <u>never</u> change.

✔ A number of Spanish adverbs are made up of more than one word.

Position of adverbs

1 Adverbs with verbs

➤ In English, adverbs can come in various places in a sentence, at the beginning, in the middle or at the end.

I'm <u>never</u> coming back.
See you <u>soon</u>!
<u>Suddenly</u>, the phone rang.
I'd <u>really</u> like to come.

➤ In Spanish, the adverb can usually go at the beginning or end of the sentence, but also immediately <u>AFTER</u> the verb or <u>BEFORE</u> it for emphasis.

No conocemos <u>todavía</u> al nuevo médico.	We still haven't met the new doctor.
<u>Todavía</u> estoy esperando.	I'm still waiting.
<u>Siempre</u> le regalaban flores.	They always gave her flowers.

➤ When the adverb goes with a verb in the perfect tense or in the pluperfect, you can <u>NEVER</u> put the adverb between **haber** and the past participle.

Lo he hecho <u>ya</u>.	I've already done it.
No ha estado <u>nunca</u> en Italia.	She's never been to Italy.

➪ For more information on the **Perfect tense**, see page 115.

2 Adverbs with adjectives and adverbs

➤ The adverb normally goes <u>BEFORE</u> any adjective or adverb it is used with.

un sombrero <u>muy</u> bonito	a very nice hat
hablar <u>demasiado</u> alto	to talk too loudly

Key points

✔ Adverbs can go at the beginning or end of a sentence.
✔ Adverbs can go immediately after verbs or before them for emphasis.
✔ You can <u>never</u> separate **haber**, **he**, **ha** and so on from the following past participle (the **-ado/-ido** form of regular verbs).
✔ Adverbs generally come just before an adjective or another adverb.

Prepositions

What is a preposition?
A **preposition** is a word such as *at*, *for*, *with*, *into* or *from*, which is usually followed by a noun, pronoun or, in English, a word ending in *-ing*. Prepositions show how people and things relate to the rest of the sentence, for example, *She's at home.*; *a tool for cutting grass*; *It's from David.*

Using prepositions

➤ Prepositions are used in front of nouns and pronouns (such as *people*, *the man*, *me*, *him* and so on), and show the relationship between the noun or pronoun and the rest of the sentence. Although prepositions can be used before verb forms ending in *-ing* in English, in Spanish, they're followed by the <u>infinitive</u> – the form of the verb ending in **-ar**, **-er**, or **-ir**.

Le enseñé el billete <u>a</u> la revisora.	I showed my ticket <u>to</u> the ticket inspector.
Ven <u>con</u> nosotros.	Come <u>with</u> us.
Sirve <u>para</u> limpiar zapatos.	It's <u>for</u> cleaning shoes.

⇨ *For more information on **Nouns**, **Pronouns** and **Infinitives**, see pages 1, 41 and 144.*

➤ Prepositions are also used after certain adjectives and verbs and link them to the rest of the sentence.

Estoy muy contento <u>con</u> tu trabajo.	I'm very happy <u>with</u> your work.
Estamos hartos <u>de</u> repetirlo.	We're fed up <u>with</u> repeating it.
¿Te gusta jugar <u>al</u> fútbol?	Do you like playing soccer?

➤ As in English, Spanish prepositions can be made up of several words instead of just one.

delante de	in front of
antes de	before

➤ In English we can end a sentence with a preposition such as *for, with* or *into*, even though some people think this is not good grammar. You can <u>NEVER</u> end a Spanish sentence with a preposition.

¿<u>Para</u> qué es?	What's it <u>for</u>?
la chica <u>con</u> la que hablaste	the girl you spoke <u>to</u>

Tip

The choice of preposition in Spanish is not always what we might expect, coming from English. It is often difficult to give just one English equivalent for a particular Spanish preposition, since prepositions are used so differently in the two languages. This means that you need to learn how they are used and look up set phrases involving prepositions (such as *to be fond of somebody* or *dressed in white*) in a dictionary in order to find an equivalent expression in Spanish.

a, de, en, para and por

1 a

> **Tip**
> When **a** is followed by **el**, the two words merge to become **al**.

➤ **a** can mean *to* with places and destinations.

Voy a Madrid.	I'm going to Madrid.
Voy al cine.	I'm going to the movies.

> **Tip**
> **de** is also used with **a** to mean *from ... to ...*
>
> | **de la mañana a la noche** | from morning to night |
> |---|---|
> | **de 10 a 12** | from 10 to 12 |

➤ **a** can mean *to* with indirect objects.

Se lo dio a María.	He gave it to María.

➤ **a** can mean *to* after **ir** when talking about what someone is *going to* do.

Voy a verlo mañana.	I'm going to see him tomorrow.

➤ **a** can mean *at* with times.

a las cinco	at five o'clock
a las dos y cuarto	at quarter past two
a medianoche	at midnight

➤ **a** can mean *at* with prices and rates.

a dos euros el kilo	(at) two euros a kilo
a 100 km por hora	at 100 km per hour

➤ **a** can mean *at* with ages.

a los 18 años	at the age of 18

➤ **a** can mean *at* with places, but generally only after verbs suggesting movement.

Te voy a buscar a la estación.	I'll meet you at the station.
cuando llegó al aeropuerto	when he arrived at the airport

> **Típ**
> You can't use **a** to mean *at* when talking about a building, area, or village where someone is. Use **en** instead.
> **Está en casa.**   He's at home.

➤ **a** can mean *onto*.
   Se cayó al suelo.   He fell onto the floor.

➤ **a** can mean *into*.
   pegar una foto al álbum   to stick a photo into the album

➤ **a** is also used to talk about distance.
   a 8 km de aquí   (at a distance of) 8 km from here

➤ **a** is also used after certain adjectives and verbs.
   parecido a esto   similar to this

➤ **a** can mean *from* after certain verbs.
   Se lo compré a mi hermano.   I bought it from my brother.
   Les robaba dinero a sus   He was stealing money from his
   compañeros de clase.   classmates.

➡ *For more information on **Prepositions after verbs**, see page 150.*

➤ **a** is used in set phrases.

a final/finales/fines de mes	at the end of the month
a veces	at times
a menudo	often
a la puerta	at the door
a mano	by hand
a caballo	on horseback
a pie	on foot
a tiempo	on time
al sol	in the sun
a la sombra	in the shade

Grammar Extra!

a is often used to talk about the manner in which something is done.

<u>a</u> la inglesa	in the English manner
<u>a</u> paso lento	slowly
poco <u>a</u> poco	little by little

The Spanish equivalent of the English construction *on* with a verb ending in *-ing* is **al** followed by the <u>infinitive</u>.

<u>al</u> levantarse	on getting up
<u>al</u> abrir la puerta	on opening the door

---

2 Personal a

➤ When the direct object of a verb is a specific person or pet animal, **a** is placed immediately before it.

Querían mucho <u>a</u> sus hijos.	They loved their children dearly.
Cuido <u>a</u> mi hermana pequeña.	I look after my little sister.

(i) Note that personal **a** is <u>NOT</u> used after the verb **tener**.

Tienen dos hijos.	They have two children.

⇨ *For more information on **Direct objects**, see page 46.*

3 de

> **Tip**
>
> When **de** is followed by **el**, the two words merge to become **del**.

➤ **de** can mean *from*.

Soy <u>de</u> Londres.	I'm <u>from</u> London.
un médico <u>de</u> Valencia	a doctor <u>from</u> Valencia

> **Tip**
>
> **de** is also used with **a** to mean *from ... to ...*
>
> | | |
> |---|---|
> | <u>de</u> la mañana <u>a</u> la noche | <u>from</u> morning <u>to</u> night |
> | <u>de</u> 10 <u>a</u> 12 | <u>from</u> 10 <u>to</u> 12 |

➤ **de** can mean *of*.

el presidente de Francia	the president of France
dos litros de leche	two liters of milk

➤ **de** shows who or what something belongs to.

el sombrero de mi padre	my father's hat (*literally: the hat of my father*)
la oficina del presidente	the president's office (*literally: the office of the president*)

➤ **de** can indicate what something is made of, what it contains or what it is used for.

un vestido de seda	a silk dress
una caja de cerillas	a box of matches
una taza de té	a cup of tea *or* a teacup
una silla de cocina	a kitchen chair
un traje de baño	a swimming costume

➤ **de** is used in comparisons when a number is mentioned.

Había más/menos de 100 personas.	There were more/fewer than 100 people.

i Note that you do <u>NOT</u> use **que** with **más** or **menos** when there is a number involved.

➤ **de** can mean *in* after superlatives (*the most..., the biggest, the least...*).

la ciudad más/menos contaminada del mundo	the most/least polluted city in the world

⇨ *For more information on **Superlative adjectives**, see page 26.*

➤ **de** is used after certain adjectives and verbs.

contento de ver	pleased to see
Es fácil/difícil de entender.	It's easy/difficult to understand.
Es capaz de olvidarlo.	He's quite capable of forgetting it.

⇨ *For more information on **Prepositions after verbs**, see page 150.*

Grammar Extra!

de is often used in descriptions.

la mujer del sombrero verde	the woman in the green hat
un chico de ojos azules	a boy with blue eyes

---

4 | **en**

➤ **en** can mean *in* with places.

en el campo	*in* the country
en Uruguay	*in* Uruguay
en la cama	*in* bed
con un libro **en** la mano	with a book *in* his hand

➤ **en** can mean *at*.

en casa	*at* home
en el colegio	*at* school
en el aeropuerto	*at* the airport
en la parada de autobús	*at* the bus stop
en Navidad	*at* Christmas

➤ **en** can mean *in* with months, years and seasons and when saying how long something takes or took.

en marzo	*in* March
en 2005	*in* 2005
Nació **en** invierno.	He was born *in* winter.
Lo hice **en** dos días.	I did it *in* two days.

ⓘ Note the following time phrase which does not use *in* in English.

en este momento	*at* this moment

> *Tip*
>
> There are two ways of talking about a length of time in Spanish which translate the same in English, but have very different meanings.
>
> Lo haré <u>dentro de</u> una semana. I'll do it *in* a week.
> Lo haré <u>en</u> una semana. I'll do it *in* a week.
>
> Though both can be translated in the same way, the first sentence means that you'll do it in a week's time; the second means that it will take you a week to do it.

➤ **en** can mean *in* with languages and in set phrases.

Está escrito **en** español.	It's written *in* Spanish.
en voz baja	*in* a low voice

➤ **en** can mean *on*.

sentado <u>en</u> una silla	sitting <u>on</u> a chair
<u>en</u> la planta baja	<u>on</u> the ground floor
Hay dos cuadros <u>en</u> la pared.	There are two pictures <u>on</u> the wall.

➤ **en** can mean *by* with most methods of transport.

<u>en</u> coche	<u>by</u> car
<u>en</u> avión	<u>by</u> plane
<u>en</u> tren	<u>by</u> train

➤ **en** can mean *into*.

No entremos <u>en</u> la casa.	Let's not go <u>into</u> the house.
Metió la mano <u>en</u> su bolso.	She put her hand <u>into</u> her handbag.

➤ **en** is also used after certain adjectives and verbs.

Es muy buena/mala <u>en</u> geografía.	She is very good/bad at geography.
Fueron los primeros/últimos/ únicos <u>en</u> llegar.	They were the first/last/only ones to arrive.

⇨ *For more information on **Prepositions after verbs**, see page 150.*

5 para

➤ **para** can mean *for* with a person, destination or purpose.

<u>Para</u> mí un zumo de naranja.	An orange juice <u>for</u> me.
Salen <u>para</u> Cádiz.	They are leaving <u>for</u> Cádiz.
¿<u>Para</u> qué lo quieres?	What do you want it <u>for</u>?

[i] Note that you cannot end a sentence in Spanish with a preposition as you can in English.

➤ **para** can mean *for* with time.

Es <u>para</u> mañana.	It's <u>for</u> tomorrow.
una habitación <u>para</u> dos noches	a room <u>for</u> two nights

➤ **para** is also used with an infinitive with the meaning of *(in order) to*.

Lo hace <u>para</u> ganar dinero.	He does it <u>to</u> earn money.
Lo hice <u>para</u> ayudarte.	I did it <u>to</u> help you.

> **Típ**
>
> **para mí** can be used to mean *in my opinion*.
>
> **Para mí, es estupendo.** In my opinion, it's great.

6 por

➤ **por** can mean *for* when it means *for the benefit of* or *because of*.

Lo hice **por** mis padres.	I did it for my parents.
Lo hago **por** ellos.	I'm doing it for them.
por la misma razón	for the same reason

➤ **por** can mean *for* when it means *in exchange for*.

¿Cuánto me darán **por** este libro?	How much will they give me for this book?
Te lo cambio **por** éste.	I'll swap you it for this one.

➤ **por** can mean *by* in passive constructions.

descubierto **por** unos niños	discovered by some children
odiado **por** sus enemigos	hated by his enemies

➪ *For more information on the **Passive** see page 122.*

➤ **por** can mean *by* with means of transport when talking about freight.

por barco	by boat
por tren	by train
por avión	by airmail
por correo aéreo	by airmail

➤ **por** can mean *along*.

Vaya **por** ese camino.	Go along that path.

➤ **por** can mean *through*.

por el túnel	through the tunnel

➤ **por** can mean *around*.

pasear **por** el campo	to walk around the countryside

➤ **por** is used to talk vaguely about where something or someone is.

Tiene que estar **por** aquí.	It's got to be around here somewhere.
Lo busqué **por** todas partes.	I looked for him everywhere.

➤ **por** is used to talk about time.

<u>por</u> la mañana	<u>in</u> the morning
<u>por</u> la tarde	<u>in</u> the afternoon/evening
<u>por</u> la noche	<u>at</u> night

➤ **por** is used to talk about rates.

90 km <u>por</u> hora	90 km an hour
un cinco <u>por</u> ciento	five percent
Ganaron <u>por</u> 3 a o.	They won by 3 to 0.

➤ **por** is used in certain phrases which talk about the reason for something.

¿<u>por</u> qué?	why?, for what reason?
<u>por</u> todo eso	because of all that
<u>por</u> lo que he oído	judging by what I've heard

➤ **por** is used to talk about how something is done.

llamar <u>por</u> teléfono	to telephone
Lo oí <u>por</u> la radio.	I heard it on the radio.

Grammar Extra!

por is often combined with other Spanish prepositions and words, usually to show movement.

Saltó <u>por encima</u> de la mesa.	She jumped over the table
Nadamos <u>por debajo del</u> puente.	We swam under the bridge.
Pasaron <u>por delante de</u> Correos.	They went past the post office.

Key points
✔ **a**, **de**, **en**, **para** and **por** are very frequently used prepositions which you will need to study carefully.

✔ Each of them has several possible meanings, which depend on the context they are used in.

Some other common prepositions

➤ The following prepositions are also frequently used in Spanish.

- **antes de**   before

  antes de las 5   before 5 o'clock

i Note that, like many other prepositions, **antes de** is used before infinitives in Spanish where in English we'd usually use the -*ing* form of the verb.

  Antes de abrir el paquete,   Before opening the packet, read
  lea las instrucciones.   the instructions.

- **bajo**   below, under

  un grado bajo cero   one degree below zero
  bajo la cama   under the bed

i Note that **debajo de** is more common than **bajo** when talking about the actual position of something.

  debajo de la cama   under the bed

- **con**   with

  Vino con su amigo.   She came with her friend.

i Note that **con** can be used after certain adjectives as well as in a few very common phrases.

  enfadado con ellos   angry with them
  un café con leche   a white coffee
  un té con limón   a (cup of) tea with a slice of lemon

- **contra**   against

  Estaba apoyado contra   He was leaning against the wall.
  la pared.
  El domingo jugamos contra   We play against Malaga on Sunday.
  el Málaga.

- **debajo de**   under

  debajo de la cama   under the bed

- **delante de**   in front of

  Iba delante de mí.   He was walking in front of me.

- **desde**   from, since

Desde aquí se puede ver.	You can see it <u>from</u> here.
Llamaron <u>desde</u> España.	They phoned <u>from</u> Spain.
<u>desde</u> otro punto de vista	<u>from</u> a different point of view
<u>desde</u> entonces	<u>from</u> then onwards
<u>desde</u> la una <u>hasta</u> las siete	<u>from</u> one o'clock <u>to</u> seven
<u>desde</u> la boda	<u>since</u> the wedding

Típ

Spanish uses the <u>present tense</u> with **desde** (meaning *since*) and
the expressions **desde hace** and **hace … que** (meaning *for*) to talk
about actions that started in the past and are still going on.

<u>Estoy</u> aquí desde las diez.	I've been here since ten o'clock.
<u>Estoy</u> aquí desde hace dos horas. *or* **Hace dos horas que <u>estoy</u> aquí.**	I've been here for two hours.

If you are saying how long something has NOT happened for, in European
Spanish you can use the <u>perfect tense</u> with **desde** and **desde hace**.

No <u>ha trabajado</u> desde el accidente.	He hasn't worked since the accident.
No <u>ha trabajado</u> desde hace dos meses.	He hasn't worked for two months.

⮑ *For more information on the **Present tense** and the **Perfect tense**, see pages 69 and 115.*

- **después de**   after

<u>después del</u> partido	<u>after</u> the match

[i] Note that, like many other prepositions, **después de** is used before
infinitives in Spanish where in English we'd usually use the *-ing* form
of the verb.

<u>Después de ver</u> la televisión me fui a la cama.	<u>After watching</u> television I went to bed.

- **detrás de**   behind

Están <u>detrás de</u> la puerta.	They are <u>behind</u> the door.

- **durante**   during, for

<u>durante</u> la guerra	<u>during</u> the war
Anduvieron <u>durante</u> 3 días.	They walked <u>for</u> 3 days.

- **entre**   between, among
  - **entre** 8 y 10
  - **Hablaban entre sí.**

  between 8 and 10
  They were talking among themselves.

- **hacia**   towards, around
  - **Van hacia ese edificio.**
  - **hacia las tres**
  - **hacia finales de enero**

  They're going towards that building.
  at around three (o'clock)
  around the end of January

Grammar Extra!

hacia can also combine with some adverbs to show movement in a particular direction.

hacia arriba	upwards
hacia abajo	downwards
hacia adelante	forwards
hacia atrás	backwards

- **hasta**   until, as far as, to, up to
  - **hasta la noche**
  - **Fueron en coche hasta Sevilla.**
  - **desde la una hasta las tres**
  - **Hasta ahora no ha llamado nadie.**

  until night
  They drove as far as Seville.
  from one o'clock to three
  No one has called up to now.

[*i*] Note that there are some very common ways of saying goodbye using **hasta**.

  - **¡Hasta luego!**
  - **¡Hasta mañana!**

  See you!
  See you tomorrow!

- **sin**   without
  - **sin agua/dinero**
  - **sin mi marido**

  without any water/money
  without my husband

Tip

Whereas in English we say *without a doubt*, *without a hat* and so on, in Spanish the indefinite article isn't given after **sin**.

  sin duda   without a doubt
  sin sombrero   without a hat

➯ *For more information on* **Articles**, *see page 10.*

_i_ Note that **sin** is used before infinitives in Spanish where in English we would use the *-ing* form of the verb.

Se fue <u>sin decir</u> nada.	He left <u>without saying</u> anything.

- **sobre** on, about

<u>sobre</u> la cama	<u>on</u> the bed
Ponlo <u>sobre</u> la mesa.	Put it <u>on</u> the table.
un libro <u>sobre</u> Shakespeare	a book <u>on</u> or <u>about</u> Shakespeare
Madrid tiene <u>sobre</u> 4 millones de habitantes.	Madrid has <u>about</u> 4 million inhabitants.
Vendré <u>sobre</u> las cuatro.	I'll come <u>about</u> four o'clock.

➤ Spanish prepositions can be made up of more than one word, for example, **antes de**, **detrás de**. Here are some more common prepositions made up of two or more words:

- **a causa de** because of

No salimos <u>a causa de</u> la lluvia.	We didn't go out <u>because of</u> the rain.

- **al lado de** beside, next to

<u>al lado de</u> la tele	<u>beside</u> the TV

- **cerca de** near, close to

Está <u>cerca de</u> la iglesia.	It's <u>near</u> the church.

- **encima de** on, on top of

Ponlo <u>encima de</u> la mesa.	Put it <u>on</u> the table.

- **por encima de** above, over

Saltó <u>por encima de</u> la mesa.	He jumped <u>over</u> the table.

- **en medio de** in the middle of

Está <u>en medio de</u> la plaza.	It's <u>in the middle of</u> the square.

- **junto a** by

Está <u>junto al</u> cine.	It's <u>by</u> the movie theater.

- **junto con** together with

Fue detenido <u>junto con</u> su hijo.	He was arrested <u>together with</u> his son.

- **lejos de** far from

No está <u>lejos de</u> aquí.	It isn't <u>far from</u> here.

Conjunctions

> **What is a conjunction?**
> A **conjunction** is a word such as *and*, *but*, *or*, *so*, *if* and *because*, that links two words or phrases of a similar type, or two parts of a sentence, for example, *Diane <u>and</u> I have been friends for years.; I left <u>because</u> I was bored.*

y, o, pero, porque and si

➤ **y**, **o**, **pero**, **porque** and **si** are the most common conjunctions that you need to know in Spanish:

- **y**   and

  el coche y la casa   the car <u>and</u> the house

i Note that you use **e** instead of **y** before words beginning with **i** or **hi** (but not **hie**).

Diana e Isabel	Diana <u>and</u> Isabel
madre e hija	mother <u>and</u> daughter
BUT	
árboles y hierba	trees <u>and</u> grass

- **o**   or

  patatas fritas o arroz   chips <u>or</u> rice

i Note that you use **u** instead of **o** before words beginning with **o** or **ho**.

diez u once	ten <u>or</u> eleven
minutos u horas	minutes <u>or</u> hours

i In the past, **ó** was routinely used instead of **o** between numerals to avoid confusion with zero, so you may come across it.

37 ó 38   37 or 38

⇨ *For more information on **Numbers**, see page 206.*

- **pero**   but

  Me gustaría ir, <u>pero</u> estoy muy   I'd like to go, <u>but</u> I am very tired.
  cansado.

i Note that you use **sino** in direct contrasts after a negative.

No es española, <u>sino</u> italiana.   She's not Spanish <u>but</u> Italian.

For further explanation of grammatical terms, please see pages viii-xii.

- **porque** because

  Ha llamado <u>porque</u> necesita un libro.
  He called <u>because</u> he needs a book.

[*i*] Note that, except in answers to **¿por qué...?** (*why...?*) questions, you don't use **porque** at the beginning of a sentence; you should use **como** instead.

  <u>Como</u> está lloviendo no podemos salir.
  <u>Because</u> *or* <u>As</u> it's raining, we can't go out.

> ## *Tip*
>
> Be careful not to mix up **porque** (meaning *because*) and **por qué** (meaning *why*).

- **que** that

  Dice <u>que</u> me quiere. He says <u>that</u> he loves me.
  Dicen <u>que</u> te han visto. They say <u>that</u> they've seen you.
  Sabe <u>que</u> estamos aquí. He knows <u>that</u> we are here.

⇨ *For more information on **que** followed by the subjunctive and **que** (meaning than) in comparisons, see pages 136 and 26.*

> ## *Tip*
>
> In English we can say both *He says he loves me* and *He says that he loves me*, or *She knows you're here* and *She knows that you're here*. You can <u>NEVER</u> leave out **que** in Spanish in the way that you can leave out *that* in English.

- **si** if, whether

  <u>Si</u> no estudias, no aprobarás. <u>If</u> you don't study, you won't pass.
  ¿Sabes <u>si</u> nos han pagado ya? Do you know <u>if</u> *or* <u>whether</u> we've been paid yet?
  Avisadme <u>si</u> no podéis venir. Let me know <u>if</u> you can't come.

⇨ *For information on **si** followed by the subjunctive, see page 143.*

> ## *Tip*
>
> There is no accent on **si** when it means *if*. Be careful not to confuse **si** (meaning *if*) with **sí** (meaning *yes* or *himself/herself/yourself/oneself/themselves/yourselves*).

Some other common conjunctions

➤ Here are some other common Spanish conjunctions:

- **como** as

Como es domingo, puedes quedarte en la cama.	<u>As</u> it's Sunday, you can stay in bed.

- **cuando** when

Cuando entré estaba leyendo.	She was reading <u>when</u> I came in.

⮕ *For information on* **cuando** *followed by the subjunctive, see page 140.*

- **pues** then, well

Tengo sueño. – ¡**Pues**, vete a la cama!	I'm tired. – <u>Then</u> go to bed!
Pues, no lo sabía.	<u>Well</u>, I didn't know.
Pues, como te iba contando ...	<u>Well</u>, as I was saying ...

- **mientras** while (*referring to time*)

Lava tú **mientras** yo seco.	You wash <u>while</u> I dry.
Él leía **mientras** yo cocinaba.	He would read <u>while</u> I cooked.

⮕ *For information on* **mientras** *followed by the subjunctive, see page 140.*

- **mientras que** whereas

Isabel es muy dinámica **mientras que** Ana es más tranquila.	Isabel is very dynamic <u>whereas</u> Ana is more laid-back.

- **aunque** although, even though

Me gusta el francés, <u>**aunque**</u> prefiero el alemán.	I like French <u>although</u> I prefer German.
Seguí andando <u>**aunque**</u> me dolía mucho la pierna.	I went on walking <u>even though</u> my leg hurt a lot.

Grammar Extra!

aunque is also used to mean *even if*. In this case, it is followed by the subjunctive.

⮕ *For more information on the* **Subjunctive**, *see page 134.*

Split conjunctions

In English we have conjunctions which are made up of two parts (*both ... and*, *neither ... nor*). Spanish also has conjunctions which have more than one part, the commonest of which are probably **ni ... ni** (meaning *neither ... nor*) and **o ... o** (meaning *either ... or*):

- **ni ... ni**   neither ... nor

  Ni Carlos ni Sofía vinieron. *or*   Neither Carlos <u>nor</u> Sofía came.
  No vinieron ni Carlos ni Sofía.

i Note that if you're putting **ni ... ni** after the verb you must put **no** before the verb.

  No tengo ni hermanos ni   I have <u>neither</u> brothers <u>nor</u>
  hermanas.   sisters.

- **o ... o**   either ... or

  Puedes tomar o helado o yogur.   You can have <u>either</u> ice cream <u>or</u> yoghurt.

Key points

✔ **y**, **o**, **pero**, **porque** and **si** are the most common conjunctions that you need to know in Spanish.

✔ Use **e** rather than **y** before words beginning with **i** or **hi** (but not with **hie**).

✔ Use **u** rather than **o** before words beginning with **o** or **ho**.

✔ **que** very often means *that*. *That* is often missed out in English, but **que** can never be left out in Spanish.

✔ Some conjunctions such as **ni ... ni** and **o ... o** consist of two parts.

Spelling

1 Sounds that are spelled differently depending on the letter that follows

➤ Certain sounds are spelled differently in Spanish depending on what letter follows them. For example, the hard [k] sound heard in the English word *car* is usually spelled:

- **c** before **a**, **o** and **u**
- **qu** before **e** and **i**

➤ This means that the Spanish word for *singer* is spelled **cantante** (pronounced [*kan-tan-tay*]); the word for *coast* is spelled **costa** (pronounced [*ko-sta*]); and the word for *cure* is spelled **cura** (pronounced [*koo-ra*]).

➤ However, the Spanish word for *cheese* is spelled **queso** (pronounced [*kay-so*]) and the word for *chemistry* is spelled **química** (pronounced [*kee-mee-ka*]).

i Note that although the letter **k** is not much used in Spanish, it is found in words relating to *kilos*, *kilometers* and *kilograms*; for example **un kilo** (meaning *a kilo*); **un kilogramo** (meaning *a kilogram*); **un kilómetro** (meaning *a kilometer*).

➤ Similarly, the [g] sound heard in the English word *gone* is spelled:

- **g** before **a**, **o** and **u**
- **gu** before **e** and **i**

➤ This means that the Spanish word for *cat* is spelled **gato** (pronounced [*ga-toe*]); the word for *goal* is spelled **gol** (pronounced [*gol*]); and the word for *worm* is spelled **gusano** (pronounced [*goo-sa-no*]).

➤ However, the Spanish word for *war* is spelled **guerra** (pronounced [*gair-ra*]) and the word for *guitar* is spelled **guitarra** (pronounced [*ghee-tar-ra*]).

2 Letters that are pronounced differently depending on what follows

➤ Certain letters are pronounced differently depending on what follows them. As we have seen, when c comes before a, o or u, it is pronounced like a [k]. When it comes before e or i, in European Spanish it is pronounced like the [th] in the English word *pith* and in Latin American Spanish it is pronounced like the [s] in *sing*.

➤ This means that casa (meaning *house*) is pronounced [ka-sa], but centro (meaning *center*) is pronounced [then-tro] in European Spanish and [sen-tro] in Latin American Spanish. Similarly, cita (meaning *date*) is pronounced [the-ta] in European Spanish and [see-ta] in Latin American Spanish.

➤ In the same way, when g comes before a, o or u, it is pronounced like the [g] in *gone*. When it comes before e or i, however, it is pronounced like the [ch] in *loch*, as it is pronounced in Scotland.

➤ This means that gas (meaning *gas*) is pronounced [gas] but gente (meaning *people*) is pronounced [chen-tay]. Similarly, gimnasio (meaning *gym*) is pronounced [cheem-na-see-o].

3 Spelling changes that are needed in verbs to reflect the pronunciation

➤ Because c sounds like [k] before a, o and u, and like [th] or [s] before e and i, you sometimes have to alter the spelling of a verb when adding a particular ending to ensure the word reads as it is pronounced:

- In verbs ending in -car (which is pronounced [kar]), you have to change the c to qu before endings starting with an e to keep the hard [k] pronunciation. So the yo form of the preterite tense of sacar (meaning *to take out*) is spelled saqué. This spelling change affects the preterite and the present subjunctive of verbs ending in -car.

- In verbs ending in -cer and -cir (which are pronounced [ther] and [thir] or [ser] and [sir]), you have to change the c to z before endings starting with a or o to keep the soft [th/s] pronunciation. So while the yo form of the preterite tense of hacer is spelled hice, the él/ella/usted form is spelled hizo. This spelling change affects the ordinary present tense as well as the present subjunctive of verbs ending in -cer or -cir.

➤ Because **g** sounds like the [*g*] of *gone* before **a**, **o** and **u**, and like the [*ch*] of *loch* before **e** and **i**, you also sometimes have to alter the spelling of a verb when adding a particular ending to ensure the verb still reads as it is pronounced:

- In verbs ending in **-gar** (which is pronounced [*gar*]), you have to change the **g** to **gu** before endings starting with an **e** or an **i** to keep the hard [*g*] pronunciation. So the **yo** form of the preterite tense of **pagar** (meaning *to pay*) is spelled **pagué**. This spelling change affects the preterite and the present subjunctive of verbs ending in **-gar**.

- In verbs ending in **-ger** and **-gir** (which are pronounced [*cher*] and [*chir*]), you have to change the **g** to **j** before endings starting with **a** or **o** to keep the soft [*ch*] pronunciation. So while the **él/ella/usted** form of the present tense of **coger** (meaning *to take* or *to catch*) is spelled **coge**, the **yo** form is spelled **cojo**. This spelling change affects the ordinary present tense as well as the present subjunctive of verbs ending in **-ger** or **-gir**.

➤ Because **gui** sounds like [*ghee*] in verbs ending in **-guir**, but **gua** and **guo** sound like [*gwa*] and [*gwo*], you have to drop the **u** before **a** and **o** in verbs ending in **-guir**. So while the **él/ella/usted** form of the present tense of **seguir** (meaning *to follow*) is spelled **sigue**, the **yo** form is spelled **sigo**. This spelling change affects the ordinary present tense as well as the present subjunctive of verbs ending in **-guir**.

➤ Finally, although **z** is always pronounced [*th*] in European Spanish and [*s*] in Latin American Spanish, in verbs ending in **-zar** the **z** spelling is changed to **c** before **e**. So, while the **él/ella/usted** form of the preterite tense of **cruzar** is spelled **cruzó**, the **yo** form is spelled **crucé**. This spelling change affects the preterite and the present subjunctive of verbs ending in **-zar**.

4 Spelling changes that are needed when making nouns and adjectives plural

➤ In the same way that you have to make some spelling changes when modifying the endings of certain verbs, you sometimes have to change the spelling of nouns and adjectives when making them plural.

➤ This affects nouns and adjectives ending in **-z**. When adding the **-es** ending of the plural, you have to change the **z** to **c**.

una vez	once, one time	→	**dos veces**	twice, two times
una luz	a light	→	**unas luces**	some lights
capaz	capable (*singular*)	→	**capaces**	capable (*plural*)

For further explanation of grammatical terms, please see pages viii-xii.

➤ The following table shows the usual spelling of the various sounds discussed above:

	Usual spelling				
	before a	before o	before u	before e	before i
[k] sound (as in *cap*)	ca: casa house	co: cosa thing	cu: cubo bucket	que: queso cheese	qui: química chemistry
[g] sound (as in *gap*)	ga: gato cat	go: gordo fat	gu: gusto taste	gue: guerra war	gui: guitarra guitar
[th] sound (as in *pith*) (pronounced [s] in Latin America)	za: zapato shoe	zo: zorro fox	zu: zumo juice	ce: cero zero	ci: cinta ribbon
[ch] sound (as in *loch*)	ja: jardín garden	jo: joven young	ju: jugar to play	ge: gente people	gi: gigante giant

[i] Note that because j is still pronounced [ch] even when it comes before e or i, there are quite a number of words that contain je or ji; for example,

el jefe/la jefa	the boss
el jerez	sherry
el jersey	jersey
el jinete	jockey
la jirafa	giraffe
el ejemplo	the example
dije/dijiste	I said/you said
dejé	I left

Similarly, because z is also pronounced [th] or [s] even when it comes before i or e, there are one or two exceptions to the spelling rules described above; for example, **el zigzag** (meaning *zigzag*) and **la zeta** (the name of the letter z in Spanish).

Stress

Which syllable to stress

➤ Most words can be broken up into <u>syllables</u>. These are the different sounds that words are broken up into. They are shown in this section by | and the stressed syllable is underlined.

➤ There are some very simple rules to help you remember which part of the word to stress in Spanish, and when to write an accent.

➤ Words <u>DON'T</u> have a written acute accent if they follow the normal stress rules for Spanish. If they do not follow the normal stress rules, they <u>DO</u> need an accent.

> *Tip*
>
> The accent that shows stress is always an <u>acute</u> accent in Spanish (´). To remember which way an acute accents slopes try thinking of this saying:
> *It's low on the left, with the height on the right.*

1 Words ending in a vowel or -n or -s

➤ Words ending in a vowel (*a*, *e*, *i*, *o* or *u*) or **-n** or **-s** are normally stressed on the <u>last syllable but one</u>. If this is the case, they do <u>NOT</u> have any written accents.

<u>ca</u>|sa	house	<u>ca</u>|sas	houses
pa|<u>la</u>|bra	word	pa|<u>la</u>|bras	words
<u>tar</u>|de	afternoon	<u>tar</u>|des	afternoons
<u>ha</u>|bla	he/she speaks	<u>ha</u>|blan	they speak
<u>co</u>|rre	he/she runs	<u>co</u>|rren	they run

➤ Whenever words ending in a vowel or **-n** or **-s** are <u>NOT</u> stressed on the last syllable but one, they have a written accent on the vowel that is stressed.

<u>úl</u>|ti|mo	last
<u>jó</u>|ve|nes	young people
<u>crí</u>|me|nes	crimes
ta|<u>bú</u>	taboo
su|<u>bí</u>	I went up

2 | Words ending in a consonant other than -n or -s

➤ Words ending in a consonant (a letter that isn't a vowel) other than -n or -s are normally stressed on the <u>last syllable</u>. If this is the case, they do <u>NOT</u> have an accent.

re|<u>loj</u>	clock, watch
ver|<u>dad</u>	truth
trac|<u>tor</u>	tractor

➤ Whenever words ending in a consonant other than -n or -s are <u>NOT</u> stressed on the last syllable, they have an accent.

ca|<u>rác</u>|ter	character
di|<u>fí</u>|cil	difficult
<u>fá</u>|cil	easy

3 | Accents on feminine and plural forms

➤ The same syllable is stressed in the plural form of adjectives and nouns as in the singular. To show this, you need to:

- add an accent in the plural in the case of unaccented nouns and adjectives of more than one syllable ending in -n

or|den	order	<u>ór</u>|de|nes	orders
e|<u>xa</u>|men	exam	e|<u>xá</u>|me|nes	exams
BUT: **tren**	train	**tre|nes**	trains

[*i*] Note that in the case of one-syllable words ending in -n or -s, such as **tren** above, no accent is needed in the plural, since the stress falls naturally on the last syllable but one thanks to the plural -es ending.

- drop the accent in the plural form of nouns and adjectives ending in -n or -s which have an accent on the last syllable in the singular

au|to|<u>bús</u>	bus	au|to|<u>bu</u>|ses	buses
re|vo|lu|<u>ción</u>	revolution	re|vo|lu|<u>cio</u>|nes	revolutions

➤ The feminine forms of nouns or adjectives whose masculine form ends in an accented vowel followed by -n or -s do <u>NOT</u> have an accent.

un franc<u>és</u>	a Frenchman
una franc<u>e</u>sa	a French woman

Tip

Just because a word has a written accent in the singular does not necessarily mean it has one in the plural, and vice versa.

jo|ven	jó|ve|nes
Ends in **n**, *so rule is to stress last syllable but one; follows rule, so* **no** *accent needed in singular*	*Ends in* **s**, *so rule is to stress last syllable but one; breaks rule, so accent* **is** *needed in plural to keep stress on* **jo-**
lec|ción	lec|cio|nes
Ends in **n**, *so rule is to stress last syllable but one; breaks rule, so accent* **is** *needed in singular*	*Ends in* **s**, *so rule is to stress last syllable but one; follows rule, so* **no** *accent needed in plural to keep stress on* **-cio-**

4 | Which vowel to stress in vowel combinations

➤ The vowels **i** and **u** are considered to be <u>weak</u>. The vowels **a**, **e** and **o** are considered to be <u>strong</u>.

➤ When a weak vowel (**i** or **u**) combines with a strong one (**a**, **e** or **o**), they form ONE sound that is part of the SAME syllable. Technically speaking, this is called a <u>diphthong</u>. The strong vowel is emphasized more.

bai|le	dance
cie|rra	he/she/it closes
boi|na	beret
pei|ne	comb
cau|sa	cause

Tip

To remember which are the weak vowels, try thinking of this saying: *U and I are weaklings and always lose out to other vowels!*

➤ When **i** combines with **u** or **u** with **i** (the two weak vowels), they form ONE sound within the SAME syllable; there is more emphasis on the second vowel.

ciu̱dad	city, town
fui̱	I went

➤ When you combine two strong vowels (**a**, **e** or **o**), they form TWO separate sounds and are part of DIFFERENT syllables.

ca|er	to fall
ca|os	chaos
fe|o	ugly

5 Adding accents to some verb forms

➤ When object pronouns are added to the end of certain verb forms, an accent is often required to show that the syllable stressed in the verb form does not change. These verb forms are:

- the <u>gerund</u> whenever one or more pronouns are added

comprando	buying
comprándo(se)lo	buying it (for him/her/them)

- the <u>infinitive</u>, when followed by two pronouns

vender	to sell
vendérselas	to sell them to him/her/them

- <u>imperative</u> forms

compra	buy
cómpralo	buy it
hagan	do
háganselo	do it for him/her/them
BUT:	
comprad	buy
compradlo	buy it

⇨ *For more information on* **Gerunds**, **Infinitives** *and the* **Imperative**, *see pages 125, 144 and 85.*

6 Accents on adjectives and adverbs

➤ Adjectives ending in **-ísimo** always have an accent on **-ísimo**. This means that any other accents are dropped.

caro	→	**carísimo**
expensive		very expensive
difícil	→	**dificilísimo**
difficult		very difficult

➤ Accents on adjectives are <u>NOT</u> affected when you add **-mente** to turn them into adverbs.

fácil	→	**fácilmente**
easy		easily

The acute accent used to show meaning

➤ The acute accent is often used to distinguish between the written forms of some words which are pronounced the same but have a different meaning or function.

Without an accent		With an accent	
mi	my	mí	me
tu	your	tú	you
te	you	té	tea
si	if	sí	yes; himself
el	the	él	he
de	of	dé	give
solo	alone; by oneself; only	sólo	only (to avoid ambiguity)
mas	but	más	more

Han robado mi coche.	They've stolen my car.
A mí no me vio.	He didn't see me.
¿Te gusta tu trabajo?	Do you like your job?
Tú, ¿qué opinas?	What do you think?
...si no viene	...if he doesn't come
Sí que lo sabe.	Yes, he does know.
El puerto está cerca.	The harbor's nearby.
Él lo hará.	He'll do it.
Vino solo.	He came alone *or* by himself.
Sale sólo los sábados.	He only goes out on Saturdays.

➤ The acute accent is sometimes used on the demonstrative pronouns (éste/ésta, aquél/aquélla, ése/ésa and so on) to distinguish them from the demonstrative adjectives (este/esta, aquel/aquella, ese/esa and so on).

¿Por qué robaban aquellos coches viejos? (= *adjective*)	Why did they steal those old cars?
¿Por qué robaban aquéllos coches viejos? (= *pronoun*)	Why did they steal old cars?

ⓘ Note that no accent is given on the neuter pronouns **esto, eso** and **aquello** since there is no adjective form with which they might be confused.

⇨ *For more information on **Demonstrative adjectives** and **Demonstrative pronouns**, see pages 30 and 67.*

➤ An accent is needed on question words in direct and indirect questions as well
as after expressions of uncertainty.

¿**Cómo** estás?	How are you?
Dime <u>cómo</u> estás.	Tell me how you are.
Me preguntó <u>cómo</u> estaba.	He asked me how I was.
¿Con <u>quién</u> viajaste?	Who did you travel with?
¿<u>Dónde</u> encontraste eso?	Where did you find that?
No sé <u>dónde</u> está.	I don't know where it is.

⇨ *For more information on **Questions**, see page 160.*

➤ An accent is also needed on exclamation words.

¡<u>Qué</u> asco!	How revolting!
¡<u>Qué</u> horror!	How awful!
¡<u>Qué</u> raro!	How strange!
¡<u>Cuánta</u> gente!	What a lot of people!

Key points

✔ When deciding whether or not to write an accent on a word, think
about how it sounds and what letter it ends in, as there are certain
rules to say when an accent should be used.

✔ The vowels **i** and **u** are considered to be weak. The vowels **a**, **e** and **o**
are considered to be strong. They can combine in a number of ways.

✔ Accents are added to written forms of words which are pronounced
the same but have a different meaning, for example, **mi/mí**, **tu/tú**
and so on.

✔ Accents are also sometimes added to masculine and feminine
singular and plural demonstrative pronouns so that they are not
confused with demonstrative adjectives.

✔ Adjectives ending in **-ísimo** always have an accent on **-ísimo**, but
accents are not affected by adding **-mente** to adjectives.

✔ Question words used in direct and indirect questions as well as
exclamation words always have an acute accent.

Numbers

1	uno (un, una)	31	treinta y uno (un, una)
2	dos	40	cuarenta
3	tres	41	cuarenta y uno (un, una)
4	cuatro	50	cincuenta
5	cinco	52	cincuenta y dos
6	seis	60	sesenta
7	siete	65	sesenta y cinco
8	ocho	70	setenta
9	nueve	76	setenta y seis
10	diez	80	ochenta
11	once	87	ochenta y siete
12	doce	90	noventa
13	trece	99	noventa y nueve
14	catorce	100	cien (ciento)
15	quince	101	ciento uno (un, una)
16	dieciséis	200	doscientos/doscientas
17	diecisiete	212	doscientos/doscientas doce
18	dieciocho	300	trescientos/trescientas
19	diecinueve	400	cuatrocientos/cuatrocientas
20	veinte	500	quinientos/quinientas
21	veintiuno (veintiún, veintiuna)	600	seiscientos/seiscientas
22	veintidós	700	setecientos/setecientas
23	veintitrés	800	ochocientos/ochocientas
24	veinticuatro	900	novecientos/novecientas
25	veinticinco	1000	mil
26	veintiséis	1001	mil (y) uno (un, una)
27	veintisiete	2000	dos mil
28	veintiocho	2500	dos mil quinientos/quinientas
29	veintinueve	1.000.000	un millón
30	treinta		(*in English*: 1,000,000)

EJEMPLOS
Vive en el número diez.
en la página diecinueve
un diez por ciento
un cien por cien(to)

EXAMPLES
He lives at number ten.
on page nineteen
10%
100%

For further explanation of grammatical terms, please see pages viii-xii.

1 uno, un or una?

➤ Use **uno** when counting, unless referring to something or someone feminine.
➤ Use **un** before a masculine noun and **una** before a feminine noun even when the nouns are plural.

<u>un</u> hombre	one man
<u>una</u> mujer	one woman
treinta y <u>un</u> días	thirty-one days
treinta y <u>una</u> noches	thirty-one nights
veinti<u>ún</u> años	twenty-one years
veinti<u>una</u> chicas	twenty-one girls

2 cien or ciento?

➤ Use **cien** before both masculine and feminine nouns as well as before **mil** (meaning *thousand*) and **millones** (meaning *million* in the plural):

<u>cien</u> libros	one hundred books
<u>cien</u> mil hombres	one hundred thousand men
<u>cien</u> millones	one hundred million

➤ Use **ciento** before other numbers.

<u>ciento</u> un perros	one hundred and one dogs
<u>ciento</u> una ovejas	one hundred and one sheep
<u>ciento</u> cincuenta	one hundred and fifty

[i] Note that you don't translate the *and* in 101, 220 and so on.

➤ Make **doscientos/doscientas**, **trescientos/trescientas**, **quinientos/quinientas** and so on agree with the noun in question.

<u>doscientas</u> veinte libras	two hundred and twenty pounds
<u>quinientos</u> alumnos	five hundred students

[i] Note that **setecientos** and **setecientas** have no **i** after the first **s**. Similarly, **novecientos** and **novecientas** have an **o** rather than the **ue** you might expect.

3 Period or comma?

➤ Use a period, not a comma, to separate thousands and millions in figures.

700.000 (setecientos mil)	700,000 (seven hundred thousand)
5.000.000 (cinco millones)	5,000,000 (five million)

➤ Use a comma instead of a decimal point to show decimals in Spanish.

0,5 (cero coma cinco)	0.5 (nought point five)
3,4 (tres coma cuatro)	3.4 (three point four)

1st	**primero (1º), primer (1ᵉʳ), primera (1ª)**
2nd	**segundo (2º), segunda (2ª)**
3rd	**tercero (3º), tercer (3ᵉʳ), tercera (3ª)**
4th	**cuarto (4º), cuarta (4ª)**
5th	**quinto (5º), quinta (5ª)**
6th	**sexto (6º), sexta (6ª)**
7th	**séptimo (7º), séptima (7ª)**
8th	**octavo (8º), octava (8ª)**
9th	**noveno (9º), novena (9ª)**
10th	**décimo (10º), décima (10ª)**
100th	**centésimo (100º), centésima (100ª)**
101st	**centésimo primero (101º), centésima primera (101ª)**
1000th	**milésimo (1000º), milésima (1000ª)**

EJEMPLOS	EXAMPLES
Vive en el quinto (piso).	He lives on the fifth floor.
Llegó tercero.	He came in third.

Tip

Shorten **primero** (meaning *first*) to **primer**, and **tercero** (meaning *third*) to **tercer** before a masculine singular noun.

su **primer** cumpleaños	his first birthday
el **tercer** premio	the third prize

---

i Note that when you are writing these numbers in figures, don't write *1st*, *2nd*, *3rd* as in English. Use **1º, 1ª, 1ᵉʳ, 2º, 2ª** and **3º, 3ª, 3ᵉʳ** as required by the noun.

la **2ª** lección	the 2nd lesson
el **3ᵉʳ** premio	the 3rd prize

4 primero, segundo, tercero or uno, dos, tres?

➤ Apart from **primero** (meaning *first*) up to **décimo** (meaning *tenth*), as well as **centésimo** (meaning *one hundredth*) and **milésimo** (meaning *one thousandth*), the ordinal numbers tend not to be used very much in Spanish. Cardinal numbers (ordinary numbers) are used instead.

Carlos **tercero**	Carlos the third
Alfonso **trece**	Alfonso the thirteenth

⇨ *For numbers used in dates, see page 211.*

For further explanation of grammatical terms, please see pages viii-xii.

LA HORA	THE TIME
¿Qué hora es?	**What time is it?**
Es la una menos veinte.	It's twenty to one.
Es la una menos cuarto.	It's (a) quarter to one.
Es la una.	It's one o'clock.
Es la una y diez.	It's ten past one.
Es la una y cuarto.	It's (a) quarter past one.
Es la una y media.	It's half past one.
Son las dos menos veinticinco.	It's twenty-five to two.
Son las dos menos cuarto.	It's (a) quarter to two.
Son las dos.	It's two o'clock.
Son las dos y diez.	It's ten past two.
Son las dos y cuarto.	It's (a) quarter past two.
Son las dos y media.	It's half past two.
Son las tres.	It's three o'clock.

Típ

Use **son las** for all times not involving **una** (meaning *one*).

¿A qué hora?	At what time?
a medianoche	at midnight
a mediodía	at midday
a la una (del mediodía)	at one o'clock (in the afternoon)
a las ocho (de la tarde)	at eight o'clock (in the evening)
a las 9:25 *or* a las nueve (y) veinticinco	at nine twenty-five
a las 16:50 *or* a las dieciséis (y) cincuenta	at 16:50 *or* sixteen fifty

[i] Note that in Spanish, as in English, you can also tell the time using the figures you see on a digital clock or watch or on a 24-hour timetable.

LA FECHA	THE DATE
Los días de la semana	**The days of the week**
lunes	Monday
martes	Tuesday
miércoles	Wednesday
jueves	Thursday
viernes	Friday
sábado	Saturday
domingo	Sunday

¿Cuándo?	When?
el lunes	on Monday
los lunes	on Mondays
todos los lunes	every Monday
el martes pasado	last Tuesday
el viernes que viene	next Friday
el sábado que viene no, el otro	a week from Saturday
dentro de tres sábados	two weeks from Saturday

[i] Note that days of the week DON'T have a capital letter in Spanish.

Los meses	Months of the year
enero	January
febrero	February
marzo	March
abril	April
mayo	May
junio	June
julio	July
agosto	August
septiembre	September
octubre	October
noviembre	November
diciembre	December

¿Cuándo?	When?
en febrero	in February
el 1 or uno de diciembre	on December 1st or first December
en 1998 (mil novecientos noventa y ocho)	in 1998 (nineteen ninety-eight)
el 15 de diciembre de 2008	on 15th December, 2008
el año dos mil	(the year) two thousand
dos mil cinco	two thousand and five

¿Qué día es hoy?	What day is it today?
Es...	It's...
lunes 26 de febrero	Monday, 26th February
domingo 1 de octubre	Sunday, 1st October
lunes veintiséis de febrero	Monday, the twenty-sixth of February
domingo uno de octubre	Sunday, the first of October

[i] Note that months of the year DON'T have a capital letter in Spanish.

For further explanation of grammatical terms, please see pages viii-xii.

> **Tip**
>
> Although in English we use *first*, *second*, *third* and so on in dates, in Spanish you use the equivalent of *one*, *two*, *three* and so on.
>
> el dos de mayo the second of May

FRASES ÚTILES — **USEFUL PHRASES**

¿Cuándo? — **When?**

hoy	today
esta mañana	this morning
esta tarde	this afternoon
esta noche	this evening

¿Con qué frecuencia? — **How often?**

todos los días	every day
cada dos días	every other day
una vez por semana	once a week
dos veces por semana	twice a week
una vez al mes	once a month

¿Cuándo pasó? — **When did it happen?**

por la mañana	in the morning
por la noche	in the evening
ayer	yesterday
ayer por la mañana	yesterday morning
ayer por la tarde	yesterday afternoon/evening
ayer por la noche	yesterday evening/last night
anoche	last night
anteayer	the day before yesterday
hace una semana	a week ago
hace quince días	two weeks ago
la semana pasada	last week
el año pasado	last year

¿Cuándo va a pasar? — **When is it going to happen?**

mañana	tomorrow
mañana por la mañana	tomorrow morning
mañana por la tarde	tomorrow afternoon/evening
mañana por la noche	tomorrow evening/night
pasado mañana	the day after tomorrow
dentro de dos días	in two days' time
dentro de una semana	in a week's time
dentro de quince días	in two weeks' time
el mes que viene	next month
el año que viene	next year

Main Index

Verb Tables

VERB TABLES

Introduction

The **Verb Tables** in the following section contain 120 tables of Spanish verbs (some regular and some irregular) in alphabetical order. Each table shows you the following forms: **Present, Present Perfect, Preterite, Imperfect, Future, Conditional, Present Subjunctive, Imperfect Subjunctive, Imperative** and the **Past Participle** and **Gerund**. For more information on these tenses and how they are formed you should look at the section on Verbs on pages 69–156.

In order to help you use the verbs shown in Verb Tables correctly, there are also a number of example phrases at the bottom of each page to show the verb as it is used in context.

In Spanish there are both **regular** verbs (their forms follow the normal rules) and **irregular** verbs (their forms do not follow the normal rules). The regular verbs in these tables that you can use as models for other regular verbs are:

hablar (regular -**ar** verb, Verb Table 336–337)
comer (regular -**er** verb, Verb Table 270–271)
vivir (regular -**ir** verb, Verb Table 452–453)

The irregular verbs are shown in full.

The **Verb Index** at the end of this section contains over 1200 verbs, each of which is cross-referred to one of the verbs given in the Verb Tables. The table shows the patterns that the verb listed in the index follows.

abolir (to abolish)

	PRESENT		PRESENT PERFECT
(yo)	abolo		he abolido
(tú)	aboles		has abolido
(él/ella/usted)	abole		ha abolido
(nosotros/as)	abolimos		hemos abolido
(vosotros/as)	abolís		habéis abolido
(ellos/ellas/ ustedes)	abolen		han abolido

	PRETERITE		IMPERFECT
(yo)	abolí		abolía
(tú)	aboliste		abolías
(él/ella/usted)	abolió		abolía
(nosotros/as)	abolimos		abolíamos
(vosotros/as)	abolisteis		abolíais
(ellos/ellas/ ustedes)	abolieron		abolían

GERUND	PAST PARTICIPLE
aboliendo	abolido

EXAMPLE PHRASES

Hay que **abolirlo**. It ought to be abolished.

¿Por qué no **abolimos** esta ley? Why don't we abolish this law?

Han abolido la pena de muerte. They have abolished the death penalty.

Abolieron la esclavitud. They abolished slavery.

Remember that subject pronouns are not used very often in Spanish.

abolir

	FUTURE	CONDITIONAL
(yo)	aboliré	aboliría
(tú)	abolirás	abolirías
(él/ella/usted)	abolirá	aboliría
(nosotros/as)	aboliremos	aboliríamos
(vosotros/as)	aboliréis	aboliríais
(ellos/ellas/ ustedes)	abolirán	abolirían

	PRESENT SUBJUNCTIVE	IMPERFECT SUBJUNCTIVE
(yo)	abola	aboliera or aboliese
(tú)	abolas	abolieras or abolieses
(él/ella/usted)	abola	aboliera or aboliese
(nosotros/as)	abolamos	aboliéramos or aboliésemos
(vosotros/as)	aboláis	abolierais or abolieseis
(ellos/ellas/ ustedes)	abolan	abolieran or aboliesen

IMPERATIVE

abolid

EXAMPLE PHRASES

Solo unidos **aboliremos** la injusticia. Only if we are united, will we abolish injustice.

Prometieron que **abolirían** la censura. They promised they'd abolish censorship.

Si lo **abolieran**, se producirían disturbios. There would be riots if it were abolished.

Remember that subject pronouns are not used very often in Spanish.

abrir (to open)

	PRESENT		PRESENT PERFECT
(yo)	abro		he abierto
(tú)	abres		has abierto
(él/ella/usted)	abre		ha abierto
(nosotros/as)	abrimos		hemos abierto
(vosotros/as)	abrís		habéis abierto
(ellos/ellas/ustedes)	abren		han abierto

	PRETERITE		IMPERFECT
(yo)	abrí		abría
(tú)	abriste		abrías
(él/ella/usted)	abrió		abría
(nosotros/as)	abrimos		abríamos
(vosotros/as)	abristeis		abríais
(ellos/ellas/ustedes)	abrieron		abrían

GERUND
abriendo

PAST PARTICIPLE
abierto

EXAMPLE PHRASES

Hoy **se abre** el plazo de matrícula. Registration begins today.

Han abierto un restaurante cerca de aquí. They've opened a new restaurant near here.

¿Quién **abrió** la ventana? Who opened the window?

La llave **abría** el armario. The key opened the cupboard.

Haz clic aquí para **abrir** una nueva pestaña. Please click here to open a new tab.

Remember that subject pronouns are not used very often in Spanish.

abrir

	FUTURE	CONDITIONAL
(yo)	abriré	abriría
(tú)	abrirás	abrirías
(él/ella/usted)	abrirá	abriría
(nosotros/as)	abriremos	abriríamos
(vosotros/as)	abriréis	abriríais
(ellos/ellas/ustedes)	abrirán	abrirían

	PRESENT SUBJUNCTIVE	IMPERFECT SUBJUNCTIVE
(yo)	abra	abriera or abriese
(tú)	abras	abrieras or abrieses
(él/ella/usted)	abra	abriera or abriese
(nosotros/as)	abramos	abriéramos or abriésemos
(vosotros/as)	abráis	abrierais or abrieseis
(ellos/ellas/ustedes)	abran	abrieran or abriesen

IMPERATIVE

abre / abrid

Use the present subjunctive in all cases other than these **tú** *and* **vosotros** *affirmative forms.*

EXAMPLE PHRASES

Abrirán todas las puertas de la catedral. They'll open all the doors of the cathedral.

Me dijo que hoy **abrirían** sólo por la tarde. He told me that today they'd be open only in the evening.

No creo que **abran** un nuevo supermercado por aquí. I don't think they'll open a new supermarket here.

No **abras** ese grifo. Don't turn on that faucet.

Remember that subject pronouns are not used very often in Spanish.

actuar (to act)

	PRESENT		PRESENT PERFECT
(yo)	actúo		he actuado
(tú)	actúas		has actuado
(él/ella/usted)	actúa		ha actuado
(nosotros/as)	actuamos		hemos actuado
(vosotros/as)	actuáis		habéis actuado
(ellos/ellas/ ustedes)	actúan		han actuado

	PRETERITE		IMPERFECT
(yo)	actué		actuaba
(tú)	actuaste		actuabas
(él/ella/usted)	actuó		actuaba
(nosotros/as)	actuamos		actuábamos
(vosotros/as)	actuasteis		actuabais
(ellos/ellas/ ustedes)	actuaron		actuaban

GERUND

actuando

PAST PARTICIPLE

actuado

EXAMPLE PHRASES

Actúa de una forma muy rara. He's acting very strangely.

Ha actuado siguiendo un impulso. He acted on impulse.

Actuó en varias películas. He was in several films.

Actuaba como si no supiera nada. She was behaving as if she didn't know anything about it.

Remember that subject pronouns are not used very often in Spanish.

actuar

	FUTURE	CONDITIONAL
(yo)	actuaré	actuaría
(tú)	actuarás	actuarías
(él/ella/usted)	actuará	actuaría
(nosotros/as)	actuaremos	actuaríamos
(vosotros/as)	actuaréis	actuaríais
(ellos/ellas/ ustedes)	actuarán	actuarían

	PRESENT SUBJUNCTIVE	IMPERFECT SUBJUNCTIVE
(yo)	actúe	actuara or actuase
(tú)	actúes	actuaras or actuases
(él/ella/usted)	actúe	actuara or actuase
(nosotros/as)	actuemos	actuáramos or actuásemos
(vosotros/as)	actuéis	actuarais or actuaseis
(ellos/ellas/ ustedes)	actúen	actuaran or actuasen

IMPERATIVE

actúa / actuad

Use the present subjunctive in all cases other than these **tú** and **vosotros** affirmative forms.

EXAMPLE PHRASES

¿Quién **actuará** en su próxima película? Who will be in his next film?

Yo nunca **actuaría** así. I'd never behave like that.

Si **actuara** de forma más lógica, sería más fácil atraparlo. It would be easier to catch him if he behaved in a more logical way.

Actuad como mejor os parezca. Do as you think best.

Remember that subject pronouns are not used very often in Spanish.

adquirir (to acquire)

	PRESENT	PRESENT PERFECT
(yo)	adquiero	he adquirido
(tú)	adquieres	has adquirido
(él/ella/usted)	adquiere	ha adquirido
(nosotros/as)	adquirimos	hemos adquirido
(vosotros/as)	adquirís	habéis adquirido
(ellos/ellas/ustedes)	adquieren	han adquirido

	PRETERITE	IMPERFECT
(yo)	adquirí	adquiría
(tú)	adquiriste	adquirías
(él/ella/usted)	adquirió	adquiría
(nosotros/as)	adquirimos	adquiríamos
(vosotros/as)	adquiristeis	adquiríais
(ellos/ellas/ustedes)	adquirieron	adquirían

GERUND	PAST PARTICIPLE
adquiriendo	adquirido

EXAMPLE PHRASES

Adquiere cada vez mayor importancia. It's becoming more and more important.

Está adquiriendo una reputación que no merece. It's getting a reputation it doesn't deserve.

Hemos adquirido nuevos ordenadores. We've bought new computers.

Con el tiempo **adquirió** cierta madurez. Over the years he gained a certain maturity.

Remember that subject pronouns are not used very often in Spanish.

adquirir

	FUTURE	CONDITIONAL
(yo)	adquiriré	adquiriría
(tú)	adquirirás	adquirirías
(él/ella/usted)	adquirirá	adquiriría
(nosotros/as)	adquiriremos	adquiriríamos
(vosotros/as)	adquiriréis	adquiriríais
(ellos/ellas/ ustedes)	adquirirán	adquirirían

	PRESENT SUBJUNCTIVE	IMPERFECT SUBJUNCTIVE
(yo)	adquiera	adquiriera or adquiriese
(tú)	adquieras	adquirieras or adquirieses
(él/ella/usted)	adquiera	adquiriera or adquiriese
(nosotros/as)	adquiramos	adquiriéramos or adquiriésemos
(vosotros/as)	adquiráis	adquirierais or adquirieseis
(ellos/ellas/ ustedes)	adquieran	adquirieran or adquiriesen

IMPERATIVE
adquiere / adquirid

Use the present subjunctive in all cases other than these tú and vosotros affirmative forms.

EXAMPLE PHRASES

Al final **adquirirán** los derechos de publicación. They will get the publishing rights in the end.

¿Lo **adquirirías** por ese precio? Would you buy it for that price?

Adquiera o no la nacionalidad, podrá permanecer en el país. She'll be able to stay in the country whether she becomes naturalized or not.

Tenía gran interés en que **adquiriera** el cuadro. He was eager that she should buy the picture.

Remember that subject pronouns are not used very often in Spanish.

advertir (to warn, to notice)

	PRESENT	PRESENT PERFECT
(yo)	advierto	he advertido
(tú)	adviertes	has advertido
(él/ella/usted)	advierte	ha advertido
(nosotros/as)	advertimos	hemos advertido
(vosotros/as)	advertís	habéis advertido
(ellos/ellas/ustedes)	advierten	han advertido

	PRETERITE	IMPERFECT
(yo)	advertí	advertía
(tú)	advertiste	advertías
(él/ella/usted)	advirtió	advertía
(nosotros/as)	advertimos	advertíamos
(vosotros/as)	advertisteis	advertíais
(ellos/ellas/ustedes)	advirtieron	advertían

GERUND	PAST PARTICIPLE
advirtiendo	advertido

EXAMPLE PHRASES

Te **advierto** que no va a ser nada fácil. I must warn you that it won't be at all easy.

No **he advertido** nada extraño en su comportamiento. I haven't noticed anything strange about his behavior.

Ya te **advertí** que no intervinieras. I warned you not to get involved.

Las señales **advertían** del peligro. The signs warned of danger.

Remember that subject pronouns are not used very often in Spanish.

advertir

	FUTURE	CONDITIONAL
(yo)	advertiré	advertiría
(tú)	advertirás	advertirías
(él/ella/usted)	advertirá	advertiría
(nosotros/as)	advertiremos	advertiríamos
(vosotros/as)	advertiréis	advertiríais
(ellos/ellas/ ustedes)	advertirán	advertirían

	PRESENT SUBJUNCTIVE	IMPERFECT SUBJUNCTIVE
(yo)	advierta	advirtiera or advirtiese
(tú)	adviertas	advirtieras or advirtieses
(él/ella/usted)	advierta	advirtiera or advirtiese
(nosotros/as)	advirtamos	advirtiéramos or advirtiésemos
(vosotros/as)	advirtáis	advirtierais or advirtieseis
(ellos/ellas/ ustedes)	adviertan	advirtieran or advirtiesen

IMPERATIVE

advierte / advertid

Use the present subjunctive in all cases other than these tú and vosotros affirmative forms.

EXAMPLE PHRASES

Si **advirtiera** algún cambio, llámenos. If you should notice any change, give us a call.

Adviértele del riesgo que entraña. Warn him about the risk involved.

Remember that subject pronouns are not used very often in Spanish.

almorzar (to have lunch)

	PRESENT		PRESENT PERFECT
(yo)	almuerzo		he almorzado
(tú)	almuerzas		has almorzado
(él/ella/usted)	almuerza		ha almorzado
(nosotros/as)	almorzamos		hemos almorzado
(vosotros/as)	almorzáis		habéis almorzado
(ellos/ellas/ ustedes)	almuerzan		han almorzado

	PRETERITE		IMPERFECT
(yo)	almorcé		almorzaba
(tú)	almorzaste		almorzabas
(él/ella/usted)	almorzó		almorzaba
(nosotros/as)	almorzamos		almorzábamos
(vosotros/as)	almorzasteis		almorzabais
(ellos/ellas/ ustedes)	almorzaron		almorzaban

GERUND	PAST PARTICIPLE
almorzando	almorzado

EXAMPLE PHRASES

¿Dónde vais a **almorzar**? Where are you going to have lunch?

¿A qué hora **almuerzas**? What time do you have lunch?

Ya **hemos almorzado**. We've already had lunch.

Almorcé en un bar. I had lunch in a bar.

Siempre **almorzaba** un bocadillo. He always had a sandwich for lunch.

Remember that subject pronouns are not used very often in Spanish.

almorzar

	FUTURE	CONDITIONAL
(yo)	almorzaré	almorzaría
(tú)	almorzarás	almorzarías
(él/ella/usted)	almorzará	almorzaría
(nosotros/as)	almorzaremos	almorzaríamos
(vosotros/as)	almorzaréis	almorzaríais
(ellos/ellas/ ustedes)	almorzarán	almorzarían

	PRESENT SUBJUNCTIVE	IMPERFECT SUBJUNCTIVE
(yo)	almuerce	almorzara or almorzase
(tú)	almuerces	almorzaras or almorzases
(él/ella/usted)	almuerce	almorzara or almorzase
(nosotros/as)	almorcemos	almorzáramos or almorzásemos
(vosotros/as)	almorcéis	almorzarais or almorzaseis
(ellos/ellas/ ustedes)	almuercen	almorzaran or almorzasen

IMPERATIVE

almuerza / almorzad

Use the present subjunctive in all cases other than these tú and vosotros affirmative forms.

EXAMPLE PHRASES

Mañana **almorzaremos** todos juntos. We'll all have lunch together tomorrow.

Almuerce o no siempre me entra sueño a esta hora. I always feel sleepy at this time of the day, regardless of whether I've had lunch or not.

Si **almorzara** así todos los días, estaría mucho más gordo. I'd be much fatter if I had this sort of lunch every day.

Remember that subject pronouns are not used very often in Spanish.

amanecer (to get light, to wake up)

	PRESENT	**PRESENT PERFECT**
(yo)	amanezco	he amanecido
(tú)	amaneces	has amanecido
(él/ella/usted)	amanece	ha amanecido
(nosotros/as)	amanecemos	hemos amanecido
(vosotros/as)	amanecéis	habéis amanecido
(ellos/ellas/ ustedes)	amanecen	han amanecido

	PRETERITE	**IMPERFECT**
(yo)	amanecí	amanecía
(tú)	amaneciste	amanecías
(él/ella/usted)	amaneció	amanecía
(nosotros/as)	amanecimos	amanecíamos
(vosotros/as)	amanecisteis	amanecíais
(ellos/ellas/ ustedes)	amanecieron	amanecían

GERUND

amaneciendo

PAST PARTICIPLE

amanecido

EXAMPLE PHRASES

Siempre **amanece** nublado. The day always starts off cloudy.

Justo en ese momento **estaba amaneciendo**. Just then dawn was breaking.

Hoy **ha amanecido** a las ocho. Today it got light at eight o'clock.

La ciudad **amaneció** desierta. In the morning the town was deserted.

Amanecía de un humor de perros. She would wake up in a really bad mood.

Remember that subject pronouns are not used very often in Spanish.

amanecer

	FUTURE	CONDITIONAL
(yo)	amaneceré	amanecería
(tú)	amanecerás	amanecerías
(él/ella/usted)	amanecerá	amanecería
(nosotros/as)	amaneceremos	amaneceríamos
(vosotros/as)	amaneceréis	amaneceríais
(ellos/ellas/ ustedes)	amanecerán	amanecerían

	PRESENT SUBJUNCTIVE	IMPERFECT SUBJUNCTIVE
(yo)	amanezca	amaneciera or amaneciese
(tú)	amanezcas	amanecieras or amanecieses
(él/ella/usted)	amanezca	amaneciera or amaneciese
(nosotros/as)	amanezcamos	amaneciéramos or amaneciésemos
(vosotros/as)	amanezcáis	amanecierais or amanecieseis
(ellos/ellas/ ustedes)	amanezcan	amanecieran or amaneciesen

IMPERATIVE
amanece / amaneced

Use the present subjunctive in all cases other than these tú and vosotros affirmative forms.

EXAMPLE PHRASES
Pronto **amanecerá**. It will soon be daylight.

Saldremos en cuanto **amanezca**. We'll set off as soon as it gets light.

Si **amanecieras** con fiebre, toma una de estas pastillas. If you should wake up with a temperature, take one of these pills.

Remember that subject pronouns are not used very often in Spanish.

andar (to walk)

	PRESENT		PRESENT PERFECT
(yo)	ando		he andado
(tú)	andas		has andado
(él/ella/usted)	anda		ha andado
(nosotros/as)	andamos		hemos andado
(vosotros/as)	andáis		habéis andado
(ellos/ellas/ ustedes)	andan		han andado

	PRETERITE		IMPERFECT
(yo)	anduve		andaba
(tú)	anduviste		andabas
(él/ella/usted)	anduvo		andaba
(nosotros/as)	anduvimos		andábamos
(vosotros/as)	anduvisteis		andabais
(ellos/ellas/ ustedes)	anduvieron		andaban

GERUND

andando

PAST PARTICIPLE

andado

EXAMPLE PHRASES

Andar es un ejercicio muy sano. Walking is very good exercise.

Hemos andado todo el camino hasta aquí. We walked all the way here.

Anduvimos al menos 10 km. We walked at least 10 km.

Por aquel entonces **andaban** mal de dinero. Back then they were short of money.

Voy **andando** al trabajo todos los días. I walk to work every day.

Remember that subject pronouns are not used very often in Spanish.

andar

	FUTURE	CONDITIONAL
(yo)	andaré	andaría
(tú)	andarás	andarías
(él/ella/usted)	andará	andaría
(nosotros/as)	andaremos	andaríamos
(vosotros/as)	andaréis	andaríais
(ellos/ellas/ ustedes)	andarán	andarían

	PRESENT SUBJUNCTIVE	IMPERFECT SUBJUNCTIVE
(yo)	ande	anduviera or anduviese
(tú)	andes	anduvieras or anduvieses
(él/ella/usted)	ande	anduviera or anduviese
(nosotros/as)	andemos	anduviéramos or anduviésemos
(vosotros/as)	andéis	anduvierais or anduvieseis
(ellos/ellas/ ustedes)	anden	anduvieran or anduviesen

IMPERATIVE

anda / andad

Use the present subjunctive in all cases other than these tú and vosotros affirmative forms.

EXAMPLE PHRASES

Andará por los cuarenta. He must be about forty.

Yo **me andaría** con pies de plomo. I'd tread very carefully.

El médico le ha aconsejado que **ande** varios kilómetros al día. The doctor has advised him to walk several kilometers a day.

Si **anduvieras** con más cuidado, no te pasarían esas cosas. If you were more careful, this sort of thing wouldn't happen to you.

Remember that subject pronouns are not used very often in Spanish.

apoderarse (to take possession)

	PRESENT		PRESENT PERFECT
(yo)	me apodero		me he apoderado
(tú)	te apoderas		te has apoderado
(él/ella/usted)	se apodera		se ha apoderado
(nosotros/as)	nos apoderamos		nos hemos apoderado
(vosotros/as)	os apoderáis		os habéis apoderado
(ellos/ellas/ ustedes)	se apoderan		se han apoderado

	PRETERITE		IMPERFECT
(yo)	me apoderé		me apoderaba
(tú)	te apoderaste		te apoderabas
(él/ella/usted)	se apoderó		se apoderaba
(nosotros/as)	nos apoderamos		nos apoderábamos
(vosotros/as)	os apoderasteis		os apoderabais
(ellos/ellas/ ustedes)	se apoderaron		se apoderaban

GERUND

apoderándose, etc

PAST PARTICIPLE

apoderado

EXAMPLE PHRASES

En esas situaciones, el miedo **se apodera** de mí. In situations like that,
   I find myself gripped by fear.

Poco a poco **se han ido apoderando** de las riquezas del país. Little by little,
   they've taken possession of the country's riches.

Se apoderaron de las joyas y huyeron. They ran off with the jewels.

El desánimo **se apoderaba** de nosotros por momentos. We were feeling more
   and more discouraged by the minute.

Remember that subject pronouns are not used very often in Spanish.

apoderarse

	FUTURE	CONDITIONAL
(yo)	me apoderaré	me apoderaría
(tú)	te apoderarás	te apoderarías
(él/ella/usted)	se apoderará	se apoderaría
(nosotros/as)	nos apoderaremos	nos apoderaríamos
(vosotros/as)	os apoderaréis	os apoderaríais
(ellos/ellas/ ustedes)	se apoderarán	se apoderarían

	PRESENT SUBJUNCTIVE	IMPERFECT SUBJUNCTIVE
(yo)	me apodere	me apoderara or apoderase
(tú)	te apoderes	te apoderaras or apoderases
(él/ella/usted)	se apodere	se apoderara or apoderase
(nosotros/as)	nos apoderemos	nos apoderáramos or apoderásemos
(vosotros/as)	os apoderéis	os apoderarais or apoderaseis
(ellos/ellas/ ustedes)	se apoderen	se apoderaran or apoderasen

IMPERATIVE

apodérate / apoderaos

Use the present subjunctive in all cases other than these tú and vosotros affirmative forms.

EXAMPLE PHRASES

No dejes que los nervios **se apoderen** de ti en el examen. Don't let your nerves get the better of you in the exam.

Dejaron que el equipo argentino **se apoderara** del balón. They let the Argentinian team get control of the ball.

Remember that subject pronouns are not used very often in Spanish.

aprobar (to pass, to approve of)

	PRESENT		PRESENT PERFECT
(yo)	apruebo		he aprobado
(tú)	apruebas		has aprobado
(él/ella/usted)	aprueba		ha aprobado
(nosotros/as)	aprobamos		hemos aprobado
(vosotros/as)	aprobáis		habéis aprobado
(ellos/ellas/ustedes)	aprueban		han aprobado

	PRETERITE		IMPERFECT
(yo)	aprobé		aprobaba
(tú)	aprobaste		aprobabas
(él/ella/usted)	aprobó		aprobaba
(nosotros/as)	aprobamos		aprobábamos
(vosotros/as)	aprobasteis		aprobabais
(ellos/ellas/ustedes)	aprobaron		aprobaban

GERUND

aprobando

PAST PARTICIPLE

aprobado

EXAMPLE PHRASES

No **apruebo** esa conducta. I don't approve of that sort of behavior.

Este año lo **estoy aprobando** todo. So far this year I've passed everything.

Han aprobado una ley antitabaco. They've passed an anti-smoking law.

¿**Aprobaste** el examen? Did you pass the exam?

La decisión **fue aprobada** por mayoría. The decision was approved by a majority.

Remember that subject pronouns are not used very often in Spanish.

aprobar

	FUTURE	CONDITIONAL
(yo)	aprobaré	aprobaría
(tú)	aprobarás	aprobarías
(él/ella/usted)	aprobará	aprobaría
(nosotros/as)	aprobaremos	aprobaríamos
(vosotros/as)	aprobaréis	aprobaríais
(ellos/ellas/ustedes)	aprobarán	aprobarían

	PRESENT SUBJUNCTIVE	IMPERFECT SUBJUNCTIVE
(yo)	apruebe	aprobara or aprobase
(tú)	apruebes	aprobaras or aprobases
(él/ella/usted)	apruebe	aprobara or aprobase
(nosotros/as)	aprobemos	aprobáramos or aprobásemos
(vosotros/as)	aprobéis	aprobarais or aprobaseis
(ellos/ellas/ustedes)	aprueben	aprobaran or aprobasen

IMPERATIVE

aprueba / aprobad

Use the present subjunctive in all cases other than these tú and vosotros affirmative forms.

EXAMPLE PHRASES

El ayuntamiento **aprobará** un nuevo impuesto ecológico. The council will approve a new green tax.

arrancar (to pull up)

	PRESENT	PRESENT PERFECT
(yo)	arranco	he arrancado
(tú)	arrancas	has arrancado
(él/ella/usted)	arranca	ha arrancado
(nosotros/as)	arrancamos	hemos arrancado
(vosotros/as)	arrancáis	habéis arrancado
(ellos/ellas/ ustedes)	arrancan	han arrancado

	PRETERITE	IMPERFECT
(yo)	arranqué	arrancaba
(tú)	arrancaste	arrancabas
(él/ella/usted)	arrancó	arrancaba
(nosotros/as)	arrancamos	arrancábamos
(vosotros/as)	arrancasteis	arrancabais
(ellos/ellas/ ustedes)	arrancaron	arrancaban

GERUND

arrancando

PAST PARTICIPLE

arrancado

EXAMPLE PHRASES

Lo tienes que **arrancar** de raíz. You must pull it up by its roots.

Estaba arrancando malas hierbas. I was pulling up weeds.

Me has arrancado un botón. You've pulled off one of my buttons.

El viento **arrancó** varios árboles. Several trees were uprooted in the wind.

Remember that subject pronouns are not used very often in Spanish.

arrancar

	FUTURE	CONDITIONAL
(yo)	arrancaré	arrancaría
(tú)	arrancarás	arrancarías
(él/ella/usted)	arrancará	arrancaría
(nosotros/as)	arrancaremos	arrancaríamos
(vosotros/as)	arrancaréis	arrancaríais
(ellos/ellas/ ustedes)	arrancarán	arrancarían

	PRESENT SUBJUNCTIVE	IMPERFECT SUBJUNCTIVE
(yo)	arranque	arrancara *or* arrancase
(tú)	arranques	arrancaras *or* arrancases
(él/ella/usted)	arranque	arrancara *or* arrancase
(nosotros/as)	arranquemos	arrancáramos *or* arrancásemos
(vosotros/as)	arranquéis	arrancarais *or* arrancaseis
(ellos/ellas/ ustedes)	arranquen	arrancaran *or* arrancasen

IMPERATIVE
arranca / arrancad

Use the present subjunctive in all cases other than these tú and vosotros affirmative forms.

EXAMPLE PHRASES

No **arranques** hojas del cuaderno. Don't go tearing pages out of the exercise book.

Arranca y vámonos. Start the engine and let's get going.

Remember that subject pronouns are not used very often in Spanish.

arrepentirse (to be sorry)

	PRESENT	PRESENT PERFECT
(yo)	me arrepiento	me he arrepentido
(tú)	te arrepientes	te has arrepentido
(él/ella/usted)	se arrepiente	se ha arrepentido
(nosotros/as)	nos arrepentimos	nos hemos arrepentido
(vosotros/as)	os arrepentís	os habéis arrepentido
(ellos/ellas/ ustedes)	se arrepienten	se han arrepentido

	PRETERITE	IMPERFECT
(yo)	me arrepentí	me arrepentía
(tú)	te arrepentiste	te arrepentías
(él/ella/usted)	se arrepintió	se arrepentía
(nosotros/as)	nos arrepentimos	nos arrepentíamos
(vosotros/as)	os arrepentisteis	os arrepentíais
(ellos/ellas/ ustedes)	se arrepintieron	se arrepentían

GERUND

arrepintiéndose, etc

PAST PARTICIPLE

arrepentido

EXAMPLE PHRASES

¡Te vas a **arrepentir** de esto! You'll be sorry you did that!

No **me arrepiento** de nada. I don't regret anything.

¿Nunca **te has arrepentido** de haberte ido de casa? Haven't you ever regretted leaving home?

Se arrepintieron y decidieron no vender la casa. They changed their minds and decided not to sell the house.

Remember that subject pronouns are not used very often in Spanish.

arrepentirse

	FUTURE	CONDITIONAL
(yo)	me arrepentiré	me arrepentiría
(tú)	te arrepentirás	te arrepentirías
(él/ella/usted)	se arrepentirá	se arrepentiría
(nosotros/as)	nos arrepentiremos	nos arrepentiríamos
(vosotros/as)	os arrepentiréis	os arrepentiríais
(ellos/ellas/ ustedes)	se arrepentirán	se arrepentirían

	PRESENT SUBJUNCTIVE	IMPERFECT SUBJUNCTIVE
(yo)	me arrepienta	me arrepintiera or arrepintiese
(tú)	te arrepientas	te arrepintieras or arrepintieses
(él/ella/usted)	se arrepienta	se arrepintiera or arrepintiese
(nosotros/as)	nos arrepintamos	nos arrepintiéramos or arrepintiésemos
(vosotros/as)	os arrepintáis	os arrepintierais or arrepintieseis
(ellos/ellas/ ustedes)	se arrepientan	se arrepintieran or arrepintiesen

IMPERATIVE
arrepiéntete / arrepentíos

Use the present subjunctive in all cases other than these tú and vosotros affirmative forms.

EXAMPLE PHRASES

Algún día **se arrepentirá** de no haber estudiado una carrera. One day he'll be sorry he didn't go to university.

No **te arrepientas** nunca de haber dicho la verdad. Don't ever regret having told the truth.

atravesar (to cross, to go through)

	PRESENT	PRESENT PERFECT
(yo)	atravieso	he atravesado
(tú)	atraviesas	has atravesado
(él/ella/usted)	atraviesa	ha atravesado
(nosotros/as)	atravesamos	hemos atravesado
(vosotros/as)	atravesáis	habéis atravesado
(ellos/ellas/ ustedes)	atraviesan	han atravesado

	PRETERITE	IMPERFECT
(yo)	atravesé	atravesaba
(tú)	atravesaste	atravesabas
(él/ella/usted)	atravesó	atravesaba
(nosotros/as)	atravesamos	atravesábamos
(vosotros/as)	atravesasteis	atravesabais
(ellos/ellas/ ustedes)	atravesaron	atravesaban

GERUND	PAST PARTICIPLE
atravesando	atravesado

EXAMPLE PHRASES

Atravesamos un mal momento. We're going through a bad patch.

En este momento **está atravesando** la ciudad en un coche descubierto. Right know he's being driven through the city in an open-topped vehicle.

Hemos atravesado el río a nado. We swam across the river.

La bala le **atravesó** el cráneo. The bullet went through his skull.

Un camión **se** nos **atravesó** en la carretera. A truck came out into the road in front of us.

Remember that subject pronouns are not used very often in Spanish.

atravesar

	FUTURE	CONDITIONAL
(yo)	atravesaré	atravesaría
(tú)	atravesarás	atravesarías
(él/ella/usted)	atravesará	atravesaría
(nosotros/as)	atravesaremos	atravesaríamos
(vosotros/as)	atravesaréis	atravesaríais
(ellos/ellas/ ustedes)	atravesarán	atravesarían

	PRESENT SUBJUNCTIVE	IMPERFECT SUBJUNCTIVE
(yo)	atraviese	atravesara or atravesase
(tú)	atravieses	atravesaras or atravesases
(él/ella/usted)	atraviese	atravesara or atravesase
(nosotros/as)	atravesemos	atravesáramos or atravesásemos
(vosotros/as)	atraveséis	atravesarais or atravesaseis
(ellos/ellas/ ustedes)	atraviesen	atravesaran or atravesasen

IMPERATIVE
atraviesa / atravesad

Use the present subjunctive in all cases other than these tú and vosotros affirmative forms.

EXAMPLE PHRASES
El túnel **atravesará** la montaña. The tunnel will go under the mountain.

aunar (to join together)

	PRESENT	PRESENT PERFECT
(yo)	aúno	he aunado
(tú)	aúnas	has aunado
(él/ella/usted)	aúna	ha aunado
(nosotros/as)	aunamos	hemos aunado
(vosotros/as)	aunáis	habéis aunado
(ellos/ellas/ ustedes)	aúnan	han aunado

	PRETERITE	IMPERFECT
(yo)	auné	aunaba
(tú)	aunaste	aunabas
(él/ella/usted)	aunó	aunaba
(nosotros/as)	aunamos	aunábamos
(vosotros/as)	aunasteis	aunabais
(ellos/ellas/ ustedes)	aunaron	aunaban

GERUND	PAST PARTICIPLE
aunando	aunado

EXAMPLE PHRASES

En esta obra **se han aunado** imaginación y técnica. This play combines imagination and technique.

Aunaron esfuerzos. They joined forces.

La pintura barroca **aunaba** conocimientos de geometría y anatomía. Baroque painting brought knowledge of geometry and anatomy together.

Remember that subject pronouns are not used very often in Spanish.

aunar

	FUTURE	CONDITIONAL
(yo)	aunaré	aunaría
(tú)	aunarás	aunarías
(él/ella/usted)	aunará	aunaría
(nosotros/as)	aunaremos	aunaríamos
(vosotros/as)	aunaréis	aunaríais
(ellos/ellas/ ustedes)	aunarán	aunarían

	PRESENT SUBJUNCTIVE	IMPERFECT SUBJUNCTIVE
(yo)	aúne	aunara or aunase
(tú)	aúnes	aunaras or aunases
(él/ella/usted)	aúne	aunara or aunase
(nosotros/as)	aunemos	aunáramos or aunásemos
(vosotros/as)	aunéis	aunarais or aunaseis
(ellos/ellas/ ustedes)	aúnen	aunaran or aunasen

IMPERATIVE

aúna / aunad

Use the present subjunctive in all cases other than these tú and vosotros affirmative forms.

Remember that subject pronouns are not used very often in Spanish.

avergonzar (to shame)

	PRESENT		PRESENT PERFECT
(yo)	avergüenzo		he avergonzado
(tú)	avergüenzas		has avergonzado
(él/ella/usted)	avergüenza		ha avergonzado
(nosotros/as)	avergonzamos		hemos avergonzado
(vosotros/as)	avergonzáis		habéis avergonzado
(ellos/ellas/ ustedes)	avergüenzan		han avergonzado

	PRETERITE		IMPERFECT
(yo)	avergoncé		avergonzaba
(tú)	avergonzaste		avergonzabas
(él/ella/usted)	avergonzó		avergonzaba
(nosotros/as)	avergonzamos		avergonzábamos
(vosotros/as)	avergonzasteis		avergonzabais
(ellos/ellas/ ustedes)	avergonzaron		avergonzaban

GERUND

avergonzando

PAST PARTICIPLE

avergonzado

EXAMPLE PHRASES

Tendrías que **avergonzarte**. You should be ashamed of yourself.

Le **avergüenza** no tener dinero. He's ashamed of having no money.

Cuando me lo dijo **me avergoncé**. I was embarrassed when he told me.

Se avergonzaba de su familia. He was ashamed of his family.

Avergonzándote no arreglas nada. Being ashamed doesn't solve anything.

Remember that subject pronouns are not used very often in Spanish.

avergonzar

	FUTURE	CONDITIONAL
(yo)	avergonzaré	avergonzaría
(tú)	avergonzarás	avergonzarías
(él/ella/usted)	avergonzará	avergonzaría
(nosotros/as)	avergonzaremos	avergonzaríamos
(vosotros/as)	avegonzaréis	avergonzaríais
(ellos/ellas/ ustedes)	avergonzarán	avergonzarían

	PRESENT SUBJUNCTIVE	IMPERFECT SUBJUNCTIVE
(yo)	avergüence	avergonzara or avergonzase
(tú)	avergüences	avergonzaras or avergonzases
(él/ella/usted)	avergüence	avergonzara or avergonzase
(nosotros/as)	avergoncemos	avergonzáramos or avergonzásemos
(vosotros/as)	avergoncéis	avergonzarais or avergonzaseis
(ellos/ellas/ ustedes)	avergüencen	avergonzaran or avergonzasen

IMPERATIVE

avergüenza / avergonzad

Use the present subjunctive in all cases other than these tú and vosotros affirmative forms.

EXAMPLE PHRASES

Si hubiera sabido que **te avergonzarías** tanto, no te lo habría dicho.
   I wouldn't have told you if I'd known you'd be so embarrassed.

Si de verdad **se avergonzaran**, no se comportarían así. They wouldn't behave
   like that if they were really ashamed.

Remember that subject pronouns are not used very often in Spanish.

averiguar (to find out)

	PRESENT		PRESENT PERFECT
(yo)	averiguo		he averiguado
(tú)	averiguas		has averiguado
(él/ella/usted)	averigua		ha averiguado
(nosotros/as)	averiguamos		hemos averiguado
(vosotros/as)	averiguáis		habéis averiguado
(ellos/ellas/ ustedes)	averiguan		han averiguado

	PRETERITE		IMPERFECT
(yo)	averigüé		averiguaba
(tú)	averiguaste		averiguabas
(él/ella/usted)	averiguó		averiguaba
(nosotros/as)	averiguamos		averiguábamos
(vosotros/as)	averiguasteis		averiguabais
(ellos/ellas/ ustedes)	averiguaron		averiguaban

GERUND

averiguando

PAST PARTICIPLE

averiguado

EXAMPLE PHRASES

Trataron de **averiguar** su paradero. They tried to find out his whereabouts.

Poco a poco van **averiguando** más cosas sobre su vida. They're gradually
   finding out more about his life.

¿Cómo **has averiguado** dónde vivo? How did you find out where I lived?

¿Cuándo lo **averiguaron**? When did they find out?

Remember that subject pronouns are not used very often in Spanish.

averiguar

	FUTURE	CONDITIONAL
(yo)	averiguaré	averiguaría
(tú)	averiguarás	averiguarías
(él/ella/usted)	averiguará	averiguaría
(nosotros/as)	averiguaremos	averiguaríamos
(vosotros/as)	averiguaréis	averiguaríais
(ellos/ellas/ustedes)	averiguarán	averiguarían

	PRESENT SUBJUNCTIVE	IMPERFECT SUBJUNCTIVE
(yo)	averigüe	averiguara or averiguase
(tú)	averigües	averiguaras or averiguases
(él/ella/usted)	averigüe	averiguara or averiguase
(nosotros/as)	averigüemos	averiguáramos or averiguásemos
(vosotros/as)	averigüéis	averiguarais or averiguaseis
(ellos/ellas/ustedes)	averigüen	averiguaran or averiguasen

IMPERATIVE

averigua / averiguad

Use the present subjunctive in all cases other than these tú and vosotros affirmative forms.

EXAMPLE PHRASES

Lo **averiguaré** pronto. I'll find out soon.

Dijo que si le dábamos tiempo lo **averiguaría**. She said that she'd find out if we gave her time.

En cuanto lo **averigüe** te lo digo. I'll tell you as soon as I find out.

¡**Averígualo** inmediatamente! Check it out immediately!

Remember that subject pronouns are not used very often in Spanish.

bendecir (to bless)

	PRESENT	PRESENT PERFECT
(yo)	bendigo	he bendecido
(tú)	bendices	has bendecido
(él/ella/usted)	bendice	ha bendecido
(nosotros/as)	bendecimos	hemos bendecido
(vosotros/as)	bendecís	habéis bendecido
(ellos/ellas/ustedes)	bendicen	han bendecido

	PRETERITE	IMPERFECT
(yo)	bendije	bendecía
(tú)	bendijiste	bendecías
(él/ella/usted)	bendijo	bendecía
(nosotros/as)	bendijimos	bendecíamos
(vosotros/as)	bendijisteis	bendecíais
(ellos/ellas/ustedes)	bendijeron	bendecían

GERUND	PAST PARTICIPLE
bendiciendo	bendecido

EXAMPLE PHRASES

Su padre **bendice** siempre la mesa. His father always says grace.

La vida me **ha bendecido** con unos hijos maravillosos. I've been blessed with wonderful children.

Jesús **bendijo** los panes y los peces. Jesus blessed the loaves and the fishes.

Bendecía el día en que lo conoció. She blessed the day she met him.

Remember that subject pronouns are not used very often in Spanish.

bendecir

	FUTURE	CONDITIONAL
(yo)	bendeciré	bendeciría
(tú)	bendecirás	bendecirías
(él/ella/usted)	bendecirá	bendeciría
(nosotros/as)	bendeciremos	bendeciríamos
(vosotros/as)	bendeciréis	bendeciríais
(ellos/ellas/ ustedes)	bendecirán	bendecirían

	PRESENT SUBJUNCTIVE	IMPERFECT SUBJUNCTIVE
(yo)	bendiga	bendijera or bendijese
(tú)	bendigas	bendijeras or bendijeses
(él/ella/usted)	bendiga	bendijera or bendijese
(nosotros/as)	bendigamos	bendijéramos or bendijésemos
(vosotros/as)	bendigáis	bendijerais or bendijeseis
(ellos/ellas/ ustedes)	bendigan	bendijeran or bendijesen

IMPERATIVE

bendice / bendecid

Use the present subjunctive in all cases other than these tú and vosotros affirmative forms.

EXAMPLE PHRASES

El Papa **bendecirá** a los fieles desde el balcón. The Pope will bless the faithful from the balcony.

Quieren que sea él quien **bendiga** su unión. They want him to marry them.

Pidieron a un sacerdote que **bendijera** su nueva casa. They asked a priest to bless their new house.

Remember that subject pronouns are not used very often in Spanish.

caber (to fit)

	PRESENT		PRESENT PERFECT
(yo)	quepo		he cabido
(tú)	cabes		has cabido
(él/ella/usted)	cabe		ha cabido
(nosotros/as)	cabemos		hemos cabido
(vosotros/as)	cabéis		habéis cabido
(ellos/ellas/ ustedes)	caben		han cabido

	PRETERITE		IMPERFECT
(yo)	cupe		cabía
(tú)	cupiste		cabías
(él/ella/usted)	cupo		cabía
(nosotros/as)	cupimos		cabíamos
(vosotros/as)	cupisteis		cabíais
(ellos/ellas/ ustedes)	cupieron		cabían

GERUND

cabiendo

PAST PARTICIPLE

cabido

EXAMPLE PHRASES

No te preocupes, que va a **caber**. Don't worry, it will fit.

Aquí no **cabe**. There isn't enough room for it here.

Al final **ha cabido** todo. In the end everything went in.

No le **cupo** la menor duda. She wasn't in any doubt.

No **cabía** en sí de gozo. She was beside herself with joy.

caber

	FUTURE	CONDITIONAL
(yo)	cabré	cabría
(tú)	cabrás	cabrías
(él/ella/usted)	cabrá	cabría
(nosotros/as)	cabremos	cabríamos
(vosotros/as)	cabréis	cabríais
(ellos/ellas/ ustedes)	cabrán	cabrían

	PRESENT SUBJUNCTIVE	IMPERFECT SUBJUNCTIVE
(yo)	quepa	cupiera or cupiese
(tú)	quepas	cupieras or cupieses
(él/ella/usted)	quepa	cupiera or cupiese
(nosotros/as)	quepamos	cupiéramos or cupiésemos
(vosotros/as)	quepáis	cupierais or cupieseis
(ellos/ellas/ ustedes)	quepan	cupieran or cupiesen

IMPERATIVE

cabe / cabed

Use the present subjunctive in all cases other than these tú and vosotros affirmative forms.

EXAMPLE PHRASES

¿Crees que **cabrá**? Do you think there will be enough room for it?

Cabría cuestionarse si es la mejor solución. We should ask ourselves whether it's the best solution.

Hizo lo imposible para que le **cupiera** la redacción en una página.
  He did everything he could to fit the composition onto one page.

Remember that subject pronouns are not used very often in Spanish.

caer (to fall)

	PRESENT		PRESENT PERFECT
(yo)	caigo		he caído
(tú)	caes		has caído
(él/ella/usted)	cae		ha caído
(nosotros/as)	caemos		hemos caído
(vosotros/as)	caéis		habéis caído
(ellos/ellas/ustedes)	caen		han caído

	PRETERITE		IMPERFECT
(yo)	caí		caía
(tú)	caíste		caías
(él/ella/usted)	cayó		caía
(nosotros/as)	caímos		caíamos
(vosotros/as)	caísteis		caíais
(ellos/ellas/ustedes)	cayeron		caían

GERUND

cayendo

PAST PARTICIPLE

caído

EXAMPLE PHRASES

Su cumpleaños **cae** en viernes. Her birthday falls on a Friday.

Ese edificio se **está cayendo**. That building's falling down.

Se me **ha caído** un guante. I've dropped one of my gloves.

Me **caí** por las escaleras. I fell down the stairs.

Me **caía** muy bien. I really liked him.

Remember that subject pronouns are not used very often in Spanish.

caer

	FUTURE	CONDITIONAL
(yo)	caeré	caería
(tú)	caerás	caerías
(él/ella/usted)	caerá	caería
(nosotros/as)	caeremos	caeríamos
(vosotros/as)	caeréis	caeríais
(ellos/ellas/ ustedes)	caerán	caerían

	PRESENT SUBJUNCTIVE	IMPERFECT SUBJUNCTIVE
(yo)	caiga	cayera or cayese
(tú)	caigas	cayeras or cayeses
(él/ella/usted)	caiga	cayera or cayese
(nosotros/as)	caigamos	cayéramos or cayésemos
(vosotros/as)	caigáis	cayerais or cayeseis
(ellos/ellas/ ustedes)	caigan	cayeran or cayesen

IMPERATIVE

cae / caed

Use the present subjunctive in all cases other than these tú and vosotros affirmative forms.

EXAMPLE PHRASES

Tarde o temprano, la capital **caerá** en manos del enemigo. Sooner or later, the capital will fall into enemy hands.

Yo me **caería** con esos tacones. I'd fall over if I wore heels like those.

Necesitamos que no **caigan** más los salarios. We need salaries to stop falling.

No **caigas** tan bajo. Don't stoop so low.

Remember that subject pronouns are not used very often in Spanish.

cambiar (to change)

	PRESENT	PRESENT PERFECT
(yo)	cambio	he cambiado
(tú)	cambias	has cambiado
(él/ella/usted)	cambia	ha cambiado
(nosotros/as)	cambiamos	hemos cambiado
(vosotros/as)	cambiáis	habéis cambiado
(ellos/ellas/ustedes)	cambian	han cambiado

	PRETERITE	IMPERFECT
(yo)	cambié	cambiaba
(tú)	cambiaste	cambiabas
(él/ella/usted)	cambió	cambiaba
(nosotros/as)	cambiamos	cambiábamos
(vosotros/as)	cambiasteis	cambiabais
(ellos/ellas/ustedes)	cambiaron	cambiaban

GERUND	PAST PARTICIPLE
cambiando	cambiado

EXAMPLE PHRASES

Necesito **cambiar** de ambiente. I need a change of scenery.

Te **cambio** mi tableta por tu iPad. I'll swap my tablet for your iPad.

He cambiado de idea. I've changed my mind.

Cambié varias veces de trabajo. I changed jobs several times.

Cambiaban de coche cada año. They changed their car every year.

Remember that subject pronouns are not used very often in Spanish.

cambiar

	FUTURE	CONDITIONAL
(yo)	cambiaré	cambiaría
(tú)	cambiarás	cambiarías
(él/ella/usted)	cambiará	cambiaría
(nosotros/as)	cambiaremos	cambiaríamos
(vosotros/as)	cambiaréis	cambiaríais
(ellos/ellas/ustedes)	cambiarán	cambiarían

	PRESENT SUBJUNCTIVE	IMPERFECT SUBJUNCTIVE
(yo)	cambie	cambiara or cambiase
(tú)	cambies	cambiaras or cambiases
(él/ella/usted)	cambie	cambiara or cambiase
(nosotros/as)	cambiemos	cambiáramos or cambiásemos
(vosotros/as)	cambiéis	cambiarais or cambiaseis
(ellos/ellas/ustedes)	cambien	cambiaran or cambiasen

IMPERATIVE
cambia / cambiad

Use the present subjunctive in all cases other than these tú and vosotros affirmative forms.

EXAMPLE PHRASES
Cuando la conozcas, **cambiarás** de idea. You'll change your mind when you meet her.

Si pudiéramos, **nos cambiaríamos** de casa. If we could, we'd move houses.

No quiero que **cambies**. I don't want you to change.

Cámbiate, que se nos hace tarde. Get changed, it's getting late.

Remember that subject pronouns are not used very often in Spanish.

cazar (to hunt, to shoot)

	PRESENT	PRESENT PERFECT
(yo)	cazo	he cazado
(tú)	cazas	has cazado
(él/ella/usted)	caza	ha cazado
(nosotros/as)	cazamos	hemos cazado
(vosotros/as)	cazáis	habéis cazado
(ellos/ellas/ustedes)	cazan	han cazado

	PRETERITE	IMPERFECT
(yo)	cacé	cazaba
(tú)	cazaste	cazabas
(él/ella/usted)	cazó	cazaba
(nosotros/as)	cazamos	cazábamos
(vosotros/as)	cazasteis	cazabais
(ellos/ellas/ustedes)	cazaron	cazaban

GERUND

cazando

PAST PARTICIPLE

cazado

EXAMPLE PHRASES

Salieron a **cazar** ciervos. They went deer-hunting.

Caza las cosas al vuelo. She's very quick on the uptake.

No **he cazado** nada de lo que ha dicho. I didn't understand a word he said.

Los **cacé** robando. I caught them stealing.

Cazaban con lanza. They hunted with spears.

Remember that subject pronouns are not used very often in Spanish.

cazar

	FUTURE	CONDITIONAL
(yo)	cazaré	cazaría
(tú)	cazarás	cazarías
(él/ella/usted)	cazará	cazaría
(nosotros/as)	cazaremos	cazaríamos
(vosotros/as)	cazaréis	cazaríais
(ellos/ellas/ustedes)	cazarán	cazarían

	PRESENT SUBJUNCTIVE	IMPERFECT SUBJUNCTIVE
(yo)	cace	cazara or cazase
(tú)	caces	cazaras or cazases
(él/ella/usted)	cace	cazara or cazase
(nosotros/as)	cacemos	cazáramos or cazásemos
(vosotros/as)	cacéis	cazarais or cazaseis
(ellos/ellas/ustedes)	cacen	cazaran or cazasen

IMPERATIVE

caza / cazad

Use the present subjunctive in all cases other than these tú and vosotros affirmative forms.

EXAMPLE PHRASES

¡Quién **cazara** a un millonario! I wish I could land myself a millionaire!

Remember that subject pronouns are not used very often in Spanish.

cerrar (to close)

	PRESENT	**PRESENT PERFECT**
(yo)	cierro	he cerrado
(tú)	cierras	has cerrado
(él/ella/usted)	cierra	ha cerrado
(nosotros/as)	cerramos	hemos cerrado
(vosotros/as)	cerráis	habéis cerrado
(ellos/ellas/ustedes)	cierran	han cerrado

	PRETERITE	**IMPERFECT**
(yo)	cerré	cerraba
(tú)	cerraste	cerrabas
(él/ella/usted)	cerró	cerraba
(nosotros/as)	cerramos	cerrábamos
(vosotros/as)	cerrasteis	cerrabais
(ellos/ellas/ustedes)	cerraron	cerraban

GERUND

cerrando

PAST PARTICIPLE

cerrado

EXAMPLE PHRASES

No puedo **cerrar** la maleta. I can't shut this suitcase.

No **cierran** al mediodía. They don't close at midday.

Ha cerrado la puerta con llave. She's locked the door.

Cerró el libro. He closed the book.

Se le **cerraban** los ojos. She couldn't keep her eyes open.

Remember that subject pronouns are not used very often in Spanish.

cerrar

	FUTURE	CONDITIONAL
(yo)	cerraré	cerraría
(tú)	cerrarás	cerrarías
(él/ella/usted)	cerrará	cerraría
(nosotros/as)	cerraremos	cerraríamos
(vosotros/as)	cerraréis	cerraríais
(ellos/ellas/ ustedes)	cerrrarán	cerrarían

	PRESENT SUBJUNCTIVE	IMPERFECT SUBJUNCTIVE
(yo)	cierre	cerrara or cerrase
(tú)	cierres	cerraras or cerrases
(él/ella/usted)	cierre	cerrara or cerrase
(nosotros/as)	cerremos	cerráramos or cerrásemos
(vosotros/as)	cerréis	cerrarais or cerraseis
(ellos/ellas/ ustedes)	cierren	cerraran or cerrasen

IMPERATIVE

cierra / cerrad

Use the present subjunctive in all cases other than these tú and vosotros affirmative forms.

EXAMPLE PHRASES

La facturación **se cerrará** 45 minutos antes de la salida del vuelo. Check-in will close 45 minutes before flight departure.

No dejes que **se cierre** la puerta de golpe. Don't let the door slam shut.

No **cierres** la ventana. Don't close the window.

Cierra el grifo. Turn off the faucet.

Remember that subject pronouns are not used very often in Spanish.

cocer (to boil, to cook)

	PRESENT	PRESENT PERFECT
(yo)	cuezo	he cocido
(tú)	cueces	has cocido
(él/ella/usted)	cuece	ha cocido
(nosotros/as)	cocemos	hemos cocido
(vosotros/as)	cocéis	habéis cocido
(ellos/ellas/ustedes)	cuecen	han cocido

	PRETERITE	IMPERFECT
(yo)	cocí	cocía
(tú)	cociste	cocías
(él/ella/usted)	coció	cocía
(nosotros/as)	cocimos	cocíamos
(vosotros/as)	cocisteis	cocíais
(ellos/ellas/ustedes)	cocieron	cocían

GERUND	PAST PARTICIPLE
cociendo	cocido

EXAMPLE PHRASES

Las gambas **se cuecen** en un momento. Prawns take no time to cook.

Aquí nos **estamos cociendo**. It's boiling in here.

He cocido todo junto. I've cooked everything together.

Coció el pan en el horno. He baked the bread in the oven.

Remember that subject pronouns are not used very often in Spanish.

cocer

	FUTURE	CONDITIONAL
(yo)	coceré	cocería
(tú)	cocerás	cocerías
(él/ella/usted)	cocerá	cocería
(nosotros/as)	coceremos	coceríamos
(vosotros/as)	coceréis	coceríais
(ellos/ellas/ ustedes)	cocerán	cocerían

	PRESENT SUBJUNCTIVE	IMPERFECT SUBJUNCTIVE
(yo)	cueza	cociera or cociese
(tú)	cuezas	cocieras or cocieses
(él/ella/usted)	cueza	cociera or cociese
(nosotros/as)	cozamos	cociéramos or cociésemos
(vosotros/as)	cozáis	cocierais or cocieseis
(ellos/ellas/ ustedes)	cuezan	cocieran or cociesen

IMPERATIVE
cuece / coced

Use the present subjunctive in all cases other than these tú and vosotros affirmative forms.

EXAMPLE PHRASES

Así se **cocerá** antes. This way it will be ready sooner.

Te dije que lo **cocieras** tapado. I told you to cook it with the lid on.

No lo **cuezas** demasiado. Don't overcook it.

Cuécelo a fuego lento. Cook it over a gentle heat.

Remember that subject pronouns are not used very often in Spanish.

coger (to take, to catch)

	PRESENT		PRESENT PERFECT
(yo)	cojo		he cogido
(tú)	coges		has cogido
(él/ella/usted)	coge		ha cogido
(nosotros/as)	cogemos		hemos cogido
(vosotros/as)	cogéis		habéis cogido
(ellos/ellas/ ustedes)	cogen		han cogido

	PRETERITE		IMPERFECT
(yo)	cogí		cogía
(tú)	cogiste		cogías
(él/ella/usted)	cogió		cogía
(nosotros/as)	cogimos		cogíamos
(vosotros/as)	cogisteis		cogíais
(ellos/ellas/ ustedes)	cogieron		cogían

GERUND	PAST PARTICIPLE
cogiendo	cogido

EXAMPLE PHRASES

¿Por qué no **coges** el tren de las seis? Why don't you catch the six o'clock train?

Estuvimos cogiendo setas. We were picking mushrooms.

Le **he cogido** cariño al gato. I've grown fond of the cat.

La **cogí** entre mis brazos. I took her in my arms.

Cogía el metro todos los días. I used to take the subway every day.

Remember that subject pronouns are not used very often in Spanish.

coger

	FUTURE	CONDITIONAL
(yo)	cogeré	cogería
(tú)	cogerás	cogerías
(él/ella/usted)	cogerá	cogería
(nosotros/as)	cogeremos	cogeríamos
(vosotros/as)	cogeréis	cogeríais
(ellos/ellas/ ustedes)	cogerán	cogerían

	PRESENT SUBJUNCTIVE	IMPERFECT SUBJUNCTIVE
(yo)	coja	cogiera or cogiese
(tú)	cojas	cogieras or cogieses
(él/ella/usted)	coja	cogiera or cogiese
(nosotros/as)	cojamos	cogiéramos or cogiésemos
(vosotros/as)	cojáis	cogierais or cogieseis
(ellos/ellas/ ustedes)	cojan	cogieran or cogiesen

IMPERATIVE

coge / coged

Use the present subjunctive in all cases other than these tú and vosotros affirmative forms.

EXAMPLE PHRASES

Se cogerá un resfriado. He'll catch a cold.

Yo **cogería** el azul. I'd take the blue one.

No le **cojas** los juguetes a tu hermana. Don't take your sister's toys.

Coja la primera calle a la derecha. Take the first street on the right.

Remember that subject pronouns are not used very often in Spanish.

colgar (to hang)

	PRESENT	PRESENT PERFECT
(yo)	cuelgo	he colgado
(tú)	cuelgas	has colgado
(él/ella/usted)	cuelga	ha colgado
(nosotros/as)	colgamos	hemos colgado
(vosotros/as)	colgáis	habéis colgado
(ellos/ellas/ustedes)	cuelgan	han colgado

	PRETERITE	IMPERFECT
(yo)	colgué	colgaba
(tú)	colgaste	colgabas
(él/ella/usted)	colgó	colgaba
(nosotros/as)	colgamos	colgábamos
(vosotros/as)	colgasteis	colgabais
(ellos/ellas/ustedes)	colgaron	colgaban

GERUND

colgando

PAST PARTICIPLE

colgado

EXAMPLE PHRASES

Cada día **cuelgan** el cartel de "no hay billetes". Every day the "sold out" sign goes up.

Hay telarañas **colgando** del techo. There are cobwebs hanging from the ceiling.

Te **he colgado** la chaqueta en la percha. I've hung your jacket on the hanger.

Me **colgó** el teléfono. He hung up on me.

De la pared **colgaba** un espejo. There was a mirror hanging on the wall.

Remember that subject pronouns are not used very often in Spanish.

colgar

	FUTURE	CONDITIONAL
(yo)	colgaré	colgaría
(tú)	colgarás	colgarías
(él/ella/usted)	colgará	colgaría
(nosotros/as)	colgaremos	colgaríamos
(vosotros/as)	colgaréis	colgaríais
(ellos/ellas/ ustedes)	colgarán	colgarían

	PRESENT SUBJUNCTIVE	IMPERFECT SUBJUNCTIVE
(yo)	cuelgue	colgara or colgase
(tú)	cuelgues	colgaras or colgases
(él/ella/usted)	cuelgue	colgara or colgase
(nosotros/as)	colguemos	colgáramos or colgásemos
(vosotros/as)	colguéis	colgarais or colgaseis
(ellos/ellas/ ustedes)	cuelguen	colgaran or colgasen

IMPERATIVE

cuelga / colgad

Use the present subjunctive in all cases other than these tú and vosotros affirmative forms.

EXAMPLE PHRASES

Colgaremos el cuadro en esa pared. We'll hang the picture on that wall.

Dile que no **cuelgue** el jersey en la silla. Tell her not to hang her sweater on the back of the chair.

No **cuelgue**, por favor. Please don't hang up.

¡**Cuelga**, por favor, que quiero hacer una llamada! Please hang up. I want to use the phone!

Remember that subject pronouns are not used very often in Spanish.

comer (to eat)

	PRESENT	PRESENT PERFECT
(yo)	como	he comido
(tú)	comes	has comido
(él/ella/usted)	come	ha comido
(nosotros/as)	comemos	hemos comido
(vosotros/as)	coméis	habéis comido
(ellos/ellas/ustedes)	comen	han comido

	PRETERITE	IMPERFECT
(yo)	comí	comía
(tú)	comiste	comías
(él/ella/usted)	comió	comía
(nosotros/as)	comimos	comíamos
(vosotros/as)	comisteis	comíais
(ellos/ellas/ustedes)	comieron	comían

GERUND	PAST PARTICIPLE
comiendo	comido

EXAMPLE PHRASES

No **come** carne. He doesn't eat meat.

Se lo **ha comido** todo. He's eaten it all.

Comimos en un restaurante. We had lunch in a restaurant.

Siempre **comían** demasiado. They always ate too much.

Remember that subject pronouns are not used very often in Spanish.

comer

	FUTURE	CONDITIONAL
(yo)	comeré	comería
(tú)	comerás	comerías
(él/ella/usted)	comerá	comería
(nosotros/as)	comeremos	comeríamos
(vosotros/as)	comeréis	comeríais
(ellos/ellas/ ustedes)	comerán	comerían

	PRESENT SUBJUNCTIVE	IMPERFECT SUBJUNCTIVE
(yo)	coma	comiera or comiese
(tú)	comas	comieras or comieses
(él/ella/usted)	coma	comiera or comiese
(nosotros/as)	comamos	comiéramos or comiésemos
(vosotros/as)	comáis	comierais or comieseis
(ellos/ellas/ ustedes)	coman	comieran or comiesen

IMPERATIVE

come / comed

Use the present subjunctive in all cases other than these tú and vosotros affirmative forms.

EXAMPLE PHRASES

Me lo **comeré** yo. I'll eat it.

Si no fuera por mí, no **comeríamos**. We wouldn't eat if it weren't for me.

Si **comieras** más, no estarías tan delgado. You wouldn't be so thin if you ate more.

No **comas** tan deprisa. Don't eat so fast.

Remember that subject pronouns are not used very often in Spanish.

conducir (to drive, to lead)

	PRESENT	PRESENT PERFECT
(yo)	conduzco	he conducido
(tú)	conduces	has conducido
(él/ella/usted)	conduce	ha conducido
(nosotros/as)	conducimos	hemos conducido
(vosotros/as)	conducís	habéis conducido
(ellos/ellas/ustedes)	conducen	han conducido

	PRETERITE	IMPERFECT
(yo)	conduje	conducía
(tú)	condujiste	conducías
(él/ella/usted)	condujo	conducía
(nosotros/as)	condujimos	conducíamos
(vosotros/as)	condujisteis	conducíais
(ellos/ellas/ustedes)	condujeron	conducían

GERUND	PAST PARTICIPLE
conduciendo	conducido

EXAMPLE PHRASES

No sé **conducir**. I can't drive.

Conduces muy bien. You're a very good driver.

Enfadarte no te **ha conducido** a nada. Getting angry hasn't got you anywhere.

La pista nos **condujo** hasta él. The clue led us to him.

¿**Conducías** tú? Was it you driving?

Remember that subject pronouns are not used very often in Spanish.

conducir

	FUTURE	CONDITIONAL
(yo)	conduciré	conduciría
(tú)	conducirás	conducirías
(él/ella/usted)	conducirá	conduciría
(nosotros/as)	conduciremos	conduciríamos
(vosotros/as)	conduciréis	conduciríais
(ellos/ellas/ ustedes)	conducirán	conducirían

	PRESENT SUBJUNCTIVE	IMPERFECT SUBJUNCTIVE
(yo)	conduzca	condujera or condujese
(tú)	conduzcas	condujeras or condujeses
(él/ella/usted)	conduzca	condujera or condujese
(nosotros/as)	conduzcamos	condujéramos or condujésemos
(vosotros/as)	conduzcáis	condujerais or condujeseis
(ellos/ellas/ ustedes)	conduzcan	condujeran or condujesen

IMPERATIVE
conduce / conducid

Use the present subjunctive in all cases other than these tú and vosotros affirmative forms.

EXAMPLE PHRASES
El camarero les **conducirá** a su mesa. The waiter will show you to your table.

Si bebes, no **conduzcas**. Don't drink and drive.

Le pedí que **condujera** más despacio. I asked him to drive more slowly.

Conduzca con cuidado. Drive carefully.

Remember that subject pronouns are not used very often in Spanish.

conocer (to know)

	PRESENT		PRESENT PERFECT
(yo)	conozco		he conocido
(tú)	conoces		has conocido
(él/ella/usted)	conoce		ha conocido
(nosotros/as)	conocemos		hemos conocido
(vosotros/as)	conocéis		habéis conocido
(ellos/ellas/ustedes)	conocen		han conocido

	PRETERITE		IMPERFECT
(yo)	conocí		conocía
(tú)	conociste		conocías
(él/ella/usted)	conoció		conocía
(nosotros/as)	conocimos		conocíamos
(vosotros/as)	conocisteis		conocíais
(ellos/ellas/ustedes)	conocieron		conocían

GERUND

conociendo

PAST PARTICIPLE

conocido

EXAMPLE PHRASES

Conozco un restaurante donde se come bien. I know a restaurant where the food is very good.

Nunca **he conocido** a nadie así. I've never met anybody like that.

La **conocí** en una fiesta. I met her at a party.

Nos conocíamos desde hacía años. We'd known each other for years.

Remember that subject pronouns are not used very often in Spanish.

conocer

	FUTURE	CONDITIONAL
(yo)	conoceré	conocería
(tú)	conocerás	conocerías
(él/ella/usted)	conocerá	conocería
(nosotros/as)	conoceremos	conoceríamos
(vosotros/as)	conoceréis	conoceríais
(ellos/ellas/ ustedes)	conocerán	conocerían

	PRESENT SUBJUNCTIVE	IMPERFECT SUBJUNCTIVE
(yo)	conozca	conociera or conociese
(tú)	conozcas	conocieras or conocieses
(él/ella/usted)	conozca	conociera or conociese
(nosotros/as)	conozcamos	conociéramos or conociésemos
(vosotros/as)	conozcáis	conocierais or conocieseis
(ellos/ellas/ ustedes)	conozcan	conocieran or conociesen

IMPERATIVE

conoce / conoced

Use the present subjunctive in all cases other than these tú and vosotros affirmative forms.

EXAMPLE PHRASES

No sé si la **conocerás** cuando la veas. I don't know if you'll recognize her when you see her.

No quiero que mis padres lo **conozcan**. I don't want my parents to meet him.

Si no la **conociera**, pensaría que lo hizo queriendo. If I didn't know her better, I'd think she had done it on purpose.

Remember that subject pronouns are not used very often in Spanish.

construir (to build)

	PRESENT	PRESENT PERFECT
(yo)	construyo	he construido
(tú)	construyes	has construido
(él/ella/usted)	construye	ha construido
(nosotros/as)	construimos	hemos construido
(vosotros/as)	construís	habéis construido
(ellos/ellas/ ustedes)	construyen	han construido

	PRETERITE	IMPERFECT
(yo)	construí	construía
(tú)	construiste	construías
(él/ella/usted)	construyó	construía
(nosotros/as)	construimos	construíamos
(vosotros/as)	construisteis	construíais
(ellos/ellas/ ustedes)	construyeron	construían

GERUND	PAST PARTICIPLE
construyendo	construido

EXAMPLE PHRASES

Construyen casas de madera. They build wooden houses.

Están construyendo una escuela. They're building a school.

Ha construido la casa él solo. He built the house on his own.

Lo **construyó** sin planos. He built it without any plans.

Su empresa **construía** puentes. His company built bridges.

Remember that subject pronouns are not used very often in Spanish.

construir

	FUTURE	CONDITIONAL
(yo)	construiré	construiría
(tú)	construirás	construirías
(él/ella/usted)	construirá	construiría
(nosotros/as)	construiremos	construiríamos
(vosotros/as)	construiréis	construiríais
(ellos/ellas/ustedes)	construirán	construirían

	PRESENT SUBJUNCTIVE	IMPERFECT SUBJUNCTIVE
(yo)	construya	construyera or construyese
(tú)	construyas	construyeras or construyeses
(él/ella/usted)	construya	construyera or construyese
(nosotros/as)	construyamos	construyéramos or construyésemos
(vosotros/as)	construyáis	construyerais or construyeseis
(ellos/ellas/ustedes)	construyan	construyeran or construyesen

IMPERATIVE

construye / construid

Use the present subjunctive in all cases other than these tú and vosotros affirmative forms.

EXAMPLE PHRASES

Aquí **construirán** una autopista. They're going to build a new highway here.

Yo **construiría** la oración de otra forma. I'd construct the sentence differently.

Le pedí que lo **construyera** así. I asked him to build it like this.

Remember that subject pronouns are not used very often in Spanish.

contar (to tell, to count)

	PRESENT		PRESENT PERFECT
(yo)	cuento		he contado
(tú)	cuentas		has contado
(él/ella/usted)	cuenta		ha contado
(nosotros/as)	contamos		hemos contado
(vosotros/as)	contáis		habéis contado
(ellos/ellas/ ustedes)	cuentan		han contado

	PRETERITE		IMPERFECT
(yo)	conté		contaba
(tú)	contaste		contabas
(él/ella/usted)	contó		contaba
(nosotros/as)	contamos		contábamos
(vosotros/as)	contasteis		contabais
(ellos/ellas/ ustedes)	contaron		contaban

GERUND

contando

PAST PARTICIPLE

contado

EXAMPLE PHRASES

Sabe **contar** hasta diez. She can count up to ten.

Estoy contando los días. I'm counting the days.

¿**Has contado** el dinero? Have you counted the money?

Nos **contó** un secreto. He told us a secret.

Para él sólo **contaba** su carrera. The only thing that mattered to him was his career.

Remember that subject pronouns are not used very often in Spanish.

contar

	FUTURE	CONDITIONAL
(yo)	contaré	contaría
(tú)	contarás	contarías
(él/ella/usted)	contará	contaría
(nosotros/as)	contaremos	contaríamos
(vosotros/as)	contaréis	contaríais
(ellos/ellas/ ustedes)	contarán	contarían

	PRESENT SUBJUNCTIVE	IMPERFECT SUBJUNCTIVE
(yo)	cuente	contara or contase
(tú)	cuentes	contaras or contases
(él/ella/usted)	cuente	contara or contase
(nosotros/as)	contemos	contáramos or contásemos
(vosotros/as)	contéis	contarais or contaseis
(ellos/ellas/ ustedes)	cuenten	contaran or contasen

IMPERATIVE
cuenta / contad

Use the present subjunctive in all cases other than these tú and vosotros affirmative forms.

EXAMPLE PHRASES

Prométeme que no se lo **contarás** a nadie. Promise you won't tell anyone.

Quiero que me **cuente** exactamente qué pasó. I want you to tell me exactly what happened.

Quería que le **contara** un cuento. She wanted me to tell her a story.

No **cuentes** conmigo. Don't count on me.

Venga, **cuéntamelo**. Come on, tell me.

Remember that subject pronouns are not used very often in Spanish.

crecer (to grow)

	PRESENT	PRESENT PERFECT
(yo)	crezco	he crecido
(tú)	creces	has crecido
(él/ella/usted)	crece	ha crecido
(nosotros/as)	crecemos	hemos crecido
(vosotros/as)	crecéis	habéis crecido
(ellos/ellas/ ustedes)	crecen	han crecido

	PRETERITE	IMPERFECT
(yo)	crecí	crecía
(tú)	creciste	crecías
(él/ella/usted)	creció	crecía
(nosotros/as)	crecimos	crecíamos
(vosotros/as)	crecisteis	crecíais
(ellos/ellas/ ustedes)	crecieron	crecían

GERUND
creciendo

PAST PARTICIPLE
crecido

EXAMPLE PHRASES

Esas plantas **crecen** en Chile. Those plants grow in Chile.

¡Cómo **has crecido**! Haven't you grown!

Crecimos juntos. We grew up together.

La ciudad **crecía** a pasos agigantados. The city was growing by leaps and bounds.

Sigue **creciendo** la inflación. Inflation is still going up.

Remember that subject pronouns are not used very often in Spanish.

crecer

	FUTURE	CONDITIONAL
(yo)	creceré	crecería
(tú)	crecerás	crecerías
(él/ella/usted)	crecerá	crecería
(nosotros/as)	creceremos	creceríamos
(vosotros/as)	creceréis	creceríais
(ellos/ellas/ustedes)	crecerán	crecerían

	PRESENT SUBJUNCTIVE	IMPERFECT SUBJUNCTIVE
(yo)	crezca	creciera or creciese
(tú)	crezcas	crecieras or crecieses
(él/ella/usted)	crezca	creciera or creciese
(nosotros/as)	crezcamos	creciéramos or creciésemos
(vosotros/as)	crezcáis	crecierais or crecieseis
(ellos/ellas/ustedes)	crezcan	crecieran or creciesen

IMPERATIVE

crece / creced

Use the present subjunctive in all cases other than these tú and vosotros affirmative forms.

EXAMPLE PHRASES

Este año la economía **crecerá** un 2%. The economy will grow by 2% this year.

Crecería mejor en un ambiente húmedo. It would grow better in a humid environment.

Cuando **crezca**, ya verás. When he grows up, you'll see.

Quería que sus hijos **crecieran** en otro ambiente. She wanted her children to grow up in a different environment.

Remember that subject pronouns are not used very often in Spanish.

cruzar (to cross)

	PRESENT		PRESENT PERFECT
(yo)	cruzo		he cruzado
(tú)	cruzas		has cruzado
(él/ella/usted)	cruza		ha cruzado
(nosotros/as)	cruzamos		hemos cruzado
(vosotros/as)	cruzáis		habéis cruzado
(ellos/ellas/ ustedes)	cruzan		han cruzado

	PRETERITE		IMPERFECT
(yo)	crucé		cruzaba
(tú)	cruzaste		cruzabas
(él/ella/usted)	cruzó		cruzaba
(nosotros/as)	cruzamos		cruzábamos
(vosotros/as)	cruzasteis		cruzabais
(ellos/ellas/ ustedes)	cruzaron		cruzaban

GERUND		PAST PARTICIPLE
cruzando		cruzado

EXAMPLE PHRASES

Hace tiempo que no **me cruzo** con él. I haven't seen him for a long time.

La piscina está **cruzando** los jardines. The swimming pool is on the other side of the gardens.

Se me **han cruzado** los cables. I got mixed up.

Cruzaron insultos a través de Twitter. They tweeted abuse at each other.

La carretera **cruzaba** la urbanización. The road went through the housing development.

Remember that subject pronouns are not used very often in Spanish.

cruzar

	FUTURE	CONDITIONAL
(yo)	cruzaré	cruzaría
(tú)	cruzarás	cruzarías
(él/ella/usted)	cruzará	cruzaría
(nosotros/as)	cruzaremos	cruzaríamos
(vosotros/as)	cruzaréis	cruzaríais
(ellos/ellas/ ustedes)	cruzarán	cruzarían

	PRESENT SUBJUNCTIVE	IMPERFECT SUBJUNCTIVE
(yo)	cruce	cruzara or cruzase
(tú)	cruces	cruzaras or cruzases
(él/ella/usted)	cruce	cruzara or cruzase
(nosotros/as)	crucemos	cruzáramos or cruzásemos
(vosotros/as)	crucéis	cruzarais or cruzaseis
(ellos/ellas/ ustedes)	crucen	cruzaran or cruzasen

IMPERATIVE

cruza / cruzad

Use the present subjunctive in all cases other than these tú and vosotros affirmative forms.

EXAMPLE PHRASES

Cruzarán varias especies distintas. They'll cross several different species.

Crucemos los dedos. Let's keep our fingers crossed.

Le dije que **cruzara** por el paso de cebra. I told her to cross at the pedestrian crossing.

No **cruces** la calle con el semáforo en rojo. Don't cross the road when the signal's at red.

Remember that subject pronouns are not used very often in Spanish.

cubrir (to cover)

	PRESENT		PRESENT PERFECT
(yo)	cubro		he cubierto
(tú)	cubres		has cubierto
(él/ella/usted)	cubre		ha cubierto
(nosotros/as)	cubrimos		hemos cubierto
(vosotros/as)	cubrís		habéis cubierto
(ellos/ellas/ ustedes)	cubren		han cubierto

	PRETERITE		IMPERFECT
(yo)	cubrí		cubría
(tú)	cubriste		cubrías
(él/ella/usted)	cubrió		cubría
(nosotros/as)	cubrimos		cubríamos
(vosotros/as)	cubristeis		cubríais
(ellos/ellas/ ustedes)	cubrieron		cubrían

GERUND

cubriendo

PAST PARTICIPLE

cubierto

EXAMPLE PHRASES

Esto no **cubre** los gastos. This isn't enough to cover expenses.

Le **han cubierto** con una manta. They've covered him with a blanket.

Se cubrió la cara con las manos. She covered her face with her hands.

La nieve **cubría** la montaña. The mountain was covered in snow.

Remember that subject pronouns are not used very often in Spanish.

cubrir

	FUTURE	CONDITIONAL
(yo)	cubriré	cubriría
(tú)	cubrirás	cubrirías
(él/ella/usted)	cubrirá	cubriría
(nosotros/as)	cubriremos	cubriríamos
(vosotros/as)	cubriréis	cubriríais
(ellos/ellas/ ustedes)	cubrirán	cubrirían

	PRESENT SUBJUNCTIVE	IMPERFECT SUBJUNCTIVE
(yo)	cubra	cubriera *or* cubriese
(tú)	cubras	cubrieras *or* cubrieses
(él/ella/usted)	cubra	cubriera *or* cubriese
(nosotros/as)	cubramos	cubriéramos *or* cubriésemos
(vosotros/as)	cubráis	cubrierais *or* cubrieseis
(ellos/ellas/ ustedes)	cubran	cubrieran *or* cubriesen

IMPERATIVE

cubre / cubrid

Use the present subjunctive in all cases other than these tú and vosotros affirmative forms.

EXAMPLE PHRASES

Los corredores **cubrirán** una distancia de 2 km. The runners will cover a distance of 2 km.

¿Quién **cubriría** la vacante? Who'd fill the vacancy?

Quiero que **cubras** la noticia. I want you to cover that news story.

Remember that subject pronouns are not used very often in Spanish.

dar (to give)

	PRESENT	PRESENT PERFECT
(yo)	doy	he dado
(tú)	das	has dado
(él/ella/usted)	da	ha dado
(nosotros/as)	damos	hemos dado
(vosotros/as)	dais	habéis dado
(ellos/ellas/ ustedes)	dan	han dado

	PRETERITE	IMPERFECT
(yo)	di	daba
(tú)	diste	dabas
(él/ella/usted)	dio	daba
(nosotros/as)	dimos	dábamos
(vosotros/as)	disteis	dabais
(ellos/ellas/ ustedes)	dieron	daban

GERUND

dando

PAST PARTICIPLE

dado

EXAMPLE PHRASES

Me **da** miedo la oscuridad. I'm afraid of the dark.

Le **han dado** varios premios a su película. His film has been awarded several prizes.

Nos **dieron** un par de entradas gratis. They gave us a couple of free tickets.

Mi ventana **daba** al jardín. My window looked out on the garden.

Remember that subject pronouns are not used very often in Spanish.

dar

	FUTURE	CONDITIONAL
(yo)	daré	daría
(tú)	darás	darías
(él/ella/usted)	dará	daría
(nosotros/as)	daremos	daríamos
(vosotros/as)	daréis	daríais
(ellos/ellas/ ustedes)	darán	darían

	PRESENT SUBJUNCTIVE	IMPERFECT SUBJUNCTIVE
(yo)	dé	diera or diese
(tú)	des	dieras or dieses
(él/ella/usted)	dé	diera or diese
(nosotros/as)	demos	diéramos or diésemos
(vosotros/as)	deis	dierais or dieseis
(ellos/ellas/ ustedes)	den	dieran or diesen

IMPERATIVE

da / dad

Use the present subjunctive in all cases other than these tú and vosotros affirmative forms.

EXAMPLE PHRASES

Te **daré** el número de mi móvil. I'll give you my cell phone number.

Me **daría** mucha alegría volver a verla. It would be really good to see her again.

Quiero que me lo **des** ahora mismo. I want you to give it to me right now.

Déme 2 kilos. 2 kilos please.

Remember that subject pronouns are not used very often in Spanish.

decir (to say, to tell)

	PRESENT	PRESENT PERFECT
(yo)	digo	he dicho
(tú)	dices	has dicho
(él/ella/usted)	dice	ha dicho
(nosotros/as)	decimos	hemos dicho
(vosotros/as)	decís	habéis dicho
(ellos/ellas/ ustedes)	dicen	han dicho

	PRETERITE	IMPERFECT
(yo)	dije	decía
(tú)	dijiste	decías
(él/ella/usted)	dijo	decía
(nosotros/as)	dijimos	decíamos
(vosotros/as)	dijisteis	decíais
(ellos/ellas/ ustedes)	dijeron	decían

GERUND

diciendo

PAST PARTICIPLE

dicho

EXAMPLE PHRASES

Pero ¿qué **dices**? What are you saying?

¿Te **ha dicho** lo de la boda? Has he told you about the wedding?

Me lo **dijo** ayer. He told me yesterday.

Siempre nos **decía** que tuviéramos cuidado. She always used to tell us to be careful.

Remember that subject pronouns are not used very often in Spanish.

decir

	FUTURE	CONDITIONAL
(yo)	diré	diría
(tú)	dirás	dirías
(él/ella/usted)	dirá	diría
(nosotros/as)	diremos	diríamos
(vosotros/as)	diréis	diríais
(ellos/ellas/ ustedes)	dirán	dirían

	PRESENT SUBJUNCTIVE	IMPERFECT SUBJUNCTIVE
(yo)	diga	dijera or dijese
(tú)	digas	dijeras or dijeses
(él/ella/usted)	diga	dijera or dijese
(nosotros/as)	digamos	dijéramos or dijésemos
(vosotros/as)	digáis	dijerais or dijeseis
(ellos/ellas/ ustedes)	digan	dijeran or dijesen

IMPERATIVE

di / decid

Use the present subjunctive in all cases other than these tú and **vosotros** *affirmative forms.*

EXAMPLE PHRASES

Yo **diría** que miente. I'd say he's lying.

Diga lo que **diga** no le voy a creer. Whatever he says I won't believe him.

Si me **dijeras** lo que pasa, a lo mejor podría ayudar. If you told me what was going on, I could maybe help.

No le **digas** que me has visto. Don't tell him you've seen me.

Remember that subject pronouns are not used very often in Spanish.

despreocuparse (to stop worrying)

	PRESENT	PRESENT PERFECT
(yo)	me despreocupo	me he despreocupado
(tú)	te despreocupas	te has despreocupado
(él/ella/usted)	se despreocupa	se ha despreocupado
(nosotros/as)	nos despreocupamos	nos hemos despreocupado
(vosotros/as)	os despreocupáis	os habéis despreocupado
(ellos/ellas/ ustedes)	se despreocupan	se han despreocupado

	PRETERITE	IMPERFECT
(yo)	me despreocupé	me despreocupaba
(tú)	te despreocupaste	te despreocupabas
(él/ella/usted)	se despreocupó	se despreocupaba
(nosotros/as)	nos despreocupamos	nos despreocupábamos
(vosotros/as)	os despreocupasteis	os despreocupabais
(ellos/ellas/ ustedes)	se despreocuparon	se despreocupaban

GERUND

despreocupándose, etc

PAST PARTICIPLE

despreocupado

EXAMPLE PHRASES

Deberías **despreocuparte** un poco más de las cosas. You shouldn't worry so much about things.

Se despreocupa de todo. He shows no concern for anything.

Se despreocupó del asunto. He forgot about the matter.

despreocuparse

	FUTURE	CONDITIONAL
(yo)	me despreocuparé	me despreocuparía
(tú)	te despreocuparás	te despreocuparías
(él/ella/usted)	se despreocupará	se despreocuparía
(nosotros/as)	nos despreocuparemos	nos despreocuparíamos
(vosotros/as)	os despreocuparéis	os despreocuparíais
(ellos/ellas/ ustedes)	se despreocuparán	se despreocuparían

	PRESENT SUBJUNCTIVE	IMPERFECT SUBJUNCTIVE
(yo)	me despreocupe	me despreocupara or
despreocupase		
(tú)	te despreocupes	te despreocuparas or
despreocupases		
(él/ella/usted)	se despreocupe	se despreocupara or despreocupase
(nosotros/as)	nos despreocupemos	nos despreocupáramos or despreocupásemos
(vosotros/as)	os despreocupéis	os despreocuparais or
despreocupaseis		
(ellos/ellas/	se despreocupen	se despreocuparan or
despreocupasen ustedes		

IMPERATIVE

despreocúpate / despreocupaos

Use the present subjunctive in all cases other than these tú and vosotros affirmative forms.

EXAMPLE PHRASES

Yo **me despreocuparía** de él. I wouldn't worry about him.

Despreocúpate porque ya no tiene remedio. Stop worrying because there's nothing we can do about it now.

Remember that subject pronouns are not used very often in Spanish.

detener (to stop, to arrest)

	PRESENT		PRESENT PERFECT
(yo)	detengo		he detenido
(tú)	detienes		has detenido
(él/ella/usted)	detiene		ha detenido
(nosotros/as)	detenemos		hemos detenido
(vosotros/as)	detenéis		habéis detenido
(ellos/ellas/ ustedes)	detienen		han detenido

	PRETERITE		IMPERFECT
(yo)	detuve		detenía
(tú)	detuviste		detenías
(él/ella/usted)	detuvo		detenía
(nosotros/as)	detuvimos		deteníamos
(vosotros/as)	detuvisteis		deteníais
(ellos/ellas/ ustedes)	detuvieron		detenían

GERUND

deteniendo

PAST PARTICIPLE

detenido

EXAMPLE PHRASES

Han detenido a los ladrones. They've arrested the thieves.

Nos detuvimos en el semáforo. We stopped at the lights.

¡Queda **detenido**! You are under arrest!

Remember that subject pronouns are not used very often in Spanish.

detener

	FUTURE	CONDITIONAL
(yo)	detendré	detendría
(tú)	detendrás	detendrías
(él/ella/usted)	detendrá	detendría
(nosotros/as)	detendremos	detendríamos
(vosotros/as)	detendréis	detendríais
(ellos/ellas/ ustedes)	detendrán	detendrían

	PRESENT SUBJUNCTIVE	IMPERFECT SUBJUNCTIVE
(yo)	detenga	detuviera or detuviese
(tú)	detengas	detuvieras or detuvieses
(él/ella/usted)	detenga	detuviera or detuviese
(nosotros/as)	detengamos	detuviéramos or detuviésemos
(vosotros/as)	detengáis	detuvierais or detuvieseis
(ellos/ellas/ ustedes)	detengan	detuvieran or detuviesen

IMPERATIVE
detén / detened

*Use the present subjunctive in all cases other than these **tú** and **vosotros** affirmative forms.*

EXAMPLE PHRASES

Nada la **detendrá**. Nothing will stop her.

Si **te detuvieras** a pensar, nunca harías nada. If you stopped to think, you'd never do anything.

¡**Deténgase**! Stop!

¡No **te detengas**! Don't stop!

Remember that subject pronouns are not used very often in Spanish.

dirigir (to direct, to run)

	PRESENT		PRESENT PERFECT
(yo)	dirijo		he dirigido
(tú)	diriges		has dirigido
(él/ella/usted)	dirige		ha dirigido
(nosotros/as)	dirigimos		hemos dirigido
(vosotros/as)	dirigís		habéis dirigido
(ellos/ellas/ ustedes)	dirigen		han dirigido

	PRETERITE		IMPERFECT
(yo)	dirigí		dirigía
(tú)	dirigiste		dirigías
(él/ella/usted)	dirigió		dirigía
(nosotros/as)	dirigimos		dirigíamos
(vosotros/as)	dirigisteis		dirigíais
(ellos/ellas/ ustedes)	dirigieron		dirigían

GERUND	PAST PARTICIPLE
dirigiendo	dirigido

EXAMPLE PHRASES

Dirijo esta empresa desde hace dos años. I've been running this company for two years.

Ha dirigido varias películas. She has directed several films.

No le **dirigió** la palabra. She didn't say a word to him.

Se **dirigía** a la parada de autobús. He was making his way to the bus stop.

Remember that subject pronouns are not used very often in Spanish.

dirigir

	FUTURE	CONDITIONAL
(yo)	dirigiré	dirigiría
(tú)	dirigirás	dirigirías
(él/ella/usted)	dirigirá	dirigiría
(nosotros/as)	dirigiremos	dirigiríamos
(vosotros/as)	dirigiréis	dirigiríais
(ellos/ellas/ ustedes)	dirigirán	dirigirían

	PRESENT SUBJUNCTIVE	IMPERFECT SUBJUNCTIVE
(yo)	dirija	dirigiera or dirigiese
(tú)	dirijas	dirigieras or dirigieses
(él/ella/usted)	dirija	dirigiera or dirigiese
(nosotros/as)	dirijamos	dirigiéramos or dirigiésemos
(vosotros/as)	dirijáis	dirigierais or dirigieseis
(ellos/ellas/ ustedes)	dirijan	dirigieran or dirigiesen

IMPERATIVE

dirige / dirigid

Use the present subjunctive in all cases other than these tú and vosotros affirmative forms.

EXAMPLE PHRASES

Dirigirá la expedición. He'll be leading the expedition.

Para más información **diríjase** al apartado de correos número 1002.
  For further information write to PO Box 1002.

Remember that subject pronouns are not used very often in Spanish.

distinguir (to distinguish)

	PRESENT	PRESENT PERFECT
(yo)	distingo	he distinguido
(tú)	distingues	has distinguido
(él/ella/usted)	distingue	ha distinguido
(nosotros/as)	distinguimos	hemos distinguido
(vosotros/as)	distinguís	habéis distinguido
(ellos/ellas/ustedes)	distinguen	han distinguido

	PRETERITE	IMPERFECT
(yo)	distinguí	distinguía
(tú)	distinguiste	distinguías
(él/ella/usted)	distinguió	distinguía
(nosotros/as)	distinguimos	distinguíamos
(vosotros/as)	distinguisteis	distinguíais
(ellos/ellas/ustedes)	distinguieron	distinguían

GERUND

distinguiendo

PAST PARTICIPLE

distinguido

EXAMPLE PHRASES

No lo **distingo** del azul. I can't tell the difference between it and the blue one.

Nos **ha distinguido** con su presencia. He has honored us with his presence.

Se **distinguió** por su gran valentía. He distinguished himself by his bravery.

Se **distinguía** desde lejos. You could see it from the distance.

Remember that subject pronouns are not used very often in Spanish.

distinguir

	FUTURE	CONDITIONAL
(yo)	distinguiré	distinguiría
(tú)	distinguirás	distinguirías
(él/ella/usted)	distinguirá	distinguiría
(nosotros/as)	distinguiremos	distinguiríamos
(vosotros/as)	distinguiréis	distinguiríais
(ellos/ellas/ustedes)	distinguirán	distinguirían

	PRESENT SUBJUNCTIVE	IMPERFECT SUBJUNCTIVE
(yo)	distinga	distinguiera or distinguiese
(tú)	distingas	distinguieras or distinguieses
(él/ella/usted)	distinga	distinguiera or distinguiese
(nosotros/as)	distingamos	distinguiéramos or distinguiésemos
(vosotros/as)	distingáis	distinguierais or distinguieseis
(ellos/ellas/ustedes)	distingan	distinguieran or distinguiesen

IMPERATIVE

distingue / distinguid

Use the present subjunctive in all cases other than these tú and vosotros affirmative forms.

EXAMPLE PHRASES

Al final **distinguirás** unas notas de otras. Eventually you'll be able to tell one note from another.

No los **distinguiría**. I wouldn't be able to tell them apart.

Remember that subject pronouns are not used very often in Spanish.

divertir (to entertain)

	PRESENT		PRESENT PERFECT
(yo)	divierto		he divertido
(tú)	diviertes		has divertido
(él/ella/usted)	divierte		ha divertido
(nosotros/as)	divertimos		hemos divertido
(vosotros/as)	divertís		habéis divertido
(ellos/ellas/ ustedes)	divierten		han divertido

	PRETERITE		IMPERFECT
(yo)	divertí		divertía
(tú)	divertiste		divertías
(él/ella/usted)	divirtió		divertía
(nosotros/as)	divertimos		divertíamos
(vosotros/as)	divertisteis		divertíais
(ellos/ellas/ ustedes)	divirtieron		divertían

GERUND	PAST PARTICIPLE
divirtiendo	divertido

EXAMPLE PHRASES

Cantamos sólo para **divertirnos**. We sing just for fun.

Me **divierte** verlos tan serios. It's amusing to see them looking so serious.

¿**Os habéis divertido** en la fiesta? Did you enjoy the party?

Nos **divirtió** con sus anécdotas. He entertained us with his stories.

Nos divertíamos mucho jugando en la playa. We had a great time playing on the beach.

Remember that subject pronouns are not used very often in Spanish.

divertir

	FUTURE	CONDITIONAL
(yo)	divertiré	divertiría
(tú)	divertirás	divertirías
(él/ella/usted)	divertirá	divertiría
(nosotros/as)	divertiremos	divertiríamos
(vosotros/as)	divertiréis	divertiríais
(ellos/ellas/ustedes)	divertirán	divertirían

	PRESENT SUBJUNCTIVE	IMPERFECT SUBJUNCTIVE
(yo)	divierta	divirtiera *or* divirtiese
(tú)	diviertas	divirtieras *or* divirtieses
(él/ella/usted)	divierta	divirtiera *or* divirtiese
(nosotros/as)	divirtamos	divirtiéramos *or* divirtiésemos
(vosotros/as)	divirtáis	divirtierais *or* divirtieseis
(ellos/ellas/ustedes)	diviertan	divirtieran *or* divirtiesen

IMPERATIVE

divierte / divertid

Use the present subjunctive in all cases other than these **tú** *and* **vosotros** *affirmative forms.*

EXAMPLE PHRASES

Si vieras esta serie, **te divertirías** mucho. If you watched this series you'd really enjoy it.

Hizo lo posible por que **se divirtieran**. He did everything he could to make it fun for them.

¡Que **te diviertas**! Have a good time!

Remember that subject pronouns are not used very often in Spanish.

dormir (to sleep)

	PRESENT		PRESENT PERFECT
(yo)	duermo		he dormido
(tú)	duermes		has dormido
(él/ella/usted)	duerme		ha dormido
(nosotros/as)	dormimos		hemos dormido
(vosotros/as)	dormís		habéis dormido
(ellos/ellas/ ustedes)	duermen		han dormido

	PRETERITE		IMPERFECT
(yo)	dormí		dormía
(tú)	dormiste		dormías
(él/ella/usted)	durmió		dormía
(nosotros/as)	dormimos		dormíamos
(vosotros/as)	dormisteis		dormíais
(ellos/ellas/ ustedes)	durmieron		dormían

GERUND	PAST PARTICIPLE
durmiendo	dormido

EXAMPLE PHRASES

No **duermo** muy bien. I don't sleep very well.

Está durmiendo. She's asleep.

He dormido de un tirón. I slept like a log.

Se me **durmió** la pierna. My leg went to sleep.

Se dormía en clase. She would fall asleep in class.

Remember that subject pronouns are not used very often in Spanish.

dormir

	FUTURE	CONDITIONAL
(yo)	dormiré	dormiría
(tú)	dormirás	dormirías
(él/ella/usted)	dormirá	dormiría
(nosotros/as)	dormiremos	dormiríamos
(vosotros/as)	dormiréis	dormiríais
(ellos/ellas/ ustedes)	dormirán	dormirían

	PRESENT SUBJUNCTIVE	IMPERFECT SUBJUNCTIVE
(yo)	duerma	durmiera or durmiese
(tú)	duermas	durmieras or durmieses
(él/ella/usted)	duerma	durmiera or durmiese
(nosotros/as)	durmamos	durmiéramos or durmiésemos
(vosotros/as)	durmáis	durmierais or durmieseis
(ellos/ellas/ ustedes)	duerman	durmieran or durmiesen

IMPERATIVE

duerme / dormid

Use the present subjunctive in all cases other than these tú and vosotros affirmative forms.

EXAMPLE PHRASES

Si no tomo café, **me dormiré**. I'll fall asleep if I don't have some coffee.

Yo no **dormiría** en esa casa. I wouldn't sleep in that house.

Quiero que **duermas** la siesta. I want you to have a nap.

Si **durmieras** más horas, no estarías tan cansada. You wouldn't be so tired if you slept for longer.

Remember that subject pronouns are not used very often in Spanish.

elegir (to choose)

	PRESENT	PRESENT PERFECT
(yo)	elijo	he elegido
(tú)	eliges	has elegido
(él/ella/usted)	elige	ha elegido
(nosotros/as)	elegimos	hemos elegido
(vosotros/as)	elegís	habéis elegido
(ellos/ellas/ ustedes)	eligen	han elegido

	PRETERITE	IMPERFECT
(yo)	elegí	elegía
(tú)	elegiste	elegías
(él/ella/usted)	eligió	elegía
(nosotros/as)	elegimos	elegíamos
(vosotros/as)	elegisteis	elegíais
(ellos/ellas/ ustedes)	eligieron	elegían

GERUND
eligiendo

PAST PARTICIPLE
elegido

EXAMPLE PHRASES

Te dan a **elegir** entre dos modelos. You get a choice of two models.

Nosotros no **elegimos** a nuestros padres, ni ellos nos **eligen** a nosotros.
    We don't choose our parents and they don't choose us either.

Creo que **ha elegido** bien. I think he's made a good choice.

No lo **eligieron** ellos. It wasn't they who chose it.

Remember that subject pronouns are not used very often in Spanish.

elegir

	FUTURE	CONDITIONAL
(yo)	elegiré	elegiría
(tú)	elegirás	elegirías
(él/ella/usted)	elegirá	elegiría
(nosotros/as)	elegiremos	elegiríamos
(vosotros/as)	elegiréis	elegiríais
(ellos/ellas/ ustedes)	elegirán	elegirían

	PRESENT SUBJUNCTIVE	IMPERFECT SUBJUNCTIVE
(yo)	elija	eligiera or eligiese
(tú)	elijas	eligieras or eligieses
(él/ella/usted)	elija	eligiera or eligiese
(nosotros/as)	elijamos	eligiéramos or eligiésemos
(vosotros/as)	elijáis	eligierais or eligieseis
(ellos/ellas/ ustedes)	elijan	eligieran or eligiesen

IMPERATIVE

elige / elegid

Use the present subjunctive in all cases other than these **tú** *and* **vosotros** *affirmative forms.*

EXAMPLE PHRASES

Yo **elegiría** el más caro. I'd choose the most expensive one.

Elija una carta. Choose a card.

Remember that subject pronouns are not used very often in Spanish.

empezar (to begin)

	PRESENT		PRESENT PERFECT
(yo)	empiezo		he empezado
(tú)	empiezas		has empezado
(él/ella/usted)	empieza		ha empezado
(nosotros/as)	empezamos		hemos empezado
(vosotros/as)	empezáis		habéis empezado
(ellos/ellas/ ustedes)	empiezan		han empezado

	PRETERITE		IMPERFECT
(yo)	empecé		empezaba
(tú)	empezaste		empezabas
(él/ella/usted)	empezó		empezaba
(nosotros/as)	empezamos		empezábamos
(vosotros/as)	empezasteis		empezabais
(ellos/ellas/ ustedes)	empezaron		empezaban

GERUND

empezando

PAST PARTICIPLE

empezado

EXAMPLE PHRASES

Está a punto de **empezar**. It's about to start.

¿Cuándo **empiezas** a trabajar en el sitio nuevo? When do you start work at the new place?

Ha empezado a nevar. It's begun to snow.

Las vacaciones **empezaron** el quince. The vacation started on the fifteenth.

Empezaba por *p*. It began with *p*.

Remember that subject pronouns are not used very often in Spanish.

empezar

	FUTURE	CONDITIONAL
(yo)	empezaré	empezaría
(tú)	empezarás	empezarías
(él/ella/usted)	empezará	empezaría
(nosotros/as)	empezaremos	empezaríamos
(vosotros/as)	empezaréis	empezaríais
(ellos/ellas/ ustedes)	empezarán	empezarían

	PRESENT SUBJUNCTIVE	IMPERFECT SUBJUNCTIVE
(yo)	empiece	empezara or empezase
(tú)	empieces	empezaras or empezases
(él/ella/usted)	empiece	empezara or empezase
(nosotros/as)	empecemos	empezáramos or empezásemos
(vosotros/as)	empecéis	empezarais or empezaseis
(ellos/ellas/ ustedes)	empiecen	empezaran or empezasen

IMPERATIVE

empieza / empezad

Use the present subjunctive in all cases other than these tú and vosotros affirmative forms.

EXAMPLE PHRASES

La semana que viene **empezaremos** un curso nuevo. We'll start a new course next week.

Yo **empezaría** desde cero. I'd start from scratch.

Quiero que **empieces** ya. I want you to start now.

Si **empezáramos** ahora, acabaríamos a las diez. If we started now, we'd be finished by ten.

Empieza por aquí. Start here.

Remember that subject pronouns are not used very often in Spanish.

enfrentarse (a to face)

	PRESENT	PRESENT PERFECT
(yo)	me enfrento	me he enfrentado
(tú)	te enfrentas	te has enfrentado
(él/ella/usted)	se enfrenta	se ha enfrentado
(nosotros/as)	nos enfrentamos	nos hemos enfrentado
(vosotros/as)	os enfrentáis	os habéis enfrentado
(ellos/ellas/ ustedes)	se enfrentan	se han enfrentado

	PRETERITE	IMPERFECT
(yo)	me enfrenté	me enfrentaba
(tú)	te enfrentaste	te enfrentabas
(él/ella/usted)	se enfrentó	se enfrentaba
(nosotros/as)	nos enfrentamos	nos enfrentábamos
(vosotros/as)	os enfrentasteis	os enfrentabais
(ellos/ellas/ ustedes)	se enfrentaron	se enfrentaban

GERUND

enfrentándose, etc

PAST PARTICIPLE

enfrentado

EXAMPLE PHRASES

Tienes que **enfrentarte** al problema. You have to face up to the problem.

Hoy **se enfrentan** los dos semifinalistas. The two semifinalists meet today.

Padre e hijo **se han enfrentado** varias veces. Father and son have had several confrontations.

Se enfrentaban a un futuro incierto. They faced an uncertain future.

enfrentarse

	FUTURE	CONDITIONAL
(yo)	me enfrentaré	me enfrentaría
(tú)	te enfrentarás	te enfrentarías
(él/ella/usted)	se enfrentará	se enfrentaría
(nosotros/as)	nos enfrentaremos	nos enfrentaríamos
(vosotros/as)	os enfrentaréis	os enfrentaríais
(ellos/ellas/ ustedes)	se enfrentarán	se enfrentarían

	PRESENT SUBJUNCTIVE	IMPERFECT SUBJUNCTIVE
(yo)	me enfrente	me enfrentara or enfrentase
(tú)	te enfrentes	te enfrentaras or enfrentases
(él/ella/usted)	se enfrente	se enfrentara or enfrentase
(nosotros/as)	nos enfrentemos	nos enfrentáramos or enfrentásemos
(vosotros/as)	os enfrentéis	os enfrentarais or enfrentaseis
(ellos/ellas/ ustedes)	se enfrenten	se enfrentaran or enfrentasen

IMPERATIVE

enfréntate / enfrentaos

Use the present subjunctive in all cases other than these tú and vosotros affirmative forms.

EXAMPLE PHRASES

El héroe **se enfrentará** a todo tipo de peligros. The hero will have to face all kinds of dangers.

No **te enfrentes** con él. Don't confront him.

Remember that subject pronouns are not used very often in Spanish.

entender (to understand)

	PRESENT	PRESENT PERFECT
(yo)	entiendo	he entendido
(tú)	entiendes	has entendido
(él/ella/usted)	entiende	ha entendido
(nosotros/as)	entendemos	hemos entendido
(vosotros/as)	entendéis	habéis entendido
(ellos/ellas/ ustedes)	entienden	han entendido

	PRETERITE	IMPERFECT
(yo)	entendí	entendía
(tú)	entendiste	entendías
(él/ella/usted)	entendió	entendía
(nosotros/as)	entendimos	entendíamos
(vosotros/as)	entendisteis	entendíais
(ellos/ellas/ ustedes)	entendieron	entendían

GERUND

entendiendo

PAST PARTICIPLE

entendido

EXAMPLE PHRASES

No lo vas a **entender**. You won't understand.

No **entiendo** las instrucciones. I don't understand the instructions.

Estás entendiéndolo todo al revés. You're getting the wrong end of the stick.

Creo que lo **he entendido** mal. I think I've misunderstood.

¿**Entendiste** lo que dijo? Did you understand what she said?

Mi hermano **entendía** mucho de videojuegos. My brother knew a lot about video games.

Remember that subject pronouns are not used very often in Spanish.

entender

	FUTURE	CONDITIONAL
(yo)	entenderé	entendería
(tú)	entenderás	entenderías
(él/ella/usted)	entenderá	entendería
(nosotros/as)	entenderemos	entenderíamos
(vosotros/as)	entenderéis	entenderíais
(ellos/ellas/ustedes)	entenderán	entenderían

	PRESENT SUBJUNCTIVE	IMPERFECT SUBJUNCTIVE
(yo)	entienda	entendiera or entendiese
(tú)	entiendas	entendieras or entendieses
(él/ella/usted)	entienda	entendiera or entendiese
(nosotros/as)	entendamos	entendiéramos or entendiésemos
(vosotros/as)	entendáis	entendierais or entendieseis
(ellos/ellas/ustedes)	entiendan	entendieran or entendiesen

IMPERATIVE

entiende / entended

*Use the present subjunctive in all cases other than these **tú** and **vosotros** affirmative forms.*

EXAMPLE PHRASES

Con el tiempo lo **entenderás**. You'll understand one day.

Yo no lo **entendería** así. I wouldn't interpret it like that.

Si **entendieras** español, te encantaría el libro. If you understood Spanish, you'd love the book.

No me **entiendas** mal. Don't misunderstand me.

Remember that subject pronouns are not used very often in Spanish.

enviar (to send)

	PRESENT	PRESENT PERFECT
(yo)	envío	he enviado
(tú)	envías	has enviado
(él/ella/usted)	envía	ha enviado
(nosotros/as)	enviamos	hemos enviado
(vosotros/as)	enviáis	habéis enviado
(ellos/ellas/ustedes)	envían	han enviado

	PRETERITE	IMPERFECT
(yo)	envié	enviaba
(tú)	enviaste	enviabas
(él/ella/usted)	envió	enviaba
(nosotros/as)	enviamos	enviábamos
(vosotros/as)	enviasteis	enviabais
(ellos/ellas/ustedes)	enviaron	enviaban

GERUND

enviando

PAST PARTICIPLE

enviado

EXAMPLE PHRASES

¿Cómo lo vas a **enviar**? How are you going to send it?

Les **envío** el trabajo por correo electrónico. I send them my work by email.

Ya **está enviando** las invitaciones. She has already started sending out the invitations.

La **han enviado** a Guatemala. They've sent her to Guatemala.

Le **envió** el regalo por correo. He posted her the present.

Me **enviaba** siempre a mí a hacer los recados. She always sent me to do the errands.

Remember that subject pronouns are not used very often in Spanish.

enviar

	FUTURE	CONDITIONAL
(yo)	enviaré	enviaría
(tú)	enviarás	enviarías
(él/ella/usted)	enviará	enviaría
(nosotros/as)	enviaremos	enviaríamos
(vosotros/as)	enviaréis	enviaríais
(ellos/ellas/ustedes)	enviarán	enviarían

	PRESENT SUBJUNCTIVE	IMPERFECT SUBJUNCTIVE
(yo)	envíe	enviara or enviase
(tú)	envíes	enviaras or enviases
(él/ella/usted)	envíe	enviara or enviase
(nosotros/as)	enviemos	enviáramos or enviásemos
(vosotros/as)	enviéis	enviarais or enviaseis
(ellos/ellas/ustedes)	envíen	enviaran or enviasen

IMPERATIVE

envía / enviad

Use the present subjunctive in all cases other than these tú and vosotros affirmative forms.

EXAMPLE PHRASES

Nos **enviarán** más información. They'll send us further information.

Yo lo **enviaría** por mensajero. I'd send it by courier.

Necesitamos que lo **envíes** inmediatamente. We need you to send it immediately.

Si lo **enviaras** ahora, llegaría el lunes. If you sent it now it would get there on Monday.

No lo **envíes** sin repasarlo antes. Don't send it in without checking it first.

Envíe sus datos personales. Send in your details.

Remember that subject pronouns are not used very often in Spanish.

equivocarse (to make a mistake, to be wrong)

	PRESENT	PRESENT PERFECT
(yo)	me equivoco	me he equivocado
(tú)	te equivocas	te has equivocado
(él/ella/usted)	se equivoca	se ha equivocado
(nosotros/as)	nos equivocamos	nos hemos equivocado
(vosotros/as)	os equivocáis	os habéis equivocado
(ellos/ellas/ ustedes)	se equivocan	se han equivocado

	PRETERITE	IMPERFECT
(yo)	me equivoqué	me equivocaba
(tú)	te equivocaste	te equivocabas
(él/ella/usted)	se equivocó	se equivocaba
(nosotros/as)	nos equivocamos	nos equivocábamos
(vosotros/as)	os equivocasteis	os equivocabais
(ellos/ellas/ ustedes)	se equivocaron	se equivocaban

GERUND
equivocándose, etc

PAST PARTICIPLE
equivocado

EXAMPLE PHRASES

Si crees que voy a dejarte ir, **te equivocas**. If you think I'm going to let you go, you're wrong.

Perdone, **me he equivocado** de número. Sorry, I've got the wrong number.

Se equivocaron de tren. They got the wrong train.

Siempre **se equivocaba** de calle. He was always taking the wrong turning.

Remember that subject pronouns are not used very often in Spanish.

equivocarse

	FUTURE	CONDITIONAL
(yo)	me equivocaré	me equivocaría
(tú)	te equivocarás	te equivocarías
(él/ella/usted)	se equivocará	se equivocaría
(nosotros/as)	nos equivocaremos	nos equivocaríamos
(vosotros/as)	os equivocaréis	os equivocaríais
(ellos/ellas/ustedes)	se equivocarán	se equivocarían

	PRESENT SUBJUNCTIVE	IMPERFECT SUBJUNCTIVE
(yo)	me equivoque	me equivocara or equivocase
(tú)	te equivoques	te equivocaras or equivocases
(él/ella/usted)	se equivoque	se equivocara or equivocase
(nosotros/as)	nos equivoquemos	nos equivocáramos or equivocásemos
(vosotros/as)	os equivoquéis	os equivocarais or equivocaseis
(ellos/ellas/ustedes)	se equivoquen	se equivocaran or equivocasen

IMPERATIVE

equivócate / equivocaos

Use the present subjunctive in all cases other than these **tú** *and* **vosotros** *affirmative forms.*

EXAMPLE PHRASES

Sobre todo, no **te equivoques** de hora. Above all, don't get the time wrong.

Si **te equivocaras**, quedarías eliminado del juego. If you made a mistake, you'd be out of the game.

erguir (to erect)

	PRESENT	PRESENT PERFECT
(yo)	yergo	he erguido
(tú)	yergues	has erguido
(él/ella/usted)	yergue	ha erguido
(nosotros/as)	erguimos	hemos erguido
(vosotros/as)	erguís	habéis erguido
(ellos/ellas/ustedes)	yerguen	han erguido

	PRETERITE	IMPERFECT
(yo)	erguí	erguía
(tú)	erguiste	erguías
(él/ella/usted)	irguió	erguía
(nosotros/as)	erguimos	erguíamos
(vosotros/as)	erguisteis	erguías
(ellos/ellas/ustedes)	irguieron	erguían

GERUND

irguiendo

PAST PARTICIPLE

erguido

EXAMPLE PHRASES

El perro **irguió** las orejas. The dog pricked up its ears.

La montaña **se erguía** majestuosa sobre el valle. The mountain rose majestically above the valley.

Tú mantén siempre la cabeza bien **erguida**. You must always hold your head high.

Remember that subject pronouns are not used very often in Spanish.

erguir

	FUTURE	CONDITIONAL
(yo)	erguiré	erguiría
(tú)	erguirás	erguirías
(él/ella/usted)	erguirá	erguiría
(nosotros/as)	erguiremos	erguiríamos
(vosotros/as)	erguiréis	erguiríais
(ellos/ellas/ ustedes)	erguirán	erguirían

	PRESENT SUBJUNCTIVE	IMPERFECT SUBJUNCTIVE
(yo)	yerga	irguiera or irguiese
(tú)	yergas	irguieras or irguieses
(él/ella/usted)	yerga	irguiera or irguiese
(nosotros/as)	irgamos	irguiéramos or irguiésemos
(vosotros/as)	irgáis	irguierais or irguieseis
(ellos/ellas/ ustedes)	yergan	irguieran or irguiesen

IMPERATIVE
yergue / erguid

Use the present subjunctive in all cases other than these tú and vosotros affirmative forms.

errar (to err)

	PRESENT	PRESENT PERFECT
(yo)	yerro	he errado
(tú)	yerras	has errado
(él/ella/usted)	yerra	ha errado
(nosotros/as)	erramos	hemos errado
(vosotros/as)	erráis	habéis errado
(ellos/ellas/ ustedes)	yerran	han errado

	PRETERITE	IMPERFECT
(yo)	erré	erraba
(tú)	erraste	errabas
(él/ella/usted)	erró	erraba
(nosotros/as)	erramos	errábamos
(vosotros/as)	errasteis	errabais
(ellos/ellas/ ustedes)	erraron	erraban

GERUND	PAST PARTICIPLE
errando	errado

EXAMPLE PHRASES

Errar es humano. To err is human.

Ha errado en su decisión. She has made the wrong decision.

Erró el tiro. He missed.

errar

	FUTURE	CONDITIONAL
(yo)	erraré	erraría
(tú)	errarás	errarías
(él/ella/usted)	errará	erraría
(nosotros/as)	erraremos	erraríamos
(vosotros/as)	erraréis	erraríais
(ellos/ellas/ustedes)	errarán	errarían

	PRESENT SUBJUNCTIVE	IMPERFECT SUBJUNCTIVE
(yo)	yerre	errara or errase
(tú)	yerres	erraras or errases
(él/ella/usted)	yerre	errara or errase
(nosotros/as)	erremos	erráramos or errásemos
(vosotros/as)	erréis	errarais or erraseis
(ellos/ellas/ustedes)	yerren	erraran or errasen

IMPERATIVE

yerra / errad

Use the present subjunctive in all cases other than these tú and vosotros affirmative forms.

escribir (to write)

	PRESENT	PRESENT PERFECT
(yo)	escribo	he escrito
(tú)	escribes	has escrito
(él/ella/usted)	escribe	ha escrito
(nosotros/as)	escribimos	hemos escrito
(vosotros/as)	escribís	habéis escrito
(ellos/ellas/ ustedes)	escriben	han escrito

	PRETERITE	IMPERFECT
(yo)	escribí	escribía
(tú)	escribiste	escribías
(él/ella/usted)	escribió	escribía
(nosotros/as)	escribimos	escribíamos
(vosotros/as)	escribisteis	escribíais
(ellos/ellas/ ustedes)	escribieron	escribían

GERUND

escribiendo

PAST PARTICIPLE

escrito

EXAMPLE PHRASES

¿Cómo **se escribe** su nombre? How do you spell your name?

¿**Estás escribiendo** un correo? Are you writing an email?

Eso lo **he escrito** yo. I wrote that.

Nos escribimos durante un tiempo. We wrote to each other for a while.

Escribía canciones. She wrote songs.

El horario de apertura estaba **escrito** en un cartel. The opening hours were written on a sign.

Remember that subject pronouns are not used very often in Spanish.

escribir

	FUTURE	CONDITIONAL
(yo)	escribiré	escribiría
(tú)	escribirás	escribirías
(él/ella/usted)	escribirá	escribiría
(nosotros/as)	escribiremos	escribiríamos
(vosotros/as)	escribiréis	escribiríais
(ellos/ellas/ustedes)	escribirán	escribirían

	PRESENT SUBJUNCTIVE	IMPERFECT SUBJUNCTIVE
(yo)	escriba	escribiera or escribiese
(tú)	escribas	escribieras or escribieses
(él/ella/usted)	escriba	escribiera or escribiese
(nosotros/as)	escribamos	escribiéramos or escribiésemos
(vosotros/as)	escribáis	escribierais or escribieseis
(ellos/ellas/ustedes)	escriban	escribieran or escribiesen

IMPERATIVE

escribe / escribid

Use the present subjunctive in all cases other than these tú and vosotros affirmative forms.

EXAMPLE PHRASES

¿Me **escribirás**? Will you write to me?

Yo lo **escribiría** con mayúscula. I'd write it with a capital letter.

Te he dicho que no **escribas** en la mesa. I've told you not to write on the table.

Si de verdad **escribiera** bien, ya le habrían publicado algún libro. If he really wrote well, he'd have had a book published by now.

Escríbelo en la pizarra. Write it on the blackboard.

Remember that subject pronouns are not used very often in Spanish.

esforzarse (to make an effort)

	PRESENT		PRESENT PERFECT
(yo)	me esfuerzo		me he esforzado
(tú)	te esfuerzas		te has esforzado
(él/ella/usted)	se esfuerza		se ha esforzado
(nosotros/as)	nos esforzamos		nos hemos esforzado
(vosotros/as)	os esforzáis		os habéis esforzado
(ellos/ellas/ ustedes)	se esfuerzan		se han esforzado

	PRETERITE		IMPERFECT
(yo)	me esforcé		me esforzaba
(tú)	te esforzaste		te esforzabas
(él/ella/usted)	se esforzó		se esforzaba
(nosotros/as)	nos esforzamos		nos esforzábamos
(vosotros/as)	os esforzasteis		os esforzabais
(ellos/ellas/ ustedes)	se esforzaron		se esforzaban

GERUND

esforzándose, etc

PAST PARTICIPLE

esforzado

EXAMPLE PHRASES

Tienes que **esforzarte** si quieres ganar. You have to make an effort if you want to win.

No **te esfuerzas** lo suficiente. You don't make enough effort.

Me he esforzado, pero nada. I've tried my best but haven't got anywhere.

Se esforzó todo lo que pudo por aprobar el examen. He did everything he could to get through the exam.

Me esforzaba por entenderla. I tried hard to understand her.

Remember that subject pronouns are not used very often in Spanish.

esforzarse

	FUTURE	CONDITIONAL
(yo)	me esforzaré	me esforzaría
(tú)	te esforzarás	te esforzarías
(él/ella/usted)	se esforzará	se esforzaría
(nosotros/as)	nos esforzaremos	nos esforzaríamos
(vosotros/as)	os esforzaréis	os esforzaríais
(ellos/ellas/ ustedes)	se esforzarán	se esforzarían

	PRESENT SUBJUNCTIVE	IMPERFECT SUBJUNCTIVE
(yo)	me esfuerce	me esforzara or esforzase
(tú)	te esfuerces	te esforzaras or esforzases
(él/ella/usted)	se esfuerce	se esforzara or esforzase
(nosotros/as)	nos esforcemos	nos esforzáramos or esforzásemos
(vosotros/as)	os esforcéis	os esforzarais or esforzaseis
(ellos/ellas/ ustedes)	se esfuercen	se esforzaran or esforzasen

IMPERATIVE

esfuérzate / esforzaos

Use the present subjunctive in all cases other than these **tú** and **vosotros** affirmative forms.

EXAMPLE PHRASES

No **te esfuerces**, no me vas a convencer. Stop struggling, you're not going to convince me.

Si **te esforzaras** un poco más, lo conseguirías. You'd manage it if you made a bit more of an effort.

Remember that subject pronouns are not used very often in Spanish.

establecer (to establish)

	PRESENT	PRESENT PERFECT
(yo)	establezco	he establecido
(tú)	estableces	has establecido
(él/ella/usted)	establece	ha establecido
(nosotros/as)	establecemos	hemos establecido
(vosotros/as)	establecéis	habéis establecido
(ellos/ellas/ustedes)	establecen	han establecido

	PRETERITE	IMPERFECT
(yo)	establecí	establecía
(tú)	estableciste	establecías
(él/ella/usted)	estableció	establecía
(nosotros/as)	establecimos	establecíamos
(vosotros/as)	establecisteis	establecíais
(ellos/ellas/ustedes)	establecieron	establecían

GERUND
estableciendo

PAST PARTICIPLE
establecido

EXAMPLE PHRASES

Han logrado **establecer** contacto con el barco. They've managed to make contact with the boat.

La ley **establece** que... The law states that...

Se ha establecido una buena relación entre los dos países. A good relationship has been established between the two countries.

En 1945, la familia **se estableció** en Madrid. In 1945, the family settled in Madrid.

Remember that subject pronouns are not used very often in Spanish.

establecer

	FUTURE	CONDITIONAL
(yo)	estableceré	establecería
(tú)	establecerás	establecerías
(él/ella/usted)	establecerá	establecería
(nosotros/as)	estableceremos	estableceríamos
(vosotros/as)	estableceréis	estableceríais
(ellos/ellas/ ustedes)	establecerán	establecerían

	PRESENT SUBJUNCTIVE	IMPERFECT SUBJUNCTIVE
(yo)	establezca	estableciera or estableciese
(tú)	establezcas	establecieras or establecieses
(él/ella/usted)	establezca	estableciera or estableciese
(nosotros/as)	establezcamos	estableciéramos or estableciésemos
(vosotros/as)	establezcáis	establecierais or establecieseis
(ellos/ellas/ ustedes)	establezcan	establecieran or estableciesen

IMPERATIVE

establece / estableced

Use the present subjunctive in all cases other than these tú and vosotros affirmative forms.

EXAMPLE PHRASES

El año que viene **se establecerá** por su cuenta. Next year she'll set up on her own.

estar (to be)

	PRESENT	PRESENT PERFECT
(yo)	estoy	he estado
(tú)	estás	has estado
(él/ella/usted)	está	ha estado
(nosotros/as)	estamos	hemos estado
(vosotros/as)	estáis	habéis estado
(ellos/ellas/ ustedes)	están	han estado

	PRETERITE	IMPERFECT
(yo)	estuve	estaba
(tú)	estuviste	estabas
(él/ella/usted)	estuvo	estaba
(nosotros/as)	estuvimos	estábamos
(vosotros/as)	estuvisteis	estabais
(ellos/ellas/ ustedes)	estuvieron	estaban

GERUND	PAST PARTICIPLE
estando	estado

EXAMPLE PHRASES

Estoy cansado. I'm tired.

¿Cómo **estás**? How are you?

¿**Has estado** alguna vez en París? Have you ever been to Paris?

Estuvimos en casa de mis padres. We were at my parents'.

¿Dónde **estabas**? Where were you?

Remember that subject pronouns are not used very often in Spanish.

estar

	FUTURE	CONDITIONAL
(yo)	estaré	estaría
(tú)	estarás	estarías
(él/ella/usted)	estará	estaría
(nosotros/as)	estaremos	estaríamos
(vosotros/as)	estaréis	estaríais
(ellos/ellas/ustedes)	estarán	estarían

	PRESENT SUBJUNCTIVE	IMPERFECT SUBJUNCTIVE
(yo)	esté	estuviera or estuviese
(tú)	estés	estuvieras or estuvieses
(él/ella/usted)	esté	estuviera or estuviese
(nosotros/as)	estemos	estuviéramos or estuviésemos
(vosotros/as)	estéis	estuvierais or estuvieseis
(ellos/ellas/ustedes)	estén	estuvieran or estuviesen

IMPERATIVE

está / estad

*Use the present subjunctive in all cases other than these **tú** and **vosotros** affirmative forms.*

EXAMPLE PHRASES

¿A qué hora **estarás** en casa? What time will you be home?

Dijo que **estaría** aquí a las ocho. She said she'd be here at eight o'clock.

Avísame cuando **estés** lista. Let me know when you're ready.

No sabía que **estuviera** tan lejos. I didn't know it was so far.

¡**Estáte** quieto! Stay still!

Remember that subject pronouns are not used very often in Spanish.

evacuar (to evacuate)

	PRESENT	PRESENT PERFECT
(yo)	evacuo	he evacuado
(tú)	evacuas	has evacuado
(él/ella/usted)	evacua	ha evacuado
(nosotros/as)	evacuamos	hemos evacuado
(vosotros/as)	evacuáis	habéis evacuado
(ellos/ellas/ustedes)	evacuan	han evacuado

	PRETERITE	IMPERFECT
(yo)	evacué	evacuaba
(tú)	evacuaste	evacuabas
(él/ella/usted)	evacuó	evacuaba
(nosotros/as)	evacuamos	evacuábamos
(vosotros/as)	evacuasteis	evacuabais
(ellos/ellas/ustedes)	evacuaron	evacuaban

GERUND	PAST PARTICIPLE
evacuando	evacuado

EXAMPLE PHRASES

Van a **evacuar** a los heridos. They're going to evacuate the injured.

Han evacuado la zona. The area has been evacuated.

Remember that subject pronouns are not used very often in Spanish.

evacuar

	FUTURE	CONDITIONAL
(yo)	evacuaré	evacuaría
(tú)	evacuarás	evacuarías
(él/ella/usted)	evacuará	evacuaría
(nosotros/as)	evacuaremos	evacuaríamos
(vosotros/as)	evacuaréis	evacuaríais
(ellos/ellas/ustedes)	evacuarán	evacuarían

	PRESENT SUBJUNCTIVE	IMPERFECT SUBJUNCTIVE
(yo)	evacue	evacuara or evacuase
(tú)	evacues	evacuaras or evacuases
(él/ella/usted)	evacue	evacuara or evacuase
(nosotros/as)	evacuemos	evacuáramos or evacuásemos
(vosotros/as)	evacuéis	evacuarais or evacuaseis
(ellos/ellas/ustedes)	evacuen	evacuaran or evacuasen

IMPERATIVE

evacua / evacuad

Use the present subjunctive in all cases other than these tú and vosotros affirmative forms.

EXAMPLE PHRASES

Seguirá existiendo peligro mientras no **evacuen** el edificio. The danger won't be over while there are still people inside the building.

freír (to fry)

	PRESENT		PRESENT PERFECT
(yo)	frío		he frito
(tú)	fríes		has frito
(él/ella/usted)	fríe		ha frito
(nosotros/as)	freímos		hemos frito
(vosotros/as)	freís		habéis frito
(ellos/ellas/ ustedes)	fríen		han frito

	PRETERITE		IMPERFECT
(yo)	freí		freía
(tú)	freíste		freías
(él/ella/usted)	frio		freía
(nosotros/as)	freímos		freíamos
(vosotros/as)	freísteis		freíais
(ellos/ellas/ ustedes)	frieron		freían

GERUND

friendo

PAST PARTICIPLE

frito, freído

EXAMPLE PHRASES

No sabe ni **freír** un huevo. He can't even fry an egg.

He frito el pescado. I've fried the fish.

Se está friendo demasiado por ese lado. It's getting overdone on that side.

Lo **frió** en manteca. She fried it in lard.

Nos **freíamos** de calor. We were roasting in the heat.

Remember that subject pronouns are not used very often in Spanish.

freír

	FUTURE	CONDITIONAL
(yo)	freiré	freiría
(tú)	freirás	freirías
(él/ella/usted)	freirá	freiría
(nosotros/as)	freiremos	freiríamos
(vosotros/as)	freiréis	freiríais
(ellos/ellas/ ustedes)	freirán	freirían

	PRESENT SUBJUNCTIVE	IMPERFECT SUBJUNCTIVE
(yo)	fría	friera or friese
(tú)	frías	frieras or frieses
(él/ella/usted)	fría	friera or friese
(nosotros/as)	friamos	friéramos or friésemos
(vosotros/as)	friais	frierais or frieseis
(ellos/ellas/ ustedes)	frían	frieran or friesen

IMPERATIVE

fríe / freíd

Use the present subjunctive in all cases other than these tú and vosotros affirmative forms.

EXAMPLE PHRASES

Yo lo **freiría** con menos aceite. I'd fry it using less oil.

Fríelo en esa sartén. Fry it in that pan.

gruñir (to grumble, to growl)

	PRESENT		PRESENT PERFECT
(yo)	gruño		he gruñido
(tú)	gruñes		has gruñido
(él/ella/usted)	gruñe		ha gruñido
(nosotros/as)	gruñimos		hemos gruñido
(vosotros/as)	gruñís		habéis gruñido
(ellos/ellas/ ustedes)	gruñen		han gruñido

	PRETERITE		IMPERFECT
(yo)	gruñí		gruñía
(tú)	gruñiste		gruñías
(él/ella/usted)	gruñó		gruñía
(nosotros/as)	gruñimos		gruñíamos
(vosotros/as)	gruñisteis		gruñíais
(ellos/ellas/ ustedes)	gruñeron		gruñían

GERUND	PAST PARTICIPLE
gruñendo	gruñido

EXAMPLE PHRASES

¿A quién **gruñe** el perro? Who's the dog growling at?

Siempre **está gruñendo**. He's always grumbling.

El oso nos **gruñía** sin parar. The bear kept growling at us.

gruñir

	FUTURE	CONDITIONAL
(yo)	gruñiré	gruñiría
(tú)	gruñirás	gruñirías
(él/ella/usted)	gruñirá	gruñiría
(nosotros/as)	gruñiremos	gruñiríamos
(vosotros/as)	gruñiréis	gruñiríais
(ellos/ellas/ ustedes)	gruñirán	gruñirían

	PRESENT SUBJUNCTIVE	IMPERFECT SUBJUNCTIVE
(yo)	gruña	gruñera or gruñese
(tú)	gruñas	gruñeras or gruñeses
(él/ella/usted)	gruña	gruñera or gruñese
(nosotros/as)	gruñamos	gruñéramos or gruñésemos
(vosotros/as)	gruñáis	gruñerais or gruñeseis
(ellos/ellas/ ustedes)	gruñan	gruñeran or gruñesen

IMPERATIVE

gruñe / gruñid

Use the present subjunctive in all cases other than these tú and vosotros affirmative forms.

EXAMPLE PHRASES

¡No **gruñas** tanto! Don't grumble so much.

guiar (to guide)

	PRESENT		PRESENT PERFECT
(yo)	guío		he guiado
(tú)	guías		has guiado
(él/ella/usted)	guía		ha guiado
(nosotros/as)	guiamos		hemos guiado
(vosotros/as)	guiais		habéis guiado
(ellos/ellas/ustedes)	guían		han guiado

	PRETERITE		IMPERFECT
(yo)	guie		guiaba
(tú)	guiaste		guiabas
(él/ella/usted)	guio		guiaba
(nosotros/as)	guiamos		guiábamos
(vosotros/as)	guiasteis		guiabais
(ellos/ellas/ustedes)	guiaron		guiaban

GERUND

guiando

PAST PARTICIPLE

guiado

EXAMPLE PHRASES

Los perros **se guían** por su olfato. Dogs follow their sense of smell.

Me he guiado por el instinto. I followed my instinct.

Nos guiamos por un mapa que teníamos. We found our way using a map we had.

Siempre me protegía y me **guiaba**. He always protected me and guided me.

Remember that subject pronouns are not used very often in Spanish.

guiar

	FUTURE	CONDITIONAL
(yo)	guiaré	guiaría
(tú)	guiarás	guiarías
(él/ella/usted)	guiará	guiaría
(nosotros/as)	guiaremos	guiaríamos
(vosotros/as)	guiaréis	guiaríais
(ellos/ellas/ ustedes)	guiarán	guiarían

	PRESENT SUBJUNCTIVE	IMPERFECT SUBJUNCTIVE
(yo)	guíe	guiara or guiase
(tú)	guíes	guiaras or guiases
(él/ella/usted)	guíe	guiara or guiase
(nosotros/as)	guiemos	guiáramos or guiásemos
(vosotros/as)	guieis	guiarais or guiaseis
(ellos/ellas/ ustedes)	guíen	guiaran or guiasen

IMPERATIVE

guía / guiad

Use the present subjunctive in all cases other than these tú and vosotros affirmative forms.

EXAMPLE PHRASES

Les **guiaré** hasta allí. I'll take you there.

Guíate por la razón. Use reason as your guide.

haber (to have – *auxiliary*)

	PRESENT	PRESENT PERFECT
(yo)	he	*not used except impersonally*
(tú)	has	*See* hay
(él/ella/usted)	ha	
(nosotros/as)	hemos	
(vosotros/as)	habéis	
(ellos/ellas/ ustedes)	han	

	PRETERITE	IMPERFECT
(yo)	hube	había
(tú)	hubiste	habías
(él/ella/usted)	hubo	había
(nosotros/as)	hubimos	habíamos
(vosotros/as)	hubisteis	habíais
(ellos/ellas/ ustedes)	hubieron	habían

GERUND	PAST PARTICIPLE
habiendo	habido

EXAMPLE PHRASES

De **haberlo** sabido, **habría** ido. If I'd known, I would have gone.

¿**Has** hablado con el orientador del colegio? Have you talked to the school's careers adviser?

Eso nunca **había** pasado antes. That had never happened before.

Esta tarde va a **haber** una manifestación. There's going to be a demonstration this evening.

Remember that subject pronouns are not used very often in Spanish.

haber

	FUTURE	CONDITIONAL
(yo)	habré	habría
(tú)	habrás	habrías
(él/ella/usted)	habrá	habría
(nosotros/as)	habremos	habríamos
(vosotros/as)	habréis	habríais
(ellos/ellas/ustedes)	habrán	habrían

	PRESENT SUBJUNCTIVE	IMPERFECT SUBJUNCTIVE
(yo)	haya	hubiera or hubiese
(tú)	hayas	hubieras or hubieses
(él/ella/usted)	haya	hubiera or hubiese
(nosotros/as)	hayamos	hubiéramos or hubiésemos
(vosotros/as)	hayáis	hubierais or hubieseis
(ellos/ellas/ustedes)	hayan	hubieran or hubiesen

IMPERATIVE

not used

EXAMPLE PHRASES

Habrá que repasarlo. We'll have to check it.

Habría que limpiarlo. We should clean it.

Como se **hayan** olvidado los mato. I'll kill them if they've forgotten.

Si me lo **hubieras** dicho, te lo **habría** traído. I'd have brought it, if you'd said.

Remember that subject pronouns are not used very often in Spanish.

hablar (to speak, to talk)

	PRESENT		PRESENT PERFECT
(yo)	hablo		he hablado
(tú)	hablas		has hablado
(él/ella/usted)	habla		ha hablado
(nosotros/as)	hablamos		hemos hablado
(vosotros/as)	habláis		habéis hablado
(ellos/ellas/ ustedes)	hablan		han hablado

	PRETERITE		IMPERFECT
(yo)	hablé		hablaba
(tú)	hablaste		hablabas
(él/ella/usted)	habló		hablaba
(nosotros/as)	hablamos		hablábamos
(vosotros/as)	hablasteis		hablabais
(ellos/ellas/ ustedes)	hablaron		hablaban

GERUND

hablando

PAST PARTICIPLE

hablado

EXAMPLE PHRASES

María no **habla** inglés. María doesn't speak English.

No **nos hablamos** desde hace tiempo. We haven't spoken to each other for a long time.

Está hablando por teléfono. He's on the phone.

Hoy **he hablado** con mi hermana. I've spoken to my sister today.

¿**Has hablado** ya con el profesor? Have you spoken to the teacher yet?

Remember that subject pronouns are not used very often in Spanish.

hablar

	FUTURE	CONDITIONAL
(yo)	hablaré	hablaría
(tú)	hablarás	hablarías
(él/ella/usted)	hablará	hablaría
(nosotros/as)	hablaremos	hablaríamos
(vosotros/as)	hablaréis	hablaríais
(ellos/ellas/ ustedes)	hablarán	hablarían

	PRESENT SUBJUNCTIVE	IMPERFECT SUBJUNCTIVE
(yo)	hable	hablara or hablase
(tú)	hables	hablaras or hablases
(él/ella/usted)	hable	hablara or hablase
(nosotros/as)	hablemos	habláramos or hablásemos
(vosotros/as)	habléis	hablarais or hablaseis
(ellos/ellas/ ustedes)	hablen	hablaran or hablasen

IMPERATIVE

habla / hablad

Use the present subjunctive in all cases other than these tú and vosotros affirmative forms.

EXAMPLE PHRASES

Luego **hablaremos** de ese tema. We'll talk about that later.

Recuérdame que **hable** con Daniel. Remind me to speak to Daniel.

¿Quieres que **hablemos**? Shall we talk?

Hay que darles una oportunidad para que **hablen**. We need to give them an opportunity to speak.

Remember that subject pronouns are not used very often in Spanish.

hacer (to do, to make)

	PRESENT	PRESENT PERFECT
(yo)	hago	he hecho
(tú)	haces	has hecho
(él/ella/usted)	hace	ha hecho
(nosotros/as)	hacemos	hemos hecho
(vosotros/as)	hacéis	habéis hecho
(ellos/ellas/ustedes)	hacen	han hecho

	PRETERITE	IMPERFECT
(yo)	hice	hacía
(tú)	hiciste	hacías
(él/ella/usted)	hizo	hacía
(nosotros/as)	hicimos	hacíamos
(vosotros/as)	hicisteis	hacíais
(ellos/ellas/ustedes)	hicieron	hacían

GERUND

haciendo

PAST PARTICIPLE

hecho

EXAMPLE PHRASES

¿Qué **hace** tu padre? What does your father do?

Están haciendo mucho ruido. They're making a lot of noise.

¿Quién **hizo** eso? Who did that?

Hicieron pintar la fachada del colegio. They had the front of the school painted.

Lo **hacía** para fastidiarme. He did it to annoy me.

Remember that subject pronouns are not used very often in Spanish.

hacer

	FUTURE	CONDITIONAL
(yo)	haré	haría
(tú)	harás	harías
(él/ella/usted)	hará	haría
(nosotros/as)	haremos	haríamos
(vosotros/as)	haréis	haríais
(ellos/ellas/ ustedes)	harán	harían

	PRESENT SUBJUNCTIVE	IMPERFECT SUBJUNCTIVE
(yo)	haga	hiciera or hiciese
(tú)	hagas	hicieras or hicieses
(él/ella/usted)	haga	hiciera or hiciese
(nosotros/as)	hagamos	hiciéramos or hiciésemos
(vosotros/as)	hagáis	hicierais or hicieseis
(ellos/ellas/ ustedes)	hagan	hicieran or hiciesen

IMPERATIVE

haz / haced

Use the present subjunctive in all cases other than these tú and vosotros affirmative forms.

EXAMPLE PHRASES

Lo **haré** yo mismo. I'll do it myself.

Dijiste que lo **harías.** You said you'd do it.

¿Quieres que **haga** las camas? Do you want me to make the beds?

Preferiría que **hiciera** menos calor. I'd rather it weren't so hot.

Hazlo como te he dicho. Do it the way I told you.

Remember that subject pronouns are not used very often in Spanish.

hay (there is, there are)

PRESENT
hay

PRESENT PERFECT
ha habido

PRETERITE
hubo

IMPERFECT
había

GERUND
habiendo

PAST PARTICIPLE
habido

EXAMPLE PHRASES

Hay una iglesia en la esquina. There's a church on the corner.

Ha habido una tormenta. There's been a storm.

Hubo una guerra. There was a war.

Había mucha gente. There were a lot of people.

Remember that subject pronouns are not used very often in Spanish.

hay

FUTURE
habrá

CONDITIONAL
habría

PRESENT SUBJUNCTIVE
haya

IMPERFECT SUBJUNCTIVE
hubiera *or* hubiese

IMPERATIVE
not used

EXAMPLE PHRASES

¿**Habrá** suficiente? Will there be enough?

De este modo **habría** menos accidentes. That way there would be fewer accidents.

No creo que **haya** mucha gente en el recital. I don't think there'll be many people at the concert.

Si **hubiera** más espacio, pondría un sofá. I'd have a sofa if there were more room.

Remember that subject pronouns are not used very often in Spanish.

herir (to injure)

	PRESENT		PRESENT PERFECT
(yo)	hiero		he herido
(tú)	hieres		has herido
(él/ella/usted)	hiere		ha herido
(nosotros/as)	herimos		hemos herido
(vosotros/as)	herís		habéis herido
(ellos/ellas/ ustedes)	hieren		han herido

	PRETERITE		IMPERFECT
(yo)	herí		hería
(tú)	heriste		herías
(él/ella/usted)	hirió		hería
(nosotros/as)	herimos		heríamos
(vosotros/as)	heristeis		heríais
(ellos/ellas/ ustedes)	hirieron		herían

GERUND	PAST PARTICIPLE
hiriendo	herido

EXAMPLE PHRASES

Vas a **herir** sus sentimientos. You're going to hurt her feelings.

Me **hiere** que me digas eso. I'm hurt that you should say such a thing.

La **han herido** en el brazo. Her arm's been injured.

Lo **hirieron** en el pecho. He was wounded in the chest.

La **hería** en lo más hondo. She was deeply hurt.

Remember that subject pronouns are not used very often in Spanish.

herir

	FUTURE	CONDITIONAL
(yo)	heriré	heriría
(tú)	herirás	herirías
(él/ella/usted)	herirá	heriría
(nosotros/as)	heriremos	heriríamos
(vosotros/as)	heriréis	heriríais
(ellos/ellas/ ustedes)	herirán	herirían

	PRESENT SUBJUNCTIVE	IMPERFECT SUBJUNCTIVE
(yo)	hiera	hiriera or hiriese
(tú)	hieras	hirieras or hirieses
(él/ella/usted)	hiera	hiriera or hiriese
(nosotros/as)	hiramos	hiriéramos or hiriésemos
(vosotros/as)	hiráis	hirierais or hirieseis
(ellos/ellas/ ustedes)	hieran	hirieran or hiriesen

IMPERATIVE

hiere / herid

Use the present subjunctive in all cases other than these tú and vosotros affirmative forms.

Remember that subject pronouns are not used very often in Spanish.

huir (to escape)

	PRESENT	PRESENT PERFECT
(yo)	huyo	he huido
(tú)	huyes	has huido
(él/ella/usted)	huye	ha huido
(nosotros/as)	huimos	hemos huido
(vosotros/as)	huis	habéis huido
(ellos/ellas/ustedes)	huyen	han huido

	PRETERITE	IMPERFECT
(yo)	hui	huía
(tú)	huiste	huías
(él/ella/usted)	huyó	huía
(nosotros/as)	huimos	huíamos
(vosotros/as)	huisteis	huíais
(ellos/ellas/ustedes)	huyeron	huían

GERUND	PAST PARTICIPLE
huyendo	huido

EXAMPLE PHRASES

No sé por qué me **huye**. I don't know why he's avoiding me.

Salió **huyendo.** He ran away.

Ha huido de la cárcel. He has escaped from prison.

Huyeron del país. They fled the country.

Remember that subject pronouns are not used very often in Spanish.

huir

	FUTURE	CONDITIONAL
(yo)	huiré	huiría
(tú)	huirás	huirías
(él/ella/usted)	huirá	huiría
(nosotros/as)	huiremos	huiríamos
(vosotros/as)	huiréis	huiríais
(ellos/ellas/ ustedes)	huirán	huirían

	PRESENT SUBJUNCTIVE	IMPERFECT SUBJUNCTIVE
(yo)	huya	huyera *or* huyese
(tú)	huyas	huyeras *or* huyeses
(él/ella/usted)	huya	huyera *or* huyese
(nosotros/as)	huyamos	huyéramos *or* huyésemos
(vosotros/as)	huyáis	huyerais *or* huyeseis
(ellos/ellas/ ustedes)	huyan	huyeran *or* huyesen

IMPERATIVE
huye / huid

*Use the present subjunctive in all cases other than these **tú** and **vosotros** affirmative forms.*

EXAMPLE PHRASES

No quiero que **huyas** como un cobarde. I dont wont you to run away like a coward.

¡**Huye**! Si te atrapan, te matarán. Run! If they catch you, they'll kill you.

Remember that subject pronouns are not used very often in Spanish.

imponer (to impose)

	PRESENT	PRESENT PERFECT
(yo)	impongo	he impuesto
(tú)	impones	has impuesto
(él/ella/usted)	impone	ha impuesto
(nosotros/as)	imponemos	hemos impuesto
(vosotros/as)	imponéis	habéis impuesto
(ellos/ellas/ ustedes)	imponen	han impuesto

	PRETERITE	IMPERFECT
(yo)	impuse	imponía
(tú)	impusiste	imponías
(él/ella/usted)	impuso	imponía
(nosotros/as)	impusimos	imponíamos
(vosotros/as)	impusisteis	imponíais
(ellos/ellas/ ustedes)	impusieron	imponían

GERUND	PAST PARTICIPLE
imponiendo	impuesto

EXAMPLE PHRASES

La vista desde el acantilado **impone** un poco. The view from the cliff top is quite impressive.

La minifalda **se está imponiendo** de nuevo. The miniskirt is in fashion again.

Han impuesto la enseñanza religiosa. They have made religious education compulsory.

El corredor nigeriano **se impuso** en la segunda carrera. The Nigerian runner triumphed in the second race.

Mi abuelo **imponía** mucho respeto. My grandfather commanded a lot of respect.

Remember that subject pronouns are not used very often in Spanish.

imponer

	FUTURE	CONDITIONAL
(yo)	impondré	impondría
(tú)	impondrás	impondrías
(él/ella/usted)	impondrá	impondría
(nosotros/as)	impondremos	impondríamos
(vosotros/as)	impondréis	impondríais
(ellos/ellas/ustedes)	impondrán	impondrían

	PRESENT SUBJUNCTIVE	IMPERFECT SUBJUNCTIVE
(yo)	imponga	impusiera or impusiese
(tú)	impongas	impusieras or impusieses
(él/ella/usted)	imponga	impusiera or impusiese
(nosotros/as)	impongamos	impusiéramos or impusiésemos
(vosotros/as)	impongáis	impusierais or impusieseis
(ellos/ellas/ustedes)	impongan	impusieran or impusiesen

IMPERATIVE
impón / imponed

Use the present subjunctive in all cases other than these tú and vosotros affirmative forms.

EXAMPLE PHRASES
Impondrán multas de hasta 50 euros. They'll impose fines of up to 50 euros.

imprimir (to print)

	PRESENT		PRESENT PERFECT
(yo)	imprimo		he imprimido
(tú)	imprimes		has imprimido
(él/ella/usted)	imprime		ha imprimido
(nosotros/as)	imprimimos		hemos imprimido
(vosotros/as)	imprimís		habéis imprimido
(ellos/ellas/ustedes)	imprimen		han imprimido

	PRETERITE		IMPERFECT
(yo)	imprimí		imprimía
(tú)	imprimiste		imprimías
(él/ella/usted)	imprimió		imprimía
(nosotros/as)	imprimimos		imprimíamos
(vosotros/as)	imprimisteis		imprimíais
(ellos/ellas/ustedes)	imprimieron		imprimían

GERUND

imprimiendo

PAST PARTICIPLE

imprimido, impreso

EXAMPLE PHRASES

Una experiencia así **imprime** carácter. An experience like that is character-building.

¿**Has imprimido** el archivo? Have you printed out the file?

Se imprimieron sólo doce copias del libro. Only twelve copies of the book were printed.

El sillón **imprimía** un cierto aire de distinción al salón. The chair gave the living room a certain air of distinction.

Remember that subject pronouns are not used very often in Spanish.

imprimir

	FUTURE	CONDITIONAL
(yo)	imprimiré	imprimiría
(tú)	imprimirás	imprimirías
(él/ella/usted)	imprimirá	imprimiría
(nosotros/as)	imprimiremos	imprimiríamos
(vosotros/as)	imprimiréis	imprimiríais
(ellos/ellas/ ustedes)	imprimirán	imprimirían

	PRESENT SUBJUNCTIVE	IMPERFECT SUBJUNCTIVE
(yo)	imprima	imprimiera or imprimiese
(tú)	imprimas	imprimieras or imprimieses
(él/ella/usted)	imprima	imprimiera or imprimiese
(nosotros/as)	imprimamos	imprimiéramos or imprimiésemos
(vosotros/as)	imprimáis	imprimierais or imprimieseis
(ellos/ellas/ ustedes)	impriman	imprimieran or imprimiesen

IMPERATIVE
imprime / imprimid

*Use the present subjunctive in all cases other than these **tú** and **vosotros** affirmative forms.*

Remember that subject pronouns are not used very often in Spanish.

ir (to go)

	PRESENT		PRESENT PERFECT
(yo)	voy		he ido
(tú)	vas		has ido
(él/ella/usted)	va		ha ido
(nosotros/as)	vamos		hemos ido
(vosotros/as)	vais		habéis ido
(ellos/ellas/ustedes)	van		han ido

	PRETERITE		IMPERFECT
(yo)	fui		iba
(tú)	fuiste		ibas
(él/ella/usted)	fue		iba
(nosotros/as)	fuimos		íbamos
(vosotros/as)	fuisteis		ibais
(ellos/ellas/ustedes)	fueron		iban

GERUND

yendo

PAST PARTICIPLE

ido

EXAMPLE PHRASES

¿Puedo **ir** contigo? Can I come with you?

¿**Vamos** a comer al campo? Shall we have a picnic in the country?

Estoy yendo a clases de natación. I'm taking swimming lessons.

Ha ido a comprar el pan. She's gone to buy some bread.

Anoche **fuimos** al cine. We went to the movies last night.

Remember that subject pronouns are not used very often in Spanish.

ir

	FUTURE	**CONDITIONAL**
(yo)	iré	iría
(tú)	irás	irías
(él/ella/usted)	irá	iría
(nosotros/as)	iremos	iríamos
(vosotros/as)	iréis	iríais
(ellos/ellas/ ustedes)	irán	irían

	PRESENT SUBJUNCTIVE	**IMPERFECT SUBJUNCTIVE**
(yo)	vaya	fuera *or* fuese
(tú)	vayas	fueras *or* fueses
(él/ella/usted)	vaya	fuera *or* fuese
(nosotros/as)	vayamos	fuéramos *or* fuésemos
(vosotros/as)	vayáis	fuerais *or* fueseis
(ellos/ellas/ ustedes)	vayan	fueran *or* fuesen

IMPERATIVE

ve / id

Use the present subjunctive in most cases other than these tú and vosotros affirmative forms.
However, in the 'let's' affirmative form, vamos is more common than vayamos.

EXAMPLE PHRASES

El domingo **iré** a Edimburgo. I'll go to Edinburgh on Sunday.

Dijeron que **irían** andando. They said they'd walk.

¡Que te **vaya** bien! Take care of yourself!

Quería pedirte que **fueras** en mi lugar. I wanted to ask you if you'd take my place.

No **te vayas** sin despedirte. Don't go without saying goodbye.

Vete a hacer los deberes. Go and do your homework.

Remember that subject pronouns are not used very often in Spanish.

jugar (to play)

	PRESENT		PRESENT PERFECT
(yo)	juego		he jugado
(tú)	juegas		has jugado
(él/ella/usted)	juega		ha jugado
(nosotros/as)	jugamos		hemos jugado
(vosotros/as)	jugáis		habéis jugado
(ellos/ellas/ustedes)	juegan		han jugado

	PRETERITE		IMPERFECT
(yo)	jugué		jugaba
(tú)	jugaste		jugabas
(él/ella/usted)	jugó		jugaba
(nosotros/as)	jugamos		jugábamos
(vosotros/as)	jugasteis		jugabais
(ellos/ellas/ustedes)	jugaron		jugaban

GERUND

jugando

PAST PARTICIPLE

jugado

EXAMPLE PHRASES

Juego al fútbol todos los domingos. I play soccer every Sunday.

Están jugando en el jardín. They're playing in the yard.

Le **han jugado** una mala pasada. They played a dirty trick on him.

Después de cenar **jugamos** a las cartas. After dinner we played cards.

Se jugaba la vida continuamente. She was constantly risking her life.

Remember that subject pronouns are not used very often in Spanish.

jugar

	FUTURE	CONDITIONAL
(yo)	jugaré	jugaría
(tú)	jugarás	jugarías
(él/ella/usted)	jugará	jugaría
(nosotros/as)	jugaremos	jugaríamos
(vosotros/as)	jugaréis	jugaríais
(ellos/ellas/ ustedes)	jugarán	jugarían

	PRESENT SUBJUNCTIVE	IMPERFECT SUBJUNCTIVE
(yo)	juegue	jugara or jugase
(tú)	juegues	jugaras or jugases
(él/ella/usted)	juegue	jugara or jugase
(nosotros/as)	juguemos	jugáramos or jugásemos
(vosotros/as)	juguéis	jugarais or jugaseis
(ellos/ellas/ ustedes)	jueguen	jugaran or jugasen

IMPERATIVE

juega / jugad

Use the present subjunctive in all cases other than these tú and vosotros affirmative forms.

EXAMPLE PHRASES

Jugarán contra el Real Madrid. They'll play Real Madrid.

Jugarías mejor si estuvieras más relajado. You'd play better if you were more relaxed.

No **juegues** con tu salud. Don't take risks with your health.

El profesor le aconsejó que **jugara** menos y leyera más. The teacher advised him to play less and read more.

Remember that subject pronouns are not used very often in Spanish.

leer (to read)

	PRESENT		PRESENT PERFECT
(yo)	leo		he leído
(tú)	lees		has leído
(él/ella/usted)	lee		ha leído
(nosotros/as)	leemos		hemos leído
(vosotros/as)	leéis		habéis leído
(ellos/ellas/ ustedes)	leen		han leído

	PRETERITE		IMPERFECT
(yo)	leí		leía
(tú)	leíste		leías
(él/ella/usted)	leyó		leía
(nosotros/as)	leímos		leíamos
(vosotros/as)	leísteis		leíais
(ellos/ellas/ ustedes)	leyeron		leían

GERUND	PAST PARTICIPLE
leyendo	leído

EXAMPLE PHRASES

Hace mucho tiempo que no **leo** nada. I haven't read anything for ages.

Estoy leyendo un libro muy interesante. I'm reading a very interesting book.

¿**Has leído** esta novela? Have you read this novel?

Lo **leí** hace tiempo. I read it a while ago.

Antes **leía** mucho más. I used to read much more than now.

Remember that subject pronouns are not used very often in Spanish.

leer

	FUTURE	CONDITIONAL
(yo)	leeré	leería
(tú)	leerás	leerías
(él/ella/usted)	leerá	leería
(nosotros/as)	leeremos	leeríamos
(vosotros/as)	leeréis	leeríais
(ellos/ellas/ ustedes)	leerán	leerían

	PRESENT SUBJUNCTIVE	IMPERFECT SUBJUNCTIVE
(yo)	lea	leyera or leyese
(tú)	leas	leyeras or leyeses
(él/ella/usted)	lea	leyera or leyese
(nosotros/as)	leamos	leyéramos or leyésemos
(vosotros/as)	leáis	leyerais or leyeseis
(ellos/ellas/ ustedes)	lean	leyeran or leyesen

IMPERATIVE

lee / leed

Use the present subjunctive in all cases other than these tú and vosotros affirmative forms.

EXAMPLE PHRASES

Si os portáis bien, os **leeré** un cuento. If you behave yourselves, I'll read you a story.

Yo **leería** también la letra pequeña. I'd read the small print as well.

Quiero que lo **leas** y me digas qué piensas. I want you to read it and tell me what you think.

No **leas** tan deprisa. Don't read so fast.

Remember that subject pronouns are not used very often in Spanish.

levantar (to lift)

	PRESENT		PRESENT PERFECT
(yo)	levanto		he levantado
(tú)	levantas		has levantado
(él/ella/usted)	levanta		ha levantado
(nosotros/as)	levantamos		hemos levantado
(vosotros/as)	levantáis		habéis levantado
(ellos/ellas/ ustedes)	levantan		han levantado

	PRETERITE		IMPERFECT
(yo)	levanté		levantaba
(tú)	levantaste		levantabas
(él/ella/usted)	levantó		levantaba
(nosotros/as)	levantamos		levantábamos
(vosotros/as)	levantasteis		levantabais
(ellos/ellas/ ustedes)	levantaron		levantaban

GERUND	PAST PARTICIPLE
levantando	levantado

EXAMPLE PHRASES

No me importa **levantarme** temprano. I don't mind getting up early.

Siempre **se levanta** de mal humor. He's always in a bad mood when he gets up.

Hoy **me he levantado** temprano. I got up early this morning.

Levantó la maleta como si no pesara nada. He lifted up the suitcase as if it weighed nothing.

Me levanté y seguí caminando. I got up and carried on walking.

Remember that subject pronouns are not used very often in Spanish.

levantar

	FUTURE	CONDITIONAL
(yo)	levantaré	levantaría
(tú)	levantarás	levantarías
(él/ella/usted)	levantará	levantaría
(nosotros/as)	levantaremos	levantaríamos
(vosotros/as)	levantaréis	levantaríais
(ellos/ellas/ustedes)	levantarán	levantarían

	PRESENT SUBJUNCTIVE	IMPERFECT SUBJUNCTIVE
(yo)	levante	levantara or levantase
(tú)	levantes	levantaras or levantases
(él/ella/usted)	levante	levantara or levantase
(nosotros/as)	levantemos	levantáramos or levantásemos
(vosotros/as)	levantéis	levantarais or levantaseis
(ellos/ellas/ustedes)	levanten	levantaran or levantasen

IMPERATIVE

levanta / levantad

Use the present subjunctive in all cases other than these tú and vosotros affirmative forms.

EXAMPLE PHRASES

La noticia le **levantará** el ánimo. This news will raise her spirits

Si pudiera **me levantaría** siempre tarde. I'd sleep in every day, if I could.

No me **levantes** la voz. Don't raise your voice to me.

Levanta la tapa. Lift the lid.

Levantad la mano si tenéis alguna duda. Put up your hands if you are unclear about anything.

Remember that subject pronouns are not used very often in Spanish.

llover (to rain)

PRESENT
llueve
llueven

PRESENT PERFECT
ha llovido
han llovido

PRETERITE
llovió
llovieron

IMPERFECT
llovía
llovían

GERUND
lloviendo

PAST PARTICIPLE
llovido

EXAMPLE PHRASES

Hace semanas que no **llueve**. It hasn't rained for weeks.

Está lloviendo. It's raining.

Le **han llovido** las ofertas. He's received lots of offers.

Llovió sin parar. It rained non-stop.

Llovía a cántaros. It was pouring down.

Remember that subject pronouns are not used very often in Spanish.

llover

FUTURE
lloverá
lloverán

CONDITIONAL
llovería
lloverían

PRESENT SUBJUNCTIVE
llueva
lluevan

IMPERFECT SUBJUNCTIVE
lloviera *or* lloviese
llovieran *or* lloviesen

IMPERATIVE
not used

EXAMPLE PHRASES

Sabía que le **lloverían** las críticas. She knew she would be much criticized.

Espero que no **llueva** este fin de semana. I hope it won't rain this weekend.

Si no **lloviera**, podríamos salir a dar una vuelta. We could go for a walk if it weren't raining.

Remember that subject pronouns are not used very often in Spanish.

lucir (to shine)

	PRESENT		PRESENT PERFECT
(yo)	luzco		he lucido
(tú)	luces		has lucido
(él/ella/usted)	luce		ha lucido
(nosotros/as)	lucimos		hemos lucido
(vosotros/as)	lucís		habéis lucido
(ellos/ellas/ ustedes)	lucen		han lucido

	PRETERITE		IMPERFECT
(yo)	lucí		lucía
(tú)	luciste		lucías
(él/ella/usted)	lució		lucía
(nosotros/as)	lucimos		lucíamos
(vosotros/as)	lucisteis		lucíais
(ellos/ellas/ ustedes)	lucieron		lucían

GERUND
luciendo

PAST PARTICIPLE
lucido

EXAMPLE PHRASES

Ahí no **luce** nada. It doesn't look very good there.

¡Anda, que **te has lucido**! Well, you've excelled yourself!

Lucían las estrellas. The stars were shining.

Remember that subject pronouns are not used very often in Spanish.

lucir

	FUTURE	CONDITIONAL
(yo)	luciré	luciría
(tú)	lucirás	lucirías
(él/ella/usted)	lucirá	luciría
(nosotros/as)	luciremos	luciríamos
(vosotros/as)	luciréis	luciríais
(ellos/ellas/ustedes)	lucirán	lucirían

	PRESENT SUBJUNCTIVE	IMPERFECT SUBJUNCTIVE
(yo)	luzca	luciera or luciese
(tú)	luzcas	lucieras or lucieses
(él/ella/usted)	luzca	luciera or luciese
(nosotros/as)	luzcamos	luciéramos or luciésemos
(vosotros/as)	luzcáis	lucierais or lucieseis
(ellos/ellas/ustedes)	luzcan	lucieran or luciesen

IMPERATIVE
luce / lucid

Use the present subjunctive in all cases other than these tú and vosotros affirmative forms.

EXAMPLE PHRASES

Lucirá un traje muy elegante. She will be wearing a very elegant dress.

Luciría más con otros zapatos. It would look much better with another pair of shoes.

Quiero que esta noche **luzcas** tú el collar. I want you to wear the necklace tonight.

Remember that subject pronouns are not used very often in Spanish.

morir (to die)

	PRESENT	PRESENT PERFECT
(yo)	muero	he muerto
(tú)	mueres	has muerto
(él/ella/usted)	muere	ha muerto
(nosotros/as)	morimos	hemos muerto
(vosotros/as)	morís	habéis muerto
(ellos/ellas/ustedes)	mueren	han muerto

	PRETERITE	IMPERFECT
(yo)	morí	moría
(tú)	moriste	morías
(él/ella/usted)	murió	moría
(nosotros/as)	morimos	moríamos
(vosotros/as)	moristeis	moríais
(ellos/ellas/ustedes)	murieron	morían

GERUND
muriendo

PAST PARTICIPLE
muerto

EXAMPLE PHRASES

¡**Me muero** de hambre! I'm starving!

Se está muriendo. She's dying.

Se le **ha muerto** el gato. His cat has died.

Se murió el mes pasado. He died last month.

Me moría de ganas de contárselo. I was dying to tell her.

Remember that subject pronouns are not used very often in Spanish.

morir

	FUTURE	CONDITIONAL
(yo)	moriré	moriría
(tú)	morirás	morirías
(él/ella/usted)	morirá	moriría
(nosotros/as)	moriremos	moriríamos
(vosotros/as)	moriréis	moriríais
(ellos/ellas/ustedes)	morirán	morirían

	PRESENT SUBJUNCTIVE	IMPERFECT SUBJUNCTIVE
(yo)	muera	muriera or muriese
(tú)	mueras	murieras or murieses
(él/ella/usted)	muera	muriera or muriese
(nosotros/as)	muramos	muriéramos or muriésemos
(vosotros/as)	muráis	murierais or murieseis
(ellos/ellas/ustedes)	mueran	murieran or muriesen

IMPERATIVE
muere / morid

Use the present subjunctive in all cases other than these tú and vosotros affirmative forms.

EXAMPLE PHRASES

Cuando te lo cuente, **te morirás** de risa. You'll kill yourself laughing when I tell you.

Yo **me moriría** de vergüenza. I'd die of shame.

Cuando **me muera**... When I die...

Riega las plantas para que no **se** te **mueran**. You need to water the plants so they don't die.

Estoy muerto de miedo. I'm scared stiff.

Remember that subject pronouns are not used very often in Spanish.

mover (to move)

	PRESENT		PRESENT PERFECT
(yo)	muevo		he movido
(tú)	mueves		has movido
(él/ella/usted)	mueve		ha movido
(nosotros/as)	movemos		hemos movido
(vosotros/as)	movéis		habéis movido
(ellos/ellas/ ustedes)	mueven		han movido

	PRETERITE		IMPERFECT
(yo)	moví		movía
(tú)	moviste		movías
(él/ella/usted)	movió		movía
(nosotros/as)	movimos		movíamos
(vosotros/as)	movisteis		movíais
(ellos/ellas/ ustedes)	movieron		movían

GERUND

moviendo

PAST PARTICIPLE

movido

EXAMPLE PHRASES

Para **mover** el archivo, haga clic y arrastre. Click and drag to move the file.

Están moviendo las fechas de los exámenes. They're changing the dates of the exams.

¿**Has movido** ese mueble de sitio? Have you moved that piece of furniture?

No **se movieron** de casa. They didn't leave the house.

Antes **se movía** en esos ambientes. He used to move in those circles.

Remember that subject pronouns are not used very often in Spanish.

mover

	FUTURE	CONDITIONAL
(yo)	moveré	movería
(tú)	moverás	moverías
(él/ella/usted)	moverá	movería
(nosotros/as)	moveremos	moveríamos
(vosotros/as)	moveréis	moveríais
(ellos/ellas/ ustedes)	moverán	moverían

	PRESENT SUBJUNCTIVE	IMPERFECT SUBJUNCTIVE
(yo)	mueva	moviera or moviese
(tú)	muevas	movieras or movieses
(él/ella/usted)	mueva	moviera or moviese
(nosotros/as)	movamos	moviéramos or moviésemos
(vosotros/as)	mováis	movierais or movieseis
(ellos/ellas/ ustedes)	muevan	movieran or moviesen

IMPERATIVE

mueve / moved

Use the present subjunctive in all cases other than these tú and vosotros affirmative forms.

EXAMPLE PHRASES

Prométeme que no **te moverás** de aquí. Promise me you won't move from here.

No **te muevas**. Don't move.

Mueve un poco las cajas para que podamos pasar. Move the boxes a bit so that we can get past.

Remember that subject pronouns are not used very often in Spanish.

nacer (to be born)

	PRESENT	PRESENT PERFECT
(yo)	nazco	he nacido
(tú)	naces	has nacido
(él/ella/usted)	nace	ha nacido
(nosotros/as)	nacemos	hemos nacido
(vosotros/as)	nacéis	habéis nacido
(ellos/ellas/ ustedes)	nacen	han nacido

	PRETERITE	IMPERFECT
(yo)	nací	nacía
(tú)	naciste	nacías
(él/ella/usted)	nació	nacía
(nosotros/as)	nacimos	nacíamos
(vosotros/as)	nacisteis	nacíais
(ellos/ellas/ ustedes)	nacieron	nacían

GERUND
naciendo

PAST PARTICIPLE
nacido

EXAMPLE PHRASES

Nacen cuatro niños por minuto. Four children are born every minute.

Ha nacido antes de tiempo. It was premature.

Nació en 1980. He was born in 1980.

¿Cuándo **naciste**? When were you born?

En aquella época había muchos más niños que **nacían** en casa. Many more babies were born at home in those days.

Remember that subject pronouns are not used very often in Spanish.

nacer

	FUTURE	CONDITIONAL
(yo)	naceré	nacería
(tú)	nacerás	nacerías
(él/ella/usted)	nacerá	nacería
(nosotros/as)	naceremos	naceríamos
(vosotros/as)	naceréis	naceríais
(ellos/ellas/ustedes)	nacerán	nacerían

	PRESENT SUBJUNCTIVE	IMPERFECT SUBJUNCTIVE
(yo)	nazca	naciera or naciese
(tú)	nazcas	nacieras or nacieses
(él/ella/usted)	nazca	naciera or naciese
(nosotros/as)	nazcamos	naciéramos or naciésemos
(vosotros/as)	nazcáis	nacierais or nacieseis
(ellos/ellas/ustedes)	nazcan	nacieran or naciesen

IMPERATIVE

nace / naced

Use the present subjunctive in all cases other than these tú and vosotros affirmative forms.

EXAMPLE PHRASES

Nacerá el año que viene. It will be born next year.

Queremos que **nazca** en España. We want it to be born in Spain.

Si **naciera** hoy, sería tauro. He'd be a Taurus if he were born today.

Remember that subject pronouns are not used very often in Spanish.

negar (to deny, to refuse)

	PRESENT		PRESENT PERFECT
(yo)	niego		he negado
(tú)	niegas		has negado
(él/ella/usted)	niega		ha negado
(nosotros/as)	negamos		hemos negado
(vosotros/as)	negáis		habéis negado
(ellos/ellas/ ustedes)	niegan		han negado

	PRETERITE		IMPERFECT
(yo)	negué		negaba
(tú)	negaste		negabas
(él/ella/usted)	negó		negaba
(nosotros/as)	negamos		negábamos
(vosotros/as)	negasteis		negabais
(ellos/ellas/ ustedes)	negaron		negaban

GERUND

negando

PAST PARTICIPLE

negado

EXAMPLE PHRASES

No lo puedes **negar**. You can't deny it.

Me niego a creerlo. I refuse to believe it.

Me **ha negado** el favor. He wouldn't do me this favor.

Se negó a venir con nosotros. She refused to come with us.

Decían que era el ladrón, pero él lo **negaba**. They said that he was the thief, but he denied it.

Remember that subject pronouns are not used very often in Spanish.

negar

	FUTURE	CONDITIONAL
(yo)	negaré	negaría
(tú)	negarás	negarías
(él/ella/usted)	negará	negaría
(nosotros/as)	negaremos	negaríamos
(vosotros/as)	negaréis	negaríais
(ellos/ellas/ ustedes)	negarán	negarían

	PRESENT SUBJUNCTIVE	IMPERFECT SUBJUNCTIVE
(yo)	niegue	negara or negase
(tú)	niegues	negaras or negases
(él/ella/usted)	niegue	negara or negase
(nosotros/as)	neguemos	negáramos or negásemos
(vosotros/as)	neguéis	negarais or negaseis
(ellos/ellas/ ustedes)	nieguen	negaran or negasen

IMPERATIVE
niega / negad

Use the present subjunctive in all cases other than these **tú** *and* **vosotros** *affirmative forms.*

EXAMPLE PHRASES
No me **negarás** que es barato. You can't say it's not cheap.

Si lo **negaras**, nadie te creería. If you denied it, nobody would believe you.

No lo **niegues**. Don't deny it.

Remember that subject pronouns are not used very often in Spanish.

Oír (to hear)

	PRESENT	PRESENT PERFECT
(yo)	oigo	he oído
(tú)	oyes	has oído
(él/ella/usted)	oye	ha oído
(nosotros/as)	oímos	hemos oído
(vosotros/as)	oís	habéis oído
(ellos/ellas/ ustedes)	oyen	han oído

	PRETERITE	IMPERFECT
(yo)	oí	oía
(tú)	oíste	oías
(él/ella/usted)	oyó	oía
(nosotros/as)	oímos	oíamos
(vosotros/as)	oísteis	oíais
(ellos/ellas/ ustedes)	oyeron	oían

GERUND
oyendo

PAST PARTICIPLE
oído

EXAMPLE PHRASES

No **oigo** nada. I can't hear anything.

Hemos estado oyendo las noticias. We've been listening to the news.

¿**Has oído** eso? Did you hear that?

Lo **oí** por casualidad. I heard it by chance.

No **oía** muy bien. He couldn't hear very well.

Remember that subject pronouns are not used very often in Spanish.

oír

	FUTURE	CONDITIONAL
(yo)	oiré	oiría
(tú)	oirás	oirías
(él/ella/usted)	oirá	oiría
(nosotros/as)	oiremos	oiríamos
(vosotros/as)	oiréis	oiríais
(ellos/ellas/ustedes)	oirán	oirían

	PRESENT SUBJUNCTIVE	IMPERFECT SUBJUNCTIVE
(yo)	oiga	oyera or oyese
(tú)	oigas	oyeras or oyeses
(él/ella/usted)	oiga	oyera or oyese
(nosotros/as)	oigamos	oyéramos or oyésemos
(vosotros/as)	oigáis	oyerais or oyeseis
(ellos/ellas/ustedes)	oigan	oyeran or oyesen

IMPERATIVE

oye / oíd

Use the present subjunctive in all cases other than these tú and vosotros affirmative forms.

EXAMPLE PHRASES

Oirías mal. You must have misheard.

¡**Oiga**! ¡A ver si mira por dónde va! Excuse me! Why don't you look where you're going?

Óyeme bien, no vuelvas a hacer eso. Now listen carefully; don't do that again.

Remember that subject pronouns are not used very often in Spanish.

oler (to smell)

	PRESENT	PRESENT PERFECT
(yo)	huelo	he olido
(tú)	hueles	has olido
(él/ella/usted)	huele	ha olido
(nosotros/as)	olemos	hemos olido
(vosotros/as)	oléis	habéis olido
(ellos/ellas/ustedes)	huelen	han olido

	PRETERITE	IMPERFECT
(yo)	olí	olía
(tú)	oliste	olías
(él/ella/usted)	olió	olía
(nosotros/as)	olimos	olíamos
(vosotros/as)	olisteis	olíais
(ellos/ellas/ustedes)	olieron	olían

GERUND
oliendo

PAST PARTICIPLE
olido

EXAMPLE PHRASES

Huele a pescado. It smells of fish.

El perro **estaba oliendo** la basura. The dog was sniffing the garbage.

Se ha olido algo. He's started to suspect.

A mí el asunto me **olió** mal. I thought there was something fishy about it.

Olía muy bien. It smelled really nice.

oler

	FUTURE	CONDITIONAL
(yo)	oleré	olería
(tú)	olerás	olerías
(él/ella/usted)	olerá	olería
(nosotros/as)	oleremos	oleríamos
(vosotros/as)	oleréis	oleríais
(ellos/ellas/ustedes)	olerán	olerían

	PRESENT SUBJUNCTIVE	IMPERFECT SUBJUNCTIVE
(yo)	huela	oliera or oliese
(tú)	huelas	olieras or olieses
(él/ella/usted)	huela	oliera or oliese
(nosotros/as)	olamos	oliéramos or oliésemos
(vosotros/as)	oláis	olierais or olieseis
(ellos/ellas/ustedes)	huelan	olieran or oliesen

IMPERATIVE
huele / oled

Use the present subjunctive in all cases other than these **tú** and **vosotros** affirmative forms.

EXAMPLE PHRASES
Con esto ya no **olerá**. This will take the smell away.

Si te **oliera** a quemado, apágalo. If you smell burning, turn it off.

pagar (to pay, to pay for)

	PRESENT	PRESENT PERFECT
(yo)	pago	he pagado
(tú)	pagas	has pagado
(él/ella/usted)	paga	ha pagado
(nosotros/as)	pagamos	hemos pagado
(vosotros/as)	pagáis	habéis pagado
(ellos/ellas/ustedes)	pagan	han pagado

	PRETERITE	IMPERFECT
(yo)	pagué	pagaba
(tú)	pagaste	pagabas
(él/ella/usted)	pagó	pagaba
(nosotros/as)	pagamos	pagábamos
(vosotros/as)	pagasteis	pagabais
(ellos/ellas/ustedes)	pagaron	pagaban

GERUND	PAST PARTICIPLE
pagando	pagado

EXAMPLE PHRASES

Se puede **pagar** la reserva con tarjeta de crédito. You can pay for your reservation by credit card.

¿Cuánto te **pagan** al mes? How much do they pay you a month?

Han pagado pensión completa. You've paid for full board.

Lo **pagué** en efectivo. I paid for it in cash.

Me **pagaban** muy poco. I got paid very little.

Remember that subject pronouns are not used very often in Spanish.

pagar

	FUTURE	CONDITIONAL
(yo)	pagaré	pagaría
(tú)	pagarás	pagarías
(él/ella/usted)	pagará	pagaría
(nosotros/as)	pagaremos	pagaríamos
(vosotros/as)	pagaréis	pagaríais
(ellos/ellas/ustedes)	pagarán	pagarían

	PRESENT SUBJUNCTIVE	IMPERFECT SUBJUNCTIVE
(yo)	pague	pagara or pagase
(tú)	pagues	pagaras or pagases
(él/ella/usted)	pague	pagara or pagase
(nosotros/as)	paguemos	pagáramos or pagásemos
(vosotros/as)	paguéis	pagarais or pagaseis
(ellos/ellas/ustedes)	paguen	pagaran or pagasen

IMPERATIVE

paga / pagad

Use the present subjunctive in all cases other than these tú and vosotros affirmative forms.

EXAMPLE PHRASES

Yo te **pagaré** la entrada. I'll pay for your ticket.

¡Quiero que **pague** por lo que me ha hecho! I want him to pay for what he's done to me!

Si **pagase** sus deudas, se quedaría sin nada. He'd be left with nothing if he paid his debts.

No les **pagues** hasta que lo hayan hecho. Don't pay them until they've done it.

Págame lo que me debes. Pay me what you owe me.

Remember that subject pronouns are not used very often in Spanish.

partir (to leave)

	PRESENT	PRESENT PERFECT
(yo)	parto	he partido
(tú)	partes	has partido
(él/ella/usted)	parte	ha partido
(nosotros/as)	partimos	hemos partido
(vosotros/as)	partís	habéis partido
(ellos/ellas/ ustedes)	parten	han partido

	PRETERITE	IMPERFECT
(yo)	partí	partía
(tú)	partiste	partías
(él/ella/usted)	partió	partía
(nosotros/as)	partimos	partíamos
(vosotros/as)	partisteis	partíais
(ellos/ellas/ ustedes)	partieron	partían

GERUND	PAST PARTICIPLE
partiendo	partido

EXAMPLE PHRASES

¿Te **parto** un trozo de queso? Shall I cut you a piece of cheese?

Partiendo de la base de que... Assuming that...

El remo **se partió** en dos. The oar broke in two.

Se partían de risa. They were splitting their sides laughing.

Remember that subject pronouns are not used very often in Spanish.

partir

	FUTURE	CONDITIONAL
(yo)	partiré	partiría
(tú)	partirás	partirías
(él/ella/usted)	partirá	partiría
(nosotros/as)	partiremos	partiríamos
(vosotros/as)	partiréis	partiríais
(ellos/ellas/ ustedes)	partirán	partirían

	PRESENT SUBJUNCTIVE	IMPERFECT SUBJUNCTIVE
(yo)	parta	partiera or partiese
(tú)	partas	partieras or partieses
(él/ella/usted)	parta	partiera or partiese
(nosotros/as)	partamos	partiéramos or partiésemos
(vosotros/as)	partáis	partierais or partieseis
(ellos/ellas/ ustedes)	partan	partieran or partiesen

IMPERATIVE

parte / partid

Use the present subjunctive in all cases other than these tú and vosotros affirmative forms.

EXAMPLE PHRASES

La expedición **partirá** mañana de París. The expedition is to leave from Paris
    tomorrow.

Eso le **partiría** el corazón. That would break his heart.

No **partas** todavía el pan. Don't slice the bread yet.

Pártelo por la mitad. Cut it in half.

Remember that subject pronouns are not used very often in Spanish.

pedir (to ask for, to ask)

	PRESENT	PRESENT PERFECT
(yo)	pido	he pedido
(tú)	pides	has pedido
(él/ella/usted)	pide	ha pedido
(nosotros/as)	pedimos	hemos pedido
(vosotros/as)	pedís	habéis pedido
(ellos/ellas/ ustedes)	piden	han pedido

	PRETERITE	IMPERFECT
(yo)	pedí	pedía
(tú)	pediste	pedías
(él/ella/usted)	pidió	pedía
(nosotros/as)	pedimos	pedíamos
(vosotros/as)	pedisteis	pedíais
(ellos/ellas/ ustedes)	pidieron	pedían

GERUND

pidiendo

PAST PARTICIPLE

pedido

EXAMPLE PHRASES

¿Cuánto **pide** por el coche? How much is he asking for the car?

La casa **está pidiendo** a gritos una mano de pintura. The house is crying out to be painted.

Hemos pedido dos cervezas. We've ordered two beers.

No nos **pidieron** el pasaporte. They didn't ask us for our passports.

Pedían dos millones de rescate. They were demanding a two-million ransom.

Remember that subject pronouns are not used very often in Spanish.

pedir

	FUTURE	CONDITIONAL
(yo)	pediré	pediría
(tú)	pedirás	pedirías
(él/ella/usted)	pedirá	pediría
(nosotros/as)	pediremos	pediríamos
(vosotros/as)	pediréis	pediríais
(ellos/ellas/ ustedes)	pedirán	pedirían

	PRESENT SUBJUNCTIVE	IMPERFECT SUBJUNCTIVE
(yo)	pida	pidiera or pidiese
(tú)	pidas	pidieras or pidieses
(él/ella/usted)	pida	pidiera or pidiese
(nosotros/as)	pidamos	pidiéramos or pidiésemos
(vosotros/as)	pidáis	pidierais or pidieseis
(ellos/ellas/ ustedes)	pidan	pidieran or pidiesen

IMPERATIVE

pide / pedid

Use the present subjunctive in all cases other than these tú and vosotros affirmative forms.

EXAMPLE PHRASES

Si se entera, te **pedirá** explicaciones. If he finds out, he'll ask you for an explanation.

Nunca te **pediría** que hicieras una cosa así. I'd never ask you to do anything like that.

Y que sea lo último que me **pidas**. And don't ask me for anything else.

Pídele el teléfono. Ask her for her phone number.

Remember that subject pronouns are not used very often in Spanish.

pensar (to think)

	PRESENT	PRESENT PERFECT
(yo)	pienso	he pensado
(tú)	piensas	has pensado
(él/ella/usted)	piensa	ha pensado
(nosotros/as)	pensamos	hemos pensado
(vosotros/as)	pensáis	habéis pensado
(ellos/ellas/ ustedes)	piensan	han pensado

	PRETERITE	IMPERFECT
(yo)	pensé	pensaba
(tú)	pensaste	pensabas
(él/ella/usted)	pensó	pensaba
(nosotros/as)	pensamos	pensábamos
(vosotros/as)	pensasteis	pensabais
(ellos/ellas/ ustedes)	pensaron	pensaban

GERUND

pensando

PAST PARTICIPLE

pensado

EXAMPLE PHRASES

¿**Piensas** que vale la pena? Do you think it's worth it?

¿Qué **piensas** del aborto? What do you think about abortion?

Está pensando en comprarse un piso. He's thinking about buying an apartment.

¿Lo **has pensado** bien? Have you thought about it carefully?

Pensaba que vendrías. I thought you'd come.

Remember that subject pronouns are not used very often in Spanish.

pensar

	FUTURE	CONDITIONAL
(yo)	pensaré	pensaría
(tú)	pensarás	pensarías
(él/ella/usted)	pensará	pensaría
(nosotros/as)	pensaremos	pensaríamos
(vosotros/as)	pensaréis	pensaríais
(ellos/ellas/ ustedes)	pensarán	pensarían

	PRESENT SUBJUNCTIVE	IMPERFECT SUBJUNCTIVE
(yo)	piense	pensara *or* pensase
(tú)	pienses	pensaras *or* pensases
(él/ella/usted)	piense	pensara *or* pensase
(nosotros/as)	pensemos	pensáramos *or* pensásemos
(vosotros/as)	penséis	pensarais *or* pensaseis
(ellos/ellas/ ustedes)	piensen	pensaran *or* pensasen

IMPERATIVE

piensa / pensad

Use the present subjunctive in all cases other than these **tú** *and* **vosotros** *affirmative forms.*

EXAMPLE PHRASES

Yo no me lo **pensaría** dos veces. I wouldn't think about it twice.

Me da igual lo que **piensen**. I don't care what they think.

Si **pensara** eso, te lo diría. If I thought that, I'd tell you.

No **pienses** que no quiero ir. Don't think that I don't want to go.

No lo **pienses** más. Don't think any more about it.

Remember that subject pronouns are not used very often in Spanish.

perder (to lose)

	PRESENT		PRESENT PERFECT
(yo)	pierdo		he perdido
(tú)	pierdes		has perdido
(él/ella/usted)	pierde		ha perdido
(nosotros/as)	perdemos		hemos perdido
(vosotros/as)	perdéis		habéis perdido
(ellos/ellas/ ustedes)	pierden		han perdido

	PRETERITE		IMPERFECT
(yo)	perdí		perdía
(tú)	perdiste		perdías
(él/ella/usted)	perdió		perdía
(nosotros/as)	perdimos		perdíamos
(vosotros/as)	perdisteis		perdíais
(ellos/ellas/ ustedes)	perdieron		perdían

GERUND

perdiendo

PAST PARTICIPLE

perdido

EXAMPLE PHRASES

Siempre **pierde** las llaves. He's always losing his keys.

Ana es la que saldrá **perdiendo**. Ana is the one who will lose out.

He perdido dos kilos. I've lost two kilos.

Perdimos dos a cero. We lost two nil.

Perdían siempre. They always used to lose.

Remember that subject pronouns are not used very often in Spanish.

perder

	FUTURE	CONDITIONAL
(yo)	perderé	perdería
(tú)	perderás	perderías
(él/ella/usted)	perderá	perdería
(nosotros/as)	perderemos	perderíamos
(vosotros/as)	perderéis	perderíais
(ellos/ellas/ ustedes)	perderán	perderían

	PRESENT SUBJUNCTIVE	IMPERFECT SUBJUNCTIVE
(yo)	pierda	perdiera or perdiese
(tú)	pierdas	perdieras or perdieses
(él/ella/usted)	pierda	perdiera or perdiese
(nosotros/as)	perdamos	perdiéramos or perdiésemos
(vosotros/as)	perdáis	perdierais or perdieseis
(ellos/ellas/ ustedes)	pierdan	perdieran or perdiesen

IMPERATIVE

pierde / perded

Use the present subjunctive in all cases other than these tú and vosotros affirmative forms.

EXAMPLE PHRASES

Date prisa o **perderás** el tren. Hurry up or you'll miss the train.

¡No **te** lo **pierdas**! Don't miss it!

No **pierdas** esta oportunidad. Don't miss this opportunity.

Remember that subject pronouns are not used very often in Spanish.

poder (to be able to)

	PRESENT	PRESENT PERFECT
(yo)	puedo	he podido
(tú)	puedes	has podido
(él/ella/usted)	puede	ha podido
(nosotros/as)	podemos	hemos podido
(vosotros/as)	podéis	habéis podido
(ellos/ellas/ustedes)	pueden	han podido

	PRETERITE	IMPERFECT
(yo)	pude	podía
(tú)	pudiste	podías
(él/ella/usted)	pudo	podía
(nosotros/as)	pudimos	podíamos
(vosotros/as)	pudisteis	podíais
(ellos/ellas/ustedes)	pudieron	podían

GERUND	PAST PARTICIPLE
pudiendo	podido

EXAMPLE PHRASES

¿**Puedo** entrar? Can I come in?

Puede que llegue mañana. He may arrive tomorrow.

No **he podido** venir antes. I couldn't come before.

Pudiste haberte hecho daño. You could have hurt yourself.

¡Me lo **podías** haber dicho! You could have told me!

Remember that subject pronouns are not used very often in Spanish.

poder

	FUTURE	CONDITIONAL
(yo)	podré	podría
(tú)	podrás	podrías
(él/ella/usted)	podrá	podría
(nosotros/as)	podremos	podríamos
(vosotros/as)	podréis	podríais
(ellos/ellas/ ustedes)	podrán	podrían

	PRESENT SUBJUNCTIVE	IMPERFECT SUBJUNCTIVE
(yo)	pueda	pudiera or pudiese
(tú)	puedas	pudieras or pudieses
(él/ella/usted)	pueda	pudiera or pudiese
(nosotros/as)	podamos	pudiéramos or pudiésemos
(vosotros/as)	podáis	pudierais or pudieseis
(ellos/ellas/ ustedes)	puedan	pudieran or pudiesen

IMPERATIVE

puede / poded

Use the present subjunctive in all cases other than these tú and vosotros affirmative forms.

EXAMPLE PHRASES

Estoy segura de que **podrá** conseguirlo. I'm sure he'll succeed.

¿**Podrías** ayudarme? Could you help me?

Ven en cuanto **puedas**. Come as soon as you can.

Si no **pudiera** encontrar la casa, te llamaría al móvil. If I weren't able to find the house, I'd call you on your cell phone.

Remember that subject pronouns are not used very often in Spanish.

poner (to put)

	PRESENT		PRESENT PERFECT
(yo)	pongo		he puesto
(tú)	pones		has puesto
(él/ella/usted)	pone		ha puesto
(nosotros/as)	ponemos		hemos puesto
(vosotros/as)	ponéis		habéis puesto
(ellos/ellas/ ustedes)	ponen		han puesto

	PRETERITE		IMPERFECT
(yo)	puse		ponía
(tú)	pusiste		ponías
(él/ella/usted)	puso		ponía
(nosotros/as)	pusimos		poníamos
(vosotros/as)	pusisteis		poníais
(ellos/ellas/ ustedes)	pusieron		ponían

GERUND

poniendo

PAST PARTICIPLE

puesto

EXAMPLE PHRASES

¿Dónde **pongo** mis cosas? Where shall I put my things?

¿Qué **pone** en la carta? What does the letter say?

¿Le **has puesto** azúcar a mi café? Did you put any sugar in my coffee?

Todos **nos pusimos** de acuerdo. We all agreed.

poner

	FUTURE	CONDITIONAL
(yo)	pondré	pondría
(tú)	pondrás	pondrías
(él/ella/usted)	pondrá	pondría
(nosotros/as)	pondremos	pondríamos
(vosotros/as)	pondréis	pondríais
(ellos/ellas/ ustedes)	pondrán	pondrían

	PRESENT SUBJUNCTIVE	IMPERFECT SUBJUNCTIVE
(yo)	ponga	pusiera *or* pusiese
(tú)	pongas	pusieras *or* pusieses
(él/ella/usted)	ponga	pusiera *or* pusiese
(nosotros/as)	pongamos	pusiéramos *or* pusiésemos
(vosotros/as)	pongáis	pusierais *or* pusieseis
(ellos/ellas/ ustedes)	pongan	pusieran *or* pusiesen

IMPERATIVE

pon / poned

Use the present subjunctive in all cases other than these tú and vosotros affirmative forms.

EXAMPLE PHRASES

Lo **pondré** aquí. I'll put it here.

¿Le **pondrías** más sal? Would you add more salt?

Ponlo ahí encima. Put it on there.

Remember that subject pronouns are not used very often in Spanish.

prohibir (to ban, to prohibit)

	PRESENT		PRESENT PERFECT
(yo)	prohíbo		he prohibido
(tú)	prohíbes		has prohibido
(él/ella/usted)	prohíbe		ha prohibido
(nosotros/as)	prohibimos		hemos prohibido
(vosotros/as)	prohibís		habéis prohibido
(ellos/ellas/ ustedes)	prohíben		han prohibido

	PRETERITE		IMPERFECT
(yo)	prohibí		prohibía
(tú)	prohibiste		prohibías
(él/ella/usted)	prohibió		prohibía
(nosotros/as)	prohibimos		prohibíamos
(vosotros/as)	prohibisteis		prohibíais
(ellos/ellas/ ustedes)	prohibieron		prohibían

GERUND

prohibiendo

PAST PARTICIPLE

prohibido

EXAMPLE PHRASES

Deberían **prohibirlo**. It should be banned.

Te **prohíbo** que me hables así. I won't have you talking to me like that!

Han prohibido el acceso a la prensa. The press have been banned.

Le **prohibieron** la entrada en el estadio. He was not allowed into the stadium.

El tratado **prohibía** el uso de armas químicas. The treaty prohibited the use of chemical weapons.

Remember that subject pronouns are not used very often in Spanish.

prohibir

	FUTURE	CONDITIONAL
(yo)	prohibiré	prohibiría
(tú)	prohibirás	prohibirías
(él/ella/usted)	prohibirá	prohibiría
(nosotros/as)	prohibiremos	prohibiríamos
(vosotros/as)	prohibiréis	prohibiríais
(ellos/ellas/ ustedes)	prohibirán	prohibirían

	PRESENT SUBJUNCTIVE	IMPERFECT SUBJUNCTIVE
(yo)	prohíba	prohibiera or prohibiese
(tú)	prohíbas	prohibieras or prohibieses
(él/ella/usted)	prohíba	prohibiera or prohibiese
(nosotros/as)	prohibamos	prohibiéramos or prohibiésemos
(vosotros/as)	prohibáis	prohibierais or prohibieseis
(ellos/ellas/ ustedes)	prohíban	prohibieran or prohibiesen

IMPERATIVE
prohíbe / prohibid

Use the present subjunctive in all cases other than these tú and vosotros affirmative forms.

EXAMPLE PHRASES
Lo **prohibirán** más tarde o más temprano. Sooner or later they'll ban it.
Yo esa música la **prohibiría**. If it were up to me, that music would be banned.
"**prohibido** fumar" "no smoking"

Remember that subject pronouns are not used very often in Spanish.

querer (to want, to love)

	PRESENT	PRESENT PERFECT
(yo)	quiero	he querido
(tú)	quieres	has querido
(él/ella/usted)	quiere	ha querido
(nosotros/as)	queremos	hemos querido
(vosotros/as)	queréis	habéis querido
(ellos/ellas/ ustedes)	quieren	han querido

	PRETERITE	IMPERFECT
(yo)	quise	quería
(tú)	quisiste	querías
(él/ella/usted)	quiso	quería
(nosotros/as)	quisimos	queríamos
(vosotros/as)	quisisteis	queríais
(ellos/ellas/ ustedes)	quisieron	querían

GERUND
queriendo

PAST PARTICIPLE
querido

EXAMPLE PHRASES

Lo hice sin **querer**. I didn't mean to do it.

Te **quiero**. I love you.

Quiero que vayas. I want you to go.

No **ha querido** montar en la tirolina. He didn't want to go on the zip wire.

Quería una bicicleta para su cumpleaños. She wanted a bicycle for her birthday.

Remember that subject pronouns are not used very often in Spanish.

querer

	FUTURE	CONDITIONAL
(yo)	querré	querría
(tú)	querrás	querrías
(él/ella/usted)	querrá	querría
(nosotros/as)	querremos	querríamos
(vosotros/as)	querréis	querríais
(ellos/ellas/ ustedes)	querrán	querrían

	PRESENT SUBJUNCTIVE	IMPERFECT SUBJUNCTIVE
(yo)	quiera	quisiera or quisiese
(tú)	quieras	quisieras or quisieses
(él/ella/usted)	quiera	quisiera or quisiese
(nosotros/as)	queramos	quisiéramos or quisiésemos
(vosotros/as)	queráis	quisierais or quisieseis
(ellos/ellas/ ustedes)	quieran	quisieran or quisiesen

IMPERATIVE
quiere / quered

Use the present subjunctive in all cases other than these tú and vosotros affirmative forms.

EXAMPLE PHRASES
¿**Querrá** firmarme un autógrafo? Will you give me your autograph?
Querría que no hubiera pasado nunca. I wish it had never happened.
¡Por lo que más **quieras**! ¡Cállate! For goodness' sake, shut up!
Quisiera preguntar una cosa. I'd like to ask something.

Remember that subject pronouns are not used very often in Spanish.

reducir (to reduce)

	PRESENT		PRESENT PERFECT
(yo)	reduzco		he reducido
(tú)	reduces		has reducido
(él/ella/usted)	reduce		ha reducido
(nosotros/as)	reducimos		hemos reducido
(vosotros/as)	reducís		habéis reducido
(ellos/ellas/ ustedes)	reducen		han reducido

	PRETERITE		IMPERFECT
(yo)	reduje		reducía
(tú)	redujiste		reducías
(él/ella/usted)	redujo		reducía
(nosotros/as)	redujimos		reducíamos
(vosotros/as)	redujisteis		reducíais
(ellos/ellas/ ustedes)	redujeron		reducían

GERUND
reduciendo

PAST PARTICIPLE
reducido

EXAMPLE PHRASES

Al final todo **se reduce** a eso. In the end it all comes down to that.

Han reducido las emisiones de CO2. They've reduced carbon emissions.

Se ha reducido la tasa de natalidad. The birth rate has fallen.

Sus gastos **se redujeron** a la mitad. Their expenses were cut by half.

Remember that subject pronouns are not used very often in Spanish.

reducir

	FUTURE	CONDITIONAL
(yo)	reduciré	reduciría
(tú)	reducirás	reducirías
(él/ella/usted)	reducirá	reduciría
(nosotros/as)	reduciremos	reduciríamos
(vosotros/as)	reduciréis	reduciríais
(ellos/ellas/ ustedes)	reducirán	reducirían

	PRESENT SUBJUNCTIVE	IMPERFECT SUBJUNCTIVE
(yo)	reduzca	redujera or redujese
(tú)	reduzcas	redujeras or redujeses
(él/ella/usted)	reduzca	redujera or redujese
(nosotros/as)	reduzcamos	redujéramos or redujésemos
(vosotros/as)	reduzcáis	redujerais or redujeseis
(ellos/ellas/ ustedes)	reduzcan	redujeran or redujesen

IMPERATIVE
reduce / reducid

Use the present subjunctive in all cases other than these tú and vosotros affirmative forms.

EXAMPLE PHRASES
Reducirán la producción en un 20%. They'll cut production by 20%.
Reduzca la velocidad. Reduce speed.

rehusar (to refuse)

	PRESENT		PRESENT PERFECT
(yo)	rehúso		he rehusado
(tú)	rehúsas		has rehusado
(él/ella/usted)	rehúsa		ha rehusado
(nosotros/as)	rehusamos		hemos rehusado
(vosotros/as)	rehusáis		habéis rehusado
(ellos/ellas/ ustedes)	rehúsan		han rehusado

	PRETERITE		IMPERFECT
(yo)	rehusé		rehusaba
(tú)	rehusaste		rehusabas
(él/ella/usted)	rehusó		rehusaba
(nosotros/as)	rehusamos		rehusábamos
(vosotros/as)	rehusasteis		rehusabais
(ellos/ellas/ ustedes)	rehusaron		rehusaban

GERUND
rehusando

PAST PARTICIPLE
rehusado

EXAMPLE PHRASES

Rehúso tomar parte en esto. I refuse to take part in this.
Ha rehusado la oferta de trabajo. He declined the job offer.
Su familia **rehusó** hacer declaraciones. His family refused to comment.

rehusar

	FUTURE	CONDITIONAL
(yo)	rehusaré	rehusaría
(tú)	rehusarás	rehusarías
(él/ella/usted)	rehusará	rehusaría
(nosotros/as)	rehusaremos	rehusaríamos
(vosotros/as)	rehusaréis	rehusaríais
(ellos/ellas/ustedes)	rehusarán	rehusarían

	PRESENT SUBJUNCTIVE	IMPERFECT SUBJUNCTIVE
(yo)	rehúse	rehusara or rehusase
(tú)	rehúses	rehusaras or rehusases
(él/ella/usted)	rehúse	rehusara or rehusase
(nosotros/as)	rehusemos	rehusáramos or rehusásemos
(vosotros/as)	rehuséis	rehusarais or rehusaseis
(ellos/ellas/ustedes)	rehúsen	rehusaran or rehusasen

IMPERATIVE

rehúsa / rehusad

Use the present subjunctive in all cases other than these tú and vosotros affirmative forms.

Remember that subject pronouns are not used very often in Spanish.

reír (to laugh)

	PRESENT	PRESENT PERFECT
(yo)	río	he reído
(tú)	ríes	has reído
(él/ella/usted)	ríe	ha reído
(nosotros/as)	reímos	hemos reído
(vosotros/as)	reís	habéis reído
(ellos/ellas/ustedes)	ríen	han reído

	PRETERITE	IMPERFECT
(yo)	reí	reía
(tú)	reíste	reías
(él/ella/usted)	rio	reía
(nosotros/as)	reímos	reíamos
(vosotros/as)	reísteis	reíais
(ellos/ellas/ustedes)	rieron	reían

GERUND

riendo

PAST PARTICIPLE

reído

EXAMPLE PHRASES

Se echó a **reír**. She burst out laughing.

Se ríe de todo. She doesn't take anything seriously.

¿De qué **te ríes**? What are you laughing at?

Siempre **están riéndose** en clase. They're always laughing in class.

Me reía mucho con él. I always had a good laugh with him.

reír

	FUTURE	CONDITIONAL
(yo)	reiré	reiría
(tú)	reirás	reirías
(él/ella/usted)	reirá	reiría
(nosotros/as)	reiremos	reiríamos
(vosotros/as)	reiréis	reiríais
(ellos/ellas/ustedes)	reirán	reirían

	PRESENT SUBJUNCTIVE	IMPERFECT SUBJUNCTIVE
(yo)	ría	riera or riese
(tú)	rías	rieras or rieses
(él/ella/usted)	ría	riera or riese
(nosotros/as)	riamos	riéramos or riésemos
(vosotros/as)	riais	rierais or rleseis
(ellos/ellas/ustedes)	rían	rieran or riesen

IMPERATIVE

ríe / reíd

Use the present subjunctive in all cases other than these tú and vosotros affirmative forms.

EXAMPLE PHRASES

Te reirás cuando te lo cuente. You'll have a laugh when I tell you about it.

Que **se rían** lo que quieran. Let them laugh all they want.

No **te rías** de mí. Don't laugh at me.

¡Tú **ríete**, pero he pasado muchísimo miedo! You may laugh, but I was really frightened.

Remember that subject pronouns are not used very often in Spanish.

reñir (to scold, to quarrel)

	PRESENT		PRESENT PERFECT
(yo)	riño		he reñido
(tú)	riñes		has reñido
(él/ella/usted)	riñe		ha reñido
(nosotros/as)	reñimos		hemos reñido
(vosotros/as)	reñís		habéis reñido
(ellos/ellas/ustedes)	riñen		han reñido

	PRETERITE		IMPERFECT
(yo)	reñí		reñía
(tú)	reñiste		reñías
(él/ella/usted)	riñó		reñía
(nosotros/as)	reñimos		reñíamos
(vosotros/as)	reñisteis		reñíais
(ellos/ellas/ustedes)	riñeron		reñían

GERUND	PAST PARTICIPLE
riñendo	reñido

EXAMPLE PHRASES

Se pasan el día entero **riñendo**. They spend the whole day quarreling.

Ha reñido con su novio. She has fallen out with her boyfriend.

Les **riñó** por llegar tarde a casa. She told them off for getting home late.

Nos **reñía** sin motivo. She used to tell us off for no reason.

reñir

	FUTURE	CONDITIONAL
(yo)	reñiré	reñiría
(tú)	reñirás	reñirías
(él/ella/usted)	reñirá	reñiría
(nosotros/as)	reñiremos	reñiríamos
(vosotros/as)	reñiréis	reñiríais
(ellos/ellas/ ustedes)	reñirán	reñirían

	PRESENT SUBJUNCTIVE	IMPERFECT SUBJUNCTIVE
(yo)	riña	riñera *or* riñese
(tú)	riñas	riñeras *or* riñeses
(él/ella/usted)	riña	riñera *or* riñese
(nosotros/as)	riñamos	riñéramos *or* riñésemos
(vosotros/as)	riñáis	riñerais *or* riñeseis
(ellos/ellas/ ustedes)	riñan	riñeran *or* riñesen

IMPERATIVE

riñe / reñid

Use the present subjunctive in all cases other than these tú and vosotros affirmative forms.

EXAMPLE PHRASES

Si se entera, te **reñirá**. He'll tell you off if he finds out.

No la **riñas**, no es culpa suya. Don't tell her off, it's not her fault.

¡Niños, no **riñáis**! Children, don't quarrel!

Remember that subject pronouns are not used very often in Spanish.

repetir (to repeat)

	PRESENT		PRESENT PERFECT
(yo)	repito		he repetido
(tú)	repites		has repetido
(él/ella/usted)	repite		ha repetido
(nosotros/as)	repetimos		hemos repetido
(vosotros/as)	repetís		habéis repetido
(ellos/ellas/ ustedes)	repiten		han repetido

	PRETERITE		IMPERFECT
(yo)	repetí		repetía
(tú)	repetiste		repetías
(él/ella/usted)	repitió		repetía
(nosotros/as)	repetimos		repetíamos
(vosotros/as)	repetisteis		repetíais
(ellos/ellas/ ustedes)	repitieron		repetían

GERUND
repitiendo

PAST PARTICIPLE
repetido

EXAMPLE PHRASES

¿Podría **repetirlo**, por favor? Could you repeat that, please?

Le **repito** que es imposible. I repeat that it is impossible.

Se lo **he repetido** mil veces, pero no escucha. I've told him hundreds of times but he won't listen.

Repetía una y otra vez que era inocente. He kept repeating that he was innocent.

Remember that subject pronouns are not used very often in Spanish.

repetir

	FUTURE	CONDITIONAL
(yo)	repetiré	repetiría
(tú)	repetirás	repetirías
(él/ella/usted)	repetirá	repetiría
(nosotros/as)	repetiremos	repetiríamos
(vosotros/as)	repetiréis	repetiríais
(ellos/ellas/ ustedes)	repetirán	repetirían

	PRESENT SUBJUNCTIVE	IMPERFECT SUBJUNCTIVE
(yo)	repita	repitiera or repitiese
(tú)	repitas	repitieras or repitieses
(él/ella/usted)	repita	repitiera or repitiese
(nosotros/as)	repitamos	repitiéramos or repitiésemos
(vosotros/as)	repitáis	repitierais or repitieseis
(ellos/ellas/ ustedes)	repitan	repitieran or repitiesen

IMPERATIVE
repite / repetid

Use the present subjunctive in all cases other than these tú and vosotros affirmative forms.

EXAMPLE PHRASES
Si sigue así, **repetirá** curso. If she goes on like this, she'll end up having to repeat the year.

Espero que no **se repita**. I hope this won't happen again.

Repetid conmigo... Repeat after me...

Remember that subject pronouns are not used very often in Spanish.

resolver (to solve)

	PRESENT		PRESENT PERFECT
(yo)	resuelvo		he resuelto
(tú)	resuelves		has resuelto
(él/ella/usted)	resuelve		ha resuelto
(nosotros/as)	resolvemos		hemos resuelto
(vosotros/as)	resolvéis		habéis resuelto
(ellos/ellas/ ustedes)	resuelven		han resuelto

	PRETERITE		IMPERFECT
(yo)	resolví		resolvía
(tú)	resolviste		resolvías
(él/ella/usted)	resolvió		resolvía
(nosotros/as)	resolvimos		resolvíamos
(vosotros/as)	resolvisteis		resolvíais
(ellos/ellas/ ustedes)	resolvieron		resolvían

GERUND

resolviendo

PAST PARTICIPLE

resuelto

EXAMPLE PHRASES

Trataré de **resolver** tus dudas. I'll try to answer your questions.

Enfadarse no **resuelve** nada. Getting angry doesn't help at all.

No **hemos resuelto** los problemas. We haven't solved the problems.

Resolvimos el problema entre todos. We solved the problem together.

Remember that subject pronouns are not used very often in Spanish.

resolver

	FUTURE	CONDITIONAL
(yo)	resolveré	resolvería
(tú)	resolverás	resolverías
(él/ella/usted)	resolverá	resolvería
(nosotros/as)	resolveremos	resolveríamos
(vosotros/as)	resolveréis	resolveríais
(ellos/ellas/ ustedes)	resolverán	resolverían

	PRESENT SUBJUNCTIVE	IMPERFECT SUBJUNCTIVE
(yo)	resuelva	resolviera *or* resolviese
(tú)	resuelvas	resolvieras *or* resolvieses
(él/ella/usted)	resuelva	resolviera *or* resolviese
(nosotros/as)	resolvamos	resolviéramos *or* resolviésemos
(vosotros/as)	resolváis	resolvierais *or* resolvieseis
(ellos/ellas/ ustedes)	resuelvan	resolvieran *or* resolviesen

IMPERATIVE

resuelve / resolved

Use the present subjunctive in all cases other than these tú and vosotros affirmative forms.

EXAMPLE PHRASES

No te preocupes, ya lo **resolveremos**. Don't worry, we'll get it sorted.

Yo lo **resolvería** de otra forma. I'd sort it out another way.

Hasta que no lo **resuelva** no descansaré. I won't rest until I've sorted it out.

Remember that subject pronouns are not used very often in Spanish.

reunir (to put together, to gather)

	PRESENT		PRESENT PERFECT
(yo)	reúno		he reunido
(tú)	reúnes		has reunido
(él/ella/usted)	reúne		ha reunido
(nosotros/as)	reunimos		hemos reunido
(vosotros/as)	reunís		habéis reunido
(ellos/ellas/ ustedes)	reúnen		han reunido

	PRETERITE		IMPERFECT
(yo)	reuní		reunía
(tú)	reuniste		reunías
(él/ella/usted)	reunió		reunía
(nosotros/as)	reunimos		reuníamos
(vosotros/as)	reunisteis		reuníais
(ellos/ellas/ ustedes)	reunieron		reunían

GERUND
reuniendo

PAST PARTICIPLE
reunido

EXAMPLE PHRASES

Hemos conseguido **reunir** suficiente dinero. We've managed to raise enough money.

Hace tiempo que no **me reúno** con ellos. I haven't seen them for ages.

Reunió a todos para comunicarles la noticia. He called them all together to tell them the news.

No **reunía** los requisitos. She didn't satisfy the requirements.

Remember that subject pronouns are not used very often in Spanish.

reunir

	FUTURE	CONDITIONAL
(yo)	reuniré	reuniría
(tú)	reunirás	reunirías
(él/ella/usted)	reunirá	reuniría
(nosotros/as)	reuniremos	reuniríamos
(vosotros/as)	reuniréis	reuniríais
(ellos/ellas/ustedes)	reunirán	reunirían

	PRESENT SUBJUNCTIVE	IMPERFECT SUBJUNCTIVE
(yo)	reúna	reuniera or reuniese
(tú)	reúnas	reunieras or reunieses
(él/ella/usted)	reúna	reuniera or reuniese
(nosotros/as)	reunamos	reuniéramos or reuniésemos
(vosotros/as)	reunáis	reunierais or reunieseis
(ellos/ellas/ustedes)	reúnan	reunieran or reuniesen

IMPERATIVE

reúne / reunid

Use the present subjunctive in all cases other than these tú and vosotros affirmative forms.

EXAMPLE PHRASES

Se reunirán el viernes. They'll meet on Friday.

Necesito encontrar un local que **reúna** las condiciones. I need to find premises that will meet the requirements.

Consiguió que su familia **se reuniera** tras una larga separación. She managed to get her family back together again after a long separation.

Antes de acusarle, **reúne** las pruebas suficientes. Get enough evidence together before accusing him.

Remember that subject pronouns are not used very often in Spanish.

rogar (to beg, to pray)

	PRESENT		PRESENT PERFECT
(yo)	ruego		he rogado
(tú)	ruegas		has rogado
(él/ella/usted)	ruega		ha rogado
(nosotros/as)	rogamos		hemos rogado
(vosotros/as)	rogáis		habéis rogado
(ellos/ellas/ustedes)	ruegan		han rogado

	PRETERITE		IMPERFECT
(yo)	rogué		rogaba
(tú)	rogaste		rogabas
(él/ella/usted)	rogó		rogaba
(nosotros/as)	rogamos		rogábamos
(vosotros/as)	rogasteis		rogabais
(ellos/ellas/ustedes)	rogaron		rogaban

GERUND

rogando

PAST PARTICIPLE

rogado

EXAMPLE PHRASES

Les **rogamos** acepten nuestras disculpas. Please accept our apologies.

Te **ruego** que me lo devuelvas. Please give it back to me.

"**Se ruega** no fumar" "No smoking, please"

Me **rogó** que le perdonara. He begged me to forgive him.

Le **rogaba** a Dios que se curara. I prayed to God to make him better.

Remember that subject pronouns are not used very often in Spanish.

rogar

	FUTURE	CONDITIONAL
(yo)	rogaré	rogaría
(tú)	rogarás	rogarías
(él/ella/usted)	rogará	rogaría
(nosotros/as)	rogaremos	rogaríamos
(vosotros/as)	rogaréis	rogaríais
(ellos/ellas/ ustedes)	rogarán	rogarían

	PRESENT SUBJUNCTIVE	IMPERFECT SUBJUNCTIVE
(yo)	ruegue	rogara or rogase
(tú)	ruegues	rogaras or rogases
(él/ella/usted)	ruegue	rogara or rogase
(nosotros/as)	roguemos	rogáramos or rogásemos
(vosotros/as)	roguéis	rogarais or rogaseis
(ellos/ellas/ ustedes)	rueguen	rogaran or rogasen

IMPERATIVE

ruega / rogad

Use the present subjunctive in all cases other than these tú and vosotros affirmative forms.

EXAMPLE PHRASES

Ruega por mí. Pray for me.

romper (to break)

	PRESENT	PRESENT PERFECT
(yo)	rompo	he roto
(tú)	rompes	has roto
(él/ella/usted)	rompe	ha roto
(nosotros/as)	rompemos	hemos roto
(vosotros/as)	rompéis	habéis roto
(ellos/ellas/ustedes)	rompen	han roto

	PRETERITE	IMPERFECT
(yo)	rompí	rompía
(tú)	rompiste	rompías
(él/ella/usted)	rompió	rompía
(nosotros/as)	rompimos	rompíamos
(vosotros/as)	rompisteis	rompíais
(ellos/ellas/ustedes)	rompieron	rompían

GERUND
rompiendo

PAST PARTICIPLE
roto

EXAMPLE PHRASES

La cuerda **se** va a **romper**. The rope is going to break.

Siempre **están rompiendo** cosas. They're always breaking things.

Se me **ha roto** la pantalla del móvil. My cell phone screen got broken.

Se rompió el jarrón. The vase broke.

Él y su novia **han roto**. He and his girlfriend have broken up.

Remember that subject pronouns are not used very often in Spanish.

romper

	FUTURE	CONDITIONAL
(yo)	romperé	rompería
(tú)	romperás	romperías
(él/ella/usted)	romperá	rompería
(nosotros/as)	romperemos	romperíamos
(vosotros/as)	romperéis	romperíais
(ellos/ellas/ustedes)	romperán	romperían

	PRESENT SUBJUNCTIVE	IMPERFECT SUBJUNCTIVE
(yo)	rompa	rompiera or rompiese
(tú)	rompas	rompieras or rompieses
(él/ella/usted)	rompa	rompiera or rompiese
(nosotros/as)	rompamos	rompiéramos or rompiésemos
(vosotros/as)	rompáis	rompierais or rompieseis
(ellos/ellas/ustedes)	rompan	rompieran or rompiesen

IMPERATIVE

rompe / romped

*Use the present subjunctive in all cases other than these **tú** and **vosotros** affirmative forms.*

EXAMPLE PHRASES

Yo nunca **rompería** una promesa. I'd never break a promise.

Si lo **rompieras**, **tendrías** que pagarlo. If you broke it, you'd have to pay for it.

Rompe con él, si ya no le quieres. If you don't love him any more, finish with him.

Cuidado, no lo **rompas**. Careful you don't break it.

Remember that subject pronouns are not used very often in Spanish.

saber (to know)

	PRESENT		PRESENT PERFECT
(yo)	sé		he sabido
(tú)	sabes		has sabido
(él/ella/usted)	sabe		ha sabido
(nosotros/as)	sabemos		hemos sabido
(vosotros/as)	sabéis		habéis sabido
(ellos/ellas/ ustedes)	saben		han sabido

	PRETERITE		IMPERFECT
(yo)	supe		sabía
(tú)	supiste		sabías
(él/ella/usted)	supo		sabía
(nosotros/as)	supimos		sabíamos
(vosotros/as)	supisteis		sabíais
(ellos/ellas/ ustedes)	supieron		sabían

GERUND

sabiendo

PAST PARTICIPLE

sabido

EXAMPLE PHRASES

No lo **sé**. I don't know.

¿**Sabes** una cosa? Do you know what?

¿Cuándo lo **has sabido**? When did you find out?

No **supe** qué responder. I didn't know what to answer.

Pensaba que lo **sabías**. I thought you knew.

Remember that subject pronouns are not used very often in Spanish.

saber

	FUTURE	CONDITIONAL
(yo)	sabré	sabría
(tú)	sabrás	sabrías
(él/ella/usted)	sabrá	sabría
(nosotros/as)	sabremos	sabríamos
(vosotros/as)	sabréis	sabríais
(ellos/ellas/ ustedes)	sabrán	sabrían

	PRESENT SUBJUNCTIVE	IMPERFECT SUBJUNCTIVE
(yo)	sepa	supiera or supiese
(tú)	sepas	supieras or supieses
(él/ella/usted)	sepa	supiera or supiese
(nosotros/as)	sepamos	supiéramos or supiésemos
(vosotros/as)	sepáis	supierais or supieseis
(ellos/ellas/ ustedes)	sepan	supieran or supiesen

IMPERATIVE
sabe / sabed

Use the present subjunctive in all cases other than these tú and vosotros affirmative forms.

EXAMPLE PHRASES

Nunca se **sabrá** quién la mató. We'll never know who killed her.

Si no le tuvieras tanto miedo al agua, ya **sabrías** nadar. If you weren't so afraid of water, you'd already be able to swim.

Que yo **sepa**, vive en París. As far as I know, she lives in Paris.

¡Si **supiéramos** al menos dónde está! If only we knew where he was!

Remember that subject pronouns are not used very often in Spanish.

sacar (to take out)

	PRESENT	PRESENT PERFECT
(yo)	saco	he sacado
(tú)	sacas	has sacado
(él/ella/usted)	saca	ha sacado
(nosotros/as)	sacamos	hemos sacado
(vosotros/as)	sacáis	habéis sacado
(ellos/ellas/ustedes)	sacan	han sacado

	PRETERITE	IMPERFECT
(yo)	saqué	sacaba
(tú)	sacaste	sacabas
(él/ella/usted)	sacó	sacaba
(nosotros/as)	sacamos	sacábamos
(vosotros/as)	sacasteis	sacabais
(ellos/ellas/ustedes)	sacaron	sacaban

GERUND	PAST PARTICIPLE
sacando	sacado

EXAMPLE PHRASES

¿**Me sacas** una foto? Will you take a photo of me?

Estás sacando las cosas de quicio. You're blowing things out of all proportion.

Ya **he sacado** las entradas. I've already bought the tickets.

No **saqué** las basura ayer. I didn't take the garbage out last night.

¿De dónde **sacaba** tanto dinero? Where did he get so much money from?

Remember that subject pronouns are not used very often in Spanish.

sacar

	FUTURE	CONDITIONAL
(yo)	sacaré	sacaría
(tú)	sacarás	sacarías
(él/ella/usted)	sacará	sacaría
(nosotros/as)	sacaremos	sacaríamos
(vosotros/as)	sacaréis	sacaríais
(ellos/ellas/ustedes)	sacarán	sacarían

	PRESENT SUBJUNCTIVE	IMPERFECT SUBJUNCTIVE
(yo)	saque	sacara or sacase
(tú)	saques	sacaras or sacases
(él/ella/usted)	saque	sacara or sacase
(nosotros/as)	saquemos	sacáramos or sacásemos
(vosotros/as)	saquéis	sacarais or sacaseis
(ellos/ellas/ustedes)	saquen	sacaran or sacasen

IMPERATIVE
saca / sacad

Use the present subjunctive in all cases other than these tú and vosotros affirmative forms.

EXAMPLE PHRASES

Yo no **sacaría** todavía ninguna conclusión. I wouldn't draw any conclusions yet.

Quiero que **saques** inmediatamente esa bicicleta de casa. I want you to get that bike out of the house immediately.

Si te **sacaras** el carnet de conducir, serías mucho más independiente. You'd be much more independent if you got your driving licence.

No **saques** la cabeza por la ventanilla. Don't lean out of the window.

Remember that subject pronouns are not used very often in Spanish.

salir (to go out)

	PRESENT	PRESENT PERFECT
(yo)	salgo	he salido
(tú)	sales	has salido
(él/ella/usted)	sale	ha salido
(nosotros/as)	salimos	hemos salido
(vosotros/as)	salís	habéis salido
(ellos/ellas/ ustedes)	salen	han salido

	PRETERITE	IMPERFECT
(yo)	salí	salía
(tú)	saliste	salías
(él/ella/usted)	salió	salía
(nosotros/as)	salimos	salíamos
(vosotros/as)	salisteis	salíais
(ellos/ellas/ ustedes)	salieron	salían

GERUND	PAST PARTICIPLE
saliendo	salido

EXAMPLE PHRASES

Hace tiempo que no **salimos**. We haven't been out for a while.

Está saliendo con un compañero de trabajo. She's going out with a colleague from work.

Ha salido. She's gone out.

Su foto **salió** en todos los periódicos. Her picture appeared in all the newspapers.

Salía muy tarde de trabajar. He used to finish work very late.

Remember that subject pronouns are not used very often in Spanish.

salir

	FUTURE	CONDITIONAL
(yo)	saldré	saldría
(tú)	saldrás	saldrías
(él/ella/usted)	saldrá	saldría
(nosotros/as)	saldremos	saldríamos
(vosotros/as)	saldréis	saldríais
(ellos/ellas/ustedes)	saldrán	saldrían

	PRESENT SUBJUNCTIVE	IMPERFECT SUBJUNCTIVE
(yo)	salga	saliera or saliese
(tú)	salgas	salieras or salieses
(él/ella/usted)	salga	saliera or saliese
(nosotros/as)	salgamos	saliéramos or saliésemos
(vosotros/as)	salgáis	salierais or salieseis
(ellos/ellas/ustedes)	salgan	salieran or saliesen

IMPERATIVE
sal / salid

Use the present subjunctive in all cases other than these tú and vosotros affirmative forms.

EXAMPLE PHRASES
Te dije que **saldría** muy caro. I told you it would work out very expensive.

Espero que todo **salga** bien. I hope everything works out all right.

Si **saliera** elegido... If I were elected...

Por favor, **salgan** por la puerta de atrás. Please leave via the back door.

satisfacer (to satisfy)

	PRESENT		PRESENT PERFECT
(yo)	satisfago		he satisfecho
(tú)	satisfaces		has satisfecho
(él/ella/usted)	satisface		ha satisfecho
(nosotros/as)	satisfacemos		hemos satisfecho
(vosotros/as)	satisfacéis		habéis satisfecho
(ellos/ellas/ ustedes)	satisfacen		han satisfecho

	PRETERITE		IMPERFECT
(yo)	satisfice		satisfacía
(tú)	satisficiste		satisfacías
(él/ella/usted)	satisfizo		satisfacía
(nosotros/as)	satisficimos		satisfacíamos
(vosotros/as)	satisficisteis		satisfacíais
(ellos/ellas/ ustedes)	satisficieron		satisfacían

GERUND

satisfaciendo

PAST PARTICIPLE

satisfecho

EXAMPLE PHRASES

No me **satisface** nada el resultado. I'm not at all satisfied with the result.

Ha satisfecho mis expectativas. It came up to my expectations.

Eso **satisfizo** mi curiosidad. That satisfied my curiosity.

Aquella vida **satisfacía** todas mis necesidades. That lifestyle satisfied all my needs.

Remember that subject pronouns are not used very often in Spanish.

satisfacer

	FUTURE	CONDITIONAL
(yo)	satisfaré	satisfaría
(tú)	satisfarás	satisfarías
(él/ella/usted)	satisfará	satisfaría
(nosotros/as)	satisfaremos	satisfaríamos
(vosotros/as)	satisfaréis	satisfaríais
(ellos/ellas/ ustedes)	satisfarán	satisfarían

	PRESENT SUBJUNCTIVE	IMPERFECT SUBJUNCTIVE
(yo)	satisfaga	satisficiera or satisficiese
(tú)	satisfagas	satisficieras or satisficieses
(él/ella/usted)	satisfaga	satisficiera or satisficiese
(nosotros/as)	satisfagamos	satisficiéramos or satisficiésemos
(vosotros/as)	satisfagáis	satisficierais or satisficieseis
(ellos/ellas/ ustedes)	satisfagan	satisficieran or satisficiesen

IMPERATIVE

satisfaz or satisface / satisfaced

Use the present subjunctive in all cases other than these tú and vosotros affirmative forms.

EXAMPLE PHRASES

Le **satisfará** saber que hemos cumplido nuestros objetivos. You'll be happy
to know that we have achieved our objectives.

Me **satisfaría** mucho más que estudiaras una carrera. I'd be far happier if
you went to university.

Remember that subject pronouns are not used very often in Spanish.

seguir (to follow)

	PRESENT	PRESENT PERFECT
(yo)	sigo	he seguido
(tú)	sigues	has seguido
(él/ella/usted)	sigue	ha seguido
(nosotros/as)	seguimos	hemos seguido
(vosotros/as)	seguís	habéis seguido
(ellos/ellas/ustedes)	siguen	han seguido

	PRETERITE	IMPERFECT
(yo)	seguí	seguía
(tú)	seguiste	seguías
(él/ella/usted)	siguió	seguía
(nosotros/as)	seguimos	seguíamos
(vosotros/as)	seguisteis	seguíais
(ellos/ellas/ustedes)	siguieron	seguían

GERUND	PAST PARTICIPLE
siguiendo	seguido

EXAMPLE PHRASES

Si **sigues** así, acabarás mal. If you go on like this you'll end up badly.

¿Te **han seguido**? Have you been followed?

Siguió cantando como si nada. He went on singing as if nothing was the matter.

El ordenador **seguía** funcionando a pesar del apagón. The computer went on working in spite of the power cut.

La **estuve siguiendo** en Twitter un tiempo. I was following her on Twitter for a while.

Remember that subject pronouns are not used very often in Spanish.

seguir

	FUTURE	CONDITIONAL
(yo)	seguiré	seguiría
(tú)	seguirás	seguirías
(él/ella/usted)	seguirá	seguiría
(nosotros/as)	seguiremos	seguiríamos
(vosotros/as)	seguiréis	seguiríais
(ellos/ellas/ ustedes)	seguirán	seguirían

	PRESENT SUBJUNCTIVE	IMPERFECT SUBJUNCTIVE
(yo)	siga	siguiera or siguiese
(tú)	sigas	siguieras or siguieses
(él/ella/usted)	siga	siguiera or siguiese
(nosotros/as)	sigamos	siguiéramos or siguiésemos
(vosotros/as)	sigáis	siguierais or siguieseis
(ellos/ellas/ ustedes)	sigan	siguieran or siguiesen

IMPERATIVE
sigue / seguid

Use the present subjunctive in all cases other than these tú and vosotros affirmative forms.

EXAMPLE PHRASES
Nos seguiremos viendo. We will go on seeing each other.

Quiero que **sigas** estudiando. I want you to go on with your studies.

Si **siguieras** mis consejos, te iría muchísimo mejor. You'd be much better off if you followed my advice.

Siga por esta calle hasta el final. Go on till you get to the end of the street.

Remember that subject pronouns are not used very often in Spanish.

sentir (to feel, to be sorry)

	PRESENT		PRESENT PERFECT
(yo)	siento		he sentido
(tú)	sientes		has sentido
(él/ella/usted)	siente		ha sentido
(nosotros/as)	sentimos		hemos sentido
(vosotros/as)	sentís		habéis sentido
(ellos/ellas/ ustedes)	sienten		han sentido

	PRETERITE		IMPERFECT
(yo)	sentí		sentía
(tú)	sentiste		sentías
(él/ella/usted)	sintió		sentía
(nosotros/as)	sentimos		sentíamos
(vosotros/as)	sentisteis		sentíais
(ellos/ellas/ ustedes)	sintieron		sentían

GERUND

sintiendo

PAST PARTICIPLE

sentido

EXAMPLE PHRASES

Te vas a **sentir** sola. You'll feel lonely.

Siento mucho lo que pasó. I'm really sorry about what happened.

Ha sentido mucho la muerte de su padre. He has been greatly affected by his father's death.

Sentí un pinchazo en la pierna. I felt a sharp pain in my leg.

Me sentía muy mal. I felt terrible.

Remember that subject pronouns are not used very often in Spanish.

sentir

	FUTURE	CONDITIONAL
(yo)	sentiré	sentiría
(tú)	sentirás	sentirías
(él/ella/usted)	sentirá	sentiría
(nosotros/as)	sentiremos	sentiríamos
(vosotros/as)	sentiréis	sentiríais
(ellos/ellas/ustedes)	sentirán	sentirían

	PRESENT SUBJUNCTIVE	IMPERFECT SUBJUNCTIVE
(yo)	sienta	sintiera or sintiese
(tú)	sientas	sintieras or sintieses
(él/ella/usted)	sienta	sintiera or sintiese
(nosotros/as)	sintamos	sintiéramos or sintiésemos
(vosotros/as)	sintáis	sintierais or sintieseis
(ellos/ellas/ustedes)	sientan	sintieran or sintiesen

IMPERATIVE

siente / sentid

Use the present subjunctive in all cases other than these tú and vosotros affirmative forms.

EXAMPLE PHRASES

Al principio **te sentirás** un poco raro. You'll feel a bit strange at first.

Yo **sentiría** mucho que usted se fuera de la empresa. I'd be really sorry if you left the firm.

No creo que lo **sienta**. I don't think she's sorry.

Sería mucho más preocupante si no **sintiera** la pierna. It would be much more worrying if he couldn't feel his leg.

Remember that subject pronouns are not used very often in Spanish.

ser (to be)

	PRESENT	PRESENT PERFECT
(yo)	soy	he sido
(tú)	eres	has sido
(él/ella/usted)	es	ha sido
(nosotros/as)	somos	hemos sido
(vosotros/as)	sois	habéis sido
(ellos/ellas/ ustedes)	son	han sido

	PRETERITE	IMPERFECT
(yo)	fui	era
(tú)	fuiste	eras
(él/ella/usted)	fue	era
(nosotros/as)	fuimos	éramos
(vosotros/as)	fuisteis	erais
(ellos/ellas/ ustedes)	fueron	eran

GERUND
siendo

PAST PARTICIPLE
sido

EXAMPLE PHRASES

Soy español. I'm Spanish.

Estás siendo muy paciente con él. You're being very patient with him.

Ha sido un duro golpe. It was a major blow.

¿**Fuiste** tú el que llamó? Was it you who phoned?

Era de noche. It was dark.

Remember that subject pronouns are not used very often in Spanish.

ser

	FUTURE	CONDITIONAL
(yo)	seré	sería
(tú)	serás	serías
(él/ella/usted)	será	sería
(nosotros/as)	seremos	seríamos
(vosotros/as)	seréis	seríais
(ellos/ellas/ustedes)	serán	serían

	PRESENT SUBJUNCTIVE	IMPERFECT SUBJUNCTIVE
(yo)	sea	fuera or fuese
(tú)	seas	fueras or fueses
(él/ella/usted)	sea	fuera or fuese
(nosotros/as)	seamos	fuéramos or fuésemos
(vosotros/as)	seáis	fuerais or fueseis
(ellos/ellas/ustedes)	sean	fueran or fuesen

IMPERATIVE
sé / sed

Use the present subjunctive in all cases other than these tú and vosotros affirmative forms.

EXAMPLE PHRASES
Será de Joaquín. It must be Joaquin's.

Eso **sería** estupendo. That would be great.

O **sea**, que no vienes. So you're not coming.

No **seas** tan perfeccionista. Don't be such a perfectionist.

¡**Sed** buenos! Behave yourselves!

Remember that subject pronouns are not used very often in Spanish.

soler (to be wont to)

	PRESENT	PRESENT PERFECT
(yo)	suelo	*not used*
(tú)	sueles	
(él/ella/usted)	suele	
(nosotros/as)	solemos	
(vosotros/as)	soléis	
(ellos/ellas/ ustedes)	suelen	

	PRETERITE	IMPERFECT
(yo)	*not used*	solía
(tú)		solías
(él/ella/usted)		solía
(nosotros/as)		solíamos
(vosotros/as)		solíais
(ellos/ellas/ ustedes)		solían

GERUND	PAST PARTICIPLE
soliendo	*not used*

EXAMPLE PHRASES

Suele salir a las ocho. He usually leaves at eight.

Solíamos ir todos los años a la playa. We used to go to the beach every year.

soler

	FUTURE	CONDITIONAL
(yo)	*not used*	*not used*
(tú)		
(él/ella/usted)		
(nosotros/as)		
(vosotros/as)		
(ellos/ellas/ ustedes)		

	PRESENT SUBJUNCTIVE	IMPERFECT SUBJUNCTIVE
(yo)	suela	soliera *or* soliese
(tú)	suelas	solieras *or* solieses
(él/ella/usted)	suela	soliera *or* soliese
(nosotros/as)	solamos	soliéramos *or* soliésemos
(vosotros/as)	soláis	solierais *or* solieseis
(ellos/ellas/ ustedes)	suelan	solieran *or* soliesen

IMPERATIVE

not used

Remember that subject pronouns are not used very often in Spanish.

soltar (to let go of, to release)

	PRESENT		PRESENT PERFECT
(yo)	suelto		he soltado
(tú)	sueltas		has soltado
(él/ella/usted)	suelta		ha soltado
(nosotros/as)	soltamos		hemos soltado
(vosotros/as)	soltáis		habéis soltado
(ellos/ellas/ ustedes)	sueltan		han soltado

	PRETERITE		IMPERFECT
(yo)	solté		soltaba
(tú)	soltaste		soltabas
(él/ella/usted)	soltó		soltaba
(nosotros/as)	soltamos		soltábamos
(vosotros/as)	soltasteis		soltabais
(ellos/ellas/ ustedes)	soltaron		soltaban

GERUND
soltando

PAST PARTICIPLE
soltado

EXAMPLE PHRASES

Al final logró **soltarse**. Eventually she managed to break free.

No para de **soltar** tacos. He swears all the time.

¿Por qué no **te sueltas** el pelo? Why don't you have your hair loose?

Han soltado a los rehenes. They've released the hostages.

Soltó una carcajada. He burst out laughing.

Remember that subject pronouns are not used very often in Spanish.

soltar

	FUTURE	CONDITIONAL
(yo)	soltaré	soltaría
(tú)	soltarás	soltarías
(él/ella/usted)	soltará	soltaría
(nosotros/as)	soltaremos	soltaríamos
(vosotros/as)	soltaréis	soltaríais
(ellos/ellas/ ustedes)	soltarán	soltarían

	PRESENT SUBJUNCTIVE	IMPERFECT SUBJUNCTIVE
(yo)	suelte	soltara or soltase
(tú)	sueltes	soltaras or soltases
(él/ella/usted)	suelte	soltara or soltase
(nosotros/as)	soltemos	soltáramos or soltásemos
(vosotros/as)	soltéis	soltarais or soltaseis
(ellos/ellas/ ustedes)	suelten	soltaran or soltasen

IMPERATIVE
suelta / soltad

Use the present subjunctive in all cases other than these tú and vosotros affirmative forms.

EXAMPLE PHRASES

Te **soltaré** el brazo si me dices dónde está. I'll let go of your arm if you tell me where he is.

Te dije que lo **soltaras**. I told you to let it go.

No **sueltes** la cuerda. Don't let go of the rope.

¡**Suéltame**! Let me go!

Remember that subject pronouns are not used very often in Spanish.

sonar (to sound, to ring)

	PRESENT		PRESENT PERFECT
(yo)	sueno		he sonado
(tú)	suenas		has sonado
(él/ella/usted)	suena		ha sonado
(nosotros/as)	sonamos		hemos sonado
(vosotros/as)	sonáis		habéis sonado
(ellos/ellas/ustedes)	suenan		han sonado

	PRETERITE		IMPERFECT
(yo)	soné		sonaba
(tú)	sonaste		sonabas
(él/ella/usted)	sonó		sonaba
(nosotros/as)	sonamos		sonábamos
(vosotros/as)	sonasteis		sonabais
(ellos/ellas/ustedes)	sonaron		sonaban

GERUND

sonando

PAST PARTICIPLE

sonado

EXAMPLE PHRASES

¿**Te suena** su nombre? Does her name sound familiar?

Ha sonado tu móvil. Your mobile rang.

Justo en ese momento **sonó** el timbre. Just then the bell rang.

Sonabas un poco triste por teléfono. You sounded a bit sad on the phone.

Estaba sonando el teléfono. The phone was ringing.

Remember that subject pronouns are not used very often in Spanish.

sonar

	FUTURE	CONDITIONAL
(yo)	sonaré	sonaría
(tú)	sonarás	sonarías
(él/ella/usted)	sonará	sonaría
(nosotros/as)	sonaremos	sonaríamos
(vosotros/as)	sonaréis	sonaríais
(ellos/ellas/ustedes)	sonarán	sonarían

	PRESENT SUBJUNCTIVE	IMPERFECT SUBJUNCTIVE
(yo)	suene	sonara or sonase
(tú)	suenes	sonaras or sonases
(él/ella/usted)	suene	sonara or sonase
(nosotros/as)	sonemos	sonáramos or sonásemos
(vosotros/as)	sonéis	sonarais or sonaseis
(ellos/ellas/ustedes)	suenen	sonaran or sonasen

IMPERATIVE
suena / sonad

Use the present subjunctive in all cases other than these tú and vosotros affirmative forms.

EXAMPLE PHRASES
Hay que esperar a que **suene** un pitido. We have to wait until we hear a beep.

¡**Suénate** la nariz! Blow your nose!

temer (to be afraid)

	PRESENT	PRESENT PERFECT
(yo)	temo	he temido
(tú)	temes	has temido
(él/ella/usted)	teme	ha temido
(nosotros/as)	tememos	hemos temido
(vosotros/as)	teméis	habéis temido
(ellos/ellas/ ustedes)	temen	han temido

	PRETERITE	IMPERFECT
(yo)	temí	temía
(tú)	temiste	temías
(él/ella/usted)	temió	temía
(nosotros/as)	temimos	temíamos
(vosotros/as)	temisteis	temíais
(ellos/ellas/ ustedes)	temieron	temían

GERUND
temiendo

PAST PARTICIPLE
temido

EXAMPLE PHRASES

Me temo que no. I'm afraid not.

Se temen lo peor. They fear the worst.

–Ha empezado a llover. –**Me** lo **temía**. "It's started raining." – "I was afraid it would."

Temí ofenderles. I was afraid of offending them.

Temían por su seguridad. They feared for their safety.

Remember that subject pronouns are not used very often in Spanish.

temer

	FUTURE	CONDITIONAL
(yo)	temeré	temería
(tú)	temerás	temerías
(él/ella/usted)	temerá	temería
(nosotros/as)	temeremos	temeríamos
(vosotros/as)	temeréis	temeríais
(ellos/ellas/ ustedes)	temerán	temerían

	PRESENT SUBJUNCTIVE	IMPERFECT SUBJUNCTIVE
(yo)	tema	temiera or temiese
(tú)	temas	temieras or temieses
(él/ella/usted)	tema	temiera or temiese
(nosotros/as)	temamos	temiéramos or temiésemos
(vosotros/as)	temáis	temierais or temieseis
(ellos/ellas/ ustedes)	teman	temieran or temiesen

IMPERATIVE
teme / temed

Use the present subjunctive in all cases other than these tú and vosotros affirmative forms.

EXAMPLE PHRASES
No **temas**. Don't be afraid.

Remember that subject pronouns are not used very often in Spanish.

tener (to have)

	PRESENT		PRESENT PERFECT
(yo)	tengo		he tenido
(tú)	tienes		has tenido
(él/ella/usted)	tiene		ha tenido
(nosotros/as)	tenemos		hemos tenido
(vosotros/as)	tenéis		habéis tenido
(ellos/ellas/ ustedes)	tienen		ha tenido

	PRETERITE		IMPERFECT
(yo)	tuve		tenía
(tú)	tuviste		tenías
(él/ella/usted)	tuvo		tenía
(nosotros/as)	tuvimos		teníamos
(vosotros/as)	tuvisteis		teníais
(ellos/ellas/ ustedes)	tuvieron		tenían

GERUND	PAST PARTICIPLE
teniendo	tenido

EXAMPLE PHRASES

Tengo sed. I'm thirsty.

Están teniendo muchos problemas con el coche. They're having a lot of trouble with the car.

En recepción **tienen** planos de la ciudad. There are street maps at reception.

Tuvimos que irnos. We had to leave.

Tenía muchos amigos en Facebook. She had a lot of friends on Facebook.

Remember that subject pronouns are not used very often in Spanish.

tener

	FUTURE	CONDITIONAL
(yo)	tendré	tendría
(tú)	tendrás	tendrías
(él/ella/usted)	tendrá	tendría
(nosotros/as)	tendremos	tendríamos
(vosotros/as)	tendréis	tendríais
(ellos/ellas/ustedes)	tendrán	tendrían

	PRESENT SUBJUNCTIVE	IMPERFECT SUBJUNCTIVE
(yo)	tenga	tuviera or tuviese
(tú)	tengas	tuvieras or tuvieses
(él/ella/usted)	tenga	tuviera or tuviese
(nosotros/as)	tengamos	tuviéramos or tuviésemos
(vosotros/as)	tengáis	tuvierais or tuvieseis
(ellos/ellas/ustedes)	tengan	tuvieran or tuviesen

IMPERATIVE
ten / tened

Use the present subjunctive in all cases other than these tú and vosotros affirmative forms.

EXAMPLE PHRASES

Tendrás que pagarlo tú. You'll have to pay for it yourself.

Tendrías que comer más. You should eat more.

No creo que **tenga** suficiente dinero. I don't think I've got enough money.

Si **tuviera** tiempo, haría un curso de catalán. If I had time, I'd do a Catalan course.

Ten cuidado. Be careful.

No **tengas** miedo. Don't be afraid.

Remember that subject pronouns are not used very often in Spanish.

tocar (to touch, to play)

	PRESENT	PRESENT PERFECT
(yo)	toco	he tocado
(tú)	tocas	has tocado
(él/ella/usted)	toca	ha tocado
(nosotros/as)	tocamos	hemos tocado
(vosotros/as)	tocáis	habéis tocado
(ellos/ellas/ ustedes)	tocan	han tocado

	PRETERITE	IMPERFECT
(yo)	toqué	tocaba
(tú)	tocaste	tocabas
(él/ella/usted)	tocó	tocaba
(nosotros/as)	tocamos	tocábamos
(vosotros/as)	tocasteis	tocabais
(ellos/ellas/ ustedes)	tocaron	tocaban

GERUND
tocando

PAST PARTICIPLE
tocado

EXAMPLE PHRASES

Toca el violín. He plays the violin.

Te **toca** fregar los platos. It's your turn to do the dishes.

Me **ha tocado** el peor asiento. I've ended up with the worst seat.

Le **tocó** la lotería. He won the lottery.

Me **tocaba** tirar a mí. It was my turn.

Remember that subject pronouns are not used very often in Spanish.

tocar

	FUTURE	CONDITIONAL
(yo)	tocaré	tocaría
(tú)	tocarás	tocarías
(él/ella/usted)	tocará	tocaría
(nosotros/as)	tocaremos	tocaríamos
(vosotros/as)	tocaréis	tocaríais
(ellos/ellas/ ustedes)	tocarán	tocarían

	PRESENT SUBJUNCTIVE	IMPERFECT SUBJUNCTIVE
(yo)	toque	tocara or tocase
(tú)	toques	tocaras or tocases
(él/ella/usted)	toque	tocara or tocase
(nosotros/as)	toquemos	tocáramos or tocásemos
(vosotros/as)	toquéis	tocarais or tocaseis
(ellos/ellas/ ustedes)	toquen	tocaran or tocasen

IMPERATIVE
toca / tocad

Use the present subjunctive in all cases other than these tú and vosotros affirmative forms.

EXAMPLE PHRASES

Sabía que me **tocaría** ir a mí. I knew I'd be the one to have to go.

No lo **toques**. Don't touch it.

Tócalo, verás qué suave. Touch it and see how soft it is.

Remember that subject pronouns are not used very often in Spanish.

torcer (to twist)

	PRESENT		PRESENT PERFECT
(yo)	tuerzo		he torcido
(tú)	tuerces		has torcido
(él/ella/usted)	tuerce		ha torcido
(nosotros/as)	torcemos		hemos torcido
(vosotros/as)	torcéis		habéis torcido
(ellos/ellas/ ustedes)	tuercen		han torcido

	PRETERITE		IMPERFECT
(yo)	torcí		torcía
(tú)	torciste		torcías
(él/ella/usted)	torció		torcía
(nosotros/as)	torcimos		torcíamos
(vosotros/as)	torcisteis		torcíais
(ellos/ellas/ ustedes)	torcieron		torcían

GERUND

torciendo

PAST PARTICIPLE

torcido

EXAMPLE PHRASES

Acaba de **torcer** la esquina. She has just turned the corner.

El sendero **tuerce** luego a la derecha. Later on the path bends around to the right.

Se le **ha torcido** la muñeca. She's sprained her wrist.

Se me **torció** el tobillo. I twisted my ankle.

Remember that subject pronouns are not used very often in Spanish.

torcer

	FUTURE	CONDITIONAL
(yo)	torceré	torcería
(tú)	torcerás	torcerías
(él/ella/usted)	torcerá	torcería
(nosotros/as)	torceremos	torceríamos
(vosotros/as)	torceréis	torceríais
(ellos/ellas/ ustedes)	torcerán	torcerían

	PRESENT SUBJUNCTIVE	IMPERFECT SUBJUNCTIVE
(yo)	tuerza	torciera or torciese
(tú)	tuerzas	torcieras or torcieses
(él/ella/usted)	tuerza	torciera or torciese
(nosotros/as)	torzamos	torciéramos or torciésemos
(vosotros/as)	torzáis	torcierais or torcieseis
(ellos/ellas/ ustedes)	tuerzan	torcieran or torciesen

IMPERATIVE
tuerce / torced

Use the present subjunctive in all cases other than these tú and vosotros affirmative forms.

EXAMPLE PHRASES
Tuerza a la izquierda. Turn left.
Tuércelo un poco más. Twist it a little more.

Remember that subject pronouns are not used very often in Spanish.

traer (to bring)

	PRESENT		PRESENT PERFECT
(yo)	traigo		he traído
(tú)	traes		has traído
(él/ella/usted)	trae		ha traído
(nosotros/as)	traemos		hemos traído
(vosotros/as)	traéis		habéis traído
(ellos/ellas/ ustedes)	traen		han traído

	PRETERITE		IMPERFECT
(yo)	traje		traía
(tú)	trajiste		traías
(él/ella/usted)	trajo		traía
(nosotros/as)	trajimos		traíamos
(vosotros/as)	trajisteis		traíais
(ellos/ellas/ ustedes)	trajeron		traían

GERUND

trayendo

PAST PARTICIPLE

traído

EXAMPLE PHRASES

¿Me puedes **traer** una toalla? Can you bring me a towel?

Nos **está trayendo** muchos problemas. It's causing us a lot of trouble.

¿**Has traído** lo que te pedí? Have you brought what I asked for?

Traía un vestido nuevo. She was wearing a new dress.

No **trajo** el dinero. He didn't bring the money.

Remember that subject pronouns are not used very often in Spanish.

traer

	FUTURE	CONDITIONAL
(yo)	traeré	traería
(tú)	traerás	traerías
(él/ella/usted)	traerá	traería
(nosotros/as)	traeremos	traeríamos
(vosotros/as)	traeréis	traeríais
(ellos/ellas/ustedes)	traerán	traerían

	PRESENT SUBJUNCTIVE	IMPERFECT SUBJUNCTIVE
(yo)	traiga	trajera or trajese
(tú)	traigas	trajeras or trajeses
(él/ella/usted)	traiga	trajera or trajese
(nosotros/as)	traigamos	trajéramos or trajésemos
(vosotros/as)	traigáis	trajerais or trajeseis
(ellos/ellas/ustedes)	traigan	trajeran or trajesen

IMPERATIVE

trae / traed

*Use the present subjunctive in all cases other than these **tú** and **vosotros** affirmative forms.*

EXAMPLE PHRASES

Me pregunto qué **se traerán** entre manos. I wonder what they're up to.

Se lo **traería** de África. He must have brought it over from Africa.

Dile que **traiga** a algún amigo. Tell him to bring a friend with him.

Trae eso. Give that here.

Remember that subject pronouns are not used very often in Spanish.

valer (to be worth)

	PRESENT	PRESENT PERFECT
(yo)	valgo	he valido
(tú)	vales	has valido
(él/ella/usted)	vale	ha valido
(nosotros/as)	valemos	hemos valido
(vosotros/as)	valéis	habéis valido
(ellos/ellas/ ustedes)	valen	han valido

	PRETERITE	IMPERFECT
(yo)	valí	valía
(tú)	valiste	valías
(él/ella/usted)	valió	valía
(nosotros/as)	valimos	valíamos
(vosotros/as)	valisteis	valíais
(ellos/ellas/ ustedes)	valieron	valían

GERUND
valiendo

PAST PARTICIPLE
valido

EXAMPLE PHRASES

No puede **valerse** por sí mismo. He can't look after himself.

¿Cuánto **vale** eso? How much is that?

¿**Vale**? OK?

No le **valió** de nada suplicar. Begging got her nowhere.

No **valía** la pena. It wasn't worth it.

valer

	FUTURE	CONDITIONAL
(yo)	valdré	valdría
(tú)	valdrás	valdrías
(él/ella/usted)	valdrá	valdría
(nosotros/as)	valdremos	valdríamos
(vosotros/as)	valdréis	valdríais
(ellos/ellas/ ustedes)	valdrán	valdrían

	PRESENT SUBJUNCTIVE	IMPERFECT SUBJUNCTIVE
(yo)	valga	valiera or valiese
(tú)	valgas	valieras or valieses
(él/ella/usted)	valga	valiera or valiese
(nosotros/as)	valgamos	valiéramos or valiésemos
(vosotros/as)	valgáis	valierais or valieseis
(ellos/ellas/ ustedes)	valgan	valieran or valiesen

IMPERATIVE
vale / valed

Use the present subjunctive in all cases other than these tú and vosotros affirmative forms.

EXAMPLE PHRASES
Valdrá unos 500 euros. It must cost around 500 euros.

Yo no **valdría** para enfermera. I'd make a hopeless nurse.

Valga lo que **valga**, lo compro. I'll buy it, no matter how much it costs.

Remember that subject pronouns are not used very often in Spanish.

vencer (to win, to beat)

	PRESENT	PRESENT PERFECT
(yo)	venzo	he vencido
(tú)	vences	has vencido
(él/ella/usted)	vence	ha vencido
(nosotros/as)	vencemos	hemos vencido
(vosotros/as)	vencéis	habéis vencido
(ellos/ellas/ ustedes)	vencen	han vencido

	PRETERITE	IMPERFECT
(yo)	vencí	vencía
(tú)	venciste	vencías
(él/ella/usted)	venció	vencía
(nosotros/as)	vencimos	vencíamos
(vosotros/as)	vencisteis	vencíais
(ellos/ellas/ ustedes)	vencieron	vencían

GERUND

venciendo

PAST PARTICIPLE

vencido

EXAMPLE PHRASES

Tienes que **vencer** el miedo. You must overcome your fear.

El plazo de matrícula **vence** mañana. Tomorrow is the last day for registration.

Finalmente le **ha vencido** el sueño. At last, he was overcome by sleep.

Vencimos por dos a uno. We won two-one.

Le **vencía** la curiosidad. His curiosity got the better of him.

Remember that subject pronouns are not used very often in Spanish.

vencer

	FUTURE	CONDITIONAL
(yo)	venceré	vencería
(tú)	vencerás	vencerías
(él/ella/usted)	vencerá	vencería
(nosotros/as)	venceremos	venceríamos
(vosotros/as)	venceréis	venceríais
(ellos/ellas/ustedes)	vencerán	vencerían

	PRESENT SUBJUNCTIVE	IMPERFECT SUBJUNCTIVE
(yo)	venza	venciera or venciese
(tú)	venzas	vencieras or vencieses
(él/ella/usted)	venza	venciera or venciese
(nosotros/as)	venzamos	venciéramos or venciésemos
(vosotros/as)	venzáis	vencierais or vencieseis
(ellos/ellas/ustedes)	venzan	vencieran or venciesen

IMPERATIVE

vence / venced

Use the present subjunctive in all cases other than these tú and vosotros affirmative forms.

EXAMPLE PHRASES

Nuestro ejército **vencerá**. Our army will be victorious.

No dejes que te **venza** la impaciencia. Don't let your impatience get the better of you.

venir (to come)

	PRESENT	PRESENT PERFECT
(yo)	vengo	he venido
(tú)	vienes	has venido
(él/ella/usted)	viene	ha venido
(nosotros/as)	venimos	hemos venido
(vosotros/as)	venís	habéis venido
(ellos/ellas/ustedes)	vienen	han venido

	PRETERITE	IMPERFECT
(yo)	vine	venía
(tú)	viniste	venías
(él/ella/usted)	vino	venía
(nosotros/as)	vinimos	veníamos
(vosotros/as)	vinisteis	veníais
(ellos/ellas/ustedes)	vinieron	venían

GERUND	PAST PARTICIPLE
viniendo	venido

EXAMPLE PHRASES

Vengo andando desde la playa. I've walked all the way from the beach.

La casa **se está viniendo** abajo. The house is falling apart.

Ha venido en taxi. He came by taxi.

Vinieron a verme al hospital. They came to see me in hospital.

La noticia **venía** en el periódico. The news was in the paper.

Remember that subject pronouns are not used very often in Spanish.

venir

	FUTURE	CONDITIONAL
(yo)	vendré	vendría
(tú)	vendrás	vendrías
(él/ella/usted)	vendrá	vendría
(nosotros/as)	vendremos	vendríamos
(vosotros/as)	vendréis	vendríais
(ellos/ellas/ustedes)	vendrán	vendrían

	PRESENT SUBJUNCTIVE	IMPERFECT SUBJUNCTIVE
(yo)	venga	viniera or viniese
(tú)	vengas	vinieras or vinieses
(él/ella/usted)	venga	viniera or viniese
(nosotros/as)	vengamos	viniéramos or viniésemos
(vosotros/as)	vengáis	vinierais or vinieseis
(ellos/ellas/ustedes)	vengan	vinieran or viniesen

IMPERATIVE

ven / venid

Use the present subjunctive in all cases other than these tú and vosotros affirmative forms.

EXAMPLE PHRASES

¿**Vendrás** conmigo al cine? Will you come to the movies with me?

A mí me **vendría** mejor el sábado. Saturday would be better for me.

¡**Venga**, vámonos! Come on, let's go!

No **vengas** si no quieres. Don't come if you don't want to.

¡**Ven** aquí! Come here!

Remember that subject pronouns are not used very often in Spanish.

ver (to see)

	PRESENT		PRESENT PERFECT
(yo)	veo		he visto
(tú)	ves		has visto
(él/ella/usted)	ve		ha visto
(nosotros/as)	vemos		hemos visto
(vosotros/as)	veis		habéis visto
(ellos/ellas/ ustedes)	ven		han visto

	PRETERITE		IMPERFECT
(yo)	vi		veía
(tú)	viste		veías
(él/ella/usted)	vio		veía
(nosotros/as)	vimos		veíamos
(vosotros/as)	visteis		veíais
(ellos/ellas/ ustedes)	vieron		veían

GERUND	PAST PARTICIPLE
viendo	visto

EXAMPLE PHRASES

No **veo** muy bien. I can't see very well.

Están viendo la televisión. They're watching television.

No **he visto** esa película. I haven't seen that movie.

¿**Viste** lo que pasó? Did you see what happened?

Los **veía** a todos desde la ventana. I could see them all from the window.

Remember that subject pronouns are not used very often in Spanish.

ver

	FUTURE	CONDITIONAL
(yo)	veré	vería
(tú)	verás	verías
(él/ella/usted)	verá	vería
(nosotros/as)	veremos	veríamos
(vosotros/as)	veréis	veríais
(ellos/ellas/ ustedes)	verán	verían

	PRESENT SUBJUNCTIVE	IMPERFECT SUBJUNCTIVE
(yo)	vea	viera or viese
(tú)	veas	vieras or vieses
(él/ella/usted)	vea	viera or viese
(nosotros/as)	veamos	viéramos or viésemos
(vosotros/as)	veáis	vierais or vieseis
(ellos/ellas/ ustedes)	vean	vieran or viesen

IMPERATIVE

ve / ved

*Use the present subjunctive in all cases other than these **tú** and **vosotros** affirmative forms.*

EXAMPLE PHRASES

Eso ya se **verá**. We'll see.

No **veas** cómo se puso. He got incredibly worked up.

¡Si **vieras** cómo ha cambiado todo aquello! If you could see how everything has changed.

Veamos, ¿qué le pasa? Let's see now, what's the matter?

Remember that subject pronouns are not used very often in Spanish.

verter (to pour)

	PRESENT		PRESENT PERFECT
(yo)	vierto		he vertido
(tú)	viertes		has vertido
(él/ella/usted)	vierte		ha vertido
(nosotros/as)	vertemos		hemos vertido
(vosotros/as)	vertéis		habéis vertido
(ellos/ellas/ ustedes)	vierten		han vertido

	PRETERITE		IMPERFECT
(yo)	vertí		vertía
(tú)	vertiste		vertías
(él/ella/usted)	vertió		vertía
(nosotros/as)	vertimos		vertíamos
(vosotros/as)	vertisteis		vertíais
(ellos/ellas/ ustedes)	vertieron		vertían

GERUND	PAST PARTICIPLE
vertiendo	vertido

EXAMPLE PHRASES

Primero **viertes** el contenido del sobre en un recipiente. First you empty out the contents of the package into a container.

Han vertido graves acusaciones contra la ministra. They've made serious allegations against the minister.

Vertió un poco de leche en el cazo. He poured some milk into the saucepan.

Se **vertían** muchos residuos radiactivos en el mar. A lot of nuclear waste was dumped in the sea.

Remember that subject pronouns are not used very often in Spanish.

verter

	FUTURE	CONDITIONAL
(yo)	verteré	vertería
(tú)	verterás	verterías
(él/ella/usted)	verterá	vertería
(nosotros/as)	verteremos	verteríamos
(vosotros/as)	verteréis	verteríais
(ellos/ellas/ustedes)	verterán	verterían

	PRESENT SUBJUNCTIVE	IMPERFECT SUBJUNCTIVE
(yo)	vierta	vertiera or vertiese
(tú)	viertas	vertieras or vertieses
(él/ella/usted)	vierta	vertiera or vertiese
(nosotros/as)	vertamos	vertiéramos or vertiésemos
(vosotros/as)	vertáis	vertierais or vertieseis
(ellos/ellas/ustedes)	viertan	vertieran or vertiesen

IMPERATIVE

vierte / verted

Use the present subjunctive in all cases other than these tú *and* vosotros *affirmative forms.*

EXAMPLE PHRASES

Se vertirán muchas lágrimas por esto. A lot of tears will be shed over this.

Ten cuidado no **viertas** el café. Be careful you don't knock over the coffee.

Por favor, **vierta** el contenido del bolso sobre la mesa. Please empty out your bag on the table.

Remember that subject pronouns are not used very often in Spanish.

vestir (to dress)

	PRESENT		PRESENT PERFECT
(yo)	visto		he vestido
(tú)	vistes		has vestido
(él/ella/usted)	viste		ha vestido
(nosotros/as)	vestimos		hemos vestido
(vosotros/as)	vestís		habéis vestido
(ellos/ellas/ ustedes)	visten		han vestido

	PRETERITE		IMPERFECT
(yo)	vestí		vestía
(tú)	vestiste		vestías
(él/ella/usted)	vistió		vestía
(nosotros/as)	vestimos		vestíamos
(vosotros/as)	vestisteis		vestíais
(ellos/ellas/ ustedes)	vistieron		vestían

GERUND

vistiendo

PAST PARTICIPLE

vestido

EXAMPLE PHRASES

Tengo una familia que **vestir** y que alimentar. I have a family to feed and clothe.

Viste bien. She's a smart dresser.

Estaba **vistiendo** a los niños. I was dressing the children

Me he vestido en cinco minutos. It took me five minutes to get dressed.

Remember that subject pronouns are not used very often in Spanish.

vestir

	FUTURE	CONDITIONAL
(yo)	vestiré	vestiría
(tú)	vestirás	vestirías
(él/ella/usted)	vestirá	vestiría
(nosotros/as)	vestiremos	vestiríamos
(vosotros/as)	vestiréis	vestiríais
(ellos/ellas/ustedes)	vestirán	vestirían

	PRESENT SUBJUNCTIVE	IMPERFECT SUBJUNCTIVE
(yo)	vista	vistiera or vistiese
(tú)	vistas	vistieras or vistieses
(él/ella/usted)	vista	vistiera or vistiese
(nosotros/as)	vistamos	vistiéramos or vistiésemos
(vosotros/as)	vistáis	vistierais or vistieseis
(ellos/ellas/ustedes)	vistan	vistieran or vistiesen

IMPERATIVE
viste / vestid

Use the present subjunctive in all cases other than these tú and vosotros affirmative forms.

EXAMPLE PHRASES
Se vestirá de princesa. She'll be dressing up as a princess.

Para un acto formal, yo no **vestiría** pantalones vaqueros y una camiseta.
I wouldn't wear jeans and a T-shirt at a formal event.

Su padre **vestirá** de uniforme. Her father will wear a uniform.

¡**Vístete** de una vez! For the last time, go and get dressed!

Remember that subject pronouns are not used very often in Spanish.

vivir (to live)

	PRESENT	PRESENT PERFECT
(yo)	vivo	he vivido
(tú)	vives	has vivido
(él/ella/usted)	vive	ha vivido
(nosotros/as)	vivimos	hemos vivido
(vosotros/as)	vivís	habéis vivido
(ellos/ellas/ustedes)	viven	han vivido

	PRETERITE	IMPERFECT
(yo)	viví	vivía
(tú)	viviste	vivías
(él/ella/usted)	vivió	vivía
(nosotros/as)	vivimos	vivíamos
(vosotros/as)	vivisteis	vivíais
(ellos/ellas/ustedes)	vivieron	vivían

GERUND	PAST PARTICIPLE
viviendo	vivido

EXAMPLE PHRASES

Me gusta **vivir** sola. I like living on my own.

¿Dónde **vives**? Where do you live?

Siempre **han vivido** muy bien. They've always had a very comfortable life.

Vivían de su pensión. They lived on his pension.

Remember that subject pronouns are not used very often in Spanish.

vivir

	FUTURE	CONDITIONAL
(yo)	viviré	viviría
(tú)	vivirás	vivirías
(él/ella/usted)	vivirá	viviría
(nosotros/as)	viviremos	viviríamos
(vosotros/as)	viviréis	viviríais
(ellos/ellas/ustedes)	vivirán	vivirían

	PRESENT SUBJUNCTIVE	IMPERFECT SUBJUNCTIVE
(yo)	viva	viviera or viviese
(tú)	vivas	vivieras or vivieses
(él/ella/usted)	viva	viviera or viviese
(nosotros/as)	vivamos	viviéramos or viviésemos
(vosotros/as)	viváis	vivierais or vivieseis
(ellos/ellas/ustedes)	vivan	vivieran or viviesen

IMPERATIVE
vive / vivid

Use the present subjunctive in all cases other than these tú and vosotros affirmative forms.

EXAMPLE PHRASES

Viviremos en el centro de la ciudad. We'll live in the city center.

Si pudiéramos, **viviríamos** en el campo. We'd live in the country if we could.

Si **vivierais** más cerca, nos veríamos más a menudo. We'd all see one another more often if you lived nearer.

!**Viva**! Hurray!

Remember that subject pronouns are not used very often in Spanish.

volcar (to overturn)

	PRESENT	PRESENT PERFECT
(yo)	vuelco	he volcado
(tú)	vuelcas	has volcado
(él/ella/usted)	vuelca	ha volcado
(nosotros/as)	volcamos	hemos volcado
(vosotros/as)	volcáis	habéis volcado
(ellos/ellas/ ustedes)	vuelcan	han volcado

	PRETERITE	IMPERFECT
(yo)	volqué	volcaba
(tú)	volcaste	volcabas
(él/ella/usted)	volcó	volcaba
(nosotros/as)	volcamos	volcábamos
(vosotros/as)	volcasteis	volcabais
(ellos/ellas/ ustedes)	volcaron	volcaban

GERUND	PAST PARTICIPLE
volcando	volcado

EXAMPLE PHRASES

Se vuelca en su trabajo. She throws herself into her work.

Se han volcado con nosotros. They've been very kind to us.

El camión **volcó**. The truck overturned.

Remember that subject pronouns are not used very often in Spanish.

volcar

	FUTURE	CONDITIONAL
(yo)	volcaré	volcaría
(tú)	volcarás	volcarías
(él/ella/usted)	volcará	volcaría
(nosotros/as)	volcaremos	volcaríamos
(vosotros/as)	volcaréis	volcaríais
(ellos/ellas/ustedes)	volcarán	volcarían

	PRESENT SUBJUNCTIVE	IMPERFECT SUBJUNCTIVE
(yo)	vuelque	volcara or volcase
(tú)	vuelques	volcaras or volcases
(él/ella/usted)	vuelque	volcara or volcase
(nosotros/as)	volquemos	volcáramos or volcásemos
(vosotros/as)	volquéis	volcarais or volcaseis
(ellos/ellas/ustedes)	vuelquen	volcaran or volcasen

IMPERATIVE

vuelca / volcad

Use the present subjunctive in all cases other than these tú and vosotros affirmative forms.

EXAMPLE PHRASES

Si sigues moviéndote, harás que **vuelque** el bote. If you keep on moving like that, you'll make the boat capsize.

Ten cuidado, no **vuelques** el vaso. Be careful not to knock over the glass.

Vuelca el contenido sobre la cama. Empty the contents onto the bed.

Remember that subject pronouns are not used very often in Spanish.

volver (to return)

	PRESENT		PRESENT PERFECT
(yo)	vuelvo		he vuelto
(tú)	vuelves		has vuelto
(él/ella/usted)	vuelve		ha vuelto
(nosotros/as)	volvemos		hemos vuelto
(vosotros/as)	volvéis		habéis vuelto
(ellos/ellas/ustedes)	vuelven		han vuelto

	PRETERITE		IMPERFECT
(yo)	volví		volvía
(tú)	volviste		volvías
(él/ella/usted)	volvió		volvía
(nosotros/as)	volvimos		volvíamos
(vosotros/as)	volvisteis		volvíais
(ellos/ellas/ustedes)	volvieron		volvían

GERUND

volviendo

PAST PARTICIPLE

vuelto

EXAMPLE PHRASES

Mi padre **vuelve** mañana. My father's coming back tomorrow.

Se **está volviendo** muy pesado. He's becoming a real pain in the neck.

Ha vuelto a casa. He's gone back home.

Me **volví** para ver quién era. I turned round to see who it was.

Volvía agotado de trabajar. I used to come back exhausted from work.

Remember that subject pronouns are not used very often in Spanish.

volver

	FUTURE	CONDITIONAL
(yo)	volveré	volvería
(tú)	volverás	volverías
(él/ella/usted)	volverá	volvería
(nosotros/as)	volveremos	volveríamos
(vosotros/as)	volveréis	volveríais
(ellos/ellas/ ustedes)	volverán	volverían

	PRESENT SUBJUNCTIVE	IMPERFECT SUBJUNCTIVE
(yo)	vuelva	volviera or volviese
(tú)	vuelvas	volvieras or volvieses
(él/ella/usted)	vuelva	volviera or volviese
(nosotros/as)	volvamos	volviéramos or volviésemos
(vosotros/as)	volváis	volvierais or volvieseis
(ellos/ellas/ ustedes)	vuelvan	volvieran or volviesen

IMPERATIVE

vuelve / volved

Use the present subjunctive in all cases other than these tú and vosotros affirmative forms.

EXAMPLE PHRASES

Todo **volverá** a la normalidad. Everything will go back to normal.

Yo **volvería** a intentarlo. I'd try again.

No quiero que **vuelvas** a las andadas. I don't want you to go back to your old ways.

No **vuelvas** por aquí. Don't come back here.

¡**Vuelve** a la cama! Go back to bed!

Remember that subject pronouns are not used very often in Spanish.

zurcir (to darn)

	PRESENT		PRESENT PERFECT
(yo)	zurzo		he zurcido
(tú)	zurces		has zurcido
(él/ella/usted)	zurce		ha zurcido
(nosotros/as)	zurcimos		hemos zurcido
(vosotros/as)	zurcís		habéis zurcido
(ellos/ellas/ ustedes)	zurcen		han zurcido

	PRETERITE		IMPERFECT
(yo)	zurcí		zurcía
(tú)	zurciste		zurcías
(él/ella/usted)	zurció		zurcía
(nosotros/as)	zurcimos		zurcíamos
(vosotros/as)	zurcisteis		zurcíais
(ellos/ellas/ ustedes)	zurcieron		zurcían

GERUND
zurciendo

PAST PARTICIPLE
zurcido

EXAMPLE PHRASES

¿Quién le **zurce** las camisas? Who darns his shirts?

Pasa horas **zurciéndose** la ropa. He spends hours darning his clothes.

Remember that subject pronouns are not used very often in Spanish.

zurcir

	FUTURE	CONDITIONAL
(yo)	zurciré	zurciría
(tú)	zurcirás	zurcirías
(él/ella/usted)	zurcirá	zurciría
(nosotros/as)	zurciremos	zurciríamos
(vosotros/as)	zurciréis	zurciríais
(ellos/ellas/ustedes)	zurcirán	zurcirían

	PRESENT SUBJUNCTIVE	IMPERFECT SUBJUNCTIVE
(yo)	zurza	zurciera or zurciese
(tú)	zurzas	zurcieras or zurcieses
(él/ella/usted)	zurza	zurciera or zurciese
(nosotros/as)	zurzamos	zurciéramos or zurciésemos
(vosotros/as)	zurzáis	zurcierais or zurcieseis
(ellos/ellas/ustedes)	zurzan	zurcieran or zurciesen

IMPERATIVE

zurce / zurcid

*Use the present subjunctive in all cases other than these **tú** and **vosotros** affirmative forms.*

EXAMPLE PHRASES

¡Que te **zurzan**! Get lost!

Remember that subject pronouns are not used very often in Spanish.

How to use the Verb Index

The verbs in bold are the model verbs which you will find in the verb tables. All the other verbs follow one of these patterns, so the number next to each verb indicates which pattern fits this particular verb. For example, **acampar** (*to camp*) follows the same pattern as **hablar** (number 336 in the verb tables).

All the verbs are in alphabetical order. Superior numbers (¹ etc) refer you to notes on page 464. These notes explain any differences between verbs and their model.

Notes

[1] The verbs **anochecer**, **atardecer**, **granizar**, **helar**, **llover**, **nevar**, **nublarse** and **tronar** are used almost exclusively in the infinitive and third person singular forms.

[2] The **past participle** of the verb **pudrir** is **podrido**.

Vocabulary

contents

468 contents

This vocabulary section is divided into 50 topics, arranged in alphabetical order. This thematic approach enables you to learn related words and phrases together, so that you can become confident in using particular vocabulary in context.

Vocabulary within each topic is divided into nouns and useful phrases which are aimed at helping you to express yourself in idiomatic Spanish. Vocabulary within each topic is graded to help you prioritize your learning. Essential words include the basic words you will need to be able to communicate effectively, important words help expand your knowledge, and useful words provide additional vocabulary which will enable you to express yourself more fully.

Nouns are grouped by gender: masculine ("el") nouns are given on the left-hand page, and feminine ("la") nouns on the right-hand page, enabling you to memorize words according to their gender. In addition, all feminine forms of adjectives are shown, as are irregular plurals.

At the end of the section you will find a list of supplementary vocabulary, grouped according to part of speech – adjective, verb, noun and so on. This is vocabulary which you will come across in many everyday situations.

ABBREVIATIONS

adj	adjective
adv	adverb
algn	alguien
conj	conjunction
f	feminine
inv	invariable
LAm	word used in Latin America
m	masculine
m+f	masculine and feminine form
Mex	word used in Mexico
n	noun
pl	plural
prep	preposition
sb	somebody
sing	singular
Sp	word used in Spain
sth	something

The swung dash ~ is used to indicate the basic elements of the compound and appropriate endings are then added.

PLURALS AND GENDER

In Spanish, if a noun ends in a vowel it generally takes –s in the plural (casa > casas). If it ends in a consonant (including y) it generally takes –es in the plural (reloj > relojes). If it doesn't follow these rules, then the plural will be given in the text.

Although most masculine nouns take "el" and most feminine nouns take "la", you will find a few nouns grouped under feminine words which take "el" (el agua water; el arca chest; el aula classroom) because they are actually feminine.

ESSENTIAL WORDS (*masculine*)

el	**aeropuerto**	airport
el	**agente de viajes**	travel agent
el	**alquiler de coches**	car rental
el	**avión** (*pl* aviones)	plane
el	**billete** (*Sp*), el **boleto** (*LAm*)	ticket
el	**bolso**	bag
el	**carnet** (*or* carné) **de identidad**	ID card
	(*pl* carnets *or* carnés ~~)	
el	**enlace**	connection
el	**equipaje**	luggage
el	**equipaje de mano**	hand luggage
el	**horario**	timetable
el	**número**	number
el	**oficial de aduanas**	customs officer
el	**pasajero**	passenger
el	**pasaporte**	passport
el	**(precio del) billete** (*Sp*) *or* **boleto** (*LAm*)	fare
el	**retraso**	delay
los	**servicios**	toilets
el	**taxi**	taxi
el	**turista**	tourist
el	**viaje**	trip
el	**viajero**	traveler

USEFUL PHRASES

viajar en avión to travel by plane
un billete (*Sp*) *or* **boleto** (*LAm*) **de ida** a single ticket
un billete (*Sp*) *or* **boleto** (*LAm*) **de ida y vuelta, un boleto redondo** (*Mex*)
  a return ticket
reservar un billete (*Sp*) *or* **boleto** (*LAm*) **de avión** to book a plane ticket
"por avión" "by airmail"
facturar el equipaje to check one's bags
perdí el enlace I missed my connection
el avión ha despegado/ha aterrizado the plane has taken off/has landed
el panel de llegadas/salidas the arrivals/departures board
el vuelo número 776 procedente de Madrid/con destino Madrid flight
  number 776 from Madrid/to Madrid

ESSENTIAL WORDS *(feminine)*

la	**aduana**	customs
la	**agente de viajes**	travel agent
la	**cabina (del avión)**	(passenger) cabin
la	**cabina (del piloto)**	cockpit
la	**cancelación** (*pl* cancelaciones)	cancellation
la	**duty free**	duty-free (shop)
la	**entrada**	entrance
la	**facturación**	check-in
la	**información** (*pl* informaciones)	information desk; information
la	**llegada**	arrival
la	**maleta**	bag; suitcase
la	**oficial de aduanas**	customs officer
la	**pasajera**	passenger
la	**puerta de embarque**	departure gate
la	**reserva**	reservation
la	**salida**	departure; exit
la	**salida de emergencia**	emergency exit
la	**tarifa**	fare
la	**tarjeta de embarque**	boarding card
la	**turista**	tourist
la	**viajera**	traveler

USEFUL PHRASES

recoger el equipaje to collect one's bags
"recogida de equipajes" "baggage claim"
pasar por la aduana to go through customs
tengo algo que declarar I have something to declare
no tengo nada que declarar I have nothing to declare
registrar el equipaje to search the luggage

IMPORTANT WORDS *(masculine)*

el	accidente de avión	plane crash
el	billete electrónico *(Sp)*	e-ticket
el	boleto electrónico *(LAm)*	e-ticket
el	carrito	cart
el	cinturón de seguridad	seat belt
	(pl cinturones ~~)	
el	helicóptero	helicopter
el	mapa	map
el	mareo *(en avión)*	airsickness
el	piloto	pilot
el	vuelo	flight

USEFUL WORDS *(masculine)*

el	asiento	seat
el	aterrizaje	landing
el	auxiliar de vuelo	steward; flight attendant
el	cambiador para bebés	baby changing station
el	control de pasaportes	passport control
el	control de seguridad	security check
el	controlador aéreo	air-traffic controller
los	derechos de aduana	customs duty
el	despegue	takeoff
el	detector de metales	metal detector
el	embarque	boarding
el	horario	timetable
los	mandos	controls
el	paracaídas *(pl inv)*	parachute
el	radar	radar
el	reactor	jet plane/engine
el	satélite	satellite terminal
el	veraneante	vacationer

USEFUL PHRASES

a bordo on board; **"prohibido fumar"** "no smoking"
"abróchense el cinturón de seguridad" "fasten your seat belts"
estamos sobrevolando Londres we are flying over London
me estoy mareando I am feeling sick; **secuestrar un avión** to hijack a plane

IMPORTANT WORDS *(feminine)*

la	**duración** *(pl* duraciones)	length; duration
la	**escalera mecánica**	escalator
la	**piloto**	pilot
la	**sala de embarque**	departure lounge
la	**velocidad**	speed

USEFUL WORDS *(feminine)*

el	**ala** *(pl f* las alas)	wing
la	**altitud**	altitude
la	**altura**	height
la	**auxiliar de vuelo**	flight attendant
la	**barrera del sonido**	sound barrier
la	**bolsa de aire**	air pocket
la	**caja negra**	black box
la	**cinta transportadora**	carousel
la	**controladora aérea**	air-traffic controller
la	**escala**	stopover
la	**etiqueta**	label
la	**hélice**	propeller
la	**línea aérea**	airline
la	**pista (de aterrizaje)**	runway
la	**terminal**	terminal
la	**tienda libre de impuestos**	duty-free shop
la	**torre de control**	control tower
la	**tripulación** *(pl* tripulaciones)	crew
la	**turbulencia**	turbulence
la	**ventanilla**	window
la	**veraneante**	vacationer

USEFUL PHRASES

"pasajeros del vuelo AB251 con destino Madrid, embarquen por la puerta 51" "flight AB251 to Madrid now boarding at gate 51"
hicimos escala en Nueva York we stopped over in New York
un aterrizaje forzoso *or* **de emergencia** an emergency landing
un aterrizaje violento a crash landing
tabaco libre de impuestos duty-free cigarettes

ESSENTIAL WORDS (masculine)

el **animal**	animal
el **buey** (pl ~es)	ox
el **caballo**	horse
el **cachorro**	puppy
el **cerdo**	pig
el **conejo**	rabbit
el **cordero**	lamb
el **elefante**	elephant
el **gatito**	kitten
el **gato**	cat
el **hámster** (pl ~s)	hamster
el **león** (pl leones)	lion
el **pájaro**	bird
el **pelaje**	fur, coat
el **pelo**	coat, hair
el **perrito**	puppy
el **perro**	dog
el **pescado**	fish
el **pez** (pl peces)	fish
el **potro**	foal
el **ratón** (pl ratones)	mouse
el **ternero**	calf
el **tigre**	tiger
el **zoo**	zoo
el **zoológico**	zoo

USEFUL PHRASES

me gustan los gatos, odio las serpientes, prefiero los ratones I like cats, I hate snakes, I prefer mice

tenemos 12 animales en casa we have 12 pets in our house

no tenemos mascotas en casa we have no pets in our house

los animales salvajes wild animals

los animales domésticos or **las mascotas** pets

el ganado livestock

meter un animal en una jaula to put an animal in a cage

liberar a un animal to set an animal free

ESSENTIAL WORDS *(feminine)*

el	**ave** *(pl f* las aves)	bird
la	**gata**	cat *(female)*
la	**oveja**	ewe
la	**perra**	dog *(female)*
la	**tortuga**	tortoise
la	**vaca**	cow

IMPORTANT WORDS *(feminine)*

la	**cola**	tail
la	**jaula**	cage

USEFUL PHRASES

el perro ladra the dog barks; **gruñe** it growls
el gato maulla the cat meows; **ronronea** it purrs
me gusta la equitación *or* **montar a caballo** I like horseback riding
a caballo on horseback
"cuidado con el perro" "beware of the dog"
"no se admiten perros" "no dogs allowed"
"¡quieto!" *(to dog)* "down!"
los derechos de los animales animal rights

USEFUL WORDS (masculine)

el	asno	donkey
el	burro	donkey
el	camello	camel
el	canguro	kangaroo
el	caparazón (pl caparazones)	shell (of tortoise)
el	casco	hoof
el	ciervo	deer; stag
el	cocodrilo	crocodile
el	colmillo	tusk
el	conejillo de Indias	guinea pig
el	cuerno	horn
el	erizo	hedgehog
el	hipopótamo	hippopotamus
el	hocico	snout
el	lobo	wolf
el	macho	male
el	macho cabrío	billy goat
el	mono	monkey
el	mulo	mule
el	murciélago	bat
el	oso	bear
el	oso polar	polar bear
el	pavo	turkey
el	pony (pl ~s)	pony
el	rinoceronte	rhinoceros
el	sapo	toad
el	tiburón (pl tiburones)	shark
el	topo	mole
el	toro	bull
el	zorro	fox

USEFUL WORDS *(feminine)*

la	ardilla	squirrel
el	asta *(pl f* las astas*)*	antler
la	ballena	whale
la	boca	mouth
la	bolsa	pouch *(of kangaroo)*
la	cabra	(nanny) goat
la	crin	mane
la	culebra	(grass) snake
la	foca	seal
la	garra	claw
la	jirafa	giraffe
la	joroba	hump *(of camel)*
la	leona	lioness
la	liebre	hare
la	melena	mane
la	mula	mule
la	pajarería	pet shop
la	pata	paw
la	pezuña	hoof
la	piel	fur; hide *(of cow, elephant etc)*
la	rana	frog
las	rayas	stripes *(of zebra)*
la	serpiente	snake
la	tienda de animales	pet shop
la	tigresa	tigress
la	trampa	trap
la	trompa	trunk *(of elephant)*
la	yegua	mare
la	zebra	zebra

ESSENTIAL WORDS *(masculine)*

el	casco	helmet
el	ciclismo	cycling
el	ciclista	cyclist
el	faro	light
el	freno	brake
el	neumático	tire

IMPORTANT WORDS *(masculine)*

el	pinchazo	puncture

USEFUL WORDS *(masculine)*

el	ascenso	climb
el	candado	padlock
el	carril bici	bike lane
el	descenso	descent
el	eje	hub
el	guardabarros *(pl inv) (Sp)*	mudguard
el	kit de reparación de pinchazos *(pl ~s ~~~~)*	puncture repair kit
el	manillar	handlebars
el	pedal	pedal
el	plato	sprocket
el	portaequipajes *(pl inv)*	carrier
el	radio	spoke
el	reflector	reflector
el	sillín *(pl sillines)*	saddle
el	timbre	bell

USEFUL PHRASES
ir en bici(cleta), montar en bici(cleta) to go by bike, to cycle
vine en bici(cleta) I came by bike
viajar to travel
a toda velocidad at full speed
cambiar de marchas to change gears
pararse to stop
frenar bruscamente to brake suddenly

bikes

ESSENTIAL WORDS *(feminine)*

la	**bici**	bike
la	**bicicleta**	bicycle
la	**bicicleta de montaña**	mountain bike
la	**ciclista**	cyclist
la	**Vuelta Ciclista a España**	Tour of Spain

IMPORTANT WORDS *(feminine)*

la	**rueda**	wheel
la	**velocidad**	speed; gear

USEFUL WORDS *(feminine)*

la	**alforja**	saddlebag
la	**barra**	crossbar
la	**bomba**	pump
la	**cadena**	chain
la	**cuesta**	slope
la	**cumbre**	top *(of hill)*
la	**dinamo**	generator
la	**llanta**	rim
la	**luz delantera** (*pl* luces ~s)	front light
la	**pendiente**	slope
la	**salpicadera** (*Mex*)	mudguard
la	**subida**	climb
la	**válvula**	valve

USEFUL PHRASES

dar una vuelta *or* **pasear en bici(cleta)** to go for a bike ride
tener un pinchazo *or* **una rueda pinchada** to have a flat
arreglar un pinchazo to fix a flat
la rueda delantera/trasera the front/back wheel
inflar las ruedas to blow up the tires
brillante, reluciente shiny
oxidado(a) rusty
fluorescente fluorescent

ESSENTIAL WORDS *(masculine)*

el	**cielo**	sky
el	**gallo**	cock
el	**ganso**	goose
el	**loro**	parrot
el	**pájaro**	bird
el	**pato**	duck
el	**pavo**	turkey
el	**periquito**	parakeet

USEFUL WORDS *(masculine)*

el	**avestruz** *(pl* avestruces)	ostrich
el	**búho**	owl
el	**buitre**	vulture
el	**canario**	canary
el	**chochín** *(pl* chochines)	wren
el	**cisne**	swan
el	**cuervo**	raven; crow
el	**cuco**	cuckoo
el	**estornino**	starling
el	**faisán** *(pl* faisanes)	pheasant
el	**gorrión** *(pl* gorriones)	sparrow
el	**halcón** *(pl* halcones)	falcon
el	**huevo**	egg
el	**martín pescador**	kingfisher
	(pl martines ~es)	
el	**mirlo**	blackbird
el	**nido**	nest
el	**pájaro carpintero**	woodpecker
el	**pavo real**	peacock
el	**petirrojo**	robin
el	**pico**	beak
el	**pingüino**	penguin
el	**ruiseñor**	nightingale
el	**tordo**	thrush
el	**urogallo**	grouse

ESSENTIAL WORDS *(feminine)*

la **gallina** — hen

USEFUL WORDS *(feminine)*

el **águila** *(pl f las águilas)* — eagle
el **ala** *(pl f las alas)* — wing
la **alondra** — lark
el **ave** *(pl f las aves)* — bird
el **ave de rapiña** *(pl f las ~s ~ ~)* — bird of prey
el **ave rapaz** *(pl f las ~s rapaces)* — bird of prey
la **cigüeña** — stork
la **codorniz** *(pl codornices)* — quail
la **gaviota** — seagull
la **golondrina** — swallow
la **jaula** — cage
la **paloma** — pigeon; dove
la **perdiz** *(pl perdices)* — partridge
la **pluma** — feather
la **urraca** — magpie

USEFUL PHRASES

volar to fly
emprender vuelo to fly away
construir un nido to build a nest
silbar to whistle
cantar to sing
la gente los mete en jaulas people put them in cages
hibernar to hibernate
poner un huevo to lay an egg
un ave migratoria a migratory bird

ESSENTIAL WORDS *(masculine)*

el	**brazo**	arm
el	**cabello**	hair
el	**corazón** (*pl* corazones)	heart
el	**cuerpo**	body
el	**dedo**	finger
el	**diente**	tooth
el	**estómago**	stomach
el	**ojo**	eye
el	**pelo**	hair
el	**pie**	foot
el	**rostro**	face

IMPORTANT WORDS *(masculine)*

el	**cuello**	neck
el	**hombro**	shoulder
el	**pecho**	chest; bust
el	**pulgar**	thumb
el	**tobillo**	ankle

USEFUL PHRASES
de pie standing
sentado(a) sitting
tumbado(a) lying

ESSENTIAL WORDS *(feminine)*

la	**boca**	mouth
la	**cabeza**	head
la	**espalda**	back
la	**garganta**	throat
la	**mano**	hand
la	**nariz** *(pl narices)*	nose
la	**oreja**	ear
la	**pierna**	leg
la	**rodilla**	knee

IMPORTANT WORDS *(feminine)*

la	**barbilla**	chin
la	**cara**	face
la	**ceja**	eyebrow
la	**frente**	forehead
la	**lengua**	tongue
la	**mejilla**	cheek
la	**piel**	skin
la	**sangre**	blood
la	**voz** *(pl voces)*	voice

USEFUL PHRASES

grande big
alto(a) tall
pequeño(a) small
bajo(a) short
gordo(a) fat
flaco(a) skinny
delgado(a) slim
bonito(a) pretty
feo(a) ugly

USEFUL WORDS *(masculine)*

el	cerebro	brain
el	codo	elbow
el	cutis *(pl inv)*	skin, complexion
el	dedo (del pie)	toe
el	dedo índice	forefinger
el	dedo gordo	the big toe
el	(dedo) meñique	little finger
el	esqueleto	skeleton
el	gesto	gesture
el	hígado	liver
el	hueso	bone
el	labio	lip
el	músculo	muscle
el	muslo	thigh
el	párpado	eyelid
el	pulmón *(pl* pulmones)	lung
el	puño	fist
el	rasgo	feature
el	riñón *(pl* riñones)	kidney
el	seno	breast
el	talle	waist
el	talón *(pl* talones)	heel
el	trasero	bottom

USEFUL PHRASES

sonarse (la nariz) to blow one's nose
cortarse las uñas to cut one's nails
cortarse el pelo to have one's hair cut
encogerse de hombros to shrug one's shoulders
asentir/decir que sí con la cabeza to nod one's head
negar/decir que no con la cabeza to shake one's head
ver to see; **oir** to hear; **sentir** to feel
oler to smell; **tocar** to touch; **probar** to taste
estrechar la mano a alguien to shake hands with somebody
saludar a alguien con la mano to wave at somebody
señalar algo to point at something

USEFUL WORDS *(feminine)*

la	**arteria**	artery
la	**cadera**	hip
la	**carne**	flesh
la	**columna (vertebral)**	spine
la	**costilla**	rib
la	**facción** *(pl* facciones)	feature
la	**mandíbula**	jaw
la	**muñeca**	wrist
la	**nuca**	nape of the neck
la	**pantorrilla**	calf *(of leg)*
la	**pestaña**	eyelash
la	**planta del pie**	sole of the foot
la	**pupila**	pupil *(of the eye)*
la	**sien**	temple *(of head)*
la	**talla**	size
la	**tez** *(pl* teces)	complexion
la	**uña**	nail
la	**vena**	vein

USEFUL PHRASES

contorno de caderas hip measurement

medida de cintura waist measurement

contorno de pecho chest measurement

sordo(a) deaf

ciego(a) blind

mudo(a) mute

discapacitado(a) disabled

discapacitado(a) psíquico(a) person with learning difficulties

él es más alto que tú he is taller than you

ella ha crecido mucho she has grown a lot

estoy demasiado gordo(a) or **tengo sobrepeso** I am overweight

ella ha engordado/adelgazado she has put on/lost weight

ella mide 1,47 she is 1.47 meters tall

él pesa 40 kilos he weighs 40 kilos

SEASONS

la **primavera**	spring
el **verano**	summer
el **otoño**	autumn
el **invierno**	winter

MONTHS

enero	January	**julio**	July
febrero	February	**agosto**	August
marzo	March	**septiembre**	September
abril	April	**octubre**	October
mayo	May	**noviembre**	November
junio	June	**diciembre**	December

DAYS OF THE WEEK

lunes	Monday
martes	Tuesday
miércoles	Wednesday
jueves	Thursday
viernes	Friday
sábado	Saturday
domingo	Sunday

USEFUL PHRASES

en primavera/verano/otoño/invierno in spring/summer/autumn/
   winter
en mayo in May
el 10 de julio de 2006 on July 10, 2006
es 3 de diciembre on December 3rd
los sábados voy a la piscina on Saturdays I go to the swimming pool
el sábado fui a la piscina on Saturday I went to the swimming pool
el próximo sábado/el sábado pasado next/last Saturday
el sábado anterior/siguiente the previous/following Saturday

CALENDAR

el	**calendario**	calendar
el	**día**	day
los	**días de la semana**	days of the week
el	**día festivo**	public holiday
la	**estación** (*pl* estaciones)	season
el	**mes**	month
la	**semana**	week

USEFUL PHRASES

el día de los (Santos) Inocentes April Fool's Day (*celebrated on 28 December in Spain*)

la broma del día de los (Santos) Inocentes April fool's trick

el primero de mayo May Day

el día de la Hispanidad Columbus Day (*Spain's national day, celebrated on 12 October*)

el himno nacional de España the Spanish national anthem

el día D D-Day

el día de San Valentín *or* **de los enamorados** St Valentine's Day

el día de Todos los Santos All Saints' Day

la Semana Santa Easter

el Domingo de Resurrección *or* **Pascua** Easter Sunday

el Lunes de Pascua Easter Monday

el Miércoles de Ceniza Ash Wednesday

el Viernes Santo Good Friday

la Cuaresma Lent

la Pascua judía Passover

el Ramadán Ramadan

el Hanukkah Hanukkah *or* Hanukah

el Divali *or* **el Festival de la Luz** Divali *or* Diwali

el Adviento Advent

la Nochebuena Christmas Eve

la Navidad Christmas

en Navidad at Christmas

el día de Navidad Christmas Day

la Nochevieja New Year's Eve

el día de Año Nuevo New Year's Day

la cena/fiesta de Fin de Año New Year's Eve dinner/party

ESSENTIAL WORDS (*masculine*)

el	**aniversario de boda**	wedding anniversary
el	**cumpleaños** (*pl inv*)	birthday
el	**(día del) santo**	saint's day
el	**divorcio**	divorce
el	**matrimonio**	marriage
el	**regalo**	present

IMPORTANT WORDS (*masculine*)

el	**compromiso**	engagement
el	**festival**	festival
los	**fuegos artificiales**	fireworks; firework display
el	**nacimiento**	birth

USEFUL WORDS (*masculine*)

el	**bautismo**	christening
el	**cementerio**	cemetery
el	**entierro**	funeral
el	**festival folclórico**	folk festival
el	**patrón**	patron saint
el	**testigo**	witness
el	**regalo de Navidad**	Christmas present

USEFUL PHRASES

celebrar el cumpleaños to celebrate one's birthday
mi hermana nació en 1995 my sister was born in 1995
ella acaba de cumplir 17 años she's just turned 17
él me dio este regalo he gave me this present
¡te lo regalo! it's a present!, it's yours!
gracias thank you
divorciarse to get divorced
casarse to get married
comprometerse (con algn) to get engaged (to sb)
mi padre murió hace dos años my father died two years ago
enterrar to bury

ESSENTIAL WORDS (feminine)

la **boda**	wedding
la **cita**	appointment, date
la **fecha**	date
la **fiesta**	festival; fair; party

IMPORTANT WORDS (feminine)

las **fiestas**	festivities
la **feria**	fair
la **muerte**	death
la **hoguera**	bonfire

USEFUL WORDS (feminine)

la **ceremonia**	ceremony
la **dama de honor**	bridesmaid
la **invitación de boda**	wedding invitation
(*pl* invitaciones ~~)	
la **jubilación** (*pl* jubilaciones)	retirement
la **luna de miel**	honeymoon
la **procesión** (*pl* procesiones)	procession; march
la **tarjeta de felicitación**	greetings card
la **testigo**	witness

USEFUL PHRASES

bodas de plata/oro/diamante silver/golden/diamond wedding anniversary
desear a algn (un) Feliz Año to wish sb a happy New Year
dar *or* **hacer una fiesta** to have a party
invitar a los amigos to invite one's friends
elegir un regalo to choose a gift
¡Feliz Navidad! *or* **¡Felices Pascuas!** Merry Christmas!
¡Feliz cumpleaños! happy birthday!
(con) nuestros mejores deseos best wishes

ESSENTIAL WORDS (masculine)

los	**aseos**	toilets
los	**baños** (LAm)	washrooms; toilets
el	**bote**	can
el	**camping** (pl ~s)	camping; campsite
el	**campista**	camper
el	**cerillo** (LAm)	match
el	**cubo de la basura**	garbage can
el	**cuchillo**	knife
el	**emplazamiento**	site
el	**espejo**	mirror
el	**gas**	gas
el	**gas butano**	butane gas
el	**guarda**	warden
el	**lavabo**	washbasin
el	**plato**	plate
los	**servicios** (Sp)	washrooms; toilets
el	**suplemento**	extra charge
el	**tenedor**	fork
el	**tráiler** (pl ~s) (LAm)	trailer
el	**vehículo**	vehicle

IMPORTANT WORDS (masculine)

el	**abrelatas** (pl inv)	can opener
el	**colchón inflable** (pl colchones ~s)	airbed
el	**detergente**	detergent
el	**enchufe**	plug; socket
el	**hornillo**	stove
el	**sacacorchos** (pl inv)	corkscrew
el	**saco de dormir**	sleeping bag

USEFUL PHRASES

ir de or **hacer camping** to go camping
acampar to camp
bien equipado(a) well equipped
hacer una hoguera to make a fire

ESSENTIAL WORDS (feminine)

el	**agua (no) potable** (f)	(non-)drinking water
la	**alberca** (*Mex*)	swimming pool
la	**caja**	box
la	**cama plegable**	camp bed
la	**campista**	camper
la	**caravana**	trailer
la	**carpa** (*LAm*)	tent
la	**cerilla**	match
la	**comida enlatada**	canned food
la	**cuchara**	spoon
la	**ducha**	shower
la	**hoguera**	campfire
la	**lata**	can
la	**lavadora**	washing machine
la	**linterna**	flashlight
la	**mesa**	table
la	**navaja**	penknife
la	**noche**	night
la	**piscina** (*Sp*)	swimming pool
la	**sala**	room; hall
la	**tienda (de campaña)** (*Sp*)	tent
la	**tumbona**	deckchair

IMPORTANT WORDS (feminine)

la	**barbacoa**	barbecue
la	**bombona de butano/de gas**	butane/gas cylinder
la	**colada**	washing
las	**instalaciones sanitarias**	washing facilities
la	**lavandería**	Laundromat®
la	**mochila**	backpack
las	**normas**	rules
la	**sombra**	shade; shadow
la	**toma de corriente**	socket

USEFUL PHRASES

montar una tienda to pitch a tent
asar unas salchichas (a la parrilla) to grill some sausages

ESSENTIAL WORDS (*masculine*)

el	aeromozo (*LAm*)	steward; flight attendant
el	agricultor	farmer
el	auxiliar de vuelo (*Sp*)	steward; flight attendant
el	bombero	firefighter
el	cajero	checkout clerk; cashier
el	cartero	mail carrier
el	diseñador de páginas web	web designer
el	electricista	electrician
el	empleado	employee
el	empresario	employer; entrepreneur; businessman
el	enfermero	nurse
el	farmacéutico	druggist
el	informático	computer expert
el	jefe	boss
el	maquinista	engineer; train driver
el	mecánico	mechanic
el	médico	doctor
el	minero	miner
el	oficio	trade
el	orientador profesional	career advisor
el	policía	police officer
el	profesor	teacher
el	recepcionista	receptionist
el	redactor	editor
el	salario mínimo	minimum wage
el	soldado	soldier
el	sueldo	wages
el	taxista	taxi driver
el	trabajador	worker
el	trabajo	job; work
el	vendedor	sales assistant

USEFUL PHRASES

él es cartero he is a postman; **él/ella es dentista** he/she is a dentist
trabajar en turismo/publicidad *or* **dedicarse al turismo/a la publicidad**
  to work in tourism/advertising
hacerse to become; **se hizo soldado** he/she became a soldier

ESSENTIAL WORDS *(feminine)*

la	**aeromoza** *(LAm)*	stewardess; flight attendant
la	**agricultora**	farmer
la	**auxiliar de vuelo**	stewardess; flight attendant
la	**cajera**	checkout clerk; cashier
la	**cartera**	mail carrier
la	**diseñadora de páginas web**	web designer
la	**doctora**	doctor
la	**empleada**	employee
la	**empresaria**	employer; entrepreneur; businesswoman
la	**enfermera**	nurse
la	**estrella** *(m+f)*	star
la	**fábrica**	factory
la	**farmacéutica**	druggist
la	**informática**	computer expert; computing *or* IT
la	**jefa**	boss
la	**jubilación** *(pl* jubilaciones)	retirement
la	**médica**	doctor
la	**oficina**	office
la	**orientadora profesional**	career advisor
la	**policía**	police officer; police
la	**profesión** *(pl* profesiones)	profession
la	**profesora**	teacher
la	**recepcionista**	receptionist
la	**redactora**	editor
la	**secretaria**	secretary
la	**soldado**	soldier
la	**taxista**	taxi driver
la	**trabajadora**	worker
la	**vendadora**	sales assistant
la	**vida laboral**	working life

USEFUL PHRASES

trabajar para ganarse la vida to work for one's living
mi ambición es ser juez(a) it is my ambition to be a judge
¿en qué trabajas? what do you do (for a living)?
solicitar un trabajo to apply for a job

IMPORTANT WORDS *(masculine)*

el	aprendizaje	apprenticeship; learning
el	asalariado	wage earner
el	aumento	(pay) raise
el	autor	author
el	becario	intern
el	cocinero	cook
el	comerciante	storekeeper
el	compañero de trabajo	colleague; coworker
el	conserje	caretaker
el	contrato	contract
el	currículum vitae	CV
el	desempleado	unemployed person
el	desempleo	unemployment
el	empleo	job
el	eventual	temp
el	fontanero *(Sp)*	plumber
el	gerente	manager
el	hombre de negocios	businessman
el	horario flexible	flextime
el	ingeniero	engineer
el	interiorista	interior designer
el	mercado laboral	job market
el	negocio *or* los negocios	business
el	óptico	optician
el	peluquero	hairdresser
el	piloto	pilot
el	pintor	painter
el	plomero *(Mex)*	plumber
el	presentador de televisión	TV newscaster
el	presidente	president; chairperson
el	sindicato	trade union

USEFUL PHRASES

estar desempleado(a) *or* **en paro** to be unemployed
despedir a algn to lay sb off
contrato indefinido/temporal/por obra permanent/temporary/
   fixed-term contract

IMPORTANT WORDS *(feminine)*

la	agencia de trabajo temporal	temping agency
la	asalariada	wage earner
la	autora	author
la	becaria	intern
la	carrera	career
la	carta de presentación	cover letter
la	cocinera	cook
la	comerciante	storekeeper
la	compañera de trabajo	colleague; coworker
la	conserje	caretaker
la	entrevista (de trabajo)	(job) interview
la	eventual	temp
la	gerente	manager
la	huelga	strike
la	ingeniera	engineer
la	interiorista	interior designer
la	limpiadora	cleaner
la	mujer de negocios	businesswoman
la	oficina de empleo	employment office
la	peluquera	hairdresser
la	piloto	pilot
la	política	politician; politics
la	presentadora de televisión	TV newscaster
la	presidenta	president; chairperson
la	solicitud	application

USEFUL PHRASES

"**demandas de empleo**" "job application"
"**ofertas de empleo**" "help wanted"
estar en/pertenercer a un sindicato to be in a union
ganar 250 dólars a la semana to earn $250 a week
una subida *or* **un aumento de sueldo** a pay raise
ponerse *or* **declararse/estar en huelga** to go/be on strike
trabajar a tiempo completo/a tiempo parcial to work full-time/part-time
trabajar horas extra(s) to work overtime
reducción de la jornada laboral reduction in working hours

USEFUL WORDS (*masculine*)

el	**abogado**	lawyer
el	**(agente) comercial**	sales rep
el	**albañil**	mason
el	**arquitecto**	architect
el	**artista**	artist; artiste
el	**astronauta**	astronaut
el	**carpintero**	carpenter
el	**cirujano**	surgeon
el	**contable** (*Sp*), el **contador** (*LAm*)	accountant
el	**cura**	priest
el	**curso de formación**	training course
el	**diputado**	MP
el	**director gerente** *or* **ejecutivo**	managing director
el	**diseñador (de moda)**	fashion designer
el	**ejecutivo**	executive
el	**escritor**	writer
el	**fotógrafo**	photographer
el	**funcionario**	civil servant
el	**horario**	schedule
el	**ingeniero civil**	civil engineer
el	**intérprete**	interpreter
el	**investigador**	researcher
el	**juez** (*pl* jueces)	judge
el	**marinero**	sailor
el	**modelo**	model (*person*)
el	**monitor de tiempo libre**	activity leader
el	**notario**	notary
el	**paro**	unemployment; unemployment benefit
el	**periodista**	journalist
el	**(período de) trabajo en prácticas**	work placement
el	**personal**	staff
el	**político**	politician
el	**procurador**	solicitor
el	**representante**	rep; sales rep
el	**sacerdote**	priest
el	**traductor**	translator
el	**veterinario**	vet
el	**viticultor**	wine grower

USEFUL WORDS *(feminine)*

la	**abogada**	lawyer
la	**administración** (*pl* administraciones)	administration
el	**ama de casa** (*pl f* amas ~~)	housewife
la	**arquitecta**	architect
la	**artista**	artist; artiste
la	**compañía**	company
la	**contable** (*Sp*), la **contadora** (*LAm*)	accountant
la	**empresa**	company
la	**formación**	training
la	**funcionaria**	civil servant
la	**huelga de celo**	work-to-rule; go-slow
la	**indemnización por despido**	severance pay
la	**intérprete**	interpreter
la	**jueza** *or* la **juez** (*pl* jueces)	judge
la	**locutora**	announcer
la	**modelo**	model (*person*)
la	**modista**	dressmaker
la	**monitora de tiempo libre**	activity leader
la	**monja**	nun
la	**orientación profesional**	careers guidance
la	**periodista**	journalist
la	**religiosa**	nun
la	**representante**	rep; sales rep
la	**traductora**	translator
la	**veterinaria**	vet

USEFUL PHRASES

el trabajo estacional seasonal work
un empleo temporal/permanente a temporary/permanent job
un trabajo a tiempo parcial (*Sp*) *or* **a medio tiempo** (*LAm*) a part-time job
ser contratado(a) to be taken on; **ser despedido(a)** to be dismissed
despedir *or* **echar a algn** to fire sb
buscar trabajo to look for work
hacer un curso de formación profesional to go on a training course
fichar al entrar a/al salir de trabajar to clock in/out
trabajar en horario flexible to work flextime

ESSENTIAL WORDS (masculine)

el	aceite	oil
el	agente de policía	police officer
el	aparcamiento (Sp)	parking lot; parking space
el	atasco	traffic jam
el	autoestop	hitchhiking
el	autoestopista	hitchhiker
el	automóvil	car
el	aventón (Mex)	hitchhiking
el	callejero	street map
el	camión (pl camiones)	truck
el	carnet or carné de conducir (Sp) (pl ~s or ~s ~~)	driver's license
el	carro (LAm)	car
el	chófer (Sp), el chofer (LAm)	driver; chauffeur
el	ciclista	cyclist
el	coche (Sp)	car
el	conductor	driver
el	cruce	crossroads
el	diésel	diesel
el	estacionamiento (LAm)	parking lot; parking space
los	faros	headlights
el	freno	brake
el	garaje	garage
el	gasoil	diesel (oil)
el	kilómetro	kilometer
el	litro	liter
el	mapa de carreteras	road map
el	mecánico	mechanic
el	neumático	tire
el	número	number
el	parking (pl ~s)	parking lot
el	peaje	toll
el	peatón (pl peatones)	pedestrian
el	radar	speed camera
el	semáforo	traffic lights
el	tráiler (pl ~s) (LAm)	trailer
el	viaje	journey

ESSENTIAL WORDS *(feminine)*

el **agua** *(f)*	water
la **autoestopista**	hitchhiker
la **autopista**	highway
la **autopista de peaje**	toll road
la **caravana** *(Sp)*	trailer
la **carretera**	road
la **carretera nacional**	main road
la **chófer** *(Sp)*, la **chofer** *(LAm)*	driver; chauffeur
la **ciclista**	cyclist
la **cochera**	garage
la **conductora**	driver
la **desviación** *(pl desviaciones)*	diversion
la **dirección** *(pl direcciones)*	direction
la **dirección asistida** *(pl direcciones ~s)*	power steering
la **distancia**	distance
la **estación de servicio** *(pl estaciones ~ ~)*	gas station
la **gasolina**	gasoline
la **gasolina sin plomo**	unleaded gasoline
la **libreta de manejar** *(Mex)*	driver's license
la **matrícula** *(Sp)*, la **placa** *(LAm)*	registration number; number plate
la **policía**	police

USEFUL PHRASES

frenar bruscamente to brake suddenly
100 kilómetros por hora 100 kilometers an hour
¿tienes carné (or carnet) de conducir? do you have a driver's license?
vamos a dar una vuelta (en coche) we're going for a drive (in the car)
¡lleno, por favor!, ¡llénelo, por favor! fill her up please!
tomar la carretera a/hacia Córdoba to take the road to Córdoba
es un viaje de tres horas it's a 3-hour trip
¡buen viaje! have a good trip!
¡vámonos!, ¡en marcha! let's go!
de camino vimos ... on the way we saw ...
adelantar a un coche to overtake a car

IMPORTANT WORDS *(masculine)*

el	**accidente (de carretera)**	(traffic) accident
el	**automovilista**	motorist
el	**camionero**	truck driver
el	**choque**	collision
el	**cinturón de seguridad**	seat belt
	(pl cinturones ~~)	
el	**claxon** *(pl* cláxones *or* ~s)	horn
el	**(coche) híbrido**	hybrid car
el	**código de la circulación**	traffic code; motor vehicle code
el	**daño**	damage
el	**embrague**	clutch
el	**empleado de una gasolinera**	gas station attendant
el	**maletero** *(Sp)*	trunk
el	**monovolumen**	minivan
el	**motor**	engine
el	**motorista**	motorcyclist
los	**papeles (del coche)**	official papers
el	**pinchazo**	puncture
el	**pito**	horn
el	**salpicadero**	dashboard
el	**seguro**	insurance
el	**surtidor (de gasolina)**	gas pump
el	**taller (mecánico** *or* **de reparaciones)**	garage
el	**tráfico**	traffic
el	**túnel de lavado**	car wash

USEFUL PHRASES

primero enciendes el motor *or* **pones el motor en marcha** first you turn on the engine

el motor arranca *or* **se pone en marcha** the engine starts up

el coche se pone en marcha the car moves off

estamos circulando we're driving along

acelerar to accelerate; **continuar** to continue

reducir *or* **aminorar la velocidad** *or* **la marcha** to slow down

detenerse to stop; **aparcar (el coche)** to park (the car)

apagar el motor to turn off the engine

parar con el semáforo en rojo to stop at the red light

IMPORTANT WORDS (*feminine*)

la	**autoescuela** (*Sp*)	driving school
la	**automovilista**	motorist
la	**avería**	breakdown
la	**batería**	battery
la	**cajuela** (*Mex*)	trunk
la	**calle de sentido único**	one-way street
la	**carrocería**	body work
la	**colisión** (*pl* colisiones)	collision
la	**documentación (del coche)**	vehicle documents
la	**esculela de conductores** (*LAm*) *or* de manejo (*Mex*)	driving school
la	**frontera**	border
la	**glorieta**	traffic circle
la	**grúa**	tow truck
la	**ITV (inspección técnica de vehículos)** (*Sp*)	motor vehicle inspection
la	**marca**	make (*of car*)
la	**motorista**	motorcyclist
la	**pieza de repuesto**	spare part
la	**póliza de seguros**	insurance policy
la	**prioridad**	right of way
la	**prueba del alcohol**	Breathalyzer® test
la	**puerta**	(*car*) door
la	**rotonda**	traffic circle
la	**rueda**	tire
la	**rueda de repuesto**	spare tire
la	**velocidad**	speed; gear
la	**zona azul**	restricted parking zone

USEFUL PHRASES

ha habido un accidente there's been an accident
hubo seis heridos en el accidente six people were injured in the accident
¿puedo ver la documentación *or* **los papeles del coche, por favor?** may I see your vehicle documents, please?
pinchar, tener un pinchazo to have a flat; **arreglar** to fix
averiarse *or* **tener una avería** to break down
me he quedado sin gasolina I've run out of gas

USEFUL WORDS (*masculine*)

el	**acelerador**	accelerator
el	**arcén** (*pl* arcenes)	hard shoulder
el	**autolavado**	car wash
el	**botón de arranque** (*pl* botones ~~)	starter
el	**capó**	hood
el	**carburador**	carburetor
el	**carril**	lane
el	**catalizador**	catalytic converter
el	**conductor novel**	student driver
el	**consumo de gasolina**	gas consumption
el	**cuentakilómetros** (*pl inv*)	speedometer
el	**desvío**	detour
el	**guardia de tráfico**	traffic officer
el	**herido**	casualty
el	**intermitente**	indicator
el	**lavacoches** (*pl inv*)	car wash
el	**límite de velocidad**	speed limit
el	**limpiaparabrisas** (*pl inv*)	windshield wiper
el	**parabrisas** (*pl inv*)	windshield
el	**parachoques** (*pl inv*)	bumper
el	**parquímetro**	parking meter
el	**pedal**	pedal
el	**policía motorizado**	motorcycle officer
el	**profesor de autoescuela**	driving instructor
el	**remolque**	trailer
el	**retrovisor**	rear-view mirror
el	**(sistema de navegación) GPS**	satellite navigation system
el	**volante**	steering wheel

USEFUL PHRASES

en la hora punta at rush hour
le pusieron una multa de 100 euros he got a 100-euro fine
¿está asegurado? are you insured?
no olviden ponerse los cinturones de seguridad don't forget to put on
  your seat belts
en la frontera at the border
hacer autoestop to hitchhike

USEFUL WORDS *(feminine)*

el	**área de descanso** (*pl f* las áreas ~~)	turnout
el	**área de servicio** (*pl f* las áreas ~~)	service area
la	**baca**	roof rack
la	**caja de cambios**	gearbox
la	**carretera de circunvalación**	bypass
la	**clase de conducir**	driving lesson
la	**curva**	bend
la	**electrolinera**	EV charging station
la	**estación de servicio** (*pl* estaciones ~~)	filling station
la	**gasolinera**	filling station
la	**guardia de tráfico**	traffic officer
la	**infracción de tráfico** (*pl* infracciones ~~)	traffic offense
las	**luces cortas**	low beams
las	**luces de emergencia**	hazard lights
las	**luces largas**	high beams
la	**mediana**	median strip
la	**multa**	fine
la	**presión**	pressure
la	**señal de tráfico**	road sign
la	**vía**	way, road; lane (*on road*)
la	**vía de acceso**	access ramp
la	**víctima** (*m+f*)	casualty
la	**zona urbanizada**	built-up area

USEFUL PHRASES

la rueda delantera/trasera the front/back wheel
tenemos que desviarnos we have to make a detour
una multa por exceso de velocidad a fine for speeding
contratar a un chófer to book a driver

"ceda el paso a la derecha" "give way to the right"
"circule por la derecha" "keep to the right"
"prohibido el paso" "no entry"
"prohibido aparcar" "no parking"
"obras" "roadwork"

ESSENTIAL WORDS (masculine)

el	abrigo	overcoat; coat
el	anorak (pl inv or ~s)	anorak
el	bañador	swimming trunks; swimsuit
el	bolso	bag
el	botón (pl botones)	button
el	calcetín (pl calcetines)	sock
los	calzoncillos	pants; boxer shorts
los	calzones (LAm)	underpants; panties
el	camisón (pl camisones)	nightdress
el	chubasquero	raincoat
el	cuello	collar
el	jersey (pl jerséis)	jumper
el	número (de pie)	(shoe) size
el	pantalón (pl pantalones)	trousers
los	(pantalones) vaqueros	jeans
el	pañuelo	handkerchief; scarf
el	paraguas (pl inv)	umbrella
el	pijama	pajamas
el	sombrero	hat
el	talle	waist
el	traje	suit (for man); costume
el	traje de chaqueta	suit
el	vestido	dress
el	zapato	shoe

IMPORTANT WORDS (masculine)

el	bolsillo	pocket
el	bolso	handbag
el	cinturón (pl cinturones)	belt
el	guante	glove
el	impermeable	raincoat
los	pantalones cortos	shorts
el	uniforme	uniform

ESSENTIAL WORDS *(feminine)*

la	**braga (del bikini)**	bikini bottoms
las	**bragas** *(Sp)*	underpants; panties
la	**camisa**	shirt
la	**camiseta**	T-shirt
la	**capucha**	hood
la	**chaqueta**	jacket
la	**corbata**	tie
la	**falda**	skirt
las	**medias**	tights
la	**moda**	fashion
la	**parka**	parka
la	**ropa**	clothes
la	**ropa interior**	underwear
la	**sandalia**	sandal
la	**talla**	size

IMPORTANT WORDS *(feminine)*

la	**americana**	jacket *(for man)*
la	**blusa**	blouse
la	**bota**	boot
las	**prendas de vestir**	clothes
la	**zapatilla**	slipper

USEFUL PHRASES

por la mañana me visto in the morning I get dressed
por la tarde me desvisto in the evening I get undressed
cuando llego a casa del colegio me cambio when I get home from school
    I get changed
llevar, llevar puesto to wear
ponerse to put on
eso es muy elegante that's very smart
(eso) te queda bien that suits you
¿qué talla tienes (*or* tiene)? what size do you take?
¿qué número de pie tienes (*or* tiene)? what shoe size do you take?
tengo un 38 (de pie), calzo un 38 I take size 38 in shoes

USEFUL WORDS (masculine)

los	accesorios	accessories
el	bastón (pl bastones)	walking stick
el	body	bodysuit
el	bolso bandolera (pl ~s ~)	shoulder bag
el	cárdigan (pl ~s)	cardigan
el	chaleco	vest; waistcoat
el	chándal (pl ~s)	tracksuit
los	cordones	(shoe)laces
el	delantal	apron
el	desfile de moda	fashion show
el	(forro) polar	fleece
el	fular	scarf
el	lazo	ribbon
el	mono	overalls
el	ojal	buttonhole
los	pantis	tights
el	peto	overalls; dungarees
el	polo	polo shirt
el	probador	fitting room
el	sujetador	bra
el	tocado (de plumas, flores o cintas)	fascinator
el	top	tube top
el	traje de etiqueta	evening dress (for man)
el	traje de noche	evening dress (for woman)
el	traje pantalón (pl ~s ~)	pants suit
los	tirantes	suspenders
el	vestido de novia	wedding dress
los	zapatos de tacón	high heels
los	zapatos de tacón de aguja	stiletto heels

USEFUL WORDS *(feminine)*

la	alpargata	espadrille
la	alta costura	haute couture
la	bandolera	shoulder bag
la	bata	dressing gown
las	bermudas	Bermuda shorts
la	boina	beret
la	bufanda	scarf
la	camiseta con capucha	hooded top
la	camiseta sin mangas	tank top
las	chanclas	flip-flops
la	cinta	ribbon
la	colada	washing
la	combinación *(pl* combinaciones)	underskirt
la	cremallera	zip
la(s)	enagua(s)	underskirt
la	falda pantalón *(pl* ~s ~)	culottes
la	gorra	cap
la	limpieza en seco	dry cleaning
la	manga	sleeve
las	medias	stockings
la	pajarita	bow tie
la	rebeca	cardigan
la	ropa blanca/de color	whites/coloreds
la	sudadera	sweatshirt
las	zapatillas de deporte	sneakers

USEFUL PHRASES

largo(a) long; **corto(a)** short
un vestido de manga corta/larga a short-sleeved/long-sleeved dress
estrecho(a), ajustado(a), ceñido(a) tight
amplio(a), suelto(a) loose
una falda ajustada *or* **ceñida** a tight skirt
a rayas, de rayas striped; **a cuadros, de cuadros** checked; **de lunares** spotted
ropa de sport, ropa informal casual clothes
con vestido de noche in evening dress
a la moda, de moda fashionable; **moderno(a)** trendy
pasado(a) de moda, anticuado(a) old-fashioned

amarillento(a)	yellowish
amarillo(a)	yellow
amarillo limón (*inv*)	lemon yellow
azul	blue
azulado(a)	bluish
azul celeste (*inv*)	sky blue
azul claro (*inv*)	pale blue
azul marino (*inv*)	navy blue
azul oscuro (*inv*)	dark blue
beige, beis (*inv*)	beige
blanco(a)	white
blanquecino(a)	whitish
burdeos (*inv*)	maroon
castaño(a)	chestnut, brown
crudo(a)	natural
dorado(a)	golden
granate (*inv*)	maroon
gris	gray
grisáceo(a)	grayish
malva (*inv*)	mauve
marrón (*pl* marrones)	brown
morado(a)	purple
naranja (*inv*)	orange
negro(a)	black
negruzco(a)	blackish
plateado(a)	silver
rojizo(a)	reddish
rojo(a)	red
rojo fuerte *or* intenso (*inv*)	bright red
rosa (*inv*)	pink
turquesa (*inv*)	turquoise
verde	green
verdoso(a), verduzco(a)	greenish
violeta (*inv*)	violet

USEFUL PHRASES

el color color

¿de qué color tienes (*or* tiene) los ojos/el pelo? what color are your eyes/ is your hair?

el azul te sienta bien blue suits you; the blue one suits you

pintar algo de azul to paint sth blue

los zapatos azules blue shoes

los zapatos azul claro light blue shoes

(ella) tiene los ojos verdes she has green eyes

cambiar de color to change color

la Casa Blanca the White House

blanco como la nieve as white as snow

Blancanieves Snow White

Caperucita Roja Little Red Riding Hood

ponerse colorado(a) *or* rojo(a) to turn red

sonrojarse de vergüenza to blush with shame

blanco(a) como el papel as white as a sheet

muy moreno(a), muy bronceado(a) as brown as a berry

(él) estaba cubierto de cardenales he was black and blue

un ojo morado a black eye

un filete muy poco hecho a very rare steak, an underdone steak

ESSENTIAL WORDS (*masculine*)

el **ordenador (personal)**	(personal) computer
el **programa**	program
el **programador**	programmer
el **ratón** (*pl* ratones)	mouse

USEFUL WORDS (*masculine*)

el **adaptador**	dongle
el **antivirus**	antivirus
el **blog** (*pl* ~s)	blog
el **corrector ortográfico**	spellchecker
el **correo basura**	spam
el **correo electrónico/web**	email
el **cursor**	cursor
los **datos**	data
el **desarrollador (de software)**	software developer
el **disco duro**	hard disk
el **documento**	document
el **fichero**	file
el **guion bajo**	underscore
el **icono**	icon
el **Internet**	internet
el **juego de ordenador**	computer game
el **mail** (*pl* ~s)	email
los **medios sociales**	social media
el **mensaje (de texto)**	text message
el **menú**	menu
el **navegador**	browser
el **(nombre de) usuario**	user(name)
el **(ordenador) portátil**	laptop
el **pirata informático**	hacker
el **puerto USB**	USB port
el **red social**	social networking site
los **seguidores (en Twitter®)**	(Twitter®) followers
el **servidor**	server
el **sitio web**	website
el **teclado**	keyboard
el **virus** (*pl inv*)	virus
el **wifi**	Wi-Fi

ESSENTIAL WORDS *(feminine)*

la	**impresora**	printer
la	**informática**	computer science/studies
la	**programadora**	programmer

USEFUL WORDS *(feminine)*

la	**aplicación** *(pl* aplicaciones)	app; program
la	**arroba**	@ (sign)
la	**banda ancha**	broadband
la	**base de datos**	database
la	**computadora (personal)** *(LAm)*	(personal) computer
la	**copia de seguridad**	back-up
la	**copia impresa**	print-out
la	**dirección de correo (electrónico)**	email address
	(pl direcciones ~~ (~))	
la	**hoja de cálculo**	spreadsheet
la	**Internet**	internet
la	**intranet**	intranet
la	**(memoria) RAM**	RAM, random-access memory
la	**memoria USB**	USB flash drive, USB stick
la	**mensajería instantánea**	instant messaging
la	**nube**	cloud
la	**página de inicio**	home page
la	**(página) web**	web page
la	**pantalla**	screen
la	**papelera**	recycle bin
la	**red**	network
las	**redes sociales**	social media
la	**tableta**	tablet
la	**webcam** *(pl* ~s)	webcam
la	**wifi**	Wi-Fi

USEFUL PHRASES

copiar to copy; **eliminar, suprimir** to delete; **formatear** to format
bajar *or* **descargar/subir un archivo** to download/upload a file
guardar to save; **imprimir** to print; **teclear** to key
navegar por Internet to surf the internet; **inalámbrico** wireless
seguir a algn en Twitter® to follow sb on Twitter®

COUNTRIES

ESSENTIAL WORDS (*masculine*)

Canadá	Canada
EE. UU.	USA
Estados Unidos	United States
país	country
Países Bajos	Netherlands
Reino Unido	United Kingdom

USEFUL WORDS (*masculine*)

Brasil	Brazil
Chile	Chile
Ecuador	Ecuador
El Salvador	El Salvador
Japón	Japan
Marruecos	Morocco
México	Mexico
Pakistán	Pakistan
Panamá	Panama
Paraguay	Paraguay
Perú	Peru
Puerto Rico	Puerto Rico
Túnez	Tunisia
Uruguay	Uruguay

USEFUL PHRASES

mi país de origen my native country
la capital de España the capital of Spain
¿de qué país eres (*or* es)? what country do you come from?
soy de (los) Estados Unidos/de Canadá I'm from the United States/ from Canada
nací en Ecuador I was born in Ecuador
me voy a los Países Bajos I'm going to the Netherlands
acabo de regresar de (los) Estados Unidos I have just come back from the United States
los países en (vías de) desarrollo the developing countries
países de habla hispana Spanish-speaking countries

ESSENTIAL WORDS *(feminine)*

Alemania	Germany
América	America
América del Sur	South America
Bélgica	Belgium
Escocia	Scotland
España	Spain
Europa	Europe
Francia	France
Gran Bretaña	Great Britain
Holanda	Holland
Inglaterra	England
Irlanda (del Norte)	(Northern) Ireland
Italia	Italy
(el País de) Gales	Wales
Sudamérica	South America
Suiza	Switzerland
USA	USA

USEFUL WORDS *(feminine)*

África	Africa
Argelia	Algeria
Argentina	Argentina
Asia	Asia
Bolivia	Bolivia
Colombia	Colombia
Costa Rica	Costa Rica
Cuba	Cuba
Francia	France
Grecia	Greece
Guatemala	Guatemala
Honduras	Honduras
la India	India
Nicaragua	Nicaragua
la República Dominicana	the Dominican Republic
la Unión Europea, UE	the European Union, the EU
Venezuela	Venezuela

NATIONALITIES

ESSENTIAL WORDS *(masculine)*

un	**alemán** *(pl* alemanes)	a German
un	**americano**	an American
un	**belga**	a Belgian
un	**británico**	a Briton
un	**canadiense**	a Canadian
un	**escocés** *(pl* escoceses)	a Scot
un	**español**	a Spaniard
un	**europeo**	a European
un	**francés** *(pl* franceses)	a Frenchman
un	**galés** *(pl* galeses)	a Welshman
un	**holandés** *(pl* holandeses)	a Dutchman
un	**inglés** *(pl* ingleses)	an Englishman
un	**irlandés** *(pl* irlandeses)	an Irishman
un	**italiano**	an Italian
un	**pakistaní** *(pl* ~es *or* ~s)	a Pakistani
un	**suizo**	a Swiss (man *or* boy)

USEFUL PHRASES
(él) es irlandés he is Irish
(ella) es irlandesa she is Irish
la campiña irlandesa the Irish countryside
una ciudad irlandesa an Irish town

ESSENTIAL WORDS *(feminine)*

una	**alemana**	a German
una	**americana**	an American
una	**belga**	a Belgian
una	**británica**	a Briton, a British woman *or* girl
una	**canadiense**	a Canadian
una	**escocesa**	a Scot
una	**española**	a Spaniard
una	**europea**	a European
una	**francesa**	a Frenchwoman, a French girl
una	**galesa**	a Welshwoman, a Welsh girl
una	**holandesa**	a Dutchwoman, a Dutch girl
una	**inglesa**	an Englishwoman, an English girl
una	**irlandesa**	an Irishwoman, an Irish girl
una	**italiana**	an Italian
una	**pakistaní** *(pl ~es or ~s)*	a Pakistani
una	**suiza**	a Swiss girl *or* woman

USEFUL PHRASES

soy escocés – hablo inglés I am Scottish – I speak English
soy escocesa I am Scottish
un(a) extranjero(a) a foreigner
en el extranjero abroad
la nacionalidad nationality

USEFUL WORDS (*masculine*)

un **africano**	an African
un **antillano**	a West Indian
un **árabe**	an Arab
un **argelino**	an Algerian
un **argentino**	an Argentinian
un **boliviano**	a Bolivian
un **brasileño**	a Brazilian
un **chileno**	a Chilean
un **chino**	a Chinese
un **colombiano**	a Colombian
un **costarricense**	a Costa Rican
un **cubano**	a Cuban
un **dominicano**	a Dominican
un **ecuatoriano**	an Ecuadorean
un **griego**	a Greek
un **guatemalteco**	a Guatemalan
un **hondureño**	a Honduran
un **indio**	an Indian
un **japonés** (*pl* japoneses)	a Japanese
un **marroquí** (*pl* ~es *or* ~s)	a Moroccan
un **mexicano**	a Mexican
un **nicaragüense**	a Nicaraguan
un **panameño**	a Panamanian
un **paraguayo**	a Paraguayan
un **peruano**	a Peruvian
un **puertorriqueño**	a Puerto Rican
un **ruso**	a Russian
un **salvadoreño**	a Salvadorian
un **tunecino**	a Tunisian
un **turco**	a Turk
un **uruguayo**	a Uruguayan
un **venezolano**	a Venezuelan

USEFUL WORDS *(feminine)*

una	**africana**	an African
una	**antillana**	a West Indian
una	**árabe**	an Arab
una	**argelina**	an Algerian
una	**argentina**	an Argentinian
una	**boliviana**	a Bolivian
una	**brasileña**	a Brazilian
una	**chilena**	a Chilean
una	**china**	a Chinese
una	**colombiana**	a Colombian
una	**costarricense**	a Costa Rican
una	**cubana**	a Cuban
una	**dominicana**	a Dominican
una	**ecuatoriana**	an Ecuadorean
una	**griega**	a Greek
una	**guatemalteca**	a Guatemalan
una	**hondureña**	a Honduran
una	**india**	an Indian
una	**japonesa**	a Japanese
una	**marroquí** (*pl* ~es *or* ~s)	a Moroccan
una	**mexicana**	a Mexican
una	**nicaragüense**	a Nicaraguan
una	**panameña**	a Panamanian
una	**paraguaya**	a Paraguayan
una	**peruana**	a Peruvian
una	**puertorriqueña**	a Puerto Rican
una	**rusa**	a Russian
una	**salvadoreña**	a Salvadorian
una	**tunecina**	a Tunisian
una	**turca**	a Turk
una	**uruguaya**	a Uruguayan
una	**venezolana**	a Venezuelan

ESSENTIAL WORDS (*masculine*)

el	**aire**	air
el	**albergue juvenil**	youth hostel
el	**árbol**	tree
el	**arroyo**	stream
el	**bastón** (*pl* bastones)	walking stick
el	**bosque**	wood; forest
el	**camino**	way
el	**campesino**	countryman; farmer
el	**campo**	country; countryside
el	**castillo**	castle
el	**cazador**	hunter
el	**granjero**	farmer
el	**mercado**	market
el	**paisaje**	landscape, scenery
el	**paseo**	walk
el	**pícnic** (*pl inv or* ~s)	picnic
el	**prado**	field; meadow
el	**pueblo**	village
el	**puente**	bridge
el	**río**	river
el	**ruido**	noise
el	**sendero**	path; track
el	**terreno**	soil; ground
el	**turista**	tourist
el	**valle**	valley

USEFUL PHRASES

al aire libre in the open air
conozco el camino al pueblo I know the way to the village
salir en bicicleta to go cycling
los vecinos *or* **los habitantes de la zona** the locals
fuimos de pícnic we went for a picnic

ESSENTIAL WORDS *(feminine)*

la	**barrera**	gate; fence
la	**camioneta** *(Sp)*	van
la	**campesina**	countrywoman; farmer
la	**carretera**	road
la	**cazadora**	hunter
la	**excursión** *(pl* excursiones)	hike
la	**granja**	farm, farmhouse
la	**granjera**	farmer
la	**montaña**	mountain
la	**piedra**	stone; rock
la	**región** *(pl* regiones)	district
la	**tierra**	land; earth; soil; ground
la	**torre**	tower
la	**turista**	tourist
la	**vagoneta** *(Mex)*	van
la	**valla**	fence

USEFUL PHRASES

en el campo in the country
ir (de excursión) al campo to go into the country
vivir en el campo/en la ciudad to live in the country/in town
cultivar la tierra to cultivate the land

IMPORTANT WORDS *(masculine)*

el	**agricultor** *(Sp)*	farmer
el	**guardia civil**	civil guard *(person)*
el	**lago**	lake
el	**mesón** *(pl* mesones)	inn
el	**polvo**	dust
el	**ranchero** *(Mex)*	farmer

USEFUL WORDS *(masculine)*

los	**anteojos de larga vista** *(LAm)*	binoculars
el	**arbusto**	bush
el	**barro**	mud
el	**brezo**	heather
el	**charco**	puddle
el	**estanque**	pond
el	**guijarro**	pebble
el	**heno**	hay
el	**matorral**	bush
el	**molino (de viento)**	(wind)mill
el	**palo**	stick
el	**pantano**	marsh
el	**páramo**	moor
el	**poste telegráfico**	telegraph pole
el	**prado**	meadow
los	**prismáticos** *(Sp)*	binoculars
el	**seto**	hedge
el	**trigo**	corn; wheat

USEFUL PHRASES

agrícola agricultural
apacible, tranquilo(a) peaceful
en la cima de la colina at the top of the hill
caer en una trampa to fall into a trap

IMPORTANT WORDS (feminine)

la	agricultora (Sp)	farmer
la	agricultura	agriculture
las	botas de goma	rubber boots
las	botas de sierra	hiking boots
la	calzada	road surface
la	cima	top (of hill)
la	colina	hill
la	gente del campo	country people
la	guardia civil	civil guard (person)
la	Guardia Civil	Civil Guard
la	hoja	leaf
la	propiedad	property; estate
la	ranchera (Mex)	farmer
la	tranquilidad	peace

USEFUL WORDS (feminine)

la	aldea	hamlet
la	cantera	quarry
la	cascada	waterfall
la	caza	hunting; shooting
la	cosecha	crop; harvest
la	cueva	cave
la	fuente	spring; source
la	furgoneta	van
la	llanura	plain
la	orilla	bank (of river)
las	ruinas	ruins
la	senda	path; track
la	señal	signpost
la	trampa	trap
la	vendimia	grape harvest
la	zanja	ditch

USEFUL PHRASES

perderse to lose one's way
recoger la cosecha to bring in the harvest
vendimiar, hacer la vendimia to harvest the grapes

ESSENTIAL WORDS *(masculine)*

el	**aspecto**	appearance
el	**bigote**	moustache
el	**cabello**	hair
el	**color**	color
los	**ojos**	eyes
el	**talle**	waist

USEFUL PHRASES

alegre cheerful
alto(a) tall
amable nice
antiguo(a) old
asqueroso(a) disgusting
bajo(a) short
barbudo(a), con barba bearded, with a beard
bonito(a) pretty
bueno(a) kind
calvo(a) bald
delgado(a) skinny
desagradable unpleasant
dinámico(a) dynamic
divertido(a), entretenido(a) amusing, entertaining
educado(a) polite
esbelto(a) slim
estupendo(a) great
feliz (*pl* felices) happy
feo(a) ugly
gordo(a) fat
gracioso(a) funny
grosero(a) rude
guapo handsome; **guapa** beautiful
horrible hideous
infeliz (*pl* infelices), desgraciado(a) unhappy, unfortunate
inquieto(a) agitated
inteligente intelligent

ESSENTIAL WORDS (*feminine*)

la	**barba**	beard
la	**edad**	age
la	**estatura**	height; size
las	**gafas**	glasses
la	**identidad**	ID
la	**lágrima**	tear
la	**persona**	person
la	**talla**	size; height

USEFUL PHRASES

joven (*pl* **jóvenes**) young
largo(a) long
malo(a) naughty
mono(a) cute
nervioso(a), tenso(a) nervous, tense
optimista/pesimista optimistic/pessimistic
pequeño(a) small, little
que se porta bien well-behaved
serio(a) serious
tímido(a) shy
tonto(a) stupid
tranquilo(a) calm
viejo(a) old
(ella) parece triste she looks sad
(él) estaba llorando he was crying
(él) sonreía he was smiling
un hombre de estatura mediana a man of average height
mido 1 metro 70 *or* **uno setenta** *or* **1,70** I am 1 meter 70 tall
¿de qué color son tus (*or* **sus**) **ojos/es tu** (*or* **su**) **pelo?** what color are your eyes/is your hair?
tengo el pelo rubio I have fair hair
tengo los ojos azules/verdes I have blue/green eyes
pelo moreno *or* **castaño** dark *or* brown hair
pelo castaño (claro) light brown hair; **pelo rizado** curly hair; **pelirrojo(a)** red-haired
pelo negro/canoso black/gray hair
pelo teñido dyed hair

IMPORTANT WORDS *(masculine)*

el	**carácter** (*pl* caracteres)	character; nature
el	**grano**	spot
el	**humor**	mood

USEFUL WORDS *(masculine)*

el	**cerquillo** (*LAm*)	fringe
el	**defecto**	fault
el	**fleco** (*Mex*), el **flequillo** (*Sp*)	fringe
el	**gesto**	gesture
el	**gigante**	giant
los	**hoyuelos**	dimples
el	**lunar**	mole, beauty spot
el	**parecido**	resemblance
el	**peso**	weight
el	**rizo**	curl

USEFUL PHRASES

(él) tiene buen carácter he is good-tempered
(él) tiene mal genio *or* **carácter** he is bad-tempered
tener la tez pálida *or* **muy blanca** to have a pale complexion
llevar gafas/lentes de contacto *or* **lentillas** to wear glasses/contact lenses

IMPORTANT WORDS *(feminine)*

la	**belleza**	beauty
la	**calidad**	(good) quality
la	**costumbre**	habit
la	**curiosidad**	curiosity
la	**expresión** *(pl* expresiones)	expression
la	**fealdad**	ugliness
las	**lentillas**	contact lenses
la	**mirada**	look
la	**sonrisa**	smile
la	**tez** *(pl* teces)	complexion
la	**voz** *(pl* voces)	voice

USEFUL WORDS *(feminine)*

las	**arrugas**	wrinkles
la	**cicatriz** *(pl* cicatrices)	scar
la	**dentadura (postiza)**	false teeth
las	**pecas**	freckles
la	**permanente**	perm
la	**tlmidez**	shyness

USEFUL PHRASES

siempre estoy de buen humor I am always in a good mood
(él) está de mal humor he is in a bad mood
(él) se enfadó he got angry
(ella) se parece a su madre she looks like her mother
(él) se muerde las uñas he bites his nails

ESSENTIAL WORDS *(masculine)*

el	abecedario	alphabet
el	alemán	German
el	alumno	pupil; schoolboy
el	amigo	pal
el	aprendizaje	learning; apprenticeship
el	club *(pl ~s or ~es)*	club
el	colegio	school
el	comedor	dining hall
el	comienzo del curso	beginning of the course/year
el	compañero de clase	school friend
el	concierto	concert
el	cuaderno	notebook; exercise book
los	deberes	homework
el	día	day
el	dibujo	drawing
el	director	principal
el	dormitorio	dormitory
el	error	mistake
el	escolar	schoolboy
el	español	Spanish
el	estudiante	student
el	estudio (de)	study (of)
los	estudios	studies
el	examen *(pl* exámenes*)*	exam
el	examen de prueba *(pl* exámenes ~~*)*	mock exam
el	experimento	experiment
el	fallo	mistake
el	francés	French
el	gimnasio	gym
el	grupo	group
el	horario	timetable
el	IES (Instituto de Enseñanza Secundaria)	secondary school
el	inglés	English
el	instituto	secondary school
el	intercambio	exchange
el	italiano	Italian

ESSENTIAL WORDS *(feminine)*

la	**alberca** *(Mex)*	swimming pool
la	**alumna**	pupil; schoolgirl
la	**amiga**	pal
el	**aula** *(pl f las aulas)*	classroom
la	**biología**	biology
la	**cafetería**	cafeteria
las	**ciencias**	science
la	**clase**	class; lecture; year; classroom
las	**clases**	lessons; lectures
las	**clases prácticas**	lab
la	**compañera de clase**	school friend
la	**directora**	principal
la	**educación física**	PE
la	**electrónica**	electronics
la	**enseñanza**	education; teaching
la	**escolar**	schoolgirl
la	**escuela**	school
la	**escuela de primaria**	elementary school
la	**escuela infantil**	nursery school
la	**estudiante**	student
la	**excursión** *(pl excursiones)*	trip; outing
la	**exposición** *(pl exposiciones)*	presentation
la	**física**	physics
la	**frase**	sentence
la	**geografía**	geography
la	**gimnasia**	PE; gym
la	**goma (de borrar)**	eraser
la	**guardería**	nursery school
la	**historia**	history; story
la	**informática**	computer studies
la	**lección** *(pl lecciones)*	lesson
la	**lectura**	reading
la	**lengua extranjera**	foreign language
la	**maestra (de primaria** **or de infantil)**	elementary school teacher
las	**matemáticas**	mathematics
la	**materia (escolar)**	(school) subject

ESSENTIAL WORDS (*masculine continued*)

el	**laboratorio**	laboratory
el	**lápiz** (*pl* lápices)	pencil
el	**libro**	book
el	**maestro (de primaria** *or* **de infantil)**	elementary school teacher
el	**mapa**	map
el	**ordenador**	computer
el	**premio**	prize
el	**profesor**	teacher
el	**progreso**	progress
el	**recreo**	break; playtime
el	**resultado**	result
el	**semestre**	semester
el	**trabajo**	work; essay; class exam
los	**trabajos manuales**	handicrafts

USEFUL PHRASES

trabajar to work

aprender to learn

estudiar to study

¿cuánto tiempo llevas (*or* **lleva) aprendiendo español?** how long have you
been learning Spanish?

aprenderse algo de memoria to learn sth off by heart

tengo deberes/tareas todos los días *or* **a diario** I have homework every
day

mi hermana pequeña va a primaria/al colegio – yo voy a secundaria
or **al instituto** my little sister goes to elementary school – I go to middle
school

enseñar español to teach Spanish

el/la profesor(a) de alemán the German teacher

he mejorado en matemáticas I have made progress in math

hacer un examen *or* **presentarse a un examen** to take an exam

aprobar un examen to pass an exam

suspender un examen to fail an exam

sacar un aprobado to get a passing grade

ESSENTIAL WORDS *(feminine continued)*

las	**mates**	math
la	**música**	music
la	**natación**	swimming
la	**nota**	mark
la	**palabra**	word
la	**piscina**	swimming pool
la	**pizarra**	blackboard
la	**pregunta**	question
la	**profesora**	teacher
la	**química**	chemistry
la	**respuesta**	answer
la	**sala de profesores**	staffroom
la	**tarea**	homework; task
la	**universidad**	college; university
las	**vacaciones**	vacation
las	**vacaciones de verano**	summer vacation

USEFUL PHRASES

fácil easy; **difícil** difficult
interesante interesting
aburrido(a) boring
leer to read; **escribir** to write
escuchar to listen (to)
mirar to look at, watch
repetir to repeat
responder to reply
hablar to speak
es la primera *or* **mejor de la clase** she is at the top of the class
es la última *or* **peor de la clase** she is at the bottom of the class
entrar en clase to go into the classroom
cometer un error *or* **fallo** to make a mistake
corregir to correct
cometí un error gramatical I made a grammatical error
he sacado buena nota I got a good mark
¡responde a la pregunta! answer the question!
¡levantad la mano! put your hand up!

IMPORTANT WORDS (*masculine*)

el **acoso escolar**	school bullying
el **bachillerato**, el **bachiller**	GED course/certificate
el **certificado**	certificate
el **colegio concertado**	state-supported school
el **colegio privado**	private school
el **colegio público**	public school
el **control**	test
el **despacho**	office
el **día libre**	day off
el **diploma**	diploma
el **estuche**	pencil case
el **examen escrito** (*pl* exámenes ~s)	written exam
el **examen oral** (*pl* exámenes ~es)	oral exam
el **expediente**	file
el **libro electrónico**	e-book
el **papel**	paper
el **pasillo**	corridor
el **patio (de recreo)**	playground
el **título**	certificate; qualification; title

USEFUL PHRASES

mi amigo se está preparando la selectividad my friend is taking his
   university entrance exam

repasar (la lección) to review

repasaré otra vez la lección mañana I'll go over the lesson again
   tomorrow

IMPORTANT WORDS *(feminine)*

el	**aula** *(pl fl*as aulas) **de informática**	computer room
la	**ausencia**	absence
la	**carpeta**	folder; file
la	**conferencia**	lecture
la	**educación infantil**	pre-school education
la	**(educación) primaria**	elementary education
la	**(educación) secundaria**	secondary education
la	**evaluación**	assessment; assessment test
la	**falta**	absence
la	**falta de ortografía**	spelling mistake
la	**licenciatura**	bachelor's degree
la	**maestría**	master's degree
las	**normas**	rules
la	**nota (de un examen)**	(exam) mark
las	**notas**	report
la	**oposición** *(pl* oposiciones)	competitive exam
la	**regla**	rule; ruler
la	**salida (organizada)**	trip
la	**selectividad** *(Sp)*	(university) entrance examination
la	**traducción** *(pl* traducciones)	translation

USEFUL PHRASES

en segundo de primaria in second grade
en primero de ESO in seventh grade
en segundo de ESO in eighth grade
en tercero de ESO in ninth grade
en cuarto de ESO in tenth grade
en primero de bachillerato in eleventh grade

presente present
ausente absent
castigar a un(a) alumno(a) to punish a pupil
el/la profesor(a) los castigó sin recreo the teacher kept them in at break time
¡silencio!, ¡callaos! be quiet!

USEFUL WORDS (*masculine*)

el	**bedel**	janitor
el	**bloc** (*pl* ~s)	jotter
el	**boli, bolígrafo**	ballpoint pen
el	**borrador**	rough copy; eraser
el	**cálculo**	sum
el	**cañón proyector**	projector
el	**castigo**	detention; punishment
el	**comportamiento**	behavior
el	**corrector (líquido)**	correction fluid
el	**diccionario**	dictionary
el	**ejercicio**	exercise
el	**examinador**	examiner
el	**griego**	Greek
el	**inspector**	school inspector
el	**internado**	boarding school
el	**interno**	boarder
el	**jefe de estudios**	director of studies
el	**latín**	Latin
el	**libro de texto**	textbook
el	**maletín** (*pl* maletines)	briefcase
el	**orientador**	career advisor
el	**parte (de faltas** *or* **ausencias)**	absence sheet
el	**pupitre**	desk
el	**rotulador**	felt-tip pen
el	**sacapuntas** (*pl inv*)	pencil sharpener
el	**test** (*pl* ~s)	test
el	**trimestre**	term
el	**tutor**	tutor
el	**vestuario**	changing room
el	**vocabulario**	vocabulary

USEFUL WORDS *(feminine)*

el	**álgebra** *(f)*	algebra
la	**aritmética**	arithmetic
la	**bedel**	janitor
la	**calculadora**	calculator
la	**caligrafía**	handwriting
la	**carpintería**	woodwork
la	**cartera**	satchel; schoolbag; briefcase
las	**ciencias de la salud**	health sciences
las	**ciencias del medio ambiente**	natural sciences
las	**ciencias naturales**	natural sciences
las	**ciencias sociales**	social sciences
la	**entrega de premios**	awards ceremony
la	**ESO (Educación Secundaria Obligatoria)** *(Sp)*	compulsory secondary education
la	**facultad**	faculty
la	**fila**	row *(of seats etc)*
la	**FP (formación profesional)** *(Sp)*	vocational training
la	**geometría**	geometry
la	**gramática**	grammar
la	**inspectora**	school inspector
la	**interna**	boarder
la	**jefa de estudios**	director of studies
la	**mancha**	blot
la	**nota media**	passing grade; average grade
la	**orientadora**	career advisor
la	**ortografía**	spelling
la	**pizarra digital** *or* **interactiva**	interactive whiteboard
la	**poesía**	poetry; poem
la	**prueba**	test
la	**religión**	religious education
las	**TIC (tecnologías de la información y la comunicación)**	IT (information technology)
la	**tinta**	ink
la	**tiza**	chalk
la	**traducción inversa** *(pl* traducciones ~s)	prose translation
la	**tutora**	tutor

ESSENTIAL WORDS (*masculine*)

el	aerogenerador	wind turbine
el	agujero	hole
el	aire	air
los	animales	animals
los	árboles	trees
el	bosque	wood
el	coche	car
el	diésel	diesel
el	ecologista	environmentalist
el	gas	gas
los	gases de escape	exhaust fumes
el	gasoil	diesel
los	habitantes	inhabitants
el	impacto ecológico	environmental impact, carbon footprint
el	mapa	map
el	mar	sea
el	medio ambiente	environment
el	mundo	world
el	país	country
el	pez (*pl* los peces)	fish
el	tiempo	weather; time
los	Verdes	the Greens

IMPORTANT WORDS (*masculine*)

el	biocombustible	biofuel
el	calor	heat
el	cambio climático	climate change
el	clima	climate
el	contaminante	pollutant
el	daño	damage
el	detergente	detergent
el	gobierno	government
el	impuesto	tax
el	lago	lake
el	parque eólico	windfarm
el	planeta	planet
el	río	river

ESSENTIAL WORDS (feminine)

el	**agua** (f)	water
las	**botellas**	bottles
la	**contaminación**	pollution
la	**costa**	coast
la	**cuestión** (pl cuestiones)	question
la	**ecología**	ecology
la	**ecologista**	environmentalist
la	**especie**	species
la	**fábrica**	factory
la	**flor**	flower
la	**fruta**	fruit
la	**gasolina**	gasoline
la	**isla**	island
la	**lluvia**	rain
la	**montaña**	mountain
la	**planta**	plant
la	**playa**	beach
la	**región** (pl regiones)	region; area
la	**temperatura**	temperature
la	**tierra**	earth
la(s)	**verdura(s)**	vegetables

IMPORTANT WORDS (feminine)

la	**biodiversidad**	biodiversity
la	**central nuclear**	nuclear plant
la	**crisis** (pl inv)	crisis
la	**desforestación**	deforestation
las	**fuentes de energía alternativas**	alternative energy sources
la	**huella de carbono**	carbon footprint
las	**legumbres**	legumes
la	**selva**	rainforest; jungle
la	**solución** (pl soluciones)	solution
la	**zona**	zone

USEFUL WORDS *(masculine)*

el	acontecimiento	event
los	alimentos ecológicos	organic food
el	biocombustible	biofuel
el	calentamiento global	global warming
el	chapapote	oil slick
los	científicos	scientists
el	combustible	fuel
el	contenedor de vidrio	recycling container for bottles
el	continente	continent
el	desarrollo sostenible	sustainable development
el	desastre natural	natural disaster
el	desierto	desert
el	ecosistema	ecosystem
el	efecto invernadero	greenhouse effect
el	fertilizante	(artificial) fertilizer
el	futuro	future
los	gases de efecto invernadero	greenhouse gases
el	impuesto ecológico	environmental tax
el	investigador	researcher
el	océano	ocean
los	transgénicos	GMOs
los	productos químicos	chemicals
el	reciclado, el reciclaje	recycling
los	residuos nucleares/industriales	nuclear/industrial waste
el	vegano	vegan
el	vertedero	dumping ground

USEFUL PHRASES

(él) es muy respetuoso con el medio ambiente he's very environmentally minded

un producto ecológico an eco-friendly product

en el futuro in the future

reciclar to recycle

salvar to save

verde green

híbrido hybrid

USEFUL WORDS *(feminine)*

las	aguas residuales	sewage
la	capa de ozono	ozone layer
la	catástrofe	disaster
la	contaminación acústica	noise pollution
las	emisiones de CO2	carbon emissions
la	energía eólica	wind power
la	energía nuclear	nuclear power
la	energía renovable	renewable energy
la	energía solar	solar power
las	especies en peligro de extinción	endangered species
las	especies protegidas	protected species
la	huella de carbono	carbon footprint
la	lluvia ácida	acid rain
la	luna	moon
la	marea negra	oil slick
la	planta de reciclado *or* reciclaje	recycling plant
la	población (*pl* poblaciones)	population
la	selva tropical	tropical rainforest
la	sostenibilidad	sustainability
la	vegana	vegan

USEFUL PHRASES

biodegradable biodegradable

nocivo(a) *or* **dañino(a) para el medio ambiente** harmful to the environment

orgánico(a), biológico(a), ecológico(a) organic

destruir to destroy

contaminar to contaminate; to pollute

prohibir to ban

ESSENTIAL WORDS *(masculine)*

el	**abuelo**	grandfather
los	**abuelos**	grandparents
los	**adultos**	adults
el	**apellido**	surname
el	**apellido de soltera**	maiden name
el	**bebé**	baby
el	**compañero**	partner
el	**hermano**	brother
el	**hijo**	son
el	**hombre**	man
el	**joven** (*pl* jóvenes)	youth, young man
los	**jóvenes**	young people
el	**marido**	husband
los	**mayores**	grown-ups
el	**niño**	child, boy
el	**nombre**	name
el	**nombre (de pila)**	first *or* Christian name
el	**novio**	boyfriend; fiancé; (bride)groom
el	**padre**	father
los	**padres**	parents
el	**papá**	daddy
el	**pariente**	relative
el	**primo**	cousin
el	**prometido**	fiancé
el	**tío**	uncle

USEFUL PHRASES

¿qué edad tiene (or** tienes)?, ¿cuántos años tiene (**or** tienes)?** how old are you?

tengo 15 años – él tiene 40 años I'm 15 – he is 40

¿cómo se llama (or** te llamas)?** what is your name?

me llamo Daniela my name is Daniela

él se llama Paco his name is Paco

prometido(a) engaged

casado(a) married; **divorciado(a)** divorced; **separado(a)** separated

casarse con algn to marry sb

casarse to get married; **divorciarse** to get divorced

ESSENTIAL WORDS *(feminine)*

la	**abuela**	grandmother
la	**compañera**	partner
la	**edad**	age
la	**familia**	family
la	**gente**	people
la	**hermana**	sister
la	**hija**	daughter; girl
la	**joven** (*pl* jóvenes)	youth
la	**madre**	mother
la	**mamá**	mom, mommy
los	**mayores**	grown-ups
la	**mujer**	woman; wife
la	**niña**	child, girl
la	**novia**	girlfriend; fiancée; bride
la	**pareja** (*m+f*)	couple; partner
la	**persona**	person
la	**prima**	cousin
la	**prometida**	fiancée
la	**señora**	lady
la	**tía**	aunt

USEFUL PHRASES

más joven/mayor que yo younger/older than me
¿tiene (*or* **tienes**) **hermanos?** do you have any brothers or sisters?
tengo un hermano y una hermana I have one brother and one sister
no tengo hermanos I don't have any brothers or sisters
soy hijo(a) único(a) I am an only child
toda la familia the whole family
crecer to grow
envejecer, hacerse viejo(a) to get old
me llevo bien con mis padres I get on well with my parents
mi madre trabaja my mother works

IMPORTANT WORDS *(masculine)*

el	**adolescente**	teenager
el	**esposo**	husband
el	**nieto**	grandson
los	**nietos**	grandchildren
el	**padrastro**	stepfather
los	**padres adoptivos**	adoptive parents
el	**sobrino**	nephew
el	**soltero**	bachelor
el	**subsidio familiar (por hijos)**	child benefit
el	**suegro**	father-in-law
el	**vecino**	neighbor
el	**viudo**	widower

USEFUL WORDS *(masculine)*

el	**ahijado**	godson
el	**amo de casa**	house husband
el	**anciano**	old man
el	**chaval,** el **chico**	kid
el	**cuñado**	brother-in-law
los	**gemelos**	identical twins
el	**hermanastro**	stepbrother
el	**hijastro**	stepson
el	**huérfano**	orphan
el	**marido**	husband
el	**matrimonio gay**	same-sex marriage
los	**mellizos**	twins
el	**padrino**	godfather
los	**recién casados**	newlyweds
los	**trillizos**	triplets
el	**viejo**	old man
el	**yerno**	son-in-law

USEFUL PHRASES

nacer to be born; **vivir** to live; **morir** to die
nací en 1990 I was born in 1990
mi abuela murió or **está muerta** my grandmother is dead
ella murió en 1995 she died in 1995

IMPORTANT WORDS *(feminine)*

la **adolescente**	teenager
la **au pair** *(pl inv)*	au pair
la **esposa**	wife
la **madrastra**	stepmother
la **nieta**	granddaughter
la **sobrina**	niece
la **soltera**	single woman
la **suegra**	mother-in-law
la **vecina**	neighbor
la **viuda**	widow

USEFUL WORDS *(feminine)*

la **ahijada**	goddaughter
el **ama de casa** *(pl f las amas ~~)*	housewife
la **anciana**	old woman
la **chavala**, la **chica**	kid
la **cuñada**	sister-in-law
la **familia monoparental**	single-parent family
las **gemelas**	identical twins
la **hermanastra**	stepsister
la **hijastra**	stepdaughter
la **huérfana**	orphan
la **madrina**	godmother
las **mellizas**	twins, twin sisters
la **niñera**	nanny
la **nuera**	daughter-in-law
la **pareja de hecho**	unmarried couple
la **vejez**	old age
la **vieja**	old woman

USEFUL PHRASES

él/ella es soltero(a) he/she is single
él es viudo he is a widower; **ella es viuda** she is a widow
soy el/la más joven I am the youngest; **soy el/la mayor** I am the eldest
mi hermana mayor my older sister; **mi familia de acogida** my foster family

ESSENTIAL WORDS *(masculine)*

el	**agricultor** *(Sp)*	farmer
el	**animal**	animal
el	**bosque**	forest
el	**buey**	ox
el	**caballo**	horse
el	**cabrito**	kid
el	**campo**	field; country
el	**cerdo**	pig
el	**chivo**	kid
el	**gato**	cat
el	**granjero**	farmer
el	**invernadero**	greenhouse
el	**pato**	duck
el	**pavo**	turkey
el	**perro**	dog
el	**perro pastor** *(pl~s~)*	sheepdog
el	**pollo**	chicken
el	**pueblo**	village
el	**ranchero** *(Mex)*	farmer
el	**ternero**	calf

IMPORTANT WORDS *(masculine)*

el	**campesino**	countryman
el	**cordero**	lamb
el	**gallo**	cock
el	**tractor**	tractor

USEFUL PHRASES

un trigal, un maizal a cornfield
la agricultura ecológica organic farming
los pollos de corral free-range chickens
los huevos de corral free-range eggs
cuidar a los animales to look after the animals
recolectar to harvest
recoger la cosecha to bring in the harvest/crops

ESSENTIAL WORDS *(feminine)*

la	**agricultora** *(Sp)*	farmer
la	**camioneta** *(Sp)*	van
la	**cerda**	sow
la	**finca**	farm
la	**gallina**	hen
la	**granja**	farm; farmhouse
la	**granjera**	farmer
la	**oveja**	sheep; ewe
la	**puerta**	gate
la	**ranchera** *(Mex)*	farmer
la	**tierra**	earth; ground
la	**vaca**	cow
la	**vagoneta** *(Mex)*	van
la	**valla**	fence
la	**verja**	gate
la	**yegua**	mare

IMPORTANT WORDS *(feminine)*

la	**agricultura ecológica**	organic farming
la	**agricultura intensiva**	intensive farming
la	**campesina**	countrywoman
la	**colina**	hill

USEFUL PHRASES
vivir en el campo to live in the country
trabajar en una granja to work on a farm
recolectar el heno to make hay

USEFUL WORDS (*masculine*)

el	**abono**	manure; fertilizer
el	**almiar**	haystack
el	**arado**	plow
el	**barro**	mud
el	**burro**	donkey
el	**carnero**	ram
el	**centeno**	rye
el	**cerdo**	pig
el	**cereal**	cereal, crop
el	**cobertizo**	shed
el	**corral**	farmyard
el	**espantapájaros** (*pl inv*)	scarecrow
el	**establo**	barn
el	**estanque**	pond
el	**estiércol**	manure
el	**gallinero**	henhouse
el	**ganado**	cattle
el	**ganso**	goose
el	**granero**	barn
el	**grano**	grain, seed
el	**heno**	hay
el	**maíz** (*pl* maices)	corn, maize
el	**molino (de viento)**	(wind)mill
el	**paisaje**	landscape
el	**pajar**	loft
el	**páramo**	moor, heath
el	**pastor**	shepherd
el	**pollito**	chick
el	**potro**	foal
el	**pozo**	well
el	**prado**	meadow
el	**rebaño**	(*sheep*) flock; (*cattle*) herd
el	**suelo**	ground, earth
el	**surco**	furrow
el	**toro**	bull
el	**trigo**	corn; wheat

USEFUL WORDS *(feminine)*

la **avena**	oats
la **cabra**	goat
la **cabritilla**	kid
la **carretilla**	cart
la **casita (con el tejado de paja)**	(thatched) cottage
la **cebada**	barley
la **cosecha**	crop
la **cosechadora**	combine harvester
la **cuadra**	stable
la **escalera**	ladder
la **ganadería**	cattle farm
la **lana**	wool
la **lonja**	market
la **paja**	straw
la **pocilga**	pigsty
la **recolección** *(pl* recolecciones)	harvest
la **uva**	grapes; grape
la **vendimia**	grape harvest, grape picking
la **viña**	vine
la **zanja**	ditch

ESSENTIAL WORDS (masculine)

el	**marisco**	seafood
el	**pez** (pl peces)	fish
el	**pez de colores** (pl peces ~~)	goldfish

IMPORTANT WORDS (masculine)

el	**cangrejo**	crab
el	**insecto**	insect

USEFUL WORDS (masculine)

el	**acuario**	aquarium
el	**arenque**	herring
el	**atún** (pl atunes)	tuna
el	**avispón** (pl avispones)	hornet
el	**bacalao**	cod
el	**calamar**	squid
el	**camarón** (pl camarones)	shrimp
el	**cangrejo de río**	crayfish
el	**chinche**	bug
el	**eglefino**	haddock
el	**grillo**	cricket
el	**gusano**	worm
el	**gusano de seda**	silkworm
los	**langostinos**	scampi
el	**lenguado**	sole
el	**lucio**	pike
el	**mejillón** (pl mejillones)	mussel
el	**mosquito**	mosquito
el	**pulpo**	octopus
el	**renacuajo**	tadpole
el	**salmón** (pl salmones)	salmon
el	**saltamontes** (pl inv)	grasshopper
el	**tiburón** (pl tiburones)	shark

USEFUL PHRASES

nadar to swim
volar to fly
vamos a ir a pescar we're going fishing

ESSENTIAL WORDS (feminine)

el **agua** (f)	water

IMPORTANT WORDS (feminine)

la **mosca**	fly
la **sardina**	sardine
la **trucha**	trout

USEFUL WORDS (feminine)

la **abeja**	bee
el **ala** (pl f las alas)	wing
la **anguila**	eel
la **araña**	spider
la **avispa**	wasp
la **cigala**	crayfish
la **cigarra**	cicada
la **cucaracha**	cockroach
la **hormiga**	ant
la **langosta**	lobster
la **libélula**	dragonfly
la **mariposa**	butterfly
la **mariquita**	ladybird
la **medusa**	jellyfish
la **mosquilla**	midge
la **mosquita**	midge
la **oruga**	caterpillar
la **ostra**	oyster
la **pescadilla**	whiting
la **polilla**	moth
la **pulga**	flea
la **rana**	frog

USEFUL PHRASES
una picadura de avispa a wasp sting
una tela de araña a spider's web

ESSENTIAL WORDS *(masculine)*

el	aceite	oil
el	aceite de oliva	olive oil
el	agua mineral	(mineral) water
el	alcohol	alcohol
el	almuerzo	lunch
el	aperitivo	appetizer; apertif
el	arroz	rice
el	asado	roast
el	autoservicio	self-service restaurant
el	azúcar	sugar
el	bar	bar
el	bistec *(pl inv or ~s)*	steak
el	bol	bowl
el	bote	can; jar
el	café	coffee; café
el	café con leche	coffee with milk
el	café largo de leche	coffee with milk, light coffee
el	camarero *(Sp)*	waiter
los	caramelos	candy
el	cerdo	pork
los	cereales	cereal
el	chocolate (caliente)	(hot) chocolate
el	cocinero	cook
el	consomé	clear soup, consommé
el	cruasán *(pl cruasanes)*	croissant
el	cuarto	quarter *(bottle/liter etc)*
el	cuchillo	knife
el	cuenco	bowl
el	desayuno	breakfast
el	dueño	owner
los	entrantes	hors d'œuvres, appetizers
el	entrecot *(pl inv or ~s)*	sirloin steak
el	filete	steak
el	helado	ice cream
el	huevo	egg
el	huevo duro *or* cocido	hard-boiled egg
el	huevo pasado por agua	soft-boiled egg
el	jamón *(pl jamones)*	ham

ESSENTIAL WORDS (*feminine*)

la	aceituna	olive
la	baguette	French bread
la	bandeja	tray
la	bebida	drink
la	botella	bottle
la	caja	box
la	carne	meat
la	carne de ternera	beef
la	carta	menu
la	cena	dinner
la	cerveza	beer
la	Coca-Cola® (*pl* ~s)	Coke®
la	cocinera	cook
la	comida	lunch; meal
la	comida precocinada *or* preparada	ready-made food *or* meals
las	conservas	canned food
la	cuchara	spoon
la	cuenta	bill
la	ensalada	salad
la	ensalada mixta	mixed salad
la	fruta	fruit
el	hambre (*f*)	hunger
la	hamburguesa	hamburger
la	lata	can
la	leche	milk
la	limonada	lemonade
la	loncha (de)	slice (of)
la	mantequilla	butter
la	mermelada	jam
la	mermelada de cítricos	marmalade
la	mesa	table
la	pastelería	pastry shop
las	patatas fritas	French fries; potato chips
la	pescadería	fish store
la	pieza de fruta	piece of fruit
la	repostería	pastry; cake shop
la	sal	salt
la	salchicha	sausage

ESSENTIAL WORDS (*masculine continued*)

el	**marisco**	seafood
el	**menú del día**	fixed-price menu
el	**mesero** (*LAm*)	waiter
el	**pan**	bread
el	**paté**	pâté
el	**pescado**	fish
el	**pícnic** (*pl inv or* ~s)	picnic
el	**platillo**	saucer
el	**plato**	plate; dish; course
el	**plato del día**	today's special
el	**pollo (asado)**	(roast) chicken
el	**postre**	dessert
el	**primero,** el **primer plato**	first course, appetizer
el	**queso**	cheese
el	**quiche** (*pl inv*)	quiche
el	**restaurante**	restaurant
el	**salchichón** (*pl* salchichones)	salami
el	**sándwich** (*pl* ~s *or* ~es)	sandwich
el	**segundo (plato)**	main course
el	**servicio**	service
el	**té**	tea
el	**tenedor**	fork
el	**vaso**	glass
el	**vinagre**	vinegar
el	**vino**	wine
el	**yogur(t)**	yogurt
el	**zumo de fruta**	fruit juice

USEFUL PHRASES

cocinar to cook; **comer** to eat

beber to drink; **tragar** to swallow

mi plato favorito my favorite dish

¿qué vas (*or* **va) a beber?** what are you having to drink?

está bueno *or* **rico** it's nice

estar hambriento, tener hambre to be hungry

estar sediendo, tener sed to be thirsty

ESSENTIAL WORDS *(feminine continued)*

la	sidra	cider
la	sopa	soup
la	tarta	cake
la	taza	cup
la	ternera	veal; beef
la	tortilla (de patatas)	Spanish omelet *(made with potatoes)*
la	tortilla francesa	omelet
la	tortita	pancake
la	tostada	toast
la	vajilla	dishes
las	verduras	vegetables

IMPORTANT WORDS *(feminine)*

la	cafetería	cafeteria
la	camarera	waitress
la	carne asada *or* a la parrilla	grilled meat
la	cerveza de barril	draft beer
la	chef *(pl inv or ~s)*	chef
la	chuleta de cerdo	pork chop
la	cuchara de postre	dessertspoon
la	cuchara de servir	tablespoon
la	cucharilla	teaspoon
la	garrafa	carafe
la	harina	flour
la	jefa de cocina	chef
la	mayonesa	mayonnaise
la	mesera *(LAm)*	waitress
la	mostaza	mustard
la	nata	cream
la	pimienta	pepper
la	pizza	pizza
la	propina	tip
la	receta	recipe
la	selección *(pl* selecciones*)*	choice
la	tarta	tart
la	tetera	teapot
la	vainilla	vanilla

IMPORTANT WORDS *(masculine)*

el	**ajo**	garlic
el	**almíbar**	syrup
los	**caracoles**	snails
el	**carrito**	cart
el	**chef** *(pl inv or ~s)*	chef
el	**comercio justo**	fair trade
el	**conejo**	rabbit
el	**cordero**	lamb; mutton
el	**cubierto**	cover charge; place setting
el	**gusto**	taste
el	**jefe de cocina**	chef
el	**olor**	smell
el	**precio con todo incluido**	inclusive price
el	**precio fijo**	set price
el	**refresco**	soft drink
el	**restaurante**	restaurant
el	**sabor**	flavor
el	**suplemento**	extra charge
el	**tentempié**	snack

USEFUL WORDS *(masculine)*

el	**abrelatas** *(pl inv)*	can opener
el	**beicon**	bacon
el	**biscote**	Melba toast
el	**bollito**	roll
el	**bollo**	bun
el	**cacao**	cocoa
el	**champán** *(pl champanes)*	champagne
el	**coñac** *(pl inv)*	brandy
el	**corcho**	cork
el	**cubito (de hielo)**	ice cube
el	**estofado**	stew
el	**fuagrás** *(pl fuagrases)*	liver pâté
el	**hígado**	liver
el	**ketchup** *(pl inv)*	ketchup

USEFUL WORDS *(feminine)*

las	**aves**	poultry
la	**carta de vinos**	wine list
la	**caza**	game
la	**chuleta**	chop
la	**clara (de cerveza)**	shandy
la	**comida**	food
la	**gelatina**	jelly
la	**infusión** (*pl* infusiones)	herbal tea
la	**jarra**	jug
la	**margarina**	margarine
la	**miel**	honey
la	**miga**	crumb
la	**nata montada**	whipped cream
las	**natillas**	custard
la	**pajita**	straw
la	**pasta**	pasta
la	**rebanada (de pan)**	slice of bread
la	**salsa**	sauce
la	**salsa de jugo de carne**	gravy
la	**servilleta**	napkin
la	**tisana**	herbal tea
la	**tostada**	slice of toast
las	**tripas**	tripe
la	**vinagreta**	vinaigrette dressing

USEFUL PHRASES

fregar los platos to do the dishes
cuando volvemos del colegio, merendamos we have a snack when we
   come back from school
desayunar, tomar el desayuno to have breakfast
delicioso(a) delicious; **repugnante** disgusting
¡que aproveche! enjoy your meal!; **¡salud!** cheers!
¡la cuenta, por favor! the bill please!
"servicio (no) incluido" "service (not) included"
comer fuera to eat out
invitar a algn a comer to invite sb to lunch
tomar algo de beber, beber algo to have drinks

USEFUL WORDS (*masculine continued*)

el	mantel	tablecloth
los	mejillones	mussels
el	panecillo	roll
el	paté de carne	potted meat
el	paté de hígado	liver pâté
el	paté de oca	goose pâté
el	puré de patatas	mashed potatoes
los	riñones	kidneys
el	rosbif (*pl inv or* ~s)	roast beef
el	sacacorchos (*pl inv*)	corkscrew
el	tapón (*pl* tapones)	cork
el	termo	flask
el	torrezno	slice of bacon
el	whisky, whiskey (*pl* ~s)	whisky
el	zumo natural de limón	freshly squeezed lemon juice

USEFUL PHRASES

poner la mesa to set the table; **quitar la mesa** to clear the table

comer, almorzar to have lunch

cenar to have dinner

probar algo to taste sth

¡eso huele bien! that smells good!

vino blanco/rosado/tinto white/rosé/red wine

un filete poco hecho/en su punto/bien hecho a rare/medium/
well-done steak

un sándwich (tostado) de jamón y queso toasted ham and cheese sandwich

SMOKING

el	cenicero	ashtray
la	cerilla	match
el	cigarrillo	cigarette
el	cigarrillo electrónico	e-cigarette
el	cigarro	cigar; cigarette
el	(cigarro) puro	cigar
el	estanco	tobacconist's
el	mechero	lighter
el	papel de fumar	cigarette paper
el	paquete de tabaco	pack of cigarettes
el	parche de nicotina	nicotine patch
la	pipa	pipe
el	tabaco	tobacco
el	vaporizador	vaporizer
la	zona de fumadores	smoking area

USEFUL PHRASES

una caja de cerillas a box of matches
¿tienes (or tiene) fuego? do you have a light?
encender un cigarrillo to light up
"prohibido fumar" "no smoking"
no fumo I don't smoke
he dejado de fumar, he dejado el tabaco I've stopped smoking
fumar es perjudicial para ti or **para la salud** smoking is very bad for you
vapear to vape

ESSENTIAL WORDS *(masculine)*

el	**ajedrez**	chess
los	**amigos (en Facebook)**	(Facebook) friends
el	**billete** (*Sp*)	ticket
el	**boleto** (*LAm*)	ticket
el	**cantante**	singer
el	**canto**	singing
el	**CD** (*pl inv or* ~s)	CD
el	**cine**	movie theater, cinema
el	**concierto**	concert
los	**deportes**	sports
los	**deportes extremos**	extreme sports
el	**disco**	record
el	**DVD** (*pl inv or* ~s)	DVD
el	**espectáculo**	show
el	**fin de semana**	weekend
el	**folleto**	leaflet
el	**futbolín** (*pl* futbolines)	foosball
el	**hobby** (*pl* hobbies)	hobby
el	**Internet**	internet
el	**juego**	game
el	**juego de rol**	role-playing game
el	**lector de CD/DVD/MP3**	CD/DVD/MP3 player
el	**museo**	museum; art gallery
el	**paseo**	walk
el	**periódico**	newspaper
el	**programa**	program
el	**reproductor de Blu-ray®/DVD/ CD/MP3**	Blu-ray®/DVD/CD/MP3 player
los	**seguidores (en Twitter®)**	(Twitter®) followers
el	**socio**	member
el	**teatro**	theater
el	**(teléfono) móvil** (*Sp*) *or* **celular** (*LAm*)	cell (phone)
el	**tiempo libre**	free time
el	**videojuego**	video game
el	**videojugador**	video game player, gamer

ESSENTIAL WORDS (feminine)

la	afición (pl aficiones)	hobby
la	cadena de televisión	TV channel
la	cámara (de fotos)	camera
la	canción (pl canciones)	song
la	cantante	singer
las	cartas	cards
la	discoteca	disco
la	diversión (pl diversiones)	entertainment
la	estrella (de cine) (m+f)	(movie) star
la	excursión (pl excursiones)	trip; outing; hike
la	fiesta	party
la	foto	photo
la	historieta	comic strip
la	lectura	reading
la	música (pop/clásica)	(pop/classical) music
las	noticias	news
la	novela	novel
la	novela policíaca or policiaca	detective novel
la	película	film
la	pista de patinaje	skating rink
la	prensa	the press
la	publicidad	publicity
la	radio	radio
la	revista	magazine
la	tele(visión) (pl teles, televisiones)	television, TV
la	videoconsola	games console
la	videojugadora	video game player, gamer

USEFUL PHRASES

salgo con mis amigos I go out with my friends
leo la revista I read the magazine
veo la televisión I watch television
juego al fútbol/al tenis/a las cartas I play soccer/tennis/cards
hacer bricolaje to do-it-yourself
hacer de canguro to baby-sit
hacer zapping to channel surf
ir de marcha (Sp) to go clubbing

IMPORTANT WORDS *(masculine)*

el	**anuncio**	notice; poster; advertisement
el	**concurso**	competition
los	**dibujos animados**	cartoon
el	**juguete**	toy
los	**megapíxeles**	megapixels
el	**mensaje de texto**	text message
el	**noticiero** *(LAm)*	news
el	**novio**	boyfriend
el	**ordenador (personal)** *(Sp)*	personal computer
los	**pasatiempos**	leisure activities
el	**PC** *(pl inv)*	PC
el	**periódico en línea**	online newspaper
el	**podcast**	podcast
el	**programa**	program
el	**reality show**	reality show
el	**SMS** *(pl inv)*	text message
el	**telediario** *(Sp)*	news
el	**vídeo** *(Sp)*, el **video** *(LAm)*	video recorder

USEFUL WORDS *(masculine)*

el	**aficionado**	fan
el	**blog**	blog
el	**campamento de verano**	holiday camp
el	**chat**	chat; chatroom
el	**club nocturno** *(pl ~s or ~es ~s)*	night club
el	**coro**	choir
el	**juego de mesa**	board game
el	**monopatín** *(pl monopatines)*	skateboard
el	**navegador**	browser
el	**patinador**	skater
el	**parque de atracciones**	amusement park
el	**snowboard**	snowboarding

USEFUL PHRASES

emocionante exciting; **aburrido(a)** boring; **divertido(a)** funny
bloguear *or* **escribir un blog** to blog
llamar a algn por Skype® to Skype sb

IMPORTANT WORDS *(feminine)*

las	**actividades extraescolares**	after-school activities
la	**cámara digital**	digital camera
la	**colección** *(pl* colecciones)	collection
la	**computadora (personal)** *(LAm)*	personal computer
la	**exposición** *(pl* exposiciones)	exhibition
la	**filmadora** *(LAm)*	camcorder
la	**pintura**	painting
la	**play**	Playstation®
la	**revista del corazón**	celebrity magazine
la	**serie**	series; serial
las	**tapas**	tapas, snacks
la	**telenovela**	soap (opera)
la	**tirolina**	zip line, zip wire
la	**videocámara** *(Sp)*	camcorder

USEFUL WORDS *(feminine)*

la	**aficionada**	fan
la	**diapositiva**	slide
la	**fotografía**	photograph; photography
la	**lista de éxitos**	charts
la	**patinadora**	skater
la	**telerrealidad**	reality TV

USEFUL PHRASES

no está mal it's not bad
bastante bien quite good
bailar to dance
hacer fotos to take photos
estoy aburrido(a) I'm bored
quedamos los viernes we meet on Fridays
estoy ahorrando para comprarme una *play* I'm saving up to buy a
    Playstation®
me gustaría dar la vuelta al mundo I'd like to go round the world

ESSENTIAL WORDS (*masculine*)

el	**albaricoque**	apricot
el	**limón** (*pl* limones)	lemon
el	**melocotón** (*pl* melocotones)	peach
el	**plátano**	banana
el	**pomelo**	grapefruit
el	**tomate**	tomato

IMPORTANT WORDS (*masculine*)

el	**árbol frutal**	fruit tree
el	**melón** (*pl* melones)	melon

USEFUL WORDS (*masculine*)

el	**aguacate**	avocado
el	**anacardo**	cashew nut
el	**arándano**	blueberry
el	**cacahuete**	peanut
el	**coco**	coconut
el	**dátil**	date
el	**higo**	fig
el	**hueso**	stone (*in fruit*)
el	**kiwi**	kiwi fruit
el	**ruibarbo**	rhubarb

ESSENTIAL WORDS *(feminine)*

la	**castaña (asada)**	(roasted) chestnut
la	**cereza**	cherry
la	**frambuesa**	raspberry
la	**fresa**	strawberry
la	**fruta**	fruit
la	**manzana**	apple
la	**naranja**	orange
la	**pasa**	raisin
la	**pera**	pear
la	**piel**	skin
la	**(pieza de) fruta**	(piece of) fruit
la	**piña**	pineapple
la	**uva**	grape(s)

USEFUL WORDS *(feminine)*

la	**avellana**	hazelnut
la	**baya**	berry
la	**ciruela**	plum
la	**ciruela pasa**	prune
la	**granada**	pomegranate
la	**grosella espinosa**	gooseberry
la	**grosella negra**	blackcurrant
la	**grosella (roja)**	redcurrant
la	**mandarina**	tangerine
la	**mora**	blackberry
la	**nuez** (*pl* nueces)	nut; walnut
la	**pepita**	seed (*in fruit*)
la	**vid**	vine

USEFUL PHRASES

un zumo de naranja/piña an orange/a pineapple juice
un racimo de uvas a bunch of grapes
maduro(a) ripe
verde unripe
pelar una fruta to peel a fruit
resbalar al pisar una cáscara de plátano to slip on a banana peel

ESSENTIAL WORDS *(masculine)*

el	**armario** *(Sp)*	cupboard; wardrobe
el	**calefactor**	heater
el	**congelador**	freezer
el	**equipo (de música)**	stereo system
el	**espejo**	mirror
el	**frigo**	refrigerator
el	**frigorífico** *(Sp)*	refrigerator
el	**mueble**	piece of furniture
los	**muebles**	furniture
el	**radiador**	radiator; heater
el	**radiodespertador**	radio alarm
el	**refrigerador** *(LAm)*	refrigerator
el	**reloj**	clock
el	**ropero** *(LAm)*	cupboard; wardrobe
el	**sillón** *(pl* sillones)	armchair
el	**teléfono**	telephone

IMPORTANT WORDS *(masculine)*

el	**aparador**	sideboard
el	**aparato**	appliance
el	**cargador del móvil**	mobile (battery) charger
el	**cuadro**	picture
el	**escritorio**	(writing) desk
el	**hervidor eléctrico**	kettle
el	**(horno) microondas**	microwave (oven)
el	**lavavajillas** *or* **lavaplatos** *(pl inv)*	dishwasher
el	**lector de CD/DVD**	CD/DVD player
el	**lector de libros electrónicos**	ereader
el	**libro electrónico**	e-book
el	**piano**	piano
el	**portátil**	laptop
el	**reproductor MP3**	MP3 player
el	**sofá**	sofa
el	**(teléfono) inalámbrico**	cordless phone
el	**(teléfono) móvil** *(Sp) or* **celular** *(LAm)*	cell phone

ESSENTIAL WORDS (feminine)

la	balda	shelf
la	cama	bed
la	cocina (eléctrica/de gas)	(electric/gas) cooker
la	estufa	heater
la	habitación (pl habitaciones)	room
la	lámpara	lamp
la	lavadora	washing machine
la	mesa	table
la	pantalla (de lámpara)	lampshade
la	radio	radio
la	silla	chair
la	televisión (pl televisiones)	television
la	televisión inteligente	smart TV

IMPORTANT WORDS (feminine)

la	aspiradora	vacuum cleaner
la	cómoda	chest of drawers
la	librería	bookcase
la	mesa de centro	coffee table
la	mesa de comedor	dining table
la	mesa de despacho	desk
la	plancha	iron
la	radio digital	digital radio
la	secadora	clothes dryer
la	tableta	tablet

USEFUL WORDS *(masculine)*

el	**altavoz** *(pl* altavoces)	speaker
el	**aplique**	wall lamp
el	**asiento**	seat
los	**auriculares**	headphones
el	**baúl**	chest; trunk
el	**cajón** *(pl* cajones)	drawer
el	**camión de mudanzas** *(pl* camiones ~ ~)	moving van
el	**cargador**	charger
el	**carrito**	cart
el	**colchón** *(pl* colchones)	mattress
el	**futón**	futon
el	**horno**	oven
el	**mando a distancia**	remote control
el	**marco**	frame
el	**mobiliario**	furniture
el	**navegador (GPS)**	satellite navigation, GPS
el	**operario de mudanzas**	moving man
el	**paragüero**	umbrella stand
el	**robot de cocina** *(pl* ~ s ~ ~)	food processor
el	**secador (de pelo)**	hairdryer
el	**sofá cama**	sofa bed
el	**taburete**	stool
el	**teléfono inteligente**	smartphone
el	**tocador**	dressing table

USEFUL PHRASES

un apartamento *or* **piso amueblado** a furnished apartment
encender/apagar el radiador to switch the heater on/off
he hecho la cama I've made my bed
sentarse to sit down
poner *or* **meter algo en el horno** to put sth in the oven
correr las cortinas to draw the curtains
cerrar las contraventanas to close the shutters

USEFUL WORDS *(feminine)*

la	**alfombra**	rug
la	**antena**	antenna
la	**antena parabólica**	satellite dish
la	**butaca**	chair
la	**cómoda**	chest of drawers
las	**contraventanas**	shutters
la	**cortacésped**	lawn mower
la	**cuna**	cradle; cot
la	**estantería**	shelves; bookcase
la	**lámpara de pie**	standard lamp
la	**lámpara halógena**	halogen lamp
las	**literas**	bunk beds
la	**máquina de afeitar**	electric shaver
la	**máquina de coser**	sewing machine
la	**memoria USB**	USB flash drive
la	**mesilla de noche**	bedside table
la	**moqueta**	wall-to-wall carpet
la	**mudanza**	move
la	**persiana**	blind
la	**plancha de pelo**	hair straighteners
la	**tabla de planchar**	ironing board
la	**tableta**	tablet
la	**tumbona**	deckchair
la	**videocámara**	video camera, camcorder

USEFUL PHRASES

es un piso de 4 habitaciones it's a 4-room apartment

¡ya está el desayuno/la comida/la cena! breakfast/lunch/dinner is ready!

ESSENTIAL WORDS

los	Alpes	the Alps
	Andalucía	Andalusia
el	Atlántico	the Atlantic
	Barcelona	Barcelona
	Bruselas	Brussels
	Castilla	Castile
	Cataluña	Catalonia
la	Costa del Sol	the Costa del Sol
(los)	Estados Unidos	(the) United States
el	este	the east
las	Islas Baleares	the Balearic Islands
las	Islas Canarias	the Canary Islands
La	Coruña	Corunna
	Londres	London
	Los Ángeles	Los Angeles
	Málaga	Malaga
	Mallorca	Majorca
el	Mar Cantábrico	the Bay of Biscay
el	Mediterráneo	the Mediterranean
	Menorca	Minorca
	México	Mexico
el	norte	the north
	Nueva York	New York City
el	oeste	the west
el	País Vasco	the Basque Country
el	Peñón (de Gibraltar)	the Rock (of Gibraltar)
los	Pirineos	the Pyrenees
	Puerto Rico	Puerto Rico
	Sevilla	Seville
la	sierra	mountain range
el	sur	the south
	Vizcaya	Biscay
	Zaragoza	Saragossa

IMPORTANT WORDS

	Edimburgo	Edinburgh
el	Támesis	the Thames

USEFUL WORDS

	Atenas	Athens
las	Bahamas	Bahamas
	Berlín	Berlin
	Canadá	Canada
la	capital	capital
	Chicago	Chicago
la	comunidad autónoma	autonomous region (of Spain)
	Cuba	Cuba
el	Extremo Oriente	the Far East
	Guadalajara	Guadalajara
las	Islas Británicas	the British Isles
La	Haya	The Hague
	Jamaica	Jamaica
	Lisboa	Lisbon
	Marruecos	Morocco
	Moscú	Moscow
el	Oriente Medio	the Middle East
el	Oriente Próximo	the Near East
el	Pacífico	the Pacific
	París	Paris
	Pekín	Beijing
el	Polo Norte/Sur	the North/South Pole
la	provincia	province
	Roma	Rome
	Varsovia	Warsaw
	Toronto	Toronto
	Viena	Vienna

USEFUL PHRASES

ir a Londres/Sevilla to go to London/Seville
ir a Andalucía to go to Andalusia
vengo de Barcelona/del País Vasco I come from Barcelona/the Basque
  Country
en el or **al norte** in or to the north
en el or **al sur** in or to the south
en el or **al este** in or to the east
en el or **al oeste** in or to the west

GREETINGS

hola hello
¿cómo está usted (or **estás)?** how are you?
¿qué tal? how are you?
bien fine (in reply)
encantado(a) pleased to meet you
¿dígame? hello (on telephone)
buenos días good morning
buenas tardes good afternoon; good evening
buenas noches good evening; good night
adiós goodbye; hello (when passing one another)
hasta mañana see you tomorrow
hasta luego see you later

BEST WISHES

feliz cumpleaños happy birthday
feliz Navidad merry Christmas
feliz Año Nuevo happy New Year
felices Pascuas happy Easter
abrazos or **un abrazo** all the best
recuerdos best wishes
saludos best wishes
bienvenido(a) welcome
enhorabuena congratulations
que aproveche enjoy your meal
que le vaya (or **te vaya) bien** all the best
que te diviertas (or **se divierta)** enjoy yourself
buena suerte good luck
buen viaje safe journey
jesús bless you (after a sneeze)
salud cheers
a tu (or **vuestra**, etc**) salud** good health

SURPRISE

Dios mío my goodness
¿qué?, ¿cómo? what?
entiendo oh, I see
vaya well, well
pues… well…
(¿)de verdad(?), (¿)sí(?) really(?)
(¿)estás (or está) de broma(?) you're kidding; are you kidding?
¡qué suerte! how lucky!

POLITENESS

perdone I'm sorry; excuse me
por favor please
gracias thank you
no, gracias no thank you
sí, gracias yes please
de nada not at all, don't mention it, you're welcome
con mucho gusto gladly

AGREEMENT

sí yes
por supuesto of course
de acuerdo, vale (*Sp*) OK
bueno fine

DISAGREEMENT

no no
que no no (*contradicting a positive statement*)
que sí yes (*contradicting a negative statement*)
claro que no of course not
ni hablar no way
en absoluto not at all
al contrario on the contrary
no me digas you don't say
qué cara what a nerve
no te metas en lo que no te importa mind your own business

DIFFICULTIES

socorro help
fuego fire
ay ouch
perdón (I'm) sorry, excuse me, I beg your pardon
lo siento I'm sorry
qué pena what a pity
qué pesadez, qué rollo what a nuisance; how boring
estoy harto(a) I'm fed up
no aguanto más I can't stand it any more
vaya (por Dios) oh dear
qué horror how awful

ORDERS

cuidado be careful
para (*or* **pare**) stop
oiga, usted hey, you there
fuera de aquí get out of here
silencio shh
basta ya that's enough
prohibido fumar no smoking
vamos, venga come on, let's go
sigue go ahead, go on
vámonos let's go

OTHERS

no tengo ni idea no idea
quizá, quizás perhaps, maybe
no (lo) sé I don't know
¿qué desea? can I help you?
aquí tienes there, there you are
ya voy I'm coming
no te preocupes don't worry
no merece la pena it's not worth it
a propósito by the way
cariño, querido(a) darling
el (*or* **la**) **pobre** poor thing
tanto mejor so much the better
no me importa I don't mind
a mí me da igual it's all the same to me
mala suerte too bad
depende it depends
¿qué voy a hacer? what shall I do?
¿para qué? what's the point?
me molesta it annoys me
me saca de quicio it gets on my nerves

ESSENTIAL WORDS (*masculine*)

el	**accidente**	accident
el	**dentista**	dentist
el	**doctor**	doctor
el	**enfermero**	(male) nurse
el	**enfermo**	patient
el	**estómago**	stomach
el	**hospital**	hospital
el	**médico**	doctor

IMPORTANT WORDS (*masculine*)

el	**algodón (hidrófilo)**	cotton
el	**antiséptico**	antiseptic
el	**comprimido**	tablet
el	**dolor**	pain
el	**esparadrapo**	adhesive bandage
el	**farmacéutico**	pharmacist
el	**jarabe**	syrup
el	**medicamento**	medicine, drug
el	**paciente**	patient
el	**resfriado**	cold
el	**seguro**	insurance

USEFUL PHRASES

ha habido un accidente there's been an accident
ingresar en el hospital to be admitted to the hospital
debe permanecer en cama you must stay in bed
estar enfermo(a) to be ill; **sentirse mejor** to feel better
cuidar to look after
me he hecho daño I have hurt myself
me he hecho un corte en el dedo I have cut my finger
me he torcido el tobillo I have sprained my ankle
se ha roto el brazo he has broken his arm
me he quemado I have burned myself
me duele la garganta/la cabeza/ el estómago I've got a sore throat/
   a headache/a stomach ache
tener fiebre to have a temperature

ESSENTIAL WORDS *(feminine)*

la	**aspirina**	aspirin
la	**cama**	bed
la	**cita**	appointment
la	**dentista**	dentist
la	**doctora**	doctor
la	**enferma**	patient
la	**enfermera**	nurse
la	**farmacia**	drug store, pharmacy
la	**médica**	doctor
la	**pastilla**	tablet, pill
la	**salud**	health
la	**temperatura**	temperature

IMPORTANT WORDS *(feminine)*

la	**ambulancia**	ambulance
la	**camilla**	stretcher
la	**clínica**	clinic, private hospital
la	**consulta**	surgery
la	**crema**	cream, ointment
la	**cucharada**	spoonful
la	**diarrea**	diarrhea
la	**enfermedad**	illness
la	**escayola**	plaster cast
la	**farmacéutica**	pharmacist
la	**gripe**	flu
la	**gripe A**	swine flu
la	**herida**	wound, injury
la	**inyección** *(pl* inyecciones)	injection
la	**medicina**	medicine
la	**operación** *(pl* operaciones)	operation
la	**paciente**	patient
la	**píldora**	pill; the Pill
las	**quemaduras del sol**	sunburn
la	**receta**	prescription
la	**sangre**	blood
la	**tableta**	tablet
las	**urgencias**	Accident and Emergency
la	**venda**	bandage

USEFUL WORDS (*masculine*)

el	**absceso**	abscess
el	**acné**	acne
el	**analgésico**	painkiller
el	**arañazo**	scratch
el	**ataque**	fit
el	**ataque al corazón**	heart attack
el	**cáncer**	cancer
el	**cardenal**	bruise
el	**embarazo**	pregnancy
el	**estrés**	stress
el	**mareo**	dizzy spell; sickness
el	**microbio**	germ
el	**nervio**	nerve
el	**preservativo**	condom
los	**primeros auxilios**	first aid
el	**pulso**	pulse
el	**régimen**	diet
el	**reposo**	rest
el	**SAMU**	emergency medical service
el	**shock**	shock
el	**sida**	AIDS
el	**vendaje**	dressing
el	**veneno**	poison
el	**VIH**	HIV

USEFUL PHRASES

tengo sueño I'm sleepy; **tengo naúseas** I feel sick
soy diabético(a) I'm a diabetic
es alérgico al pollo he's allergic to chicken
adelgazar to lose weight; **engordar** to put on weight
estar en forma to be in good shape
curarse to get better
tragar to swallow
sangrar to bleed
toser to cough
vomitar to vomit
reposar, descansar to rest

USEFUL WORDS *(feminine)*

la	**amigdalitis**	tonsillitis
las	**anginas**	sore throat; tonsillitis
la	**apendicitis**	appendicitis
la	**astilla**	splinter
la	**cicatriz** (*pl* cicatrices)	scar
la	**dentadura postiza**	false teeth
la	**dieta**	diet
la	**epidemia**	epidemic
la	**fiebre del heno**	hay fever
la	**insolación** (*pl* insolaciones)	sunstroke
la	**migraña**	migraine
la	**muleta**	crutch
la	**náusea**	nausea
las	**paperas**	mumps
la	**pomada**	ointment
la	**radiografía**	X-ray
la	**recuperación**	recovery
la	**rubeola**	German measles
la	**silla de ruedas**	wheelchair
la	**tos**	cough
la	**tos ferina**	whooping cough
la	**transfusión (de sangre)**	blood transfusion
	(*pl* transfusiones (~~))	
la	**varicela**	chickenpox

USEFUL PHRASES

gravemente herido(a) seriously injured

¿tiene seguro? are you insured?

estoy resfriado(a) I have a cold

¡eso duele! that hurts!; **me duele** it hurts!

respirar to breathe

desmayarse to faint

morir to die

perder el conocimiento to lose consciousness

llevar el brazo en cabestrillo to have one's arm in a sling

ESSENTIAL WORDS (*masculine*)

el	**almuerzo**	lunch
el	**ascensor**	lift
el	**balcón** (*pl* balcones)	balcony
los	**baños públicos** (*LAm*)	toilets
el	**bar**	bar
el	**botones**	bellboy
el	**camarero**	waiter
el	**cambio**	change
el	**cheque**	check
el	**cliente**	guest, customer
el	**cuarto de baño**	bathroom
el	**depósito**	deposit
el	**desayuno**	breakfast
el	**director**	manager
el	**equipaje**	luggage
el	**hostal**	cheap hotel
el	**hotel**	hotel
el	**huésped**	guest
el	**impreso**	form
el	**maletero**	porter
el	**número**	number
el	**pasaporte**	passport
el	**piso**	floor; story
el	**precio**	price
el	**recepcionista**	receptionist
el	**restaurante**	restaurant
el	**ruido**	noise
el	**servicio de habitaciones**	room service
los	**servicios**	toilets
el	**teléfono**	telephone

USEFUL PHRASES

quisiera reservar una habitación I would like to book a room
una habitación con ducha/con baño a room with a shower/
with a bathroom
una habitación individual/doble a single/double room

ESSENTIAL WORDS *(feminine)*

la	caja fuerte	safe
la	cama de matrimonio	double bed
la	cama individual	single bed
la	camarera	waitress; chambermaid
las	camas separadas	twin beds
la	clienta	guest, customer
la	comida	lunch; meal
la	cuenta	bill
la	directora	manager
la	ducha	shower
la	entrada	entrance
la	escalera	stairs
la	fecha	date
la	ficha	form
la	habitación *(pl* habitaciones)	room
la	huésped	guest
la	llave	key
la	maleta	suitcase
la	media pensión	Modified American Plan
la	noche	night
la	pensión *(pl* pensiones)	guest house
la	pensión completa	full board
la	piscina	swimming pool
la	planta	floor; story
la	planta baja	ground floor
la	recepción	reception
la	recepcionista	receptionist
la	salida de incendios	fire escape
la	tarifa	rate, rates
la	televisión *(pl* televisiones)	television
la	vista	view

USEFUL PHRASES

¿lleva algún documento de identidad? do you have any ID?
¿a qué hora se sirve el desayuno? what time is breakfast served?
limpiar la habitación to clean the room
"se ruega no molestar" "do not disturb"

IMPORTANT WORDS *(masculine)*

el **albergue**	hostel
el **apart(h)otel**	aparthotel, apartment hotel
el **baño**	bathroom
el **interruptor**	switch
el **lavabo**	washbasin; bathroom
el **precio total**	inclusive price
el **recibo**	receipt

USEFUL WORDS *(masculine)*

el **cocinero**	cook
el **conserje**	concierge
el **IVA**	VAT
el **jacuzzi**®	Jacuzzi®
el **maître**	head waiter
el **metro**	underground
el **mostrador de recepción**	reception desk
el **paquete turístico**	package deal
el **parador (nacional)** *(Sp)*	state-run high-class hotel
el **plano de la ciudad**	street map
el **portero**	porter, doorman
el **spa**	spa
el **sumiller**	wine waiter
el **vestíbulo**	foyer

USEFUL PHRASES

ocupado(a) occupied
libre vacant
limpio(a) clean
sucio(a) dirty
dormir to sleep
despertar to wake
"completo" "no vacancies"
"con todas las comodidades" "with all facilities"
¿podrían despertarme (or **llamarme) mañana por la mañana a las siete?**
  I'd like a 7 o'clock alarm call tomorrow morning, please
una habitación con vistas al mar a room overlooking the sea

IMPORTANT WORDS *(feminine)*

la	**bañera**	bathtub
la	**bañera de hidromasaje**	hot tub
la	**bienvenida**	welcome
la	**camarera (de habitaciones)**	chambermaid
la	**casa de huéspedes**	guest house
la	**factura**	bill
la	**guía turística**	guidebook
la	**propina**	tip
la	**reclamación** *(pl* reclamaciones)	complaint
la	**reserva**	reservation; booking

USEFUL WORDS *(feminine)*

la	**cama supletoria**	extra bed
la	**cocinera**	cook
la	**conserje**	concierge
la	**fonda**	guest house
la	**hoja de reclamaciones**	complaint form
la	**tarjeta de crédito**	credit card
la	**tarjeta de débito**	debit card
la	**terraza**	balcony; roof

USEFUL PHRASES

hacer una reserva en línea *or* **por Internet** to book online
una habitación con media pensión room on the Modified American Plan
¿nos sentamos fuera *or* **en la terraza?** shall we sit outside?
nos sirvieron la cena fuera *or* **en la terraza** should we sit outside?
un hotel de tres estrellas a three-star hotel
IVA incluido inclusive of VAT

ESSENTIAL WORDS *(masculine)*

el	**aparcamiento** *(Sp)*	parking lot; parking space
el	**apartamento**	apartment
el	**ascensor**	elevator
el	**balcón** *(pl* balcones*)*	balcony
el	**bloque de departamentos** *(LAm)*	apartment house
el	**bloque de pisos** *(Sp)*	apartment house
el	**comedor**	dining room
el	**cuarto**	bedroom; room
el	**cuarto de baño**	bathroom
el	**cuarto de los huéspedes**	spare room
el	**departamento** *(LAm)*	apartment
el	**dormitorio**	bedroom
el	**edificio**	building
el	**estacionamiento** *(LAm)*	parking lot; parking space
el	**exterior**	exterior
el	**garaje**	garage
el	**interior**	interior
el	**jardín** *(pl* jardines*)*	yard; garden
el	**mueble**	piece of furniture
los	**muebles**	furniture
el	**numéro de teléfono**	phone number
el	**patio**	yard
el	**piso**	floor, story; *(Sp)* apartment
el	**pueblo**	village
el	**salón** *(pl* salones*)*	living room
el	**solar**	plot of land
el	**sótano**	basement
el	**terreno**	plot of land

USEFUL PHRASES

cuando vaya a casa when I go home
mirar por la ventana to look out of the window
en mi/tu/nuestra casa at my/your/our house
mudarse de casa to move house
alquilar un apartamento *or* **un piso** to rent an apartment

ESSENTIAL WORDS *(feminine)*

la	**avenida**	avenue
la	**bodega**	cellar
la	**calefacción (central)**	(central) heating
	(*pl* calefacciones (~es))	
la	**calle**	street
la	**casa**	house
la	**ciudad**	town; city
la	**cocina**	kitchen
la	**comodidad**	comfort
la	**dirección** (*pl* direcciones)	address
la	**ducha**	shower
la	**entrada**	entrance
la	**entrada para coches** (*Sp*)	drive
	or **para carros** (*LAm*)	
la	**escalera**	stairs
la	**habitación** (*pl* habitaciones)	room
la	**llave**	key
la	**parcela**	plot of land
la	**pared**	wall
la	**planta**	floor, story
la	**planta baja**	ground floor
la	**plaza de parking** *or* **de garaje**	parking space (*in parking lot*)
la	**puerta**	door
la	**puerta principal**	front door
la	**sala de estar**	living room
la	**urbanización** (*pl* urbanizaciones)	housing development
la	**ventana**	window
la	**vista**	view

USEFUL PHRASES

vivo en una casa/en un apartamento *or* **un piso** I live in a house /
  an apartment
(en el piso de) arriba upstairs
(en el piso de) abajo downstairs
en el primer piso on the first floor
en la planta baja on the ground floor
en casa at home

IMPORTANT WORDS *(masculine)*

el	alojamiento	accommodation
el	alquiler	rent
el	baño	toilet
el	césped	lawn
el	dueño	landlord; owner
el	humo	smoke
el	lavabo	toilet; washbasin
el	mantenimiento	upkeep
el	mobiliario	furniture
el	pasillo	corridor
el	piso amueblado	furnished apartment
el	portero	caretaker
el	propietario	owner; landlord
el	rellano	landing
el	tejado	roof
el	trastero	storeroom; *(Mex)* cupboard
el	vecino	neighbor

USEFUL WORDS *(masculine)*

el	ático	penthouse; attic
el	chalet *(pl ~s)*	bungalow; detached house
el	cristal	window pane
el	despacho	study
el	escalón *(pl escalones)*	step
el	estudio	studio apartment
el	inquilino	tenant; lodger
el	muro	wall
el	parquet *(pl ~s)*	parquet floor
el	piso piloto	model apartment
el	seto	hedge
el	suelo	floor
el	techo	ceiling
el	timbre	door bell
el	tragaluz *(pl tragaluces)*	skylight
el	umbral	doorstep
el	vestíbulo	hall
el	vidrio	window pane

IMPORTANT WORDS *(feminine)*

la	**casa de campo**	cottage
la	**chimenea**	chimney; fireplace
la	**dueña**	landlady; owner
la	**mudanza**	move
la	**portera**	caretaker
la	**propietaria**	owner; landlady
la	**señora de la limpieza**	cleaner
la	**vecina**	neighbor
la	**vivienda**	housing

USEFUL WORDS *(feminine)*

el	**ama de casa** *(f pl* amas ~~)	housewife
la	**antena**	antenna
la	**baldosa**	tile
la	**buhardilla**	attic
la	**caldera**	boiler
la	**contraventana**	shutter
la	**cristalera** *(Sp)*	French window
la	**decoración** *(pl* decoraciones)	decoration
la	**fachada**	front *(of house)*
la	**habitación de los invitados**	spare room
la	**inquilina**	tenant; lodger
la	**persiana**	blind
la	**portería**	caretaker's room
la	**puerta ventana**	French window
la	**teja**	roof tile; slate
la	**tubería**	pipe
la	**vivienda de protección oficial**	public housing

USEFUL PHRASES

llamar a la puerta to knock at the door
acaba de sonar el timbre the doorbell just rang
desde fuera from the outside
dentro on the inside
hasta el techo up to the ceiling

ESSENTIAL WORDS (*masculine*)

el	**armario**	cupboard; wardrobe
el	**bote de la basura** (*Mex*)	garbage can
el	**buzón** (*pl* buzones)	mailbox
el	**cazo**	saucepan
el	**cenicero**	ashtray
el	**cepillo**	brush
el	**cuadro**	picture
el	**cubo de la basura**	trash can
el	**despertador**	alarm clock
el	**espejo**	mirror
el	**felpudo**	doormat
el	**fregadero**	sink
el	**frigorífico** (*Sp*)	refrigerator
el	**gas**	gas
el	**grifo**	faucet
el	**interruptor**	switch
el	**jabón** (*pl* jabones)	soap
el	**lavabo**	washbasin; toilet
la	**pasta de dientes**	toothpaste
el	**póster** (*pl* ~es *or* ~s)	poster
el	**radiador**	radiator
el	**refrigerador** (*LAm*)	refrigerator
el	**televisor**	television set

USEFUL PHRASES
darse un baño, bañarse to have a bath
darse una ducha, ducharse to have a shower
hacer la limpieza de la casa to do the housework
me gusta cocinar I like cooking

ESSENTIAL WORDS *(feminine)*

el	**agua** *(f)*	water
la	**alfombra**	carpet, rug
la	**almohada**	pillow
la	**balanza**	scales
la	**bandeja**	tray
la	**bañera**	bath
la	**cacerola**	saucepan
la	**cafetera**	coffee pot; coffee maker
la	**cazuela**	saucepan
la	**cocina**	cooker
las	**cortinas**	curtains
la	**ducha**	shower
la	**electricidad**	electricity
la	**foto**	photo
la	**lámpara**	lamp
la	**lavadora**	washing machine
la	**luz** *(pl luces)*	light
la	**manta**	blanket
la	**radio**	radio
la	**refrigeradora** *(LAm)*	refrigerator
la	**sábana**	sheet
la	**servilleta**	napkin
las	**tareas domésticas**	housework
la	**televisión** *(pl televisiones)*	television
la	**toalla**	towel
la	**vajilla**	dishes

USEFUL PHRASES
ver la televisión to watch television
en televisión on television
encender/apagar la tele to switch on/off the TV
tirar algo al cubo de la basura to throw sth in the garbage can
lavar *or* **fregar los platos** to do the dishes

IMPORTANT WORDS (masculine)

el **bidé**	bidet
el **detergente (en polvo)**	laundry detergent
el **enchufe**	plug; socket
el **horno**	oven
el **inodoro**	toilet (bowl)
el **lavavajillas** (*pl inv*)	dishwasher; dish detergent
el **mueble de cocina**	cooker
el **polvo**	dust

USEFUL WORDS (masculine)

el **adorno**	ornament
el **almohadón** (*pl* almohadones)	bolster
el **cojín** (*pl* cojines)	cushion
el **colchón**	mattress
el **contenedor de reciclaje**	recycling bin
el **cubo**	bucket
el **edredón nórdico** (*pl* edredones ~s)	duvet
el **(horno) microondas**	microwave oven
el **jarrón** (*pl* jarrones)	vase
el **molinillo de café**	coffee grinder
el **paño de cocina**	dishcloth
el **papel pintado**	wallpaper
el **picaporte**	door handle
el **trapo (del polvo)**	duster

USEFUL PHRASES

enchufar/desenchufar to plug in/to unplug
pasar la aspiradora to hoover
hacer la colada to do the washing

IMPORTANT WORDS *(feminine)*

la	**aspiradora**	vacuum cleaner
la	**bombilla**	light bulb
la	**cerradura**	lock
la	**colada**	(clean) laundry
la	**estufa**	heater
la	**pintura**	paint; painting
la	**receta**	recipe
la	**ropa de cama**	bedclothes
la	**ropa sucia**	(dirty) laundry
la	**sartén** *(pl* sartenes)	frying pan
la	**señora de la limpieza**	cleaner

USEFUL WORDS *(feminine)*

la	**basura**	garbage
la	**batidora**	blender
la	**bayeta**	duster
la	**escalera (de mano)**	ladder
la	**escoba**	broom
la	**esponja**	sponge
la	**manta eléctrica**	electric blanket
la	**moqueta**	wall-to-wall carpet
la	**olla a presión**	pressure cooker
la	**papelera**	waste paper basket
la	**percha**	coat hanger
la	**plancha**	iron
la	**tabla de planchar**	ironing board
la	**tapa**	lid
la	**tapicería**	upholstery
la	**tostadora**	toaster

USEFUL PHRASES

barrer to sweep (up)
limpiar to clean
recoger uno sus cosas to clean up one's things
dejar uno sus cosas por ahí tiradas to leave one's things lying about

ESSENTIAL WORDS (*masculine*)

el	**banco**	bank
el	**billete (de banco)**	banknote
el	**bolígrafo**	ball-point pen
el	**buzón** (*pl* buzones)	mailbox
el	**cambio**	change
el	**carnet** *or* **carné de identidad** (*Sp*)	ID card
	(*pl* ~s ~ ~)	
el	**cartero**	mail carrier
el	**céntimo de euro**	euro cent
el	**cheque**	check
el	**código postal**	zip code
el	**contrato telefónico**	phone contract
el	**correo electrónico**	email
el	**documento de identidad**	ID card
el	**dólar**	dollar
el	**empleado**	counter clerk
el	**error**	mistake
el	**euro**	euro
el	**impreso**	form
el	**ingreso**	deposit
el	**justificante**	written proof
el	**mensaje de texto**	text message
el	**mostrador**	counter
el	**prefijo**	area code
el	**número**	number
el	**paquete**	parcel
el	**pasaporte**	passport
el	**precio**	price
el	**sello**	stamp
el	**sobre**	envelope
el	**teléfono**	telephone
el	**tono de marcado**	dial tone

USEFUL PHRASES

el banco más cercano the nearest bank

quisiera cobrar un cheque/cambiar dinero I would like to cash a check/
change some money

ESSENTIAL WORDS (feminine)

la	ambulancia	ambulance
la	caja	check-out
la	carta	letter
la	cartera	mail carrier; wallet; (LAm) handbag
la	cédula de identidad (LAm)	ID card
la	compañía de teléfonos	phone company
la	dirección (pl direcciones)	address
la	embajada	embassy
la	empleada	counter clerk
la	firma	signature
la	información	information; directory assistance
la	libra (esterlina)	pound (sterling)
la	llamada	call
la	oficina de correos	post office
la	oficina de información or turismo	tourist information office
la	policía	police
la	reclamación	complaint
la	respuesta	reply
la	tarjeta de crédito	credit card
la	tarjeta de débito	debit card
la	(tarjeta) postal	postcard

USEFUL PHRASES

una llamada telefónica a phone call
llamar a algn por teléfono, telefonear a algn to phone sb
descolgar el teléfono to lift the receiver
marcar (el número) to dial (the number)
hola – soy el Dr Pérez or **el Dr Pérez al habla** hello, this is Dr. Pérez
está comunicando or **la línea está ocupada** the line is busy
no cuelgue hold the line
me he equivocado de número I got the wrong number
colgar to hang up
hacer una llamada internacional to make an international phone call

IMPORTANT WORDS (*masculine*)

el	**archivo adjunto**	attachment
los	**bomberos**	fire department
el	**buzón de voz** (*pl* buzones ~~)	voicemail
el	**cajero automático**	cash machine, ATM
el	**cambio de divisas**	foreign exchange
el	**cibercafé**	internet café
el	**consulado**	consulate
el	**contestador (automático)**	answering machine
el	**correo**	mail
el	**crédito**	credit
el	**departamento de atención al cliente**	customer service department
el	**domicilio**	home address
el	**gasto**	expense
el	**hospital**	hospital
el	**impuesto**	tax
el	**monedero**	purse
el	**pago**	payment
el	**recargo**	extra charge
el	**SMS** (*pl inv*)	text message
el	**teléfono de información**	directory
el	**(teléfono) fijo**	landline
el	**(teléfono) móvil**	cell (phone)
los	**teléfonos de emergencias**	emergency telephone numbers
el	**tipo de cambio**	exchange rate

USEFUL WORDS (*masculine*)

el	**apartado de correos**	PO box
el	**destinatario**	addressee
el	**documento adjunto**	attachment
el	**nombre de usuario**	username
el	**papel de envolver**	wrapping paper
el	**remitente**	sender
el	**tono de llamada**	ringtone

IMPORTANT WORDS *(feminine)*

la	**banda ancha**	broadband
la	**clave de acceso**	password
la	**contraseña**	password
la	**cuenta (bancaria)**	(bank) account
la	**estampilla** *(LAm)*	stamp
la	**llamada telefónica**	phone call
la	**oficina de objetos perdidos**	lost and found
la	**ranura**	slot
la	**recogida**	collection
la	**recompensa**	reward
la	**tarjeta de recarga (del móvil)**	phone card
la	**zona wifi**	Wi-Fi hotspot

USEFUL WORDS *(feminine)*

la	**carta certificada**	registered letter
la	**destinataria**	addressee
la	**llamada de emergencia**	emergency call
la	**llamada internacional**	international call
la	**llamada local**	local call
la	**llamada nacional**	inter-city call
la	**oficina de cambio**	currency exchange
la	**remitente**	sender
las	**tarifas de itinerancia**	roaming charges
la	**tarjeta SIM** *(pl ~s ~)*	SIM card

USEFUL PHRASES

he perdido la cartera I've lost my wallet
rellenar un impreso to fill in a form
en mayúsculas in block letters
hacer una llamada a cobro revertido to make a collect call
cargar el móvil to charge your cell

GENERAL SITUATIONS

¿cuál es su dirección? what is your address?
¿cómo se escribe? how do you spell that?
¿tiene cambio de 100 euros? do you have change of 100 euros?
escribir to write
responder to reply
firmar to sign
¿me puede ayudar por favor? can you help me please?
¿cómo se va a la estación? how do I get to the station?
todo recto straight ahead
a la derecha to *or* on the right; **a la izquierda** to *or* on the left

LETTERS

Querido Carlos Dear Carlos
Querida Ana Dear Ana
Estimado señor Dear Sir
Estimada señora Dear Madam
recuerdos, saludos best wishes
un abrazo de, un beso de, besos de love from
le saluda atentamente *or* **cordialmente** kind regards
besos y abrazos love and kisses
atentamente yours faithfully
reciba un atento saludo, le saluda atentamente yours sincerely
sigue over

EMAILS

mandarle un correo electrónico a algn to mail *or* email sb

CELL PHONES

mandarle un mensaje de texto a algn to text sb

PRONUNCIATION GUIDE

Pronounced approximately as:

A	ah
B	bay
C	thay, say
CH	chay
D	day
E	ay
F	efay
G	khay
H	atchay
I	ee
J	khota
K	kah
L	elay
LL	elyay
M	emay
N	enay
Ñ	enyay
O	oh
P	pay
Q	koo
R	eray
RR	erray
S	essay
T	tay
U	oo
V	oobay (*Sp*), **bay korta** (*LAm*)
W	oobay doblay (*Sp*), **doblay bay** (*LAm*)
X	ekees
Y	ee griayga
Z	theta, seta

ESSENTIAL WORDS *(masculine)*

el	**abogado**	lawyer
el	**accidente**	accident
el	**carnet de identidad** *(Sp) (pl ~s ~ ~)*	ID card
el	**documento de identidad**	ID card
el	**incendio**	fire
el	**policía**	police officer
el	**problema**	problem
el	**robo**	burglary; theft

IMPORTANT WORDS *(masculine)*

el	**atracador**	armed robber; mugger
el	**atraco**	hold-up; mugging
el	**consulado**	consulate
el	**control policial**	checkpoint; roadblock
el	**culpable**	culprit
el	**daño** *or* **los daños**	damage
el	**ejército**	army
el	**espía**	spy
el	**gobierno**	government
el	**guardia civil**	civil guard *(person)*
los	**impuestos**	tax
el	**ladrón** *(pl* ladrones*)*	burglar; thief; robber
el	**monedero**	purse
el	**muerto**	dead man
el	**permiso**	permission
el	**propietario**	owner
el	**testigo**	witness

USEFUL PHRASES

robar to burgle; to steal; to rob
¡me han robado la cartera! someone has stolen my wallet!
ilegal illegal; **inocente** innocent
no es culpa mía it's not my fault
¡socorro! help!; **¡al ladrón!** stop thief!
¡fuego! fire!; **¡arriba las manos!** hands up!
robar un banco to rob a bank
encarcelar to imprison; **fugarse, escapar** to escape

ESSENTIAL WORDS *(feminine)*

la	**abogada**	lawyer
la	**cédula de identidad** *(LAm)*	identity card
la	**culpa**	fault
la	**documentación**	papers
la	**identidad**	identity
la	**policía**	police; police officer
la	**verdad**	truth

IMPORTANT WORDS *(feminine)*

la	**atracadora**	armed robber; mugger
la	**banda**	gang
la	**cartera**	wallet; *(LAm)* handbag
la	**comisaría**	police station
la	**culpable**	culprit
la	**denuncia**	report
la	**espía**	spy
la	**Guardia Civil**	Civil Guard
la	**guardia civil**	civil guard *(person)*
la	**ladrona**	burglar; thief; robber
la	**manifestación** *(pl* manifestaciones)	demonstration
la	**muerta**	dead woman
la	**muerte**	death
la	**multa**	fine
la	**pena de muerte**	death penalty
la	**póliza de seguros**	insurance policy
la	**propietaria**	owner
la	**recompensa**	reward
la	**testigo**	witness

USEFUL PHRASES

un atraco a mano armada a hold-up
raptar *or* **secuestrar a un niño** to abduct a child
un grupo de gamberros a bunch of hooligans
en la cárcel in prison
pelearse to fight; **arrestar** to arrest; **acusar** to charge
estar detenido(a) to be remanded in custody
acusar a algn de algo to accuse sb of sth; to charge sb with sth

USEFUL WORDS *(masculine)*

el	**acusado**	the accused
el	**arresto**	arrest
el	**asesinato**	murder
el	**asesino**	murderer
el	**botín** *(pl* botines*)*	loot
el	**cadáver**	corpse
el	**crimen** *(pl* crímenes*)*	murder; crime
el	**criminal**	criminal
el	**detective privado**	private detective
el	**disparo (de arma)**	(gun) shot
el	**drogadicto**	drug addict
el	**encarcelamiento**	imprisonment
el	**gamberro**	hooligan
el	**gángster** *(pl* ~s*)*	gangster
el	**guarda**	guard; warden
el	**guardia**	guard; police officer
el	**inmigrante ilegal**	illegal immigrant
el	**intento**	attempt
el	**juez** *(pl* jueces*)*	judge
el	**juicio**	trial
el	**jurado**	jury
el	**levantamiento**	uprising
el	**pirómano**	arsonist
el	**poli**	cop
el	**preso**	prisoner
el	**rehén** *(pl* rehenes*)*	hostage
el	**rescate**	ransom; rescue
el	**revólver**	revolver
el	**secuestrador**	kidnapper; hijacker
el	**secuestro**	kidnapping
el	**secuestro aéreo**	hijacking
el	**terrorismo**	terrorism
el	**terrorista**	terrorist
el	**traficante de drogas**	drug dealer
el	**tribunal**	court
los	**tribunales**	law courts
el	**valor**	bravery
el	**violador**	rapist

USEFUL WORDS *(feminine)*

la **acusación** (*pl* acusaciones)	the prosecution; charge
el **arma** (*pl* f las armas)	weapon
la **asesina**	murderer
la **bomba**	bomb
la **cárcel**	prison
la **celda**	cell
la **criminal**	criminal
la **declaración** (*pl* declaraciones)	statement
la **defensa**	defence
la **detective privada**	private detective
la **detención** (*pl* detenciones)	arrest
la **droga**	drug
la **drogadicta**	drug addict
la **estafadora**	crook
la **fuga**	escape
la **gamberra**	hooligan
la **guarda**	guard; warden
la **guardia**	guard; police officer
la **inmigrante ilegal**	illegal immigrant
la **investigación** (*pl* investigaciones)	inquiry
la **ley**	law
la **multa**	fine
la **pelea**	fight
la **pirómana**	arsonist
la **pistola**	gun
la **poli**	the cops; cop
la **prisión** (*pl* prisiones)	prison
la **presa**	prisoner
la **prueba**	proof
las **pruebas**	evidence
la **redada**	raid
la **rehén** (*pl* rehenes)	hostage
la **riña**	argument
la **secuestradora**	kidnapper; hijacker
la **suplantación de personalidad** (*pl* suplantaciones ~~)	identity theft
la **terrorista**	terrorist
la **traficante de drogas**	drug dealer

ESSENTIAL WORDS *(masculine)*

el	**acero**	steel
el	**algodón**	cotton
el	**caucho**	rubber
el	**cristal**	glass
el	**cuero**	leather
el	**gas**	gas
el	**gasoil**	diesel
el	**hierro**	iron
el	**metal**	metal
el	**oro**	gold
el	**plástico**	plastic
el	**vidrio**	glass

IMPORTANT WORDS *(masculine)*

el	**acero inoxidable**	stainless steel
el	**aluminio**	aluminum
el	**cartón**	cardboard
el	**estado**	condition
el	**hierro forjado**	wrought iron
el	**ladrillo**	brick
el	**papel**	paper
el	**tejido**	fabric

USEFUL PHRASES
una silla de madera a wooden chair
una caja de plástico a plastic box
un anillo de oro a gold ring
en buen estado, en buenas condiciones in good condition
en mal estado, en malas condiciones in bad condition

ESSENTIAL WORDS *(feminine)*

la	**lana**	wool
la	**madera**	wood
la	**piedra**	stone
la	**piel**	fur; leather
la	**plata**	silver
la	**tela**	fabric

IMPORTANT WORDS *(feminine)*

la	**fibra sintética**	synthetic fiber
la	**seda**	silk

USEFUL PHRASES

un abrigo de piel a fur coat
un jersey de lana a wool sweater
oxidado(a) rusty

USEFUL WORDS *(masculine)*

el	**acrílico**	acrylic
el	**alambre**	wire
el	**ante**	suede
el	**bronce**	bronze
el	**carbón**	coal
el	**cemento**	cement
el	**cobre**	copper
el	**encaje**	lace
el	**estaño**	tin
el	**hilo**	thread
el	**latón**	brass
el	**lino**	linen
el	**líquido**	liquid
el	**mármol**	marble
el	**material**	material
el	**mimbre**	wickerwork
el	**pegamento**	glue
el	**plomo**	lead
el	**raso**	satin
el	**terciopelo**	velvet
el	**tweed**	tweed

USEFUL WORDS *(feminine)*

la	**arcilla**	clay
la	**cera**	wax
la	**cerámica**	ceramics
la	**cola**	glue
la	**cuerda**	string
la	**escayola**	plaster
la	**gomaespuma**	foam rubber
la	**hojalata**	tin, tinplate
la	**lona**	canvas
la	**loza**	pottery
la	**paja**	straw
la	**pana**	corduroy
la	**porcelana**	china

ESSENTIAL WORDS *(masculine)*

el	**director de orquesta**	conductor
el	**grupo**	band
el	**instrumento musical**	musical instrument
el	**músico**	musician
el	**piano**	piano
el	**violín** *(pl* violines)	violin

USEFUL WORDS *(masculine)*

el	**acorde**	chord
el	**acordeón** *(pl* acordeones)	accordion
el	**arco**	bow
el	**atril**	music stand
el	**bajo**	bass
el	**bombo**	bass drum
el	**chelo**	cello
el	**clarinete**	clarinet
el	**contrabajo**	double bass
el	**estuche**	case
el	**estudio de grabación**	recording studio
el	**fagot**	bassoon
los	**instrumentos de cuerda**	string instruments
los	**instrumentos de percusión**	percussion instruments
los	**instrumentos de viento**	wind instruments
el	**jazz**	jazz
los	**metales**	brass
el	**micrófono**	microphone
el	**oboe**	oboe
el	**órgano**	organ
los	**platillos**	cymbals
el	**saxofón** *(pl* saxofones)	saxophone
el	**solfeo**	music theory
el	**solista**	soloist
el	**tambor**	drum
el	**teclado**	keyboard
el	**triángulo**	triangle
el	**trombón** *(pl* trombones)	trombone
el	**violonchelo**	cello

ESSENTIAL WORDS (feminine)

la	**batería**	drums, drum kit
la	**directora de orquesta**	conductor
la	**flauta**	flute
la	**flauta dulce**	recorder
la	**guitarra**	guitar
la	**música**	music; musician
la	**orquesta**	orchestra

USEFUL WORDS (feminine)

la	**armónica**	harmonica
el	**arpa** (pl las arpas)	harp
la	**batuta**	conductor's baton
la	**composición** (pl composiciones)	composition
la	**corneta**	bugle
la	**cuerda**	string
la	**gaita**	bagpipes
la	**grabación digital** (pl grabaciones ~es)	digital recording
la	**megafonía**	PA system
la	**mesa de mezclas**	mixing deck
la	**nota**	note
la	**pandereta**	tambourine
la	**solista**	soloist
la	**tecla (de piano)**	(piano) key
la	**trompeta**	trumpet
la	**viola**	viola

USEFUL PHRASES

tocar or **interpretar una pieza** to play a piece
tocar alto/bajo to play loudly/softly
tocar afinado/desafinado to play in tune/out of tune
tocar el piano/la guitarra to play the piano/the guitar
tocar la batería to play drums
Pedro a la batería Pedro on drums
practicar el piano to practice the piano
¿tocas en un grupo? do you play in a band?
una nota falsa a wrong note

CARDINAL NUMBERS

cero	0	zero
uno (*m*), una (*f*)	1	one
dos	2	two
tres	3	three
cuatro	4	four
cinco	5	five
seis	6	six
siete	7	seven
ocho	8	eight
nueve	9	nine
diez	10	ten
once	11	eleven
doce	12	twelve
trece	13	thirteen
catorce	14	fourteen
quince	15	fifteen
dieciséis	16	sixteen
diecisiete	17	seventeen
dieciocho	18	eighteen
diecinueve	19	nineteen
veinte	20	twenty
veintiuno(a)	21	twenty-one
veintidós	22	twenty-two
veintitrés	23	twenty-three
treinta	30	thirty
treinta y uno(a)	31	thirty-one
treinta y dos	32	thirty-two
cuarenta	40	forty
cincuenta	50	fifty
sesenta	60	sixty
setenta	70	seventy
ochenta	80	eighty
noventa	90	ninety
cien	100	one hundred

CARDINAL NUMBERS (*continued*)

ciento uno(a)	101	a hundred and one
ciento dos	102	a hundred and two
ciento diez	110	a hundred and ten
ciento ochenta y dos	182	a hundred and eighty-two
doscientos(as)	200	two hundred
doscientos(as) uno(a)	201	two hundred and one
doscientos(as) dos	202	two hundred and two
trescientos(as)	300	three hundred
cuatrocientos(as)	400	four hundred
quinientos(as)	500	five hundred
seiscientos(as)	600	six hundred
setecientos(as)	700	seven hundred
ochocientos(as)	800	eight hundred
novecientos(as)	900	nine hundred
mil	1000	one thousand
mil uno(a)	1001	a thousand and one
mil dos	1002	a thousand and two
dos mil	2000	two thousand
dos mil seis	2006	two thousand and six
diez mil	10000	ten thousand
cien mil	100000	one hundred thousand
un millón	1000000	one million
dos millones	2000000	two million

USEFUL PHRASES

mil euros a thousand euros
un millón de dólares one million dollars
tres coma dos (3,2) three point two (3.2)

ORDINAL NUMBERS

primero(a)	$1^{\circ}, 1^{a}$	first
segundo(a)	$2^{\circ}, 2^{a}$	second
tercero(a)	$3^{\circ}, 3^{a}$	third
cuarto(a)	$4^{\circ}, 4^{a}$	fourth
quinto(a)	$5^{\circ}, 5^{a}$	fifth
sexto(a)	$6^{\circ}, 6^{a}$	sixth
séptimo(a)	$7^{\circ}, 7^{a}$	seventh
octavo(a)	$8^{\circ}, 8^{a}$	eighth
noveno(a)	$9^{\circ}, 9^{a}$	ninth
décimo(a)	$10^{\circ}, 10^{a}$	tenth
undécimo(a)	$11^{\circ}, 11^{a}$	eleventh
duodécimo(a)	$12^{\circ}, 12^{a}$	twelfth
decimotercero(a)	$13^{\circ}, 13^{a}$	thirteenth
decimocuarto(a)	$14^{\circ}, 14^{a}$	fourteenth
decimoquinto(a)	$15^{\circ}, 15^{a}$	fifteenth
decimosexto(a)	$16^{\circ}, 16^{a}$	sixteenth
decimoséptimo(a)	$17^{\circ}, 17^{a}$	seventeenth
decimoctavo(a)	$18^{\circ}, 18^{a}$	eighteenth
decimonoveno(a), decimonono(a)	$19^{\circ}, 19^{a}$	nineteenth
vigésimo(a)	$20^{\circ}, 20^{a}$	twentieth

Note:
Ordinal numbers are hardly ever used above 10th in spoken Spanish, and rarely at all above 20th. It's normal to use the cardinal numbers instead, except for **milésimo(a)**, **millonésimo(a)**, etc.

milésimo(a)	$1000^{\circ}, 1000^{a}$	thousandth
dosmilésimo(a)	$2000^{\circ}, 2000^{a}$	two thousandth
millonésimo(a)	$1000000^{\circ}, 1000000^{a}$	millionth
dosmillonésimo(a)	$2000000^{\circ}, 2000000^{a}$	two millionth

FRACTIONS

un medio	$^1/_2$	a half
uno(a) y medio(a)	$1^1/_2$	one and a half
dos y medio(a)	$2^1/_2$	two and a half
un tercio, la tercera parte	$^1/_3$	a third
dos tercios, las dos terceras partes	$^2/_3$	two thirds
un cuarto, la cuarta parte	$^1/_4$	a quarter
tres cuartos, las tres cuartas partes	$^3/_4$	three quarters
un sexto, la sexta parte	$^1/_6$	a sixth
tres y cinco sextos	$3^5/_6$	three and five sixths
un séptimo, la séptima parte	$^1/_7$	a seventh
un octavo, la octava parte	$^1/_8$	an eighth
un noveno, la novena parte	$^1/_9$	a ninth
un décimo, la décima parte	$^1/_{10}$	a tenth
un onceavo, la onceava parte	$^1/_{11}$	an eleventh
un doceavo, la doceava parte	$^1/_{12}$	a twelfth
siete doceavos, las siete doceavas partes	$^7/_{12}$	seven twelfths
un centésimo, la centésima parte	$^1/_{100}$	a hundredth
un milésimo, la milésima parte	$^1/_{1000}$	a thousandth

USEFUL PHRASES

ambos (ƒambas), los dos (ƒlas dos) both of them
un bocado de a mouthful of
un bote de a jar of; a can of
una botella de a bottle of
un botellín (de cerveza) a small bottle (of beer)
una caja de a box of
(gran) cantidad de lots of
una caña (de cerveza) a small glass of beer
cien gramos de a hundred grams of
un centenar de (about) a hundred
un cuarto de a quarter of
tres cuartos de three quarters of
una cucharada de a spoonful of
una docena de (about) a dozen
un grupo de a group of
una jarra de a jug of; a mug of (*beer*)
un kilo de a kilo of
un litro de a liter of
la mayoría (de), la mayor parte (de) most (of)
media docena de half a dozen
medio litro de half a liter of
una loncha de jamón a slice of ham
un metro de a meter of
miles de thousands of

USEFUL PHRASES

la mitad de half of
un montón de a pile of
mucho(a) a lot of, much
muchos (f muchas) a lot of, many
multitud de, montones de loads of
un paquete de a pack of
un par de a pair of
un plato de a plate of
un poco de a little; some
una porción de a portion of
un puñado de a handful of
una rebanada de pan a slice of bread
un rebaño de a herd of (*cattle*); a flock of (*sheep*)
una rodaja de merluza a slice of hake
un sobre de sopa a pack of soup
una taza de a cup of
un tazón de a bowl of
un terrón de azúcar a lump of sugar
un tonel de a barrel of
un trozo de papel/pastel a piece of paper/cake
a unos metros de a few meters from
un vaso de a glass of
varios several
a varios kilómetros de a few kilometers from

ESSENTIAL WORDS (*masculine*)

el	anillo	ring
el	cepillo	brush
el	cepillo de dientes	toothbrush
el	champú	shampoo
el	desodorante	deodorant
el	espejo	mirror
el	maquillaje	makeup
el	peine	comb
el	perfume	perfume
el	reloj	watch

USEFUL WORDS (*masculine*)

el	aftershave	aftershave
el	broche	brooch
el	colgante	pendant
el	collar	necklace
el	dentífrico	toothpaste
el	desmaquillador	makeup remover
el	diamante	diamond
los	efectos personales	personal effects
el	esmalte (de uñas)	nail polish
el	gel de baño	shower gel
los	gemelos	cufflinks
el	klínex (*pl inv*)	tissue
el	lápiz de labios (*pl* lápices ~~)	lipstick
el	llavero	keyring
el	neceser	toilet kit, vanity case
el	papel higiénico	toilet paper
el	peinado	hairstyle
el	pendiente	earring
los	polvos compactos	face powder
el	quitaesmalte	nail polish remover
el	rímel	mascara
el	rulo	roller
el	secador	hairdryer

ESSENTIAL WORDS *(feminine)*

el	**agua de colonia** *(f)*	eau de toilette
la	**cadena**	chain
la	**colonia**	eau de toilette
la	**crema hidratante**	moisturizing cream, moisturizer
la	**crema para la cara**	face cream
la	**cuchilla de afeitar**	razor
la	**joya**	jewel
la	**maquinilla de afeitar**	(safety) razor
la	**pasta de dientes**	toothpaste
la	**pulsera**	bracelet

USEFUL WORDS *(feminine)*

la	**alianza**	wedding ring
la	**base de maquillaje**	foundation
la	**brocha de afeitar**	shaving brush
la	**crema de afeitar**	shaving cream
la	**esponja**	sponge
la	**espuma de afeitar**	shaving foam
la	**loción para después del afeitado**	aftershave
la	**manicura**	manicure
la	**perla**	pearl
la	**polvera**	(powder) compact
la	**sombra de ojos**	eye shadow

USEFUL PHRASES
maquillarse to put on one's makeup
desmaquillarse to take off one's makeup
hacerse un peinado to do one's hair
peinarse to comb one's hair
cepillarse el pelo to brush one's hair
afeitarse to shave
lavarse los dientes, limpiarse los dientes to clean *or* brush one's teeth

ESSENTIAL WORDS (*masculine*)

el	**árbol**	tree
el	**césped**	lawn
el	**jardín** (*pl* jardines)	garden
el	**jardinero**	gardener
el	**sol**	sun

IMPORTANT WORDS (*masculine*)

el	**arbusto**	bush
el	**banco**	bench
el	**camino**	path
el	**cultivo**	cultivation; crop
el	**ramo de flores**	bunch of flowers

USEFUL PHRASES

plantar to plant
quitar las malas hierbas, desherbar to weed
regalar a algn un ramo de flores to give sb a bunch of flowers
cortar el césped to mow the lawn
"no pisar el césped" "keep off the grass"
a mi padre le gusta la jardinería my father likes gardening

ESSENTIAL WORDS *(feminine)*

la	**flor**	flower
la	**hierba**	grass
la	**hoja**	leaf
la	**jardinera**	gardener; flower bed
la	**jardinería**	gardening
la	**lluvia**	rain
la	**planta**	plant
la	**rama**	branch
la	**rosa**	rose
la	**tierra**	land; soil; ground
las	**verduras**	vegetables

IMPORTANT WORDS *(feminine)*

la	**abeja**	bee
la	**avispa**	wasp
las	**malas hierbas**	weeds
la	**raíz** *(pl* raíces)	root
la	**sombra**	shade; shadow
la	**valla**	fence
la	**verja**	gate

USEFUL PHRASES

las flores están creciendo the flowers are growing
en el suelo on the ground
regar las plantas to water the flowers
coger flores to pick flowers
irse a la sombra to go into the shade
quedarse en la sombra to remain in the shade
a la sombra de un árbol in the shade of a tree

USEFUL WORDS *(masculine)*

el **arriate**	flowerbed
el **azafrán** *(pl* azafranes)	crocus
el **brote**	bud
el **clavel**	carnation
el **cortacésped**	lawnmower
el **crisantemo**	chrysanthemum
el **diente de león**	dandelion
el **estanque**	(ornamental) pool
el **follaje**	leaves
el **girasol**	sunflower
el **gusano**	worm
el **huerto**	vegetable garden
el **invernadero**	greenhouse
el **invierno**	winter
el **jacinto**	hyacinth
el **lirio**	lily
el **lirio del valle**	lily of the valley
el **narciso**	daffodil
el **otoño**	autumn, fall
el **parterre**	flowerbed
el **pensamiento**	pansy
el **ranúnculo**	buttercup
el **rocío**	dew
el **rosal**	rose bush
el **sendero**	path
el **seto**	hedge
el **suelo**	ground; soil
el **tallo**	stalk
el **tronco**	trunk *(of tree)*
el **tulipán** *(pl* tulipanes)	tulip
el **verano**	summer

USEFUL WORDS *(feminine)*

la	amapola	poppy
la	baya	berry
la	campanilla	campanula, bellflower
la	campanilla de invierno	snowdrop
la	carretilla	wheelbarrow
la	cerca	fence
la	cosecha	crop
la	espina	thorn
la	herramienta	tool
la	hiedra	ivy
la	hortensia	hydrangea
las	lilas	lilac
la	madreselva	honeysuckle
la	manguera	hose
la	margarita	daisy
la	mariposa	butterfly
la	orquídea	orchid
la	peonía	peony
la	primavera	spring; primrose
la	regadera	watering can
la	semilla	seed
la	violeta	violet

ESSENTIAL WORDS *(masculine)*

los	**anteojos de sol** *(LAm)*	sunglasses
el	**bañador**	swimming trunks; swimsuit
el	**bañista**	swimmer
el	**barco**	boat; ship
el	**barco de pesca**	fishing boat
el	**biquini** *or* **bikini**	bikini
el	**bote**	boat
el	**mar**	sea
el	**muelle**	wharf, dock
el	**paseo**	walk
el	**paseo marítimo**	promenade
el	**pescador**	fisherman
el	**pesquero**	fishing boat
el	**pícnic** *(pl~s)*	picnic
el	**puerto**	port, harbor
el	**puerto deportivo**	marina
el	**remo**	rowing; oar
el	**traje de baño**	swimsuit

IMPORTANT WORDS *(masculine)*

el	**cangrejo**	crab
el	**castillo de arena**	sandcastle
el	**fondo**	bottom
el	**horizonte**	horizon
el	**mareo**	seasickness
el	**veraneante**	vacationer

USEFUL PHRASES

en la playa at the seaside; at *or* on the beach
en el horizonte on the horizon
está mareado he is seasick
nadar to swim
ahogarse to drown
me voy a dar un baño I'm going for a swim
tirarse al agua, zambullirse to dive into the water
flotar to float

ESSENTIAL WORDS *(feminine)*

el	**agua** (*f*)	water
la	**arena**	sand
la	**bañista**	swimmer
la	**barca**	boat
la	**costa**	coast
las	**gafas de sol** (*Sp*)	sunglasses
la	**isla**	island
la	**natación**	swimming
la	**pescadora**	fisherwoman
la	**piedra**	stone
la	**playa**	beach; seaside
las	**quemaduras de sol**	sunburn
la	**toalla**	towel

IMPORTANT WORDS *(feminine)*

la	**colchoneta inflable**	air mattress
la	**crema (de protección) solar**	sunscreen
la	**tabla de windsurf**	windsurfing board
la	**travesía**	crossing
la	**tumbona**	deckchair
la	**veraneante**	vacationer

USEFUL PHRASES

en el fondo del mar at the bottom of the sea
hacer la travesía en barco to go across by boat
broncearse, ponerse moreno(a) to get a tan
estar moreno(a) to be tanned
sabe nadar he can swim

USEFUL WORDS *(masculine)*

el	acantilado	cliff
el	aire del mar	sea air
el	balde	bucket
el	balón de playa	beach ball
el	(barco de) vapor	steamer
los	binoculares	binoculars
el	bote de pedales	paddle boat
el	cabo	headland
el	crucero	cruise
el	cubo	bucket
el	embarcadero	pier
el	estuario	estuary
el	faro	lighthouse
el	ferri	ferry
el	guijarro	pebble
el	marinero	sailor
el	marino	sailor; naval officer
el	mástil	mast
el	naufragio	shipwreck
los	náufragos	shipwrecked people, castaways
el	océano	ocean
el	oleaje	swell
el	pedal *(Sp)*	paddle boat
los	prismáticos	binoculars
el	puente (de mando)	bridge *(of ship)*
los	restos de un naufragio	wreckage
el	salvavidas *(pl inv)*	lifeguard; life preserver
el	socorrista	lifeguard
el	timón *(pl* timones)	rudder
el	transbordador	ferry

USEFUL WORDS *(feminine)*

las	**algas**	seaweed
el	**ancla** *(pl f las anclas)*	anchor
la	**bahía**	bay
la	**balsa**	raft
la	**bandera**	flag
la	**barca**	small boat
la	**boya**	buoy
la	**brisa marina**	sea breeze
la	**carga**	cargo
la	**concha**	shell
la	**corriente**	current
la	**desembocadura**	mouth *(of river)*
la	**espuma**	foam
la	**gaviota**	seagull
la	**insolación** *(pl insolaciones)*	sunstroke
la	**marea**	tide
la	**marina**	navy; sailor; naval officer
la	**marinera**	sailor
la	**nave**	vessel
la	**ola**	wave
la	**orilla**	shore
la	**pala**	spade
la	**pasarela**	gangway
la	**ría**	estuary
la	**roca**	rock
la	**salvavidas** *(pl inv)* or **socorrista**	lifeguard
la	**sombrilla**	parasol
la	**tripulación** *(pl tripulaciones)*	crew
la	**vela**	sail; sailing

USEFUL PHRASES

tuve una insolación I had sunstroke
con la marea baja/alta at low/high tide
hacer vela to go sailing

ESSENTIAL WORDS *(masculine)*

el	banco	bank
el	billete (de banco)	paper money
el	cajero automático	automated teller machine
el	cambio	change
el	céntimo	cent
el	centro comercial	shopping center
el	cliente	customer
el	datáfono	card reader
el	departamento	department
el	dependiente	shop assistant, sales assistant
el	descuento	discount
el	dinero	money
el	estanco	tobacconist's
el	euro	euro
los	grandes almacenes	department store
el	hipermercado	supermarket
el	horario comercial or de apertura or de atención al público	opening hours
el	mercado	market
el	número (de zapato)	(shoe) size
el	precio	price
el	regalo	present
el	souvenir (pl~s)	souvenir
el	suelto	small change
el	supermercado	supermarket
el	vendedor	salesman

USEFUL PHRASES

comprar/vender to buy/sell
¿cuánto cuesta? how much does it cost?
¿cuánto es? how much does it come to?
pagué veinte euros por esto, esto me costó veinte euros I paid 20 euros for that
en la carnicería/la panadería at the butcher's/bakery

ESSENTIAL WORDS *(feminine)*

la	**agencia de viajes**	travel agent's
la	**alimentación**	food
la	**caja**	checkout
la	**carnicería**	butcher's
la	**charcutería**	pork butcher's
la	**clienta**	customer
la	**compra**	purchase; shopping
la	**compra online**	online shopping; online purchase
la	**dependienta**	sales assistant
la	**factura**	bill; invoice
la	**farmacia**	pharmacy
la	**floristería**	flower shop
la	**frutería**	fruit store
la	**garantía**	guarantee
la	**lista**	list
la	**oficina de correos**	post office
la	**panadería**	bakery
la	**pastelería**	cake shop
la	**perfumería**	perfume shop/department
la	**pescadería**	fish store
la	**pollería**	poultry store
la	**rebaja**	reduction
las	**rebajas**	sales
la	**sección** *(pl* secciones)	department
la	**talla**	size
la	**tarjeta de crédito**	credit card
la	**tarjeta de débito**	debit card
la	**tienda**	shop
la	**tienda de alimentación** or **de comestibles**	grocer's
la	**tienda de regalos**	gift shop
la	**tienda de ropa**	clothes store
la	**tienda virtual**	online store
la	**vendedora**	saleswoman
la	**verdulería**	produce store
la	**zapatería**	shoe store

IMPORTANT WORDS *(masculine)*

el	**artículo**	article
el	**carnicero**	butcher
el	**carrito**	cart
el	**charcutero**	pork butcher
el	**comerciante**	storekeeper
el	**comercio**	trade; store
el	**comercio electrónico**	e-commerce
el	**comercio justo**	fair trade
el	**encargado**	manager
el	**frutero**	fruit vendor
el	**mercadillo**	street market
el	**monedero**	purse
el	**mostrador**	counter
el	**panadero**	baker
el	**pastelero**	confectioner
el	**peluquero**	hairdresser
el	**pescadero**	fish vendor
el	**pollero**	poulterer
el	**probador**	fitting room
el	**rastro** *(Sp)*	flea market
el	**recibo**	receipt
el	**tícket** *(pl ~s)*	receipt; ticket
el	**vendedor de periódicos**	news dealer
el	**verdulero**	produce vendor
el	**zapatero**	cobbler

USEFUL PHRASES

solo estoy mirando I'm just looking
es demasiado caro it's too expensive
algo más barato something cheaper
es barato it's cheap
"pague en caja" "pay at the checkout"
"no se admiten cambios ni devoluciones" "no refunds or exchanges"
¿lo quiere para regalo? would you like it gift-wrapped?
debe de haber un error there must be some mistake

IMPORTANT WORDS *(feminine)*

la **biblioteca**	library
la **boutique**	boutique
la **calculadora**	calculator
la **carnicera**	butcher
la **cartera**	wallet; purse; (*LAm*) handbag
la **charcutera**	pork butcher
la **comerciante**	storekeeper
la **encargada**	manager
la **escalera mecánica**	escalator
la **etiqueta**	label
la **frutera**	fruit vendor
la **galería comercial**	shopping arcade
las **galerías de alimentación**	small indoor food market
la **gran superficie**	superstore
la **librería**	bookstore
la **marca**	brand
la **panadera**	baker
la **pastelera**	confectioner
la **peluquera**	hairdresser
la **pescadera**	fish vendor
la **planta**	floor, story
la **promoción** (*pl* promociones)	special offer
la **reclamación** (*pl* reclamaciones)	complaint
la **tintorería**	dry cleaner
la **vendedora de periódicos**	news dealer
la **verdulera**	produce vendor
la **vitrina**	display case; (*LAm*) store window

USEFUL PHRASES

¿**algo más?** anything else?

S.A. (= *Sociedad Anónima*) Ltd

S.L. (= *Sociedad Limitada*) limited liability company

y Cía & Co

"**de venta aquí**" "on sale here"

un coche de ocasión a used car

en oferta, de oferta on special offer

el café de comercio justo fair-trade coffee

USEFUL WORDS *(masculine)*

el	**agente inmobiliario**	real estate agent
el	**color**	color
el	**escaparate**	store window
el	**ferretero**	hardware store
el	**gerente**	manager
el	**joyero**	jeweler; jewelery box
el	**kiosco de periódicos**	newsstand
el	**lavado en seco**	dry cleaning
el	**librero**	bookseller
el	**medio de pago**	method of payment
el	**óptico**	optician
el	**producto**	product
los	**productos**	produce
el	**recado**	errand
el	**relojero**	watchmaker; clockmaker
el	**salón de belleza**	beauty parlor
el	**sitio de comparación de precios**	price comparison site
el	**tendero**	grocer
el	**trato**	deal
el	**vale de compra**	credit note
el	**vale regalo**	gift voucher

USEFUL PHRASES

ir a ver escaparates, ir de escaparates to go window shopping
¿tiene cambio de cien euros? have you got change for a hundred euros?
pagar en metálico to pay cash
pagar con un cheque to pay by check
pagar con tarjeta de crédito to pay by credit card
una moneda de una libra/de dos euros/de cincuenta céntimos
a one-pound/two-euro/fifty-cent coin

USEFUL WORDS *(feminine)*

la	**agencia de viajes**	travel agent's
la	**agencia inmobiliaria**	real estate agent
la	**agente inmobiliaria**	real estate agent
la	**banca electrónica**	e-banking
la	**banca por Internet**	internet banking, online banking
la	**cola**	line
las	**compras**	shopping
la	**confitería**	candy store
la	**devolución**	return (*of product*); refund (*of money*)
la	**droguería**	store selling household goods and cleaning products
la	**ferretera**	hardware store
la	**ferretería**	hardware store
la	**gerente**	manager
la	**joyera**	jeweler
la	**joyería**	jewelry store
la	**lavandería**	laundry
la	**librera**	bookseller
la	**mercancía**	goods
la	**óptica**	optician; optician's
la	**papelería**	stationer's
la	**relojera**	watchmaker; clockmaker
la	**relojería**	watchmaker's; clockmaker's
la	**sucursal**	branch
la	**talla de cuello**	collar size
la	**tarjeta de cliente**	loyalty card
la	**tendera**	grocer
la	**venta**	sale
la	**venta online**	online shopping

USEFUL PHRASES

en el escaparate in the window
ir de compras to go shopping
hacer la compra to do the shopping
gastar to spend

ESSENTIAL WORDS *(masculine)*

el **aeróbic**	aerobics
el **ajedrez**	chess
el **arco** *(LAm)*	goal
el **automovilismo**	motor racing
el **balón** *(pl* balones*)*	ball *(large)*
el **baloncesto**	basketball
el **balonmano**	handball *(game)*
el **billar**	billiards
el **campeón** *(pl* campeones*)*	champion
el **campeonato**	championship
el **campo**	field; *(golf)* course; *(basketball)* court
el **ciclismo**	cycling
el **deporte**	sport
el **equipo**	team
el **esquí**	skiing; ski
el **estadio**	stadium
el **fútbol**	soccer
el **gimnasta**	gymnast
el **golf**	golf
el **hockey**	hockey
el **juego**	game; play
el **jugador**	player
el **motociclismo**	motorcycling
el **partido**	match, game
el **resultado**	result; score
el **rugby**	rugby
el **tenis**	tennis
el **voleibol**	volleyball

USEFUL PHRASES

jugar al fútbol/tenis to play soccer/tennis
marcar un gol/anotar un punto to score a goal/a point
llevar la cuenta de los tantos to keep the score
ganar/perder un partido to win/lose a match
mi deporte preferido my favorite sport

ESSENTIAL WORDS *(feminine)*

las	**artes marciales**	martial arts
la	**campeona**	champion
la	**cancha**	(*basketball/tennis*) court; (*LAm*) field
la	**equitación**	horseback riding
la	**gimnasia (artística/rítmica)**	(artistic/rhythmic) gymnastics
la	**gimnasta**	gymnast
la	**jugadora**	player
la	**lucha libre**	wrestling
la	**natación**	swimming
la	**partida**	game (*chess etc*)
la	**pelota**	ball
la	**pesca**	fishing
la	**piscina**	swimming pool
la	**pista**	track; court (*tennis*)
la	**portería**	goal
la	**tabla de windsurf**	windsurfing board
la	**vela**	sailing; sail

USEFUL PHRASES

empatar to equalize; to draw

correr to run; **saltar** to jump; **lanzar** to throw

ganar *or* **derrotar** *or* **vencer a algn** to beat sb

entrenarse to train

LA Galaxy gana por 2 a 1 LA Galaxy is leading by 2 goals to 1

un partido de tenis a game of tennis

es socio de un club he belongs to a club

ir a nadar to go swimming; **ir de pesca** to go fishing

ir a la piscina to go to the swimming pool

¿sabes nadar? can you swim?

hacer deporte to do sport

montar en bicicleta *or* **hacer ciclismo** to go cycling

hacer vela/footing/alpinismo to go sailing/jogging/climbing

patín de cuchilla/de ruedas/en línea (ice) skate/roller skate/Rollerblade®

tiro con arco/al blanco archery/target practice

IMPORTANT WORDS (*masculine*)

los	bolos	bowling
el	encuentro	match

USEFUL WORDS (*masculine*)

el	adversario	opponent
el	alpinismo	climbing; mountaineering
el	árbitro	referee; umpire (*tennis*)
el	atletismo	athletics
el	bádminton	badminton
el	boxeo	boxing
el	buceo	diving
el	circuito	circuit; racetrack
el	cronómetro	stopwatch
el	defensa	defender
el	delantero	forward
el	descanso	halftime
el	entrenador	trainer; coach
el	espectador	spectator
el	footing	jogging
el	ganador	winner
el	gol	goal
los	Juegos Olímpicos	Olympic Games
el	maratón	marathon
el	Mundial (de fútbol)	World Cup
el	pádel	paddle tennis
el	parapente	paragliding
el	patín	skate
el	patinaje sobre hielo	(ice) skating
el	perdedor	loser
el	portero	goalkeeper
el	remo	rowing; oar
el	salto de altura	high jump
el	salto de longitud	long jump
el	senderismo	trekking; hill walking
el	tiro	shot; shooting
el	torneo	tournament
el	windsurf *or* windsurfing	windsurfing
el	yudo	judo

IMPORTANT WORDS (feminine)

la	bola	ball (small)
la	carrera	race
la	carrera de relevos	relay race
las	carreras (de caballos)	horse racing
la	defensa	defense
la	delantera	forward line; forward
la	pista de esquí	ski slope

USEFUL WORDS (feminine)

la	adversaria	opponent
la	árbitra	referee; umpire (tennis)
la	camiseta (de deporte)	jersey, shirt
la	caña de pescar	fishing rod
la	caza	hunting
la	copa	cup
la	Copa del Mundo	World Cup
la	eliminatoria	heat; qualifying round
la	entrenadora	trainer, coach
la	esgrima	fencing
la	espectadora	spectator
la	estación de esquí (pl estaciones de ~)	ski resort
la	etapa	stage
la	final	final
la	ganadora	winner
la	halterofilia	weightlifting
la	jabalina	javelin
la	lucha libre	wrestling
la	pelota vasca	jai alai
la	perdedora	loser
la	pista de hielo/de patinaje	ice/skating rink
la	portera	goalkeeper
la	prórroga	overtime
la	raqueta	racket
la	red	net
las	zapatillas de deporte	athletic shoes
las	zapatillas de tenis	tennis shoes

ESSENTIAL WORDS (*masculine*)

el	actor	actor
el	ambiente	atmosphere
el	anfiteatro	amphitheater
el	asiento	seat
el	auditorio	auditorium; audience
el	boleto (*LAm*)	ticket
el	cine	movie theater
el	circo	circus
el	cómico	comedian
el	espectáculo	show
el	patio de butacas	seats on the main level, orchestra
el	payaso	clown
el	programa	program
el	público	audience
el	teatro	theater
el	telón	curtain
el	vestuario	costume
el	videoclip (*pl* ~s)	music video
el	wéstern (*pl* ~s)	western

IMPORTANT WORDS (*masculine*)

el	acomodador	usher
el	actor principal	leading man
el	ballet (*pl* ~s)	ballet
el	cartel	notice; poster
el	director	director
el	entreacto	intermission
el	intermedio	intermission
el	maquillaje	make-up

USEFUL PHRASES

ir al teatro/al cine to go to the theater/to the movies
reservar un asiento *or* **una butaca** to reserve a seat in the orchestra
mi actor preferido/actriz preferida my favorite actor/actress
durante el intermedio during the intermission
salir a escena to come on stage
interpretar el papel de to play the part of

ESSENTIAL WORDS *(feminine)*

la	**actriz** *(pl* actrices*)*	actress
la	**banda sonora**	soundtrack
la	**boletería** *(LAm)*	box office
la	**cómica**	comedian
la	**entrada**	ticket
la	**especialista**	stuntwoman
la	**estrella de cine** *(m+f)*	film star
la	**música**	music
la	**obra (de teatro)**	play
la	**ópera**	opera
la	**orquesta**	orchestra
la	**payasa**	clown
la	**película**	film
la	**película de animación**	cartoon, animated film
la	**sala**	auditorium; theater
la	**salida**	exit
la	**sesión** *(pl* sesiones*)*	performance; showing
la	**taquilla**	box office

USEFUL PHRASES

interpretar to play
bailar to dance
cantar to sing
filmar una película to shoot a movie
"próxima sesión: 21 horas" "next showing: 9 p.m."
"versión original" "original version"
"subtitulada" "subtitled"
"localidades agotadas" "full house"
aplaudir to clap
¡otra! encore!
¡bravo! bravo!
una película de ciencia ficción/de amor a science fiction movie/a romance
una película de aventuras/de terror an adventure/horror movie

IMPORTANT WORDS *(masculine continued)*

el	primer actor	leading man
el	protagonista	star
el	subtítulo	subtitle
el	título	title

USEFUL WORDS *(masculine)*

los	aplausos	applause
el	argumento	plot
los	bastidores	wings
los	créditos	credits
el	crítico	critic
el	decorado	scenery
el	director de escena	producer; stage manager
el	dramaturgo	playwright
el	elenco	cast
el	ensayo (general)	(dress) rehearsal
el	escenario	stage; scene
el	escenógrafo	stage/set designer
el	especialista	stuntman
el	espectador	member of the audience
el	estreno	first night, premiere
el	foco	spotlight
el	foso de la orquesta	orchestra pit
el	gallinero	the highest and least expensive seats; peanut gallery *(informal)*
el	guardarropa	checkroom
el	guion	script
el	guionista	scriptwriter
el	monologuista (cómico)	stand-up comedian
el	musical	musical
el	palco	box
el	papel	part
el	personaje	character
el	productor	producer
el	realizador	director *(movie)*; producer *(TV)*
el	regidor	stage manager
el	reparto	cast
el	vestíbulo	foyer

IMPORTANT WORDS *(feminine)*

la	**acomodadora**	usher
la	**actriz principal** *(pl* actrices ~es)	leading lady
la	**butaca**	seat
la	**cartelera**	listings, billboard, marquee
la	**comedia**	comedy
la	**directora**	director
la	**platea**	seats on the main level, orchestra
la	**primera actriz** *(pl* ~s actrices)	leading lady
la	**protagonista**	star
la	**reserva**	booking

USEFUL WORDS *(feminine)*

la	**actuación** *(pl* actuaciones)	acting, performance
la	**crítica**	review; critics; critic
la	**directora de escena**	producer; stage manager
la	**dramaturga**	playwright
la	**escena**	scene
la	**escenógrafa**	stage/set designer
la	**escenografía**	scenery
la	**espectadora**	member of the audience
la	**farsa**	farce
la	**función** *(pl* funciones)	performance
la	**guionista**	scriptwriter
la	**interpretación**	acting, performance
la	**monologuista (cómica)**	stand-up comedian
la	**pantalla**	screen
la	**precuela**	prequel
la	**productora**	producer
la	**puesta en escena**	production
la	**realizadora**	director *(movie)*; producer *(TV)*
la	**regidora**	stage manager
la	**representación** *(pl* representaciones)	performance
la	**secuela**	sequel
la	**serie**	series
la	**tragedia**	tragedy

ESSENTIAL WORDS *(masculine)*

el	**año**	year
el	**cuarto de hora**	quarter of an hour
el	**despertador**	alarm clock
el	**día**	day
el	**fin de semana**	weekend
el	**instante**	moment
el	**mes**	month
el	**minuto**	minute
el	**momento**	moment
el	**reloj**	watch; clock
el	**segundo**	second
el	**siglo**	century
el	**tiempo**	time

USEFUL PHRASES

a mediodía at midday
a medianoche at midnight
pasado mañana the day after tomorrow
hoy today
hoy en día nowadays
anteayer, antes de ayer the day before yesterday
mañana tomorrow
ayer yesterday
hace dos días 2 days ago
dentro de dos días in 2 days
una semana a week
una quincena two weeks
todos los días every day
¿a qué día estamos?, ¿qué día es hoy? what day is it?
¿cuál es la fecha de hoy?, ¿qué fecha es hoy? what's the date today?
de momento for the time being, for the moment
las tres menos cuarto a quarter to 3
las tres y cuarto a quarter past 3
en el siglo XXI in the 21st century
ayer por la noche last night, yesterday evening

ESSENTIAL WORDS *(feminine)*

la	**hora**	hour; time *(in general)*
la	**jornada**	day
la	**mañana**	morning
la	**media hora**	half an hour
la	**noche**	night; evening
la	**quincena**	two weeks
la	**semana**	week
la	**tarde**	afternoon; evening

USEFUL PHRASES

el año pasado/próximo last/next year
la semana/el año que viene next week/year
dentro de media hora in half an hour
una vez once
dos/tres veces two/three times
varias veces several times
tres veces al año three times a year
nueve de cada diez veces nine times out of ten
érase una vez once upon a time there was
diez a la vez ten at a time
¿qué hora es? what time is it?
¿tiene hora? have you got the time?
son las seis/las seis menos diez/las seis y media it is 6 o'clock/10 to 6/
    half past 6
son las dos en punto it is 2 o'clock exactly
hace un rato a while ago
dentro de un rato in a while
temprano early
tarde late
esta noche *(past)* last night; *(to come)* tonight

IMPORTANT WORDS *(masculine)*

el	**día siguiente**	next day
el	**futuro**	future; future tense
el	**pasado**	past; past tense
el	**presente**	present *(time)*; present tense
el	**retraso**	delay

USEFUL WORDS *(masculine)*

el	**año bisiesto**	leap year
el	**calendario**	calendar
el	**cronómetro**	stopwatch
el	**lustro**	five years
el	**reloj de pie**	grandfather clock
el	**reloj de pulsera**	wristwatch

USEFUL PHRASES

dos días después two days later
el día antes *or* **el día anterior** the day before
un día sí y otro no every other day
en el futuro in the future
un día libre a day off
un día de fiesta a public holiday
un día laborable a weekday
en un día de lluvia, en un día lluvioso on a rainy day
al amanecer, al alba at dawn
la mañana/tarde siguiente the following morning/evening
ahora now

USEFUL WORDS *(feminine)*

las	**agujas**	hands (*of clock*)
la	**década**	decade
la	**Edad Media**	Middle Ages
la	**época**	time; era
la	**esfera**	face (*of clock*)
las	**manecillas**	hands (*of clock*)

USEFUL PHRASES

llegas tarde you are late

llegas temprano you are early

este reloj adelanta/atrasa this watch is fast/slow

llegar a tiempo, llegar a la hora to arrive on time

¿cuánto tiempo? how long?

el tercer milenio the third millennium

no levantarse hasta tarde to sleep in, to sleep late

de un momento a otro any minute now

dentro de una semana in a week's time

el lunes que viene no, el otro a week from Monday

la noche antes, la noche anterior the night before

en esa época at that time

ESSENTIAL WORDS (*masculine*)

el	**bricolaje**	do-it-yourself
el	**manitas** (*pl inv*)	handyman
el	**taller**	workshop

USEFUL WORDS (*masculine*)

el	**alambre (de espino)**	(barbed) wire
los	**alicates**	pliers
el	**andamio**	scaffolding
el	**candado**	padlock
el	**celo** (*Sp*)	Scotch® tape
el	**chinche** (*LAm*)	thumb tack
el	**cincel**	chisel
el	**clavo**	nail
el	**destornillador**	screwdriver
el	**durex®** (*LAm*)	Scotch® tape
el	**martillo**	hammer
el	**muelle**	spring
el	**pico**	pickax
el	**pincel**	paintbrush
el	**taladro**	drill
el	**tornillo**	screw

USEFUL PHRASES
hacer bricolaje, hacer chapuzas to do odd jobs
clavar un clavo con el martillo to hammer in a nail
"recién pintado(a)" "wet paint"
pintar to paint
empapelar to wallpaper

ESSENTIAL WORDS (feminine)

la	**cuerda**	rope
la	**herramienta**	tool
la	**llave**	key; (LAm) tap
la	**llave inglesa**	wrench
la	**manitas** (pl inv)	handywoman
la	**máquina**	machine

USEFUL WORDS (feminine)

la	**aguja**	needle
la	**batería**	battery (in car)
la	**caja de herramientas**	toolbox
la	**cerradura**	lock
la	**chinche** (LAm)	thumb tack
la	**chincheta** (Sp)	thumb tack
la	**cola**	glue
la	**escalera (de mano)**	ladder
la	**goma (elástica)**	rubber band
la	**horca**	(garden) fork
la	**lima**	file
la	**obra**	construction site
la	**pala**	spade
la	**pila**	battery (in radio etc)
la	**sierra**	saw
la	**tabla**	plank
la	**taladradora**	pneumatic drill
las	**tijeras**	scissors

USEFUL PHRASES

"prohibido el paso a la obra" "construction site: keep out"
práctico(a) handy
cortar to cut
reparar to repair
atornillar to screw (in)
desatornillar to unscrew

ESSENTIAL WORDS (*masculine*)

los	**alrededores**	surroundings
el	**aparcamiento** (*Sp*)	parking lot; parking space
el	**autobús** (*pl* autobuses)	bus
el	**ayuntamiento**	town hall; town council
el	**banco**	bank; bench
el	**barrio**	district
el	**bloque de departamentos** (*LAm*)	apartment house
el	**bloque de pisos** (*Sp*)	apartment house
el	**café**	café; coffee
el	**carro** (*LAm*)	car
el	**casco viejo**	old town
el	**centro de la ciudad**	town center
el	**cine**	movie theater
el	**coche** (*Sp*)	car
el	**edificio**	building
el	**estacionamiento** (*LAm*)	parking lot; parking space
el	**habitante**	inhabitant
el	**hotel**	hotel
el	**mercado**	market
el	**metro**	subway
el	**museo**	museum; art gallery
el	**parking** (*pl* ~s)	parking lot
el	**parque**	park
el	**peatón** (*pl* peatones)	pedestrian
el	**policía**	police officer
el	**puente**	bridge
el	**restaurante**	restaurant
los	**suburbios**	suburbs; slum areas
el	**taxi**	taxi
el	**teatro**	theater
el	**tour** (*pl* ~s)	tour
el	**turista**	tourist

ESSENTIAL WORDS *(feminine)*

la	**boutique**	boutique
la	**calle**	street
la	**carretera**	road
la	**catedral**	cathedral
la	**ciudad**	town, city
la	**comisaría**	police station
la	**contaminación**	air pollution
la	**esquina**	corner
la	**estación (de trenes)**	(train) station
	(*pl* estaciones (~~))	
la	**estación de autobuses**	bus station
	(*pl* estaciones ~~)	
la	**fábrica**	factory
la	**gasolinera**	gas station
la	**habitante**	inhabitant
la	**lavandería automática**	launderette
la	**oficina**	office
la	**oficina de correos**	post office
la	**parada de autobús**	bus stop
la	**parada de taxis**	taxi stand
la	**piscina**	swimming pool
la	**plaza**	square
la	**policía**	police officer; police
la	**tienda**	shop
la	**torre**	tower
la	**turista**	tourist
la	**vista**	view
la	**vivienda de protección oficial**	public housing

USEFUL PHRASES

voy a la ciudad *or* **al centro** I'm going into town
en el centro (de la ciudad) in the town center
en la plaza in the square
una calle de sentido único a one-way street
una zona muy urbanizada a built-up area
"dirección prohibida" "no entry"
cruzar la calle to cross the street

IMPORTANT WORDS *(masculine)*

el	abono (de transportes)	season ticket
el	agente (de policía)	police officer
el	alcalde	mayor
el	atasco	traffic jam
el	cartel	notice; poster
el	castillo	castle
el	cibercafé	internet café
el	cruce	crossroads
los	jardines públicos	park
el	lugar	place
el	monumento	monument
el	parquímetro	parking meter
el	quiosco de periódicos	newsstand
el	semáforo	traffic lights
el	sitio	place
el	tráfico	traffic
el	transeúnte	passer-by
el	zoológico	zoo

USEFUL PHRASES

en la esquina de la calle at the corner of the street
vivir en las afueras to live in the outskirts
andar, caminar to walk
tomar el autobús/el metro, coger el autobús/el metro (*Sp*) to take the bus/the subway
comprar una tarjeta multiviajes to buy a multiple-journey ticket
picar to punch (*ticket*)

IMPORTANT WORDS *(feminine)*

la	**acera**	pavement
la	**agente (de policía)**	police officer
la	**alcaldesa**	mayor
la	**biblioteca**	library
la	**calle principal**	main street
la	**calzada**	road
la	**circulación**	traffic
la	**circunvalación**	ring road
la	**desviación** (*pl* desviaciones)	detour
la	**estación de servicio** (*pl* estaciones ~ ~)	gas station
la	**iglesia**	church
la	**máquina expendedora de billetes** (*Sp*) *or* **de boletos** (*LAm*)	ticket machine
la	**mezquita**	mosque
la	**parte antigua**	old town
la	**polución**	air pollution
la	**sinagoga**	synagogue
la	**tarjeta multiviajes**	multiple-trip ticket
la	**transeúnte**	passer-by
la	**zona azul**	restricted parking zone
la	**zona industrial**	industrial park
la	**zona peatonal**	pedestrian mall
la	**zona verde**	green space

USEFUL PHRASES
industrial industrial
histórico(a) historic
bonito(a) pretty
feo(a) ugly
limpio(a) clean
sucio(a) dirty

USEFUL WORDS *(masculine)*

el	**adoquín** *(pl* adoquines)	cobblestone
el	**barrio residencial**	residential area
el	**callejón sin salida** *(pl* callejones ~~)	cul-de-sac, dead end
el	**camino de bicicletas**	bike path
el	**carril bici**	bike lane
el	**cementerio**	cemetery
el	**ciudadano**	citizen
el	**cochecito (de niño)**	pram, buggy
el	**concejo municipal**	town council
el	**desfile**	parade
el	**distrito**	district
el	**edificio**	building
el	**embotellamiento**	traffic jam
el	**folleto**	leaflet
los	**lugares de interés**	sights, places of interest
el	**paradero de autobús** *(LAm)*	bus stop
el	**parque de bomberos** *(Sp)*	fire station
el	**paso de cebra**	pedestrian crossing
el	**paso de peatones**	pedestrian crossing
el	**pavimento**	road surface
el	**rascacielos** *(pl inv)*	skyscraper
el	**sondeo de opinión**	opinion poll

USEFUL WORDS *(feminine)*

las	**afueras**	outskirts
la	**alcantarilla**	sewer
la	**cafetería**	coffee shop, café
la	**calle cortada** *or* **sin salida**	cul-de-sac, dead end
la	**camioneta de reparto**	delivery truck
la	**cárcel**	prison
la	**ciudadana**	citizen
la	**cola**	line
la	**ciudad universitaria**	university campus
la	**curva**	bend
la	**estación de bomberos** *(pl* estaciones ~ ~) *(LAm)*	fire station
la	**estatua**	statue
la	**farola**	streetlight
la	**flecha**	arrow
la	**galería de arte**	art gallery
la	**glorieta**	traffic circle; square
la	**isla peatonal**	traffic island
la	**muchedumbre**	crowd
la	**multitud**	crowd
la	**muralla**	rampart
la	**población** *(pl* poblaciones)	population
la	**rotonda**	traffic circle
la	**señal de tráfico**	road sign

ESSENTIAL WORDS (*masculine*)

el	**andén** (*pl* andenes)	platform
el	**asiento**	seat
el	**AVE**	high-speed train
el	**billete** (*Sp*)	ticket
el	**billete de ida** (*Sp*)	single ticket
el	**billete de ida y vuelta** (*Sp*)	return ticket
el	**billete electrónico** (*Sp*)	e-ticket
el	**billete sencillo** (*Sp*)	single ticket
el	**boleto** (*LAm*)	ticket
el	**boleto de ida** (*LAm*)	single ticket
el	**boleto de ida y vuelta** (*LAm*)	return ticket
el	**boleto electrónico** (*LAm*)	e-ticket
el	**bolso** (*Sp*)	handbag
el	**compartimento**	compartment
el	**descuento**	discount
el	**enlace**	connection
el	**equipaje**	luggage
el	**expreso**	fast train
el	**freno**	brake
el	**horario**	timetable
el	**maletero**	porter
el	**metro**	subway
el	**número**	number
el	**oficial de aduanas**	customs officer
el	**pasaporte**	passport
el	**plano**	map
el	**precio del billete** (*Sp*)	fare
	or **del boleto** (*LAm*)	
el	**puente**	bridge
el	**recargo**	extra charge
el	**retraso**	delay
el	**taxi**	taxi
el	**tícket** (*pl* ~s)	ticket; receipt
el	**tren**	train
el	**vagón** (*pl* vagones)	coach, car
el	**viaje**	journey
el	**viajero**	traveler

ESSENTIAL WORDS (feminine)

la **aduana**	customs
la **bici**	bike
la **bicicleta**	bicycle
la **boletería** (LAm)	ticket office
la **bolsa**	bag
la **cafetería (de la estación)**	snack bar
la **cantina (de la estación)**	snack bar
la **cartera**	wallet; (LAm) handbag
la **clase**	class
la **conexión** (pl conexiones)	connection
la **consigna**	checkroom
la **consigna automática**	luggage locker
la **dirección** (pl direcciones)	direction
la **entrada**	entrance
la **estación** (pl estaciones)	station
la **estación de metro** (pl estaciones ~~)	subway station
la **información**	information
la **línea**	line
la **llegada**	arrival
la **maleta**	suitcase
la **oficial de aduanas**	customs officer
la **oficina de objetos perdidos**	lost and found
la **parada de taxis**	taxi stand
la **petaca** (Mex)	suitcase
la **reserva**	reservation
la **sala de espera**	waiting room
la **salida**	departure; exit
la **taquilla**	ticket office; locker
la **vía**	track, line
la **viajera**	traveler

USEFUL PHRASES

reservar un asiento to book a seat

pagar un recargo, pagar un suplemento to pay an extra charge, to pay a surcharge

hacer/deshacer el equipaje to pack/unpack

IMPORTANT WORDS *(masculine)*

el **coche-cama** *(pl ~s~)*	sleeping car
el **coche-comedor** *(pl ~s~)*	dining car
el **conductor**	driver
el **destino**	destination
el **ferrocarril**	railway
el **revisor**	ticket collector
el **vagón restaurante**	dining car

USEFUL WORDS *(masculine)*

el **abono**	season ticket
el **baúl**	trunk
el **carnet joven** *(pl ~s ~)*	young persons' discount card
el **coche**	carriage
el **descarrilamiento**	derailment
el **jefe de estación**	stationmaster
el **maquinista**	engineer
el **panel informativo**	bulletin board
el **paso a nivel**	railroad crossing
el **silbato**	whistle
el **suplemento**	extra charge, supplement
el **trayecto**	journey
el **(tren de) cercanías** *(pl (~es~)~)*	suburban train; commuter train
el **(tren de) mercancías** *(pl (~es ~) ~)*	freight train

USEFUL PHRASES

tomar el tren, coger el tren *(Sp)* to take the train

perder el tren to miss the train

montarse en el tren to get on the train

bajar del tren to get off the train

¿está libre este asiento? is this seat free?

el tren lleva retraso the train is late

un vagón de fumadores/no fumadores a smoking/ non-smoking compartment

"prohibido asomarse por la ventanilla" "do not lean out of the window"

IMPORTANT WORDS *(feminine)*

la	**barrera**	barrier
la	**conductora**	driver
la	**duración** *(pl* duraciones)	length (of time)
la	**escalera mecánica**	escalator
la	**frontera**	border
la	**litera**	couchette *(basic sleeping accommodation on a train in Europe)*
la	**propina**	tip
la	**RENFE**	Spanish Railway
la	**revisora**	ticket collector
la	**tarifa**	fare

USEFUL WORDS *(feminine)*

la	**alarma**	alarm
la	**etiqueta**	label
la	**jefa de estación**	station master
la	**locomotora**	locomotive
la	**maquinista**	engineer
la	**vía férrea**	(railroad) line or track
las	**vías**	rails

USEFUL PHRASES

te acompañaré a la estación I'll go to the station with you
iré a buscarte a la estación I'll come and pick you up at the station
el tren de las diez con destino a/procedente de Madrid the 10 o'clock train to/from Madrid

ESSENTIAL WORDS *(masculine)*

el **árbol**	tree
el **bosque**	wood

USEFUL WORDS *(masculine)*

el **abedul**	birch
el **abeto**	fir tree
el **acebo**	holly
el **albaricoque**	apricot tree
el **árbol frutal**	fruit tree
el **arbusto**	bush
el **arce**	maple
el **boj**	box tree
el **brote**	bud
el **castaño**	chestnut tree
el **cerezo**	cherry tree
el **chabacano** (*Mex*)	apricot tree
el **chopo**	poplar
el **duraznero** (*LAm*)	peach tree
el **espino**	hawthorn
el **follaje**	foliage
el **fresno**	ash
el **huerto**	orchard
el **limonero**	lemon tree
el **manzano**	apple tree
el **melocotonero** (*Sp*)	peach tree
el **naranjo**	orange tree
el **nogal**	walnut tree
el **olmo**	elm
el **peral**	pear tree
el **pino**	pine
el **platanero**	banana tree
el **plátano**	plane tree
el **roble**	oak
el **sauce llorón** (*pl* ~s llorones)	weeping willow
el **tejo**	yew
el **tilo**	lime tree
el **tronco**	trunk
el **viñedo**	vineyard

ESSENTIAL WORDS (*feminine*)

la	**hoja**	leaf
la	**rama**	branch
la	**selva** (tropical)	rain forest

USEFUL WORDS (*feminine*)

la	**baya**	berry
la	**corteza**	bark
la	**encina**	evergreen oak
el	**haya** (*pl f* las hayas)	beech
la	**higuera**	fig tree
la	**raíz** (*pl* raíces)	root
la	**viña**	vineyard

ESSENTIAL WORDS (masculine)

el	**ajo**	garlic
los	**champiñones**	mushrooms
los	**chícharos** (Mex)	peas
los	**ejotes** (Mex)	French beans
los	**guisantes** (Sp)	peas
el	**pimiento**	pepper
el	**tomate**	tomato

USEFUL WORDS (masculine)

el	**apio**	celery
el	**berro**	watercress
el	**brécol** or **brócoli**	broccoli
el	**calabacín** (pl calabacines)	zucchini
el	**elote** (Mex)	sweetcorn
los	**espárragos**	asparagus
los	**frijoles** or **fríjoles** (LAm)	beans
los	**garbanzos**	chickpeas
el	**maíz (dulce** or **tierno)**	sweetcorn
el	**nabo**	turnip
el	**pepino**	cucumber
el	**perejil**	parsley
el	**pimiento morrón** (pl ~s morrones)	(sweet) pepper
el	**puerro**	leek
el	**rábano**	radish
el	**repollo**	cabbage

USEFUL PHRASES
cultivar verduras to grow vegetables
una mazorca de maíz (Sp), **una mazorca de choclo** (Mex) corn on the cob

ESSENTIAL WORDS *(feminine)*

las	**acelgas**	Swiss chard, spinach beet
las	**arvejas** *(LAm)*	peas
la	**cebolla**	onion
la	**coliflor**	cauliflower
la	**ensalada**	salad
las	**habichuelas** *(LAm)*	green beans
las	**hortalizas**	vegetables
las	**judías verdes** *(Sp)*	green beans
la	**papa** *(LAm, Southern Sp)*	potato
la	**patata** *(Sp)*	
las	**verduras**	vegetables
la	**zanahoria**	carrot

USESFUL WORDS *(feminine)*

la	**alcachofa**	artichoke
las	**alubias** *(Sp)*	beans
la	**berenjena**	eggplant
la	**calabacita** *(Mex)*	zucchini
la	**calabaza**	pumpkin
la	**cebolleta**	scallion
la	**col**	cabbage
las	**coles de Bruselas**	Brussels sprouts
la	**endibia**	endive, chicory
la	**escarola**	escarole
las	**espinacas**	spinach
las	**judías**	beans
las	**judías blancas**	navy beans
la	**lechuga**	lettuce
las	**legumbres**	legumes
las	**lentejas**	lentils
la	**remolacha**	beet
la	**rúcula**	arugula

USEFUL PHRASES

zanahoria rallada grated carrot
biológico(a) organic
vegetariano(a) vegetarian; **vegano(a)** vegan

ESSENTIAL WORDS *(masculine)*

el	**autobús** *(pl* autobuses*)*	bus
el	**autocar**	coach
el	**avión** *(pl* aviones*)*	plane
el	**barco de vela**	sailing ship; sailing boat
el	**bote**	boat
el	**bote de remos**	rowboat
el	**camión** *(pl* camiones*)*	truck
el	**carro**	cart; *(LAm)* car
el	**casco**	helmet
el	**ciclomotor**	moped
el	**coche** *(Sp)*	car
el	**coche de línea**	coach
el	**helicóptero**	helicopter
el	**medio de transporte**	means of transport
el	**metro**	subway
el	**precio del billete** *(Sp) or* **del boleto** *(LAm)*	fare
el	**taxi**	taxi
el	**transbordador**	ferry
el	**transporte público**	public transport
el	**tren**	train
el	**vehículo**	vehicle
el	**vehículo pesado**	large truck

IMPORTANT WORDS *(masculine)*

el	**coche de bomberos**	fire engine

USEFUL PHRASES

viajar to travel
ha ido a Barcelona en avión he flew to Barcelona
tomar el autobús/el metro/el tren, coger *(Sp)* **el autobús/el metro/el tren** to take the bus/the subway/the train
montar en bicicleta to go cycling
se puede ir en coche you can go there by car

ESSENTIAL WORDS *(feminine)*

la	bici	bike
la	bicicleta	bicycle
la	camioneta	van
la	caravana	camper
la	distancia	distance
la	moto	motorbike
la	motocicleta	motorcycle, motorbike
la	parte de atrás	back
la	parte de delante	front
la	parte delantera	front
la	parte trasera	back
la	vespa®	scooter

IMPORTANT WORDS *(feminine)*

la	ambulancia	ambulance
la	grúa	tow truck

USEFUL PHRASES

reparar el coche de algn to repair sb's car
un coche de alquiler a rental car
un coche deportivo a sports car
un coche de carreras a race car
un coche de empresa a company car
"coches de ocasión" "used cars"
arrancar to start, to move off

USEFUL WORDS (masculine)

el	aerodeslizador	hovercraft
el	(barco de) vapor	steamship
el	bulldozer (pl ~s)	bulldozer
el	buque	ship
el	camión articulado (pl camiones ~s)	tractor trailer
el	camión cisterna (pl camiones ~)	tanker
el	cochecito (de niño)	baby carriage, stroller
el	cohete	rocket
el	hidroavión (pl hidroaviones)	seaplane
el	jeep (pl ~s)	jeep
el	monovolumen	minivan
el	navío	ship
el	ovni (objeto volador no identificado)	UFO (unidentified flying object)
el	petrolero	oil tanker (ship)
el	planeador	glider
el	platillo volante	flying saucer
el	portaaviones (pl inv)	aircraft carrier
el	remolcador	tug
el	remolque	trailer
el	riesgo	risk
el	submarino	submarine
el	tanque	tank
el	teleférico	cable car
el	telesilla	chairlift
el	todoterreno	SUV
el	tractor	tractor
el	tranvía	tram
el	velero	sailboat
el	velomotor	moped
el	yate	yacht; pleasure cruiser

USEFUL WORDS *(feminine)*

la	**autocaravana**	motor home
la	**barcaza**	barge
la	**camioneta de reparto**	delivery truck
la	**canoa**	canoe
la	**carreta**	wagon; cart
la	**excavadora**	excavator
la	**golondrina**	pleasure boat
la	**lancha**	boat (*small*); launch
la	**lancha de salvamento**	lifeboat
la	**lancha de socorro**	lifeboat
la	**lancha neumática**	rubber dinghy
la	**lancha rápida**	speedboat
la	**locomotora**	locomotive
la	**ranchera**	station wagon

the weather

USEFUL PHRASES

¿qué tiempo hace? what's the weather like?
hace calor/frío it's hot/cold
hace un día estupendo, hace un día precioso it's a lovely day
hace un día horrible it's a horrible day
al aire libre in the open air
hay niebla it's foggy
30° a la sombra 30° in the shade
escuchar el pronóstico del tiempo to listen to the weather forecast
llover to rain
nevar to snow
llueve it's raining
nieva it's snowing

ESSENTIAL WORDS (feminine)

la	**estación** (pl estaciones)	season
la	**lluvia**	rain
la	**niebla**	fog
la	**nieve**	snow
la	**nube**	cloud
la	**primavera**	spring
la	**región** (pl regiones)	region, area
la	**temperatura**	temperature

USEFUL PHRASES

brilla el sol the sun is shining
sopla el viento the wind is blowing
hace un frío que pela it's freezing
helarse to freeze
ha helado there's been a frost
fundirse to melt
soleado(a) sunny
tormentoso(a) stormy
lluvioso(a) rainy
frío(a) cool
variable changeable
húmedo(a)humid
el cielo está cubierto the sky is overcast

IMPORTANT WORDS *(masculine)*

el	**chaparrón** *(pl* chaparrones)	shower
el	**claro**	sunny spell
el	**humo**	smoke
el	**polvo**	dust

USEFUL WORDS *(masculine)*

el	**aguacero**	downpour
el	**amanecer**	dawn, daybreak
el	**anochecer**	nightfall, dusk
el	**arco iris** *(pl inv)*	rainbow
el	**barómetro**	barometer
el	**cambio**	change
el	**carámbano**	icicle
el	**charco**	puddle
el	**ciclón**	cyclone
el	**copo de nieve**	snowflake
el	**crepúsculo**	twilight
el	**deshielo**	thaw
el	**granizo**	hail
el	**huracán** *(pl* huracanes)	hurricane
el	**pararrayos** *(pl inv)*	lightning rod
el	**quitanieves** *(pl inv)*	snowplow
el	**rayo**	lightning
el	**rayo de sol**	ray of sunshine
el	**relámpago**	flash of lightning
el	**rocío**	dew
el	**trueno**	thunder
el	**tsunami**	tsunami

IMPORTANT WORDS (feminine)

las	precipitaciones	rainfall
la	previsión meteorológica	(weather) forecast
	(pl previsiones ~s)	
la	sombrilla	parasol
la	tormenta	storm
la	visibilidad	visibility

USEFUL WORDS (feminine)

el	alba (pl f las albas)	dawn
la	atmósfera	atmosphere
la	brisa	breeze
la	bruma	mist
la	corriente (de aire)	draught
la	escarcha	frost (on the ground)
la	gota de lluvia	raindrop
la	helada	frost (weather)
la	inundación (pl inundaciones)	flood
la	luz de la luna	moonlight
la	mejora or mejoría	improvement
la	nevada	snowfall
la	ola de calor	heatwave
la	ola de frío	cold spell
la	oscuridad	darkness
la	puesta de sol	sunset
la	ráfaga de viento	gust of wind
la	sequía	drought
la	tormenta	thunderstorm
la	ventisca	snowdrift

youth hostelling

ESSENTIAL WORDS (masculine)

el	albergue juvenil	youth hostel
los	baños públicos (LAm)	toilets
el	bote de la basura (Mex)	garbage can
el	comedor	dining room
el	cuarto de baño	bathroom
el	cubo de la basura	garbage can
el	desayuno	breakfast
el	dormitorio	dormitory
los	lavabos	toilets
el	mapa	map
los	servicios (Sp)	toilets
el	silencio	silence
el	visitante	visitor

IMPORTANT WORDS (masculine)

el	carnet de socio (pl ~s ~~)	membership card
el	lavabo	washbasin; toilet
el	saco de dormir	sleeping bag

ESSENTIAL WORDS (feminine)

la	cama	bed
la	(cama) litera	bunk bed
la	cocina	kitchen; cooking
la	comida	meal
la	ducha	shower
la	estancia	stay
la	lista de precios	price list
la	noche	night
la	oficina	office
la	sábana	sheet
la	sala de juegos	game room
la	tarifa	rate(s)
las	vacaciones	vacation
la	visitante	visitor

IMPORTANT WORDS (feminine)

la	caminata	hike
la	excursión (pl excursiones)	trip
la	guía	guidebook
la	mochila	backpack
las	normas	rules
la	ropa de cama	bed linen

USEFUL PHRASES

pasar una noche en el albergue juvenil to spend a night at the youth hostel

quisiera alquilar un saco de dormir I would like to rent a sleeping bag

está todo ocupado there's no more room

The vocabulary items on pages 666 to 703 have been grouped under parts of speech rather than topics because they can apply in a wide range of circumstances. Use them just as freely as the vocabulary already given.

ARTICLES AND PRONOUNS

What is an article?
In English, an **article** is one of the words *the*, *a* and *an* which is given in front of a noun.

What is a pronoun?
A **pronoun** is a word you use instead of a noun, when you do not need or want to name someone or something directly, for example, *it*, *you*, *none*.

algo something; anything
alguien somebody, someone; anybody, anyone
alguno/alguna one; someone, somebody
algunos/algunas some, some of them; some of us, some of you, some of them
ambos/ambas both
aquel/aquella; aquél/aquélla that
aquellos/aquellas; aquéllos/aquéllas those
cada each; every
cual which; who; whom
  lo cual which
cuál what, which one
cualquiera any one; anybody, anyone
  cualquiera de los dos/las dos either (*see also* Adjectives)
cualesquiera (*pl*) any (*see also* Adjectives)
cuanto/cuanta as much as
cuánto/cuánta how much
cuantos/cuantas as many as
cuántos/cuántas how many
cuyo/cuya/cuyos/cuyas whose

  en cuyo caso in which case
demasiado/demasiada too much
demasiados too many
dos: los/las dos both
el/la the
él he; him; it
  de él his
ella she; her; it
  de ella hers
ello it
ellos/ellas they; them
  de ellos/ellas theirs
ese/esa; ése/ésa that
esos/esas; ésos/ésas those
este/esta; éste/ésta this
estos/estas; éstos/éstas these
la her; it; you
las them; you
le him; her; it; you
les them; you
lo him; it; you
los/las the
los them; you
me me; myself
mi/mis my
(el)mío/(la) mía/(los) míos/(las) mías mine

supplementary vocabulary

mismo/misma/mismos/mismas
same
  mí mismo/misma; yo mismo/
  misma myself; nosotros mismos/
  nosotras mismas ourselves;
  sí misma; ella misma herself;
  sí mismo; él mismo himself;
  sí mismos/sí mismas; ellos
  mismos/ellas mismas themselves;
  ti mismo/ti misma; tú mismo/
  tú misma; usted mismo/
  usted misma yourself; vosotros
  mismos/vosotras mismas;
  ustedes mismos/ustedes
  mismas yourselves; uno mismo/
  una misma oneself
mucho/mucha a lot, lots; much
  (see also Adjectives; Adverbs)
muchos/muchas a lot, lots; many
  (see also Adjectives)
nada nothing
  nada más nothing else
nadie nobody, no one; anybody,
  anyone
  nadie más nobody else
ninguno/ninguna any; neither;
  either; none; no one, nobody
  ninguno de los dos/ninguna
  de las dos neither (see also
  Adjectives)
ningunos/ningunas any; none
  (see also Adjectives)
nos us; ourselves; each other
nosotros/nosotras we; us
nuestro/nuestra/nuestros/
  nuestras our; ours
  el nuestro/la nuestra/
  los nuestros/las nuestras ours
os you; yourselves; each other
otro/otra another, another one
  (see also Adjectives)

otros/otras others (see also
  Adjectives)
poco/poca un poco a bit, a little
  dentro de poco shortly
pocos/pocas not many, few
que who; that
qué what; what a
quien/quienes who; whoever
quién/quiénes who
se him; her; them; you; himself;
  herself; itself; themselves;
  yourself; yourselves; oneself; each
  other
su/sus his; her; its; their; your; one's
(el) suyo/(la) suya /(los) suyos/
  (las) suyas his; her; its; their; your;
  hers; theirs; yours; one's own
tal/tales such
tampoco not...either, neither
te you; yourself
ti you
todo/toda (it) all
  todo el mundo everybody,
  everyone (see also Adjectives)
todos/todas all; every; everybody;
  everyone (see also Adjectives)
tu/tus your
tú you
usted you
ustedes you
(el) tuyo/ (la) tuya/ (los) tuyos/
  (las) tuyas yours
un/una a; an; one
unos/unas some; a few; about,
  around
varios/varias several
vosotros/vosotras you
vuestro/vuestra/vuestros/
  vuestras your; yours
  los vuestros/las vuestras yours
yo I; me

supplementary vocabulary

CONJUNCTIONS

What is a conjunction?
A **conjunction** is a word such as *and*, *but*, *or*, *so*, *if* and *because*, that links two words or phrases of a similar type, or two parts of a sentence, for example, *Diane <u>and</u> I have been friends for years*; *I left <u>because</u> I was bored*.

ahora though
  ahora bien however; **ahora que** now that
antes: antes de que before
así: así (es) que so
  así pues so
aunque although, though
como as
conque so, so then
consiguiente: por consiguiente so, therefore
cuando when; whenever; if
cuanto: en cuanto as soon as; as
dar: dado que since
decir: es decir that is to say
desde: desde que since
después: después de que after
e and
embargo: sin embargo still, however
entonces then
fin: a fin de que so that, in order that
forma: de forma que so that
hasta: hasta que until, till
luego therefore
manera: de manera que so that
mas but
más: más que more than
menos: menos que less than
mientras while; as long as

mientras que whereas; **mientras (tanto)** meanwhile
modo: de modo que so that
momento: en el momento en que just as
ni or; nor; even
  ni...ni neither...nor
o or
  o ... o ... either ... or ...
para: para que so that
pero but
porque because
pronto: tan pronto como as soon as
pues then; well; since
puesto: puesto que since
que that
ser: o sea that is
  a no ser que unless
si if; whether
  si no otherwise
siempre: siempre que whenever; as long as, provided that
sino but; except; only
tal: con tal (de) que as long as, provided that
tanto: por (lo) tanto so, therefore
u or
vez: una vez que once
vista: en vista de que seeing that
y and
ya: ya que as, since

supplementary vocabulary

ADJECTIVES

> **What is an adjective?**
> An **adjective** is a descriptive word that tells you about a person or thing, such as their appearance, color, size or other qualities, for example, *pretty*, *blue*, *big*.

abierto(a) open
absoluto(a) absolute
absurdo(a) absurd
académico(a) academic
accesible accessible; approachable
aceptable acceptable
acondicionado(a) fitted out
  con aire acondicionado
  air-conditioned
acostumbrado(a) accustomed
activo(a) active
acusado(a) accused; marked
adecuado(a) appropriate
admirable admirable
aéreo(a) aerial
aficionado(a) keen
afilado(a) sharp
afortunado(a) fortunate, lucky
agitado(a) rough; agitated; hectic
agotado(a) exhausted
agradable pleasant, agreeable
agresivo(a) aggressive
agrícola agricultural
agudo(a) sharp; acute
aislado(a) isolated
alegre happy; bright; lively; merry
alguno/alguna (*before masc sing***
  algún)** some; any (*see also* Articles
  and Pronouns)
algunos/algunas some; several
  (*see also* Articles and Pronouns)
alternativo(a) alternating; alternative

alto(a) high; tall
amargo(a) bitter
ancho(a) broad; wide
anciano(a) elderly
animado(a) lively; cheerful
anónimo(a) anonymous
anormal abnormal
anterior former
antiguo(a) old; vintage; antique
anual annual
apagado(a) out; off; muffled; dull
aparente apparent
apasionado(a) passionate
apropiado(a) appropriate, suitable
aproximado(a) rough
arriba: de arriba top
asequible affordable
asombrado(a) amazed, astonished
asombroso(a) amazing,
  astonishing
áspero(a) rough
atestado(a) crowded; popular
atento(a) attentive; watchful
atractivo(a) attractive
automático(a) automatic
avanzado(a) advanced
bajo(a) low; short
barba: con barba bearded
barbudo(a) bearded
básico(a) basic
bastante enough; quite a lot of
  (*see also* Adverbs)

supplementary vocabulary

...en well-to-do
bienvenido(a) welcome
blando(a) soft
breve brief
brillante shining; bright
brutal brutal
bruto(a) rough; stupid; uncouth;
  gross
bueno(a) good
cada each; every
caliente hot; warm
callado(a) quiet
cansado(a) tired
capaz capable
cariñoso(a) affectionate
caro(a) expensive
cauteloso(a) cautious
central central
ceñido(a) tight
cercano(a) close; nearby
cerrado(a) closed; off
científico(a) scientific
cierto(a) true; certain
civil civil; civilian
claro(a) clear; light; bright
clásico(a) classical; classic
climatizado(a) air-conditioned
cobarde cowardly
comercial commercial
cómodo(a) comfortable
complejo(a) complex
completo(a) complete
complicado(a) complicated; complex
comprensivo(a) understanding
común common; mutual
concreto(a) specific; concrete
concurrido(a) crowded; popular
conmovedor(a) moving
consciente conscious; aware

conservador(a) conservative
considerable considerable
constante constant
contemporáneo(a) contemporary
contento(a) happy; pleased
continuo(a) continuous
convencional conventional
correcto(a) correct, right
corriente ordinary; common
cortado(a) cut; closed; off; shy
creativo(a) creative
cristiano(a) Christian
crítico(a) critical
crudo(a) raw
cuadrado(a) square
cualquiera (*before masc and fem sing*
  cualquier) any (*see also* Articles
  and Pronouns)
cualesquiera any (*see also* Articles
  and Pronouns)
cuanto/cuanta as much as
cuánto/cuánta how much
cuantos/cuantas as many as
cuántos/cuántas how many
cultural cultural
curioso(a) curious
debido(a) due, proper
decepcionante disappointing
decidido(a) determined
delicado(a) delicate
delicioso(a) delicious
demasiado/demasiada too much
demasiados too many
democrático(a) democratic
derecho(a) right
desafortunado(a) unfortunate
desagradable unpleasant
desconocido(a) unknown
desesperado(a) desperate

desierto(a) deserted
desnudo(a) naked; bare
despejado(a) clear
despierto(a) awake; sharp; alert
despreocupado(a) carefree; careless
destruido(a) destroyed
detallado(a) detailed
diestro(a) skillful
difícil difficult
digno(a) worthy; dignified
diminuto(a) tiny
directo(a) direct
disgustado(a) upset
disponible available
dispuesto(a) arranged; willing
distinguido(a) distinguished
distinto(a) different; various
divertido(a) funny, amusing; fun;
  entertaining
dividido(a) divided
divino(a) divine
doble double
domesticado(a) tame
doméstico(a) domestic
dos: los/las dos both
dulce sweet
duro(a) hard
económico(a) economic; economical
efectivo(a) effective
eficaz effective; efficient
eficiente efficient
eléctrico(a) electric
electrónico(a) electronic
elemental elementary
emocionante exciting
emotivo(a) emotional; moving
encantador(a) charming; lovely
enmascarado(a) masked
enorme enormous, huge

enterado(a) knowledgeable;
  well-informed; aware
entero(a) whole
equivalente equivalent
equivocado(a) wrong
escandaloso(a) shocking
esencial essential
especial special
específico(a) specific
espectacular spectacular
espeso(a) thick
espiritual spiritual
estrecho(a) narrow
estricto(a) strict
estropeado(a) broken (off); off
estupendo(a) marvelous, great
estúpido(a) stupid
étnico(a) ethnic
evidente obvious, evident
exacto(a) exact; accurate
excelente excellent
excepcional outstanding
exclusivo(a) exclusive
exigente demanding, exacting
experto(a) experienced
éxito: de éxito successful
exitoso(a) successful
exquisito(a) delicious; exquisite
extra extra; top-quality
extranjero(a) foreign
extraño(a) strange; foreign
extraordinario(a) extraordinary;
  outstanding; special
extremo(a) extreme
fácil easy
falso(a) false
familiar family; familiar
famoso(a) famous
fatigoso(a) tiring

federal federal
feroz fierce
fijo(a) fixed; permanent
final final
financiero(a) financial
fino(a) fine; smooth; refined
firme firm; steady
físico(a) physical
flexible flexible
fluido(a) fluid; fluent
formal reliable; formal; official
frágil fragile; frail
frecuente frequent
fresco(a) fresh; cool; cheeky
fuerte strong; loud
futuro(a) future
general general
generoso(a) generous
genial brilliant; wonderful
gentil kind
genuino(a) genuine
global global
gordo(a) fat; big
grande (*before masc sing* **gran**) big; great
grandioso(a) grand; grandiose
habitual usual
herido(a) injured; wounded; hurt
hermoso(a) beautiful
histórico(a) historic; historical
holgado(a) loose
honrado(a) honest; respectable
horrible horrific; hideous; terrible
horroroso(a) dreadful; hideous; terrible
humano(a) human; humane
ideal ideal
idéntico(a) identical
igual equal

ilegal illegal
iluminado(a) illuminated, lit; enlightened
ilustrado(a) illustrated
imaginario(a) imaginary
impar odd
importante important
imposible impossible
imprescindible indispensable
impresionante impressive; moving; shocking
inaguantable unbearable
incapaz (de) incapable (of)
increíble incredible; unbelievable
inculto(a) uncultured
indefenso(a) defenseless
independiente independent
indiferente unconcerned
individual individual; single
industrial industrial
inesperado(a) unexpected
inevitable inevitable
infantil childlike; childish
inflable inflatable
injusto(a) unfair
inmediato(a) immediate
inmenso(a) immense
inmune immune
inquieto(a) anxious; restless
intacto(a) intact
intencionado(a) deliberate
intenso(a) intense; intensive
interior interior; inside; inner; domestic
interminable endless
internacional international
interno(a) internal
interrumpido(a) interrupted
inútil useless

supplementary vocabulary

invisible invisible
izquierdo(a) left
junto(a) together
justo(a) just, fair; exact; tight
largo(a) long
legal legal
lento(a) slow
libre free
ligero(a) light; slight; agile
limpio(a) clean
liso(a) smooth; straight; plain
listo(a) ready; bright
llamativo(a) bright; striking
llano(a) flat; straightforward
lleno(a) (de) full (of)
lluvioso(a) rainy, wet
loco(a) mad, crazy
lujo: de lujo luxurious
lujoso(a) luxurious
magnífico(a) magnificent;
  wonderful, superb
maligno(a) malignant; evil, malicious
malo(a) bad
malvado(a) wicked
manso(a) meek; tame
maravilloso(a) marvelous,
  wonderful; magic
marcado(a) marked
más more of a
máximo(a) maximum
mayor bigger; elder
  el/la…mayor the biggest…;
  the eldest…
mecánico(a) mechanical
médico(a) medical
medio(a) half; average
medioambiental environmental
mejor better
  el/la mejor the best

menor smaller; younger
  el/la…menor the smallest;
  the youngest
menos less of a
mental mental
militar military
minucioso(a) thorough; very
  detailed
mismo(a) same
misterioso(a) mysterious
moderado(a) moderate
moderno(a) modern
mojado(a) wet; soaked
molesto(a) annoying; annoyed;
  awkward; uncomfortable
montañoso(a) mountainous
mucho/mucha a lot of, lots of;
  much (see also Pronouns; Adverbs)
muchos/muchas a lot of, lots of;
  many (see also Pronouns)
muerto(a) dead
mundial worldwide, global
mutuo(a) mutual
nacido(a) born
nacional national; domestic
nativo(a) native
natural natural
necesario(a) necessary
negativo(a) negative
**ninguno/ninguna (before masc sing
  ningún)** no; any (see also
  Pronouns)
ningunos/ningunas no; any
  (see also Pronouns)
normal normal; standard
nuclear nuclear
nuevo(a) new
numeroso(a) numerous
obediente obedient

supplementary vocabulary

objetivo(a) objective
obligatorio(a) compulsory,
  obligatory
obvio(a) obvious
ocupado(a) busy; taken; engaged;
  occupied
oficial official
oportuno(a) opportune;
  appropriate
original original
oscuro(a) dark; obscure
otro/otra another
  a/en otro lugar somewhere else;
  otra cosa something else; otra
  persona somebody else; otra vez
  again (see also Pronouns); otros/
  otras other (see also Pronouns)
pacífico(a) peaceful; peaceable
pálido(a) pale
par even
particular special; particular; private
patético(a) pathetic
peligroso(a) dangerous
peor worse
  el peor the worst
perdido(a) lost; stray; remote
perfecto(a) perfect
personal personal
pesado(a) heavy; tedious
picante hot
pie: de pie standing (up)
poco/poca not much, little
pocos/pocas not many, few
poderoso(a) powerful
polémico(a) controversial
polvoriento(a) dusty; powdery
popular popular
portátil portable
posible possible; potential

positivo(a) positive
práctico(a) practical
precioso(a) lovely, beautiful;
  precious
preciso(a) precise; necessary
preferido(a) favorite
preliminar preliminary
presentable presentable
presunto(a) alleged
previo(a) previous
primario(a) primary
principal main
privado(a) private
privilegiado(a) privileged
profundo(a) deep
prometido(a) promised; engaged
propio(a) own
próximo(a) near, close; next
psicológico(a) psychological
público(a) public
pueril childish
pulcro(a) neat
puntiagudo(a) pointed; sharp
puntual punctual
puro(a) pure
qué what; which; what a
querido(a) dear
químico(a) chemical
racial racial
radical radical
rápido(a) fast, quick
raro(a) strange, odd; rare
razonable reasonable
reacio(a) reluctant
real actual; royal
reciente recent
recto(a) straight; honest
redondo(a) round
refrescante refreshing

regional regional
regular regular
religioso(a) religious
repentino(a) sudden
repuesto: de repuesto spare
reservado(a) reserved
resistente resistant; tough
responsable (de) responsible (for)
revolucionario(a) revolutionary
ridículo(a) ridiculous
rival rival
romántico(a) romantic
rubio(a) fair, blond
ruidoso(a) noisy
rural rural
sabio(a) wise
sagrado(a) sacred
salvaje wild
salvo: a salvo safe
sanitario(a) sanitary; health
sano(a) healthy
  sano(a) y salvo(a) safe and sound
santo(a) holy
satisfecho(a) (de) satisfied (with)
seco(a) dry
secreto(a) secret
secundario(a) secondary
seguro(a) safe; secure; certain; sure
semejante similar
sencillo(a) simple; natural; single
sensacional sensational
sentado(a) sitting, seated
señalado(a) special
separado(a) separate
servicial helpful
severo(a) severe
sexual sexual
significativo(a) significant;
  meaningful

siguiente next, following
silencioso(a) silent; quiet
sincero(a) sincere
singular singular; outstanding
siniestro(a) sinister
situado(a) situated
sobra: de sobra spare
sobrante spare
social social
solemne solemn
sólido(a) solid
solo(a) alone; lonely; black;
  straight, neat
soltero(a) single
sombrío(a) somber; dim
sonriente smiling
soportable bearable
sorprendente surprising
sospechoso(a) suspicious
suave smooth; gentle; mild; slight
sucio(a) dirty
superior top; upper; superior
supremo(a) supreme
supuesto(a) assumed; supposed
tal/tales such
tanto/tanta so much
tantos/tantas so many
técnico(a) technical
terrible terrible
típico(a) typical
tirante tight; tense
todo/toda all (see also Pronouns)
todos/todas all; every (see also
  Pronouns)
tolerante broad-minded
total total
tradicional traditional
tremendo(a) tremendous
triste sad

último(a) last
  el último the latest
ultrajante offensive; outrageous
único(a) only; unique
urgente urgent
útil useful, helpful
vacante vacant
vacío(a) empty
valiente brave, ourageous
valioso(a) valuable
valor: de valor valuable
variado(a) varied

varios/varias several
vecino(a) neighboring
verdad: de verdad real
verdadero(a) real; true
viejo(a) old
vil villainous; vile
violento(a) violent; awkward
visible visible
vital vital
vivo(a) living; alive; lively
voluntario(a) voluntary

supplementary vocabulary

ADVERBS AND PREPOSITIONS

> **What is an adverb?**
> An **adverb** is a word usually used with verbs, adjectives or other adverbs that gives more information about when, how, where, or in what circumstances something happens, or to what degree something is true, for example, *quickly, happily, now, extremely, very*.
>
> **What is a preposition?**
> A **preposition** is a word such as *at, for, with, into* or *from*, which is usually followed by a noun, pronoun, or, in English, a word ending in -ing. Prepositions show how people or things relate to the rest of the sentence, for example, *She's at home; a tool for cutting grass; It's from David*.

a to; at; into: onto
abajo down; downstairs; below
  allá abajo down there
absolutamente absolutely
acá here, over here; now
acerca: acerca de about
actualmente at present
acuerdo: de acuerdo OK, okay
adelante forward
  en adelante from now on
  hacia adelante forward
además also; furthermore, moreover, in addition
  además de as well as; besides
admirablemente admirably
afortunadamente fortunately
agradablemente nicely
ahora now; in a minute
  hasta ahora so far
alcance: al alcance within reach
allá there, over there
allí there
alrededor de around
ansiosamente anxiously
ante before; in the face of; faced with

ante todo above all
antemano: de antemano beforehand, in advance
anteriormente previously, before
antes before **antes de** before
  cuanto antes as soon as possible
  lo antes posible as soon as possible
apartado: apartado de away from
aparte: aparte de apart from
apenas hardly, scarcely; only
aproximadamente approximately
aquí here; now
arriba up; upstairs; above
  allá arriba up there
así like that; like this
  así como as well as
atentamente attentively, carefully; kindly
atrás behind; at the back; backwards; ago
  hacia atrás backwards
aun even **aun así** even so
  aun cuando even if
aún still, yet; even
azar: al azar at random

supplementary vocabulary

ajo low; quietly; under
básicamente basically
bastante enough; quite a lot; quite
  (*see also* Adjectives)
bien well; carefully; very; easily
brevemente briefly
bruscamente abruptly
cambio: a cambio de in exchange
  for; in return for
  en cambio instead
camino: de camino on the way
casi almost, nearly
caso: en el caso de (que) in the case of
  en todo caso in any case
casualidad: por casualidad by
  chance
causa: a causa de because of
cerca (de) close (to); near (to)
claramente clearly
cómo how
como like; such as; as; about
completamente completely
con with
concreto: en concreto specifically,
  in particular
continuamente constantly
contra against
correctamente correctly
cortésmente politely
cuando when
cuándo when
cuanto: en cuanto a as regards, as for
cuánto how much; how far; how
cuenta: a fin de cuentas ultimately
  teniendo en cuenta considering
cuidado: con cuidado carefully
cuidadosamente carefully
curiosamente curiously
curso: en el curso de in the course of

de of; from; about; by; than; in; if
debajo underneath
  debajo de under; **por debajo**
  underneath; **por debajo de** under;
  below
débilmente faintly; weakly
delante in front; at the front;
  opposite
  delante de in front of; opposite
  hacia delante forward
  por delante ahead; at the front
demasiado too; too much
dentro inside
  dentro de inside; in; within
deprisa quickly, hurriedly
derecha: a la derecha on the right
desde from; since
desgraciadamente unfortunately
despacio slowly
después later; after(wards); then
  después de after
detrás behind; at the back; on the
  back; after
  detrás de behind; **por detrás** from
  behind; on the back
día: al día per day
diariamente on a daily basis
diario: a diario daily
donde where; wherever
dónde where
dondequiera anywhere
duda: sin duda definitely,
  undoubtedly
dulcemente sweetly; gently
durante during; for
  durante todo/toda throughout
efecto: en efecto in fact
ejemplo: por ejemplo for example
en in; on; at; into; by

encima on top
  encima de above; on top of; **por**
  encima over; **por encima de** over;
  above
enfrente (de) opposite
enseguida right away
entonces then
  desde entonces since then; **hasta**
  entonces until then
entre among(st); between
especialmente especially,
  particularly; specially
evidentemente obviously, evidently
exactamente exactly
excepción: con la excepción de
  with the exception of
excepto except (for)
extranjero: en el extranjero
  overseas; abroad
extremadamente extremely
fácilmente easily
fielmente faithfully
fin: por fin finally; at last
finalmente eventually
forma: de alguna forma somehow
  de esta forma like that; like this;
  de ninguna forma in no way;
  de otra forma otherwise;
  de todas formas anyway
francamente frankly; really
frecuentemente frequently
frente: frente a opposite, facing;
  against
fuera outside; out
  fuera de outside
gana: de buena gana willingly,
  happily
  de mala gana reluctantly
general: por lo general as a rule

generalmente generally
gracias: gracias a thanks to
gradualmente gradually
hacia towards
hasta to, as far as; up to; down to;
  until
honradamente honestly
igualmente equally; likewise
incluido including
inmediatamente immediately
intensamente intensely
izquierda: a la izquierda on the left
jamás never; ever
junto: junto a close to, near; next
  to; together with
  junto con together with
justamente just; exactly; justly
lado: al lado (de) next door (to); near
  al lado de alongside; **al otro lado de**
  across; **de un lado a otro** to and fro;
  por este lado (de) on this side (of)
largo: a lo largo de along
lejos (de) far (from)
ligeramente lightly; slightly
luego then; later, afterwards
  desde luego certainly
mal badly; poorly; ill
manera: de alguna manera
  somehow
  de esta manera like that; like this;
  de ninguna manera in no way; **de**
  otra manera otherwise; **de todas**
  maneras anyway
más more; plus
  el/la más the most; **más allá de**
  beyond; **más bien** rather; **más**
  cerca closer; **más lejos** further;
  más o menos about; **más...que**
  more...than; **no más** no more

medio: **en medio de** in the middle of
por medio de by means of
mejor better
el mejor the best
menos less; minus
el/la menos the least; **menos...**
que less than; **por lo menos** at
least
mentalmente mentally
menudo: **a menudo** often
misteriosamente mysteriously
modo: **de algún modo** somehow
de este modo like that; like this; **de**
ningún modo in no way; **de otro**
modo otherwise; **de todos modos**
anyway
momento: **en este momento** at
the moment
en ese mismo momento at that
very moment
mucho a lot
no mucho not much (see also
Pronouns; Adjectives)
muy very
naturalmente naturally
nerviosamente nervously
no no; not
nombre: **en nombre de** on behalf of
normalmente normally; usually
novedad: **sin novedad** safely
nunca never; ever
paciencia: **con paciencia** patiently
para for; to
para atrás backwards; **para la**
derecha towards the right; **para**
siempre forever
parte: **de mi parte** on my behalf
en cualquier parte anywhere;
en gran parte largely

en otra parte elsewhere
en parte partly, in part; **en todas**
partes everywhere; **por otra parte**
on the other hand
peligrosamente dangerously
peor worse
el peor the worst
perfectamente perfectly
persona: **por persona** per person
personalmente personally
pesadamente heavily
pesar: **a pesar de** despite; in spite of
a pesar de que even though
pie: **a pie** on foot
poco not very; not a lot; not much
poco a poco little by little, bit by bit
por because of; for; by; through
por qué why
precisamente precisely, exactly
primero first
principalmente mainly
principio: **al principio** at first
probable likely
probablemente probably
profundamente deeply
pronto soon
propósito: **a propósito** deliberately;
on purpose
qué how
querer: **sin querer** accidentally
quién: **de quién/de quiénes** whose
rápidamente fast, quickly
rápido quickly
realidad: **en realidad** in fact, actually
realmente really
recientemente recently, lately
regularmente regularly, on a
regular basis
relativamente relatively

repente: de repente suddenly
seguida: en seguida right away
seguido straight on
  todo seguido straight on
según according to; depending on
seguramente probably; surely
sencillamente simply
sentido: en este sentido in this
  respect
separado: por separado separately
ser: a no ser que unless
serio: en serio seriously
sí yes
siempre always
  como siempre as usual
siguiente: al/el día siguiente next
  day
silencio: en silencio quietly; in
  silence
silenciosamente quietly, silently
sin without **sin embargo** still,
  however, nonetheless
siquiera: ni siquiera not even
sitio: en algún sitio somewhere
  en ningún sitio nowhere
sobre on; over; about
solamente only; solely
sólo only; solely
  tan sólo only, just
suavemente gently; softly; smoothly
suelo: al suelo to the ground
  en el suelo on the ground
sumamente highly, extremely
supuesto: por supuesto of course
tal: tal como just as
  tal y como están las cosas
  under the circumstances; **tal vez**
  perhaps, maybe
también also, too

tampoco not...either, neither
tan so; such
  tan ... como as ... as
tanto so much; so often
  tanto más all the more
tarde late
  más tarde later; afterwards
temprano early
  más temprano earlier
tiempo: a tiempo in time; on time
  al mismo tiempo at the same
  time; **mucho tiempo** long
todavía still; yet; even
todo: en todo/toda throughout
  todo lo más at (the) most
total in short; at the end of the day
  en total altogether, in all
totalmente totally, completely
través: a través de through; across
vano: en vano in vain
velocidad: a toda velocidad at full
  speed, at top speed
ver: por lo visto apparently
vez: algunas veces sometimes
  cada vez más more and more;
  cada vez menos less and less; **de
  vez en cuando** from time to time,
  now and then; **en vez de** instead
  of; **rara vez** rarely, seldom; **una
  vez** once; **una vez más** once more
vía: en vías de on its way to
  en vías de desarrollo developing;
  en vías de extinción endangered
vista: de vista by sight
  en vista de in view of
voz: en voz alta aloud; loudly
  en voz baja in a low voice
ya already
  ya mismo at once; **ya no** not any
  more, no longer

SOME EXTRA NOUNS

> **What is a noun?**
> A noun is a 'naming' word for a living being, thing or idea, for example, *woman, desk, happiness, Andrew.*

la abertura opening
el abismo gulf
el aburrimiento boredom
el abuso abuse
el acceso access
la acción (*pl* acciones) action
el acento accent
el ácido acid
el acontecimiento event
la actitud attitude
la actividad activity
el acuerdo agreement; settlement
la advertencia warning
la afirmación (*pl* afirmaciones) claim
la agencia agency
la agenda diary
el/la agente agent
la agitación (*pl* agitaciones) stir
el agujero hole
la alcantarilla drain
la alcayata hook
la alegría joy
el alfabeto alphabet
el alfiler pin
el/la aliado/a ally
el aliento breath
el alivio relief
el alma (*f*) soul
el almacén (*pl* almacenes) store
el/la amante lover
la ambición (*pl* ambiciones) ambition
la amenaza threat
el/la amigo(a) mate

la amistad friendship
el amor love
el análisis (*pl inv*) analysis
la anchura breadth; width
el/la anfitrión(ona) host
el ángel angel
el ángulo angle
la angustia anguish
el animal doméstico pet
la antigüedad antique
el anuncio announcement
el anzuelo hook
el apoyo support
la aprobación (*pl* aprobaciones) approval
la apuesta bet; stake
la armada navy
el arreglo compromise
la artesanía craft
el artículo article; item
la asociación (*pl* asociaciones) association
el asombro astonishment
el aspecto aspect
la astilla splinter
el asunto affair
el atajo short-cut
el ataúd coffin
la atención (*pl* atenciones) attention
el atentado attempt
la atracción; el atractivo attraction
la ausencia absence
la autoridad authority

la **aventura** adventure; affair
el **aviso** notice
la **ayuda** assistance, help
el/la **ayudante** assistant
el **ayuntamiento** council
el **azar** chance
la **bala** bullet
la **bañera** tub
la **barandilla** rail
la **barrera** barrier
el **barril** barrel
la **base** base
la **batalla** battle
la **batería** battery
la **beca** grant
el **beso** kiss
la **Biblia** Bible
el/la **blogero(a)** blogger
la **bolsa** bag
la **bomba** bomb
la **bondad** kindness
el **borde** edge
la **broma** joke
el **brote** outbreak
el **bullicio** bustle
la **burbuja** bubble
el **cable** cable
la **caja** box
la **calcomanía** transfer
el **cálculo** calculation
el **caldo** stock
la **calidad** quality
la **calma** calm
el **camino** path; way
el **campamento** camp
la **campaña** campaign
el **camping** (*pl* ~s) site
el **canal** channel
el/la **canguro** babysitter

la **cantidad** amount
el **caos** chaos
la **capa** layer
la **capacidad** ability; capacity
el **capítulo** chapter
la **característica** characteristic; feature
la **caridad** charity
el **cartucho de tinta** ink cartridge
el/la **catedrático(a)** professor
el **cazo** pot
los **celos** jealousy (*sing*)
el **centro** center; focus; middle
el **centro turístico** resort
la **cesta** basket
el **chiste** joke
el **cielo** heaven
la **cima** top
el **círculo** circle
las **circunstancias** circumstances
la **cita** quote; extract; appointment
el/la **civil** civilian
la **civilización** (*pl* civilizaciones) civilization
la **clase** sort; period
la **clasificación** (*pl* clasificaciones) classification
la **codicia** greed
la **columna** column
el **columpio** swing
la **combinación** (*pl* combinaciones) combination
el **combustible** fuel
el **comentario** comment, remark
el/la **comentarista** commentator
las **comillas: entre comillas** quotation marks; in quotes
la **comisión** (*pl* comisiones) commission

el **comité** (*pl* comités) committee
el **compañero** fellow
la **comparación** (*pl* comparaciones)
  comparison
la **compasión** (*pl* compasiones)
  sympathy
la **competición** (*pl* competiciones)
  contest
el/la **competidor(a)** rival
la **comprensión** (*pl* comprensiones)
  sympathy
el **compromiso** commitment
la **comunicación** (*pl*
  comunicaciones) communication
la **comunidad** community
la **concentración** (*pl*
  concentraciones) concentration
la **conciencia** conscience
la **condecoración** (*pl*
  condecoraciones) honor
la **condición** (*pl* condiciones)
  condition; status
la **conducta** conduct
la **conexión** (*pl* conexiones)
  connection
la **conferencia** conference
la **confianza** confidence
el **conflicto** conflict
el **confort** comfort
el **congreso** conference
la **conmoción** (*pl* conmociones)
  shock; disturbance
el **conocimiento** consciousness;
  knowledge
la **consecuencia** consequence
el **consejo** advice
la **construcción** (*pl* construcciones)
  construction; structure
el/la **consumidor(a)** consumer

el **contacto** contact
el **contenido** content
el **contexto** context
el **contorno** outline
el **contraste** contrast
la **contribución** (*pl* contribución)
  contribution
la **conversación** (*pl* conversaciones)
  conversation
la **copia** copy
el **corazón** (*pl* corazones) heart; core
la **corona** crown
el/la **corresponsal** correspondent
la **corrupción** (*pl* corrupciones)
  corruption
la **cortesía** politeness
la **cosa** thing
las **cosas** stuff (*sing*)
la **costumbre** custom
el **crecimiento** growth
el/la **criado(a)** servant
la **crisis** (*pl inv*) crisis
la **crítica** criticism
el **cuadro** picture
la **cuba** tub
el **cubierto** place
el **cuchicheo** whispering
la **cuenta** count
  por su cuenta of his own accord
el **cuento** tale
la **cuestión** (*pl* cuestiones) question
la **cueva** cave
el **cuidado** care
la **culpa** blame
la **cultura** culture
la **cuota** fee
la **curiosidad** curiosity
los **datos** data (*pl*)
el **debate** debate

el **deber** duty
la **decepción** (pl decepciones) disappointment
la **decisión** (pl decisiones) decision
el **defecto** fault
la **definición** (pl definiciones) definition
el/la **dependiente(a)** assistant
la **depresión** (pl depresiones) depression
el/la **derecho(a)** right
  los **derechos** fee
el **desagüe** drain
el **desarrollo** development
el **desastre** disaster
el **descanso** break
el/la **desconocido(a)** stranger
la **desdicha** unhappiness
el **deseo** desire; wish; urge
el **desgarrón** (pl desgarrones) tear
la **desgracia** misfortune
el **desorden** disorder; mess
el **destino** destiny; fate
la **destreza** skill
la **destrucción** (pl destrucciones) destruction
la **desventaja** disadvantage
el **detalle** detail
la **devolución** (pl devoluciones) refund; return
el **diagrama** diagram
el **diálogo** dialogue
la **diana** target
el **diario** diary; journal
la **diferencia** difference
la **dificultad** difficulty
la **dimensión** (pl dimensiones) dimension
el **Dios** God

el/la **diplomático(a)** diplomat
el/la **diputado(a)** deputy
la **dirección** (pl direcciones) direction
la **disciplina** discipline
el **discurso** speech
la **discusión** (pl discusiones) argument; discussion
el **diseño** design
el **dispositivo** device
la **disputa** dispute
la **distancia** distance
la **división** (pl divisiones) division
el **drama** drama
la **duda** doubt
el **eco** echo
la **economía** economics (sing); economy
la **edición** (pl ediciones) edition
el **efecto** effect
el **ejemplar** copy
el **ejemplo** example
  por **ejemplo** for instance
el/la **elector(a)** elector
la **elegancia** elegance
el **elemento** element
la **encuesta** survey
el/la **enemigo(a)** enemy
la **energía** energy
el **entusiasmo** enthusiasm; excitement
la **envidia** envy
la **época** period
el **equilibrio** balance
el **equipo** equipment
el **error** mistake
el **escándalo** scandal
el **escape** leak
la **escasez** shortage
la **escritura** writing

el **esfuerzo** effort
el **espacio** space
la **espalda** back
la **especie** species (*sing*)
el **espectáculo** show; sight
la **esperanza** hope
el **espesor; la espesura** thickness
el **esquema** outline; diagram
la **estaca** stake
la **estancia** stay
la **estatua** statue
el **estilo** style
la **estrategia** strategy
el **estrés** stress
la **estructura** structure
el **estudio** studio
la **estupidez** (*pl* estupideces) stupidity
la **etapa** stage
la **excepción** (*pl* excepciones) exception
el **exceso** excess
la **excusa** excuse
el/la **exiliado(a)** exile
el **exilio** exile
las **existencias** stock
el **éxito** success
la **experiencia** experience
el/la **experto(a)** expert
la **explicación** (*pl* explicaciones) explanation
la **explosión** (*pl* explosiones) explosion
una **explosión** a bomb blast
las **exportaciones** exports
la **exposición** (*pl* exposiciones) exhibition
la **expresión** (*pl* expresiones) expression

la **extensión** (*pl* extensiones) extent
el **extracto** extract
el/la **extranjero(a)** foreigner
la **fabricación** (*pl* fabricaciones) manufacture
la **facilidad** facility
el **factor** factor
el **fallo** failure
la **falta:** absence
   falta (de) lack (of)
la **fama** reputation
el **favor** favor
la **fe** faith
la **felicidad** happiness
la **fila** row
la **filosofía** philosophy
el **fin** end
la **flecha** arrow
el **fondo** background; bottom; fund
el/la **forastero(a)** stranger
la **forma** form; shape
la **fortuna** fortune
el **fracaso** failure
la **frase** sentence; phrase
la **frente** front
el **frescor, la frescura** freshness
la **fuente** source
la **fuerza** force; strength
la **función** (*pl* funciones) function
la **ganancia** gain
el **gancho** hook
los **gastos** expenses
la **generación** (*pl* generaciones) generation
el **gol** goal
el **golfo** gulf
el **golpe** bang; blow; knock
la **gotera** leak
el **grado** degree

el **gráfico** chart
el **grito** cry
el **grupo** group
la **guía** guide
el **hambre** (f) hunger
el **hecho** fact
la **higiene** hygiene
la **hilera** row
el **honor** honor
los **honorarios** fee
la **honra** honor
el **hueco** gap
el **humo** fumes (pl); smoke
el **humor** humor
la **idea** idea
  no tengo ni idea I haven't a clue
el **idioma** language
el/la **idiota** fool; idiot
la **imagen** (pl imágenes) image
la **imaginación** (pl imaginaciones)
  imagination
el **impacto** impact
el **imperio** empire
las **importaciones** imports
la **importancia** importance
la **impresión** (pl impresiones)
  impression
el **impuesto** duty
el **impulso** urge
la **inauguración** (pl inauguraciones)
  opening
el **incidente** incident
la **independencia** independence
el **índice** index
la **indirecta** hint
la **infancia** childhood
el **infierno** hell
la **influencia** influence
los **ingresos** earnings

el/la **inspector(a)** inspector
el **instante** instant
la **institución** (pl instituciones)
  institution
el **instituto** institute
las **instrucciones** instructions
el **instrumento** instrument
la **intención** (pl intenciones)
  intention; aim
el **interés** (pl intereses) interest
el/la **internauta** internet user
la **interrupción** (pl interrupciones)
  interruption
el **intervalo** gap
la **investigación** (pl investigaciones)
  research
la **invitación** (pl invitaciones)
  invitation
la **ira** anger
el **jaleo** row
el/la **jefe(a)** chief
el **juego** gambling
los **juegos del ordenador** gaming
el **juguete** toy
la **lágrima** tear
la **lata** can
el/la **lector(a)** reader
la **leyenda** legend; caption
la **libertad** freedom
la **licenciatura** degree
el/la **líder** leader
la **liga** league
el **límite** boundary; limit
la **limpieza** cleanliness
la **línea** line
la **liquidación** (pl liquidaciones)
  settlement
la **lista** list
la **literatura** literature

el **local** premises (*pl*)
la **locura** madness
el **logro** achievement
la **loncha** slice
la **longitud** length
el **lugar** site
el **lujo** luxury
la **luz** (*pl* luces) light
  luz de la luna moonlight
el/la **maestro(a)** master
la **magia** magic
la **manera** manner
la **máquina** machine
la **marca** brand; mark
el **marco** frame
el **margen** (*pl* márgenes) margin
la **máscara** mask
la **matrícula** fee
el **máximo** maximum
la **mayoría** majority
el **medio (de)** means (of)
la **mejora, la mejoría** improvement
la **memoria** memory
la **mente** mind
el **método** method
la **mezcla** mixture
el **miedo** fear
el **milagro** miracle
la **mina** mine
el **mínimo** minimum
el **ministerio** ministry
la **minoría** minority
la **mirada** glance
la **misa** mass
la **misión** (*pl* misiones) mission
el **misterio** mystery
el **mitin** (*pl* mítines) rally
el **mito** myth
la **moda** fashion; trend

la **molestia** annoyance
el **molino** mill
el **montón** (*pl* montones) mass; pile
la **moral** morals (*pl*)
el **mordisco** bite
el **motivo** pattern
el **motor** motor
el **muchacho** boy; young man
la **muchedumbre** crowd
la **muestra** sample
la **muñeca** doll
la **naturaleza** nature
el **naufragio** wreckage (*sing*)
la **negociación** (*pl* negociaciones)
  negotiation
el **nervio** nerve
la **niñez** childhood
el **nivel** level
el **nombramiento** appointment
la **nota** note
el **número** number; issue
la **objeción** (*pl* objeciones) objection
el **objetivo** objective; purpose;
  target
el **objeto** object; goal
las **obras** works
el **odio** hate
el/la **oficial** officer
la **olla** pot
el **olor** smell
la **opción** (*pl* opciones) option
la **opinión** (*pl* opiniones) opinion
la **oportunidad** chance; opportunity
la **oposición** (*pl* oposiciones)
  opposition
la **orden** (*pl* órdenes) order
la **organización** (*pl* organizaciones)
  organization
  organización benéfica charity

el **orgullo** pride
el **origen** (*pl* orígenes) origin
la **oscuridad** darkness
la **paciencia** patience
la **página** page
la **paja** straw
la **palabra** word
el **palacio** palace
el **palo** stick
el **pánico** panic
el **paquete** pack; packet; package
el **paquete de programas** software
  package
la **pareja** pair
la **parte** part
  parte de arriba top; **parte**
  delantera front; **parte trasera** rear;
  de parte de algn on behalf of sb
la **partida** item
el **parto** labor
  estar de parto to be in labor
el **pasaje**; el **pasillo** passage
la **pasión** (*pl* pasiones) passion
el **paso** footstep
el **patrón** (*pl* patrones) pattern
la **pausa** pause
el **pedazo** piece
el **pedido** order
el **peligro** danger
la **pena** distress; penalty
el **penalty** (*pl* penalties) penalty
el **pensamiento** thought
el **periódico** journal
el **periodo** period
el/la **perito(a)** expert
el **permiso** permission
la **persona** person
el **personal** personnel
la **perspectiva** prospect

la **pesadilla** nightmare
la **picadura** bite
la **pieza** piece; item
la **pila** battery; pile
la **pista** clue
el **placer** delight; pleasure
el **plan** plan; scheme
el **plato** dish
la **plaza** place
el **poder** power
el **poema** poem
la **política** politics (*sing*); policy
la **póliza** policy
el **polvo** dust
la **pompa** bubble
el **porcentaje** percentage
la **porción** (*pl* porciones) portion
el **portavoz** (*pl* portavoces)
  spokesperson
la **posibilidad** possibility
la **posición** (*pl* posiciones) position
el **post** post (*on forum or blog*)
la **práctica** practice
la **preferencia** choice
el **prefijo** code
la **pregunta** question
el **premio** award
la **preparación** (*pl* preparaciones)
  preparation
los **preparativos** arrangements
la **presencia** presence
la **presión** (*pl* presiones) pressure
el **presupuesto** budget; quote
la **princesa** princess
el **príncipe** prince
el **principio** beginning; principle
la **prioridad** priority
el **problema** problem; trouble
el **proceso** process

el/la **profesor(a)** master
la **profundidad** depth
el **programa** schedule
la **prohibición** (*pl* prohibiciones) ban
el **propósito** purpose
  a **propósito** on purpose
la **propuesta** proposal
la **prosperidad** prosperity
la **protección** (*pl* protecciones)
  protection
la **protesta** protest
las **provisiones** provisions
el **proyecto** plan
la **publicidad** publicity
la **puja** bid
la **punta** point
la **puntería** aim
el **punto** item; point
  punto de partida starting point;
  punto de vista point of view
el/la **querido(a)** darling
la **rabia** rage
la **raja** crack
el **rato** while
la **razón** (*pl* razones) reason
la **reacción** (*pl* reacciones) reaction;
  response
la **realidad** reality
la **rebanada** slice
el/la **rebelde** rebel
el **recado** message
la **recepción** (*pl* recepciones)
  reception
la **recesión** (*pl* recesiones) recession
la **reclamación** (*pl* reclamaciones)
  claim
el **recuerdo** souvenir
el **recurso** resource
  como último recurso as a last resort

la **red** network
la **reducción** (*pl* reducciones)
  reduction
la **reforma** reform
la **regla** period
la **reina** queen
la **relación** (*pl* relaciones) relationship
la **religión** (*pl* religiones) religion
la **reputación** (*pl* reputaciones) status
el **requisito** requirement
la **reserva** fund; stock
la **resistencia** resistance
la **resolución** (*pl* resoluciones)
  resolution
el **respecto: con respecto a** with
  regard to
el **respeto** respect
la **respiración** (*pl* respiraciones) breath
la **responsabilidad** responsibility
la **respuesta** reply; response
los **restos** remains; wreckage (*sing*)
el **resultado** outcome
el **reto** challenge
el **retrato** portrait
la **reunión** (*pl* reuniones) meeting
la **revista** magazine; journal
el **rey** (*pl* ~es) king
el **riel** rail
el **ritmo** pace
el/la **rival** rival
la **rodaja** slice
el **ruido** noise
la **ruina** ruin
el **rumor** rumor
la **ruptura** break
la **rutina** routine
el **sacrificio** sacrifice
el/la **santo(a)** saint
la **sección** (*pl* secciones) section

el **secreto** secret
el **sector** sector
la **sed** thirst
la **seguridad** security; safety
la **selección** (pl selecciones)
  selection; choice
el **sentido** sense; way
el **sentimiento** feeling
la **señal** sign; mark
el **señor** lord
el **servicio** service
la **sesión** (pl sesiones) session
el **significado** meaning
el **silbato** whistle
el **silencio** silence
el **símbolo** symbol
el **sindicato** trade union
el **sistema** system
el **sitio** place
la **situación** (pl situaciones)
  situation
el/la **socio(a)** member
la **soledad** loneliness
la **solución** (pl soluciones) solution
la **sombra** shadow
el **sondeo (de opinión)** poll
el **sonido** sound
el **soporte (físico)** hardware
la **sorpresa** surprise
la **sospecha** suspicion
la **subasta** auction
el **subtítulo** caption
la **subvención** (pl subvenciones)
  grant
la **suciedad** dirtiness
el **sueño** sleep
la **suerte** luck
  buena/mala suerte good/bad
  luck

la **sugerencia** suggestion
el **suicidio** suicide
la **suma** sum
la **superficie** surface
la **supervisión** (pl supervisiones)
  supervision
el/la **superviviente** survivor
el/la **suplente** substitute
el **surtido** choice
la **sustancia** substance
el/la **sustituto(a)** substitute
la **táctica** tactics (pl)
el **talento** talent
la **tapa** top
la **tapicería, el tapiz** (pl tapices)
  tapestry
el **tapón** (pl tapones) top
la **tarea** task
la **tarifa; la tasa** rate
el **teatro** theater; drama
la **técnica** technique
la **tecnología** technology
el **tema** theme; issue
la **tendencia** trend
la **tensión** (pl tensiones) tension;
  strain
la **tentativa** attempt; bid
la **teoría** theory
el **territorio** territory
el **terrón** (pl terrones) lump
el **texto** text
la **tienda** store
la **timidez** shyness
el **tipo** type; kind; fellow, guy
el **tío** (Sp) guy
la **tirada** edition
el **título** title
el **tomo** volume
la **tortura** torture

el **total** total
la **tradición** (*pl* tradiciones)
  tradition
la **trampa** trap
la **tranquilidad** calmness
la **transferencia** transfer
el **tratamiento** treatment
el **trato** deal; treatment
la **tristeza** sadness
el **trozo** bit; piece; slice
el **truco** trick
el **tubo** tube
la **tumba** grave
el **tumor** growth
el **turno** turn
la **unidad** unit
la **valentía** bravery, courage
el **valor** value
el **vapor** steam
la **variedad** variety; range

la **vela** candle
el **veneno** poison
la **ventaja** advantage; asset
la **verdad** truth
la **vergüenza** shame
la **versión** (*pl* versiones) version
la **victoria** victory
la **vida** life
el **vínculo** bond
la **violencia** violence
la **visita;** visit; visitor
el/la **visitante** visitor
la **vista** sight
el **volumen** (*pl* volúmenes) volume
el/la **voluntario(a)** volunteer
el/la **votante** voter
la **vuelta** turn; return
  dar una vuelta to go for a stroll;
  dar una vuelta en bicicleta to go
  for a bike ride

VERBS

What is a verb?
A **verb** is a 'doing' word which describes what someone or something does, what someone or something is, or what happens to them, for example, *be*, *sing*, *live*.

abandonar to abandon
abrigar(se) to shelter
abrir to turn on
  abrir(se) to open
abrochar to fasten
aburrir to bore
  aburrirse to get bored
acabar de hacer algo to have just done sth
acampar to camp
aceptar to accept
acercarse (a) to approach
  acercarse a to go towards
aclarar(se) to clear
acompañar to accompany; to go with
aconsejar to advise; to suggest
acordarse de to remember
acostarse to lie down
acostumbrarse a algo/algn to get used to sth/sb
actuar to act; to operate
acusar to accuse
adaptar to adapt
adelantar to go forward; to overtake
adivinar to guess
admirar to admire
admitir to admit
adoptar to adopt
adorar to adore
adquirir to acquire; to purchase
afectar to affect
afirmar to assert; to state

agarrar to catch; to grab; to grasp
agradecer to thank (for)
aguantar to bear
ahorrar to save
ahuyentar to chase (off)
alcanzar to reach
  alcanzar a algn to catch up with sb;
  alcanzar a ver to catch sight of
alimentar to nourish
aliviar to relieve
almacenar to store
alojarse to put up
  alojarse con to lodge with
alquilar to hire; to rent: to let
amar to love
amenazar to threaten
amontonar to stack
andar to walk
anhelar to long for
animar to encourage
  animar a algn a hacer algo to urge sb to do sth
anunciar to advertise; to announce
añadir to add
apagar to switch off; to turn off; to put out
apagar to turn off
  apagarse to fade
aparecer to appear
apetecer to crave; to want
  me apetece un helado I would like an ice cream

aplastar to crush
aplaudir to applaud; to cheer; to clap
aplazar to postpone; to put back
aplicar a to apply to
apostar (a) to bet (on)
apoyar to support; to endorse
  apoyar(se) to lean
apreciar to appreciate
aprender to learn
apretar to press; to squeeze
aprobar to approve of; to endorse
aprovechar to take advantage (of)
apuntar to take down
arañar to scratch
arrancar to pull out
arrastrar to drag
  arrastrarse to crawl
arreglar to fix (up); to arrange; to settle
  arreglárselas to cope; to manage
arrepentirse de to regret
arriesgar to risk
arrojar to hurl
arruinar to ruin
asar to bake
ascender to promote
asegurar to assure; to ensure;
  to secure
asentir con la cabeza to nod
asfixiar(se) to suffocate
asistir (a) to attend
asombrar to amaze; to astonish
asustar to alarm; to frighten;
  to startle
atacar to attack
atar to attach; to tie
atender to treat
  atender a to attend to
atraer to attract
atrasar to hold up

atreverse (a hacer algo) to dare
  (to do sth)
aumentar to increase; to raise
avanzar to advance
averiarse to break down
averiguar to check
avisar to warn
ayudar to help
azotar to whip
bailar to dance
bajar: to come down; to go down;
  to lower
  bajar (de): to get off; bajar de to
  get out of
balbucir to stammer
barrer to sweep
basar algo en to base sth on
batir to whip; to beat
besar to kiss
bombardear to bomb
brillar to shine; to sparkle
bromear to joke
burlarse de to make fun of
buscar to look for; to search; to seek
caerse to fall (down)
  se me cayó I dropped it
calcular to estimate
calentar(se) to heat (up)
callarse to be quiet
cambiar to alter; to exchange
  cambiar(se) to change
cancelar to cancel
cantar to sing
capturar to capture
carecer de to lack
cargar (de) to load (with)
causar to cause
cavar to dig
celebrar to celebrate

centellear to sparkle
cerrar: to turn off: to close; to fasten
  cerrar(se): to shut; cerrar con
  llave to lock
charlar to chat
chillar to scream
chismear to gossip
chocar con to bump into
chupar to suck
citar to quote
clasificarse to qualify
cobrar to claim; to get
coger to catch; to grab; to seize
colaborar to collaborate
coleccionar to collect
colgar to hang (up)
colocar to place
combinar to combine
comenzar (a) to start (to)
cometer to commit
compaginar to combine
comparar to compare
compartir to share
compensar to compensate (for)
  compensar por to make up for
competir en to compete in
complacer to please
completar to complete; to make up
comprar (a) to buy (from)
comprender to comprise
comunicar to communicate
conceder to grant
concentrarse to concentrate
concertar to arrange
concluir to conclude; to accomplish
condenar to condemn; to sentence
conducir to lead
conectar to connect
confesar to confess

confiar to trust
  confiar en to rely on
confirmar to confirm
confundir (con) to confuse (with)
  confundir a algn con to mistake
  sb for
congelar to freeze
conocer to know
conseguir to achieve; to get; to secure
  conseguir (hacer) to succeed (in
  doing)
considerar to consider; to rate
constar de to consist of
  hacer constar to record
constituir to constitute; to make up
construir to build; to put up
consultar to consult
consumir to consume
contar to count
  contar con to depend on
contemplar to contemplate
contener to contain; to hold
contestar to answer
continuar to continue; to keep;
  to resume
contribuir to contribute
controlar to control
convencer to convince
convenir to suit
convertir to convert
copiar to copy
correr to run
cortar to cut (off); to mow
costar to cost
crear to create
crecer to grow
creer to believe; to reckon
criar to bring up
criticar to criticize

cruzar to cross
cubrir (de) to cover (with)
cuchichear to whisper
cuidar to look after; to take care of;
 to mind
 cuidar de to take care of
cultivar to cultivate
cumplir to accomplish; to carry out
curar to heal
dañar to harm
dar to give:
 dar a to overlook; dar asco a to
 disgust; dar de comer a to feed;
 dar la bienvenida to welcome;
 dar marcha atrás to reverse;
 dar saltitos to hop; dar un paseo
 to go for a stroll; dar un puñetazo
 a to punch; dar una bofetada a to
 slap; dar vergüenza a to embarrass;
 dar vuelta a to turn; darse cuenta
 de algo to become aware of sth;
 darse por vencido to give up;
 darse prisa to hurry;
deber must; to owe
 deber hacer algo to be supposed
 to do sth; debo hacerlo I must do it
decepcionar to disappoint
decidir(se) (a) to decide (to)
decidirse (a) to make up one's mind
 (to)
decir to say; to tell
declarar to declare
 declarar culpable to convict;
 declararse en huelga to (go on)
 strike
decorar to decorate
dedicar to devote
defender to defend
definir to define

dejar to leave
 dejar caer to drop
deletrear to spell
demorar(se) to delay
demostrar to demonstrate
depender de to depend on
derribar to demolish
desanimar to discourage
desaparecer to disappear
desarrollar(se) to develop
descansar to rest
descargar to unload
describir to describe
descubrir to discover; to find out
desear to desire; to wish
deshacerse de to get rid of
deslizar(se) to slip
desnudarse to strip
despedir to dismiss
despegar to take off
despejar(se) to clear
despertar(se) to wake up
desprenderse to come off
desteñirse to fade
destruir to smash
desviar to divert
detener to arrest
determinar to determine
detestar to detest
devolver to bring back; to give back;
 to send back
 devolver a su sitio to put back
dibujar to draw
diferenciarse (de) to differ (from)
dimitir to resign
dirigir to conduct; to direct; to
 manage
disculparse (de) to apologize (for)
discutir to argue; to debate; to discuss

diseñar to design
disfrazar to disguise
disfrutar to enjoy
disminuir to decline; to decrease;
to diminish
distinguir to distinguish
distribuir to distribute
divertir to divert
divertirse to enjoy oneself
dividir to divide; to split
doblar to fold
doblar(se) to double
dominar to dominate; to master
ducharse to shower
dudar to doubt
durar to last
echar to pour:
echar a algn to throw sb out;
echar a algn la culpa de algo
to blame sb for sth; **echar al correo**
to post; **echar de menos** to miss;
echar una mirada a algo to glance
at sth; **echarse** to lie; **echarse a**
llorar to burst into tears; **echarse**
a reír to burst out laughing
educar to bring up; to educate
ejecutar to execute
elegir to choose; to select; to elect
elogiar to praise
emocionar to excite
empatar to draw, to tie
empezar (a) to begin (to)
emplear to employ
empujar to push
encarcelar to imprison
encender to switch on; to turn on;
to light
encerrar to shut in
encontrar to find; to meet

enfocar to focus
enjugar to wipe
enseñar to teach; to show
entender to understand
enterarse de to hear about
enterrar to bury
entrar (en) to enter
entregarse to give oneself up;
to surrender
entrevistar to interview
enviar to send
envolver to wrap up
equivocarse to make a mistake;
to be mistaken
erigir to erect
escapar (de) to escape (from)
escarbar to dig
escoger to choose; to pick
esconderse to hide
escuchar to listen (to)
especializarse en to specialize in
especular to gamble
esperar to wait (for); to expect;
to hope
establecer to establish; to set up
establecerse to settle
estallar to blow up
estar to be
estar acostumbrado a algo/
algn to be used to sth/sb; **estar**
de acuerdo to agree; **estar de pie**
to be standing; **estar dispuesto**
a hacer algo to be prepared to do
sth; to be willing to do sth;
estar equivocado to be wrong;
estar involucrado en algo to be
involved in sth
estirar(se) to stretch (out)
estrecharse la mano to shake hands

estrellar(se) to crash
estropear to ruin
  estropear(se) to spoil
estudiar to study; to investigate
evitar (hacer) to avoid (doing)
exagerar to exaggerate
examinar to examine
  examinarse to take an exam
excitar to excite
exclamar to exclaim
excluir to exclude; to suspend
existir to exist
experimentar to experience
explicar to explain
explorar to explore
explotar to explode
exponer to display
exportar to export
expresar to express
exprimir to squeeze
expulsar temporalmente to suspend
extender to spread: to extend
  extender(se) to spread out
extrañar (*LAm*) to miss
fabricar to manufacture
faltar to be lacking; to fail
felicitar to congratulate
fiarse de to trust
financiar to finance
fingir to pretend (to)
firmar to sign
flotar to float
fluir to flow
formar(se) to form
forzar a algn a hacer (algo) to force
  sb to do (sth)
fotografiar to photograph
frecuentar to frequent
freír to fry

funcionar to work
  (hacer) funcionar to operate
fustigar to whip
ganar to earn; to gain
garantizar to guarantee
gastar to spend: to waste
  gastar(se) to wear (out)
gemir to groan
golpear to knock; to beat
grabar to record
gritar to shout; to scream; to cry
guardar to keep; to store
guiar to guide
gustar to like
haber to have
hablar to speak; to talk
hacer to do; to make; to bake
  hacer añicos to shatter; **hacer
  campaña** to campaign; **hacer
  comentarios** to comment; **hacer
  daño a** to hurt; **hacer las maletas**
  to pack; **hacer preguntas** to ask
  questions; **hacer público** to issue;
  hacer señas *or* **una señal** to
  signal; **hacer una lista de** to list;
  hacer una oferta to bid; **hacer una
  pausa** to pause; **hacer una señal
  con la mano** to wave; **hacerse** to
  become; to get; **hacerse adulto**
  to grow up; **hacer(se) pedazos** to
  smash
helarse to freeze
herir to injure
hervir to boil
huir to flee; to run away *or* off
identificar to identify
iluminar(se) to light
imaginar to imagine
impedir to prevent (from)

implicar to imply; to involve
imponer to impose
importar to matter; to mind; to care
  ¡no me importa! I don't care!;
  ¿y a quién le importa? who cares?
impresionar to impress
imprimir to print
inclinar to bend
  inclinarse to bend down
incluir to include
indicar to point out; to indicate
influir to influence
informar to inform
inscribirse to register
insinuar to hint
insinuar to imply
insistir en to insist on
instruir to educate
insultar to insult
intentar to attempt to
interesar to interest
  interesarse por to be interested in
interrogar to question
interrumpir to interrupt
introducir to introduce
invadir to invade
investigar to investigate
invitar to invite
  invitar a algn a algo to treat sb to sth
ir to go
  ir a buscar a algn to fetch sb;
  ir bien a to suit; **ir deprisa** to dash;
  ir en bicicleta to ride a bike
irse to go away
irritar to irritate; to aggravate
jugar to play; to gamble
juntarse con to join
jurar to swear
justificar to justify

juzgar to judge
lamentarse to moan
lamer to lick
lanzar to throw; to launch
  lanzarse a to rush into
leer to read
levantar to raise; to put up; to lift
  levantarse to get up; to rise
limpiar to clean
llamar to call
  llamar por teléfono: to ring;
  llamarse to be called
llegar to arrive
llenar (de) to fill (with)
llevar: to carry; to bear; to wear
  llevar a cabo to carry out;
  llevarse to take
llorar to cry, weep
llover to rain
  llover a cántaros to pour
luchar to fight; to struggle
maltratar to abuse
manchar to dirty
mandar to command, to order
manifestarse to demonstrate
mantener to maintain; to support
  mantener el equilibrio to balance
marcharse to depart; to leave
medir to measure
mejorar(se) to improve
mencionar to mention
mentir to lie
merecer to deserve
meterse en to get into
mezclar to mix
mimar to spoil
mirar to look (at); to watch
  mirar fijamente to stare at
modificar to adjust

molestar to annoy; to disturb;
to trouble
montar a caballo to ride
morder to bite
morir to die
mostrar to hold up
mostrar(se) to show
mover to move
multiplicar to multiply
nacer to be born
necesitar to need
negar to deny
negarse (a) to refuse (to)
negociar to negotiate
notar to note
obedecer to obey
obligar a algn a to oblige sb to
observar to notice; to observe
obstruir to block
obtener to obtain
ocasionar to bring about
ocultar to hide
ocupar to occupy
ocuparse de to deal with
ocurrir to occur
odiar to hate
ofender to offend
ofrecer to offer
ofrecerse a hacer algo to volunteer
to do sth
oír to hear
oler to smell
olvidar to forget
operar a algn to operate on sb
oponerse a to oppose; to object to
organizar(se) to organize
otorgar to award
pagar to pay
pararse to come to a halt, to stop

parecer to seem (to); to look
parecerse a to look like, to resemble
participar en to take part in
partir to share
partir(se) to split
pasar to pass; to overtake; to spend
pedir to request; to order
pedir a algn que haga algo to ask
sb to do sth; **pedir algo a algn** to
ask sb for sth; **pedir algo prestado
a algn** to borrow sth from sb
pegar to hit; to stick; to strike
pensar to think
pensar en to think about; **pensar
hacer** to intend to do
perder to miss:
perder a algn de vista to lose
sight of sb
perdonar a to forgive
perdurar to survive
permitir to allow, to permit, to let
permitirse to afford
perseguir to pursue
persuadir to persuade
pertenecer a to belong to
pesar to weigh
picar to bite
pinchar(se) to burst
planchar to iron
plegar to fold
poder to be able to; can; might
¿puedo llamar por teléfono?: can I
use your phone?; **el profesor podría
venir ahora:** the teacher might
come now; **puede que venga más
tarde** he might come later
poner to put; to lay
poner de relieve to highlight;
poner en duda to question; **poner**

en el suelo to put down; **poner en orden** to tidy; **ponerse** to put on; **ponerse de pie** to stand up; **ponerse en contacto con** to contact
portarse to behave
poseer to own, to possess
practicar to practice
precipitarse to rush
predecir to predict
preferir to prefer
preguntar (por) to inquire (about)
  preguntarse to wonder
prender fuego to catch fire
preocupar to trouble; to bother
  preocuparse (por) to worry (about)
preparar(se) to prepare
prescindir de to do without
presentar to present; to introduce
prestar to lend
prevenir to warn
prever to foresee
privar to deprive
probar to prove
producir to produce
prohibir to ban; to forbid
prometer to promise
pronosticar to predict
pronunciar to pronounce
propagarse to spread
proponer to propose
proteger to protect
protestar to protest
proveer to provide
publicar to publish
quedar to remain
  quedarse to stay
quejarse (de) to complain (about)
quemar to burn

querer to want (to); to love; to like
quitar to remove
  quitar algo a algn to take sth from sb; **quitarse** to take off
reaccionar to react; to respond
realizar to fulfil; to realize
reanudar to resume
recalcar to emphasize; to stress
rechazar to reject
recibir to receive
  recibirse (*LAm*) to qualify
reclamar to demand; to claim
recoger to pick (up); to collect; to gather
recomendar to recommend
reconocer to recognize
recordar to recall
  recordarle a algn to remind sb of
recuperarse to recover
reducir(se) to reduce
reembolsar to refund
referirse a to refer (to)
  en lo que se refiere a ... as regards ...
reflejar, reflexionar to reflect
reformar to reform
regañar to tell off
regar to water
registrar to register; to examine
reír to laugh
  reírse de to laugh at
relajarse to relax
relatar to report
renovar to renew
reñir to quarrel
reparar to repair, to mend
repartir to deal; to deliver
repetir(se) to repeat
reponer to replace
  reponerse to mend

representar to perform; to represent
requerir to require
resbalar to slide
reservar to book; to reserve
resistir to hold out
  resistir(se) to resist
resolver to solve
respetar to respect
respirar to breathe
responder to reply, to answer;
  to respond
restaurar to restore
resultar to prove
retar to challenge
retirar(se) to withdraw
reunir(se) to collect
  reunirse to gather; reunirse con
  to rejoin
revelar to reveal
rodear (de) to surround (with)
romper(se) to break; to tear;
  to burst
ruborizarse to blush
saber a to taste of
saber to know
  sé nadar I can swim
sacar to bring out; to take out
  sacar brillo to polish; sacarse el
  título to qualify
sacudir to shake
salir to emerge
saltar to leap
saludar to greet
  saludar con la cabeza to nod
salvar to rescue; to save
secar(se) to dry
seguir to follow
  seguir haciendo algo to go on
  doing sth

sentarse to sit (down)
sentir to be sorry
  sentir(se) to feel
señalizar to indicate
ser to be
servir to serve
significar to mean
sobrevivir to survive
solicitar to apply to; to seek
soltar to release
sonar to sound
  (hacer) sonar to ring
sonreír to smile
sorprender to surprise
sospechar to suspect
subir to climb; to come up; to go up
  subir a to board; to get on
suceder to happen
sufrir (de) to suffer (from)
  sufrir un colapso to collapse
sugerir to suggest
sujetar to fix
suministrar to supply
suponer to assume; to suppose;
  to involve
surgir to emerge
suspender to suspend; to fail
suspirar to sigh
sustituir to replace
telefonear to telephone
temblar to shake
temer to fear
tender to hold out
tener to have; to hold
  tener antipatía a to dislike; tener
  cuidado to be careful; tener éxito
  to be successful; tener lugar
  to take place; to come off; tener
  mala suerte to be unlucky; tener

miedo to be afraid; **tener que** to have to; **tener que ver con** to concern; **tener razón** to be right; **tener suerte** to be lucky; **tener tendencia a hacer algo** to tend to do sth
terminar to end; to finish
tirar to throw away
  tirar de to pull
tocar to touch; to play; to ring
tomar to take
torcer to twist
trabajar to work
traducir to translate
traer to bring
traicionar to betray
tranquilizar(se) to calm down
trasladar to transfer
tratar to treat
  tratar (de) to try (to); **tratar con** to deal with
unir to join
  unir(se) to unite

untar to spread
usar to use
vaciar(se) to empty
vacilar to hesitate
valer to be worth
variar to vary
vencer to conquer, to defeat, to overcome
vender to stock
  vender(se) to sell
venir to come
  venirse abajo to collapse
ver to see
visitar to visit
vislumbrar to catch sight of
vivir to live
volar to fly
volcar to overturn
volver to come back; to go back; to return
  volver(se) to turn round; **volverse hacia** to turn towards
votar to vote